Advance praise for *The Mind of the Censor and the Eye of the Beholder*

"Corn-Revere's extraordinary THE MIND OF THE CENSOR AND THE EYE OF THE BEHOLDER offers a riveting review and astute analysis of the evolution of free expression – and censorship of free speech – in the USA through the eras of Anthony Comstock, 'offensive' comic books, porn rock, the FCC's regulation of the 'vast wasteland,' fleeting expletives, and the indecency wars of the twenty-first century. Corn-Revere brings to life the absurdities of censorship and the dangers such views pose to American liberty and democracy. This original work is informative, insightful, and often wildly entertaining."

Geoffrey R. Stone, Professor of Law, University of Chicago and author of SEX AND THE CONSTITUTION SEX AND THE CONSTITUTION (2017)

"Bob Corn-Revere has written a book of stunning originality and importance. By tracing the efforts at censorship in American history, Corn-Revere shows us that temptations for censorship exist in every generation. Inevitably, the censors self-righteously think that they are doing good for society by stopping harmful speech. And inevitably in hindsight, we realize that the efforts at censorship were a huge mistake. Corn-Revere's engagingly written book provides a powerful defense of freedom of speech and of freedom of thought."

Erwin Chemerinsky, Dean and Jesse H. Choper Distinguished Professor of Law, University of California, Berkeley School of Law

"As a longtime student and advocate of free speech, it is a rare joy to encounter a new work that so greatly enhances my understanding and appreciation of this precious freedom, providing renewed encouragement and ammunition for continuing the never-ending efforts that are required to resist constant censorial pressures. Regardless of how much or how little you know or care about free speech when you begin this book, you will be enlightened, inspired, and galvanized by every page!"

Nadine Strossen, immediate past President, American Civil Liberties Union, and author of HATE: WHY WE SHOULD RESIST IT WITH FREE SPEECH, NOT CENSORSHIP (2018)

"Bob Corn-Revere is my friend and I love this book. I'm not saying I love this book because Bob's my friend – he's my friend because I love this book. A lot of what's good about Bob is in this book. It tells great stories. It's smart, funny, knowledgeable, honest, freedom-loving and works for truth, justice, and the American way. This book will prove to you that Bob is as groovy as Superman, without the stupid cape. Shit, piss, fuck, cunt, cocksucker, motherfucker, tits! Read it."

Penn Jillette, the taller, louder half of Penn & Teller

"Somebody once said: "Censorship is the strongest drive in human nature; sex is a weak second." Everybody who wants to get a better understanding of this powerful force of human nature should read Corn-Revere's brilliant book. It's funny, well written, and a superb guide to the mechanisms of censorship in the Land of the Free. Corn-Revere's insightful exploration and deconstruction of the censor's mind will equip the reader to see through the rhetorical fog of arguments for shutting down unpopular speech. It's the best available medicine against any pandemic of censorship."

Flemming Rose, Senior Fellow at the Cato Institute and former editor
at Jyllands-Posten

"Philosophy, psychology, sociology, and history set the backdrop for an arresting narrative and a profound exploration of the law of free speech. The result is a thought-provoking book destined to have a long shelf life and an even longer digital one. A momentous contribution to First Amendment literature!"

Ronald K. L. Collins, co-author of We Must Not Be Afraid to
Be Free The Trials of Lenny Bruce

THE MIND OF THE CENSOR AND THE EYE OF THE BEHOLDER

Beginning in the nineteenth century with Anthony Comstock, America's "censor in chief," *The Mind of the Censor and the Eye of the Beholder* explores how censors operate and why they wore out their welcome in society at large. This book explains how the same tactics were tried and eventually failed in the twentieth century, with efforts to censor music, comic books, television, and other forms of popular entertainment. The historic examples illustrate not just the mindset and tactics of censors, but why they are the ultimate counterculture warriors and why, in free societies, censors never occupy the moral high ground. This book is for anyone who wants to know more about why freedom of speech is important and how protections for free expression became part of the American identity.

Robert Corn-Revere is a leading First Amendment lawyer whose career has spanned over thirty-eight years. He has argued cases in the Supreme Court, defeated the FCC in the Super Bowl "wardrobe malfunction" case, and obtained a posthumous pardon for the late comedian Lenny Bruce from the Governor of New York.

FIGURE 0.1: Caricature of Anthony Comstock
Source: The Public I blog (http://thepublici.blogspot.com/2015/
08/the-profession-al-prig.html).

The Mind of the Censor and the Eye of the Beholder

THE FIRST AMENDMENT AND THE CENSOR'S DILEMMA

ROBERT CORN-REVERE

CAMBRIDGE UNIVERSITY PRESS

CAMBRIDGE
UNIVERSITY PRESS

University Printing House, Cambridge CB2 8BS, United Kingdom

One Liberty Plaza, 20th Floor, New York, NY 10006, USA

477 Williamstown Road, Port Melbourne, VIC 3207, Australia

314–321, 3rd Floor, Plot 3, Splendor Forum, Jasola District Centre,
New Delhi – 110025, India

103 Penang Road, #05–06/07, Visioncrest Commercial, Singapore 238467

Cambridge University Press is part of the University of Cambridge.

It furthers the University's mission by disseminating knowledge in the pursuit of
education, learning, and research at the highest international levels of excellence.

www.cambridge.org
Information on this title: www.cambridge.org/9781107129948
DOI: 10.1017/9781316417065

First published 2021

Printed in the United Kingdom by TJ Books, Limited, Padstow Cornwall

A catalogue record for this publication is available from the British Library.

Library of Congress Cataloging-in-Publication Data
NAMES: Corn-Revere, Robert, author.
TITLE: The Mind of the Censor and the Eye of the Beholder : the First Amendment and the
Censor's Dilemma / Robert Corn-Revere.
DESCRIPTION: Cambridge, United Kingdom ; New York, NY : Cambridge University Press,
2021. | Includes index.
IDENTIFIERS: LCCN 2021017164 (print) | LCCN 2021017165 (ebook) | ISBN 9781107129948
(hardback) | ISBN 9781107570375 (paperback) | ISBN 9781316417065 (ebook)
SUBJECTS: LCSH: Freedom of expression – United States – History. | Censorship – United
States – History. | Obscenity (Law) – United States – History. | Comstock, Anthony,
1844–1915 – Influence.
CLASSIFICATION: LCC KF4770 .C67 2021 (print) | LCC KF4770 (ebook) | DDC 342.7308/5–dc23
LC record available at https://lccn.loc.gov/2021017164
LC ebook record available at https://lccn.loc.gov/2021017165

ISBN 978-1-107-12994-8 Hardback
ISBN 978-1-107-57037-5 Paperback

Contents

Figures

For Sigrid

Foreword

For all the protections that the First Amendment of the US Constitution provides, we have never had immunity from the censorship virus. One of the early statutes of the new republic was the Sedition Act of 1798, which made criminal the publication of "disloyal, profane, scurrilous or abusive language" about the President and various other high-ranking officials as well as speech that led others "to view the United States government or its institutions with contempt." That ugly and repressive piece of legislation, signed into law by President John Adams, expired by its terms in 1801 and Adams' successor, Thomas Jefferson, pardoned those found guilty of violating the law and returned fines paid by those convicted.

But censorship of one sort or another has frequently recurred, and censors and would-be censors have played a major role throughout the history of the country in affecting and often limiting what Americans could see, hear, and read. That is what Robert Corn-Revere's irresistibly readable new book The Mind of the Censor and the Eye of the Beholder is about.

Of course, American censorship, at its worst, has never approached that too often imposed abroad. We do not seize dissident newspapers and execute editors. We have never reached the point that China did in 1991 when the manufacture and sale of T-shirts with inscriptions saying "I'm fed up!" was banned and a state-owned newspaper urged that the shirts should have said "I must train myself for the construction of the motherland." Our editors have never been told, as those in Nazi Germany were, that the role of the press was "not to inform but to shake up and spur onward" in a manner instructed by the government. We do not live in a totalitarian state.

But, as Corn-Revere's book makes clear, we have never been without prominent and often admired advocates for significant limitations on what speech should be permitted. Anthony Comstock, for example, is discussed at length in the book. He was an enormously significant advocate in the late nineteenth and early twentieth centuries of limiting the sale of books and other materials that he viewed as immoral. While he was mocked by more First Amendment–oriented commentators of his day, he was a serious force in American life, so serious that, as Corn-Revere's book reveals, his obituary in the *New York Times* described him as "having served a good cause with tireless devotion."

Similarly, Dr. Fredric Wertham, also considered at length in the book, led a much-publicized personal crusade against comic books in the 1950s. Wertham testified before Congress that Superman was "particularly injurious to the education of children" and urged draconian limitations on the sale of comic books. He too was controversial in his day and, even more than Comstock, was generally viewed as a significant contributor to public discourse. The review in the *New York Times* of his bestselling book SEDUCTION OF THE INNOCENT praised him for a "most commendable use of the professional mind." He would not be so viewed today, and Corn-Revere's highly critical treatment of him is particularly powerful.

For me, the analysis in THE MIND OF THE CENSOR AND THE EYE OF THE BEHOLDER of governmental pressures on radio and television entities that were subject to a high level of government regulation is particularly insightful. There is no doubt that radio and television have endured governmental oversight that would plainly be unconstitutional if applied to the print press. For a number of years commencing in the late 1960s, I represented NBC on a number of matters in which its decisions about what to broadcast were subject to extreme pressure from the Nixon administration. Earlier in that decade, the Kennedy administration had sought to use the "fairness doctrine," which required broadcasters that had broadcast positions of one side of issues of public importance to put the "other" side across as well, to harass right-wing broadcasters by filing complaints to the Federal Communications Commission (FCC) about editorials that the administration considered "irrationally hostile to the President and his programs."

The Nixon administration marched further down that road. Under President Nixon, a number of fairness doctrine complaints were filed by a conservative group called Accuracy in Media (AIM) in which claims were made that the broadcasts – often documentaries – violated the fairness doctrine. The cases filed were both time-consuming and expensive to defend, and they were meant to be just that. My role was to defend NBC when it was accused of some sort of unfairness. Not until I read Corn-Revere's book did I learn that what we suspected of the claims was true – that the Nixon administration had itself worked with AIM in planning the filing of these complaints. Indeed, the book quotes one Nixon aide as saying that "working through AIM was perfect because it was 'a mechanism under which private non-government pressures can be brought.'" Was that a form of censorship – or at least attempted censorship? You bet.

There is a broader aspect of FCC regulation of the broadcast media described in the book that resonates well beyond that particular area of law. That was the repeated assurance by the FCC that it was not engaged in censorship or anything akin to it. From the time, in 1927, when the first legislation was adopted regulating radio and the Federal Radio Commission (forerunner of the FCC) was created, the statute made explicit that the new entity could not engage in censorship. At the same time, the legislation provided that the FCC should take account of "the public interest" in awarding licenses. The tension between those two lodestar principles has been at the heart of debate about broadcast regulation from the start and, as the book makes indisputably clear, has often led to a not-quite-censorship regime of the FCC when it raised its eyebrows enough to affect – and sometimes determine – what would and would not be broadcast. At the same time, through all the years of broadcast regulation, the FCC has maintained that it was not acting as a censor.

That assertion, sometimes dubious, sometimes simply false, has been a common refrain throughout history, even from individuals who were playing nothing but a censorial role. That is one of the most striking lessons of the book. No one – not the FCC, not Anthony Comstock, not Dr. Wertham, and not any of the other would-be censors described in the book – has chosen to describe themselves as a censor. Dr. Wertham, for example, testified before a Senate committee that "regulating what is being forced down children's throats in the way of corrupting pictures and words" was not censorship at all. It was, he testified, simply a "public health" measure.

Just that sort of verbal gymnastics had been engaged in years before by George Alexander Redford, the London censor of the theater in the first half of the twentieth century. Having banned George Bernard Shaw's 1893 play *Mrs. Warren's Profession* from being performed, he memorably explained his role as a non-censor this way:

> I am not a censor. I never censorize over anybody. I merely used the experience I have gained from a long association with theatrical matters to administer the Regulations of my office. There is no such thing as an offhand decision about interdicting a play. No play is ever prohibited without the most careful thought, and every chance is given to authors to tone down their work whenever it is possible.

Not a censor? Read carefully. What Mr. Redford was saying in the most elegant manner was that he was a helpful censor, a thoughtful censor, a good censor. But the most telling words in his explanation of why he was not a censor are "No work is ever prohibited without the most careful thought …." I cannot think of any censor who would not say that of their own censorial conduct.

Every year the international organization Reporters Without Borders publishes a list that ranks the nations of the world based on the degree to which they protect freedom of the press. In 2020, the United States has fallen to number forty-five, between OECS (the Organization of East Caribbean States) and Papua New Guinea. We would all do well to learn about the nature of censorship, and Robert Corn-Revere's new book is a most valuable step in that direction.

Floyd Abrams
Senior Counsel, Cahill Gordon & Reindel LLP
Founding Sponsor, The Floyd Abrams Institute for Free Expression at Yale Law
School

Acknowledgments

Writing may be a solitary pursuit, but this book would not have been written or seen the light of day without the help of many people. I am especially thankful for the partnership with my wife of thirty-seven years, Sigrid Fry-Revere, my greatest supporter and most perceptive critic, whose keen observations made this a better book. I would not have been able to summon the effort to write this if not for her love, support, and patience. It is to her that I dedicate this book.

I am also deeply indebted to Ron Collins, my coconspirator on a range of First Amendment projects, who first connected me with John Berger, my commissioning editor at Cambridge University Press. Ron's sage advice has guided me every step of the way. I had previously conspired with Ron and his long-time writing partner, David Skover, in seeking a posthumous pardon for Lenny Bruce, the groundbreaking comedian who was convicted of obscenity by the State of New York in 1963 for his stand-up routines. The pardon petition was inspired by Ron and David's wonderful book THE TRIALS OF LENNY BRUCE, and we were floored when New York Governor George Pataki granted the pardon in December 2003. Ron, David, and I have often brainstormed about free speech issues in the years since (usually when they were working on one of their many book projects), and those discussions helped shape some of the ideas I explore in this book. I thank them for their friendship, good humor, and collaboration.

I am especially honored that Floyd Abrams, the greatest First Amendment advocate of our time, wrote a foreword, and that other giants in our field kindly agreed to read the manuscript and offer words of support, including Nadine Strossen, Geoffrey Stone, Erwin Chemerinsky, and, again, Ron Collins and David Skover. I am grateful that my friend Penn Jillette, whose life and work are an inspiration to all who value freedom of thought and speech, kindly agreed to review the book and offer his reactions. Thanks as well to Flemming Rose, the prominent journalist and former editor of the Danish newspaper *Jyllands-Posten*, who personally has felt the heat of the assassin's veto and therefore certainly knows censorship when he sees it. I also owe a debt of gratitude to Charles Brownstein for his perceptive comments on the history of comic book censorship and help in securing permissions for some of the images in the chapter on the comic book panic. In that regard, my thanks to Denis Kitchen, David Hajdu, and Kelly Carlin for their generosity in granting permission to use some of the images in this book. Speaking of images, I owe a special debt of gratitude to Alex Lubertozzi, whose brilliant cover design captured the theme and spirit of the book and who helped track down some of the other images that appear in the book. Thanks as well to Ronnie London, my brother-in-arms in many First Amendment battles over the past two decades, and to Carol Kaltenbaugh, our long-standing (and long-suffering) assistant for most of that time, who prepared the book's index.

Permissions

1

The Censor's Dilemma

Pity the plight of poor Anthony Comstock. The man H. L. Mencken described as "the Copernicus of a quite new art and science," who literally invented the profession of anti-obscenity crusader in the waning days of the nineteenth century, ultimately got, as legendary comic Rodney Dangerfield would say, "No respect. No respect at all." As head of the New York Society for the Suppression of Vice and special agent for the US Post Office under a law that popularly bore his name, Comstock was, in Mencken's words, the one "who first capitalized moral endeavor like baseball or the soap business, and made himself the first of its kept professors."

For more than four decades, Comstock terrorized writers, publishers, and artists – driving some to suicide – yet he also was the butt of public ridicule. George Bernard Shaw popularized the term "Comstockery" to mock the unique blend of militant sanctimony and fascination with the lurid that marks American prudishness. Comstock frequently was lampooned in illustrated comics, and in his final days, even his supporters distanced themselves from his excessive zeal. In this respect, Comstock personified the censor's dilemma in a free society – the capacity to wield great power combined with the inability to shake off the taint of illegitimacy.

Comstock's mindset lives on, both in the extension of his law to modern communications technologies and in the army of Lilliputian Comstocks pursuing the same profession, but who, like Elvis impersonators, can never quite come close to the real thing. His outsized shadow looms over the likes of Dr. Fredric Wertham, the psychiatrist who stoked a national panic about comic books (Chapter 5), and Tipper Gore of the Parents Music Resource Center, who leveraged her political connections to cow the music industry (Chapter 6). It dwarfs the impact of Newton Minow, JFK's Federal Communications Commission (FCC) Chairman, who endeavored to tell Americans that the television medium they so love is nothing but a "vast wasteland" and who used the power of the FCC to homogenize broadcasting (Chapter 7). Comstock's accomplishments also overshadow such lesser zealots as Brent Bozell, founding president of the Parents Television Council (PTC), an organization created to keep the world safe from fleeting expletives and wardrobe malfunctions (Chapter 8).

This book examines the work of these and other would-be censors and explores reasons why, while destructive to freedom in their time, they had no permanent impact in the United States. Or, more accurately, they didn't achieve their intended impact. This is not a partisan argument. No political philosophy has a monopoly on sanctimony, or on the belief that revealed truth – as its adherents define it – should be enforced as a matter of public policy. Progressives and conservatives are united in the common conviction that they know what speech should be banned (or required) and that their choices should be enforced by law; they only differ in their preferences. In this respect, the eye of the beholder governs the mind of the censor. But, in part because the arbiters of propriety wish to suppress or supplant what the public embraces, they are the ultimate counterculture warriors and therefore doomed, in the end, to failure and disrepute.

A FUNDAMENTAL(IST) DISCONNECT

A more fundamental reason for the censor's harsh fate is that his very existence contradicts the arc of history among societies that value freedom. From the time Anthony Comstock shuffled off into the void in 1915 to the present day, constitutional protections for the freedom of imagination and expression have become well-established to a degree Comstock could never have anticipated, and that would have horrified him. The year Comstock died, the Supreme Court held that the First Amendment's protections do not extend to the then-new medium of cinema. It reasoned that "the exhibition of moving pictures is a business, pure and simple, originated and conducted for profit," and, more to the point, "capable of evil, having power for it, the greater because of their attractiveness and manner of exhibition."

The Court's opinion produced a result and employed a rhetorical style worthy of the great morals crusader himself, but it would not stand the test of time. As both the sophistication and artistry of film evolved, the public enthusiastically embraced it, as did – eventually – the courts. When Comstock passed, the Supreme Court had not yet issued a single decision upholding any First Amendment claim. But over the next fifty years, the Court would decide that the medium of film was constitutionally protected in the same way as newspapers and books; that the government's ability to impose prior restraints – to censor expression in advance of publication – was strictly limited; that sex and obscenity are not synonymous; and that discussions of intimate subjects could be banned only if they were "prurient" and utterly lacked redeeming social value. At the same time, both public and judicial estimations of what is socially valuable shifted radically. Since then, the legal component of the so-called culture war has continued to be waged along the border, and it is an ever-expanding frontier.

It is tempting to think of Comstock's Victorian Era reign of censorship as a limited episode in our history – like the Red Scare and McCarthyism – that erupted for a time only to be left behind as law and social understandings evolved. But the reality is not so simple, if only because no such phenomenon is ever a one-time thing when we fail to learn from history. Even at the height of his power, Comstock was ridiculed almost as much as he was feared, and his death did not signal the end of the profession of morals crusader. Far from it. The names and faces may change, as do the specific problems that represent the latest threat to civil society (and usually to our children), but there has never been a shortage of volunteers eager to save us from our own bad taste and poor manners.

One defining moment for what we have come to know as the "culture war" at the start of the twenty-first century was the Janet Jackson/Justin Timberlake "wardrobe malfunction" that ended the halftime show of Super Bowl XXVIII in 2004. Although the broadcast network immediately apologized for what turned out to be a poorly planned and flawed execution of a last-minute stunt secretly contrived by Jackson and her choreographer, policy entrepreneurs like Brent Bozell immediately pounced on the nine-sixteenths-of-a-second flash of bejeweled breast flesh as a sign of the End of Days and a call to arms. The FCC instantly launched a major investigation; Congress convened a series of hearings; and Michael Powell, the FCC's chairman at the time, initiated a number of steps designed, as he put it, to "sharpen our enforcement blade." The Commission ultimately fined CBS over half a million dollars for the unplanned and unauthorized moment which the agency nevertheless decreed "was designed to pander to, titillate and shock the viewing audience." After eight years of litigation, however, that penalty was thrown out as "arbitrary and capricious," and the fine was refunded.

But the FCC's problem wasn't just with the courts. The public had a quite different reaction to the "wardrobe malfunction." Most people didn't see the blink-and-you-miss-it moment that ended the Super Bowl halftime show, and those who did weren't immediately clear about what they had seen. Even inside the network control room at Reliant Stadium, amidst the managed chaos that accompanies any live broadcast, directors of the show turned to one another after witnessing the show's climax and asked, "What was *that?*" But the curiosity of the audience had been piqued. The "wardrobe malfunction," as it was later called by a hapless Justin Timberlake, was the most TiVoed moment in television history up to that point and the most searched event online according to Google.

It wasn't as if the public was rising up in outrage so it could flood the FCC with complaints. That task would be left to Bozell's PTC and other pro-censorship groups whose bread and butter is whipping up spam email campaigns to energize regulators and legislators. No, the viewing audience was more curious than outraged about this strange and unprecedented event. In fact, a nationwide poll sponsored by the Associated Press in the weeks after the Super Bowl revealed that 80 percent of respondents believed that the federal investigation was a waste of taxpayer dollars.

Therein lies the censor's dilemma.

Censors may wield great power and enjoy political favor – for a time – and can ravage individual lives and reputations. But they are also the subject of popular derision and generally end up on the wrong side of history – in the United States, at least. This is why those who actively seek to suppress speech try vehemently to deny that their actions amount to "censorship," and why they often feel beleaguered even as they marshal the power of the state to serve their purposes. Defensiveness pervades their occupation. Those who engage in the business of censorship have an inferiority complex for a reason – at some level they understand that their enterprise is fundamentally un-American.

WHAT DO YOU MEAN, CENSORSHIP?

Censorship is a word people use to mean many different things. Parents censor their children when they tell them not to make too much noise in the house or when they tell them they mustn't say out loud that Aunt Maude is fat, or that Grandpa smells funny. But that isn't the sort of censorship that is the primary focus of this book, as it does not implicate the law or state action. Nor is the use of private ratings systems, such as the Motion Picture Association of America's ratings for movies or the Electronic Software Association's ratings for electronic games. People often confuse such private editorial commentary with unconstitutional censorship.

There are those who claim to be censored by what they call "political correct-ness," when their intolerant or racist rants are met with disdain and social ostracism. When LA Clippers owner Donald Sterling was banned from the National Basketball Association for life after he was recorded making mindlessly bigoted remarks to a young woman friend in 2014, it may have been an act of censorship, but it wasn't *illegal* censorship. The First Amendment provides that "Congress shall make no law . . . abridging the freedom of speech, or of the press." It does not say "the NBA shall make no rules." Same goes for the NFL when it decreed that players must either stay in the locker room or stand and salute during the national anthem (although the league later vacillated on that policy). For censorship to violate the Constitution, there must be an element of government action.

Such questions sometimes become complicated when public officials throw their weight around. Donald Trump launched his presidential campaign in 2015 with attacks on undocumented immigrants as rapists and murderers and defending his inflammatory rhetoric by saying he had no time for "political correctness." As President, Trump trashed any and all perceived critics, dredging up the Stalinist tag "enemy of the people" to describe established news organizations. Although he bristles at any suggestion that his own speech should be limited in any way, Trump also said that we should "open up" the libel laws (whatever that means), that flag burners should be stripped of their citizenship, and that late-night comedy shows and the networks that air them should be investigated for lampooning him. Of course, it is one thing for a president to speak like a sixth grader who flunked civics, but when he acted to block critics from his official social media account, or revoked White House press credentials of reporters or news organizations he dislikes, that was another matter entirely. Courts correctly understood that such official actions were censorship and held that not even the President can use his office in this way.

The question of what constitutes censorship also has arisen in the context of social media platforms that restrict speech through their terms of service. Regardless of size, however, when online services such as Facebook or Google apply their moderation policies, they are not engaged in unconstitutional censorship, as there is no state action. To the contrary, enforcement of terms of use is the exercise of their First Amendment rights as electronic publishers. But the issue becomes convoluted when policy advocates or legislators try to insert the government into such decisions. Some argue that online intermediaries should be forced to identify and remove "hate speech" or "fake news" (as is done under European law), while some opportunistic politicians in the United States advocate regulating online platforms to prevent them from enforcing such policies on their own. A social media platform, like Twitter, is not a public forum that is subject to First Amendment rules, but a public official's Twitter account that he uses as an extension of his or her office is.

The ways in which free speech questions arise are myriad and complex, but what may constitute censorship in a legal sense is straightforward – the issue is whether governmental power is being used to limit or compel speech. Such censorship can take many forms, including not only government actions to suppress particular expression but also rules requiring speech, such as a pledge or loyalty oath. As a constitutional matter, compelled speech and coerced silence are indistinguishable. Thus, when the FCC requires broadcasters to air certain programs it deems to be in the "public interest" in order to obtain a government license to operate a radio or television station, it necessarily raises First Amendment questions. A censor is one who seeks to exert control over the culture through law, based on the idea that he or she, speaking for the community, has a right to draw the boundary lines for speech. Few have ever had the power that Comstock wielded, serving as both anti-speech activist and law enforcer. But those Comstock wannabes who merely advocate the use of state power to silence others certainly share his heart and soul.

THE COMMON THREAD

Ultimately, censorship results from the conviction that some forms of expression are so vile or dangerous that they should be restricted, or so valuable that they should be compelled. Censors claim the moral sanction to speak for the collective, either by enforcing "community standards" against evil expression or by mandating speech that they believe serves the "public interest." They are willing to legislate their preferences and to brand as outlaws those who would transgress their standards. You can't really argue taste – or, as the Latin maxim would have it, *de gustibus non est disputandum*, but at some times or places in America, people have gone to jail – or lost their broadcast licenses – over such disputes.

The message of the censor is clear and unmistakable: I (or we) know the truth, and must control the ideas or influences to which you may become exposed to protect you from falling into error (or sin). Truth may be revealed by whispers from god, by political theory, by popular vote, or by social science, but once it has been determined, the time for debate is over. Anthony Comstock did not invent censorship, but his DNA may be found in the genetic code of every would-be censor who walks the earth. As Supreme Court Justice Anthony Kennedy put it: "Self-assurance has always been the hallmark of a censor." In this respect, he echoed Mencken's assessment of vice crusaders that "[t]heir very cocksureness is their chief source of strength."

The arbiters of culture are sustained and emboldened by their moral fervor, but at least in this country they can never shake a certain defensiveness since they live in a nation where the Supreme Court affirmed as far back as 1943 that one "fixed star in our constitutional constellation" is that "no official, high or petty, can prescribe what shall be orthodox in politics, nationalism, religion, or other matters of opinion." One might quickly add, as the Court did within a few years, that this principle applies equally to matters of taste and that "a requirement that literature or art conform to some norm prescribed by an official smacks of an ideology foreign to our system." As Justice John Marshall Harlan would later write, "one man's vulgarity is another man's lyric." Thus, in a free society, the censor cannot claim moral superiority, no matter how sanctimonious he may be.

JUST CAN'T GET ENOUGH

The internal conflict is not just a question of law. There appears to be a psychological dimension to the censor's dilemma as well. What can one say about the type of person who devotes his or her life to denouncing certain types of expression and advocating its prohibition while choosing a profession in which he immerses himself in it? Purity crusaders claim to hate the stuff they want to suppress and argue that it will ruin all who are exposed, but invariably they can't get enough of it. They search it out, collect it, study it, categorize it, archive it, talk about it, and display it to others, all for the ostensible purpose of making such expression cease to exist.

Comstock created what he called a Chamber of Horrors – his personal collection of lewd publications and "obscene" objects – that he would show Members of Congress to persuade them of the need for his 1873 federal obscenity law. More than 120 years later, Senator James Exon crafted his "Blue Book" to illustrate early examples of Internet porn, which he showed to colleagues to persuade them of the need to restrict online "indecency." Congress responded by adopting the indecency prohibitions of the Communications Decency Act (CDA) by an overwhelming margin in 1996.

Activists of all political stripes surround themselves with the type of speech they believe must be suppressed for the good of others yet mysteriously claim to be immune to its dangerously toxic effects. Could it be that such people are drawn to their work because of the opportunity to spend countless hours communing with the forbidden? As Sydney Smith, a noted British writer and cleric of the nineteenth century, observed: "Men whose trade is rat-catching love to catch rats; the bug destroyer seizes upon the bug with delight; and the suppressor is gratified by finding his vice." It is not beyond belief that censorship is an ultimate act of self-gratification, and that our rights are sacrificed on an altar of the censor's guilty pleasure.

Morris L. Ernst, a cofounder of the American Civil Liberties Union (ACLU), noted this phenomenon in his 1928 study of obscenity and the censor entitled To The Pure: "Recall those men who belong to vice societies but enjoy showing, of course in a scientific manner, postal cards of homosexual acts." He concluded that examples of such public hypocrisy "are too multitudinous to permit a detailed inventory." Ernst observed that Anthony Comstock was an "obvious psychopath" whose diaries provided "precious morsels for any psychiatrist" because his writings made it obvious that "he suffered from extreme feelings of guilt because of a habit of masturbation." This may help explain why Comstock devoted a lifetime to collecting, cataloguing, and destroying all that he found to be shameful.

A VAST BIPARTISAN CONSPIRACY

Because the urge to censor derives from personal preferences or policy positions, no political party or philosophy is immune from the impulse to suppress contrary views. One oft-expressed stereotype is that conservatives favor censorship while liberals oppose it, but one needn't search long to find numerous counterexamples, as later chapters will explore. Liberals and conservatives alike, regardless of how one might define those philosophies, appear to agree that the machinery of government can rightfully be used to restrict speech, provided the targeted expression is sufficiently vile (from their point of view) or insufficiently valuable (using their scale as a measure). The problem is that the competing factions never can seem to agree on which speech should be banned.

A common assumption is that conservatives want to censor sex, while liberals want to censor depictions of violence and "hate" speech, and both want to restrict speech about abortion – so long as it is the other side that gets muzzled. Veteran journalist and free speech advocate Nat Hentoff summed up the mindset quite nicely in his book Free Speech For Me But Not For Thee, noting that "the lust to suppress can come from any direction." Hentoff credited to a fellow journalist the insight that censorship "is the strongest drive in human nature; sex is a weak second."

Some social conservatives seek to limit access to information about abortion (just as earlier generations sought to suppress discussions of contraceptives), while some progressives try to restrict "sidewalk counseling" and other efforts outside clinics to dissuade women from terminating their pregnancies. Both sides justify their actions in the name of public health and decry their adversary's tactics as censorial. Liberals generally favor placing limits on political campaign expenditures and contributions, while conservatives tend to oppose them as a violation of free speech. But the roles switch when restrictions are imposed on providing "material support" (aka "contributions") to organizations branded by the government as supporting terrorism (or, in earlier days, Communism). Liberals recoil at the courts' increasing recognition of constitutional protection for commercial speech (unless it involves the commercial promotion of contraceptives), while conservatives (and some progressives) claim authority to ban or restrict sexually oriented entertainment because it is "commercialized."

These are generalizations, of course. Not all liberals think alike on these issues, just as conservatives may take different positions. The problem may lie in the left–right labels themselves, notwithstanding the polarization of our current political culture that resembles a giant game of "shirts versus skins." The two sides divide into self-selected factions and reflexively oppose whatever the other team is proposing as the solution to society's ills. But the one point on which most of the combatants in these political controversies agree is that they don't want to be tarred as "censors." Censorship is what the other side is doing. Those *bastards*.

IMPLAUSIBLE DENIABILITY

Just as hypocrisy is the homage that vice pays to virtue, as seventeenth-century French writer Francois de La Rochefoucauld put it, so is euphemistic evasion. George Orwell, in his 1946 essay *Politics and the English Language*, wrote that political euphemism "is designed to make lies sound truthful and murder respectable, and to give the appearance of solidity to pure wind." He observed that "[d]efenseless villages are bombarded from the air, the inhabitants driven out into the countryside, the cattle machine-gunned, the huts set on fire with incendiary bullets: this is called *pacification*." "In our time," Orwell concluded, "political speech and writing are largely [employed in] defense of the indefensible." Updating Orwell's example, genocide came to be known in the 1990s as "ethnic cleansing."

The corruption of language for political ends is a central premise of Orwell's fictional masterpiece, Nineteen Eighty-Four. In that novel he described the nation of Oceania in which the apparatus of government was divided between the Ministry of Truth, which concerned itself with news, entertainment, education, and the fine arts; the Ministry of Peace, which concerned itself with war; the Ministry of Love, which maintained law and order by torturing dissidents; and the Ministry of Plenty, which was responsible for economic affairs and rationing. Newspeak, the official language of Oceania, was designed to meet the ideological needs of the State. Its purpose, Orwell wrote, was "to make all other modes of thought impossible," which was accomplished by eliminating superfluous words from the dictionary and stripping all remaining words of "unorthodox meanings." These principles were the basis for the official slogans of the Party over which Big Brother presided:

War is Peace
Freedom is Slavery
Ignorance is Strength

Orwell's vision would seem outlandish if real-world examples of language corruption were not so common. "America's Mayor" (and later Trump consigliere) Rudolph Giuliani was seemingly channeling Big Brother in a 1994 speech in which he said that "[f]reedom is about authority. Freedom is about the willingness of every single human being to cede to lawful authority a great deal of discretion about what you do."

Giuliani at least was clear that he was all about control. Others obfuscate more (or at least are a little more artful about it). In 2017, officials at American University refused to approve a sorority fundraiser they believed may have been insensitively "appropriating culture." They were wrong about that, but couldn't bring themselves to cop to the censor label. Instead, Colin Geeker, the school's assistant director of fraternity and sorority life, wrote to Sigma Alpha Mu to say: "I want to continue empowering a culture of controversy prevention among [Greek] groups," advising the sorority to "stay away from gender, culture, or sexuality for thematic titles." Evidently feeling empowered by this exchange, Sigma Alpha Mu canceled the fundraiser.

Public officials routinely use language creatively to expand their power. As a candidate, Donald Trump asserted that no one has greater respect for the First Amendment while simultaneously condemning reporters and advocating "opening up" the libel laws. As President, he and his senior staff members labeled unfriendly stories "fake news" while at the same time offering a different version of reality based on what they unblushingly described as "alternative facts." In this parallel universe, words simply don't have the meanings they once did. Such people would be right at home in Orwell's Oceania.

Given the long history of misdirection by those seeking to avoid the appearance of misusing power, it is no wonder that euphemism is the weapon of choice among censors in America. Ever since Anthony Comstock gave censorship a bad name, his philosophical descendants have gone to great lengths to describe their actions as something else. The vehemence of their denials and rationalizations is a pretty reliable measure of the grip of the censor's dilemma.

THE LAW EVOLVES

Supreme Court Justice Oliver Wendell Holmes identified the mindset of the censor early on. He wrote in 1919 that "[p]ersecution for the expression of opinions seems to me perfectly logical. If you have no doubt of your premises or your power and want a certain result with all your heart you naturally express your wishes in law and sweep away all opposition." But he ultimately realized that this impulse to censor, and the sense certainty that drives it, must be leavened with historical perspective:

> When men have realized that time has upset many fighting faiths, they may come to believe even more than they believe the very foundations of their own conduct that the ultimate good desired is better reached by free trade in ideas – that the best test of truth is the power of the thought to get itself accepted in the competition of the market, and that truth is the only ground upon which their wishes safely can be carried out.

This insight came from Holmes' dissent in *Abrams* v. *United States*, the fourth decision that year in which the Supreme Court upheld prosecutions of anti-war dissenters under the Espionage Act of 1917. That law made it a crime to cause or attempt to cause insubordination, disloyalty, mutiny, or refusal of duty in the military or naval forces of the United States. An amendment to the law, the Sedition Act of 1918, prohibited "disloyal, profane, scurrilous, or abusive language" about the United States government, its flag, or its armed forces, or that caused others to view the American government or its institutions with contempt. These sweeping prohibitions on dissent begged courts to answer the question of what the framers of the Constitution meant when they wrote the First Amendment. And if the law's suppressive language weren't enough to force the question, the sheer number of prosecutions – nearly 2,000 during the Great War alone (and over a thousand convictions) – made it critically important that the Supreme Court create doctrine defining freedom of speech.

There was little the Court could draw on from earlier precedents. In the few cases that had come up in preceding years, the Court was not quite sure what to make of the First Amendment. Among other things, it had allowed the deportation of anarchists, permitted the Post Office to exclude certain publications from the US mail, upheld a state flag "misuse" law, as well as a law that prohibited any publication that tended to incite crime or disrespect for the law. In most cases the Court simply sidestepped First Amendment controversies by ruling that free speech issues were outside its jurisdiction, or by categorizing the behavior at issue as conduct and not speech. In a 1911 case, for example, it held that union advocacy of a boycott was a "verbal act," not protected expression.

But the Court's ability to avoid First Amendment questions came to an abrupt end with America's involvement in World War I and the Espionage Act cases that followed. It was inevitable that the issue would come to the Court, and, in quick succession, it upheld convictions of members of the Socialist Party for circulating anti-draft pamphlets, a newspaper publisher for articles that criticized the war effort, and a speech by socialist (and presidential candidate) Eugene Debs for purportedly obstructing the draft. Justice Holmes authored each of those opinions. But then he began to reconsider. The *Abrams* case was much like the others the Court had decided just months earlier. It involved the circulation of leaflets by socialists questioning the war. But Justice Holmes was now coming to believe that the "cure" of a criminal prosecution was worse than the disease. This time he dissented, writing that "Congress certainly cannot forbid all effort to change the mind of the country," much less criminalize "publishing of a silly leaflet by an unknown man." But Holmes' main argument was not based on the practical consideration that speech should be allowed just because it is impotent and harmless. Quite to the contrary, he maintained that we must be "eternally vigilant against attempts to check the expression of opinions we loathe and believe to be fraught with death" unless "an immediate check is required to save the country."

He then posited his marketplace of ideas metaphor for the First Amendment. It was not that he believed that free trade in ideas guaranteed that truth necessarily would emerge but just that it provided the "best test" of truth over time compared to some "authoritative selection." This notion, Holmes suggested, "is the theory of our Constitution." He cautioned that it is "an experiment, as all life is an experiment. Every year if not every day we have to wager our salvation upon some prophecy based upon imperfect knowledge." From this basic premise that flowed from Holmes' pen in 1919, First Amendment law evolved through the twentieth century.

But it didn't happen immediately. Another dozen years would pass before the Supreme Court would begin to uphold First Amendment claims – 140 years after the Bill of Rights was ratified. From that point on, First Amendment law developed through a process of case-by-case adjudication, with each decision drawing on or distinguishing the reasoning of prior rulings. As a consequence, First Amendment law reflects the times in which it was crafted. Just as an archeologist may better understand modern society by studying prior civilizations on which it is built, those who want to grasp the American imperative of free expression – and our innate aversion to censorship as a people – should examine the many circumstances in which these principles were developed and applied.

Disputes involving radical politics as well as labor disputes underlie many of the cases that the Supreme Court confronted in the 1930s and 1940s. The rights of minority religious groups like the Jehovah's Witnesses gave rise to a series of cases through the 1940s and 1950s. During this period and continuing into the 1960s, the Red Scare and McCarthyism generated numerous cases involving academic freedom, loyalty oaths, and the general right to question political orthodoxy. The cultural and political upheavals of the 1950s through the 1970s led to a series of landmark cases that set the standards for doctrines involving defamation, public protest, and obscenity. In this sense, the development of the law of free speech is intertwined with the rise and fall of the Cold War, the civil rights movement, antiwar demonstrations, and widespread cultural changes. In more recent years, cases have extended legal protections for commercial speech and have subjected political campaign regulations to constitutional scrutiny.

It has been an evolutionary process that has trended toward greater levels of tolerance for – and legal protection of – divergent expression. And it is a level of tolerance that tends to mirror what society is prepared to accept. There are exceptions, of course, since evolution generally does not progress in a straight line. And it often takes years – and sometimes decades – for courts to catch up with the culture.

But the interconnected nature of legal and social attitudes toward free expression was well articulated by Justice Anthony Kennedy in a 2000 case, *United States v. Playboy Entertainment Group, Inc.*:

> When a student first encounters our free speech jurisprudence, he or she might think it is influenced by the philosophy that one idea is as good as any other, and that in art and literature objective standards of style, taste, decorum, beauty, and esthetics are deemed by the Constitution to be inappropriate, indeed unattainable. Quite the opposite is true. The Constitution no more enforces a relativistic philosophy or moral nihilism than it does any other point of view. The Constitution exists precisely so that opinions and judgments, including esthetic and moral judgments about art and literature, can be formed, tested, and expressed. What the Constitution says is that these judgments are for the individual to make, not for the Government to decree, even with the mandate or approval of a majority.

This growing level of tolerance for free expression, and by extension an inherent distaste for arbitrary authority, means that many current battles over free expression are being fought along the fringes of the culture war and involve issues that expose fault lines in our polarized society. Current cases ask whether some types of expression are simply too offensive to merit the protection of the Constitution or too trivial to qualify for a First Amendment shield. They reframe the question posed by Justice Holmes in 1919 – whether "enough can be squeezed from these poor and puny anonymities to turn the color of legal litmus paper."

This book does not seek to present a grand theory of freedom of expression, nor does it engage in the ongoing academic debate about how to interpret the First Amendment. Its purpose is more modest – to understand something about the nature of free speech by exploring the mind of the censor. The First Amendment may best be understood by examining what it was designed to *prevent* rather than by speculating about what it was intended to promote. And, quite apart from what the framers may have intended originally, modern First Amendment doctrine developed as a response to episodes of suppression and the excesses of censors. What came from this may not be a perfectly consistent or coherent body of law, but it has produced increasing levels of protection against would-be censors as it continues to evolve.

The ensuing chapters explore various incarnations of censorship in American history, beginning with the rise and decline of Anthony Comstock, the nation's first professional anti-vice crusader. His career set the standard, and, for many, the rhetorical tone, for those seeking to condemn various forms of speech. Although all who follow in Comstock's outsized footsteps try to claim moral superiority – characterizing the speech they would restrict as distasteful, trivial, valueless, or downright harmful – the plain fact is that the censor in a free society never has the moral high ground. The censor's dilemma is that somewhere, down deep inside, he – or she – is painfully aware of it.

Anthony Comstock: Professional Anti-vice Crusader

In December 1872, twenty-eight-year-old Anthony Comstock, a dry goods salesman and volunteer for a special project of the New York Young Men's Christian Association (YMCA), packed his great cloth bag for a trip to Washington, DC. He gathered various items from his personal collection especially for the journey, including contraceptive "rubber goods," racy playing cards, filthy pictures, and steamy half-dime novels, such as THE LUSTFUL TURK. As Major T. J. "King" Kong from the 1964 film *Dr. Strangelove* would say of his B-52 survival kit that stocked condoms, lipstick, and nylon stockings, "shoot, a fella could have a pretty good weekend in Vegas with all that stuff." But Comstock wasn't aiming to live out the punchlines of the myriad traveling salesman jokes that would be furtively shared by generations of schoolboys. No, he was sallying forth to change the world.

And so he did.

THE CHAMBER OF HORRORS

On this and subsequent trips to the nation's capital in early 1873, Comstock stalked the halls of Congress as a special lobbyist for a secret committee of the YMCA – the Committee for the Suppression of Vice. His mission was to secure passage of a law to strengthen the federal prohibition against mailing obscene or lewd matter. He displayed his lurid exhibits – his "Chamber of Horrors" as he called it – before various committees and met several times with James C. Blaine, the Speaker of the House. The young Comstock even set up shop in the office of Vice President Schuyler Colfax, where he showed off his collection to demonstrate the perils of "evil reading."

Comstock may have been new at this game, but there was no doubt about his seriousness of purpose. He regaled the legislators with tales of his vigilante exploits in vice-busting, and his stories packed a wallop. As Comstock wrote in a January 1873 letter to Representative Clinton L. Merriam of New York, of the four publishers of obscene books in business as of last March, "today three of these are in their graves, and it is charged by their friends that I worried them to death. Be that as it may, I am sure that the world is better off without them." If not admirers, these war stories at least won him congressional assistance, as did his Chamber of Horrors.

Comstock's diary entry of February 6, 1873, recounts that "[a]bout 11:30 went up to the Senate with my exhibits. A.H. Byington of Norwalk very kindly aided me by securing the Vice-President's room and inviting Senators out to see me. I spent an hour or two talking and explaining the extent of the nefarious business and answering questions. . . . All were very much excited, and declared themselves ready to give me any law I might ask for, if it was only within the bounds of the Constitution." He had earlier spent nearly a full day on the floor of the House of Representatives showing off his collection to the horror of many legislators. D. M. Bennett, a publisher and free thought advocate who later became a repeated target of Comstock's purity campaigns, wrote that "[a]fter the lawmakers had been regaled with a view of these unclean curiosities, they seemed to be prepared to vote, Aye, on almost any kind of laws for which their vote might be solicited."

Ultimately, Congress gave Comstock the law he wanted, and the legislation was so closely connected with the young anti-vice crusader that it ever since has been known as the "Comstock Law." For his part, Comstock always called it "my law." And the connection went both ways. One admiring biographer wrote that for the forty-two years of the crusader's career, "Anthony Comstock himself *was* the Comstock Act."

Needless to say, the neophyte lobbyist from New York was an unlikely power broker in the District of Columbia. Somewhat pudgy, balding, and with a faint mustache (his trademark mutton-chop whiskers would come a year later to cover a scar from a wound inflicted by a nemesis), Comstock didn't exactly cut a dashing figure (Figure 2.1). His Puritan instincts were offended by Washington society, with which he was forced to do business to achieve his objectives. He attended a White House function as he waited impatiently for his bill to wend its way through Congress, and vented his disgust to his diary:

> Attended the President's reception with Maggie [his wife] and Miss Abby Burchard. Shook hands with Grant. There were a large number present, among them certain ones who were almost caricatures of everything but what a modest lady ought to be. They were brazen – dressed extremely silly – enameled faces and powdered hair – low dresses – hair most ridiculous and altogether most extremely disgusting to every lover of pure, noble, modest woman. What are they? Who do they belong to? How can we respect them? They disgrace our land and *yet* consider themselves ladies.

But Comstock's visceral revulsion at Washington's wicked ways did not derail his campaign for two very important reasons. First, he had the backing and support of powerful friends who secured access to the right people, and second, Washington was in the throes of a bribery scandal and badly needed a distraction. For this, Comstock's purity crusade was tailor-made.

FIGURE 2.1 Portrait of young Anthony Comstock
Source: *Hue Magazine* (Fashion Institute of NYC) (https://news.fitnyc.edu/2018/12/13/lust-on-trial/).

Some of the richest men in New York bankrolled Comstock's mission to the nation's Capitol, including financier J. P. Morgan, mining magnate William E. Dodge, Jr., soap tycoon Samuel Colgate, real estate baron J. M. Cornell, publisher Alfred Barnes (the "Barnes" of what was later to become Barnes & Noble), and NEW YORK SUN publisher Moses S. Beech. Morris K. Jesup, the wealthy banker and president of the YMCA, had personally taken Comstock under his wing and provided the initial funds for what would become, first, a special project of the YMCA and, later, an independent organization, the New York Society for the Suppression of Vice.

With such influential backing naturally came political connections that opened doors for the young and zealous activist. He enlisted the aid of Benjamin Abbott, a prominent lawyer, to draft the bill, and his financial patrons secured the cooperation of prominent members of Congress and other high officials to shepherd it through the Byzantine legislative process. Jesup and Dodge sent telegrams to House Speaker Blaine stressing their "personal interest" in the legislation. Representative Merriam, who had invited Comstock to display his "exhibits" on the floor of Congress, agreed to introduce the bill in the House, and Senator William Windom introduced it in the Senate.

Supreme Court Justice William Strong reviewed the measure to ensure that it was legally sound, and Representative Benjamin Butler of Massachusetts, who sat on the House Judiciary Committee, took the bill home to work on it and to combine it with other legislative proposals. Justice Strong was a natural (if somewhat conflicted) choice for this project – he had once backed an amendment to add references to god and Jesus to the Constitution's Preamble and had supported resolutions that would have allowed legal presumptions to enforce Christian morality.

Congressman Butler, by contrast, was a most ironic choice. As a Union General during the Civil War, Butler had acquired the nickname the "Beast of New Orleans" for his alleged atrocities against the virtue of numerous southern ladies when he was commandant of that southern city. But then, why should personal hypocrisy stand in the way of a good cause? The bill that emerged was all encompassing.

The draft was subjected to the types of procedural wrangling and delays that are common in Washington but baffling to those unaccustomed to the legislative process. An exasperated Comstock filled his diary with lamentations over the ups and downs of the political maneuvering. His words, though, resonate today as proof that some things never change:

> The exebitions [sic] today in the Halls of legislation has been one that outrages all decency. Men assailing one another's character while legislation goes begging. Malice fills the air. Party bitterness and venom. Loud talk of constitution, law, justice. It seems a burlesque on our Forefathers. . . . They tear out all principle and leave the skeleton, and where then is the Constitution. [sic] . . . It seems as if every man almost, acted from personal motives or party interests, regardless of right or Justice. It is a dead law, without vitality, without Justice. As I look over the House of R., I see few, very few men here that the young men of today can safely pattern after.

No doubt Comstock's salacious exhibits, coupled with his odd-duck appearance and wrath-of-god demeanor, were a source of bawdy humor in the congressional cloakroom. But he was not criticized publicly – at least not by the politicians. They knew he was there at the behest of powerful benefactors. But more to the point, Comstock and his cause were useful to them.

When the zealous envoy from the New York YMCA arrived in Washington, the Capitol was in the midst of the greatest scandal yet to hit the city known for its intrigues and peccadillos. Allegations of bribery and influence peddling swirled around *Crédit Mobilier of America*, a joint-stock company organized to finance the building of the transcontinental railroad. The NEW YORK SUN had broken the story during the presidential campaign of 1872 that Congressman Oakes Ames had distributed shares of *Crédit Mobilier* stock to other congressmen, in addition to making cash bribes, in exchange for support of the Union Pacific Railroad. An investigation would later reveal that thirty members of Congress had received *Crédit Mobilier* stock. The scandal even touched Vice President Colfax, whose political career ultimately would be ruined by the association.

So when Comstock rolled into town in a flurry of righteous indignation carrying his great cloth bag of obscenities, the timing could not have been more perfect. As journalism professor Margaret Blanchard would write, in the midst of the *Crédit Mobilier* affair "Congress needed an issue that could help clean up its much tarnished reputation; Comstock's purity campaign was just the ticket." The country was also facing an industrial depression in the wake of Reconstruction, fueled by reckless speculation, inflation, and defaults on federal loans by the railroad and steel industries. All this made talking about smut a welcome distraction.

And so Congress acted quickly to deflect attention from its ethical lapses and real-world economic problems. Comstock's diaries from the time are filled with complaints about what he saw as the interminable delays by the legislators, but, even by the standard of the time, the bill's progression from introduction to passage was lightning-fast – less than three months elapsed from the time Comstock arrived in Washington before his bill became law.

After Congressman Merriam introduced the measure, there was virtually no floor debate and most members of Congress did not know what was in the legislation. It was one of 260 bills passed on March 3, 1873, the eve of President Grant's second inauguration, and it was combined with 15 other proposals that were adopted in a vote at 2 a.m. At one point, Congressman William Niblack of Indiana complained of the lateness of the hour and objected to further legislative action because "[s]ome members are sleepy" and "members are not [even] listening to what is said." An effort to send the bill back to committee failed by seven votes, and the measure passed despite the fact that, as Congressman Niblack observed, it is "now Sunday morning."

In fact, the Comstock Law and the bills to which it was attached *were* passed in the wee hours of Sunday morning, but the clock in the chamber was stopped to preserve the fiction that it was still Saturday night. Free-thought publisher D. M. Bennett described the scene as being "extremely discreditable to American legislation." He wrote that the bill was presented in the early morning "when within a few hours, and when the house was in the wildest state of confusion, and numbers of the members were under the influence of ardent spirits, some two hundred and sixty acts were hurried through without inquiry or consideration." In many instances, Bennett wrote, "even the titles of the bills voted upon were unknown to members," let alone their content. President Grant signed the newly passed bills "in the same hurried, reckless manner," affixing his signature as quickly as an attendant could hand him each one and without the slightest examination.

A LAW IS BORN

The achievement was astonishing. The bill was signed into law exactly one year to the day from when Comstock made his first high-profile "citizen's arrest" under local ordinances at two stationery stores in New York. Accompanied by a reporter from the *New York Tribune* and a police captain, Comstock had purchased books and pictures that he believed were obscene and promptly demanded the arrest of the culprits who had fulfilled his order. The haul in his net on that first day consisted of six employees, including two boys aged eleven and thirteen. One year later, with the stroke of President Grant's pen, Comstock gained official sanction for such police actions.

The new law was everything Comstock had hoped for. It provided that "[n]o obscene, lewd, or lascivious book, pamphlet, picture, paper, print, or other publication of an indecent character, or any article or thing designed or intended for the prevention of conception or procuring of an abortion, nor any article or thing intended or adapted for any indecent or immoral use or nature ... shall be carried in the mail." The cherry on top was that Comstock was designated a "special agent" of the Post Office Department, vested with the power to enforce the law and to seize offending items. On March 6, 1873 – one day shy of his twenty-ninth birthday – Comstock was given his postal commission which carried not just the power to arrest but also free passage on all rail lines that carried the mail.

Initial press reports indicated that the law's enactment had the intended political effect. The *New York Times* proclaimed that Congress should not be blamed for the *Crédit Mobilier* scandal because it had "powerfully sustained the cause of morality. ... These wretches who are debauching the youth of the country and murdering women and unborn babies, will soon be in the strong grip of government." Likewise, the *Journal of Commerce* of March 7, 1873, declared that "[s]omething will be forgiven to a Congress which thus powerfully sustains the cause of morality."

For his part, the tireless Comstock wasted no time in exerting his new authority. During his first ten months as a special agent, he traveled 23,000 miles in search of contraband. By December 1873 he had made fifty-five arrests and obtained twenty convictions under the new federal law. The following month the YMCA issued a confidential pamphlet to its supporters touting Comstock's success, reporting that those convicted under the law had been sentenced to an aggregate twenty-four years in prison and ordered to pay $9,250 in fines. But even more importantly, Comstock had seized and destroyed 134,000 pounds of books "of an improper character," as well as 194,000 obscene pictures, 14,200 pounds of stereotype plates, 5,500 indecent playing cards, 60,300 "rubber articles," and 3,150 boxes of pills and powders.

Over the years Comstock purported to keep detailed records of his conquests, meticulously cataloging the types of materials seized and destroyed, the numbers of people arrested and convicted, and even their nationalities. Near the end of his forty-two-year career as an anti-vice crusader, he claimed to have convicted enough people "to fill a passenger train of sixty-one coaches, sixty coaches containing sixty passengers each and the sixty-first almost full." He also took credit for destroying 160 tons of obscene literature and 4 million pictures.

In a 1915 interview with *Harper's Weekly*, just a few months before he died, Comstock provided more specific claims that even exceeded his colorful allusion to a trainload of literary convicts. He said he had arrested over 3,800 people during his career and had obtained guilty pleas or convictions in 2,881 cases, resulting in imprisonments "to the length of 565 years, 11 months, and 20 days" and fines amounting to $237,134.30. Another grisly aspect of Comstock's career was the pride he felt when he hounded adversaries to their deaths. He openly boasted of

causing at least fifteen suicides. After Comstock was gone, a final macabre accounting placed his career totals as suppressing 3 million pictures and postcards, 30,000
printing plates for books, 700 pictures that had hung in saloons, 3.5 million circulars,
88,000 newspapers with ads for "sexual materials," and 20,000 "figures and images."

But Comstock's success wasn't really reflected in these numbers. Most were
probably fabricated anyway, as his claims seemed to shift pretty randomly. This
suggested that the figures were less an actual exercise in accounting than a public
relations (PR) device. His flamboyant references to trainloads of criminals and
calculations of prison terms down to the number of days mostly were ploys to clothe
his claims in memorable, if somewhat questionable, specifics. Suffice it to say, there
were lots and lots of arrests and convictions.

RISE OF THE ANTI-VICE SOCIETIES

There was no denying Comstock's influence, as measured by the expansion of the
anti-vice movement generally and by the network of "mini-Comstock laws" that
were passed after the federal law was enacted. States passed legislation emulating the
new federal law, with twenty-four states adopting what were called "mini-Comstock"
statutes by 1885. By 1920, all but two states had passed such laws. Anti-vice societies
also sprang up across the country to emulate Comstock's formula for enforcing
moral purity. The New England Society for the Suppression of Vice, later to become
the Watch and Ward Society, was established in Boston in 1878. It was patterned
after his work in New York, and, within a decade, sister organizations sprang up from
coast to coast, in cities such as Philadelphia, Cincinnati, Louisville, Chicago,
St. Louis, and San Francisco.

But the first was the New York Society for the Suppression of Vice, also known as
"the Comstock Society." It was incorporated as an entity separate from the YMCA in
May 1873, just after the legislative victory in Washington. Comstock was appointed
its Secretary, and he finally was able to quit his day job as a dry goods salesman. The
same gentlemen who had formed the YMCA committee served as incorporators of
the new organization, and the list read "like a *Who's Who* of the day." Depending on
which account you read, the separation occurred either because the campaign to
suppress vice had grown to justify a separate organization or because some of
Comstock's methods were considered overzealous and the YMCA wanted some
distance from the fray. But one thing was beyond dispute: the incorporation (combined with the new law) brought with it expanded powers. The official seal of the
Society said it all: It depicted, on one side, a constable ushering a miscreant to jail,
and, on the other, a top-hatted Victorian gentleman stoking a large fire with
armloads of books (Figure 2.2).

The incorporation documents filed with the New York legislature provided that
"[t]he police force of the city of New York, as well as of other places, where police
organizations exist, shall, as occasion may require, aid this corporation, its members or

FIGURE 2.2 Official seal of the New York Society for the Suppression of Vice
Source: Public domain image from the National Postal Museum (https://postalmuseum
.si.edu/research-articles/all-bets-are-off/the-makings-of-a-crusader).

agents, in the enforcement of all laws which now exist or which may hereafter be enacted for the suppression" of vice. So Comstock was not just vested with federal authority as a postal agent; he had state and local police forces placed at his disposal. Two years later, when New York adopted its own "mini-Comstock" law, the legislation authorized agents of the vice society to be deputized and to "make arrests and bring before any court ... offenders found violating the provisions of any" state or federal obscenity law.

But while agents of the Society for the Suppression of Vice were to be "deputies," there was no question about who was to take the leading role and call the shots. The charter provided that the police "as occasion may require" will "aid this corporation, its members or agents." That is, the police were to act to serve and support the Society, not the other way around. After describing the task confronting them, Comstock wrote in the Society's second annual report that "[s]uch are some of the difficulties in the way of a speedy and complete suppression of this vice, showing conclusively that we must not trust to the ordinary officers of the law, and the police to deal with it." So as Comstock saw things, the police simply could not be trusted to stamp out evil. No, that task would fall to one man – a man on a mission. A mission from god.

SEX AND EMERGING LEGAL STANDARDS

When Congress adopted the Comstock Act, there was no established body of First Amendment law, much less cases that defined what was meant by obscenity. Obscenity was not a concept that was known to the Constitution's architects, although they were familiar with European censorship of sedition and heresy. No colonial obscenity laws existed at the time of the country's founding, and the framers of the Constitution rejected a proposal that the First Amendment's protections for freedom of speech and press be limited just to "decent" expression. Roger Sherman of Connecticut had proposed alternative language to James Madison's draft of what became the First Amendment so that it would protect only "rights . . . of Speaking, writing and publishing their Sentiments with decency and freedom," but this proposal was rejected in favor of the more expansive command that "Congress shall make no law . . . abridging the freedom of speech, or of the press."

This, of course, did not prevent Anthony Comstock from claiming to know what was in the minds of the Constitution's framers. "Where is the life, or property interest to debauch the morals of the young to be found in the Constitution?" he asked. He confidently asserted that "[n]o man will dare libel our forefathers by suggesting that even for one moment they dreamed such a claim could be made under their form of government." And he purported to know not only what the framers intended but also what they *should* have intended: "Had they suspected the barest possibility of such an outrage, they would have framed an iron-bound section to prevent it."

Comstock's certitude notwithstanding, it is impossible to know what the men who wrote the Bill of Rights might have done if they had debated the issue of obscenity. But it seems pretty clear that – unlike the great moralist – they would not have worked themselves into a lather over the dangers of "evil reading." These were educated, well-read people, who were quite familiar with "foreign literature," such as Ovid's ART OF LOVE and Henry Fielding's TOM JONES (both of which Comstock unsuccessfully tried to suppress in 1894). Morris Ernst, co-founder and former general counsel of the American Civil Liberties Union, went so far as to suggest that "[m]ost of the men who framed the Constitution were lovers of what today [in 1928] is deemed obscenity." The papers and diaries they left behind listed among their favorite writers Fielding, Sterne, and Smollett, leading Ernst to conclude that "[a]ll of the early Presidents enjoyed the frankness and vulgarity of fleshly novels." Ernst wrote that "[t]hose men who drafted our federal Constitution bulged their cheeks in naughty giggles when reading the works of Fielding or Sterne."

The nation's founders' affinity for salty language or bawdy tales was even more direct. Benjamin Franklin's 1745 letter *Advice to a Young Man on Choosing a Mistress*, his 1747 fictional story, *Speech of Polly Baker*, about a young woman put on trial for having an illegitimate child, or his impish 1781 essay on farting, entitled *A Letter to the Royal Academy at Brussels*, were just the sort of writings Comstock would later prosecute, but they hardly bothered our Constitution's framers.

The first obscenity cases in the United States did not occur until twenty-four years after the Bill of Rights was ratified. In 1815, Jesse Sharpless and two companions were charged in the Mayor's Court in Philadelphia with a common-law offense of circulating "an obscene painting, representing a man in an obscene, impudent, and indecent posture with a woman." Six years later, Massachusetts would bring the first US obscenity case involving a book, prosecuting a publisher for the novel FANNY

HILL. Although the book contains no coarse language, it is the memoir of a prostitute, and the court was scandalized. It declined to even enter a copy of the novel into evidence because, as the court explained, "said printed book is so lewd, wicked and obscene, that the same would be offensive to the court here, and improper to be placed upon the records thereof."

Because early American obscenity cases were scant and creatures of common law, Comstock had little domestic precedent to guide him as he launched his career against vice in all its forms – the hydra-headed monster, as he called it. But no matter, Comstock had little need of precedent, since he had god on his side. But as a Special Agent of the Post Office, he sometimes found it useful to draw on the law as well. And for that, he turned to (where else?) Victorian England.

England had adopted an Obscene Publications Act in 1857, also known as Lord Campbell's Act, which allowed material found obscene under common law to be seized and destroyed. An 1868 prosecution under that law in the case of *Regina* v. *Hicklin* would set that standard for obscenity, not just in Great Britain but also in the USA. Comstock quickly picked up on the *Hicklin* rule and successfully applied it in numerous prosecutions. It became the prevailing standard in American law for three-quarters of a century until the Supreme Court finally abandoned it in 1957 because of evolving First Amendment concerns.

In *Hicklin*, the publisher of an anti-Catholic booklet entitled *The Confessional Unmasked* was prosecuted under Lord Campbell's Act. He was convicted, but this was set aside on appeal. The matter then went to the Court of the Queen's Bench, which reinstated the conviction. In doing so, Chief Judge Cockburn laid down a definition of obscenity as anything that "depraves and corrupts those whose minds are open to such immoral influences and into whose hands a publication of this sort might fall." Under this broad definition of obscenity, a single tainted word or passage was enough to convict. The court was unconcerned with community standards or a book's literary merit. Nor did it matter whether the work as a whole was worthwhile. The *Hicklin* rule asked only "whether the tendency of the matter charged as obscenity is to deprave and corrupt those whose minds are open to such immoral influences."

Comstock enthusiastically embraced the *Hicklin* decision, calling it "one of the most remarkable cases on record." He cited it as justification for suppressing "the evil effect of certain matter, whether printed, written, engraved, drawn, or painted," and hinted that it was divinely inspired, claiming that the test was "laid down before our society ever started." Comstock took full advantage of Judge Cockburn's expansive legal reasoning, persuading American judges to apply it in case after case. Apart from the specific requirements of the legal test, such as what elements the government had to prove and what evidence would suffice to make a case, the sheer breadth of *Hicklin's* concept of obscenity was unbounded. It gave the government a free hand to enforce "morality," however that notion may be conceived. In some cases, judges would not even permit jurors to review the books themselves, holding that the titles alone were enough to support a conviction.

Obscenity is a difficult enough concept to grasp even when it is narrowed to "patently offensive" depictions of specified sex acts (as it later came to be in American law) along with other limiting requirements. A few years after the US Supreme Court stepped in to "constitutionalize" obscenity law in the late 1950s, Justice Potter Stewart cautioned that the Court was "faced with the task of trying to define what may be indefinable." But, he added – memorably, if not so helpfully – "I know it when I see it."

Anthony Comstock could say the same thing, except he saw obscenity *everywhere*. Unlike Potter Stewart, who in 1964 believed that obscenity encompassed only "hard core pornography" and who ten years later would abandon even that idea as unconstitutional, Comstock's law applied to all that was obscene, lewd, or lascivious, anything intended for the prevention of conception or for procuring an abortion, or anything "intended or adapted for any indecent or immoral use." Everything that Comstock considered immoral was – by definition – obscene, and therefore illegal. And his concept of immorality was very expansive indeed. In addition to "pornography," it included blasphemy, sensational novels and news stories, art, and even scientific and medical texts.

Comstock considered the danger of "evil reading" to be worse than yellow fever or smallpox. Which is to say, Comstock considered sex to be worse than deadly diseases because he saw sex (and the risk of masturbation) in everything. This danger even lay hidden as a trap for the young in newspaper accounts of crime or in stories about public speeches given by freethinkers. Such newspapers should be intercepted and destroyed, Comstock wrote, lest the stories breed "scoffers" of "the sweet influences of religion." He explained the connection to sex: "Remove the thought of the certainty of a final judgment or the existence of God from the mind of many youth, and you will have a bid for a life of self-gratification and sin."

He used similar logic to link pornography, contraception, and abortion. To him the equation was simple logic: Illicit images and stories cause temptation, which not infrequently leads to action, that is, sex. As Comstock put it, "infidelity and obscenity occupy the same bed." Contraceptives are then necessary to prevent pregnancy and to hide the fact of the extra- or nonmarital relations from public view. And if contraceptives fail, abortion then becomes necessary. So, in Comstock's twisted reasoning, porn equals dead babies. (This, by the way, is not unlike the logic of some opponents of same-sex marriage in 2015. A group calling itself "100 Scholars of Marriage" filed an amicus brief at the Supreme Court in *Obergefell* v. *Hodges* to argue that approval of gay marriage would be so disheartening to straights that it would lead to almost 600,000 children being born out of wedlock and an additional 900,000 abortions over a thirty-year period.)

The lax legal standard of the *Hicklin* rule enabled Comstock to make these lazy connections. Quite simply, he did not see prosecution of obscenity as raising any free speech concerns at all. Comstock maintained that he accorded "every man the fullest scope for his views and convictions. He may shout them from the housetop, or print them over the face of every fence and building for all I care. But the common law and statutes both declare he must do it in a decent and lawful manner or not at all." His assessment of the state of the law at that time was correct; there was no recognized constitutional limit on the government's authority to prescribe what was "decent and lawful." And this broad latitude was played out repeatedly, eventually culminating in both public and judicial reactions.

ATTACKS ON FREE LOVERS AND FREE THINKERS

Comstock's energies were devoted largely to stamping out anything related to sex, and it was not a narrowly defined concern. He viewed his mandate to stamp out "sin" quite broadly to include all that he saw as "ungodly," and he reserved a special wrath for those who questioned his religious convictions. Of "free lovers" and "freethinkers" Comstock wrote that "they loudly blaspheme the holy name of God, and seem to take especial delight in printing God, Lord, or Jesus Christ, commencing each with small letters." He was incensed that they "ridicule the Savior of mankind, and scoff at His teachings," while "what they intend leads directly to sin and shame." Accordingly, free thinkers were his natural targets, and to him indistinguishable from pornographers. In fact, to him they were worse – "more offensive to decency" and "more revolting to good morals" than pornographers because, in his mind, they "added hypocrisy to vice," and he used such terms as "infidel," "free luster," and "abortionist's pimp" interchangeably.

Of course, their real sin – in Comstock's view – was that they opposed him and his purity crusade. He wrote that "*no sect or class*, as a sect or class, has ever publicly sided with the smut-dealer, and defended his nefarious business, except the Infidels, the Liberals, and the Free Lovers" (his emphasis). Still, he did draw some distinctions. Of the levels of depravity, advocates of free love were the worst, and he wrote that they are "of course in their natural element, and I make no exception for them." As to "Liberals" and "Infidels," however, he observed that there "are many infidels who abhor this cursed traffic," and so did not include in his condemnation "that large class known as liberals, which includes the Unitarian, the Universalist, or the decent infidel, etc." The way to tell a "good" infidel from a "bad" one was by whether they wanted to overturn the Comstock Act, and he dubbed the latter group "the howling, ranting, blaspheming mob of repealers."

Whether Comstock actually believed that free-thought publications were obscene is debatable. Some have written that Comstock merely used obscenity allegations as pretext in order to close down publications that offended his religious sensibilities. But he explicitly linked the issues of obscenity and atheism in his Fourth Annual Report for the New York Society for the Suppression of Vice:

> The public generally can scarcely be aware of the extent that blasphemy and filth commingled have found vent through these [publications issued by free-lovers and

freethinkers]. Under a plausible pretense, men who raise a howl, about 'free press,' 'free speech,' etc., ruthlessly trample under feet the most sacred things, breaking down the altars of religion, bursting asunder the fires of home, and seeking to overthrow every social restraint.

Whatever Comstock may or may not have believed about the obscenity of free-thought publications, it is clear that he used prosecutions to crush political enemies and to settle personal grievances. And he was dismissive of the free speech arguments made by the freethinkers. Their advocacy certainly had nothing to do with the Constitution or freedom of speech, according to Comstock, because "[f]reedom to speak or print does not imply the right to say or print that which shocks decency, corrupts the morals of the young, or destroys all faith in God."

Comstock attracted attention early on by instigating obscenity prosecutions against advocates of women's rights and free love. Even before his triumph in Washington, DC, Comstock's name hit the front pages of the New York papers in late 1872 for his role in the obscenity prosecutions of the flamboyant sisters Victoria Woodhull and Tennessee Clafin. It was a mixed blessing for the emerging champion of rectitude, for he received at least as much scorn as praise for his efforts. But the episode inspired Comstock's demand for stronger federal legislation and catapulted him to a position of some prominence from which to continue his larger crusade. Opposition to advocates of free love and other unconventional ideas became a central tenet of Comstock's early campaigns, because he considered them utterly immoral and anti-Christian.

The Bewitching Brokers and the Hypocritical Preacher

If one were to conjure an opposite counterpart to Comstock's repressed religious fanaticism, it would be in the form of Victoria Woodhull. She personified everything he hated: Contrary to Biblical commands (and Victorian convention) that women should be chaste, silent, and homebound, Woodhull was a twice-divorced, outspoken woman who lived under the same roof with her then-current husband, Colonel Harvey Blood, and her former husband, Canning Woodhull. Victoria and her sister, Tennessee Clafin, had taken New York by storm after moving to the City in 1868, where, under the patronage of Cornelius Vanderbilt, they set up shop as the first women stockbrokers on Wall Street. Known as the "queens of finance" or the "bewitching brokers," Victoria and Tennie's exploits became instant tabloid fodder. The sisters often dressed alike in bold and fashionable clothes, and their feminine figures and garb garnered nearly as much press coverage as their unconventional lifestyles and controversial views. It also was reputed at the time that the widower Vanderbilt became Tennie's lover.

Woodhull was a candidate for president in 1872 on the Equal Rights ticket, and she was the first woman to testify before Congress – addressing the House Judiciary

Committee in 1871 on behalf of the Women's Rights Association. Her argument for women's suffrage was straightforward: No constitutional amendment was needed to accord women the right to vote because of the recently enacted Fourteenth and Fifteenth Amendments. She cited the text of the Fourteenth Amendment – that "no State shall make or enforce any law which shall abridge the privileges and immunities of citizens of the United States, nor deny to any person within its jurisdiction the equal protection of the law" – along with the provision of the Fifteenth Amendment – that no citizen shall be denied the right to vote "on account of race, color, or previous servitude." When asked by committee members how the "servitude" condition applied to women, Woodhull shot back to the laughter and applause of spectators, "servitude of the hardest kind, and just for board and clothes, at that."

Women had to wait another half-century to win the right to vote, with passage of the Nineteenth Amendment, but Woodhull's 1871 testimony was a landmark achievement that elevated her profile among American feminists. It also sowed the seeds of discord and jealousy among some in the women's rights movement who felt that more experienced (and respectable) representatives of the suffragist cause should have been the ones to address Congress. Established leaders, such as Susan B. Anthony and Elizabeth Cady Stanton, could only observe Woodhull's impassioned performance before the congressional committee. And while she won their initial praise for her testimony and oratorical skills, they distanced themselves from the energetic newcomer as they came to understand her more controversial views. In contrast to the staider advocates of women's suffrage, Woodhull was a radical firebrand who championed socialism, spiritualism, labor reform, the end of the death penalty, and the total emancipation of women. She argued that women should convene a constitutional convention and elect a new government if they failed to establish their full rights as citizens. To underscore the point, she proclaimed, "We mean treason!"

If this were not bad enough (from the perspective of the more conventional leaders of the women's movement), Woodhull's advocacy of free love tainted her with the whiff of scandal. She rebelled against the Victorian code by which women were to be the sexual property of their husbands, who had license to pursue dalliances outside the home. Accordingly, Woodhull argued for the "right of sexual determination," stating frankly that "[w]hen woman rises from sexual slavery to sexual freedom, into the ownership and control of her sexual organs, and man is obliged to respect this freedom, then will this instinct become pure and holy; then will women be raised from the iniquity and morbidness in which she now wallows for existence." Nor did she shy away from the logical implications of her philosophy. When challenged, she responded forthrightly in a November 20, 1871, speech at Steinway Hall: "Yes. I am a Free Lover. I have an inalienable, constitutional and natural right to love whom I may, to love as long or as short a period as I can; to change that love every day if I please, and with that right neither you nor any law you can frame have any right to interfere."

Victoria and Tennie propagated these and other radical views in their own tabloid, the *Woodhull and Clafin Weekly*. Among other things, the *Weekly* was the first American newspaper to publish Karl Marx's COMMUNIST MANIFESTO. And, along with the promotion of everything from spiritualism and sex education to vegetarianism, the paper was also used as a vehicle for skewering Victorian hypocrisy and settling scores. As if their lifestyles and radical views were not enough, it was this editorial mission of the *Weekly* that brought the sisters into direct conflict with Anthony Comstock.

The November 2, 1872, issue of the *Woodhull and Clafin Weekly* contained two articles that Woodhull intended to "burst like a bombshell into the ranks of the moralistic social camp." The first exposed a scandalous affair between the renowned pastor of the Plymouth Congregationalist Church, Henry Ward Beecher, and Elizabeth Tilton, the wife of his close friend (and parishioner) Theodore Tilton. In a lengthy and detailed account that spanned eleven and a half double-measure columns, Woodhull took on "the most famous man in America" and charged him with preaching one set of values while practicing another. Another story in the same issue was a tale of debauchery about a prominent businessman, Luther Challis. The article, written by Tennie, alleged that Challis had seduced two underage girls at an event called the French Ball and that he openly boasted about his conquest. It reported that Challis "to prove that he had seduced a maiden carried for days on his finger, exhibiting in triumph, the red trophy of her virginity." It also claimed that Challis had kept the girls in sexual captivity for days thereafter and that he shared them with numerous friends.

The issue of the *Weekly* caused an immediate sensation. Within hours of its publication, copies of the ten-cent tabloid were being sold for $2.50. The paper had a normal circulation of 10,000, but this edition sold 150,000 copies in a matter of days, and second-hand copies fetched as much as $40 apiece. It was indeed a bombshell, but Woodhull's intended targets were not the only casualties.

All of this was too much for Comstock, who was settling into his self-appointed role as a vigilante for purity and solidifying his connection with the YMCA. He first sought to bring an action in state court, but the prosecutor balked. So Comstock promptly arranged to have clerks from Beecher's Plymouth Church purchase copies of the *Weekly* specifying that they should be delivered by mail, thus invoking the jurisdiction of federal law. Comstock then secured a federal warrant to arrest the sisters through the United States district attorney for the Southern District of New York, who, as it turned out, was a Plymouth Church parishioner and friend of Reverend Beecher. Comstock personally went to Wall Street along with two federal marshals to see that the sisters were arrested, and the women were whisked off to the Ludlow Street jail, where they languished for weeks. Federal marshals also seized their press and office equipment, and destroyed 3,000 copies of the *Weekly*. Because of the arrest, Victoria Woodhull, the first woman candidate for President of the United States, spent Election Day in jail.

Their plight could not have been more serious – two women in America imprisoned for publishing a newspaper – yet, from the beginning, the prosecution had the air of a circus. The federal marshals insisted that the sisters sit on their laps on the ride to court, and the carriage attracted a growing procession of onlookers. And, of course, the press was as much interested in the sisters' appearance as it was the charges brought against them. The *New York Dispatch* on November 3, 1872, reported that the sisters were dressed alike in "plain dark suits of alpaca" and "hats of the most jaunty style"; that Tennie "is a pretty-looking young woman, round-faced, with well-cut features, and bright, animated expression," while Victoria "is rather more sedate in appearance, and of a less lovely turn." Although they were formally charged with obscenity, the assistant prosecutor described their offense as publishing "an atrocious, abominable, and untrue libel on a gentleman whom the whole country reveres," the Reverend Henry Ward Beecher. The *New York Herald* described the case as "the sensational comedy of free love."

But it was no laughing matter for the sisters, who sat in jail for four weeks before getting out on bail, which was set initially at $8,000 apiece (about $250,000 each in 2021 dollars). The bail was paid by a wealthy benefactor, but the sisters were subjected to repeated arrests and increasing bail demands – first by Challis on a libel claim, and then again by Comstock because they refused to cease selling their newspaper. Woodhull's husband, Colonel Blood, was also arrested, as were other workers at the *Weekly*.

Comstock even arranged to have federal marshals arrest Woodhull from the stage of a January 1873 Cooper Institute lecture entitled "The Naked Truth – Thirty Days in the Ludlow Street Jail," where she denounced the prosecution as a violation of freedom of the press. The marshals had tried to prevent Woodhull from speaking, but she evaded their stake-out by entering the hall dressed as an elderly Quaker woman. After taking the stage and dramatically casting aside her disguise, Woodhull delivered a fiery speech to a packed house, but was immediately taken into custody. All told, between the initial arrest in November 1872 and their June 1873 trial, the sisters and Colonel Blood were assessed $80,000 in bail. It was higher than the bail that had been set for Boss Tweed when he was put on trial for running Tammany Hall's corrupt political machine.

The legal proceedings were no less of a spectacle than the events that led to them. Court sessions were packed to capacity by crowds of people wanting to be the first to hear every salacious detail and to catch glimpses of the scandalous sisters. And an obliging press corps reported on what the *New York Tribune* called a drama that "has seldom been surpassed for filthiness of detail." Victoria and Tennie were represented by the flamboyant attorney William F. Howe, renowned for his flashy clothes, diamond rings, and courtroom theatrics. At the arraignment in front of a US commissioner, Howe cross-examined the complainant – Comstock – on precisely why the *Weekly* was "obscene." The veteran attorney probed the young crusader on whether he was a man "of a literary turn of mind" and invited Comstock to opine on whether the BIBLE's Book of Deuteronomy might also be obscene, as well as the works of Shakespeare, Byron, and Henry Fielding. Comstock's fumbling responses were roundly mocked in the press.

The case ultimately was dismissed at the end of June, with the judge ruling that the 1872 law under which the prosecution was brought applied to books, pamphlets, and pictures but not to newspapers or advertisements. It was a stinging defeat for Comstock, but his existing concerns about the narrow scope of the law were what had inspired him to lobby Congress for expanded authority. If the Woodhull case was a disappointment, it at least vindicated his efforts to change the law, so that malefactors in the future would not escape his grasp. But the newspapers were not quite so forgiving. The *Brooklyn Eagle* dubbed the case "An Inglorious Failure."

Some in the press attacked Comstock for making a federal case about what should have been a matter of local concern. The New York *Sunday Mercury* wrote of the prosecution that "[i]t does not seem right … that the whole machinery of the Federal Government, with its courts and marshals, should be placed at the beck of a man who has, somehow or other, chosen it for his private business to deprive this woman of her liberty." The paper condemned the proceedings as a "mockery" that would gratify no one "but him who, 'solitary and alone,' has set it in motion." The *Weekly Argus* of Easton, Pennsylvania opined that liberty of the press "is ours no longer when, in the opinion of any single person, the contents of a paper are not exactly moral or high-toned, and therefore should be suspended and its publisher imprisoned." And the Troy *Daily Press* condemned Comstock for striking "a dastard's blow at liberty and law in the United States."

None of this mattered to Comstock, who believed that he answered to a higher authority. As he had written earlier in his diary, "Jesus was never moved from the path of duty, however hard, by public opinion. Why should I be?" Besides, he still had the support of the good gentlemen of the YMCA and, by the time the Woodhull-Clafin prosecution collapsed, was now armed with his new federal law that would keep newspapers and advertisers from slipping through the cracks. And so he cranked up his jihad against all he considered unholy and impure.

The Crackpot Millionaire

Comstock's campaign of suppression specifically targeted those who sympathized with Woodhull and Clafin, including an eccentric (and likely insane) millionaire. George Frances Train had amassed a fortune while still in his twenties and had become an early supporter of Susan B. Anthony and Elizabeth Cady Stanton, as well as various radical causes. By any standard, Train was a most colorful character. His trips around the world inspired the Jules Verne novel AROUND THE WORLD IN EIGHTY DAYS, and on one of these journeys Train was offered the presidency of Australia. He ran as an independent candidate for US President, and later, declared himself dictator of a new government he wanted to form for America. Train knew of

Woodhull and admired her work, although he was leery of her free love position. But such concerns evaporated in response to Comstock's aggressive prosecution.

The forty-three-year-old Train was making a speech on the steps of a Wall Street bank when he learned of Woodhull's and Clafin's arrests. He immediately promised to help and became a frequent visitor at the Ludlow Street jail. In addition to moral support, Train decided he could best serve the cause by getting arrested himself and forcing a test case. So he published his own newspaper, called *The Train Ligue*, in which he reprinted some of the more sensational accusations from *Woodhull and Clafin's Weekly*, and later some salacious passages from the Old Testament under sensational headlines. He also demanded that publishers of the BIBLE be prosecuted for "disgusting slanders on Lot, Abraham, Solomon and David."

Federal authorities declined to prosecute the quirky tycoon, but Comstock would not countenance such impudent blasphemy, and he brought an obscenity prosecution in state court. There was no question but that Train could pay his bail, yet he refused to do so. Train maintained that he was guilty as charged, but that the law was an affront to freedom of the press. He wanted to plead guilty with the proviso that it was "based on extracts from the BIBLE," but the court declined to accept a conditional plea. So it appeared that he would get the trial he wanted. In the spring of 1873, as Woodhull and Clafin awaited their own trial, proceedings began in what the New York press playfully dubbed "the Train matinees."

Comstock appeared as chief witness for the prosecution, and his April 15, 1873, diary entry about the event dripped with disgust at what he perceived as the "free love" crowd in the courtroom. He described the women as "thin-faced, cross, sour-looking, each wearing a look of 'Well, I am boss,' and 'Oh, for a man.'" One might well wonder how these vile creatures could simultaneously show expressions of domination and submissiveness, but Comstock left such things to the imagination. And he was equally repulsed by the men, who he described as "licentious looking, sneakish, mean, contemptable, making a true man blush to be seen near them." "This," Comstock proclaimed, "is Free Love." Never mind that Train had never supported the free love cause and was on trial for blasphemy; to Comstock, it was all the same.

In the end, neither Train nor Comstock got what they wanted out of the trial. Comstock was shocked that the press seemed to favor the addled defendant and was put off by the scathing cross-examination by Train's counsel, who insinuated that Comstock had acted as a paid informer. Most importantly, the trial ended without a verdict – guilty or otherwise.

This bitterly disappointed Train in more ways than one. His entire purpose for insisting on a trial was to show the injustice of the law, but it came to nothing. Train was undone by his unconventional views and theatrical flair. After one session, in which he attended court accompanied by a woman bearing a silken banner that purported to be the rainbow flag of a new nation over which Train was to be dictator, the court appointed two doctors to examine the defendant to assess his sanity. He was declared "of unsound mind, though harmless" and the judge decreed that the obscenity trial should be halted and Train sent to an insane asylum in Utica. Amidst the pandemonium that erupted when the ruling was announced, Train stood up and demanded that the judge be impeached in the name of the people. This was to no avail, of course, and a frustrated Train was led from the courtroom in tears. But he was not institutionalized as the judge had ordered. Once outside, Train was left unattended, and he slipped away to board a ship bound for England.

Even though Train eluded Comstock's net, that fact did not prevent the crusader from continuing the prosecution through surrogates. In 1875 he prosecuted John Lant, the publisher of a New York-based free-thought journal called the *Toledo Sun*, for publishing, among other things, a humorous poem by Train entitled "Beecher's Prayer," which satirized the famed but compromised clergyman by comparing his illicit affair to a naval battle. The paper also ran a letter from a Dr. E. P. Miller that discussed physiological development. Comstock pounced, throwing Lant into the Ludlow Street jail for two months and leaving the publisher's wife and three children destitute. Lant was later convicted and sentenced to eighteen months' hard labor and a $200 fine. The ordeal broke the man's spirit and ruined his health, but it no doubt gave Comstock the satisfaction that had eluded him after the Train fiasco.

Cupid's Yokes

Comstock's pursuit and cruel treatment of John Lant was typical of his early campaigns against the "free lusters," as he called them. Another was his persecution of free love activist Ezra Heywood for his publication of a twenty-three-page pamphlet entitled *Cupid's Yokes*, which decried the strictures of matrimony and extolled the virtues of sexual freedom. A contemporary reader would be hard-pressed to find anything remotely sexual in *Cupid's Yokes*, apart from a clinical reference or two mentioning words like semen and coition. By most accounts it was nothing but a "dull little sociological treatise." The pamphlet was primarily a polemic against the institution of marriage (which it compared to slavery) and in favor of "sexual self-government." It also advocated gender equality and (gasp) equal pay for equal work: "[B]y excluding woman from industrial pursuits and poisoning her mind with superstitious notions of natural weakness, delicacy, and dependence, capitalists have kept her wages down to very much less than men get for the same work."

But the pamphlet was intentionally provocative, calling out Reverend Henry Ward Beecher for hypocrisy in committing adultery, and Comstock for despotism and cruelty. Heywood did not begrudge Beecher his affair with Elizabeth Tilton, but ridiculed him for his evasions and excuses. *Cupid's Yokes* maintained that while Reverend Beecher's "natural right to commit adultery is unquestionable, his right to lie about it is not so clear." Heywood wrote that the famous preacher's half-assed denials "sadly illustrate the pathetic penitence, the sniveling cowardice, and brazen-faced falsity with which 'great men' endeavor to appease, cajole, and defy equivocal public opinion." *Cupid's Yokes* credited Congress with good intentions for passing the Comstock Act, but maintained that the legislators "probably were unaware of the unwarrantable stretch of despotism embodied in their measure, and of the abuse which would be made of it."

But of Comstock himself, Heywood was not so forgiving. Citing the prosecutions of Victoria Woodhull, George Frances Train, and John Lant, he described Comstock as "a religious monomaniac, whom the mistaken will of Congress and the lascivious fanaticism of the Young Men's Christian Association have empowered to use the Federal Courts to suppress free inquiry." He called for immediate repeal of "the National Gag-Law." Heywood also quoted correspondence written by Comstock, in which the moralist had boasted of driving several publishers to their deaths, and concluded: "This is clearly the spirit that ignited the fires of the Inquisition."

There may have been nothing obscene about *Cupid's Yokes*, but to Comstock it was an all-out declaration of war. And it was a confrontation for which he spoiled. Comstock considered *Cupid's Yokes* to be "a most obscene and loathsome book" that was "too foul for description" and Heywood to be the "chief creature" promoting the "vile creed" of free love. Perhaps it was because Heywood was a former BIBLE school teacher who studied for the ministry at Brown University, or that he was an erudite man who was respected in his community that so incensed Comstock. Or maybe it was just the fact that Heywood publicly challenged him and his world view. Whatever the reason, Comstock prosecuted him three times for publishing and selling *Cupid's Yokes*. As D. M. Bennett put it, "Comstock made up his mind that Mr. Heywood must be crushed out and sent to prison."

As was his way, Comstock pursued Heywood relentlessly and arrested him personally. The first was on November 2, 1877, as Heywood and his wife spoke at the New England Free Love League at Nassau Hall in Boston. Comstock traveled from New York to Boston for the meeting, bought a ticket, and sat in the audience unrecognized as Heywood and his wife addressed the assembly. Comstock would later record the event in his book, TRAPS FOR THE YOUNG:

> I looked over the audience of about 250 men and boys. I could see lust in every face. After a while, the wife of the president (the person I was after) took the stand, and delivered the foulest address I ever heard. She seemed lost to all shame. ... Occasionally she referred to "that Comstock." Her husband presided with great self-complacency. You would have thought he was the champion of some majestic cause instead of a mob of free-lusters.

Comstock followed Heywood as he left the stage and arrested him in an anteroom, then, with angry audience members in pursuit, hustled his captive outside to a waiting carriage. "Thus, reader," Comstock boasted, "the devil's trapper was trapped." He charged Heywood for having sent through the mail *Cupid's Yokes* and a medical text entitled SEXUAL PHYSIOLOGY.

Heywood was convicted and sentenced to two years in jail and hard labor after a trial in which *Cupid's Yokes* had not been allowed to be admitted as evidence and most of the defense arguments were disallowed. The court looked only at the factual question of whether Heywood had placed the books in the mail. The district attorney maintained that the book was too "obscene, lewd and lascivious" to be placed on the records of the court, and selected passages were provided to jurors as they entered the jury room. Judge Daniel Clark barred Heywood's lawyers from discussing the purpose of *Cupid's Yokes* or the nature of obscenity, and he invoked the *Hicklin* rule – that the jury must convict if it found that any part of the work might tend to deprave or corrupt those into whose hands it might fall. Judge Clark further instructed the jury that if Heywood's ideas were followed, "Massachusetts would become a vast house of prostitution."

The conviction came as no surprise following such a kangaroo court, and Heywood's lawyers appealed on First Amendment grounds. But the appeal was held up, and ultimately rejected, after the Supreme Court in *Ex Parte Jackson* affirmed the federal government's authority to exclude immoral materials from the US mail. *Ex Parte Jackson* involved the mailing of lottery tickets, but the Court broadly reasoned that the First Amendment does not prevent denying mailing privileges for material "deemed injurious to the public morals." The New York Society for the Suppression of Vice annual report crowed: "This has long been a mooted question, and one from which the enemy has long drawn comfort, and now by their good service has been settled in our favor." Comstock took the ruling as complete vindication of his views and a renewed license to go after the likes of Ezra Heywood.

But not everything went his way. Heywood's conviction galvanized the opposition and generated the beginnings of an organized political response. The National Liberal League, which had been formed in 1876 to oppose the law, submitted a petition to Congress after the Heywood trial with 70,000 signatures seeking repeal of the Comstock Act. The petition advocated repeal to prevent the law from being used "to abridge the freedom of the press or of conscience." The effort was particularly galling to Comstock because it was spearheaded by Robert Ingersoll, the leading orator and freethinker of the day, who had strong political connections that extended even to the White House.

The effort initially had some momentum, but ultimately it failed. The petition was presented to the House Committee on the Revision of Laws by none other than Congressmen Benjamin Butler. As if any proof were needed that politicians can be on different sides of every issue, this was the same Benjamin Butler who had secured an invitation for Victoria Woodhull to testify on women's rights before the House Judiciary Committee in 1871, and the very same congressman who had made final revisions to the bill that became the Comstock Act. Now he was presenting a petition stating that the law had been "enforced to destroy the liberty of conscience in matters of religion, against the freedom of the press and to the great hurt of the learned professions." But, of course, true to his politician's nature (if to nothing else), Butler "presented" the petition without endorsing its substance.

Comstock saw the petition as a "deep-laid plot to break down the agents of this Society, destroy their good name, and prevent their further usefulness" that was hatched by a conspiracy of ex-convicts, liberals, and free-lovers. He called it a fraudulent effort that was "backed by one of the basest conspiracies ever concocted against a holy cause." And he was alarmed that "respectable papers lent themselves to the opposition by publishing injurious insinuations against the agent." But once again he prevailed. The House Committee briefly considered the petition, but ultimately affirmed the law's constitutionality, stating that "the Post Office was not established to carry instruments of vice, or obscene writings, indecent pictures, or lewd books." A similar petition was presented to the Senate Judiciary Committee, but no action was taken.

Another organization, the National Defense Association, which was formed to aid those prosecuted under the Comstock Law, organized an August 1, 1878, "indignation meeting" at Faneuil Hall in Boston, drawing nearly six thousand people to protest Heywood's conviction. The NDA was an offshoot of the National Liberal League, and was made up of those who demanded total repeal of the Comstock Law as opposed to more moderate reforms. The "indignation meeting" produced a petition to President Rutherford B. Hayes seeking executive clemency, which was granted in December 1878, six months into Heywood's sentence. The petition sought leniency in part because of Heywood's poor health, but Hayes believed that the free love advocate had not even violated the law. He wrote in his diary that he had no doubt but that Heywood was on the wrong side of the question, yet "it is no crime by the laws of the United States to advocate the abolition of marriage." And, far worse (from Comstock's perspective), the President did not consider *Cupid's Yokes* "obscene, lascivious, lewd, or corrupting in the criminal sense."

Comstock considered this exercise of executive clemency to be "inexplicable," and he believed that the pardon extended to "the most villainous law-breakers, who make it the business of their lives to corrupt and destroy all that is lovely and of good report, and who openly boast of their crimes." He was particularly disappointed that the President "pardons this man on the petition of Infidels and liberals, free lovers and Smut dealers." He wrote in his office blotter that "[t]his action of Pres. Hayes practically licenses the sale of *Cupid's Yokes*, and is a strong encouragement for others to violate the law, as well as a great hindrance to the further enforcement of the law." The setback, however, was short-lived. Courts continued to find *Cupid's Yokes* to be obscene, and the well of political capital for further presidential pardons ran dry.

This freed Comstock to pursue Heywood in other cases, which led to additional arrests and prosecutions. In 1883, Comstock charged Heywood with violating the federal obscenity law, this time not just for selling *Cupid's Yokes* but also for reprinting in his magazine, *The Word – Extra*, two of Walt Whitman's poems from LEAVES OF GRASS: "A Woman Waits for Me," and "To a Common Prostitute." Heywood was also charged for publishing in *The Word* an advertisement for a contraceptive device, puckishly called the "Comstock Syringe." Heywood ultimately was tried only on the count involving the advertisement and the jury acquitted him. But Comstock nevertheless achieved at least part of his objective. The experience persuaded Heywood not to tempt fate, and he ceased publishing contraceptive advertisements in *The Word*, lest he be arrested again.

But this precaution proved to be insufficient. Comstock arrested Heywood shortly after the acquittal and again in 1887, but the judge in the first instance dismissed the case, and in the other the charges were dropped by the US attorney. Heywood was arrested again in 1890 (this time by the New England Watch and Ward Society) for sending issues of *The Word* through the US Mail. The offending articles included a series entitled "A Woman's View of It," penned by Angela Heywood, the defendant's wife, in which she advocated a woman's right to control her reproduction and sexuality; a letter entitled "A Physician's Testimony," which discussed oral-genital sex; and another letter from a mother discussing sex education for her children. In particular, Ms. Heywood defended the use of frank language, advocating the widespread use of such terms as "fuck," "penis," "womb," "semen," and "vagina." This time the jury convicted Ezra Heywood, who was by now sixty-one, and he was sentenced to two years' hard labor. No presidential pardon was forthcoming this time, and Heywood served all but two months of his sentence.

Heywood was often ill during his imprisonment, and he died a year after his release. An obituary in the publication *Secular Thought* blamed Comstock for "relentlessly hound[ing]" Heywood and causing his early death. "Mr. Heywood's premature death," the article read, "must be laid at the door of this man," Anthony Comstock, "who will in the future be classed with murderers."

The Truth Seeker

Comstock did not stop with Heywood but expanded his campaign to include those who supported the author of *Cupid's Yokes* and/or opposed the New York Society for the Suppression of Vice and its culture war. This naturally included DeRobigne Mortimer Bennett, who had been prominent in the petition drive to repeal the Comstock Act and who published the leading free-thought journal of the day. D. M. Bennett had run weekly appeals for signatures in *The Truth Seeker*, his tabloid devoted to "science, morals, free thought, free discussions, liberalism, sexual equality, labor reform, progression, free education and whatever tends to elevate and emancipate the human race." It is fair to say that Bennett was known at least as much for the things he opposed, and that long list included "priestcraft, ecclesiasticism, dogmas, creeds, false theology, superstition, bigotry, ignorance, monopolies, aristocracies, privileged classes, tyranny, oppression, and everything that degrades or burdens mankind mentally or physically." That is to say, Bennett was naturally opposed to everything Comstock stood for. And Comstock returned the sentiment in spades, calling Bennett the "ringleader in this fraud" of seeking repeal, and his newspaper "the mouthpiece of these moral cancer planters."

Bennett had publicly pledged to submit the repeal petition to Congress shortly after the first of the year in 1878. So it surprised no one that Comstock was moved to arrest Bennett in November 1877. The timing was as suspicious as the charges were spurious. Bennett was arrested for publishing his essay entitled "An Open Letter to Jesus Christ" and for a scientific article (written originally for *Popular Science Monthly*) by one A. B. Bradford, "How Do Marsupials Propagate Their Kind?" It is hard to tell what offended Comstock more – Bennett's opposition to the obscenity law or his outspoken atheism. His letter to Jesus Christ mocked religion, listed sexual (and other) crimes of "villainous" popes, excoriated the Inquisition, criticized the shallowness and hypocrisy of contemporary churchgoers, and ultimately asked the rhetorical question: "In a few words, is not Christianity as known and practiced in the world, a cheat, a fraud, a costly and expensive luxury which mankind could well spare, losing nothing by its rejection?" To Comstock, such views were "most horrible and obscene blasphemies," and he complained that Bennett's idea of liberty "is to do and say as he pleases without regard to the rights, morals or liberties of others."

Comstock's distaste for Bennett and his views caused him to overreach. Even by the standards of the time, the idea of prosecuting a publisher for obscenity for criticizing the Christian religion or for a scientific paper describing the mating habits of possums and kangaroos simply was too much. That, essentially, was the argument that Robert Ingersoll made to the Postmaster General when he interceded on Bennett's behalf: *"Are you serious?"* Ingersoll wrote to ask whether the United States really intended to prohibit such works from the mails, and if so, stated his intention to defend Bennett "not only in the U.S. Courts, but before the country as well." As a consequence, the case was hastily dropped in early January 1878 notwithstanding a grand jury indictment. It didn't hurt that Ingersoll had campaigned for President Hayes in 1876.

This only stoked Comstock's hatred of Bennett, and strengthened his resolve to put the "old infidel" in the dock. That anyone could support such a vile creature as Bennett was incomprehensible to Comstock, who asked in his 1880 book FRAUDS EXPOSED whether "in all Christendom, a more despicable character can be found, or a better representative of that ranting mob [of repealers], than this scoundrel Bennett?" Comstock devoted five long chapters of his score-settling tome to his fight against obscene literature and the efforts to repeal his law, paying special attention to Bennett, Ingersoll, and other "pestilent fellows" who had joined in a "monstrous conspiracy" to undo his divinely inspired law. In particular he saw Bennett as a "liberal-obscenity-martyr" and a "special pet of Ingersoll," who was nothing but a "foul-mouthed libertine" and an "apostle of nastiness."

The feeling was more than mutual. Bennett devoted a chapter of his lengthy book THE CHAMPIONS OF THE CHURCH: THEIR CRIMES AND PERSECUTIONS to Comstock under the title "Anthony Comstock, His Career of Cruelty and Crime." Of his adversary he wrote: "This man has evinced the disposition of hatred and cruelty that a few centuries ago would have made a first-class Torquemada, Calvin, Alva, Charles IX, or Matthew Hopkins." He set forth the details of many of Comstock's cases (including his own) that he wrote were characterized by prosecutions based on decoy letters, false testimony, and entrapment. He labeled these efforts "the American Inquisition," and asked "whether the Church has ever had a cruel zealot in its employ who has labored with more resolution and zest" than Comstock. And he persisted in his efforts to repeal the Comstock Law.

Even worse, Bennett lampooned some of Comstock's wealthy patrons, including Samuel Colgate, a founding supporter and president of the New York Society for Suppression of Vice. Colgate had even accompanied Comstock to Washington in 1878 to lobby against the repeal petition. In *An Open Letter to Samuel Colgate*, Bennett charged the industrialist with hypocrisy because advertisements for Colgate's product Vaseline suggested that it could be used as a contraceptive when combined with salicylic acid. Colgate's company was embarrassed and withdrew the advertisements, and for years afterward freethinkers boycotted its products on principle. The false claim that Vaseline could act as a birth control also left a legacy not just of embarrassment but of unwanted pregnancies.

It was only a matter of time before Comstock would again have Bennett in his sights, and, in some ways, Bennett made it easy for the anti-vice crusader. As Ezra Heywood sat in the Dedham, Massachusetts jail for publishing *Cupid's Yokes*, Bennett defiantly sold a copy of the pamphlet at a convention of liberals in Watkins, New York, and was arrested under state law. Although Bennett was not particularly sympathetic to Heywood's free love views, he wanted to put the Comstock Law to the test, noting that the pamphlet "was not written to excite passion, but to elicit thought." So he upped the ante, pledging in the pages of *The Truth Seeker* to send *Cupid's Yokes* to anyone who wanted it. Of course, Comstock took him up on the offer. Writing under the fictitious name of G. Brackett, the undercover moralist ordered several tracts, including "a copy of the Heywood book you advertise Cupid's something or other, you know what I mean."

To Comstock's great satisfaction, Bennett was convicted and sentenced to thirteen months' imprisonment and hard labor. Bennett mounted a spirited defense – in many ways this was the test case he sought. But he was hamstrung by the prevailing legal standards of the day. His attorney, Abram Wakefield, had tried to persuade the court to adopt a new test for assessing obscenity, in which words or images would not be considered indecent or obscene when used "in good faith, in social polemics, philosophical writings, serious arguments, or for any scientific purpose, and are not thrust forward wantonly, or for the purpose of exciting lust or disgust." He also argued that the work should be considered as a whole, and not just based on portions the prosecutor selected to read to the jury. His arguments presaged the standard that the Supreme Court ultimately would adopt in the mid-twentieth century. But for Bennett, mired in the law of the Victorian period – and caught in Comstock's clutches – they were of no avail.

The court followed the practice of the Heywood case and found that the work *Cupid's Yokes*, for which Bennett had been arrested, was "so lewd, obscene and lascivious, that the same would be offensive to the court here, and improper to be placed on the court records." Trial proceeded based on the passages of the book marked by the prosecutor, which were read to the jury. Assistant District Attorney William P. Fiero was every bit as inclined as Comstock to see that the entire work was purged because it had "dirty" parts. But he didn't want the jury to get distracted by the fact that Comstock had procured his evidence using decoy letters. So he told the jurors, "this case is not entitled 'Anthony Comstock against D.M. Bennett.'" No, he said, "it is the United States against D.M. Bennett, and the United States is one great society for the suppression of vice." For its part, the court instructed the jurors to disregard Comstock's obvious hatred of Bennett. It told them it made no difference "whether Mr. Comstock has hostile feelings against this man or not. ... The prosecution is not his. It is the prosecution of the United States."

In the end, the court rejected Bennett's attack on the constitutionality of the Comstock Law, holding that "[f]reedom of the press does not include freedom to use the mails for the purpose of distributing obscene literature, and no right or privilege of the press is infringed by the exclusion of obscene literature from the mails." And it expressly adopted the test for obscenity from *Regina* v. *Hicklin* that asks "whether the tendency of the matter is to deprave and corrupt the morals of those whose minds are open to such influences, and into whose hands a publication of this sort may fall." That is, the material is considered obscene "if it would suggest impure and libidinous thoughts in the young and the inexperienced." The conviction, inevitable under this standard, was upheld on appeal.

As before, Bennett's supporters mounted a campaign seeking executive clemency. After all, it had worked for Heywood, and Robert Ingersoll had successfully headed off Comstock's initial attempt to prosecute the publisher of *The Truth Seeker*. The National Liberal League petitioned President Hayes for a pardon, and Bennett's counsel and friends boasted that a pardon would be granted within ten days. It made sense to think they could pull it off, as the petition reportedly garnered 200,000 signatures. What's more, President Hayes had pardoned Ezra Heywood for distributing *Cupid's Yokes*, and Attorney General Charles Devens had opined that the pamphlet, although undesirable, was not obscene. How could Bennett possibly be imprisoned for the same crime for which Heywood had been pardoned?

The answer, of course, was to be found in Anthony Comstock's dogged determination to see that Bennett was punished. "I went immediately to Washington and saw the President," Comstock later wrote. He found the President to be "a thoroughly upright man" who "desired to know *facts*." He argued that Heywood's earlier pardon had been a mistake and that "[h]e was pardoned because facts were suppressed." But as to Bennett, Comstock had a secret weapon: He brought with him a bundle of indiscreet letters Bennett had written to a young woman who was not his wife. This did not sit well with Hayes, who was known to be religious. This appeal to the President (and to the President's wife) helped turn the tide, and Hayes denied the pardon petition.

That Comstock capitalized on Bennett's supposed indiscretion was more than a little ironic. He devoted a chapter of his book FRAUDS EXPOSED to what he called Bennett's "infidelity and obscenity," referring to letters he said exposed the publisher's unsuccessful attempts to "obtain control of the person of a young woman who touched his fancy and who had been induced to accept a salaried position in his office, evidently under the design, on his part, to obtain her consent to become his mistress." Comstock quoted at length from an article about the matter published in the *Religio-Philosophical Journal* of September 25, 1878, and said that the journal provided "a long list of letters too foul to reproduce here," but nevertheless printed a number of extracts that he said provided "evidences of this man's character." Of course, Comstock did not mention the Beecher-Tilton affair, or the fact that, a mere six years earlier, he had been instrumental in the prosecution of Victoria Woodhull and Tennessee Clafin for exposing Reverend Beecher's *successful* infidelity.

But the irony (and hypocrisy) of Comstock's tactics did nothing to help the aging Bennett, who nearly died in jail. Bennett's wife unsuccessfully implored the President to cut short the term because of Bennett's deteriorating health, but Hayes stood firm. Bennett survived to serve his full sentence, sending monthly dispatches to *The Truth Seeker* all the while, and friends and supporters celebrated his release from Albany Penitentiary in 1880 with a large reception at New York's Chickering Hall. Bennett died two years later and was memorialized with a monument reading "The Defender of Liberty and Its Martyr."

ATTACKS ON ART AND LITERATURE

Anthony Comstock didn't know much about art, but he knew what he didn't like. Throughout his career, the crusader took on literary figures, playwrights, artists, gallery owners, and a skeptical press because, as he put it, "Art is not above morals. *Morals stand first.*" But Comstock's determination to impose purity on the world of art and literature presented him with one of his toughest challenges. In this realm he was not just attacking those he could marginalize as representing the fringes of society – the "free lusters" and the free thinkers. Here, he had to contend with notions that art was a product of high culture and had patrons among the upper classes. So this tension pitted his innate prudishness against some in the social class that had bankrolled his crusade. Although Comstock tried to accommodate that tension, more often than not priggery won out.

Comstock's inexhaustible supply of sanctimony played best when he was rounding up the rabble. He attracted his initial support from the wealthy gentlemen of New York's YMCA for clearing the streets of back-alley pornographers and their fellow travelers among the lower classes, focusing special attention on the threat of recent immigrants. As he wrote in the Second Annual Report for the New York Society for the Suppression of Vice, "[i]t will be seen at a glance that we owe much of this demoralization to the importation of criminals from other lands. Of the 48 persons found in this traffic [of obscene materials] during the year [1875], but 17 were Americans." Years later he would still maintain that foreigners were a principal source of obscenity, and he believed that, by keeping track, he could "help thoughtful men to realize what we are up against, and sound an alarm call for the future" and to help "keep undesirable classes from our shores."

Like the dry goods clerk that he once was, Comstock kept inventory in the Society's annual reports not just of the number of arrests made and books seized but also of the nationalities of those apprehended. In its first three years of operation, the Society's records showed that nearly one-third of those prosecuted were Irish, although the numbers Comstock reported rose and fell as the source of the waves of immigrants changed over time. In 1875, 20 percent of Comstock's arrests were of Irish suspects, while this number declined to 2.5 percent by 1910. At the same time, as immigration from Italy increased, so did Comstock's arrests of Italians, amounting to 10 percent of his prosecutions in 1910. After that, immigrants (and arrestees) from Russia and Austria-Hungary picked up, so that a quarter of Comstock's prosecutions in 1915 represented these nationalities. Through it all, Comstock's unabashed xenophobia grew unchecked. His reaction to George Bernard Shaw's use of the derisive label "Comstockery" was typical: "I never heard of him in my life. Never saw one of his books, so he can't be much," he told the *New York Times*, referring to Shaw as some "Irish smut-dealer."

Comstock's attack on Shaw fizzled because his act did not play as well when he targeted art and literature favored by the upper classes. It was one thing to prosecute a free love advocate like Ezra Heywood because he happened to include work by Walt Whitman in his cursed publications, but it was quite another to go after Whitman directly. So, as he tried to clean up the art world, Comstock was forced to adapt his wrath-of-god message to the more nuanced circumstances. He argued that he had no intention of restricting legitimate art or literature – he just wanted to prevent its being "prostituted" to the lower classes. This did not blunt Comstock's efforts or diminish his enthusiasm for the task, but it did affect some of his tactics and his rationalizations.

For his part, Comstock was convinced that the artistic merit of a book or painting made matters worse, as he explained that "'art' and 'classic' are made to gild some of the most obscene representations and foulest matters in literature, regardless of their results to immature minds," and because "[m]any 'classical' writers, as the word goes today, have gained fame by catering to the animal in man, expending high genius in their efforts to deify this 'companion of every other crime.'" He called reproductions of French paintings "a foreign foe," and proclaimed, "[i]n the guise of art, this foe to moral purity comes in its most insidious, fascinating and seductive form."

In Whitman's case, Comstock was convinced by his failed initial prosecution of Heywood that he might not succeed if he tried to prosecute the poet directly. Yet he was convinced that LEAVES OF GRASS and other such works were obscene and merely "an attempt by an author of our own time to clothe the most sensual thoughts, with the flowers and fancies of poetry, making the lascivious conception only the more insidious and demoralizing." Comstock told reporters in 1882 that he would move to suppress LEAVES OF GRASS if he found it on sale in New York, but he ultimately declined to do so, perhaps to avoid the embarrassment of a high-profile loss at his home base. But he wrote to allies in the New England Society for the Suppression of Vice (which had just rebranded as the Watch and Ward Society) and from behind the scenes persuaded them to take action. The Boston group in turn leveraged its contacts with the local district attorney to pressure Whitman's publisher, James R. Osgood and Company, to drop its plans to release a new edition of the book. Whitman had the last laugh, though – he took his work to a publisher in Philadelphia and enjoyed phenomenal sales because of the controversy. The first printing in Philadelphia sold out in a single day, and Whitman reportedly said, "The Boston fools have already made me more than $2,000."

The Fifth Annual Report for the New York Society for the Suppression of Vice in 1879 included a section on what Comstock described as "a new issue" – the defense of obscenity using the veneer of classic literature. Such works, he wrote, "heretofore carefully concealed from public view, and kept by booksellers only to meet what some consider to be the legitimate demand of the student, or the gentleman's library, are now advertised and sold by certain parties as 'rich, rare and racy' books, 'amorous adventures,' 'spicy descriptions,' 'love intrigues on the sly,' etc." Such things may "have their proper and legitimate spheres" where "they are safe under the law," Comstock wrote. But they are "clearly illegal when they are so prostituted from what has heretofore been thought to be their proper and legitimate place."

So there it was: the upper classes (like some of his patrons) could keep their expensive, leather-bound racy stories in their gentlemen's libraries, but the rest of society would be quarantined. Of course, this did not suggest that Comstock was willing to accept classic literature as legitimate. He only recognized what *"some consider to be"* legitimate uses of such books, and he generally referred to classics of this sort in quotation marks. This pragmatic compromise merely illustrated Comstock's calculation that he would lose important support if he tried to ban literary works for all. But his personal revulsion for the subject matter was evident from his writings. "Unlike wine," Comstock wrote, "age does not improve the character and effect of this class of literature." As always, he was alert to what he saw as corrupting foreign influences such as "French and Italian novels, translated in popular and cheap forms," which he saw as "little better than histories of brothels and prostitutes, in these lust-cursed nations."

Comstock found it "absurd" to think that because "scenes are beautifully transferred to canvas or clothed in flowery verse or elegant prose, that their power for evil is lessened." And he could not imagine "why the filthy side of life, or the reeking imaginings of ancient writers, should be served up in beautiful form, woven out of the choicest rhetoric, or drawn in lines of beauty by minds especially endowed with highest attainments." To him, it was all just poison, and he believed that the "death-dealing powers of strychnine are the same whether administered as a sugar-coated pill or in its natural state." As he wrote in an 1891 essay, "Garbage smells none the less rank and offensive because deposited in a marble fount or a gold or silver urn. So these foul stories and unclean tales of ancient writers find no justification in the moral world simply because clothed in smooth verse or choice rhetoric."

Comstock was not impressed when works of Ovid, Boccaccio, and Balzac were defended as classics. In his 1883 book TRAPS FOR THE YOUNG, for example, he wrote that THE DECAMERON should be confined to educational institutions and "gentlemen's libraries." He conceded that the book's one hundred tales swapped between young Florentines during the time of the Black Death (including some satirical pokes at the Catholic Church) "has become part of our literary inheritance from the fourteenth century, and was considered a text-book of pure Italian of that age." But he cautioned that it must be treated "like a wild beast" and prevented "from breaking loose and destroying the youth of this land." Additionally, in a nod to his upper-crust supporters, Comstock proclaimed that "the suppression of non-genuine and cheap editions of Boccaccio's book ... should be sanctioned by every decent citizen." Thus, "gentlemen's libraries" would not be disturbed.

Comstock's acknowledgment of THE DECAMERON as a classic was grudging at best, and came with significant reservations. He observed that "literary men of all ages regard it as obscene and indecent," and claimed that Boccaccio himself repented before he died and warned the youth of Florence against reading his own works. More to the point, Comstock quoted at length from an unnamed scholar he described as "a master of English literature" for the proposition that THE DECAMERON "is simply an English book made from a filthy Italian book," and that only the Italian original could properly be considered a classic. Even if his position was based on a strategic need to compromise, this was Anthony Comstock at his most broad-minded. And it was a tiny, tiny space, indeed.

This was evident in his attacks on some of New York's finer art galleries. In November, 1887, Comstock seized 117 photographic reproductions of living French artists from the Fifth Avenue Gallery of Herman Knoedler, many of which had been displayed in the Paris Salon. The Knoedler Gallery, which catered to the rich and famous until it was closed by an art forgery scandal in 2011, had already become an established cultural institution for four decades before Comstock staged his raid. But the crusader proclaimed that "Fifth Avenue has no more rights in this respect than Centre Street or the Bowery." The controversial arrest was covered widely in the press and condemned in a statement issued by the Society of American Artists. The Society defended the gallery, proclaiming that "the study of the nude is necessary to the existence of any serious art" and that "the popularization of such works of art by photography [is] of the greatest educational benefit to the community." It declared the seizure of artworks "the work of incompetent persons" and denounced the action as "subversive to the best interests both of art and morality."

This kind of criticism stung Comstock. He was accustomed to attacks from his usual foes among freethinkers, free-lovers and some in the press. But the Knoedler raid galvanized opposition from prominent artists, public intellectuals, and respectable organizations. Concerned because some of the major newspapers had joined in condemning him, Comstock and the New York Society for the Suppression of Vice issued a tract entitled *Morals Versus Art* to explain his theories of aesthetics and censorship. True to form, Comstock claimed his action was necessary to keep what he saw as lewd materials "out of reach of the rabble." The nude in art "is not necessarily obscene, lewd, or indecent," Comstock wrote (once again displaying his hidden liberal leanings), but photographs of artistic works are another matter altogether. Such photographs "are a curse" because they "appeal to passion, and create impure imaginations." There was no contradiction here, according to Comstock, because the artist's conception "may be chaste, sweet and free from lewd posture or expression in the original painting" but when presented as a photograph "is transformed." The painting, "with its sweet harmony of blended colors and tints, is one thing to the cultured mind: but the cold reality of black and white in the photograph, where the nude figure is placed prominently before the eyes of the uncultured, is, in character and effect a very different thing."

Just as with literature, Comstock believed that his role was to serve as a guardian of public morality whose mission was to prevent artistic works from falling into the "wrong" hands. His professed goal was to keep any representation of nudity confined to galleries where it belonged and not on the open market "for all classes to gaze upon." Truth be told, Comstock seemed deeply troubled by any artistic representations that involved nudes. Such things, he wrote, "fan the flames of secret desires." But he crafted a public position that would ease tensions with his patrons. If the "wild beast" of classic literature could be kept in captivity in gentlemen's libraries, then the siren song of titillating art could be confined in galleries. Comstock's argument may not have been entirely consistent or true to his core beliefs, but it served the interests of his wealthy benefactors.

Comstock received considerable flack because of his forays into art censorship. When a court found that most of the photographs seized at Knoedler's gallery were not obscene, the *New York Times* was not alone in suggesting that perhaps the powers of "professional hunters after indecency" like Comstock should be reduced because his judgments about art were wrong 94 percent of the time. Comstock was described as a "moral scavenger," who, while perhaps performing a useful function, should not try to set himself up as "a censor of public morals" lest he become "a social nuisance almost as pestilent as that which he exists to abate." The *New York Evening Telegram* responded to the Knoedler raid by reproducing on its front page sketches of the artwork Comstock seized. Believing that the news articles were obscene, but not wanting to proceed on his own, Comstock asked District Attorney Randolph Martine to submit the matter to a grand jury. But Martine would have none of it, and instead released Comstock's letters and his response to the press. A *Life* magazine cartoon in 1888 depicted Comstock arresting an artist for depicting a woman almost totally submerged in a stream with the rebuke: "Don't you suppose I can imagine what is under the water?" (Figure 2.3).

Such critiques irritated Comstock but did nothing to persuade him that he was wrong. As biographers Broun and Leech observed, they forced him to become "more articulate than ever before" and to issue public defenses of his actions. Hence the release of *Morals Versus Art*. But "he was not dissuaded from his campaign against the arts." It was a theme to which he would return throughout his career.

FIGURE 2.3 Comstock cartoon "That Fertile Imagination"
Source: www.eden.eraudica.com/single-post/2018/08/22/Comstock-Era-20—The-Modern-Sex-Shame-Cycle.

In 1906 Comstock decided to make an example of the Art Students' League because he believed that the League was too free in distributing nude images to the public through its journal, *The American Student of Art*. Based on a complaint from a mother who said she found the artwork depicting nude figures to be "highly indecent," Comstock and his assistant went to the League's offices to arrest the person responsible for what he described as "influencing 60,000 young girls annually to turn to lives of shame." But as it was a warm August day in New York in the days before air conditioning, with most of its members out of town to avoid the heat, Comstock settled on arresting Anna Reibley, a nineteen-year-old bookkeeper who handed him a copy of the journal. He charged her with "giving away, showing, offering to give away, or having in her possession a certain obscene, indecent, filthy, and disgusting book." Comstock also seized and eventually destroyed somewhere between 2,500 and 3,650 copies of the League's pamphlet.

Comstock's adoring biographer Charles Trumbull described the raid on the Art Students' League and the prosecution of Ms. Reibley as being "the only course open to the Society in the administration of the law against a public menace." After all, Trumbull observed, it was "a plain violation of the postal laws" to send out pamphlets with drawings of nude figures made by amateurs "indiscriminately and by the thousands, apparently to people of all sorts whether known to be lovers of art or not." The young woman's arrest was justified, he wrote, because Comstock's assistant could not locate "any man who could be held responsible," and besides, Ms. Reibley was giving the pamphlets away free "to anyone who happened to call for them." Evidently, it wasn't just the postal laws that were offended.

Once again, Comstock's actions were greeted with outrage and scorn. The *New York World* published a front-page photo of Comstock, the "vice chaser," alongside photos of the Venus de Milo and the Apollo Belvedere, suggesting that he would arrest them if they were to venture outdoors. The *World* ran a half page of cartoons lampooning Comstock the day after the raid. For its part, the Art Students' League hanged a fat effigy of Comstock outside its third-floor window on West 57th Street, and students caricatured the old man "whenever they could find space on a wall for a sketch." This time public condemnations of Comstock were both more pointed and widespread. The unfortunate bookkeeper was a particularly sympathetic victim, and newspapers and magazines across the country hotly debated the case. As the case progressed, images of Comstock filled the newspapers and magazines, and most of the coverage was unflattering, with even *Life* magazine getting in on the fun. Reaction by the European press was even more scathing, calling America "the laughingstock of the world" and describing the raid on the Art Students' League as "idiotic officiousness" and "preposterous pruriency."

The case against Ms. Reibley fared almost as badly at trial as it had in the court of public opinion, and Comstock was attacked on the official record as being a "degenerate" and "blind to the beauties of life." After an unfavorable evidence ruling, Comstock offered to drop the prosecution if the court would authorize him to destroy the copies he had seized of *The American Student of Art*. The court didn't officially take him up on this offer, but dismissed the case on New Year's Eve 1906 after the League's lawyer cut a backroom deal to allow destruction of the journals.

Although Comstock was forced to make a tactical retreat, he nevertheless got what he wanted – the suppression of the offending work. And the board of the Art Students' League, not eager to repeat the experience, voted to discontinue publication of *The American Student of Art* even before the trial began. Comstock may have had to endure a torrent of criticism, but this was nothing new for him and it did not affect his attitude. His response to the Art Students' League controversy was the same as it had been nearly three decades earlier after the Knoedler's raid: "Such a work of art shut up in a salon or studios is one thing, but such a work of art prowling around in the public street or in the home where it may suggest impure thoughts, is another thing. Wild animals are all right in their cages, but when they break out, they must be suppressed." Monsters from the id, indeed.

Toward the end of his career in 1913, Comstock had the same reaction to Paul Chabas' masterpiece, *September Morn* (Figure 2.4). Noticing the work displayed in the West 46th Street window of Braun & Company, Comstock stormed into the

FIGURE 2.4 Paul Chabas' "September Morn"
Source: Wikimedia Commons (1913), from cover of sheet music for "September Morn [I'd Like to Meet Her]" (https://commons.wikimedia.org/wiki/File:September_Morn_ (I%27d_Like_to_Meet_Her).pdf).

gallery and demanded that the offending work be removed immediately. The old man was unimpressed that the Chabas painting had been awarded a medal of honor at the Spring 1912 Paris Salon, and he commanded a startled shop clerk named James Kelly to "take her out at once!" The *New York Times* reported the ensuing exchange in a tongue-in-cheek front-page account on May 11, 1913:

> Kelly looked his surprise.
> "The picture of the girl without any clothes on," Mr. Comstock said.
> "But that is the famous September morning," Kelly explained.
> "There's too little morning and too much maid," Comstock said severely. "Take it out."

When Kelly asked the visitor what authorized him to say what should be in the window, "Mr. Comstock threw back the flap of his coat, displayed his badge of office, and identified himself." Comstock busied himself perusing other works in the gallery as Kelly got the hook to remove the picture. Upon spying Jean Francois Millet's *Goose Girl*, he told the clerk, "[I]f you ever put that picture in the window I'll confiscate your whole stock."

Of the painting itself, the *Times* reported that the subject of *September Morn* was "quite unconscious that her undraped loveliness was offending." Braun & Company's manager ordered *September Morn* returned to its place of pride in the window once he learned what had happened and pledged "I will keep it on display if I have to spend the value of my entire stock in contesting the point with Mr. Comstock." The gallery kept the painting in its window a week longer than its usual practice, awaiting a return visit from the crusader, but Comstock never showed up. It finally removed the picture, the manager explained in a letter to the *Times*, because the crowds around the display window kept paying customers from entering the shop.

Even when he was not going after "high culture," some of Comstock's attacks on art could backfire badly. He threatened to have the commissioners of the 1893 Chicago World's Fair indicted for "keeping a disorderly house" because the Midway attractions included hoochie-coochie dancers who performed under the name Little Egypt. Upon witnessing the show, Comstock declared it to be "the most outrageous assault on the sacred dignity of womanhood ever endured in this country." He demanded the commissioners put a stop to it or else "[t]he whole World's Fair must be razed to the ground." Of course, the Fair, officially known as the Columbian Exposition to celebrate the 400th anniversary of the voyage of Columbus, did not come to an end because of Comstock's high dudgeon. While he managed to secure a nonunanimous report condemning the attraction from the Fair's committee of "Lady Managers," no further action was taken. The incident generated some bemused news coverage, and Thomas Edison filmed performances of the dance at his Black Maria Studios – performances that can be viewed on YouTube to this day.

ATTACKS ON MEDICAL LITERATURE AND CONTRACEPTIVES

Comstock did not confine his campaigns to suppressing lewd art or works of fiction. To him, anything even remotely connected to sex was a potential "devil trap." Medical information in particular could be a threat, because knowledge of the human body and its workings could inspire impure thoughts. Thus, one of his early prosecutions was against a popular marriage manual entitled DR. ASHTON'S BOOK OF NATURE AND MARRIAGE GUIDE, which was sold by many reputable booksellers. Comstock's objection was that the book dealt with sexual anatomy. In this regard, his reaction to medical literature was much the same as it had been to fine art: Supposedly scientific writings on sex by "a few indecent creatures calling themselves reformers," he wrote, were even "more revolting to good morals" and "more offensive to decency" than the smut he suppressed. To the end of his days the old crusader professed that his actions did not affect the work of "legitimate" doctors. In an interview just before he died, Comstock insisted that "no reputable physician has ever been prosecuted under these laws."

But his grim record showed otherwise. Comstock equated obscenity with medical writings with any connection to sexuality, no matter how remote the connection to actual sex. How else could he have prosecuted D. M. Bennett for reprinting a scientific article on the mating habits of marsupials? Thus, Comstock targeted a Dr. E. C. Abbey of Buffalo, New York, who specialized in treating sexual diseases. Abbey, aware of the risk of publishing anything on such a sensitive subject as maladies affecting the sexual system, first submitted his manuscript to the local US attorney and other legal authorities who found nothing amiss. But Comstock felt that "nothing treating upon the sexual part of our being should be allowed to pass freely to the masses," so he induced Abbey to send a copy through the mails and then promptly arrested the physician for obscenity. Abbey was convicted and given a light sentence, although it was never carried out.

An even more prominent victim of Comstock's wrath was Dr. Edward Bliss Foote, a physician who in 1858 published a popular household medical guide entitled MEDICAL COMMON SENSE. Through his book and other publications, such as FOOTE'S HEALTH MONTHLY, Dr. Foote sought to make medical information more widely and democratically available. Appalled at the health problems caused by unwanted pregnancies, uninformed methods of contraception, and botched abortions, Foote believed that women should be able to control their own sexuality and so provided information on birth control in his publications. Of course, such views did not sit well with Comstock.

Like many of Comstock's adversaries, however, Dr. Foote drew Comstock's ire as much (if not more) for his political views as for the writings for which he was prosecuted. Foote's advocacy of sexual liberation of women and birth control was bad enough, but probably more offensive to Comstock was the fact that Foote had been the only one to oppose his 1872 legislative proposal to the New York assembly for an obscenity law. This made it inevitable that the zealous Puritan would look for a chance to pounce. That opportunity presented itself in January 1876 when Comstock ordered a copy of a Foote pamphlet entitled *Words in Pearl*. It described in detail four different types of birth control devices (including "membranous envelopes" – condoms made from fish bladders) and offered them for sale. As was his usual practice, Comstock obtained a copy of the pamphlet using a decoy letter and arrested Foote.

At his trial, Foote was not allowed to enter his pamphlet as evidence, as the judge was convinced that there was no need to send medical works through the US mails. In rejecting the defense claim that such a reading of the Comstock Act would prevent doctors from sending sensitive medical information by mail, the court explained that it saw no great inconvenience that would arise if that were the result, as doctors had other ways of communicating with their patients. It reasoned that if Congress had intended to exempt doctors' medical advice from the obscenity law, it would have said so, and if the law were interpreted otherwise, it would "afford an easy way of nullifying the law." Given such rulings from the bench, the jury took only twenty minutes to return its verdict – Foote was convicted and fined $3,500.

Dr. Foote responded to the conviction by removing information about contraception from his publications (although some suggest that he just became more subtle about it). But the experience made him an implacable foe of Comstock's efforts, as it did his son, Edward Bond Foote, also a physician. The sales of his popular medical texts bankrolled the organized opposition to the Comstock Act. This resulted in a considerable war chest, as it was estimated that he sold 300,000 copies of his popular home guide MEDICAL COMMON SENSE between 1858 and 1876. The father and son physicians have been called "free speech's greatest philanthropists," and for that Comstock deserves the credit (or the blame, depending on your outlook). But such was the reaction to Comstock's excesses. The senior Dr. Foote had advocated repeal of the Comstock Act by working with the National Liberal League. He and his son later helped form the National Defense Association, which continued to call for the law's demise and provided assistance to those prosecuted under the law. They would later be influential benefactors for the Free Speech League, which continued to wage battles for freedom of expression in the early twentieth century.

Comstock's attacks on medical literature and practitioners were far from discriminate, but he devoted special attention to anything that had to do with birth control. After all, the federal law that bore his name not only prohibited publications "of an indecent character" but banned the mailing of "any article or thing designed or intended for the prevention of conception or procuring of an abortion." Accordingly, in 1873 alone he arrested thirty-five people for advocating contraceptives and secured twenty-five convictions. From the start of his career to its bitter end, Comstock exhibited particular tenacity in his attempts to stamp out contraceptives.

Once an "offender" was in his sights, Comstock would go to every effort to mete out his vision of justice. Such was the case with Dr. Sara Blakeslee Chase who advocated health reform through lectures and a journal, *The Physiologist*. Dr. Chase, a distant relative of Supreme Court Justice Salmon P. Chase, provided information on birth control and, as part of her medical practice, performed abortions. She and Comstock were legal adversaries for more than two decades, beginning with her 1878 arrest for selling "a certain article … made of India Rubber and sponge." A first grand jury unanimously voted not to indict the lady physician, and Comstock urged District Attorney Benjamin K. Phelps to raise the matter once again with a different panel. When Phelps refused, Comstock presented the matter to another grand jury on his own and obtained an indictment, but Phelps still declined to prosecute.

Dr. Chase then went on the offensive, having Comstock apprehended for false arrest, but charges were dropped without a formal hearing. In response, Comstock arrested Chase for selling a vaginal syringe, but once again the district attorney declined prosecution. Dr. Chase later served time in prison after a failed abortion resulted in a patient's death. But after resuming her medical practice in 1899, Comstock had Chase arrested the following year for selling a syringe. As before, the grand jury cleared her of the charge.

Dr. Chase's experience with Comstock's fanaticism was no anomaly. Morris Sieckel sold Comstock a condom in May 1872, only to find that the professional moralist was willing to pursue him to the ends of the earth to ensure that this "crime" was punished. The charge was initially thrown out under the previous federal law. But after Comstock secured passage of his new and improved obscenity law in 1873, he moved to rearrest Sieckel at his new location in Bridgeport, Connecticut. After securing a warrant, Comstock traveled to New England to make the arrest, only to find that Sieckel had left for New York. Comstock seized the suspect's manufacturing plant and his goods, but was more determined than ever to get his man. He tracked Sieckel's movements to Montreal, and then later to Detroit, Chicago, St. Louis, and finally to New Orleans. With a handful of warrants from far-flung locations, Comstock saw Sieckel arrested just in time for Mardi Gras. But his quarry was sprung from jail on a writ of habeas corpus issued by a sympathetic state court, and federal marshals released the suspect. Comstock then learned that Sieckel was planning to escape on the steamer *Juanita*, scheduled to stop in Cuba on its way to Philadelphia. For whatever reason, Sieckel did not disembark in Havana, and Comstock arrested him at the port in Philadelphia. Comstock got his conviction, and Sieckel was sentenced to a $500 fine and a year in prison.

HIS LAST HURRAH

Comstock's final case arose from his pursuit of pioneering feminist Margaret Sanger. As the founder of organizations that became Planned Parenthood and originator of the term "birth control," Sanger came to Comstock's attention in 1914 by advocating the broad dissemination of information about contraceptives and publicly opposing his law. Sanger wrote in the radical journal *The Woman Rebel* of the need for access to birth control and how the law prohibited "the imparting of information on this subject." She concluded, "Is it not time to defy this law?" The subject matter of the journal alone seemed calculated to inflame Comstock, dedicated as it was to the emancipation of womankind and acknowledging "No Gods or Masters." And so it did. Alarmed at the direct attack, Comstock approached Postmaster General S. Marshall Snowden and persuaded him that the publication was obscene. The federal government promptly declared *The Woman Rebel* unmailable under the Comstock Act, and secured grand jury indictments against Sanger for publishing indecent articles and for incitement to murder and riot. The first issue of *The Woman Rebel* was suppressed, and the May, July, August, September, and October issues were not just deemed unmailable; they were confiscated.

Rather than prepare a defense against a law that Sanger believed to be unconstitutional and that was being enforced "to destroy the liberty of conscience and thought in matters of religion and against the freedom of the press," she instead devoted her time to writing a new pamphlet, *Family Limitation*. Sanger had 100,000 copies of the small pamphlet distributed to factories and mines throughout the country. Comstock – predictably – was horrified, and he described *Family Limitation* as "contrary not only to the law of the State, but to the law of God." As he vented to one reporter at the time, "Are we to have homes or brothels? Can't everybody, whether rich or poor, learn to control themselves?" Just as predictably, Comstock prepared to arrest Sanger for this fresh affront, but before he could find her, she escaped to England using a Canadian passport. As she would later write, "not desiring to fritter away my time by these legal annoyances, which sap one's strength and unfit one for any useful work, I decided to take an indefinite postponement and left for London."

This, however, did not deter Comstock, who had an assistant show up at the art studio of Sanger's husband, William, purporting to be a friend who was interested in translating *Family Limitation* into several languages and distributing copies to the poor. Sanger at first demurred, but, after the caller became insistent, he looked for a copy "as a special favor to a friend of his wife." He managed to find a copy in Margaret's desk, which he gave the visitor. Within minutes, the man returned with Comstock, who promptly arrested Sanger. Comstock was as much revolted at Sanger's bohemian lifestyle as he was the pamphlet, noting in the New York Society's annual report that Sanger "lived separate from his family with many artists in the house."

The trial was tumultuous, to say the least. The courtroom was packed, with more than a hundred would-be spectators struggling to get in. Many prominent advocates of anarchism and socialism attended, including Alexander Berkman and labor activist Elizabeth Gurley Flynn, later a founding member of the ACLU. Sanger gamely defended himself, but had little chance in a three-judge bench trial in which the presiding judge would declare that the pamphlet was "awful," and who offered his "personal opinion" that "[i]f some of these women who go around advocating Women Suffrage would go around and advocate women having children, they would be rendering society a greater service."

For his part, Comstock spent much of the trial in shouting matches with Sanger and his supporters, and he accused Margaret Sanger of being "a heinous criminal who sought to turn every home into a brothel." At one point Sanger accused Comstock of mounting the prosecution only as a ploy to locate his wife, claiming that the anti-vice crusader offered him a suspended sentence if he would give up her location. Comstock loudly denied it, and fired back, "Well, I have been told that if I prosecuted this case I would be shot. I have disregarded the threat."

Judge McInerney denied Sanger permission to mount a defense based on freedom of speech and, in the end, agreed with the prosecution that *Family Limitation* was indecent, immoral, and a menace to society. As Comstock was leaving the witness chair, the judge leaned over the bench and told Sanger that he would have preferred sending him to prison but had decided only to fine him instead. After the court pronounced a sentence of "$150 or thirty days in the City Prison," Sanger shouted, "It is indeed the law on trial here today," adding, "I will never pay that fine. I would rather be in jail for my conviction than to be free at a loss of my manhood and self-respect." "Then," Judge McInerney responded, "you will go to jail." The courtroom erupted with shouts and hand-clapping. The *New York Times* reported that "[m]en and women stood on the benches and waved their hats and handkerchiefs." The red-faced judges stood up as well, and "[t]he gavel of the Chief Justice went on pounding, which

FIGURE 2.5 Anthony Comstock Source: Getty Images.

only marked time for the din in the room." Court attendants seized Sanger and "hustled him through the door to the pen and the Tombs." Police and courtroom personnel then struggled to clear the crowd into the corridor.

It was a victory for Comstock, but a pyrrhic one. Although a jail sentence was a heavy price for Sanger to pay, it was far short of the one-year imprisonment and $1,000 fine that could have been imposed. What's more, the trial did nothing to reduce circulation of *Family Limitation*, and likely had the opposite effect. Even as the trial was ending, there was discussion of raising $1,000 to publish a new edition of the pamphlet that would include a full account of the trial. And a reporter interviewed "a very small and young woman" at the courthouse who confessed to having circulated many copies of the pamphlet among her classmates and who asserted that further efforts to stop such circulation would be futile, for "as fast as one circulator was arrested[,] another would step forward and take his place."

Comstock (Figure 2.5) was worn down by the ordeal, and the day after the Sanger trial ended, the old man took to his bed with acute pneumonia. He never recovered. Comstock would live another ten days, bedridden, rallying only briefly to dictate some notes to a stenographer from the New York Society. But it was the end, and on September 21, 1915, the old crusader died. His *New York Times* obituary attributed his death to overwork and overexcitement resulting from his fight to retain his position "and from his successful efforts to convict William Sanger."

3

Comstock's Legacy: A Dilemma Is Born

By almost every measure, Anthony Comstock was an incredible success. It is arguable that no one person before or since has affected American culture so profoundly. Within a year of starting his vigilante campaign against obscenity, he had won the support of the most powerful men in New York and persuaded Congress to pass an anti-obscenity bill that would remain on the books nearly a century and a half later. And it was a law that he enforced personally. Most states followed the lead of federal law based on reform movements led or inspired by Comstock. Art historian Amy Werbel was not exaggerating when she wrote that his literary preferences "served for forty years as the national line between virtue and vice."

Through his knack for self-promotion, Comstock also became a national celebrity whose exploits were followed in the press as avidly as showman P. T. Barnum and boxing champ John L. Sullivan. Legendary journalist H. L. Mencken described Comstock as "more than the greatest Puritan gladiator of his time; he was the Copernicus of quite a new art and science." It was Comstock who "first capitalized moral endeavor like baseball or the soap business, and made himself the first of its kept professors." He was "the best known of the urban vice fighters of his day" and "the foremost policeman of private vices in America's Gilded Age." *Harper's Weekly* wrote that the name Anthony Comstock is known not just "all over the country" but "over most of the civilized world."

Upon his death, mourners called Comstock a fallen "soldier of righteousness," and the *New York World* dubbed him "the most spectacular crusader against vice that America has known." The *New York Times* ran a front-page obituary describing Comstock as a person "known the world over through the controversies that have followed his crusades against books, pictures and plays that he deemed indecent." And the *Times* praised him editorially as a "benefactor and hero" who "served a good cause with tireless devotion." Pulitzer Prize–winning biographer Carl Van Doren wrote that Comstock had earned a place in history "along with other amazing Americans like Barnum, Brigham Young, John L. Sullivan, Jesse James, Billy the Kid and Carrie Nation," and, although the man himself was gone, it was said that

"Comstockery goes on forever, always trying to organize a conspiracy of silence against certain of the major concerns of mankind." And yet, what is his true legacy?

WHAT DOES WINNING LOOK LIKE?

Would anyone suggest that American society embraces the Victorian values that Anthony Comstock devoted his life and his prodigious energy to preserving? Hardly. Even a sympathetic biographer observed that all the gains have been completely reversed in virtually every endeavor that occupied Comstock's long career – from trying to outlaw most discussions or depictions of sex, his opposition to contraceptives and abortion, and his horror at the notion of "modern marriage." If he could be revived and transported from the grave to today's America, the old crusader would find his worst fears confirmed and he would conclude "that he now stood in a very different country" in which courts and legislatures "have already given their blessings to fornication, adultery, pornography, contraception, easy divorce, abortion, and sodomy." It is easy to imagine that Comstock's head would explode at the mere mention of gay marriage.

The Supreme Court's 2015 decision striking down state restrictions on gay marriage in *Obergefell* v. *Hodges* would have left Comstock aghast and sputtering. Imagine his reaction to Justice Kennedy's soaring rhetoric:

> The nature of injustice is that we may not always see it in our own times. The generations that wrote and ratified the Bill of Rights and the Fourteenth Amendment did not presume to know the extent of freedom in all of its dimensions, and so they entrusted to future generations a charter protecting the right of all persons to enjoy liberty as we learn its meaning. When new insight reveals discord between the Constitution's central protections and a received legal stricture, a claim to liberty must be addressed. ... This analysis compels the conclusion that same-sex couples may exercise the right to marry.

Say *what?* New insight? A claim of liberty for what he believed to be the basest perversion? In Comstock's mind, truth was eternal and dictated by a Christian god. And it was this god-given mandate that must determine what the Constitution means – then and for all time. Not even Justice Scalia's intemperate dissent, in which he wrote that if he had signed on to Justice Kennedy's opinion "I would hide my head in a bag," could touch how Comstock would have reacted. That the Supreme Court could embrace this notion of liberty would have shown Comstock that the world was upside down and his failure was complete.

But Comstock's legacy is far more complex than just the failure of his own personal objectives and his long-term vision of a "pure" America. No, in many ways he is a principal source of the censor's dilemma. His dogmatic and inflexible insistence that the government has a divine mandate to censor anything even remotely related to sex forced free speech advocates to sharpen their constitutional reasoning for extending First Amendment protection, and those arguments eventually prevailed. His vociferous campaigns, such as the one against the Artists' League in New York and against belly dancers on the Midway Plaisance of the 1893 Chicago World's Fair, made him a frequent target of political cartoonists, and his face became the buffoonish image of censorship. Margaret Sanger wrote: "There is nothing which causes so much laughter or calls forth so many joking comments by people in Europe as Comstockery in America." Of course, she penned those words while safe in England at a time when her husband faced trial in America for handing out one of her pamphlets. But as Comstock's power to inflict punishment waned and eventually disappeared, the clownish aspects of his crusade were what people remembered.

Free speech scholar and advocate Marjorie Heins observed that "the historical image of Anthony Comstock is more comic than threatening." This judgment of history is harsh – and remarkable – given the vast power that Comstock wielded and his influence on American culture during his career. Yet even in his lifetime, Comstock became "a myth, a symbol, a personified reductio ad absurdum," wrote John Collier, a cofounder of the National Board of Censorship (which regulated motion pictures at the time). Upon Comstock's death in 1915, Collier wrote that the great crusader was "the whipping boy of present day public opinion." For most who still remember him, Comstock continues to perform that role.

This view of Comstock was crystalized in an anecdote involving an event that supposedly took place in 1873, shortly after he was appointed postal inspector. One rainy day, Comstock was almost run down by a wagon as he was crossing lower Broadway in Manhattan. The enraged reformer reportedly thrust his badge under the horse's nose and shouted, "Don't you know who I am? I'm Anthony Comstock!" Biographers Broun and Leech wrote that the incident involved a mail wagon, so "the horse was, in a sense, his subordinate. So, from the first, many a mail clerk smarted under the reprimands of this irascible superior."

Stories like this are so preposterous that they seemingly can't be true. But with Comstock, it is hard to separate the real from the apocryphal. In March 1888, the *New York Times* gleefully reported a prank played by Princeton University students when Comstock came to give a lecture on campus. Concerned that "nothing should be allowed to remain in such a state as to offend his well-known ideas of art and morality," puckish undergrads glued red flannel pajamas to "the lower limbs" of a statue known as "The Gladiator" so that "the wind might not visit [those parts] too roughly." The university was forced to enlist the aid of the local fire department, at considerable expense, to remove the garment. Earlier that year, *Life* magazine published a cartoon by Charles Dana Gibson entitled "A Scene in the Moral Future" (Figure 3.1) that depicted a time when Comstock's influence caused even horses, dogs, and birds to wear trousers.

Throughout his career, the humorless crusader proved almost impossible to parody, for he outdid even those who would ridicule him. In 1895, Comstock was

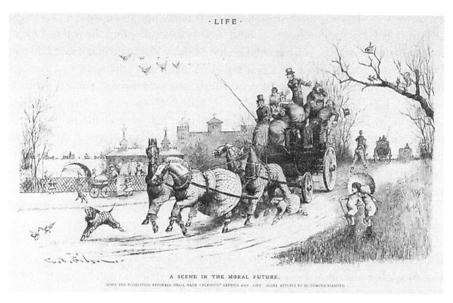

FIGURE 3.1 Charles Dana Gibson's "A Scene in the Moral Future"
Source: Art Institute of Chicago (www.artic.edu/art-works/129269/a-scene-in-the-moral-future-from-life).

seen on Brooklyn trains personally pasting black patches over parts of advertisements for an exhibit at the Metropolitan Museum of Art. He had been unable to get the advertisements removed, so he took it upon himself to cover the offending parts of artworks he considered to be lewd. Other passengers were amused by Comstock's actions, the *Times* reported, and the advertiser was thrilled by the notoriety. Self-aware Comstock was not. In recounting his outrage to a *New York World* reporter about Little Egypt's provocative dance at the 1893 Columbian Exhibition, Comstock drove home his point by trying to imitate her performance. The correspondent wryly recounted that Comstock "wreathed his arms over his head and made his ginger-colored side-whiskers shiver in the air," and when the stout old man tried to bend back like the supple young Egyptian dancer, he almost fell over on his sofa. The reporter described the display as "interesting," but added – unnecessarily – "not at all libidinous."

   Cartoonish episodes like this, combined with Comstock's overheated rhetoric and his whole-hearted embrace of the censor's mandate to enforce morality, ultimately caused even sympathetic observers to question his legitimacy and to recoil from the label "censor." What to Comstock had been the source of his greatest pride – serving as the arbiter of pure and wholesome literature – eventually would become to most Americans an embarrassment. H. L. Mencken observed that "Old Anthony ... believed his idiotic postulates as devotedly as a Tennessee Baptist believes that a horse-hair put into a bottle of water will turn into a snake" and that years of "gargantuan endeavor made him one of the national clowns – and his cause one of the national jokes." Mencken concluded that "the old imbecile" "did more than any other man to ruin Puritanism in the United States" and that he "liberated American letters from the blight of Puritanism." Mencken summed up Comstock's accomplishments as "at best, laughable," and "at worst, revolting." After Comstock, it became increasingly difficult, and is now virtually impossible, for an American organization overtly to claim censorship as its avowed purpose.

Yet, even now, Comstock has his defenders, primarily among his people: cultural conservatives and religious fundamentalists. A recent animated feature celebrating his career is entitled *Anthony Comstock: Fighter*. It is marketed not as a cartoon but as a "moving comic," which is a more accurate description, as it combines voice-over narrative with panned shots of still comic book images. *Fighter* purports to tell "the adventurous true story of how one godly man almost single-handedly fought the battle for national purity . . . and won." Produced for children, it is the origin story of a "godly moral hero." There are no superheroes, it informs its young audience – no super-strong saviors sent from dying planets, no mutants bitten by radioactive spiders, and no quirky inventors in iron suits of armor – just righteous men who put Biblical lessons in action. The story focuses on a teenage Comstock, whose exploits include saving his community from rabid dogs and avaricious saloon-keepers.

Anthony Comstock: Fighter takes its title from an adoring 1913 biography written by Reverend Charles Gallaudet Trumbull, editor of *The Sunday School Times* from 1903 to 1941, and its stories are drawn from a 2013 reissue of the old biography under the title OUTLAWED! HOW ANTHONY COMSTOCK FOUGHT & WON THE PURITY OF A NATION. The editor's preface from the new edition maintains that "Comstock was exactly right," and that the anti-vice crusader "succeeded in just about every aspect of his campaign for purity; he dramatically curtailed the pornography industry, and nearly eliminated both abortion and contraception."

But such opinions are far from the current mainstream, where "free speech" is generally considered to be good and "censorship" bad – at least in the abstract. Even Comstock is not permitted to defend himself in his own words without an overlay of the shame now attached to his profession. Reprints of his books now come with disclaimers on their *covers*, no less. A 2009 edition of Comstock's FRAUDS EXPOSED explains on its dust jacket that the New York Society for the Suppression of Vice "sounds like the satirical invention of a modern wag, but it was a very real organization dedicated to policing public morality in the late 19th century." While for most books, such blurbs are devoted to praising the book's contents, this one describes Comstock's work as "a relic of American Victorian-era prudery" that "makes for wickedly amusing reading today."

Likewise, a 1967 reissue of Comstock's 1883 book TRAPS FOR THE YOUNG reproduces on its front cover a 1915 cartoon from *The Masses* that depicts an older Comstock dragging a wretched young woman into court by her scruff. He tells the judge, "Your Honor, this woman gave birth to a naked child!" (Figure 3.2). The book also reprints a number of notable political cartoons that lampooned the crusader and his causes, and it reproduces a series of satirical exchanges from an 1884 issue of *Life* magazine purporting to collect donations for "The Comstock Polar Fund." Its objective – to send Comstock to the North Pole to start a Society for the Prevention of Ice. Robert Bremner, editor of the volume for Harvard University Press, noted that, while ardent admirers memorialized Comstock as a modern Galahad, the "more sober view" was that Comstock "both embodied and caricatured the moral sense of his epoch."

A CULTURAL SEA-CHANGE

The fact that the title "censor" has fallen into disfavor does not mean that the interest in censorship itself has waned – that impulse remains as strong as ever depending on what speech is at issue (and whose ox is gored). It's just that fewer Americans are willing to self-identify with the label because, to quote Richard Nixon, "that would

FIGURE 3.2 Comstock cartoon from *The Masses*: "Your Honor, this woman gave birth to a naked child!"
Source: Public domain image, www.cybertraps.com/2017/05/14/trumpism-is-the-new-comstockery-guest-post/.

be wrong." Unlike the New York Society for the Suppression of Vice, whose very seal depicted its twin goals of jailing people for bad words and torching vile books, modern incarnations of anti-vice societies are forced to couch their objectives in softer or misleading terms, even when their ultimate purposes are the same – perhaps *especially* when their ultimate purposes are the same.

Of course, this transformation did not happen overnight. Our history is replete with pro-censorship movements in the United States, but the tide slowly began to turn after Comstock. Like a snowball that grows to boulder-size as it rolls down a long snow-covered slope, a general distaste for censorship gathered momentum throughout the twentieth century. Much of this had to do with Comstock's puritanical excesses that wore out America's welcome for censors. Mencken observed that when Comstock began his long and brilliant career of "unwitting sabotage," practically every reputable American supported "the essential principles of Comstockery," but by the end of his tenure, the same ideas "enjoyed a degree of public esteem, at least in the big cities, halfway between that enjoyed by phrenology and that enjoyed by homosexuality."

In 1905, George Bernard Shaw described Comstockery as "the world's standing joke at the expense of the United States. Europe likes to hear of such things," he wrote, because "it confirms the deep-seated conviction of the old world that America is a provincial place, a second rate country town civilization after all." Shaw is often credited with inventing the term "Comstockery," but the word first appeared in a *New York Times* editorial ten years earlier mocking Comstock's penchant for personally covering up advertisements for the Metropolitan Museum of Art that offended him. Comstock's *New York Times* obituary observed that Shaw was simply one among "the long line of humorists and satirists who have exercised their talents on the noted Secretary of the Society for the Suppression of Vice." Such attitudes about Comstock – and censors in general – took root in the fertile soil of emerging First Amendment protections in the ensuing decades so that today, as Gerald Gardner wrote in THE CENSORSHIP PAPERS, "[m]ost people don't even like the word – especially the censors."

The backlash to Comstock was magnified by the vast scope of his achievements. If this former dry goods clerk had managed only to persuade the city fathers of New York City to adopt an anti-porn ordinance, few would remember him today and fewer still would point to him as a cautionary example of the evils of censorship. But the vast scale of Comstock's accomplishments, his lust for attention, his relish for punishing those who offended his Puritan sense of propriety, and the cruelty he showed in celebrating the deaths he caused still make would-be censors pause and reflect.

Such was the case with Anna Louise Bates, whose 1995 biography of Comstock began as a doctoral dissertation. As a feminist historian, Bates started her graduate studies with the conviction that "pornography degraded all women, and that all pornographic writing should be illegal." But after a decade of research reflected in her wonderfully detailed WEEDER IN THE GARDEN OF THE LORD: ANTHONY COMSTOCK'S LIFE AND CAREER, Bates concluded that free speech is "a liberty above price" and that efforts to enforce purity "have historically done far more harm to women than pornographic pictures." Comstock's legacy did not just set back censorship as an occupation; it forever tarnished the title "censor" – in America at least.

This is true even for those who practice censorship not by operation of law but by industry practice – commonly called "self-regulation." Industry bureaus and departments tasked with restricting speech self-consciously cloak their activities in euphemism. The censorship departments of broadcast networks are called "Standards and Practices," and in Hollywood, before the ratings system was developed, the Hays censorship office was called the "Production Code Authority." Jack Vizzard, a veteran of the Hays Office, captured the ambivalence among those whose trade is repression in the very first line of his memoir: "Being a censor is like being a whore; everyone wants to know how you got into the business." Alfred Schneider, whose account of his thirty years as a broadcast network censor frankly acknowledges that censorship was his role, nevertheless suggested that his purpose was "to try to see how to help get the program on the air rather than to just say no." Schneider described his position for a private broadcast network as being more akin to that of editor (or arbiter) than an authoritarian position, but he nevertheless wondered whether it was "strange or hypocritical to mention freedom of expression in the same breath with censorship."

THE PSYCHOLOGY OF THE CENSOR

Although the backlash against censorship was not immediate, the recognition that Comstock had more than his share of quirks and kinks was evident early on. That is, he was not a person whose foibles and excessive zeal became apparent only in retrospect when his career could be assessed through a historical prism. Biographers Broun and Leech set forth Comstock's peculiarities in detail, reproducing a number of diary entries from his youth. Of their subject they observed, "men do not greatly change. The signs of their destiny are written early, if we have the eyes to read them." As a young soldier during the Civil War, Comstock was not content just to refuse his liquor rations. Rather, he would make a show of pouring his whiskey allotment on the ground in front of his comrades. Small wonder he wasn't popular with his compatriots, and such ostentatious sanctimony forever colored others' reactions to him. Not surprisingly, the *New York Times* reported that the ridicule that was heaped on Comstock began at the very outset of his vigilante career.

This reaction was not confined to Comstock's staunch adversaries. The Unitarian Reverend O. B. Frothingham queried in an 1882 forum on the suppression of vice whether society is prepared to accept Comstock's judgment about what is obscene or indecent and what is not, and observed: "There have already been some odd – some people call them ludicrous – performances in that line." He warned that purity crusaders risked losing allies "if the policy of suppression is pushed to extremes." Others were even less comfortable with Comstock's militancy. A clergyman introduced Comstock at an 1880 meeting as someone "whose work was displeasing to the devil and whose methods were displeasing to saints." And Comstock did not, as one might say today, play well with others. His "prickly personality" and overzealous methods did not always sit well with fellow reformers. As Mrs. Harriet Pritchard, who headed the New York Department for Purity in Literature and Art for the Women's Christian Temperance Union, told the *New York Daily Tribune*, "The trouble with Mr. Comstock is that he thinks no one has the right to work for social purity without first obtaining permission from him."

Even John Sumner, who succeeded Comstock as secretary of the New York Society for the Suppression of Vice, found it necessary to distance himself from the old crusader as times changed. In the mid-1930s Sumner sought to avoid public criticism by describing Comstock – by then in his grave for two decades – as "somewhat of a religious fanatic who also loved notoriety." The Society by then had rejected what it called "Puritanical prying and snooping" and officially retired its old seal, which depicted a Victorian gentleman stoking a bonfire with books. Later, shortly before it closed its doors forever in 1950, it changed its name to the Society to Maintain Public Decency.

Other assessments of Comstock were even harsher. Famed civil liberties lawyer Morris Ernst would later write that Comstock was an "obvious psychopath" for whom "suppression gratified his hatred of everything he saw as vice," and whose self-hatred stemmed from an obsession with masturbation. Mencken was a little more charitable about this, writing that Comstock's zeal to stamp out the sin of autoeroticism was the product of the "hard, incontrovertible experience of a Puritan farm-boy, in executive session behind the barn." Others were less forgiving. Ida Craddock, a spiritualist who became a frequent target of Comstock's after 1900 and who was driven to suicide by his persecution, wrote in an open letter that she believed Comstock to be "a sex pervert; he is what physicians term a sadist – namely a person in whom the impulses of cruelty arise concurrently with the stirrings of sex emotion." Broun and Leech wrote that "the vice-hunter did little to dispel the impression that he took a cruel, almost savage satisfaction in bringing to justice the violators of the laws he had made his especial concern."

Whether or not Comstock actually felt sexual gratification from his professional exploits is anybody's guess, but it seems quite likely that the viciousness with which he pursued his victims was driven by extreme self-loathing. As a nineteen-year-old Comstock recorded in his diary:

> I debased myself in my own eyes today by my own weekness [*sic*] and sinfulness, and was strongly tempted today, and oh! I yealded [*sic*] instead of fleeing to the

"fountain" of all my strength. What sufferings I have undergone since, no one knows. Attended pr. meetings yet found no relief; instead each prayer or Hymn seemed to add to my misery.

Detailed review of these diary entries led Broun and Leech to write that Comstock was angry "at things in himself that he feared and hated," and throughout his life the zealot treated anything remotely connected with sex as a public danger. To justify confining nude paintings to artists' studios rather than permitting public display, he compared them to "wild animals" that must be "caged." Comstock acted to purge his own sinful thoughts by trying to purge the world of "sinners," and it became a lifelong habit.

D. M. Bennett, the free-thinker whom Comstock jailed and who championed the 1877 petition drive to repeal the federal obscenity law, put his finger on the censor's dilemma that eventually would sum up Comstock's career. Bennett wrote: "An honorable, good man will never willingly accept the office of a spy and informer to lie in wait and watch for the errors and weaknesses of his fellow-beings and then, by decoying them on and entrapping them, use their simplicity or their confidence to throw them into prison and effect their utter ruin." Such a man, Bennett added, "who receives weekly pay for prying into the transgressions of mankind, and bringing them to consequent punishment, will always be hated by mankind, and the office must fall to the lot of some man of desperate fortunes and ambiguous character."

Bennett prophesied that the Comstock Law would be "believed by many to be subversive of the very principles of American liberty and destructive to individual rights guaranteed by the Constitution of our country." In the end, he was proved to be right, both about the general disrepute of censors and about the constitutional standards that later would limit obscenity law. But both developments occurred far too late to help him.

It may be too much to suggest that Comstock alone could be responsible for such an enduring backlash. Public attitudes were transformed by multiple forces in the twentieth century. The nation survived two world wars and saw the birth of wondrous new media of communication – from cinema and radio to television and the Internet. The Jazz Age came and went and youth culture embraced various forms of entertainment that their parents neither understood nor countenanced. America's acceptance of free expression was tested by the labor movement, the Red Scare, the civil rights and anti-war movements, and various drives to tamp down popular entertainments – from comic books to rock music. And through it all, as society changed, the courts developed a robust body of First Amendment law that initially recognized some protections for freedom of expression and grew to embrace broad free speech values as fundamental. But these developments in the law, and many of the cultural events that shaped them, took place beneath the long shadow cast by Anthony Comstock.

THE COMSTOCK EFFECT

In his own way Comstock contributed to the cultural backlash. Think of it as a Gilded Age version of what is now called the Streisand Effect – the effort to suppress information that only makes it more sought after and available. The modern incarnation got its name from entertainer Barbra Streisand's 2003 lawsuit against the California Coastal Records Project to block access to photographs of her cliff-side Malibu home on grounds of invasion of privacy. News of the lawsuit itself sparked interest in the photos – far more than would have existed from the archive alone – and by the time the meritless case was thrown out, many thousands of people had seen the photos, which otherwise would have been unknown to them. Over 420,000 people reportedly viewed the pictures of Streisand's home in just the few weeks after she filed suit, and her name is now forever associated with comically misguided censorship efforts.

So it was with Comstock, and, as with most major developments involving American censorship, he was the pioneer. Comstock wrote about it himself in an 1891 article entitled "Vampire Literature," in which he recounted the story of a fashionably dressed young woman who came to his office seeking assistance. She was an actress in need of publicity, she explained, and said she wanted to publish a "spicy" book. She then asked if she could pay him to "attack it just a little" and to "seize a few copies" in order to "attract attention to her book and to get the newspapers to notice it." Comstock stiffly declined, and described the encounter as "sad and ludicrous." But he forgot to add that it was ironic as well, confirming that he wasn't in on the joke. As art historian and Comstock biographer Amy Werbel has written, "Comstock, as much as or perhaps even more than any other figure in American history, put art on page one." Morris Ernst aptly described vice-hunters who succeeded the old man as "the advertising agents of sex."

Of course, Comstock should have been aware of this effect from the beginning, and, to a certain extent, he was. Even before he traveled to Washington to secure passage of a federal obscenity law and prior to the formation of the New York Society for the Suppression of Vice, his efforts to prosecute Victoria Woodhull and Tennessee Clafin, and to suppress their salacious account of the Ward–Beecher affair, only stoked interest in the scandal and drove up sales (and prices) of their weekly newspaper. Comstock understood cause and effect, but the ultimate lesson that censorship is counterproductive was utterly lost on him. He later noted that when his anti-vice society attacked a book, it resulted in "a large amount of free advertising for the offensive matter." For that reason, he directed the society's efforts toward obliterating offending works entirely by arresting both the author and the publisher while seizing the publication and the printing plates and destroying them. But such scorched earth tactics inevitably failed. Despite the crackdown, Comstock observed in 1891 that New York was facing "an epidemic of lewdness through the channels of light literature" and that there was "strong competition among writers and publishers of cheap books and papers to see which one can excel the others in unclean stories." As usual, his takeaway was that he was right and the rest of the world was wrong.

And he never learned. Toward the end of his career, he attacked George Bernard Shaw's play *Mrs. Warren's Profession* because a central character in this work about women's empowerment was involved with prostitution. When Comstock sent a note demanding that the producer cancel the "filthy play," the savvy promoter leaked the ultimatum to the press and publicly invited Comstock to attend rehearsals at the Garrick Theatre. Unamused, Comstock went to court to block the "obscene" performances, but was unsuccessful. As the play's producer understood (but as Comstock failed to appreciate), the resulting publicity made the play a huge success, with overflow audiences and tickets fetching premium prices. So many people thronged to opening night that the city police had to call out the reserves to manage the crowds.

There is no doubt but that the Comstock Effect was real, although some aspects of it have taken the form of legend, including his efforts to suppress public display of prints of the painting *September Morn*. Described by biographers as his "best-known escapade in the field of art," Comstock's actual involvement was limited to bullying a store clerk into removing the print from the front window of Braun & Company, a confrontation captured in a tongue-in-cheek front-page *New York Times* account. But that story mutated and eventually took on a life of its own.

There is a legend that press agent Harry Reichenbach engineered the event specifically to boost sales of *September Morn*, and was engaged by Braun & Company to achieve that end. Reichenbach claimed he paid forty or fifty kids to stand outside the store window and gawk at the piece, then placed an anonymous call to Comstock to report the "outrage." Comstock predictably rushed to the scene, and, according to this account, ordered the print removed. The rest, as they say, was the first rough draft of history. The story made international headlines, and reportedly challenged news of the war in Europe for the public's attention. This spurred on sales of the print, and American art dealers reportedly sold seven million copies in just a few months. The value of Chabas' original painting was said to spiral from $35 to $10,000.

It is a great story, and, given Comstock's career, not an entirely incredible one. But it is more likely an example of a clever promoter exploiting general awareness of the Comstock Effect to burnish his own image. Reichenbach recounted the event in his 1931 autobiography PHANTOM FAME, in which he claimed credit for making *September Morn* the most famous painting in the world. He wrote that he had applied for work at a small art shop that had been unable to sell 2,000 surplus copies of the print, and he hit upon the idea to "introduce the immodest young maiden to Anthony Comstock." Several calls to the old man's office went unanswered, but this changed, Reichenbach wrote, after he hired a bunch of youngsters for fifty cents apiece to stand outside the display window "uttering expressions of unholy glee and making grimaces too sophisticated for their years." Comstock rushed to the scene, and the unseemly display of despoiled youth prompted the desired reaction. According to Reichenbach, Comstock first demanded the print be removed, and, when that failed, he appealed to the courts. As a direct result, according to the promoter, a lithograph that had been rejected as a brewer's calendar became an overnight sensation.

There's only one problem with Reichenbach's boast – not one word of it is true. There is nothing to indicate that he ever worked for Braun & Company, and, according to contemporary newspaper accounts, he was not looking for work at the time but was already an established publicist. More to the point, *September Morn* had already become infamous by the time Comstock learned of it, because the Chicago police had tried unsuccessfully to prosecute a small art store for selling copies of the print. An alderman known as "Bath House John Coughlin" (reputedly a "companion and protector of prostitutes, pimps, barrel house bums and saloon keepers") announced that *September Morn* could not be displayed anywhere in Chicago, but was rebuffed by the courts. None of the accounts from the time suggest any contact between Reichenbach and Comstock, and one newspaper reported that Comstock approached Braun & Company only after a schoolteacher complained to him that display of the print "might work havoc in the minds of her pupils passing that way." Even then, Comstock did not bring a legal action as Reichenbach claimed, but satisfied himself with abusing a store clerk (and getting a headline).

But as with any good fiction, just because the details were made up doesn't mean the story is false. Writing four years before Reichenbach spun his tale, Broun and Leech described as a "yarn" suggestions that "Comstock's attention was purposefully called to the picture by the proprietor who wished to boom the sales" of *September Morn*. That story was denied by the good men of the New York Society for the Suppression of Vice, who said that Comstock dispatched an assistant to look at the Braun & Company display, who reported that it was "not actionable."

Comstock likely reached the same conclusion – at least as to a criminal prosecution – but he never disavowed his encounter with the store clerk, as reported in the *Times*. Whether or not conceived as a PR stunt, there is no denying that Comstock's objection to *September Morn* and the front-page *New York Times* coverage helped stoke the work's phenomenal success. As Broun and Leech observed, "[t]he picture sold hugely, and indeed some people went into the print publishing business merely for the sake of handling this picture." The story was recounted in Comstock's obituary, and the *Times* reported that within weeks of the incident copies of the print were on sale in every part of the United States. Hoax or not, with Comstock's help the controversy made *September Morn* one of the most famous and popular paintings of the twentieth century.

A SLOW-MOTION BACKLASH IN THE LAW

One consequence of being the Bond villain of censorship is that Comstock galvanized opposition to his cause. And the reaction he inspired was as broad and deep as his universal mission to reform society. His 1880 tome FRAUDS EXPOSED devotes thirty-two chapters to his various causes, which included taking on bank fraud, gambling and lotteries, bogus mining companies, fake jewelry scams, divining rods, quack medicine, petty swindles of various kinds, dime novels, and – of course – obscenity. The subject of smut was his chief preoccupation, however, and it kept him very busy indeed, as he saw filthiness in everything from literature and art to medical texts. This mobilized a resistance that included more than just the freethinkers and free love advocates that first pushed back against his militant prudishness, and it grew over time to include mainstream publishers, artists, doctors, and merchants.

But while the social backlash was more immediate, taking the form of critical commentaries, satire, and petition drives, reform of the prevailing legal standard took far longer. And the task was formidable. Comstock was no lawyer, but he followed the controlling precedents closely and observed accurately in 1891 that the test for obscenity adopted by the British courts in *Regina* v. *Hicklin* "has been adopted and affirmed in every case of importance tried since on both continents." Under that test, he noted, "[c]lassical, standard, literary, and medical works are all indictable if sold in such a manner as to reach and corrupt the young and inexperienced." This seeming legal monolith forced Comstock's opponents to develop and refine the legal arguments to dismantle a broad obscenity standard that would prevail for decades after the crusader's death.

Comstock's indiscriminate attacks on all that he considered "unclean" sowed the seeds of his undoing. Had he confined his campaign rooting out to back-alley smut peddlers and the furtive boys behind the newsstands, it is doubtful he would have generated such widespread sympathy for his victims or inspired an articulate response to the legal doctrine of the day. But by making martyrs of the likes of Ezra Heywood and D. M. Bennett, and by equating artists, playwrights, doctors, and birth control advocates with pornographers, Comstock guaranteed that a cogent case would be made that he had gone too far. And his many goofs and gaffes provided ample ammunition to make that case persuasive. "The friends of commercialized pornography were few," Broun and Leech wrote, but for "the liberty to know, to utter, and to argue freely, according to conscience, men may be found ready to fight and suffer."

Such concerns prompted 70,000 people to sign the National Liberal League's 1878 petition asking Congress to repeal the Comstock Act, a document that began to lay an intellectual foundation for arguments against censorship. The petition described the Act as a plain violation of the letter and spirit of the First Amendment, and charged that it was being used "for the purposes of moral and religious persecution, whereby the dearest and most precious rights of the people are being grievously violated under the forms of legal inquisition, fines, forfeitures, and imprisonment." It posited that the First Amendment requires the government to remain neutral in the field of ideas, and that "all attempts of civil government, whether State or national, to enforce or to favor particular religious, social, moral, or medical opinions, or schools of thought or practice, are not only unconstitutional but ill-advised, contrary to the spirit and progress of our age, and almost certain in the end to defeat any beneficial objects intended." The petition proclaimed that society's "mental, moral, and physical health and safety" would be "better secured and preserved by virtue resting upon liberty and knowledge, than upon ignorance enforced by governmental supervision." It concluded that "even error may be safely left free, where truth is free to combat it," and that "the greatest danger to a republic is in the insidious repression of the liberties of the people."

Another of the arguments developed in this early period was that obscenity laws are incapable of precise definition and their enforcement is inherently subjective. This theme was sounded during the keynote address at an "Indignation Meeting" organized to protest Ezra Heywood's conviction for publishing *Cupid's Yokes*. The event, held at Boston's Faneuil Hall on August 1, 1878, was the first official project of the National Defense Association (NDA), which was formed after the repeal petition floundered. The new organization was created to continue the effort to end the Comstock Act and to defend those prosecuted under it. Between four and six thousand people crowded into Faneuil Hall for the event and a full account of the proceedings was later published.

In the first of many speeches denouncing Heywood's conviction, the staunch abolitionist Elizur Wright argued that few would object to the law if it could define obscenity "as not to exclude a great part of our most valuable literature, including the Bible, and so as not to violate the true and constitutional liberty of the press." That same year, D. M. Bennett, who also fell prey to the vagaries of the Comstock Act, wrote that obscenity "ought to be correctly described so that it may be known in what it consists, and so that an accused person shall not be at the mercy of a man or of a number of men who construe what is obscene, what is indecent and immoral, by their own particular opinion or notion of morality and immorality."

Arguments about the legitimacy of obscenity laws continued to be developed and refined as time went on. Pioneering free speech advocate and scholar Theodore Schroeder reviewed trials of Ezra Heywood and others for selling *Cupid's Yokes* and concluded that obscenity law boiled down to nothing more than a disagreement about literary style. He likened obscenity laws to those banning witchcraft. Schroeder surveyed five arrests by federal and state authorities involving *Cupid's Yokes*, and observed that one prosecution was abandoned, two resulted in findings of not guilty, and two resulted in convictions. He concluded that "no man on earth can tell, even now, whether it is a crime to send *Cupid's Yokes* through the mail." And, he added, "[i]f anyone claims to know whether the law condemns this book, I ask him to point to a statutory test which is decisive," noting that "[e]ven if in every case *Cupid's Yokes* had been declared not to be 'obscene,' still this would be no protection to the next vendor of the book."

Others reasoned that prevailing law destroyed freedom of expression because it could result in a conviction if a book contained a single "immoral" passage. At D. M. Bennett's trial, for example, his attorney tried to persuade the court to consider the work "as a whole," and not to dwell just on what prosecutors thought were the naughty bits. These arguments were unsuccessful at the time, but they contributed intellectual heft to concepts that eventually became the law.

THE FREE SPEECH LEAGUE

In many ways Comstock broadened the base for free speech advocacy. The NDA's key members and financial backers eventually joined with others in 1902 to create the Free Speech League, an organization committed to a more expansive defense of free expression. While the NDA had focused on Comstock's exploits on the East Coast, the Free Speech League drew members from across the United States; whereas the NDA had concentrated its efforts in defending the victims of Comstock's sex censorship, the League took on free speech issues of all kinds, whatever the subject; and where the NDA had been more associated with cultural radicals, the Free Speech League was formed to protect free speech for all, regardless of viewpoint. According to one contemporary account, the League was "a nucleus around which to rally the opponents of censorship" and was "composed of men and women of every phase of opinion, who believe in preserving the freedom of speech, press, assemblage and mails, guaranteed to us by the constitution of the United States and essential to our existence as a free people."

A forerunner of the ACLU, the Free Speech League was embroiled in almost all the major battles over free speech from the time it was formed until 1920. Its members crafted arguments to support freedom of expression, provided legal assistance to those hauled into court, organized protests, distributed pamphlets, lobbied political officials, testified before government bodies, and publicized these activities. Its organizers and members were influential, including muckraking journalist Lincoln Steffens, anarchist Emma Goldman, and birth control advocate Margaret Sanger, among others. Dr. Edward Bond Foote, who had been a prominent target of Comstock and a driving force in the NDA, was an organizer and major funder of the League. It has been aptly described by First Amendment scholar David M. Rabban as "the first organization in American history to demonstrate a principled commitment to free expression for all viewpoints on all subjects."

The League's victories in court were few. This was, after all, more than two decades before the Supreme Court would uphold a claim in any First Amendment case. But the unfavorable legal environment of the period makes the organization's persistence, and its ultimate victory, all the more remarkable. Much of this success is attributable to the work of Theodore Schroeder, the League's prolific secretary, a man H. L. Mencken described as having "done more for free expression in America than any other." Schroeder eschewed representing clients in court, both because of his temperament and because he believed the arguments made in legal briefs too impermanent. Instead, Schroeder left the courtroom arguments to others while he spoke and wrote widely and frequently on a broad range of First Amendment topics. Between 1906 and 1919 Schroeder published some 120 books, articles, pamphlets, essays, and other works on topics ranging from blasphemy, censorship of the mails, the Alien and Sedition Acts, free speech for radicals, advertising, and sex censorship. The purpose of his work, he wrote, was "to increase intellectual hospitality to the end that more truth will prevail."

Schroeder's prodigious output included his 1911 treatise, OBSCENE LITERATURE AND CONSTITUTIONAL LAW: A FORENSIC DEFENSE OF FREEDOM OF THE PRESS, a work that, like most of his writings, was well ahead of its time. How far ahead? In 1938 Schroeder recalled that, when he wrote the treatise, no publisher would touch it for fear of a Comstock raid, so he was forced to self-publish. Naturally, he couldn't sell the book, so he endeavored to give it away "in such manner and to such persons that Anthony Comstock, the 'purity' crusader in chief, would not catch me at it." Smaller research libraries accepted the gift, but others refused it, including the libraries of the New York City Bar Association and of the British Museum.

The ascendency of Schroeder's ideas on freedom of expression and the decline of Comstock's reign of terror were foreshadowed to some degree in a scheduled debate between the two men at the 1906 National Purity Federation Conference in Chicago, a gathering of social reformers billed as a united national effort to promote public virtue. Comstock and Schroeder had never met face-to-face but had debated the legitimacy of obscenity laws via extensive correspondence. So this confrontation, just after Comstock's infamous raid of the New York Art Students' League, was highly anticipated, and Schroeder did not disappoint. In an address entitled "More Liberty of Press Essential to Moral Progress," he told the assembled social reformers that more freedom for sexual expression was needed and that the present obscenity laws as they relate to adults should be repealed. He advocated increased dissemination of scientific literature on sex and called for sex education in the schools. Schroeder blasted the vagueness of the Comstock Law, noting that even Biblical quotations and passages from UNCLE TOM'S CABIN were not safe from the censors.

What did the aging champion of morality have to say in response? Nothing. Though he was a member of the National Purity Federation's Executive Committee, Comstock was a no-show. He was said to be too ill to attend. But what happened next was even more astonishing. At the close of the conference, the Federation unanimously backed a resolution calling for its president to establish a permanent committee to push for "changes in the judicial tests of obscenity" to make them less vague and arbitrary and to prevent "suppression of any scientific and educational purity literature." According to one contemporary account, as a result of the presentation, an organization which, "in the popular mind stands for organized and legalized prudery, did unanimously adopt a resolution almost as broad as Mr. Schroeder's contention." The vote was characterized as marking "a new epoch among purity workers."

SUPPORT FOR FREE SPEECH TAKES ROOT

Eventually the ideas began to percolate into judicial opinions. One of the first to incorporate free speech concepts was a 1913 case involving a novel entitled HAGAR REVELLY, about a working girl in New York who was described as "impulsive, sensuous, fond of pleasure and restive." The novel is written in sedate language but it chronicles the young woman's exploits in which "her virtue is unsuccessfully assailed by a man she does not love and later successfully by one she does." This is followed by "several amorous misadventures" ending in "a loveless marriage and the prospect of a dreary future." In short, it was a perfect target for Comstock, and one that would have given him no trouble in earlier years. But the judge in the case was the famed jurist Learned Hand, who began to chip away at the prevailing legal doctrine. Although he was constrained by precedent to apply the *Hicklin* rule that required him to instruct the jury that the book was to be judged by its tendency to corrupt those most susceptible to immoral influences, he questioned whether the test was defensible.

Recognizing that a new standard had not yet emerged, Judge Hand wondered whether the law should "forbid all which might corrupt the most corruptible, or that society is prepared to accept for its own limitations those which may perhaps be necessary to the weakest of its members." Under *Hicklin*, the court had to focus on whether any part of the book – not the work as a whole – might be considered obscene, and Hand allowed as how two pages of HAGAR REVELLY "might tend to corrupt the morals." But he asked whether society should "reduce our treatment of sex to be the standard of a child's library" and whether the current law would prevent "adequate portrayal of some of the most serious and beautiful sides of human nature." Hand wrote that "the rule as laid down, however consonant it may be with mid-Victorian morals, does not seem to me to answer to the understanding and morality of the present time, as conveyed by the words, 'obscene, lewd, or lascivious.'" The jury ultimately acquitted the publisher of the obscenity charge.

After this, judges increasingly doubted whether the prevailing standard was still valid, and some began to write opinions chipping away at the legal edifice supporting the Comstock Law. A key break occurred in 1930, when the US Court of Appeals for the Second Circuit held that the law could not be used to bar the mailing of a sex education pamphlet directed at adolescents entitled *The Sex Side of Life: An Explanation for Young People*. The pamphlet was written by Mary Ware Dennett, an ardent feminist, birth control advocate, and vocal opponent of postal censorship. Originally conceived as an educational guide for her own children, the work was first published in the medical literature and then published as a pamphlet by the YMCA – ironically the same organization that spawned Comstock's New York Society for the Suppression of Vice decades earlier.

The Post Office found Dennett's pamphlet to be "unmailable" under the Comstock Law and the district court upheld that determination. But the Court of Appeals reversed that decision in an opinion written by Judge Augustus Hand (Learned Hand's cousin). Without directly straying from the *Hicklin* rule, Judge Hand noted that even the English court in *Hicklin* had agreed that "the circumstances of the publication" should determine whether the law had been violated. And in this case, he concluded, the pamphlet was written "with sincerity of feeling and an idealization of the marriage relation and sex emotions" and that "accurate information, rather than mystery and curiosity, is better in the long run and less likely to occasion lascivious thoughts than ignorance and anxiety." Judge Hand added that there could be no doubt about the law's constitutionality, but that, properly understood, "it must not be assumed to have been designed to interfere with serious instruction regarding sex matters unless the terms in which the information is conveyed are clearly indecent." The federal obscenity law "was never thought to bar from the mails everything which might stimulate sex impulses," he concluded, for otherwise "much chaste poetry and fiction, as well as many useful medical works would be under the ban." Clearly, Judge Hand never consulted Anthony Comstock's writings on the meaning of "his" law, for those were precisely the things he thought it should – and did – ban.

But this was just the beginning. More of the central tenets of Comstock's view of the law (and of prevailing legal doctrine) were stripped away when federal courts held in the early 1930s that James Joyce's novel Ulysses could not be excluded from the United States under the Tariff Act of 1930. This showed how far the courts were willing to venture in reinterpreting the test for obscenity following the ruling on Mary Dennett's sex manual. Ulysses was fiction, not "serious instruction regarding sex matters," and it was not "an idealization of the marriage relation and sex emotions." Far from it. Ulysses was an exploration of the thoughts and feelings of certain people described as "lower middle class" as they went about their day in Dublin in 1904, and it was presented in an avant-garde, stream-of-consciousness style that would have been challenging even without any risqué subject matter. If the characters seemed to be a tad too preoccupied with sex, well, as Judge John Woolsey observed, "it must always be remembered that his locale was Celtic and his season spring."

What mattered to Judge Woolsey was not that Ulysses dealt with sex and used "dirty words" so much as the fact that it was an honest attempt to employ the writer's craft to portray genuine thoughts and feelings. Although he acknowledged that Ulysses "is not an easy book to read or understand" and that it contains language of "unusual frankness," he evaluated whether the book was obscene based on "the intent with which the book was written." In doing so, Judge Woolsey did not "detect anywhere the leer of the sensualist" and found that it would have been "artistically inexcusable" if Joyce had pulled his literary punches. He observed that the words challenged as dirty "are old Saxon words known to almost all men and, I venture, to many women, and are such words as would be naturally and habitually used, I believe, by the types of folk whose life, physical and mental, Joyce is seeking to describe." In short, the book was not pornography because it was not written with "pornographic intent."

Judge Woolsey's reasoning mirrored arguments that had been made unsuccessfully in defense of Ezra Heywood and D. M. Bennett, among others, and that had been refined by such advocates as Theodore Schroeder. And it could not have been more contrary to Comstock's world view. The old man had long railed against "artistic traps" that, in his view, only made the obscenity worse. He believed it only made the work more of an attractive nuisance and therefore more dangerous if foul thoughts were dressed up with fine words or placed in an artistic setting. Comstock wrote in his 1887 pamphlet *Morals Versus Art* that "this foe to moral purity comes in its most insidious, fascinating and seductive form" in "the guise of art," and that the motive or intention of a defendant "does not affect the tendency of a book or picture" to corrupt. In a later article, Comstock dismissed the argument about artistic intent as a "popular delusion" and cited the standard legal authorities of the time for his firm belief that "[c]lassical, standard, literary, and medical works are all indictable," regardless of the author's intent, "if sold in such a manner as to reach and corrupt the young and inexperienced."

The court of appeals disagreed that obscenity was to be determined based on "the motives of an author to promote good morals," but that reservation was not good news for the would-be censors. The opinion, penned by Judge Augustus Hand, rejected the legal reasoning previously used to convict D. M. Bennett and referred instead to the test laid down in the more recent decision involving Mary Dennett's sex manual. Although Judge Hand acknowledged that Joyce wrote with a literalism "that left nothing unsaid" and that "numerous long passages in Ulysses contain matter [that] is obscene under any fair definition of the word," he broke with decades of case law under the *Hicklin* rule and concluded that it was not enough to condemn a book based on isolated passages. Instead, he wrote, the question in each case must be "whether a publication taken as a whole has a libidinous effect." Any other rule would condemn works of Aristophanes, Chaucer, Boccaccio, Shakespeare, or even the Bible, and that, Judge Hand concluded, could not be what Congress had in mind.

The judges clearly had a different take on literary merit than did Comstock. In his hierarchy of values, "[a]rt is not above morals. *Morals stand first.*" For the vice hunter, "[p]ure morals are of first importance. They are protected by law, while art, if unclean, is not." But Judge Woolsey clearly had been moved by the artistic value of Ulysses, describing James Joyce as "a great artist in words" and his book as "an amazing tour de force." Such glowing praise typically is reserved for book reviews, not judicial opinions. It is also worth noting, as did one scholar of Ulysses, that

Judge Woolsey wrote his opinion just a few months after the Nazi book burnings, and his decision "did more than legalize a book. It turned a cultural insurgency into a civic virtue of a free and open society."

Judge Hand was somewhat less effusive in his praise than was Judge Woolsey, but he still called Joyce a "pioneer among those writers who have adopted the 'stream of consciousness' method of presenting fiction." He described ULYSSES as "a sincere portrayal with skillful artistry," and his opinion limited the scope of obscenity law by confirming that art must be given wide latitude. Judge Hand wrote that "[a]rt certainly cannot advance under compulsion to traditional forms, and nothing in such a field is more stifling to progress than limitation of the right to experiment with a new technique."

With these and other decisions, Comstock's view of obscenity law was unraveling. In 1935, for example, John Sumner, Comstock's successor, filed an action under New York obscenity law against Gustave Flaubert's book NOVEMBER. The local magistrate dismissed the complaint, pointing out that the statute "was not intended to suppress bona fide literary effort." Drawing on Judge Learned Hand's 1913 opinion regarding the novel HAGAR REVELLY and Judge Augustus Hand's decision that ULYSSES was not obscene, Magistrate Goldstein wrote that the law cannot "embalm the precise morals" of yesteryear and that obscenity has to be judged by modern standards. "Whether we like it or not," he wrote, "the fact is that the public concept of decency has changed. What was regarded as indecent in the days of the Floradora Sextette, is decent in the days of the Fan and Bubble Dances." More importantly, he stressed, it was not his job to be the judge of morality. "To change standards of morals is the task of school and church," he concluded, and it was not his role "to emulate King Canute in an effort to turn back the tide." Instead, it was his duty "to act as observer and recorder, not as regulator."

Comstock, had he still been alive, would have been aghast. *Not his job?* To the old smut-buster, judging morality was Magistrate Goldstein's *principal* job.

Judicial decisions such as these began limiting the concept of obscenity by narrowing the interpretation of the statutes and by adopting legal tests that made it harder for the government to make out a case. Writing in *The Nation* in 1932, Morris Ernst observed that, since 1915, the New York Society for the Suppression of Vice "has failed to gain a conviction in a single case where a book was published with an established publisher's imprint or where the book had been openly sold by the retailers and reviewed by the press." But it would take another two and a half decades before the Supreme Court would weigh in with a more important and lasting limitation on obscenity – a ruling that the law and any prosecutions brought thereunder must satisfy First Amendment scrutiny.

HICKLIN UNDONE

Roth v. *United States*, decided in 1957, is remembered by most as a Supreme Court holding that the First Amendment does not protect obscenity. And so it is. But

Justice William Brennan's opinion for the Court effectively "constitutionalized" the law in this area, which means that the law can be applied only so far as the First Amendment permits, and all material beyond that line is protected. Unlike Comstock, who recoiled at any mention of sex, Justice Brennan wrote that "sex and obscenity are not synonymous." He described sex as "a great and mysterious motive force in human life [that] has indisputably been a subject of absorbing interest to mankind through the ages; it is one of the vital problems of human interest and public concern."

It was one thing to find that discussions or portrayals of sex *could* be constitutionally protected, but it was something else to come up with a legal test that makes that happen. And in this regard Justice Brennan's opinion demolished what remained of Comstock's influence on the law. His opinion in *Roth* rejected the *Hicklin* standard as being "unconstitutionally restrictive of the freedoms of speech and press." Rather than judging a work by its imagined effect on "the most susceptible persons," the Supreme Court held that it must evaluate it by its impact on "the average person in the community." This review could not be limited to "isolated passages"; instead, "books, pictures and circulars must be judged as a whole, in their entire context," and courts could not dwell on "detached or separate portions in reaching a conclusion."

The analysis could not be mired in the Victorian standards of the previous century; it had to be held to the "present-day standards of the community." And at the end of this analysis, material could be adjudged obscene only if it was "utterly without redeeming social importance." That is, all ideas "having even the slightest redeeming social importance – unorthodox ideas, controversial ideas, even ideas hateful to the prevailing climate of opinion – have the full protection" of the First Amendment.

As revolutionary as the *Roth* opinion was – or evolutionary is perhaps more apt, given how long it took for the Court to get to this point – it still was not enough for some, and the decision was not unanimous. Justice John Marshall Harlan dissented in part, and Justices Hugo Black and William O. Douglas dissented in full. Justice Harlan was concerned that the test left a final determination of obscenity to juries, an outcome that he believed created grave constitutional problems. Harlan observed that many juries could find Joyce's Ulysses or Bocaccio's Decameron to be obscene, and that "no such verdict could convince me, without more, that these books are 'utterly without redeeming social importance.'"

Justices Black and Douglas were more absolutist, echoing ideas espoused by Theodore Schroeder. Their dissent, written by Douglas, argued that in a free society the government should not have the power to prosecute anyone based on "the arousing of sexual thoughts," which, he observed, "happens every day in normal life in dozens of ways." Douglas wrote that he could understand (and to a certain extent sympathize with) "the motives of the Anthony Comstocks who would impose Victorian standards on the community," but that any test "that turns on what is offensive to the community's standards is too loose, too capricious, too destructive of freedom of expression to be squared with the First Amendment." Ultimately, he concluded that "literature should not be suppressed merely because it offends the moral code of the censor."

Oddly enough, the insight that sex is "a great and mysterious motive force in human life," as Brennan wrote, and that sexual arousal "happens every day in normal life in dozens of ways," as Douglas mused, was the common link between the key players. It is what drove Comstock to suppress anything that might inspire "impure thoughts," either in himself or in anyone else; it is the very subject that made ULYSSES controversial, and it is a key part of what ultimately convinced the Supreme Court that the legal standard for obscenity had to change.

But while this "lust crime" has been greatly narrowed, it has not gone away. Some believe that the concept of obscenity no longer exists in the Internet age, yet it lives on, albeit in a greatly diminished form. In the years after *Roth*, courts tried to tweak and modify the legal test for obscenity, prompting Justice Potter Stewart to remark memorably in 1964 that he may not be able to intelligibly define the concept, but "I know it when I see it." After the Court revamped the obscenity test to its current formulation in 1973's *Miller* v. *California*, Justice Brennan was convinced that the effort to devise a meaningful obscenity standard, which started with his opinion in *Roth*, had failed. Joined by Justices Potter Stewart and Thurgood Marshall, Brennan wrote that "after 16 years of experimentation and debate I am reluctantly forced to the conclusion that none of the available formulas, including the one announced today, can reduce the vagueness to a tolerable level." By joining Brennan's opinion, Justice Stewart signaled that, as of 1973, he no longer "knew it when he saw it." And since Justice Douglas wrote separately to repeat the position he had espoused consistently since *Roth* – that the First Amendment does not permit enforcement of obscenity laws – it meant that almost half of the Supreme Court was convinced that the very concept of obscenity should be retired.

Since then, the Court has continued to put off a day of reckoning, refusing to grapple hard questions about obscenity's relevance to a global medium. In the United States today, obscenity has almost zero impact on the mainstream publishing industry and negligible impact, if any, on the culture. Yet the ghost of Anthony Comstock lingers. Because obscenity law still exists, it can still be used to go after anyone unlucky enough to be targeted by a zealous prosecutor. Federal obscenity prosecutions are now rare – a handful were brought during both the Bush and the Obama Administrations – but the issue is perennially trotted out during election seasons, which can prompt a few cases to serve as examples. State and local prosecutors are more active – mainly in a few Bible Belt states – and prosecutions can be used to limit the availability of adult entertainment and to force local businesses to shut down.

In addition, Comstock's methods and motives were emulated by Congress in the late 1990s when it enacted a law to regulate Internet "indecency" by passing the

Communications Decency Act by an overwhelming margin. In that law, Congress adopted criminal penalties for "indecent" online communications, enforceable under a standard eerily reminiscent of the *Hicklin* rule. The Supreme Court made short work of it, though, proclaiming that the First Amendment did not permit the government to reduce the adult population to reading only what is fit for children, and striking down a law that threatened "to torch a large segment of the Internet community."

COMSTOCK'S IRONIC END

Among the many ironies that characterized Comstock's career is that he was permitted a glimpse of his own irrelevance. And it came at a time when his name appeared in the newspapers and magazines more than ever and when the legal doctrines on which he relied were most secure. In the early years of the twentieth century, he already was becoming – at least to the younger generation – a "joke" and a "scapegoat."

Comstock became increasingly irritable and difficult to work with as he got older and as his disputes grew more frequent both in and out of his office. He would repeatedly fire his hapless assistant, Charles Bamberger, over some trifle, only to plead for him to return days later after he had cooled down. Stenographers didn't last long at the New York Society for the Suppression of Vice, and Comstock reportedly burned through a dozen in a single year. His courtroom quarrels became more frequent, particularly when younger prosecutors failed to share his sense of outrage, and at one point he upbraided an assistant US attorney by shouting, "You are nothing but a little boy trying to tell me my business!"

It was just another day in the office when, one morning in 1906, the long-suffering Bamberger fielded a call from a reporter for the *New York Sun*. The correspondent asked whether Comstock had been punched in the face during his court appearance that morning. Bamberger sighed. "Probably," he said. As it turned out, a former US district attorney from West Virginia named Hugh Gordon Miller had struck Comstock in response to being called a liar.

So it came as no surprise – to anyone but Comstock – that the anti-vice society eventually began to look for ways to show the old man the door. The Society's executive committee in 1913 appointed a New York attorney, John S. Sumner, to serve as Comstock's "assistant." The cover story was thin, and Sumner would later write that he had been hired to replace the crotchety crusader. The committee wanted a new image, so it sought a secretary "of a different sort." Its members sought someone who was young, moderate, and dignified, "with nothing of the fanatic about him." They also wanted someone who avoided publicity. Consequently, Sumner was everything Comstock was not, on the surface at least. Coming from a prestigious banking firm, Sumner was soft-spoken and impressed everyone with his even temper. So, naturally, he and Comstock fought often. Sumner ascended to the top job after Comstock's death, and remained in that post for thirty-five years.

With Sumner's arrival, Comstock not only had to contend still with the many enemies he had made in his years of militant smut-busting; he had to watch his back now as well. In 1915, rumors circulated that Comstock was losing his commission with the Post Office, and the old man was convinced it was the result of a plot by some in the federal building to get rid of him. He told reporters that he didn't care if the rumors were true, but of course he cared deeply. Adding to his woes, someone inside the Society leaked to the press that Comstock only had "nominal" duties since the beginning of that year and that Sumner had taken on the role of running the organization. This all happened while Comstock was preparing his prosecution of William Sanger for handing him a copy of his wife's pro-birth control pamphlet, *Family Limitation*. It was almost too much to bear.

Just as things looked bleakest, a godsend arrived. That July, President Woodrow Wilson appointed Comstock to serve as a delegate to the International Purity Congress, shoring up the old man's fraying reputation and buoying his sagging spirits. Accompanied by the president of the International Purity Federation, Comstock made the long journey by train to San Francisco, where he maintained an exhausting schedule, giving many speeches. But the strain of the trip, combined with the stress of the Sanger trial upon his return, wore him down. The day after the trial ended, Comstock became ill, and within ten days died of pneumonia. Dedicated to the end, Comstock dictated notes for use by the Society up until the day before his death.

As a final irony, Comstock's most intimate words suffered the same fate he had imposed on many thousands of books and other materials – they were put to the torch. Comstock's diaries, which he had kept since he was a lad, faithfully recording his most private thoughts and concerns, had been used to great effect in Broun and Leech's 1927 biography, ANTHONY COMSTOCK: ROUNDSMAN OF THE LORD. The authors even reproduced photostatic copies of some of the more revealing diary passages, providing what ACLU cofounder Morris Ernst would later describe as "precious morsels for any psychiatrist," documenting Comstock's deep-rooted neuroses. After the Comstock biography was published, the diaries and other papers mysteriously disappeared, and all that remains are the portions preserved in the Broun and Leech book. The biographers had borrowed the diaries and Comstock's correspondence from the New York Society for the Suppression of Vice, and returned them to John Sumner upon the book's completion. Sumner later denied any knowledge of what became of them, but correspondence located among his papers described the burning of Comstock's diaries and letters to keep them from "falling into the wrong hands."

So, a book burner's own diaries and letters were consigned to the flames. Seems fitting somehow, particularly in light of how history remembers Comstock. It is something like the (probably apocryphal) fate of Matthew Hopkins, the "Witchfinder General," who was responsible for the executions of more than 300 women for practicing witchcraft between 1644 and 1646. As legend has it – according to Schroeder – Hopkins himself was condemned as a wizard for having an "unnatural" ability to detect witches. Schroeder wrote that Hopkins was subjected to his own "swimming test," in which he was bound hand to foot and tossed into a pond to check his accusers' hypothesis. The outcome was good news, as Hopkins' sinking like a stone proved he was not consorting with the Evil One. The bad news, of course, was that he never rose again. (More mainstream accounts say that Hopkins died of tuberculosis, at home and in his bed.) What for Hopkins is merely a "pleasing legend" actually happened with Comstock, at least as to his private writings.

Even in death, Comstock can't shake off the censor's dilemma. The Evergreens Cemetery in Brooklyn, where the old moralist's bones are interred, for a time highlighted him on its official website in recognition of the magnitude of his accomplishments. That says quite a lot, since more than half a million people are buried within its 225 acres of rolling landscape. The website accurately described Comstock as "one of the nation's most important and distinguished censors of public morals." But the post-mortem recognition was suffused with the ridicule that dogged Comstock in life. Comstock's mixed legacy was highlighted by a section of the cemetery's website that was devoted to "quirky characters." It noted that "no one was as radical as Comstock," and that "many people were furious with Comstock's corruption and undeserved power." It added that his behavior provoked many nicknames, including "The One-Man Traveling Vice Squad," "The Protector of the Public Morals," "the Self Constituted Censor," and "Sir Anthony." The website has since been updated, and no longer even mentions Comstock.

As Rodney Dangerfield would say: No respect. No respect at all.

4

The Comstock Playbook

Comstock didn't invent censorship, of course. By the time he came along, suppression of information was already the standard response to what sociologists would later call a "moral panic." This describes a condition in which a threat to the social order is perceived, magnified, and stereotyped by the media of the day, and to which those holding positions of moral authority (be they clergy, politician, or other reformer) typically offer simplistic and quick-fix solutions. Moral panics provide rich and fertile soil in which the seeds of censorship may be planted. Comstock merely perfected ways to capitalize on and perpetuate such conditions. In this respect, he was not just a "weeder in the garden of the Lord," as he liked to fancy himself. He was also a sower of bad seeds.

Comstock's crusade against crime stories and dime novels was foreshadowed by mid-nineteenth-century campaigns in Europe to stamp out cheap, lurid theater productions called "Penny Dreadfuls." Named for the low price of admission, these were mass-produced serialized stories about the exploits of Gothic villains, pirates, highwaymen, thieves, and murderers, designed to appeal to a youthful and mass audience. Reformers claimed that "a very large majority" of those who turn bad "may trace the commencement of their career in crime to their attendance in Penny Theatres." Such extravagant assertions no doubt inspired Comstock and his fellow activists, who later would blame dime novels for virtually all the antisocial behavior exhibited by the youth of the period.

This cycle would be repeated throughout the twentieth century and into the twenty-first in censorship crusades targeting literature, ragtime and jazz music, movies, comic books, rock 'n' roll, television, the Internet, and video games. Generally, any time a new medium is deemed a threat to children or some other vulnerable class, we can expect campaigns to ban or censor it. But our collective memory is short. Past crusades are either forgotten or leave behind a cultural sense of curious bemusement, making it difficult to imagine what all the fuss was about. But that does not prevent social reformers and politicians from latching on to the next cause célèbre that unquestionably will lead to the ruination of America's youth unless decisive action is taken. So goes the cycle of outrage in the typical moral panic.

Such campaigns were not just the residue of Comstock's Victorian prudery, and his various tactics have been employed frequently by progressives, often in pursuit of the same goals. The anti-vice societies of the late nineteenth century were precursors of the larger reform movement that typified the Progressive Era. Morris Jesup, Comstock's primary benefactor and a driving force in the creation of the New York Society for the Suppression of Vice, also supported such causes as education of former slaves, industrial reform, and assistance for the handicapped. He helped establish and fund the American Museum of Natural History. Fighting vice was seen as a natural corollary to other reform efforts, and organizations like Comstock's Society in New York and Boston's Watch and Ward Society were considered normal fixtures on the philanthropic landscape.

Julia Ward Howe, the noted writer of "Battle Hymn of the Republic" and champion of various causes, including abolition and women's suffrage, also advocated using the law to censor bad literature. In an address to the Association for the Advancement of Women, she said she could imagine "nothing more important than the careful and rigid enforcement of the [obscenity] laws." It is for "the guardians of society to keep a watchful eye upon the press," she said, and "the flashy novels, the unclean novels, the novels that glow with the fires of impure passions, are to be relentlessly proscribed."

The American Library Association (ALA), which later in the twentieth century would become a major voice for freedom of expression, had more in common with Comstock during the Progressive Era. In a 1908 essay entitled *The Librarian as Censor*, ALA's President Arthur Bostwick advocated suppressing all books of an "immoral tendency," claiming that American literature was being threatened by immigrants whose "standards of propriety are sometimes those of an earlier and grosser age." These were not isolated examples. A leader in the social worker movement in 1903 lauded Boston's Watch and Ward Society as "a sort of Moral Board of Health." And at the National Conference of Charities and Corrections in 1906, a prominent speaker touted what was then the majority view in praising the campaign against "salacious literature."

Comstock's substantive accomplishments were impermanent, but his methods continue to be used by crusaders of all political persuasions against the latest "speech crimes." By institutionalizing censorship as an entrepreneurial endeavor, he set the tone and defined the tactics of anti-speech activists to this day. Half a century after his death, long after his name had faded from the limelight, Comstock still was described as "the *beau* ideal of the American reformer" and "the spiritual father of today's youthful suburbanites who have undertaken to cleanse newsstands and drugstore magazine racks of 'objectionable' material." In 2019, Writer Annalee Newitz dubbed Comstock "the original anti-feminist crusader," and wrote that his tactics – "a combination of media manipulation and ruthless legal strategies – are a precursor to those used by anti-feminists on social media and in Washington today." Had he left behind a playbook, these rules would have defined his strategic arsenal.

TEN RULES FOR THE MORALS ENTREPRENEUR

Rule #1: *Exhibit Moral Certainty*

Comstock didn't have to work at this attribute, as belligerent sanctimonious-ness came to him quite naturally. The thing about being on a holy mission is that the crusader never doubts the righteousness of the cause, and that certainly was true of Anthony Comstock. The man was, in the words of his biographers, "a four-square granite monument to the Puritan tradition." Comstock firmly believed "in himself and in his work to the end."

His writings exhibited an unshakable certitude. Comstock described the statutes adopted in his name as "the most righteous laws ever enacted," calling them a "barrier between youth and moral death." When he acted to suppress Margaret Sanger's pamphlet *Family Limitation*, he called the publication "contrary not only to the law of the State, but to the law of God." In his prolific writings documenting his campaign for moral purity, Comstock said his purpose in writing was "in the hope that the blind be made to see and the erring to correct their ways." He said his goal was to "appeal for greater watchfulness on the part of those whose duty is to think, act, and speak for that very large portion of the community who have neither the intellect nor [the] judgment to decide what is wisest and best for themselves."

Comstock was so wrapped up in the belief that he was on god's holy mission as to blur the distinction between deity and man. His grandiosity was revealed most when in the throes of one of his perennial bouts of self-pity brought on by what he saw as unjust and uninformed attacks on his character. When warned that his reputation would be maligned by those seeking to repeal the postal law, Comstock replied, "I cannot expect to have better treatment than our blessed Master."

Perhaps Oliver Wendell Holmes had Anthony Comstock in mind when he wrote in 1919 that persecution of disfavored ideas and expression is perfectly logical if "you have no doubt of your premises or your power and want a certain result with all your heart." But where Holmes encouraged self-doubt and caution as a hedge against tyranny, Comstock pushed in the opposite direction. Like Samson's flowing locks, the source of Comstock's strength was his cock-sureness. The way to tell a censor, according to Supreme Court Justice Anthony Kennedy, is by their level of self-assurance. So it was with Comstock. And so it is with all who believe that his or her conception of truth, morality, or sensitiv-ity to offensiveness can override the right of another individual to write or speak. Comstock's creed was the mirror opposite of words often attributed to Thomas Jefferson: "Eternal vigilance is the price of liberty." For the vice hunter, Comstock wrote, "eternal vigilance is the price of moral purity." No doubt about it.

Rule #2: *Equate Opposition with Love of Vice*

One of the chief weapons in Comstock's rhetorical arsenal was to equate his opponents with the vice he was attacking. Anyone who questioned the law or his methods was not advocating for free speech; Comstock tarred them as "pro-obscenity." It was unthinkable to him that anyone who opposed his postal legislation could have been acting out of principle or good motives. They were merely, according to Comstock, "defending 'this, their dear obscenity.'" Concern about limiting government and respect for constitutional values were not what moved them. No, Comstock proclaimed, their actions were based on "revenge, avarice, and innate depravity." As he wrote in his 1883 score-settling polemic TRAPS FOR THE YOUNG, liberals "defend obscenity and favor the repeal of the laws made to suppress it" because they want to "tear down the pure and holy" and "naturally favor the impure and base." They were, quite simply, the "enemies of moral purity."

H. L. Mencken, a keen observer of both politics and social trends, spotted the tactic for what it was. "The moral gladiators," he wrote, "know the game." "They come before a legislature with a bill ostensibly designed to cure some great admitted evil, they procure its enactment by scarcely veiled insinuations that all who stand against it must be apologists for the evil itself, and then they proceed to extend its aims by bold interferences, and to dragoon the courts into ratifying these interferences, and to employ it as a means of persecution, terrorism and blackmail." It is a tried and true tactic that is at home in the twenty-first century every bit as much as in the nineteenth.

Rule #3: *Denounce and Discredit Adversaries.*

This may not seem like much of a revelation after the Age of Trump, but it was an indispensable part of Comstock's toolkit. His mode of argument was to attack the motives and character of anyone who questioned his holy mission. It was a style that suited his demeanor, and one that he practiced throughout his career. Merely to defeat his opponents was not enough. He set out to crush them, which is one reason why he openly boasted of driving some to suicide. As he launched his bid for a federal obscenity law in January 1873, he wrote to Representative Merriam that there had been four publishers of obscene books in New York "'on the 2nd of last March,' but 'today three of these are in their graves, and it is charged by their friends that I worried them to death. Be that as it may, I am sure that the world is better off without them.'" And time did not mellow the man. Toward the end of his career, Comstock bragged that he was responsible for at least fifteen suicides.

Comstock charged the liberals behind the 1878 petition drive to repeal his law with being "liberal with the truth" and said that they "seem to care nothing for truth so long as they carry their point." He claimed that his opponents "either do not know what they are talking about or else they are governed by a corrupt motive," and asserted that some of the names on the petition were forgeries. In this regard, Comstock reserved special venom for the famed freethinker Robert Ingersoll, whom he accused of dishonest practices, describing his advocacy as "sneering, scoffing, and blasphemous lectures."

To Comstock, those who opposed him were not just misguided and dishonest; they were criminals. How did he know that? Because many of those seeking repeal of the postal censorship law had been prosecuted under it, including some he arrested personally. And what were their crimes? For many, it was simply the fact that they pushed back against Comstock and his world view. At every opportunity he called D. M. Bennett "a scoundrel whom I caught committing a felony." And in Comstock's estimation, the NDA was "composed of ex-convicted smut dealers and Liberals," created merely "to defend those so charged." There was a sinister circular logic to it all: Comstock's opponents were not credible because they were criminals, and they were criminals because they opposed him.

Rule #4: *Exploit Xenophobia and Blame "The Other"*

Comstock mastered a tactic that made a big comeback under the 45th President: blame the nation's peril on foreign influences. This was a standard part of Comstock's repertoire, and his annual reports for the New York Society for the Suppression of Vice were filled with charts showing the country of origin of the various miscreants he put behind bars. He blamed debauchery on the "importation of criminals from other lands" and he kept track of their nationalities to help "keep undesirable classes from our shores." Even though he was rough around the edges, Comstock's Victorian sensibilities would not have permitted him to refer to "shithole countries" as President Trump did, but his message was the same. He advocated banning classic works by Ovid, Boccaccio, and others, dismissing them as "little better than histories of brothels and prostitutes, in those lust-cursed nations." He described French art as "a foreign foe," and one that presents itself in a "most insidious, fascinating and seductive form." And he blocked postal access to the English publication *The Suffragette*, saying he could "see no reason why we should have the sewerage of Great Britain dumped on our shores." Comstock summed up his dispute with George Bernard Shaw by referring to him dismissively as an "Irish smut-dealer" and a "foreign writer of filth." He would have felt right at home in the Trump White House.

Rule #5: *Poison the Debate with Invective*

Turn to any page of Comstock's books or articles, or scan the annual reports of the New York Society for the Suppression of Vice and you will find them thick with colorful invective and scabrous metaphor denouncing his many targets. Comstock may have been a prude, but he was far from conservative in his use of inflammatory rhetoric. Broun and Leech explained that he "wanted to denounce the evildoers with Biblical frankness, with Anglo-Saxon clarity, with all the invective that his violent nature and colorful imagination suggested." One can only marvel at how outrageous he would have been had he been the sort to use profanity. Comstock would have made the characters on the HBO series *Deadwood* blush.

As it was, his richly metaphorical descriptions evoked the desired imagery of hellfire and eternal peril. At the end of his career, Comstock would say that for forty years he was "stationed in a swamp at the mouth of a sewer," a post he shared with "rattlesnakes and other poisonous dangers." His basic theme did not vary much during his long career. At the very beginning, during the 1872 trial of Victoria Woodhull and Tennie Claflin, he described his mission as "to vindicate the laws and protect the young of our land from the leprosy of this vile trash." Filth, poison, disease, and wild beasts – his rhetorical palette included them all – like the imaginary lions and tigers and bears (*oh, my!*) that haunted the Yellow Brick Road.

To him, pornography was a "hydra-headed monster," and obscene book and picture dealers were more dangerous beasts of prey than rabid dogs. In any guise or form, whether in trashy novels, classic works, art, or medical textbooks, any lewdness was, to Comstock, "a moral monster." He compared it to "a parasite, fattening upon carrion. Its very presence poisons the moral atmosphere. Its breath is fetid, and its touch moral prostration and death." He applied the same over-the-top imagery to all who would defend such material, comparing their arguments to advocating shooting children, cutting off their noses, sending boxes of snakes and scorpions to girls in seminaries, or lighting matches in a powder magazine. Those who traded in or defended such obscenities were "moral cancer planters," while he was just a "weeder in the garden of the Lord."

Rule #6: *Tout Pseudo Science*

Comstock primarily drew on religious faith, not science, in campaigning against vice, but he wasn't above drawing on worldly sources of support if he thought they might help. He developed his own rough notions of psychology to illustrate the dangers of evil reading. Weaving a mash-up of pop-psychology and Christianity, Comstock postulated that "in the heart of every child there is a chamber of imagery, the memory's storehouse, the commissary department in which is received, stored up and held in reserve every good or evil influence for future requisition." He warned that "[i]f you allow the devil to decorate the Chamber of Imagery in your heart with licentiousness and sensual things, you will find that he has practically thrown a noose around your neck and will forever exert himself to draw you away from the 'Lamb of God which taketh away sins of the world.'" He called this stage of development the "plastic or receptive state," a period of life when "character is forming and is most easily moulded" and when children are "open to every insidious teacher, and subject to every bad influence." The lesson, of course, was that "if you open the door to anything, the filth will all pour in and the degradation of youth will follow."

Comstock's chief concern was that such influences would lead to "impure thoughts," which naturally would be followed by lustful deeds. Works of art depicting nudity, he wrote, are a "constant menace" to young men, "cursed as thousands of the present day are, with secret vices." Comstock cited medical authorities of the time to prove his theory that masturbation was not merely sinful but unhealthy. He warned parents to take special care if they saw "the vigor of youth failing, the cheek growing pail, the eye lustreless and sunken, the step listless and faltering, the body enervated, and the desire to be much alone coming over your offspring." He saw signs of "peevishness and irritability" not just as natural attributes of adolescence but as symptoms of a deeper problem – "secret practices" that sap "the health of mind and body." As proof, he turned to an "eminent professor in a Southern college" who had concluded that "seventy-five if not ninety percent of our young men are victims of self-abuse."

His concerns extended to women's health as well, and he drew on contemporary medical authorities to support his conclusions that contraception and abortion were harmful to women. As one 1867 publication explained, "[i]ntentionally to prevent the occurrence of pregnancy" or "to bring it, when begun, to a premature close, are alike disastrous to a woman's mental, moral, and physical well-being." Professor Augustus K. Gardner of New York Medical College had written in 1870 that any use of contraceptives was "a species of self-abuse" that had serious health implications for women, including "[l]ocal congestions, nervous affections and debilities." As one current admirer of Comstock wrote, he "stood in solidarity with the cutting-edge medical authorities of his day" and thus "could see his suppression of contraceptives as an act in line with the very best medical advice and for the protection of women's health." Comstock declared that any effort to loosen restrictions on birth control or abortion would be "a crime against young women." In keeping with his wrath-of-god rhetoric, he told an interviewer in 1915 that "if you turn loose passions and break down that fear [of pregnancy,] you bring worse disaster than the war. It would debase sacred things, break down the health of women and disseminate a greater curse than the plagues and diseases of Europe."

Comstock presaged twentieth-century social scientists who would assert, successively, that jazz music, cinema, comic books, televised violence, and video games cause juvenile delinquency and crime. He complained of dime novels and sensationalized stories of crime in the daily and weekly newspapers as inspiring youthful misdeeds. One of his repeated refrains was that we are "in imminent danger from schoolboys crazed by the accursed blood-and-thunder story papers." Comstock claimed that "[m]any a boy or youth has been led to commit crimes which have brought him to the penitentiary or the State's prison, from the infection or seduction of this class of crime-breeding publications." He cited medical authorities of the time, who agreed with his theories about the pernicious effects of dime novels. But, for the most part, he relied on anecdotal accounts to prove the impact of evil reading, which he would sprinkle generously throughout his writings. Recounting tales of teens who killed a saloon keeper during a failed robbery attempt, another youth who shot a companion after arguing over a card game, and a sixteen-year-old boy who, "after reading about train wrecking, tied a log across a railroad over a culvert," Comstock concluded with a flourish that clearly these "'hurrah-for-hades' publications had done their work." He worried that the courts would be unable to keep up with the literature-induced crime wave.

Rule #7: *Crank Up the Publicity Machine*

Say what you will about Anthony Comstock, he always made for good copy. Even Mencken, who had nothing but disdain for religious fundamentalism, admitted to liking "the old imbecile" for being akin to a P. T. Barnum for the anti-vice movement. Comstock, he wrote, "could not undertake even so banal a business as raiding a dealer in abortifacient pills without giving it the melodramatic air of a battle with a brontosaurus. So a crowd always followed him, and when he made a colossal ass of himself, which was very frequently, that fact was bruited about." Broun and Leech observed that Comstock "had always possessed a genius for attracting notice" and his name had become a thing "from which to weave headlines." Whether Comstock's words were reported with the deadly seriousness with which he intended them or he was just being mocked, he always got headlines – from the beginning of his career right up to the day of his front-page *New York Times* obituary. And that was just the way he liked it.

Had he shied away from the attention, Comstock would never have made his mark. Twenty-first-century career coaches may talk about "creating your own job," but Comstock invented an entire profession. As a 1915 *Harper's Weekly* article put it, he had, "if one may borrow a stage term, 'created' his unique position." And he did so by skillfully cultivating the press. Comstock arranged for reporters to accompany him on vigilante smut raids in 1872, leveraged the resulting coverage to gain attention and funding from the YMCA, and used this backing to lobby for the federal legislation that secured his position and made his name. His work may have been conducted under the auspices of the New York Society for the Suppression of Vice, but the law he championed bore his name (informally, at least), and the press knew that "the tremendous accomplishments of the society in its fight against various publications in the past forty years have been in reality the accomplishments of Mr. Comstock."

Rule #8: *Exaggerate the Threat*

Just as Comstock's florid rhetoric was over the top, so was his estimation of the dire consequences of evil reading. His mind naturally turned toward religious allegory, so of course the stakes of his many battles were of Biblical proportions. Mixing his metaphors, Comstock wrote that "[t]hese publications, like the fishes of the sea, spawn millions of seed, and each year these seeds germinate and spring up to a harvest of death." He maintained that "[c]hildren of all grades of society, institutions of learning in all sections of the land, and the most select homes, are invaded by the evil of licentious literature." Because of the pervasiveness of the material, he warned that "evil is found everywhere."

Everywhere indeed. Comstock's catalogue of catastrophes no doubt left Victorian Era parents agitated and alarmed. What mother or father could have another peaceful moment after the nation's leading anti-vice expert warned that reading a book could be "a worse evil than yellow fever or small pox" and that "[*y*]*our child is in danger of having its pure mind cursed for life.*" Even "light literature" was "a devil-trap to captivate the child by perverting taste and fancy." And *newpapers*! Don't even get the old man started on the evils of the press. Daily newspapers "are worse than a scourge to our children," he wrote, because "[t]hey make a pure mind almost impossible." According to Comstock, a youth who reads crime stories "might almost as well pass his time in the society of criminals. He could scarcely learn more of vice if he associated with thieves, murderers, libertines, and harlots."

And as dangerous as factual accounts of mayhem may have been, fiction was even worse. Dime novels were "products of corrupt minds [that] are the eggs from which all kinds of villainies are hatched." The stories they spin "breed vulgarity, profanity, loose ideas of life, impurity of thought and deed. They render the imagination unclean, destroy domestic peace, desolate homes, cheapen women's virtue, and make foul-mouthed bullies, cheats, vagabonds, thieves, desperados, and libertines." Beyond that, the danger multiplied when imagination leapt from the printed page to the stage. "Low theater," Comstock railed, is "a plague, worse a thousandfold than locusts, flies, or frogs." He went on: "[W]orse than any cyclone or tornado is this silent influence, this breath of poison which is breaking over our youth, destroying the brightest intellects, crushing and wounding the most lovely forms, and grinding down its victims to lowest depths of shame and degradation." "These theatres," he proclaimed, "should be named 'recruiting stations for hell.'"

Of all the many terrors facing America's families, in Comstock's mind the most horrible was anything that even hinted at sex. Comstock described the sale of erotic publications as "a deadly poison, cast into the fountain of moral purity." Because of it the "family is polluted, home desecrated, and each generation born into the world is more and more cursed by the inherited weakness, the harvest of this seed-sowing of the Evil one." To Comstock, lust was "the boon companion of all other crimes." To him, there was "no evil so extensive, none doing more to destroy the institutions of free America" because such literature "sets aside the laws of God and morality; marriage bonds are broken, most sacred ties severed, State laws ignored, and dens of infamy plant themselves in almost every community, and then reaching out like immense cuttlefish, draw in, from all sides, our youth to destruction." Truly, it was the End of Days.

Rule #9: *Hype Your Accomplishments*

According to Mark Twain, there are three kinds of lies: lies, damn lies, and statistics. Twain attributed this aphorism to British Prime Minister Benjamin Disraeli, although there is no telling who said it first. It speaks to the power of hard numbers to bolster soft arguments, a technique that is a permanent fixture on the political landscape. As with many such tricks, Comstock was a pioneer. He made annual tallies of the books burned, printing plates melted, and convictions secured (along with the prison terms to be served), a centerpiece of each year's report of the New York Society for the Suppression of Vice. Like the dry good clerk that he once was, Comstock kept inventory, and he was immensely proud of his numbers. He cited them incessantly as a measure of his success – including the suicides he claimed to have caused.

But Comstock didn't confine himself just to the sterile numbers. Tables and statistics alone lacked his flair for showmanship. So he combined his raw stats – supposedly objective facts – with colorful allusions to railway cars packed with nefarious criminals being carted off to perdition. He claimed to have convicted enough people during his career to fill a long passenger train of more than sixty coaches. All told, Comstock boasted of locking away almost 3,000 people for a total of "565 years, 11 months, and 20 days." Just brilliant – calculating the prison terms down to the day. Who could doubt someone so precise?

Senator Joseph McCarthy would exploit a similar rhetorical device to great effect half a century later in his anti-communist witch hunts. In a 1950 speech to Republican women in Wheeling, West Virginia, McCarthy waved a piece of paper in the air and claimed: "I have here in my hand a list of 205 [State Department employees] that were known to the Secretary of State as being members of the Communist Party and who nevertheless are still working and shaping the policy of the State Department." McCarthy repeated his claims in subsequent speeches and statements, but his numbers would shift constantly. Sometimes he would claim that there were fifty-seven communists at State; other times he would say that it was eighty-one or as low as ten. Of course, he never provided any evidence to back up his accusations. Proof was not the point. Just using numbers made him sound authoritative.

Specifics have the ring of truth – unless one bothers to take a closer look. Comstock claimed a near-perfect conviction rate; he always got his man. And he would put a number on that too, boasting that he obtained convictions in 98.5 percent of his cases over the course of forty years. But he had a problem: simple math. Because Comstock attached numbers to everything, it was easy enough to check some of his claims, and they didn't line up. For example, Comstock's official biography reported the number of his prosecutions as 3,646, with 2,682 convictions. This works out to a conviction rate of 73 percent. Over the next couple of years, Comstock would boast to a reporter from the New York *Evening World* and an interviewer from *Harper's Weekly* that the tally was 3,697 prosecutions and 2,740 convictions, for a success rate of around 74 percent. It certainly is possible that he was conscientiously updating his figures on each occasion rather than pulling numbers out of the air. Whatever the explanation, the statistics undercut his claims of a near-perfect conviction rate.

But who cares if he cooked his books? In the end, the actual numbers didn't matter for Comstock, just as they would not matter for McCarthy five decades later. The figures were just trotted out for the sake of PR. The true impact was not captured in statistics but in lives ruined, books censored, and speech chilled. One thing is certain, though: The world would be a better place if Anthony Comstock had confined his bookkeeping to the dry goods trade.

Rule #10: *Play the Martyr*

Given Comstock's absolute certainty that he was doing god's work, and considering the magnitude of his accomplishments, he was confounded that anyone should dare criticize him. How could they even *question* him? He was so obviously right and his critics so perverse and misguided, why couldn't everyone see it? Was the truth not obvious? So, to make sure people understood that any unfavorable opinions were borne of ignorance or intentional character assassination, Comstock devoted the final three chapters of his 1880 book FRAUDS EXPOSED to calling out his critics to reveal their lies and insinuations – even to the point of rebutting a number of unfavorable articles and letters to the editor of various papers from around the country.

Never mind the many people he jailed or drove to suicide, Comstock made clear that *he* was the real victim here. No doubt any criticism was the work of his great foe, the devil, and his earthly minions. Comstock complained that prejudices mounted against him because of libels disseminated by a compliant press, and that he would not be able to prevent such lies about his methods and acts "while the father of lies lives and his horde of followers inhabit the earth." Thus, in his mind the drive to repeal the postal censorship law was "one of the most diabolical schemes to repeal a righteous statute, and ruin a good man's name and reputation." Comstock's takeaway from reports of some of the proceedings of repeal efforts was "that the prime object of interest and importance was to see who could say the bitterest things against the present writer." Naturally, it was all about him.

He complained: "I have discharged my duty faithfully, accomplishing some very important object, or securing some notorious criminal dealing in vilest matters, and yet I have received nothing but misrepresentation, odium, and abuse." In a just world there "ought to be enough honesty and fairness to protect a man, engaged in suppressing this monster evil, from being branded as a criminal, and maligned by insinuations and base charges, in reputable papers." But, he lamented, no one "outside of a very limited circle knows of the faithful and heroic conduct of the officer of the Society that has dared to confront this evil."

Comstock's playbook is distinctly nonpartisan, and its tenets have been employed over the years as much by progressives as by conservatives. Activists of every political stripe have drawn from its teachings to condemn whatever expression they considered to be beyond the pale. The common denominator is the willingness to use government power to censor the speech of others, and that impulse comes from all directions.

5

Seduction of the Innocent: The Comic Book Menace

The American crusade against comic books, which began in the late 1940s and ended in the mid-1950s, was, in many ways, an upside-down moral panic. It was the denouement of Anthony Comstock's campaign against dime novels from a half-century earlier, and it began around the same time that the US Supreme Court seemingly settled the issue – the legal issue, that is, of how far the legislature could go in banning "evil reading" among America's youth. The campaign to restrict comics certainly had grassroots precursors, but it was fueled and brought to prominence by intellectuals and social progressives. Chief among those fanning the flames was a noted psychiatrist and liberal social activist, Dr. Fredric Wertham.

To most observers, Wertham and Comstock could not have seemed more different. Wertham was a nonreligious lettered man of science while Comstock was a store clerk and Puritan fundamentalist; Wertham was a social progressive who championed civil rights and racial integration – one admiring biographer called him "a traditional left-wing European intellectual" and "a card-carrying member of the liberal intelligentsia" – while Comstock was a rock-ribbed conservative who looked down on lower classes; and Wertham was a German immigrant while Comstock was obsessed with driving out foreign influences, particularly from what he called "lust-cursed nations." But when it came to censorship, they were very much the same man. Wertham was merely Comstock in miniature, yet that was enough to wreak havoc on a flourishing comic book industry.

BEGINNING AT THE END, OR ENDING AT THE BEGINNING?

The end came on March 29, 1948. That was the day the Supreme Court struck down New York's 1884 law prohibiting publications that featured "pictures and stories of deeds of bloodshed, lust or crime." That law had direct links to Comstock, as the New York legislature adopted it in response to Comstock's 1883 polemic, TRAPS FOR THE YOUNG. Comstock had no notion of comic books, of course, as that literary form would not emerge until the 1930s, starting as compilations of newspaper comic strips. But as the new medium developed in the late 1930s and into the 1940s, with detective and crime stories driving their popularity, Comstock's words about dime novels and crime stories carried a special resonance: "Crimes are gilded, and lawlessness painted to resemble valor, making a bid for bandits, brigands, murderers, thieves, and criminals in general." He blamed "the accursed blood-and-thunder story papers" as causing many a boy or youth to commit crimes "which have brought him to the penitentiary or the State's prison." New York's lawmakers agreed, and they branded as a criminal anyone who:

> Prints, utters, publishes, sells, lends, gives away, distributes or shows, or has in his possession with intent to sell, lend, give away, distribute or show, or otherwise offers for sale, loan, gift or distribution, any book, pamphlet, magazine, newspaper or other printed paper devoted to the publication, and principally made up of criminal news, police reports, or accounts of criminal deeds, or pictures, or stories of deeds of bloodshed, lust or crime.

The law remained undisturbed on the books for six decades until Murray Winters, a New York City bookseller, was fined for offering for sale a true-crime tabloid entitled *Headquarters Detective, True Cases from the Police Blotter*. The paper was not a comic, although it might as well have been. Its lurid tales of vice, murder, and intrigue were illustrated with photographs of criminals and their victims. The New York Court of Appeals upheld the fine, but the US Supreme Court reversed, issuing an opinion that would have shocked Comstock to his core. The Court didn't just throw out the fine; it struck down the statute as unconstitutional, taking with it similar laws in over half the states.

Justice Stanley Reed's pathbreaking opinion in *Winters v. New York* rejected the state's argument that such publications were beneath the dignity (and therefore outside the protection) of the First Amendment. He specifically rejected the notion "that the constitutional protection for a free press applies only to the exposition of ideas." As he explained,

> [t]he line between the informing and the entertaining is too elusive for the protection of that basic right. Everyone is familiar with instances of propaganda through fiction. What is one man's amusement, teaches another's doctrine. Though we can see nothing of any possible value to society in these magazines, they are as much entitled to the protection of free speech as the best of literature.

After finding the type of magazine at issue to fall within the Constitution's protection, the Court held that the statute was too vague to distinguish protected from unprotected speech. "It does not seem to us that an honest distributor of publications could know" when he might cross the line, and "[c]ollections of tales of war horrors, otherwise unexceptionable, might well be found to be 'massed' so as to become 'vehicles for inciting violent and depraved crimes.'"

Such an opinion from the nation's highest court usually comes at the end of a moral panic. That certainly was the case for Comstock, who labored for nearly forty years with the law on his side, taking advantage of the *Hicklin* rule's forgiving approach to censorship. Only after Comstock was gone did the legal tide turn, and the edifice he built begin to crumble. The evolution took decades to reach fruition, and *Winters* was an important part of that course correction. But this 1948 ruling came just as the anti-comic book crusade was taking root.

No matter, on the same day the Supreme Court issued the *Winters* decision, *Time* magazine published an article on the "psychopathology of comic books" entitled "Puddles of Blood." It marked Wertham's debut in the field, reporting on a symposium organized by his Association for the Advancement of Psychotherapy to explore the effects of what the article labeled "so-called 'comic books.'" Next to a photograph of a very dour-looking Dr. Wertham in his white lab coat, the *Time* article ticked off "grisly" examples and "shuddery statistics" about children's exposure to violent imagery. One expert estimated that the average city kid reads ten to a dozen comics a month and "[i]f there is only one scene of violence a page, this gives him a diet of '300 scenes of beating, shooting, strangling, torture, and blood per month.'" Based on this tally, he projected that every city child who was six years old by 1938 had "absorbed an absolute minimum of 18,000 pictorial beatings, shootings, stranglings, and blood puddles and torturings-to-death from comic books alone." Dr. Wertham assessed the impact of this exposure, concluding that comic books "not only inspire evil but suggest a form for evil to take."

Despite these deathly serious pronouncements, the *Time* article cheekily observed that "[t]he young may also pick up a few ideas from such old-fashioned sources as fairy tales (in Hansel & Gretel, the witch is oven-crisped by a couple of kids), myths (Perseus decapitates a lady who stands in his way), [and] Bible stories (little David gives Goliath a hole in the head)." Playful sarcasm aside, the crusade against comic books was off and running.

A NATIONAL DISGRACE

Wertham didn't start the anti-comic book movement, although he leapt to the front of the parade once he had the chance. A few noted intellectuals got there before him. One of the first prominent denunciations of the medium came in a 1940 editorial in the *Chicago Daily News* by literary critic and children's author Sterling North. Entitled "A National Disgrace," the short piece painted comic books with Comstockian prose, describing them as "a poisonous mushroom growth" and "pulp-paper nightmares" that would lead to "a cultural slaughter of the innocents." North lashed out at what he saw as comics' appeal to "mayhem, murder, torture, and abduction," and, like most would-be censors, tried to distinguish the new panic from the now-passé terrors of yesteryear. As he put it, "[t]he old dime novels in which an occasional redskin bit the dust were classic literature compared to the sadistic drivel pouring from the presses today."

North's politically incorrect diatribe marked the beginning of another chapter in the long history of moral panics that even predated Comstock. These recurring campaigns are typified by exaggerated claims of adverse effects of popular culture on youth based on pseudo-scientific assertions of harm that are little more than thinly veiled moral or aesthetic preferences. They inevitably target the "latest thing," only to fade away as new media lose their novelty and are assimilated. In this respect, North's articles echoed earlier complaints against Sunday supplements in newspapers. *The Atlantic Monthly* in August 1906 blasted funnies like the "Katzenjammer Kids" for a supposed disrespect for property, parents, the law and decency, while a January 1909 piece in the *Ladies' Home Journal* labeled Sunday strips a "national crime against our children." But, of course, comic books were different according to North (who happened to write for newspapers). He claimed that "a careful examination of the 108 periodicals now on the stands" revealed that "70 percent of the total were of a nature no respectable newspaper would think of accepting."

Although it was far from original, Sterling North's challenge to America's teachers and parents to rise up and "break the 'comic' magazine" clearly struck a nerve. The *Daily News* received more than twenty-five million requests for reprints of "A National Disgrace," and forty other papers published the editorial as well. North would later supplement his critique of mass culture (and comic books specifically) in subsequent pieces. Most historians who study the anti-comic book hysteria trace its roots to these articles. What followed was a combination of highbrow critiques of low culture combined with populist rallies, including book burnings, with a common goal of destroying the ten-cent menace.

A CRUSADE TAKES SHAPE

Today, it is difficult to appreciate the extent to which comic books took America by storm in the late 1930s and early 1940s. More Americans consumed comics in those years than read regular magazines, went to the movies, or listened to radio. In 1937 there were 150 different comic book titles, and during that period superhero books began to emerge – Superman in 1938 and Batman in 1939. By 1941, 30 comic book publishers churned out 15 to 18 million books each month and had a projected readership that topped 60 million. Newsstand sales rose to 25 million copies a month by the middle of World War II, and in the decade to follow, the number of comics sold or traded each month reached 75 million copies. At the time it was estimated that comic books were read by 91 to 95 percent of children between the ages of six and eleven. Wertham described comic books as "the greatest book publishing success in history," but, of course, he saw that as the problem. In his estimation, this made comics "the greatest mass influence on children."

After North's inflammatory 1940 editorial, but before Wertham published his first pieces on comic books beginning in 1948, academic literature on the issue was more neutral. Periodicals such as the *Journal of Experimental Education* carried articles like "Reading the Comics: A Comparative Study, Children's Interest in Reading the Comics," and "Words and the Comics." The journal *Educational Administration and Supervision* in 1942 ran a piece entitled "Reading the Comics in Grades IV–XII." An entire issue of the *Journal of Educational Sociology* in December 1944 was devoted to the study of comics, with articles such as "The Comics as a Social Force," and "Comics and Instructional Methods." Articles from this period tended to be short, data-driven analyses using dry, academic language and were cautious in drawing conclusions. One exception was a 1944 *Journal of Education* article entitled "The Viciousness of the Comic Book," but even then the author warned only that comics used "over-stimulating" colors and removed readers "from the land of reality to the land of wish-fulfillment." Reading them might make kids prone to daydreaming or becoming "a loafer."

The popular press of the period began to sound more alarmist themes. A 1945 *Time* magazine article posed the question "Are Comic Books Fascist?," echoing a theme that had been bubbling up in Catholic literature during the war. A February 1943 issue of *Catholic World* described Superman comics as "very much in the style of a Nazi pamphleteer." Among the Church's concerns (ironically) was that such super beings "defy natural laws." Others made the same point. As one Jesuit priest wrote in 1944:

> There is an anti-American, dictator propaganda in the glorification of these wrong-righting supermen. If our youth get the notion that it is heroic for a private person to "take over" in matters of public order we are ready for a Hitler. Hitler took over Germany when his followers had been persuaded that he was a superman with a mission to right the wrongs of the German state.

Wertham would later pick up and exploit the same theme, as did others. Author and "cultural critic" (and, oddly, inventor of the vibrating dildo) Gershon Legman blamed Superman for "giving every American child a complete course in paranoid megalomania such as no German child ever had, a total conviction of the morality of force such as no Nazi could ever aspire to." Likewise, a 1952 United Nations report on the impact of media on children made much the same point, if a bit more obliquely. Written by a "press and radio specialist" named Professor Philippe Bauchard, who later would be described as "a dumber, French version of Fredric Wertham," the report asserted that "[b]y undermining or warping the traditional values of each country, the Superman myth is becoming a kind of international monster."

During this period, it was hard to tell whether the primary concern about comic books was aesthetic, political, or a matter of public safety, as critics tended to lump the issues together. The various complaints ranged from blaming comics for degrading reading skills and dampening appreciation for natural colors to promoting fascism, advocating homosexuality, and causing drug use and juvenile delinquency. For example, the *New York Times* quoted Frances M. Crowley, dean of Fordham

University's school of education, for the various propositions that comic books "ruined eyesight," taught "atrocious English," and (incidentally) "bred juvenile delinquency."

The intellectuals of the Frankfurt school of thought, such as Herbert Marcuse, blamed "mass culture," including comic books, for creating a false consciousness and destroying the inner life among "the masses." One such writer at the time described comic books as "intellectual marijuana" and harbingers of cultural doom. Both Wertham and Legman adopted these ideas, and their loathing of such popular culture was unbounded. Legman recommended banning comic books for "peddling the same old violence, the same old illiteracy, the same old 'passive reception of mass entertainment,' requiring of the reader nothing more than to hand over his ten cents and then sit there drugged while little effortless pictures flow over him." And, he claimed, there was "the same undercurrent of homosexuality and sadomasochism."

As Wertham came on the scene in the late 1940s, concern about comics crystallized around their supposed contribution to juvenile delinquency. This was driven by the popular press, not by scientific literature. Great weight was placed on Wertham's credentials and purported "findings" based on his clinical experience, but there were no studies and no data to support the panic. Wertham himself published articles about comics almost exclusively in popular periodicals rather than peer-reviewed journals. Even his remarks on the psychopathology of comic books presented at the 1948 symposium of Association for the Advancement of Psychotherapy were published in THE *Saturday Review of Literature*, not in a scientific journal. By contrast, the statements of others – including those of professional eccentric Gershon Legman – were collected and published in the *American Journal of Psychotherapy*. A condensed version of Wertham's article was published in the August 1948 issue of *Reader's Digest*.

But Wertham was where he wanted to be, speaking to the audience he wanted to reach. His article, entitled "The Comics ... Very Funny!," was filled with lurid illustrations and florid descriptions of comic book content, unsupported and categorical conclusions about their effects, anecdotes in place of data or research, *ad hominem* attacks on anyone who doubted him, and unabashed admiration for public burnings of comic books. In short, Dr. Wertham was channeling his inner Comstock. This was his first publication on the subject of comic books, and he never deviated from this formula in the ensuing years.

Other popular articles echoed these themes and parroted the conclusions. *Time* magazine's coverage of the Wertham's symposium appeared under the title "Puddles of Blood," and others struck the same chord. The day before the *Time* piece, *Colliers* published an article by Judith Crist entitled "Horror in the Nursery," replete with photos child models "reenacting" anecdotal accounts of misbehavior purportedly conveyed by Wertham's young patients. This, according to Crist, was the first time Wertham's "findings" were being published. The article uncritically amplified all of the good doctor's dire warnings as being the considered scientific views of his clinic's "researchers" and "experts." These included Wertham's rather unscientific pronouncements that his team had determined that the effect of comics "is definitely and completely harmful" and that the number of good comics "is not worth discussing." His conclusion: "[T]he time has come to legislate these books off the newsstands and out of the candy stores." Around the same time, Wertham told the *New York Daily News* that he would offer his services in the upcoming election to any candidate "who really wants an issue to take directly to the parents of almost every home in this country where there are children."

This was the language of the crusader, not the scientist, and the article made no bones about the fact that Wertham was launching an "attack on comic books." Wertham candidly told the writer he got involved in "the fight" against comics "not as a psychiatrist, but as a voice for the thousands of troubled parents who, like myself, are concerned primarily with their children's welfare." And he was bitterly frustrated that most child welfare organizations and the psychology community had been "silent on the subject or they have frankly or apologetically endorsed comic books." To Wertham, the lack of scientific data to support his position and the paucity of others in his profession confirming his strident views "only proves the unhealthy state of child psychiatry." All those others were just "psycho-prima donnas who sit on committees and decide the fate of children from a distance." Yeah, *they* were the problem.

The controversy surrounding comic books became a regular fixture in women's magazines of the period. A February 1949 article in *Family Circle* posed the rhetorical question "What Can YOU Do about Comic Books?" And a lengthy piece in the November 1953 issue of *Ladies' Home Journal* (again, by Dr. Wertham) appeared under the headline "What Parent's Don't Know about Comic Books." The *Family Circle* article was remarkably balanced for writings of this genre. It began by acknowledging that there was "complete disagreement" among experts about the impact of comic books and that "[t]here are many different opinions in this field but no real data." It credited Wertham for sparking "a salutary house cleaning in the comic-book industry," but questioned his simplistic conclusions that children had been led to do evil deeds by reading comics. It urged parents to "look behind" the stories of these children, suggesting that "[i]n most cases you will discover a deeper background of emotional disturbance, of home rejection, elements that even without the stimulus of the comics would have caused the children to run amuck." The article took the revolutionary step of suggesting that parents not be swayed by the conflicting pronouncement of experts and instead should look into the problem themselves, read comics of various kinds, and discuss them with their children.

Wertham, of course, could not have disagreed more, which may be one reason he titled his *Ladies' Home Journal* piece "What Parents Don't Know about Comic Books." As in previous stories, the *Ladies' Home Journal* article purported to report Wertham's "findings" (alongside another think piece entitled "Can This Marriage

Be Saved?"), but it really was more of an extended rant that concluded "[i]f one were to set out to teach children how to steal, rob, lie, cheat, assault and break into candy stores, no more insistent method could be devised" than comic books. Illustrated with salacious images and liberally quoting from comics Wertham considered the vilest, the article blamed comic books for increasing the level and intensity of juvenile crime.

He scoffed at the idea that censoring comic books conflicted in any way with civil liberties. Wertham expected the industry to invoke the First Amendment, which he derided as "their Magna Charta [sic]," and he wrote that such arguments only diverted attention from "the real issue and veils the business in an idealistic haze." In his view, using "constitutional rights against progressive legislation is . . . an old story," but was the "fatal misuse of a high principle." Echoing Comstock, he concluded "[t]he framers of the Constitution and the amendments would certainly be surprised if they knew that these guarantees are used to sell children stories with pictures in which men prowl on the streets and dismember beautiful girls." This one passage pretty much summed up his arguments on both the "science" and the "law." If the stories and pictures were bad in his estimation, they must be harmful and likewise must be outside the law's protection.

GRASSROOTS ACTION

It's not that people didn't have enough to worry about in the late 1940s and early 1950s. The USA had just gone through a world war that represented an existential threat to the free world; the nuclear age had begun, ushering in the Cold War; the nation was in the grip of a Red Scare; and American troops were dying in Korea. In this uncertain environment, popular appeals by Wertham and others about comic books found a credulous audience and had their intended effect. They gave people something immediate to fear that was close to home – indeed, *in* the home – and they provided an identifiable villain and a simple solution: Get rid of comic books and all will be right with the world. The response was predictable.

Organizations such as the Parent Teacher Association(PTA), Daughters of the American Revolution, the Catholic Church, and youth groups (including the Boy Scouts, the Girl Scouts, and the Cub Scouts) initiated anti-comic book campaigns. The responsible adults rarely acted directly, however, as memories of Nazi book burnings organized by German students and by Hitler's government were still fresh, even if the lessons of those events had failed to sink in. All that was needed was for a concerned teacher or other authority figure to drop a hint to an energetic student who was eager to do "good," which usually led to community efforts to collect comics and hold public burnings. A couple of such events took place at Catholic schools in the mid-1940s, but the practice gained greater popularity after a public burning organized by middle-school students in Spencer, West Virginia, garnered national press coverage. This inspired others to follow suit, including public burnings of comics at parochial schools in Binghamton and Auburn, New York, in the following months (Figure 5.1). The events were organized and carried out by students, but they had the full support of church and school authorities.

Variations on this theme were repeated in communities across the country. In Illinois, a rally to burn comic books was sponsored by a community police captain. In Rumson, New Jersey, the anti-comics campaign played out as a bizarre, mirthless foreshadowing of Ray Bradbury's 1953 dystopian novel FAHRENHEIT 451, in which firemen had the job of burning books. Local Cub Scouts had been galvanized to action by their scoutmaster and the town mayor, and they prowled the streets on fire trucks, sirens blaring, to collect objectionable titles. The mayor presented awards to the scouts who had collected the most comics, and the winner was given the privilege of lighting the bonfire in Victory Park.

Some weeks later, a Girl Scout troop in Cape Girardeau, Missouri, collected comics for a public burning at a local Catholic high school. Students conducted a mock trial of several notable comic characters, including Superman, who confessed to "leading young people astray and building up false conceptions in the minds of youth." At the fire that followed the scripted proceedings, the parish pastor led 400 elementary and high-school students in a pledge "neither to read nor purchase objectionable publications and to stay away from retail establishments

FIGURE 5.1 Comic book bonfire from St. Patrick's Academy Yearbook, Binghamton, NY
Source: Collection of David Hajdu. Used by permission.

where such are sold." Wertham interpreted such events as proof that, when left to their own "free choice," children would prefer to burn comic books than read them.

LOCAL ORDINANCES

Any issue that attracts this kind of attention is catnip for politicians, and the ink was not yet dry on the Supreme Court's decision in *Winters* v. *New York* when local policymakers began looking for ways to restrict comic books despite the holding. The principal flaw of the New York law struck down in *Winters* was its vagueness, and the Court had said that neither the states nor Congress are prevented by the First Amendment from regulating such publications if the language of the statute is sufficiently precise to pass constitutional muster. Cities across the country immediately began investigating ways to develop the right legal tools, some using blunter instruments than others.

The Los Angeles Board of Supervisors studied the *Winters* ruling, and County Counsel Harold Kennedy devised what he called a "pioneering" ordinance designed to navigate the legal terrain that the Supreme Court charted. In September 1948, the County of Los Angeles banned the sale to minors of "crime comics," which the law defined as any publication "in which there is prominently featured an account of crime and which depicts by the use of drawings or photographs the commission or attempted commission" of a long list of specified crimes from murder to "mayhem." The idea was to avoid the problem of vagueness by listing the specific crimes for which depictions were banned. Kennedy consulted Dr. Wertham when the time came to defend the law, who provided a thirty-four-page affidavit in support of the measure, including the good doctor's considered legal opinion that the ordinance was constitutional. In his view, such laws were "nothing but a public health measure." He wrote: "It is no more a restriction of freedom of speech than not selling whiskey to children is a restraint of trade."

Press accounts initially lauded the ordinance for cleaning up LA's newsstands, including a favorable story in the *New York Times*, and Kennedy triumphantly predicted that his approach would lead to comprehensive state legislation. That did not happen, however, as the California Superior Court, evidently less impressed with Dr. Wertham's legal analysis than was County Counsel Kennedy, held that the law violated the First Amendment and struck it down. Although the ordinance was specific as to which crimes could not be depicted, it was far from clear exactly which comic books were forbidden. The court was concerned that publications depicting such crimes as the Lincoln assassination could be prohibited by the law. Years later, still smarting from the loss, Wertham took issue with the court's concern that the LA ordinance could prohibit illustrating the Lincoln assassination in a textbook. "Would that be such a calamity?" he asked. "There are many other pictures of Lincoln's time and life that would be far more instructive."

Failure of the LA ordinance did little to stem the tide of anti-comics measures in cities across the United States. By 1949, laws to regulate comic books – mostly designed to ban the sale of crime or horror comics to minors – were pending in fourteen states, and eventually at least fifty US cities would attempt to regulate the sale of comics. Often, local authorities would explore unofficial ways to suppress comics so as to avoid court review – in a word, bullying. Different communities used various measures, including having police or local prosecutors circulate blacklists as part of organized programs "to drive certain publications from [the] community." In some jurisdictions, officials obtained informal recommendations from interested organizations, while other communities established advisory committees or "literature commissions" to identify suspect works. Such methods proved to be highly effective "establishing a virtual censorship over reading matter by keeping it from reaching newsstands or by withdrawing it afterwards." Such indirect censorship efforts almost never saw the inside of a court.

Detroit implemented a particularly active censorship drive at the urging of the National Organization for Decent Literature (NODL), a Catholic group organized in the late 1930s to suppress various forms of "bad literature." Although comics were far from NODL's main focus, titles such as *Wonder Woman* showed up on their blacklist. Detroit operated its own censorship bureau, and on the advice of community groups (like NODL) effectively banned thirty-six comic titles from city newsstands. One legal commentator observed that the city's news distributors never failed to withhold from publication anything blacklisted under this quasi-informal system. This approach was typical.

In May 1948, working with local civic groups, Indianapolis "persuaded" local news dealers to drop twenty-five comic book titles. In Quincy, Massachusetts, a three-person citizen committee would review comics and other printed material intended for distribution to those under eighteen and report its findings to the police chief, who would in turn tell distributors not to sell or display the proscribed titles. Georgia also had a three-person committee of individuals appointed by the governor to investigate sales of any publications (including comics) deemed detrimental to public morals. Oklahoma City set up a Board of Review for Juvenile Readers to advise law enforcement agencies about which publications should be investigated or restricted.

Such systems of censorship did not require prosecutions to serve as effective bans on disfavored publications. Compliance was almost universal among newsstand operators because few were willing to shoulder the cost and aggravation – not to mention the adverse publicity – of fighting "unofficial" suggestions just to save a few titles. "Cleanup" efforts in large cities like Detroit could affect readers across the country, as some publishers would withdraw disapproved publications entirely. However, given the informal methods employed, a 1955 analysis in the *Harvard Law Review* found that "legal proceedings which might impose limitations on these practices are extremely rare."

When such measures did get tested in court, however, as foreshadowed by the Supreme Court's *Winters* decision, and as experienced with the LA ordinance, the outcome was predictable. In fact, LA County later took another run at defending its approach, and in 1959 the California Supreme Court applied *Winters* to strike down the renewed comic book ordinance under the First Amendment. The Washington State Supreme Court the year before struck down a comprehensive state law licensing and regulating the sale of "crime comic books." The Court described the law as "a prior restraint in the most unrestricted form," applied *Winters* and other Supreme Court precedent, and voided the law.

The Supreme Court addressed the issue again in 1957, although (as in *Winters*) not for a law specifically directed at comic books. It struck down a Michigan statute that prohibited making available to the public any book "tending to the corruption of the morals of youth," which meant that it dealt with the same legal issues that motivated the comic book laws. And the case originated in Detroit, with its uncommonly active censorship bureau of twelve employees, who worked through both formal and informal channels to protect that city's youth from any evil influences in print (as defined by NODL). That group's "blacklist" included both comic books and books like Catcher in the Rye, From Here to Eternity, and God's Little Acre. The case that reached the Supreme Court involved the arrest and conviction of bookseller Alfred E. Butler, who was fined $100 for selling a paperback novel, The Devil Rides Outside, to a Detroit police inspector.

Michigan courts upheld the conviction, but a unanimous Supreme Court made short work of it in *Butler* v. *Michigan*. Justice Felix Frankfurter's very short opinion voiding the law explained that it "reduce[d] that adult population of Michigan to reading only what is fit for children." This, he famously wrote, "is to burn the house to roast the pig." Supreme Court opinions are this concise and unanimous only when the constitutional issues are obvious. And here, they were. Justice Frankfurter's opinion, comprising a mere six paragraphs – eight if you count the footnotes separately – takes up only five pages in the US Reports. And its bedrock principles were cited in later cases striking down state laws regulating sale of comic books.

A few years later, the Supreme Court addressed the practice of informal censorship that had been widely employed to suppress comic books, and again, it had no difficulty applying the First Amendment. In *Bantam Books, Inc.* v. *Sullivan*, the Court struck down a scheme in which the Rhode Island "Commission to Encourage Morality in Youth" would send letters to booksellers urging them to prevent the circulation of certain books that the commission deemed "objectionable." The letters were phrased as requests for "cooperation," and the commission had no authority to prosecute or take other legal action, although it said that it would provide its views to police and the state Attorney General. Nevertheless, the Supreme Court held that this coercive innuendo violated the First Amendment: "We are not the first court to look through forms to the substance and recognize that informal censorship may sufficiently inhibit the circulation of publications." It rejected the state's argument that the distributors were free to ignore the letters, finding that they were "thinly veiled threats to institute criminal proceedings against [the distributors] if they do not come around." The Court held that the informal system violated the First Amendment because the Youth Commission functioned as an "instrument[] of regulation independent of the laws."

Even before the Supreme Court rulings in *Butler* and *Bantam Books*, some elected officials understood the First Amendment issues presented by demands to regulate comic books and felt sufficiently constrained by their oath of office to uphold the Constitution. For example, in March 1952 the New York legislature passed a bill to prohibit the sale and display of crime comics to children under the age of fifteen. Wertham and others had lobbied for the measure, describing it as a "public health" law aimed at "the cause of a psychological mutilation of children." The bill did not become law, however, because Governor Thomas E. Dewey vetoed it, citing the *Winters* decision. Dewey's veto memorandum said that the bill violated the First Amendment. He had vetoed an earlier bill on the same grounds.

CUE THE INVESTIGATORS

With this level of public interest and concern, it is hardly surprising that, between 1950 and 1954, multiple congressional committees investigated comic books and their asserted link to juvenile delinquency. Congressional hearings like this are the perfect vehicle for ambitious politicians because they provide a platform for speechifying and venting concerns without having to worry too much about any constitutional ramifications. They don't even have to enact legislation to reap some benefits. Just putting on the show provides political rewards while passing the proverbial buck to others. As essayist Louis Menand put it in *The New Yorker*, "[a]n investigation by senators has been compared to a court run by kangaroos, an analogy that is not unfair, except possibly to the kangaroos." He noted that "[t]he normal rules of evidence do not apply in congressional hearings: badgering is appreciated; the verdict has frequently been arrived at in advance."

The first round of hearings was conducted in 1950 by the Senate's Special Committee to Investigate Organized Crime in Interstate Commerce. The hearings were called by Senator Estes Kefauver, a New Deal Democrat from Tennessee who won fame investigating organized crime in some of the first ever televised congressional hearings. A reported 30 million Americans tuned in to watch the hearings, elevating Kefauver to national prominence (Figure 5.2). He appeared on the cover of *Time* magazine, and in December 1951 was voted one of America's ten most admired men. Oddly, Kefauver reportedly was not much interested in the issue of organized crime when it was first suggested to him, until *Washington Post* publisher Donald Graham told him it would enhance his political future. "Estes," Graham asked him, "don't you want to be vice president?" Kefauver relented, and would go on to

FIGURE 5.2 Women and young girls entering movie theater to see Free TV of Kefauver
Senate crime hearings
Source: Photo by Michael Rougier/The LIFE Picture Collection via Getty Images.

become a two-time presidential candidate and was Adlai Stevenson's vice-
presidential running mate in 1956.

The 1950 hearings on comic books and juvenile delinquency spanned several days
and the investigation included written submissions from over a hundred witnesses,
including judges of juvenile and family courts, probation officers, court psychiatrists, social workers, comic book publishers, cartoonists, officers of national organizations, and public officials, such as FBI Director J. Edgar Hoover. Wertham was
not among them, as he claimed that he had lacked sufficient time to prepare
a written response. He would later write that he was on vacation when he heard

from the committee, so "[o]f course I refused, replying that such a hasty publication without investigation was certainly not in the interests of the public." One might be forgiven for thinking that the world's foremost expert on comic books and their effects (in his own estimation, at least), who had been studying the issue for years and publishing articles, and who had already been working with the committee, might have managed to crank out a few pages to answer the committee's questions, but it didn't happen. The committee managed nevertheless to carry on its work without Wertham's input, a transgression for which the doctor never forgave Kefauver.

The findings of the hearings were far from definitive. Although Director Hoover agreed that "crime books" that "glorify crime and the criminal" may be dangerous, "particularly in the hands of an unstable child," he saw delinquency as "a result of a combination of forces," and concluded that the causes of lawlessness "do not stem from any one source." He cited statistics indicating that arrests of youths had leveled off in the post-war years (contrary to the claims of those favoring regulation), and said that it was doubtful "that an appreciable decrease in juvenile delinquency would result if crime comic books of all types were not readily available to children." A New York judge submitted a statement that his experience with comics had been positive, and that, in his years of experience and close contact with thousands of defendants, "I never came across a single case where the delinquent or criminal act would be attributed to the reading of comic books." He surveyed other state agencies that deal with delinquency as well and reported his "considered opinion that there is no demonstrable connection between the reading of comic books and juvenile delinquency." Professor Harvey Zorbaugh of the New York University (NYU) Department of Education, among others, opined that "comics have very little to do with juvenile delinquency." The Committee issued its final report in November 1950 and, based on the evidence, found "no direct connection between the comic books dealing with crime and juvenile delinquency."

Given these findings, or, more to the point, the lack of them, the investigation produced no legislative proposals. Nevertheless, Kefauver had learned the value of this type of political theater, and in 1953 cosponsored a resolution with Republican Senator Robert C. Hendrickson of New Jersey to convene a special Subcommittee of the Senate Judiciary Committee to investigate juvenile delinquency. Just days before they introduced the resolution, the *New York Times* reported a decline in juvenile crime, but that fact did not slow the momentum for hearings. By then Kefauver had already developed a taste for the show. Like Kefauver's 1950 hearings, this inquiry was not narrowly focused on comics but included gangs, narcotics, pornography, access to guns, and child prostitution among the subjects it would explore. This did not prevent Senator Hendrickson from announcing, even before any witnesses testified, that he believed the primary cause of juvenile crime to be "the increasing emphasis on sex and crime in public entertainment." And why not? The senator's incoming mail indicated that the public was convinced that comic books caused crime, so it was just good politics to give the people what they wanted.

Accordingly, Hendrickson announced in February 1954 that he would hold televised hearings on the dangers of comic books.

SEDUCTION OF THE INNOCENT AND THE 1954 HEARINGS

Dr. Wertham was determined not to repeat the mistakes of the past: He hadn't submitted testimony for the 1950 Kefauver hearings and they came to nothing. His expert testimony helped persuade the New York state legislature to pass anticrime comics legislation in 1950 and 1951, but Governor Thomas Dewey vetoed the bills on First Amendment grounds. Before that, Wertham had provided a lengthy expert affidavit in support of the Los Angeles County ordinance regulating crime comics, only to see the law struck down in court as unconstitutional. Worse still, there was a concern that public attention to the threat posed by comic books might fade, particularly since no federal legislation was forthcoming. This time, the doctor had the perfect prescription for these problems – he published a book presenting his "findings" and made an impassioned case for banning crime comics for minors. Its Comstockian title was also perfect: SEDUCTION OF THE INNOCENT.

Wertham's timing was impeccable. The book was published on April 19, 1954, two days before he testified at Hendrickson and Kefauver's televised hearings on the perils of comic books for America's youth. Of course, it is pretty easy to get the timing right when you are a special consultant to the committee, as Wertham was. Plus, his book had been heavily promoted in the weeks and months leading up to the hearings. It was a Book-of-the-Month Club selection and was widely advertised in women's magazines, in newspapers, and even on billboards across the USA. The lead article in the November 1953 issue of *Ladies' Home Journal* (with the article "What Parents Don't Know about Comic Books") had laid the groundwork for this media blitz by previewing extended excerpts from SEDUCTION OF THE INNOCENT. *Reader's Digest* published excerpts as well in an article entitled "Comic Books – Blueprints for Delinquency."

It is little, wonder then, that Wertham's book was described as the "primer of the American campaign" against comics. The book was promoted ostensibly as a work of science, described in a publisher's note as "the result of seven years of scientific investigation," but it was far from a scientific work. It was a long-form, first-person screed denouncing comic books, inactive legislators, misguided judges, bought-off psychologists, and anyone else who dared disagree with him. The "science" in the book was nothing more than a series of descriptions of salacious comic book stories (including some illustrations), anecdotal accounts of counseling sessions with patients, and Wertham's personal opinions presented as indisputable scientific fact.

The book might have been called THE ADVENTURES OF DR. FREDRIC WERTHAM, MD (and likely would have been, had it been a comic), for much of the book is devoted to his efforts to advocate for the regulation of comics and how he had been thwarted by an evil comic book industry and spineless lawmakers. This is not the usual stuff of scientific literature. But it explains why the lead paragraph in the *New York Times* review of SEDUCTION OF THE INNOCENT described Wertham as "an angry man, who has good reasons for anger."

The *Times* review was written by C. Wright Mills, an associate professor of sociology from Columbia University, who praised Wertham for "a most commendable use of the professional mind in the service of the public." Mills accepted Wertham's conclusions about the effects of comic books uncritically, but in his praise revealed one of the book's biggest weaknesses – its lack of any scientific foundation. He quoted Wertham's lament that he shouldn't have to prove his thesis when to him its truth was self-evident, but observed: "There is needed . . . studies of the effects of comic books on children at various levels, on an adequate statistical basis," adding that "[t]his is one of the most difficult types of problems in the whole of social psychology." There were other favorable reviews, including – predictably – in *Catholic World*, which expressed the hope that the book would prompt anti-comic book legislation. *The New Yorker* described Wertham's work as "a formidable indictment" against comics that was "practically unanswerable."

But not all contemporary reviews were so forgiving of Wertham's loose methodology and florid rhetoric. Writing in *Commentary*, Robert S. Warshow described SEDUCTION OF THE INNOCENT as "a kind of crime comic book for parents" in which "the logic of personal interest is inexorable." The piece criticized Wertham's simplistic reasoning and suggested that the book may have cause-and-effect backwards, noting that "it would be a dull child indeed who could go to Dr. Wertham's clinic and not discover very quickly that most of his problematical behavior can be explained in terms of comic books." A *New Republic* review criticized the book as oversimplified and unscientific, making the fair point that Wertham sought to bolster his claims "not with his professional argument" but simply by reference to "his professional status." It observed that Wertham failed to provide evidence that children interpreted the stories in comics as he did, and described his conclusions about their effects as "a tissue of troublesome points."

Because Wertham published almost exclusively in popular magazines and not in peer-reviewed journals, his work did not have the benefit of adequate professional review at the time. And what little data he revealed in SEDUCTION OF THE INNOCENT and in his articles did not stand up to scrutiny over time. His random, undocumented, and unverifiable case studies of children who supposedly had been harmed, presented through the dramatic reconstruction of contrived dialogue, appeared selected simply to correspond to his preconceived conclusions about comics. Scholarly critiques noted that the book lacked any scientifically gathered research or systematic inventory of comic book content, and concluded that "[w]ithout such an inventory, the conjectures are biased, unreliable, and useless." Others observed that Wertham's claims were based on a "crude social learning theory model which either implicitly or explicitly assumed unmediated modeling effects."

Probably the worst blow came three decades after Wertham's death when a researcher reviewed the case files used in the writing of SEDUCTION OF THE INNOCENT. Wertham's papers were not made widely available to researchers until 2010, and when Carol Tilley, a professor of library and information science, reviewed his notes, she found that he had "manipulated, overstated, compromised, and fabricated evidence." Wertham had misstated the ages of children, combined quotations taken from many subjects to make it appear as if they came from the same person, and omitted (or even invented) key details. His accounts left out other likely factors that might explain delinquency, such as a history of family violence, substance abuse, gang membership, or low intelligence, and invariably returned to his preferred cause – comics. He exaggerated the number of patients from which he drew his conclusions, which numbered in the hundreds and not the "many thousands" as he had claimed. And some were not even his patients but instead were those of colleagues whom he had never met or personally observed. Although some critics still considered Wertham "an extremely well-intentioned liberal, progressive man," Dr. Tilley concluded that he got "carried away with his own preconceptions, his own agenda," and "became perhaps disconnected from the kids that he was treating and observing."

But this is now and that was then. Wertham's questionable methods and spurious conclusions, even had they been fully examined at the time, were not going to get in the way of a good legislative show trial. After all, surveys showed that in 1954 three-quarters of the American public believed that comic books caused juvenile delinquency. Nor were hearings going to be derailed by the developing case law suggesting it would be extremely difficult to write a law restricting crime or horror comic books that could survive a court challenge. Wertham was convinced – in his professional opinion – that the Supreme Court's First Amendment analysis on such matters was dead wrong, and he had a great deal to say about it in SEDUCTION OF THE INNOCENT. Chapters are devoted to recounting his testimony in court cases, his advice to legislative committees about the need for "public health" laws, and why the Supreme Court's decision in *Winters* was misguided. Wertham approvingly cited Comstock-era precedents and quoted lengthy passages from Justice Frankfurter's dissenting opinion in *Winters*, which he predicted would be vindicated as "one of the great documents of legal and social philosophy of our time." Spoiler alert: It wasn't. Wertham's confident prediction failed to anticipate Justice Frankfurter's 1957 opinion in *Butler* v. *Michigan*, in which a unanimous Court struck down Michigan's law to prevent the corruption of youth as an example of "burn[ing] the house to roast the pig."

But legal analysis was not the point; Wertham's purpose was to try to shame the legislators into some action to join in what Wertham immodestly described as *his* "contest with the crime-comic-book industry." He did this by recounting his disappointment with the committee's failure to adopt legislation in 1950. Wertham dejectedly reported that "it really seemed for a while that Superman had licked me," but claimed that he had become optimistic for a time, when, in preparation for his 1950 hearings, Senator Kefauver visited Wertham in his apartment seeking advice on what to do about comic books. Several years after this meeting, Wertham somehow managed to recall the conversation verbatim and wrote "[t]hen and there he appointed me as psychiatric consultant to his committee."

Wertham was encouraged by what he called Kefauver's "sincere homespun friendliness," but he listed conditions for his cooperation: The committee would have to scrutinize the "far-flung propaganda of the industry, a legal investigation of sales practices, the links to drugs, prostitution," and – of course – "illustrations from comic books would be used." Kefauver agreed to it all, and that meeting was followed by phone calls, visits from committee staffers, and Wertham's instruction on how they should proceed. He wrote in SEDUCTION OF THE INNOCENT that he could not say for certain that the efforts would result in legislation, "but I did think that there would be at least some kind of investigation." Wertham outlined in detail what he described as "preliminary steps" for the committee to take, and helped develop the questionnaire to be sent to experts. But then he refused to provide his own response.

Wertham's mysterious refusal to submit answers to the seven-point questionnaire at the committee's request was never adequately explained. His claim in SEDUCTION OF THE INNOCENT that he lacked adequate time to provide a detailed response because he was on vacation when the request arrived was absurd. The questions Wertham had helped formulate (including "Do you believe that there is any relationship between the reading of crime comic books and juvenile delinquency?" and, redundantly, "Do you believe juvenile delinquency would decrease if crime comic books were not readily available to children?") probed core allegations he had been making for years in articles, testimony, and affidavits. Could it be that Wertham simply was offended by the fact that his answers would not be given priority but instead would be lumped together with the opinions of lesser witnesses, such as juvenile court judges and FBI Director Hoover? No one knows.

But it is certain that he was using SEDUCTION OF THE INNOCENT to try to settle the score. He wrote that he was aghast when he read news reports proclaiming the committee's finding that comic books had little or nothing to do with juvenile crime. After quoting a number of headlines and editorials about the 1950 committee report, Wertham wrote (again, immodestly): "[I]t was I who had inadvertently given the crime-comic-book industry the biggest advertising it had ever had." (He uncharacteristically was willing to share the credit, though. He also called the committee report "the greatest advertisement the crime comic book industry has had to date.") Wertham denounced the committee report as incompetent and the expert witnesses cited therein as tools of the comic book industry. He also described Kefauver as a deserter in the battle against comic books, and called New York Governor Thomas Dewey "strange" for vetoing anti-comics legislation on constitutional grounds. Wertham wrote that "the decision of Governor Dewey and the lack of decision by Senator Kefauver had given the green light to the comic book industry" and "they went ahead full steam." And he described a series of gruesome comic book stories that he claimed were the natural by-products of "what might be called the Kefauver-Dewey charter" – "in short," he added sarcastically, "real freedom of expression."

So, what was Senator Kefauver to do? He had become a national celebrity for shining a spotlight on crime and had personally reached out to the foremost expert on the connection between comic books and juvenile delinquency, and now he was being blamed by that same expert for allowing children to consume a steady diet of horror, crime, and mayhem. Wertham's message was delivered in a book that did not just promise to be a bestseller; it was being excerpted in the ladies' magazines, and the author was scheduled to be the committee's star witness. This would have been a political problem any time, but it was all the more pronounced in April 1954 because Kefauver was hoping to parlay this latest round of televised hearings into the Democratic nomination for president in 1956. So the senator from Tennessee responded in a way that every modern politician would understand – he blamed someone else.

The comic book publishers had been allowed to flourish unregulated not because of his committee's inaction after the 1950 hearings, Kefauver maintained, but because he had been hoodwinked. Now, during the 1954 hearings, Kefauver proclaimed that the comic book industry had failed to reveal its connections to certain child experts. He charged that the Child Study Association of America had "deceived the public" in its reports on comic books, because it had failed to note that some of the experts it employed were consultants to comic-book publishers. The maneuver was misleading and failed to account for the previous testimony of J. Edgar Hoover, among others, who questioned the asserted link between comic books and crime. But it served its purpose. Kefauver promised that the 1954 hearings on comic books would be different. And they were.

THE SHOW

Just as Wertham had demanded as a condition of his participation in 1950, the 1954 hearings opened with a Comstockian "Chamber of Horrors," including a display of gruesome comic book covers and a discussion of their lurid storylines (Figure 5.3). Chairman Hendrickson began with the obligatory disclaimer that freedom of the press was not at issue and that the committee did not intend to become "blue-nosed censors," but then he turned the proceedings over to the committee's executive director, Richard Clendenen, to set the stage. Clendenen began with a slide show of comic book covers and selected panels from particular stories to illustrate the types of stories under investigation, providing body counts along the way. The committee heard from twenty-two witnesses in three days of

FIGURE 5.3 Display of comic book covers at Senate hearings
Source: Photo by Bettman/Getty Images.

hearings, but the main event – and what the hearings are remembered for – was the back-to-back testimony from Wertham followed by William Gaines, publisher of EC Comics.

Wertham's testimony was as advertised. He drew heavily on his credentials and claimed that SEDUCTION OF THE INNOCENT was the product of "a sober, painstaking, laborious clinical study" that provided "incontrovertible evidence of the pernicious influences on youth of crime comic books." He had even showed up "in costume," wearing a white coat in case there were any doubt of his status as a doctor. Wertham pronounced his opinion in slow, stentorian tones: "[W]ithout any reasonable doubt, and without any reservation, . . . comic books are an important contributing factor in many cases of juvenile delinquency." Despite the fact that most professional social workers, psychologists, sociologists, and criminologists denied any direct link between mass media and delinquency, Wertham told the committee "on this subject there is practically no controversy."

Citing his "case studies" and punctuating his testimony with examples from what he considered the worst comics, Wertham testified that if his task were "to teach children delinquency, to tell them how to rape and seduce girls, how to hurt people, how to break into stores, how to cheat, how to forge, how to do any known crime, if it were my task to teach that, I would have to enlist the crime comic book industry." This conclusion was self-evident to Wertham: "I will say that every crime of delinquency is described in detail and that if you teach somebody the technique of something you, of course, seduce him into it." As if any further proof were needed, Wertham added, "Nobody would believe that you teach a boy homosexuality without introducing him to it. The same thing with crime." QED.[1] Wertham reserved special scorn for his old nemesis, Superman, who he opined was "particularly injurious to the ethical development of children." He claimed that Superman comics fed children's fantasies of "sadistic joy in seeing other people punished over and over again while you yourself remain immune." Such stories, he claimed, "teach complete contempt of the police."

His testimony matched the alarmist tenor of his writings. When asked whether or not children from good homes might be less susceptible to the lure of bad comics, Wertham assured the committee "as long as the crime comic books industry exists in its present form there are no secure homes." Wertham compared comic books to communicable disease, asserting: "You cannot resist infantile paralysis in your own home alone. Must you not take into account the neighbor's children?" The senators did not seem to mind that Wertham responded to their questions with inapt metaphors rather than evidence, and this latitude only spurred the witness to greater rhetorical excesses. "Hitler was a beginner compared to the comic-book industry," he proclaimed.

The committee members asked Wertham no hard questions and for the most part simply let him talk. This deferential treatment illustrated how hearings of this type are a form of morality play. Like professional wrestling matches, they typically follow simple, preordained storylines with well-defined good guys and bad guys. Wertham, flawed as he was, had been cast as the good guy, and the senators were not about to interfere with that narrative. Briefing papers prepared by the staff before the hearing had cautioned members that Wertham represented "the extreme position among the psychiatrists," and suggested careful questions to help members nudge the doctor toward more mainstream views. While they needed Wertham's storyline, they didn't want to be embarrassed by it, either.

Notwithstanding this warning, no one challenged any of Wertham's over-the-top statements, and questions seemed designed only to underscore his conclusions. At one point, for example, Senator Kefauver asked Wertham to confirm that he, "more than any other psychiatrist in the United States," had observed children's reactions to crime and horror comic books. Wertham was happy to accept Kefauver's premise, and didn't push back as the senator suggested that the doctor's original estimate of "hundreds" of children was too low and should be

---

[1]   QED (quod erat demonstrandum) literally means "what was to be shown."

measured in the "thousands." Of course, Wertham did not reveal that many of the "patients" whose stories were recounted in SEDUCTION OF THE INNOCENT were not his, that he had not actually spoken to many of them, and that he tended to modify and embellish their stories to fit his diagnoses.

Whether or not Wertham's diatribe was convincing, the committee's selection of William Gaines to play the role of the "bad guy" proved decisive. Gaines, an outspoken defender of comic books, was the publisher of EC Comics, the market leader in the horror genre with such well-known titles as *Tales from the Crypt* and *Weird Science*. Even before the hearing, Gaines had attracted the committee's attention by providing an advance copy of an editorial cartoon soon to appear on the inside cover of several EC titles satirically linking the anti-comics crusade with Communism. Foreshadowing the type of lampoon that later would make *Mad* magazine a cultural phenomenon (with Gaines as publisher), the cartoon pointed out that the group most anxious to destroy comics are the Communists, and puckishly posed the question "Are You a Red Dupe?"

Using illustrations of a style that would be later be instantly recognizable by generations of *Mad* readers, the cartoon began by illustrating a fictitious account of Melvin Blitzinken-Skovichsky, who was hanged in the town of Gazoosky, "in the heart of Soviet Russia," for publishing a comic magazine. It observed that here in America we can still publish comics but that "there are some people in America who would *like* to censor," singling out Gershon Legman (who, the cartoon said, "claims to be a ghost writer for Dr. Fredric Wertham, the author of a recent blast against comics published in '*The Ladies Home Journal*'"). It then reported that research of newspaper files had led to the "astounding discovery" that "the group most anxious to destroy comics are the Communists!"

Gaines' cartoon quoted an actual article from the *Daily Worker* of July 13, 1953, charging that comic books brutalized America's youth and prepared them to serve the nation's goal of world domination. The *Daily Worker* article purported to link reading comics with "atrocities now being perpetrated by American soldiers and airmen in Korea." It concluded: "So, the next time some joker gets up at [a] P.T. A. meeting, or starts jabbering about the 'naughty comic books' at your local candy store, give him the *once-over*." The editorial cartoon sardonically assured its readers it wasn't actually accusing anti-comics crusaders of *being* Communists, allowing for the possibility that they "may not even *read* the *Daily Worker*." But they have "swallowed the red bait . . . hook, line, and sinker!" So Gaines' cartoon conceded the possibility that anti-comics crusaders in the USA may merely be "Red dupes."

Members of the committee were not amused. Needless to say, with the nation in the grip of McCarthyism, for this group of ambitious politicians, the parody did not sit well. The "Red dupe" comparison was an especially sore subject for the senators, as their comic book hearings coincided with those of Joseph McCarthy, who was "investigating" Communists in the US Army. With the "Red dupe" editorial cartoon in the subcommittee's possession, Gaines came into the hearing room perfectly positioned for a roasting. Several senators obliged, huffily grilling Gaines on what he had intended by the satire. Committee staffer Clendenen interpreted the editorial cartoon as an effort to forestall any inquiry into the comic book industry. Senator Kefauver in particular was outraged. Even apart from his presidential ambitions, he was in the midst of a reelection campaign in which his opponent had claimed that the Tennessee Democrat was "coddling Communists." The cartoon only served to whet the appetites of Gaines' ravenous interrogators.

Even before he was questioned, Gaines did himself (and the industry) no favors. He tried to counter Wertham's claims of harmfulness by charging that the psychiatrist saw children as "dirty, sneaky, perverted monsters who use the comics as a blueprint for action." But this wasn't true, Gaines explained: "Perverted little monsters are few and far between. They don't read comics. The chances are most of them are in schools for retarded children." While he understood that some might not like the comics he produced, he told the committee that "it would be just as difficult to explain the harmless thrill of a horror story to Dr. Wertham as it would to explain the sublimity of love to a frigid old maid." Much of his testimony was along the same lines, and, for the most part, the senators let him finish without interruption. Then came the questions. If comics could teach good moral lessons, couldn't they also teach bad ones? How did they test appropriate subjects for their stories? Did they use children? And on and on.

The pivotal moment of the hearing came in a colloquy between members of the committee and Gaines, with Kefauver using recent EC Comics covers as visual aids. Gaines had testified that he relied on his sense of "good taste" to set the limits on what he considered appropriate for children, and this opened the door for Kefauver. Earlier that day he and other committee members had posed for pictures in front of a poster-board display of comic book covers under the label "Representative Comic Book Covers; Crime, Horror, & Weird Variety." And so he was ready when Gaines offered the setup about "good taste."

The Senator from Tennessee theatrically pulled out a copy of the EC title *Crime SuspenStories* from May 1954 (which promised "Jolting tales of *tension* in the EC tradition!") and held it up for all to see. The art, which made up about two-thirds of the cover, told the story. In the background a woman's legs were sprawled on a tile floor. Standing above her was a man, visible from mid-chest to the top of his thighs. In his right hand he gripped an ax near the top of the handle, just below the blade. In his left, in the foreground, he held a woman's head, letting it dangle from his grip on the victim's blonde hair. It certainly wasn't graphic by today's standards. The woman's head was the most prominent image on the cover, but no wounds were depicted. And while the ax was stained with a dark substance that presumably was blood, it was not the crimson red one might expect. Still, it was more than enough for Kefauver's purposes.

As Kefauver held the comic aloft, the following exchange ensued:

SENATOR KEFAUVER:	Here is your May 22 issue. This seems to be a man with a bloody ax holding a woman's head up which has been severed from her body. Do you think that is in good taste?
MR. GAINES:	Yes, sir; I do, for the cover of a horror comic. A cover in bad taste, for example, might be defined as holding the head a little higher so that the neck could be seen dripping blood from it and moving the body over a little further so that the neck of the body could be seen to be bloody.
SENATOR KEFAUVER:	You have blood coming out of her mouth.
MR. GAINES:	A little.
SENATOR KEFAUVER:	Here is blood on the ax. I think most adults are shocked by that.
CHAIRMAN HENDRICKSON:	Here is another one I want to show him.
SENATOR KEFAUVER:	This is the July one. It seems to be a man with a woman in a boat and he is choking her to death with a crowbar. Is that in good taste?
MR. GAINES:	I think so.
CHIEF COUNSEL HANNOCH:	How could it be worse?

In retrospect, Gaines probably should have seen it coming. Anti-comics advocates had long maintained that the cover art alone was enough to convict comics for all the bad effects of which they had been accused. That was why Wertham had long insisted that any hearings about the evils of comic books must use the covers as exhibits. And this time it paid off. The "severed head exchange" was widely quoted in press reports across the country, including in a front-page *New York Times* story. While it did nothing to bolster Wertham's extravagant claims about the harmful effects of crime and horror comic books, it embarrassed the industry's defenders, and Gaines in particular. In the public mind, comics were convicted of bad taste.

Like the 1950 comic book investigation, the 1954 hearings produced no legislative proposals. But that had never been the point. The lawmakers were well aware that attempting to draft legislation that could meet the legal standards set forth in earlier cases like *Winters* would be difficult, and that a law that attempted to restrict comic books would be unlikely to survive a constitutional challenge (and might get them branded as censors to boot). So why bother? The political theater of the hearings had fully served their purposes without the fuss of legislative drafting or the risk of embarrassment if their work was later rejected in court. So the objective all along had been to pressure the industry into adopting a "voluntary" code of self-regulation. And it worked.

It took a while to get it right – the committee's report from the hearings was not published until 1955 – but when it finally emerged, the document was perfectly crafted to be on all sides of the issue (and to do nothing). The report adopted Wertham's scolding tone, warning that crime and horror comic books "offer short courses in murder, mayhem, robbery, rape, cannibalism, carnage, necrophilia, sex, sadism, masochism, and virtually every other form of crime, degeneracy, bestiality, and horror." It found that "these books evidence a common penchant for violent death in every form imaginable," but observed that there was disagreement among the experts in behavioral science except on one key point – "that juvenile delinquency has many causes, not just one." It consequently announced that the committee "has no proposal for censorship," finding that such a solution would be "totally out of keeping with our basic American concepts of a free press operating in a free land for a free people." Instead, it endorsed a strict system of self-regulation that, at least in the short term, would disrupt the comics industry.

THE CODE

Quite a bit happened between the time that the hearings wrapped in early summer 1954 and publication of the committee's report in March the following year. The industry was shaken by Gaines' poor performance and the corresponding negative publicity, and it took to heart Chairman Hendrickson's statement on the final day of the hearings that he believed he spoke "for the entire subcommittee" in suggesting that "[a] competent job of self-policing within the industry will achieve much." The combined pressure of local regulation, bad press, and ongoing federal investigations convinced key industry players that they had to act before they were acted upon. So in September 1954, the industry formed the Comics Magazine Association of America (CMAA), and announced that former New York City magistrate Charles F. Murphy would serve as the "comics czar." The group initially offered the "czar" position to Wertham, but he turned it down.

With all but three of the top industry publishers as members, CMAA was able to impose a strict form of industry self-regulation. CMAA announced its regulatory "code" within a couple of months after the group was formed, and it set forth forty-one requirements for approval, including the following: comics could not use terms like "horror" or "terror" in their titles, and themes including zombies, vampires, cannibals, or werewolves were banned; no lurid, unsavory, or gruesome images would be allowed; no attack on any religion would ever be permissible; comics could not present unique details or methods of crime; police, judges and other public officials could not be portrayed disrespectfully; no profanity, obscenity, smut, or vulgarity was permitted in word or image; no suggestive or salacious drawings of women would be approved; love stories must promote the sanctity of marriage; and comics should foster respect for parents, the moral code, and honorable behavior. Members agreed to submit their comics to association censors for review of the images, text, covers, and advertisements in order to obtain a seal of approval (Figure 5.4). Comic layouts were reviewed after the inking stage to ensure that they conformed.

FIGURE 5.4 Comics Code Authority Seal
Source: Comic Book Legal Defense Fund, used by permission.

Having an industry code was not a novel concept. The comic book industry merely followed the example of the movie industry's production code, established at a time when Hollywood was steeped in scandal and beset by hostile regulators. The filmmakers set up the Motion Picture Producers and Distributors of America (later to become the Motion Picture Association of America, or MPAA), adopted a production code, and installed former Postmaster General Will Hays to head the enterprise. The Production Code, adopted in 1930, established a system under which the studios agreed to self-censor their movies and to submit prints for prior approval by code authorities. This approach was very consciously emulated by the CMAA, and the comic book code was in substantial part a paraphrase of the Hays Office code.

The comic book industry had attempted s similar approach once before. The CMAA replaced a previous industry watchdog set up by the Association of Comic Magazine Publishers (ACMP) in 1948 in response to Wertham's initial attacks on the industry. ACMP had established a six-point editorial code that touted such aspirational guidelines as that "sexy" or "wanton" comics should not be published, crime should not be depicted in a sympathetic light, "sadistic torture" (is there any other kind?) should not be depicted, divorce should not be taken lightly, and there should be no vulgarities, obscenities, or attacks on religion. But ACMP was plagued from the beginning with low membership and compliance problems. Only twelve out of thirty-four comic book publishers signed up at the outset, accounting for less than a third of comic books on the newsstands, and those numbers dwindled quickly. By the time the 1954 Senate hearings convened, only three publishers remained as members.

CMAA, as the successor to this failed effort, had a very different experience. The new group had buy-in from most comic book publishers, and, more importantly, its decisions were enforced by comic book distributors, who refused to carry nonapproved comics. Plus, "comics czar" Murphy took his job quite seriously, to the surprise of some in the industry. Taking a page from Comstock's book of self-promotion by the numbers, Murphy announced shortly after the code was announced that his office already had screened 285 comic books and rejected 126 stories and 5,656 individual drawings. Murphy pledged that horror comics would be purged from the industry, and they were. Crime titles also dwindled, and were pretty much gone by the following year. The Code's impact extended beyond those who signed on to be governed by it. Although William Gaines refused to sign EC Comics up as a member of CMAA, he was finding it increasingly difficult to get distribution and announced in September 1954 that he would no longer publish horror or crime comics. He eventually would exit the business altogether to focus his energies on *Mad* magazine.

The comic book code accomplished what law could not – it had a broadly chilling effect industrywide. Although not entirely due to the code, the number of comic book titles published dropped by 40 percent, from around 500 in 1952 to approximately 300 in 1955, while the number of comics on the stands declined by more than half. More than 800 comic book artists, writers, and associated employees lost their jobs as a result. In various communities, students organized public burnings of comics that lacked CMAA's seal of approval. In 1955, for the first time since the business began, no new publishers entered the comic book market. Kefauver naturally declared victory. Coinciding with his presidential bid, Kefauver proclaimed in 1956 that "the comic book situation has been brought under control by voluntary compliance with the code of ethics."

None of this was enough to satisfy Fredric Wertham, the man who might have been czar. A year after the CMAA Code devastated the comic book industry, Wertham renewed his claim that the Kefauver committee "whitewashed the crime comic book industry," and the failure to enact legislation after the 1954 hearings showed "that Senators are more informed about subversion than about perversion." While this complaint revealed a greater gift for rhyming than for rhetorical clarity, Wertham was unambiguous about his displeasure with the industry effort. Ignoring the disappearance of entire genres of comics from the newsstands, the dwindling numbers of titles, and the resulting unemployment of hundreds of writers and artists, Wertham maintained that the industry "flourishes openly." He compared particular provisions of CMAA's Code with examples of approved comics and declared: "At present it is far safer for a mother to let her child have a comic book without a seal of approval than one with it."

To Wertham, the problem was really simple: "You either close down a house of prostitution or you leave it open." He concluded that the CMAA Code was nothing more than a "smokescreen" that "will make it more difficult to pass much-needed legislation," and renewed his call for a "public health law." In doing so, he approvingly quoted a Minnesota juvenile court judge for the proposition that "True freedom is regulation." Orwell could not have said it better.

WHO'S A CENSOR? *I'M* NOT A CENSOR!

Wertham was all about censorship, but he couldn't admit as much, not even to himself. Psychiatrists have a term for this – being in denial – but here it really was just a manifestation of the censor's dilemma. Unlike Comstock, Wertham was aware on at least some level (perhaps due to his German roots) that censorship is a bad thing. He even proclaimed to the Senate committee, "I detest censorship." Yet he managed to convince himself that if the speech he wanted to prohibit was really, *really* bad, then his methods did not amount to censorship. As Wertham put it in SEDUCTION OF THE INNOCENT, "[i]t is a widely held fallacy that civil liberties are endangered or could be curtailed via children's books. But freedom to publish comics has nothing to do with civil liberties." He went on: "Leaving everything to the individual is actually *not* democracy; it is anarchy."

Wertham saw the issue as "primarily a public health issue, not a fundamental issue of censorship," and he blamed the comic book industry for "moral bankruptcy in publishers hiding behind the First Amendment." His rationale was set forth in the thirty-four-page affidavit he submitted in support of the Los Angeles County comic book ordinance: "The word censorship in its ordinary meaning is not applicable to the control of children's reading. An ordinance regulating what is being forced down children's throats in the way of corrupting pictures and words (that is the correct sequence) is nothing but a public health measure. It is no more a restriction of freedom of speech than not selling whiskey to children is a restraint of trade. ... It shows the confusion and the precarious state of our own civil liberties, if an ordinance to protect children can be construed in *any* way as a threat to free expression for adults (his emphasis)."

Wertham felt he had been "maligned" and was angered by those who called him a censor. Historian Bradford Wright described this as the most "curious feature of a controversy plagued by peculiarities and contradictions": that "a grassroots crusade marked by calls for censorship and book burnings found scientific legitimacy and leadership in an elitist liberal psychiatrist and professed opponent of censorship." As Wertham himself wrote in SEDUCTION OF THE INNOCENT, "[c]rime comics are a severe test of the liberalism of liberals."

But censorship is not about a contest between liberals and conservatives. Regardless of political outlook, it comes down to whether or not one accepts authoritarian solutions. In this, Wertham and Anthony Comstock had much in common.

Comstock described himself as a "weeder in the garden of the Lord," and Wertham framed his task using the same metaphor. The opening words of SEDUCTION OF THE INNOCENT proclaim that "[g]ardening consists largely in protecting plants from blight and weeds, and the same is true of attending to the growth of children." He saw the job of the "good gardener" as not to worry about the health of individual plants but to "think in terms of general precaution and spray the whole field." Comstock wrote endlessly about doing battle with Satan as a literal presence in the materials he condemned. Wertham, while more allegorical, described neutrality, "especially when hidden under the cloak of scientific objectivity" as "the devil's ally." Both men believed that they were doing god's work; Comstock merely used a capital G.

Consciously or not, Wertham closely followed the rules in the Comstock play-book: He exhibited absolute moral certainty of the rightness of his cause; equated any opposition with love of the vice he was committed to destroy; denounced and discredited any adversaries (or even those who declined to fully embrace his conclusions); poisoned the debate with over-the-top rhetoric and invective; pro-pounded his aesthetic preferences as scientific fact; vigorously pursued publicity; wildly exaggerated the threat; puffed up his own importance; and portrayed himself as the victim of evil forces.

Like Comstock, one of Wertham's chief weapons was the "Chamber of Horrors." His writings were suffused with comic book panels ripped from context to prove his points, and he insisted that the senate investigators use displays of comic book covers, as if their mere presence proved the link to juvenile delinquency. The one Comstock tool he did not employ was to blame foreign influences, which might have proved awkward for a German immigrant. But, otherwise, his tactics were almost indistinguishable from Comstock's. Unlike Comstock, however, Wertham lacked the power to make arrests. But even without such authority, he leveraged those in government to threaten legislation in support of a crusade that crippled the comic book industry.

WERTHAM'S LEGACY

For all his accomplishments, Fredric Wertham is largely forgotten today. A noted psychiatrist who entered the profession after corresponding with Sigmund Freud, Wertham immigrated to the United States to join the psychiatric staff at Johns Hopkins University. After becoming a naturalized citizen, Wertham moved to New York, where he later became a professor of psychiatry at NYU and director of the Mental Hygiene Clinic at Bellevue Hospital. He also founded the Lafargue Clinic in Harlem, which provided low-cost psychiatric services to community residents. Wertham wrote numerous books, was published in peer-reviewed scien-tific journals (for his non-comic book-related work), and conducted studies docu-menting the harms of racial segregation that were cited in *Brown v. Board of Education*. Yet, for all that, he is remembered (if at all) as "a caricature at best – a footnote in the annals of cultural criticism" and "one of the most iconic censors in modern history." His *New York Times* obituary listed him as a "Foe of Violent TV and Comics," and the lead paragraphs detailed how he was "credited some 30 years ago with causing the comic book industry to soften its emphasis on horror and crime." The rest of his career was described almost as an afterthought.

Some consider this treatment unfair and have attempted to rehabilitate Wertham's reputation. Bart Beaty, a communications theorist at the University of Calgary, wrote a book-length defense entitled FREDRIC WERTHAM AND THE CRITIQUE OF MASS CULTURE that described Wertham as an important mid-century thinker who has been "unjustly marginalized" by the psychiatric and social science communities, cultural critics, and comic book fans. Likewise, media studies scholar James E. Reibman, who wrote the introduction to a 2004 reprint of SEDUCTION OF THE INNOCENT, complained that Wertham has been misunderstood and unfairly blamed for the demise of comic books. Yet both writers admit that Wertham has been relegated to historical obscurity and professional disrepute. Beaty described Wertham as a "ghostlike figure haunt[ing] the postwar debates on American popular culture" whose name "rings few bells" and whose stature as a scholar has been erased. Reibman observed that, "among comic book cognoscenti, his name has become a by-word for the censorious, the narrow-minded, and the ill-informed." And these assessments came even before a review of Wertham's papers revealed that he had manipulated, overstated, and even falsified evidence to support his dubious conclusions. Like Anthony Comstock, who exerted great influence in his lifetime, all that remains is the ridicule.

In a minor way, Wertham generated his own "Comstock Effect." Comic books he attacked are remembered largely because of him. Reibman noted that comics whose illustrations appear in SEDUCTION OF THE INNOCENT are now collector's items and in 1985 Eclipse Comics published a series of books under the title SEDUCTION OF THE INNOCENT. The same title is used for a website that archives information about Wertham's crusade against comic books, but, more to the point, it also collects and preserves covers of the many comics he condemned. Wertham even inspired artistic creations in which he became a character, including numerous unflattering portrayals in comics.

As with Comstock before him, the mocking portrayals started early in his career. Wertham was parodied in the *Spirit Sunday Supplement* in February 1949, less than a year after he first gained notoriety for his anti-comics crusades. In a piece entitled *The Deadly Comic Book*, Wertham appeared as "Dr. Wolfgang Worry." *The Deadly Comic Book* was popular, and the story was reprinted in other books at least four times over the following decades. Not surprisingly, Wertham was a target of William Gaines' *Mad* magazine, appearing in the August 1957 issue as "Dr. Fredric Werthless" in a piece called "Baseball Is Ruining Our Children." Just as Comstock once reveled in the derisive term "Comstockery," Wertham reportedly kept a framed copy of the *Mad* article in his office. But the ridicule did not end with Wertham's death in 1981. Sixty years after he was first parodied in the comics – and nearly three decades after he died – *Grave Tales* ran a piece entitled "Freddie Wertham Goes to Hell."

Such caricatures were not confined to comic books. Wertham also appeared as a character in a play entitled *The Last Days of the Brave and the Bold*, about a fictional encounter in which the good doctor sits down for a drink with fetishist and Wonder Woman creator William Moulton Marston. Another unsympathetic portrayal of Wertham is imagined in Michael Chabon's Pulitzer Prize–winning novel THE AMAZING ADVENTURES OF KAVALIER & CLAY. In a short chapter devoted to the 1954 hearings, Wertham is described as testifying "at great length, somewhat incoherently, but dignified throughout and alive, ablaze with outrage." This is better treatment than one might have expected (or than Wertham ever got in other fictional works), until one turns the page to see the senators questioning one of the book's protagonists about one of Wertham's pet theories – that Batman and Robin depicted a homosexual fantasy. In this imagined exchange, Senator Hendrickson says he credits Wertham's suggestion that the comic may be a "thinly veiled allegory of pedophilic inversion" and then asks about other dynamic duos. A little too enthusiastically, the senator asks about other "muscular, strapping young fellows in tight trousers . . . flitting around the skies together," until an exasperated Senator Kefauver finally blurts out, "For Heaven's sake, gentlemen, let us move on."

But what of his life's work? Wertham's activism had an undeniable impact, ushering in a restrictive regime of industry self-regulation that fundamentally altered the comic book landscape, wrecked businesses and destroyed lives. Entire genres of comics were swept away and those that remained were blander and more anodyne. But such effects were not permanent, because the public tastes and attitudes that made comics popular did not go away. By the mid-1960s, banned themes in comic books reemerged in the underground comix movement, including violence, illegal drug use, explicit sexuality, and even horror. The movement reflected the rise of the counterculture, but in many ways it was a direct reaction to the censorship of comic books of the previous decade. Robert Crumb, a founder of *Zap Comix* and creator of *Fritz the Cat*, described the appeal of the underground scene: "That was why we did it. We didn't have anybody standing over us saying 'No, you can't draw this' or 'You can't show that.' We could do whatever we wanted" (Figure 5.5).

Underground comics were heavily influenced by William Gaines' EC Comics, the primary target of Wertham's crusade. Although the anti-comic book campaign led to the demise of EC Comics, here it was ten years later, rising from the ashes as a far freakier phoenix. Comix gained in popularity between the mid-1960s through the mid-1970s, and even achieved some mainstream acceptance. In 1969 the Corcoran Gallery of Art in Washington, DC, hosted an exhibition of comix art, including works by Crumb and others.

Traditional comic book publishers, like Marvel, picked up on the trend in the early 1970s, publishing toned-down versions of comix. But Marvel, under the leadership of Stan Lee, also made a comeback with its superheroes, and began

FIGURE 5.5 Cover of *Zap Comix* No. 1
Source: Amazon.com, used by permission of Denis Kitchen Art Agency on behalf of Robert Crumb.

pushing back against the Code. This was followed by the emergence of graphic novels that expanded on comic book themes with an edgier and more adult approach. In the 1980s, books like Art Spiegelman's *Maus*, Frank Miller's *The Dark Knight Returns*, and Alan Moore and Dave Gibbons' *Watchmen* achieved commercial success and redefined the genre. These longer-form versions of comic narratives paved the way for broader public acceptance of a darker and more sophisticated form of graphic storytelling. Throughout these years the supervision of standard comics by the CMAA declined, and by 2011 the organization ceased to exist.

Comic books won the mainstream culture war as well. By 1972 one of EC Comics' leading titles, *Tales from the Crypt*, became a feature film as an anthology of stories, some of which were adapted from issues of the comic. The cast included established stars, including leading British actor Sir Ralph Richardson as the Crypt Keeper, and such notables as Peter Cushing and Joan Collins as characters in the various stories. This was followed by a 1973 sequel, *The Vault of Horror*. *Tales from the Crypt* reappeared as a television series that ran for seven seasons, from 1989 to 1996, and even as an animated series (*Tales from the Cryptkeeper*) in 1993–1994. Other film adaptations included *Demon Knight* (1995), *Bordello of Blood* (1996), and *Ritual* (2002). The series also inspired two 1995 rap albums, *Tales from the Crypt*, by American rapper C-Bo, and *Tales from the Crib*, by Canadian band d.b.s.

Of course, movies based on superheroes date back nearly to the beginnings of comics themselves, starting out as Saturday morning serials for kids. Some suggest that such fare even predates comics to the early days of cinema, with movies featuring characters such as Zorro, Tarzan, and Flash Gordon. But post-Wertham, movies based on comic book heroes came to dominate Hollywood's output – for better or worse – to the point that some complained they could no longer get a project greenlighted if it wasn't wearing a cape. In 2018 Wikipedia listed more than 400 films that had been made based on English language comic books with another 16 slated for release in 2019. And that does not include the many television series that were spun off. The two highest-grossing films of 2018 – the *Avengers: Infinity War* and *Black Panther* – were both superhero movies drawn from the Marvel universe that together pulled $3.4 billion globally. In 2019, *Avengers: Endgame* blew through previous box office records, grossing $1.2 billion worldwide its opening weekend.

The cultural victory of comics extends beyond popular entertainment. The academic study of graphic novels and comic books is increasingly common at the university level, with established programs at the University of Florida and the University of Toronto, among others worldwide. University libraries house collections of underground comics. Scholarly conferences abound, such as the International Comics Arts Forum, which has been held annually since 1995. Academic journals devoted to comic books include *Journal of Graphic Novels and Comics*, *Studies in Comics*, *European Comic Art*, *SANE: Sequential Art Narrative in Education* (based at the University of Nebraska–Lincoln), and *Inks: The Journal of the Comics Studies Society* (published by the Ohio State University Press). Libraries and schools use comics as classroom aids to encourage reading, and comic book characters appear on posters distributed by the ALA. Comic book publishers attend library and education conferences, and teachers and librarians likewise attend comic book conventions.

Wertham's failure could not be more complete. Whether measured in terms of cultural influence, academic acceptance, or the law, the medium he sought to crush emerged triumphant. His failure has a personal dimension as well. When Stan Lee died in November 2018, the Marvel Comics impresario was lauded in obituaries and feature articles as a visionary who helped bring comics back from the doldrums after the purges of the 1950s. By the time of Lee's death, movies based on characters he helped create (including Spiderman, Iron Man, the Incredible Hulk, the Fantastic Four, and Black Panther) had grossed more than $17.5 billion globally. Wertham, by contrast, was thoroughly discredited and largely forgotten. No statues or monuments exist for this anti-comic book crusader; only caricature and parody.

Just as George Bernard Shaw retained his luster and literary relevance for the plays and books he wrote while Anthony Comstock faded away as a barely remembered irrelevance, creators prevail while censors disappear. Those who create nothing leave nothing behind.

6

Ya Got Trouble: Censorship and Popular Music

The September 19, 1985, hearing of the Senate Committee on Commerce, Science, and Transportation on "Record Labeling" was not your typical congressional hearing. To be sure, its witness lineup included certain Washington fixtures, like Eddie Fritts, President of the National Association of Broadcasters (NAB) and Stanley Gortikov, President of the Recording Industry Association of America (RIAA). So far, so good – as Washington goes – but then things just got weird. Headlining the event were some notable Washington wives, including Tipper Gore, then-wife of then-Senator Al Gore of Tennessee, and Susan Baker, wife of James A. Baker, who had served as President Ronald Reagan's Chief of Staff and was at the time his Treasury Secretary (and who would later become Chief of Staff and Secretary of State under George Bush). Weirder still, the roster of witnesses included Frank Zappa, the gonzo rocker who in the 1960s was the driving force behind the Mothers of Invention, Dee Snider, front man for the 1980s heavy metal band Twisted Sister, and John Denver, the beloved soft rock phenomenon with a folk music background, best known for the song "Rocky Mountain High."

The subject? "Porn rock," which is what critics called the mid-1980s wave of music that contained explicit lyrics about sex, violence, fetishes, and references to the occult. The Washington wives had taken up the cause just a few months earlier and formed an organization they called the Parents Music Resource Center – PMRC – and their goal was to "persuade" the record companies to put ratings on record albums that contained bad lyrics, to establish an industry monitoring board, and to get the industry to practice self-restraint in the music it was releasing to the nation's children. This was not "censorship," as the PMRC witnesses and members of the committee stressed at every turn, because there was no legislative proposal on the table for restricting the music industry. But the interplay of Washington politics and news coverage of this circus-like event showed it to be a near perfect blend of Comstock's playbook with the censor's dilemma.

The dilemma was posed by the fact that American society had been transformed in the seventy years since Comstock's death, and even in the three decades since the comic book panic. Along with these changes, a body of First Amendment law evolved that extended constitutional protections to art, literature, and music such that freedom became the expected norm. Equally important was the distaste for censorship inspired by Comstock's excesses and perpetuated over the years by actions of his spiritual successors. By 1985, the label "censor" was to be avoided at all cost, even for the cheerleaders for censorship, like the ladies of PMRC. The hearing served as Exhibit A for that fact – which was no small feat given that this political and media extravaganza was designed for the sole purpose of leveraging government power to clamp down on popular music.

WHIPPED UP LIKE AN INSTANT PUDDING BY "THE WIVES OF 'BIG BROTHER'"

The assembled senators and pro-labeling witnesses emphatically denied any intention of engaging in censorship at least twenty-five times during the five-hour hearing, starting with Chairman John C. Danforth's opening statement. Senator Danforth, an ordained Episcopal priest (and heir to the Ralston Purina pet food fortune), assured the crowd, both in the overflowing hearing room and those watching the televised proceedings on C-SPAN, that the purpose of the proceeding was "not to promote any legislation" but "simply to provide a forum for airing the issue." He said that it was his "understanding" that "various private groups have been holding discussions with people who are in the music publishing and music industry to try to achieve some sort of understanding with respect to the labeling of records." The hearing was called just so that "the whole issue can be brought to the attention of the American people."

This was rich. However much Senator Danforth tried to distance himself from the matter by professing merely a passive "understanding" that "various private groups" had met on the matter, he knew full well that this was a classic Washington power play. PMRC had been formed just four months earlier by the wives of prominent politicians and business leaders, and its membership topped out at twenty-two individuals before it faded away in the early 1990s. It was unthinkable that the hearing would have come together without their influential connections and the behind-the-scenes pressure on the industry. According to an *LA Times* political tally, "half the original 20 PMRC members [were] married to 10% of the Senate." By contrast, the National Parent Teacher Association (PTA), with its 5.6 million members and 25,000 local affiliates, had been working the issue for over a year and had gotten nowhere with the record companies. But once the Washington wives got involved, they not only got meetings with record moguls but secured commitments from twenty-four RIAA members, who collectively released 80 percent of prerecorded music sold in the USA, to put warning labels on record albums. But PMRC wanted more, and that was the point of the hearing.

Frank Zappa put it best when he described the scene as a recipe for censorship "whipped up like an instant pudding by 'the wives of Big Brother.'" But he didn't stop there. Noting the growing number of issues that concerned the ladies, including not just lyrics but concert performances and MTV music videos, Zappa said: "[T]he complete list of PMRC demands reads like an instruction manual for some sinister kind of toilet training program to house-break all composers and performers because of the lyrics of a few." He chided them, "Ladies, how dare you?"

This was beyond the pale. Zappa may have shed his freak persona from his Mothers of Invention days and appeared on Capitol Hill sporting a short haircut and black business suit – looking more like a banker than a rocker (save for the trimmed soul patch under his mustache) – but this wasn't the deferential tone expected. People aren't supposed to talk to senators that way, much less their wives. However, Zappa's greatest transgression wasn't his tone but the substance of what he said. He had the audacity to actually name what the committee was up to.

In response, a sputtering Senator Slade Gorton of Washington could not contain himself. Describing Zappa's statement as "boorish" and "incredibly insulting" to the other witnesses, he said: "[Y]ou could manage to give the first amendment of the Constitution of the United States a bad name." He charged that Zappa lacked "the slightest understanding of the difference between Government action and private action," adding, "[Y]ou have certainly destroyed any case you might otherwise have had with this Senator." This, of course, begged the question what case? What "case" does anyone need to make with a senator if all you are talking about is private action? Or, as Zappa asked simply, "Is this private action?"

You might think so if you took at face value all the disclaimers tossed about during the hearing. On average, witnesses and senators denied any intention of engaging in censorship five times for each hour of the hearing, or about once every twelve minutes. PMRC's Tipper Gore and Susan Baker stressed that a "voluntary labeling system is not censorship," and that such a "voluntary" initiative "in no way infringes on First Amendment rights." Millie Waterman, who testified for the PTA, described the labeling initiative as a reasonable solution "that would not involve any form of censorship," and stated that her organization "would in no way encourage nor support censorship of the music industry." PMRC and the PTA would later promote mandatory labeling legislation, and it was proposed in nineteen states, but for purposes of the "porn rock" hearings, they were willing to maintain the pose that they were interested only in "voluntary" action.

The lawmakers embraced this theme and ran with it. Chairman Danforth stressed that PMRC was "not asking for censorship," and sought to assuage John Denver's concerns by saying that there was "zero chance of legislation." Senator Paul Trible of Virginia assured everyone that "the First Amendment is not under attack here," explaining that under the "classic legal definition," only "prior restraint of publication constitutes censorship." (This is wrong, by the way, as the Supreme Court made clear in 1931; First Amendment abridgments may come in many forms, and not just by previous restraint.) He was followed by Tipper's husband, Senator Al Gore of Tennessee, who emphatically denied that "any form of censorship or regulation" was afoot, and stressed that the members of PMRC were not seeking "a Government role of any kind whatsoever." This last statement had a bit of a tinny ring to it, coming as it did just seconds after Senator Trible had proclaimed that the proceedings "may well be the most important hearing conducted by the Commerce Committee this year."

This was puzzling to Senator James Exon of Nebraska, who in the coming decade would propose and secure passage of the Communications Decency Act, a bill to impose sweeping regulation of "indecent" speech on the Internet. After noting that no proposed legislation was being considered, he asked Chairman Danforth: "[I]f we are not talking about Federal regulation and we are not talking about Federal legislation, what is the reason for these hearings in front of the Commerce Committee?" Later in the proceedings Exon answered his own question, cautioning witnesses against assuming that just because "no bills have been introduced, [it didn't mean] that bills might not be introduced." Like a stand-up comic forced to explain a joke, he added: "I want to hold that threat . . . over the head [of those] trying to accomplish some free enterprise volunteerism that most people have agreed to."

Now we were getting to the point. The word "voluntary" has an entirely different meaning in Washington, DC, than almost everywhere else. In our nation's capital, when legislators or regulators speak of voluntarism, what they mean is "do what we say . . . *or else*." Some are more subtle about it than others, but the message does not vary. This was the entire point of the "porn rock" hearings – to serve as a showcase for making this not-so-veiled threat, while striving to maintain plausible deniability. Censorship? Of course not – that would be wrong.

One committee member who was particularly skilled at this form of legislative extortion (if not particularly artful) was Senator Fritz Hollings, the ranking Democrat who served as a senator from South Carolina for four decades, from 1966 to 2005. With a gift for malapropism to rival Yogi Berra and a manner like Foghorn Leghorn, Hollings rarely passed up an opportunity to lean on media companies, and this hearing was no exception. He opened by calling heavy metal rock "outrageous filth," adding: "[I]f I could find some way constitutionally to do away with it, I would." While he commended Chairman Danforth's "tempered" approach, he said that he was "asking the best of constitutional minds, if there is some way in the world to try to limit it as we go along with the voluntary labeling." Hollings wrapped up his opening statement by stressing his interest in "trying our level best to limit and control [this music] as best we can, for the tender young ears of America."

CUE THE REGULATORS

By his "level best," Hollings meant that Congress did not need to pass legislation for the government to exert control over the music. He reminded everyone that the FCC had authority to penalize radio stations under the agency's broadcast indecency rules if they aired songs such as those that PMRC found problematic, and proudly noted that the Commission had fined a radio station "in my own backyard" for "using four-letter words." And then, in a dazzling display of incoherence, he pronounced that "the aura or atmosphere developing in this particular hearing is developing to make sure that we do not do nothing, or to transmit, rather back to the original problem, pornography, suicide, all this other stuff coming out of these records." Hollings went on. The American public was not going to "go along just with a nice hearing up here in Washington." No sir. Unless "that discipline develops" – that is, unless the industry gets with the program – "with the broadcast media, we are going to be forced somewhere with regulations, through the FCC or otherwise."

Hollings may have served up a heaping helping of word salad, but his meaning was plain: The hearing was not a mere "listening session," as Chairman Danforth had claimed. Its purpose was to flex some government muscle to achieve PMRC's aims. And flex it he did. Hollings warned that "unless the industry 'cleans up their act' . . . there is likely to be legislation." But he also observed that legislation was not necessary to achieve his aim: "[W]e should not be on the defensive and we should not create the atmosphere that we are powerless." Citing *FCC* v. *Pacifica Foundation, Inc.*, the Supreme Court case that upheld the FCC's authority to sanction a broadcaster for airing George Carlin's "filthy words" monologue, Hollings recalled having the broadcast networks appear before the committee some years earlier for a similar "listening session." He said that they "demonstrated how they had this film, and then got together with the producer and removed certain scenes of violence and certain four-letter words, and did not offend the producer's sense of art in the production itself." It is doubtful that the producer would have agreed with Hollings' artistic assessment. But it is difficult not to accede to a senator's "requests" when the government's boot is on your neck.

That, of course, was the point of having the NAB president appear as a witness. Eddie Fritts was a savvy Washington operator who knew that broadcasters had nothing to gain by resisting Hollings' (or PMRC's) demands. Fritts testified that he had been in regular contact with PMRC's leaders from the beginning, so he didn't have to wait for Hollings' garbled diatribe to know that the cornpone was cooked and ready to serve. The month PMRC was formed, Fritts sent a letter to executives of the more than 800 radio and television station group owners "to alert them to the public concern that was developing over porn rock" and quickly followed it with a letter to chief executives of 45 record companies that account for 85 percent of the nation's recorded music asking them to provide copies of lyrics when they sent music to the stations. The music industry "was not overwhelmed by the idea," Fritts told the committee, but his broadcasters were responding as they should. He reported that songs that the stations found "inappropriate" were "removed from the play lists, and new songs were being monitored more carefully."

This was not censorship, he observed: "NAB will never attempt to intrude into any station's programming judgments." Rather, he called it an effort "to balance the need for voluntary industry restraint with a strong sensitivity to first amendment concerns." These sentiments were echoed by William J. Steding, a broadcaster who testified alongside Fritts, and who added an Orwellian spin to the proceedings. The issue was not about censorship, he agreed, insisting: "[I]t is about freedom of information, freedom of choice." But, he quickly added, "if all voluntary efforts fail and the problems inherent in the airing of pornographic lyrics continue unabated, it is my personal opinion that some form of legislation may be appropriate."

THE FCC AND DRUG LYRICS

Strong endorsement for free speech, indeed. However, as both Fritts and Steding knew, legislation was hardly necessary so long as broadcasters are beholden to the FCC, the federal agency that controls their broadcast licenses. The industry weathered a similar controversy in the 1970s, when the FCC cautioned radio stations to be on the lookout for "drug lyrics." The Commission had issued a Public Notice advising broadcasters that they were expected to exercise "responsibility" in deciding whether to air "drug-oriented" music. Although the FCC took no action against any particular station, its message was unmistakable, particularly since one of the commissioners issued a statement describing that the agency's purpose was to "discourage, if not eliminate, the playing of records which tend to promote and/or glorify the use of illegal drugs." And if that were not sufficiently clear, five weeks later the FCC's Bureau of Complaints and Compliance sent broadcasters a list of twenty-two recordings that had come to its attention as having "so-called drug-oriented song lyrics." The list had originated with the Department of the Army, and it included such titles as "Lucy in the Sky with Diamonds" and "With a Little Help from My Friends" by The Beatles, "Mr. Tambourine Man" by Bob Dylan, and the whimsical "Puff, the Magic Dragon" by folk trio Peter, Paul and Mary.

You didn't need to be clairvoyant to predict how broadcasters would react. The FCC's list was widely circulated as a "do not play" list, and stations moved quickly to comply. Licensees stopped playing the songs and, in some instances, banned the work of certain artists altogether regardless of the subject of the songs or lyrics. Some DJs were fired for playing "suspect" songs, and one broadcaster simply purged all Bob Dylan songs because "the management could not interpret the lyrics." The FCC subsequently issued a follow-up order to "clarify" that it was only reaffirming broadcasters' general obligation to know what they were putting on the air, explaining that the list of songs was not "official" and had only been provided by "a Commission employee" in response to "a request from a broadcast station's news department." It stressed that it was not intended as a ban on any particular song or artist, but nonetheless reaffirmed its advice that a broadcaster "could jeopardize his license by failing to exercise licensee responsibility in this area."

Yale Broadcasting challenged the FCC's pronouncements, arguing that they constituted a government effort to suppress disfavored music. However, under the less rigorous constitutional protections that applied to the broadcast medium, the US Court of Appeals for the DC Circuit upheld the FCC because the agency had not taken any official action. The Supreme Court declined review, although Justices Brennan and Douglas voted to take the case. To Douglas, it was clear that the agency had intended "to coerce broadcasters into refusing to play songs that in the Commission's judgment were somehow 'drug-related.'" The lesson was that such measures could survive judicial scrutiny if done subtly enough, but everyone knew their practical effect.

THE "FILTHY FIFTEEN" AND A CARROT

The Nixon Administration's tactics over the "drug lyrics" controversy were not lost on the participants in the "porn rock" hearings, and PMRC came prepared with its own "do not play" list. Dubbed by *Rolling Stone* as the "Filthy Fifteen," PMRC's list included songs that Tipper Gore said represented "a sick new strain of rock music." Representative examples included "Darling Nikki" by Prince, "Sugar Walls" written by Prince and performed by Sheena Easton, "Dress You Up" by Madonna, and "We're Not Gonna Take It" by Twisted Sister. PMRC's criteria for which songs made the list were far from clear, in that "We're Not Gonna Take It" was a pretty run-of-the-mill rock song celebrating teen rebellion. But PMRC's objection seemed to be less about the lyrics than about the music video that depicts a teenager and his siblings being transformed into the band members of Twisted Sister who proceed to discipline "daddy." But the reason for any particular song making the list really didn't matter that much, since PMRC's complaints achieved much of what the group intended.

Beyond making blacklists, in the carrot-and-stick routine of Washington power politics, PMRC did not rely just on the stick. The strategy included dangling a carrot in front of RIAA's members to remind them that the government was in a position to be nice to a cooperative industry. Senator Hollings had punctuated his disjointed comments about wanting to ban heavy metal (if he could constitutionally get away with it) and his musing about broadcasting's less-protected status with a cryptic reference to "a tax bill" he had noticed in a media report, adding: "I looked into that." Hollings didn't elaborate, but then, he didn't need to. Frank Zappa connected the dots, pointing out that the record industry was urging Congress to pass H.R. 2911, The Blank Tape Tax, that would impose an assessment on recording devices and blank tapes to compensate the industry for music piracy (Figure 6.1). The RIAA had drafted H. R. 2911 for Rep. Bruce Morrison of Connecticut, and it had languished in Congress for more than a year, but now reportedly it would be taken up by the Senate in a committee chaired by Strom Thurmond. Mrs. Thurmond, as it turned out, was a PMRC member.

FIGURE 6.1 American musicians Frank Zappa and Dee Snider hold up papers relating to
the PMRC Senate hearing at Capitol Hill, Washington DC, September 19, 1985
Source: Photo by Mark Weiss/Getty Images.

RIAA's Gortikov certainly knew the game. After meeting with PMRC, he urged
his association members to capitulate or risk the music industry's legislative agenda
on such issues as copyright, anti-piracy enforcements, and – of course – the Blank
Tape Tax. As he wrote at the time in a memo to the heads of the major record
companies: "Non-response by companies can have serious negative backlash effects.
Our legislation and national/international anti-piracy projects can be diluted or
jeopardized." He even recommended reviewing certain recording artists' contracts
to ensure that "future content" doesn't cause more problems. Tipper Gore would
later refer to Gortikov as her "secret ally" in the record industry.

The 1985 "porn rock" hearing came straight from the Anthony Comstock playbook, beginning with its "Chamber of Horrors." Just as Comstock helped secure
passage of his 1873 obscenity law by exhibiting "obscenities" drawn from his great
cloth bag, PRMC came prepared to shock the assembled senators into action. One
of the three PMRC witnesses to testify was a "consultant" named Jeff Ling,
a Washington area preacher who had his own anti-heavy metal road show. For his
testimony, the committee dimmed the hearing room lights so that Ling could take
the senators and the audience on a guided tour of the evils of rock, featuring the
display of album covers and lyrics of such bands as AC/DC, Twisted Sister, Ozzie

Osbourne, Judas Priest, KISS, Great White, WASP, and Mötley Crüe. Although Chairman Danforth opened the proceedings by cautioning the witnesses that this was, after all, a hearing of a US Senate committee, and not to "needlessly use expressions that may be in bad taste," Ling was not deterred in the least. The minister had a well-worn shtick, and seemed to derive perverse satisfaction from regaling the crowd with four-letter words and references to sex with Satan. He concluded his testimony by quoting lyrics from a song by an obscure band called The Mentors: "Bend up and smell my anal vapor. Your face is my toilet paper. On your face I leave a shit tower. Golden Showers."

What was the reaction to this? Did Chairman Danforth bang his gavel or admonish the witness over this breach of congressional decorum? No. Did any other senator complain? Hardly. This was the show that PMRC (and its consultant) came to present, and it had previewed the material for committee members before the hearing. So as the PMRC witnesses wrapped up, Danforth simply thanked them, adding, "I know that for all of you it was not the most pleasant of experiences to read some of the lyrics in public." The committee members saved their expressions of outrage for Frank Zappa, who had the bad taste to use an even dirtier word – censorship.

PMRC borrowed more than just the Chamber of Horrors from Comstock's playbook. Its testimony, and the response of those who supported it, was rife with colorful invective condemning the music and littered with metaphorical allusions seemingly intended to obscure the fact that it was talking about speech. Senator Paula Hawkins was not a member of the Commerce Committee, but she attended as a witness in her capacity as Chair of the Children, Family, Drugs, and Alcohol Subcommittee. Speaking from behind the dais and not the witness table, Senator Hawkins displayed a series of album covers that she said were "self-explanatory," and, echoing Comstock's use of metaphor, described the lyrics as "poison." Of course, if the covers were self-explanatory, one might wonder at the need for a label, but Hawkins' statement was an exercise in condemnation, not logic.

Hawkins' brief statement hewed to a number of Comstock's basic tenets. She exuded sanctimony (she was hardly alone in this respect), exaggerated the threat, and questioned the motives of any skeptics. She asked Frank Zappa whether he made a profit from the sale of "rock records." When he answered in the affirmative, Hawkins sat back and said, "Thank you. I think that statement tells the story to this committee."

SUICIDE SOLUTION?

Just as Comstock tied dime novels and "evil reading" to crime, PMRC tried to make the case that heavy metal and "porn rock" spawned murderers, caused teen suicide, and led to teen pregnancy. Although they tried to stay away from overtly claiming any actual causal relationship between this devil music and destruction of youth, the witnesses couldn't help suggesting that where you find one, you get the other. PMRC's Susan Baker cited a report indicating that the United States had the highest rate of teen pregnancy among developed countries and that suicide rates among those aged sixteen to twenty-four had increased 300 percent in the previous three decades. She didn't suggest that the study had asserted any possible link to music, but in her next breath she intimated that certain songs seemed to encourage suicide, reaching back more than a decade to name Blue Oyster Cult's "Don't Fear the Reaper" and listing Ozzie Osbourne's "Suicide Solution" and AC/DC's "Shoot to Thrill" among the likely culprits. She added that, just the previous week, a young man in a small Texas town "took his life while listening to the music of AC/DC."

Mrs. Baker wavered a bit when Senator Jay Rockefeller asked her if "there is a direct relationship between violence and disturbing tendencies and occurrences among young people and the proliferation of this type of material that we have seen this morning?" She said that she believed there was an influence but that we "certainly do not blame music for . . . all the ills that exist in the teenage population." Not getting the definitive answer he was fishing for, Rockefeller reframed the question: "Is the relationship between the escalation of the so-called MTV phenomenon and the things that we have seen this morning, and the problems that exist in the teenage population . . . incontrovertible in your mind?" Evidently realizing that she had not given the right answer the first time, Baker quickly got back on script. "Absolutely," she responded.

Reverend Ling, PMRC's consultant, picked up the theme, suggesting a link between several suicides and AC/DC songs, and upping the ante to include murder among the ravages of rock. He observed with a straight face that the Night Stalker was a "fan" of AC/DC. Richard Ramirez, the so-called Night Stalker, committed fourteen murders between the spring of 1984 and the summer of 1985. Of course, Ling offered no evidence to suggest that music creates serial killers, but then he didn't have to. Evidence was not the point. Later in the hearing, Ling said that he worked with young people and "listened to what they have listened to" and concluded: "I think it has great effect."

Problems like youth crime and suicide are the product of many complex causes that defy such facile claims. But subtleties like that have never deterred reformers on a mission. PMRC's witnesses were correct when they said that the rate of teen suicides was increasing in the mid-1980s, but, beyond that statistical fact, their testimony was uninformed speculation. The Centers for Disease Control reported that suicide rates for youths aged fifteen to nineteen rose from 1975 through around 1990, then dropped significantly to reach record lows around 2007. The numbers crept back up after that point, but not to the levels that existed in the mid-1980s. Many factors affect this tragic phenomenon, with depression, a perceived lack of parental interest, and eating disorders among the most frequently cited correlates, among numerous factors. But rock music – or any form of music, for that matter – has never been listed by legitimate researchers as a "cause" of teen suicide.

PMRC's claims about "porn rock" and teen pregnancy rates and suggestions about rape were even wackier. The witnesses made no pretense of actually connecting their claims to anything suggesting that heavy metal music led teens to have more sex (much less unprotected sex), and even a cursory review of the data would have dispelled any such notion. The rate of teenage pregnancy reached a peak in the mid-1950s (over 96 per 1,000 girls aged 15 to 19), when squeaky clean Pat Boone was a teen heartthrob, and dropped over 40 percent by the time of the "porn rock" hearing in 1985. It has since been cut in half again, declining to 24.2 per 1,000 teens in 2014. In more recent years, the rate at which teens have sex or have abortions has declined as well. A National Crime Victimization Survey likewise found that the crime rate for rape was cut in half between 1975 and 1985. Whatever else may explain these trends, heavy metal rock is not a prime candidate. But that made no difference to the Senate "fact-finders."

SAME AS IT EVER WAS . . .

Just as PMRC and its supportive witnesses disavowed any interest in censorship, they also tried to distance themselves from the moral panics of yesteryear that seemed deadly serious at the time, but in retrospect looked silly. Senator Hawkins noted that three decades had passed "since Elvis first shook his hips on the Ed Sullivan Show," and that "[m]uch has changed since Elvis' seemingly innocent times." According to the Senator, action was needed because "[s]ubtleties, suggestions, and innuendo" had been replaced by "descriptions of often violent sexual acts, drug taking, and flirtations with the occult." Susan Baker of PMRC agreed, describing "porn rock" and the media's impact on children as "historically unique." Other witnesses acknowledged that popular music had sparked previous concerns about youth culture and fueled earlier moral panics, but any such recognition was immediately extinguished by the claim that "heavy metal music is categorically different from previous forms of popular music." Well, not so much.

As soon as social reformers appeared on the scene, popular music became a target of would-be censors. Ragtime music was castigated in 1899 as "vulgar, filthy and suggestive music" that should be "suppressed by press and pulpit." In a 1914 call to arms, the *Musical Observer* urged its readers to "take a united stand against the Ragtime Evil as we would against bad literature." Moralists compared ragtime and jazz to alcohol and other intoxicating substances. Thus, in December 1933, a Washington State congressman introduced House Bill 194 to empower the governor to impose a ban if it was determined that "our people are becoming dangerously demented, confused, distracted or bewildered by jazz music." It also provided that those convicted of being "jazzily intoxicated shall go before the Superior Court and be sent to an insane asylum."

The moral panic over music was captured perfectly in lyrics from *The Music Man*, which told a story, set in 1912, of "Professor" Harold Hill, a con man who sought to spook the townsfolk of River City, Iowa into seeking more wholesome activities for its youth: "One fine night, they leave the pool hall, headin' for the dance at the Arm'ry! Libertine men and Scarlet women! And Rag-time, shameless music that'll grab your son and your daughter with the arms of a jungle animal instink! Mass-staria!"

The over-wrought reactions to ragtime and jazz foreshadowed later campaigns against popular music of the day, but by then the critics had forgotten how foolish those efforts looked from a historical perspective. Responding to such demands, NBC in 1940 banned from the radio more than 140 songs because they allegedly encouraged "disrespect for virginity, mocked marriage, and encouraged sexual promiscuity." Duke Ellington's "The Mooche" was blamed for inciting rape, and only the instrumental version of Cole Porter's "Love for Sale" could be aired.

THE ROCK REBELLION AND THE BIZARRE CASE OF "LOUIE, LOUIE"

The "seemingly innocent times" that Senator Paula Hawkins nostalgically invoked during the "porn rock" hearings did not seem so innocent at the time. In the mid-1950s rock music was widely condemned as a public nuisance and threat to public safety, and the junk science of the day claimed that teens were "addicted" to the music. Police officials across the country – in Connecticut, New Jersey, Maryland, Pennsylvania, Rhode Island and other states – blamed juvenile delinquency and general unrest on rock. Minneapolis in 1959 banned a show hosted by Dick Clark "for the peace and well-being of the city" because the police chief was convinced that it would spark violence. It was not an isolated overreaction. Other cities that banned rock shows based on public safety concerns included Boston, Massachusetts; Bridgeport and New Haven, Connecticut; Asbury Park, New Jersey; Santa Cruz, California; and Birmingham, Alabama.

A 1955 *Los Angeles Times* article described rock as "a violent, harsh type of music that, parents feel, incites teenagers to do all sorts of crazy things," and it quoted a psychiatrist who opined that rock and roll was a "contagious disease." Others in the psychiatric field concurred. Dr. Francis J. Braceland, an internationally known psychiatrist who testified at the Nuremberg trials and would serve as president of both the American Psychiatric Association and the World Psychiatric Association, called rock "cannibalistic and tribalistic," comparing it to a "communicable disease." The *Washington Post* in 1956 quoted Dr. Jules Masserman, another former president of the American Psychiatric Association, as saying that rock was "primitive quasi-music that can be traced back to prehistoric cultures." The notion that rock music was dangerous and could exert some mysterious power over young minds was not out of the mainstream.

Such pronouncements may help explain the bizarre overreaction by authorities to a 1963 garage-band song with almost unintelligible lyrics recorded by a Portland,

Oregon band called The Kingsmen. The song, "Louie, Louie," was written in 1956 by rhythm and blues (R&B) artist Richard Berry, but it came to prominence in the early 1960s after being recorded by several bands, including Paul Revere and the Raiders and, more notably, The Kingsmen. It was nothing more than a lovesick sailor's lament to a bartender about wanting to get back home to his girl. But because Jack Ely, The Kingsmen's lead singer, slurred the words beyond recognition, it became something of a Rorschach Test for dirty minds. Schoolyard rumors about filthy lyrics in "Louie, Louie" stoked parental fears, prompted fevered complaints, and ultimately triggered a prolonged nationwide investigation. The controversy made "Louie, Louie," in the words of rock critic Dave Marsh, the world's most famous rock 'n' roll song.

A letter from one panicked mom to then-Attorney General Robert Kennedy captured the general tone:

> My daughter brought home a record of 'LOUIE[,] LOUIE' and I . . . proceeded to try and decipher the jumble of words. The lyrics are so filthy that I can-not enclose them in this letter . . . .
>
> I would like to see these people, [t]he 'artists,' the Record company and the promoters prosecuted to the full extent of the law.
>
> We all know there is [*sic*] obscene materials available for those who seek it, but when they start sneaking in this material in the guise of the latest teen rock & roll hit record[,] these morons have gone too far.
>
> This land of ours is headed for an extreme state or moral degradation what with this record, the biggest hit movies and the sex and violence exploited on T.V.
>
> How can we stamp out this menace? ? ? ?

She was not alone. Indiana's Democratic governor, Matthew E. Welsh, claimed that the record was so obscene it made his "ears tingle," and he announced a statewide ban on both radio play and live performances of the song. (It was not an "official" ban. The Governor merely reached out to his contacts at the Indiana Broadcasters Association to make sure that the record was not played in his state.)

Official or not, the controversy triggered a two-and-a-half-year investigation that involved efforts by six FBI field offices, several US attorneys, and the FCC into the supposedly corrupting lyrics of "Louie, Louie." FBI Director J. Edgar Hoover corresponded with an anti-pornography activist about the song, and he was kept apprised of the inquiry. Record label personnel were questioned, and even the song's composer was interviewed (although not, apparently, Jack Ely, the supposedly obscene performer). Some who were interviewed were read their rights, according to the FBI's notes to the file. Recordings were shipped off to FBI laboratories where the records would be played back at various speeds with FBI agents straining to pick up a dirty word somewhere in the mix. United Press International (UPI) reported (prematurely) that the FBI, the Post Office, and the FCC had dropped their investigations in February 1964 "because they were unable to determine what the lyrics of the song were, even after listening to the records at speeds ranging from 16 rpm to 78 rpm." That report was wrong in a couple of important respects: the investigation was far from over – it was just getting underway, really – and it was never clear that the Post Office was involved (although this may have been a subconscious nod to Anthony Comstock).

The UPI report that FBI investigators could not understand the words was accurate, however, as reflected in correspondence from the FBI Laboratory returning materials submitted for review by the Tampa Field office: "The Department advised that they were unable to interpret any of the wording in the record and therefore could not make any decision concerning the matter." Yet the investigation would drag on for almost two more years. A June 1965 Justice Department memorandum summarizing the Detroit office inquiry, which included input from the record company, NAB, and the FCC (each of which found the complaints to be baseless), may have come closest to the truth. The FCC official, after approximately two years of receiving "unfounded complaints concerning the recording 'Louie Louie,'" concluded that, to the best of her knowledge, "the trouble was started by an unidentified college student, who made up a series of obscene verses for 'Louie Louie' and then sold them to fellow students." But the fact is that no one knows for sure how it all started. The rumor of "dirty lyrics" persisted, passed on by word of mouth, fueled by Jack Ely's inarticulate vocals and Governor Welsh's tingling ears. Perhaps the rumormongers can be forgiven their mistake. As FBI investigators put it, "with this type of rock and roll music, a listener might think he heard anything being said that he imagined."

The FBI was a year and a half into the investigation before someone thought to check out the lyrics on file with the US Copyright Office. Here is what they found:

> Louie, Louie, me gotta go.
> Louie, Louie, me gotta go.
>
> A fine little girl, she wait for me;
> me catch a ship across the sea.
>
> I sailed the ship all alone;
> I never think I'll make it home
>
> Louie, Louie, me gotta go.
> Louie, Louie, me gotta go.
>
> Three nights and days we sailed the sea;
> me think of girl constantly.
>
> On the ship, I dream she there;
> I smell the rose in her hair.
>
> Louie, Louie, me gotta go.
> Louie, Louie, me gotta go.

> Me see Jamaica moon above;
> It won't be long me see me love.
> Me take her in my arms and then
> I tell her I never leave again."

According to one source interviewed for the FBI's file (whose identity was redacted), "it is obvious [that] the lyrics to this record are not pornographic or objectionable in any way."

Nevertheless, reports in various other FBI files contained different variants of the "schoolyard" version of "Louie, Louie," such as:

> Oh, Louie, Louie, Oh, No,
> Get her way down low,
>
> Oh, Louie, Louie, Oh, Baby,
> Get her way down low,
>
> A fine little girl awaiting for me
> she's just a girl across the way
> Well I'll take her and park all alone
> She's never a girl I'd lay at home
>
> (Chorus repeat)
>
> At night at 10 I lay her again
> Fuck you girl, Oh, all the way
> Oh, my bed and I lay her there
> I meet a rose in her hair.
>
> (Chorus repeat)
>
> Ok Let's give it to them right now!
>
> She's got a rag on and I'll move above
> It won't be long she'll slip it off
> I'll take her in my arms again
> I'll tell her I'll never leave again.
>
> (Chorus repeat)
>
> Get that Broad out of here!

Needless to say, the imagined words of "Louie, Louie" bore little resemblance to the actual lyrics. Time and again, FBI investigators scrutinized the song and each time reached the same conclusion: They couldn't make out the words.

None of this mattered to those demanding FBI action. One anti-porn activist from Flint, Michigan, wrote to J. Edgar Hoover in June 1965 out of concern over "the alarming rise in venereal disease, perversion, promiscuity and illegitimate births in the teen groups." She said that her organization knew about the "dual set of lyrics" associated with "Louie, Louie," and she claimed that The Kingsmen had master-minded an "auditory illusion." So it was irrelevant whether you could prove which set of lyrics was being used to perform the song "since they were capitalizing on its obscenity," and "every teenager in the county 'heard' the obscene[,] not the copy-righted lyric." In other words, the song must be obscene if enough people became convinced that they had heard something "bad," no matter what words had been sung. Hoover wrote back to assure the correspondent that the FBI was actively investigating the matter and kindly enclosed copies of two Bureau publications – *Poison for Our Youth*, and *Combatting Merchants of Filth: The Role of the FBI*.

The activist responded the following month to say that her group had conducted its own investigation of "Louie, Louie" and had played back the original recording at various speeds. She reported that when the record was played "somewhere between 45 and 33-1/2 RPM . . . the obscene articulation is clearer." Her group compared the record with a recording of the song taken from a televised performance by The Kingsmen and reported that when "the copywritten lyric" was performed "intelli-gibly," then "by no stretch of the imagination is the obscene lyric audible." It is hard to tell what the zealous informant was trying to say. Was it that The Kingsmen performed a "clean" version of "Louie, Louie" for television but that the record was a subliminal "dirty" version? It is impossible to know what Hoover thought of this "field report." He wrote a cordial letter back (enclosing more FBI anti-smut pamph-lets), but also had the Detroit office investigate the woman and her group. Agents reported back that the Bureau had "nothing derogatory concerning [the] correspondent."

The FBI finally closed out its investigation on October 10, 1966, with a brief, nondescript memo from the FBI Labs to the New York office returning the record-ing and the lyrics sheet. But here's the oddest part. For all the scrutiny devoted to this song and its lyrics, the countless hours that FBI agents and lab technicians spent listening to the record at different speeds, and the many fans (and critics) obsessively searching for something dirty, no one seemed to notice that Lynn Easton, The Kingsmen's drummer, fleetingly uttered the word "fuck" just under a minute into the song. He had fumbled with his drumsticks and spontaneously vocalized his frustration at the mistake. But, because the song was recorded in one take, the accidentally improvised expletive stayed in, indistinct and in the background. There is a lesson about human nature in this: People rarely find what they do not seek, but, quite often, they can clearly see what they are looking for – even when it isn't there.

The whole "Louie, Louie" episode bore the hallmarks of a classic Comstockian debacle – it originated in a moral panic about nothing, was driven by apocalyptic rhetoric about the mortal dangers threatening youth, would-be censors ultimately were embarrassed by their actions, and, in the end, the controversy only magnified public attention and interest in the work. The FBI files documented the Comstock

Effect at work: One September 1965 memorandum said that when first released on the West Coast, record sales were poor, but, after Indiana's Governor issued his "ban" and the obscenity rumor spread, sales soared and hit the two million mark. Whether to quell the rumors (or to capitalize on them), the record label offered a $1,000 reward to anyone who could substantiate the reported obscenity. No one ever did.

Indiana Governor Matthew Welsh came to regret that "Louie, Louie" would be the only thing for which he would be remembered. He tried to downplay the incident in a 1991 interview, calling it "a tempest in a teapot," and he emphatically denied being a censor. He never banned the record, Welsh told Dave Marsh for his definitive book on the subject. Rather, he only sent a letter to Reid Chapman, president of the Indiana Broadcasters Association, suggesting that "Louie, Louie" not be played on any radio stations in the state. This wasn't censorship, Welsh insisted, as he had merely suggested to Chapman "that it might be simpler all around if it wasn't played." But "it doesn't take a First Amendment scholar to see the contradiction," Marsh concluded, for "[i]f a record isn't played at the suggestion of the state's chief executive, it has been banned."

After all this, Anthony Comstock's ghost still lingers, and Governor Welsh would not be the last public official to be burned by wading into the "Louie, Louie" controversy. In May 2005, school superintendent Paula Dawning of Benton Harbour, Michigan decreed that the middle school marching band could not perform "Louie, Louie" in the town's Grand Floral Parade. She explained that her decision was because of the song's "degrading" and "vulgar lyrics" even though the band was to perform an *instrumental* version. Her decision was reported nation-wide – and roundly mocked – and Superintendent Dawning ultimately relented. She stood by her decision, though (both of them), telling reporters that her real concern was "parental influence." She initially issued her ban, she explained, "because one parent questioned the appropriateness for that particular song," but rescinded the decision after "listening to a majority of the McCord Renaissance Middle School band parents." Dawning said that she was merely guarding "the right of parents to set standards for their children." She did not mention whether the coast-to-coast ridicule she had received or a public official's constitutional obligation not to succumb to a heckler's veto were factors.

In the end, defenders of "Louie, Louie" got the last laugh. April 11 is listed in the National Special Events Registry as International "Louie, Louie" Day, and the states of Washington and Oregon have proclaimed their own observances of "Louie, Louie" Day. The City of Seattle has done the same, and Tacoma, Washington sponsored an annual "LouieFest" from 2003 to 2012. Peoria, Illinois hosts an annual "Louie, Louie" parade and festival (answering the age-old question, will it play in Peoria?), and Philadelphia had "Louie, Louie" parades from 1985 to 1989 (until the annual event was canceled due to rowdiness). In 1985, Washington considered making "Louie, Louie" the state song, but the effort fizzled. Still, the song is played during the seventh-inning stretch at all Seattle Mariners home games. Politicians (for the most part) now embrace the once-taboo song, and Washington Governor Christine Gregoire danced to the tune at her Inaugural Ball in 2005. She did not say whether it made her ears tingle.

TORCHING THE DEVIL'S MUSIC

The year the FBI threw in the towel on the "Louie, Louie" investigation marked another milestone in the censorship of rock music, although this was not an example of government action. In a March 1966 interview with the *London Evening Standard*, John Lennon quipped that The Beatles were "more popular than Jesus now," a remark that led to a wave of protests in the American South and a number of public burnings of the band's records and memorabilia. Radio station WAQY in Birmingham, Alabama organized a "Beatles bonfire" to which outraged listeners could come to heap albums and other band merchandise onto a pyre. The idea caught on, and similar events were held in Georgia, Texas, and other states. At least thirty radio stations announced that they were banning Beatles music from the air. In South Carolina, the Imperial Wizard of the Ku Klux Klan nailed Beatles records to a flaming cross, and in Washington, DC, Klan members decked out in their robes and hoods picketed a Beatles concert.

That a gaggle of religious nut-jobs took it upon themselves to torch some records isn't unconstitutional censorship, of course, as it involved no government action. But it is notable that the outraged mobs chose a method of suppressing expression that had been preferred by official censors for millennia (and that later would be used by PMRC's allies). In ancient times, book burning was frequently done for political purposes, but, as often as not, a belief in the supernatural helped fan the flames. Antiochus IV ordered Jewish books in Jerusalem be "rent to pieces" and burned in 168 BC; the Emperor Constantine ordered the burning of works by those who disputed the Trinity; the Christian Emperor Jovian burned the library of Antioch in AD 364 because it had been stocked largely by Emperor Julian who was non-Christian; and in AD 392 the library at Alexandria was looted and burned by Christian mobs and the woman philosopher Hypatia murdered. Pope Gregory IX prevailed on King Louis IX in 1242 to destroy all copies of the Talmud in Paris, and in 1401 the English Parliament under King Henry IV passed a law that required the collection and public burning of heretical works. All of this came before the Spanish Inquisition, which ordered the wholesale burning of Jewish and Arabic texts.

Closer to our own time, Anthony Comstock boasted of having burned some 15 tons of books, as well as 284,000 pounds of printing plates for "objectionable" texts (which were melted down), and nearly 4 million pictures. In the twentieth century, book burning is most closely associated with Nazi Germany, and for good reason, the Nazis *wanted* to be known for it. On May 10, 1933, Nazi youth groups burned some 25,000 "degenerate" books at a large bonfire in Berlin, with radio broadcasts publicizing the event to those who could not attend in person. Books by such authors as Albert Einstein, Bertold Brecht, Helen Keller, Sigmund Freud, Thomas Mann, Karl Marx, Ernest Hemingway, and H. G. Wells were tossed on the flaming heap. Similar events were held throughout Germany in the 1930s and 1940s. These were followed (a little too closely for comfort) by the comic book bonfires in various US communities in the late 1940s and early 1950s.

Notwithstanding these dark associations, the practice of throwing rallies to roast rock albums and other band-related materials caught on in the 1970s. A Tallahassee, Florida preacher named Charles Boykin garnered headlines in 1975 when he conducted a record-burning campaign to save souls. Citing surveys that he said proved that 98 percent of unwed mothers were impregnated while under the influence of rock, and inspired by the command in Deuteronomy 7:25 that the graven images of false gods must be burned with fire, Boykin organized bonfires to consign evil to the flames. Given that records then were made of vinyl (and were not "graven"), Reverend Boykin evidently skipped over that part of the Bible verse that said "thou shalt not desire the silver or gold that is on them" and opted for a less-than-literal view that allows some interpretive latitude when it comes to fighting the evils of rock.

Others would emulate stunts like this from time to time. The Peters brothers, Christian evangelists from Minnesota, conducted a campaign in the late 1970s to burn rock albums. They called rock and roll music "one of Satan's grandest schemes," and claimed to have destroyed ten million dollars' worth of records and tapes. Sally Nevius of PMRC credited the Peters brothers for getting "the rock 'n['] roll wrecking ball swinging in the right direction." PMRC's "consultant" at the 1985 "porn rock" hearings, Reverend Jeff Ling, with his anti-heavy metal road show, was another direct connection with this kind of flim-flam. Such associations made PRMC's claim that its concerns about music were "historically unique" not just wrong but ludicrous.

From the earliest complaints about ragtime and jazz, through the hysteria that greeted early rock and roll, and into the ascendancy of heavy metal, the one common element is that the popular entertainment favored by the youth culture of the time confused and alarmed parents. That was the point. Fashions and styles inevitably change, and usually in ways that are not aesthetically pleasing to older ears. The fact that a musical form is new (or ugly) hardly sets it apart. And if you wait long enough, what was once obscene may become "classic."

One other commonality that has made the perceived influences on youth so threatening is that they were said to emanate from foreign influences, or from "the other." Comstock was obsessed with this, with his meticulous records of the number of defendants that had immigrated from foreign lands and his belief that bad literature and art was being imported from, as he put it, "lust-cursed nations." It is no coincidence that racist attacks were directed at ragtime, jazz, and rock and roll – music that originated with black people – and some anti-music crusaders were quite up front about their prejudices. As with book burning, the concerns had a sinister pedigree. Adolph Hitler banned jazz from the Berlin Broadcasting Station in 1933, "especially that brand produced by Negro orchestras and singers," and the Nazi party adopted an Ordinance Against Negro Culture with the intention to eliminate "all immoral and foreign racial elements in the arts." It wasn't just Nazis who held such attitudes. During the same period, the BBC banned jazz, which it described as "hot music," from the air.

The same attitudes were common in the USA, so that jazz, R&B, and early rock routinely were labeled "jungle music," "cannibalistic," and "primitive." And, given the mores of the time, the descriptions were not always couched in euphemism. Up through the end of World War II, for example, R&B had been classified by *Billboard* magazine as "race records." The emergence of rock and roll in the mid-1950s heightened the tensions over music and race because it coincided with the civil rights movement and the drive for integration. The backlash was predictable. It brought out some overtly racist reactions, exemplified by a 1954 pamphlet handed out by an Alabama White Citizens' Council warning that "rock 'n' roll will pull the white man down to the level of the negro." But even those not inclined to engage in mindless race-baiting were prone to believe the worst about the music and its dark origins. Not only did cities across the USA respond to the "threat" by banning rock shows but some passed ordinances that focused on their real concerns by banning interracial dancing.

DANGEROUS RAP

The cycle was repeated with the reactions to rap and hip-hop music in the late 1980s and early 1990s. These musical genres emerged from the inner-city, were aimed at minority audiences, and not infrequently touched on themes involving violence and macho posturing. While performers maintained that they were merely depicting life as they experienced it, the language and subjects they explored were threatening to adults – particularly white adults. Songs focusing on sex, drugs, and violence toward cops (and others) acquired their own moniker – gangsta rap – and along with it the unwelcome attention of policymakers. Concerns peaked as the music gained favor with young white audiences, just as had happened with rock thirty-some years earlier, and jazz before that. By the mid-1990s, legislation to limit access by minors to music with "obscene or erotic lyrics" had been introduced in more than twenty states.

Just as "porn rock" had been the moral panic *du jour* the decade before, "gangsta rap" became the focus of hearings before a House of Representatives subcommittee in February and May 1994. And, like "porn rock," "gangsta rap" was not a recognized subgenre of music but was merely a pejorative label used by pro-censorship activists. The lead witness was C. Delores Tucker, a former civil rights worker and Pennsylvania Secretary of State who had become chair of the National Political

Congress of Black Women, and a prominent critic of rap music. Tucker played the Comstock role at the hearings, deploying many of his standard techniques. She showed up with her own Chamber of Horrors, displaying graphic artwork from album covers and sporting examples of shocking lyrics. She denounced gangsta rap with (as Comstock would have put it) Biblical frankness, claiming that its violent references and misogynistic lyrics were "nothing more than pornographic smut" and that its influence "explains why so many of our children are out of control and why we have more black males in jail than we have in college."

Tucker advocated regulation to rein in what she called the avarice of an out-of-control record industry and dismissed any notion that doing so might raise free speech concerns. In her view, "no one has the right to poison our children's minds and poison their values," and she ticked off three reasons "that prevent gangsta rap from being a freedom of speech issue": "Number one, it is obscene; number two, it is obscene; and number three, it is obscene." To support her contention that prohibiting gangsta rap would present no censorship problem, Tucker referred to a 1992 decision of Canada's Supreme Court which held that it was "more important to ban speech that is dehumanizing to women than to protect free speech." This was reminiscent of Fredric Wertham pointing to a Canadian law banning crime comics as precedent to be followed in the USA, and Comstock embracing the British *Hicklin* decision as justification for his anti-obscenity crusades.

Of course, Canada is not the United States, and, among other things, it has no First Amendment. The decision that Tucker held up as a model, *Butler* v. *The Queen*, held that, under the Canadian Charter of Rights and Freedoms, obscenity law could be enforced against pornography that could be viewed as degrading to women or promoting violence. The rationale of *Butler* represented an interpretation of free speech law that had been rejected in the USA and for good reason: The *Butler* case became an engine for censorship in Canada, and its casualties were gay, lesbian, and women's literature. At the time that Dolores Tucker was extolling the decision's virtues before Congress, officials in Canada relied on *Butler* to confiscate or detain materials from more than half of the feminist bookstores in that country. But the "gangsta rap" hearings were not the place to bring up such inconvenient facts. Tucker was an activist on a mission, and she was on a roll.

She found some support at the hearing from Congressman Cliff Stearns of Florida, whose written statement for the record railed against "the moral erosion of society." He noted that his state had actively sought to prosecute the rap group 2 Live Crew for obscenity, but was forced to acknowledge that the government's case had failed. Nevertheless, he added that there was strong support for the notion that "something must be done to stop the production of violent, misogynistic material." Despite such rhetoric, these hearings were quite different from the PMRC show from the previous decade. This was no media circus, so politicians were not clamoring for face time, and the hearings were not used as a veiled threat to coerce concessions from the industry. Hillary Rosen, then-president of the RIAA, testified late in the proceedings, almost as an afterthought.

Something else was remarkable about the sessions. The hearings were just that – hearings. Representative Cardiss Collins, a former president of the Congressional Black Caucus who chaired the subcommittee, pursued no apparent agenda and actually listened to what the witnesses had to say. She described her purpose as being to find out what was going on in a matter of importance to the community that had been glossed over by the media. When she said that the purpose of the hearings was "not to legislate, not to censure, not to discuss abridgement of First Amendment rights," she seemed to mean it, adding that the government cannot legislate morality and if "a parent wants his child to listen to this music, that is a parent's responsibility." While her lead witness was a prominent anti-rap activist, others invited to testify included record executives, rap artists, Don Cornelius (the long-time host of the television show *Soul Train*), a DJ with expertise in hip-hop music, high-school educators, and even some young people.

Additionally, she had as a witness Representative Maxine Waters of California, who also did something almost unheard-of for a politician. Rather than grand-standing on the issue, she praised the artists for their creativity and stressed the need to listen to the assembled witnesses, including C. Delores Tucker. Representative Waters observed that humans "have always created art to express their pain, hope and despair of change," and, while many people may be offended by harsh language, the artists did not create the conditions in which they lived or the reality they tried to describe. But she understood the nature of this type of show trial in Washington. "Let's not kid ourselves," she said. Both liberals and conservatives tended to use such events for political ends to distract people from the real issues. As she put it, liberals would consider banning certain types of music as an exercise in social engineering in the hope of stopping violence, while conservatives "would point to the inordinately high number of blacks in prisons and on death row." She added that such "evil propaganda stands virtually unopposed in today's public debate over rap music."

Representative Waters' assessment of the political landscape was spot on. A year after the "gangsta rap" hearings, C. Delores Tucker teamed up with William Bennett, then co-director of a conservative advocacy group Empower America (and former Secretary of Education under President Reagan and Drug Czar under President George Bush), to crank up the heat on the anti-gangsta rap campaign. They did so with gusto and over-the-top Comstockian denunciation. "Nothing less is at stake than civilization," Bennett thundered. For her part, Tucker continued to scold the record industry, proclaiming that "these companies have the blood of children on their hands." She told *Ebony* magazine that, as a direct result of rap music, "little boys are raping little girls." Denouncing particular artists or songs became a standard culture war tactic, and President Bush (the elder) and his hapless Vice President Dan Quayle both got in on the act. So did Senator Bob Dole, who castigated songs such as Ice-T's

"Cop Killer" during his presidential campaign. Then-congressman Newt Gingrich urged people to boycott radio stations that played any rap music at all.

And it wasn't just the conservatives. In the grand tradition of most moral panics, the level of alarm was entirely bipartisan. C. Delores Tucker, who was leading the charge, was a long-time Democratic activist and civil rights worker. President Bill Clinton also joined the fray, as did Democratic senators Sam Nunn and Joe Lieberman. Lieberman in particular embraced the role of culture warrior, warning the entertainment industry in 1999: "[I]f you don't use your rights with some sense of responsibility, there is a danger [that] those very rights will be endangered." The controversy led to more congressional hearings, and eventually a major inquiry by the Federal Trade Commission (FTC) into whether the use (or misuse) of ratings in the entertainment industry constituted a "deceptive trade practice." The study addressed all forms of entertainment marketed to kids, not just music, and it was conducted by the FTC in an attempt to avoid claims that the government was threatening censorship. According to its proponents, this was not a precursor to regulating art or entertainment; it was merely directed at regulating the *marketing* of art and entertainment.

There was one big flaw with this attempt at a linguistic work-around: the FTC was a little too honest in its evaluation of the issue. The agency found that privately developed ratings worked pretty well, but, more to the point, the FTC recognized that any effort by the federal government to regulate media ratings would necessarily raise First Amendment problems, even if characterized as "trade" regulations. Robert Pitofsky, the FTC's chairman, warned senators that such regulations would be confronted with "substantial and unsettled constitutional questions," and the Commission's staff advised that "vigilant self-regulation is the best approach to ensuring that parents are provided with adequate information to guide their children's exposure to entertainment media with violent content."

Of course, none of this slowed down Senator Lieberman, who promptly introduced the Media Marketing Accountability Act of 2001, which would extend FTC authority over the marketing of motion pictures, video games, and music recordings that have been rated as "inappropriate" for children. A separate bill introduced in the House would establish a mandatory uniform ratings scheme for labeling "violent content in audio and visual media products." Neither bill went anywhere, perhaps because Congress was forced to focus on actual violence, not imaginary violence, after September 11, 2001. Another possible explanation is that Congress may have been dissuaded from acting because courts had begun to address some of the constitutional questions involved, and the decisions in those cases were not encouraging to regulatory-minded lawmakers.

MUSIC FOUGHT THE LAW, AND MUSIC WON

Following the 1985 "porn rock" hearings, PMRC continued to lobby for record labeling, and by 1990 mandatory record labeling legislation was proposed in nineteen states. This prompted the RIAA to announce a renewed agreement with PMRC in which the industry agreed to put labels of uniform size and placement on albums and CDs when lyrics touched on sex, violence, or substance abuse. Space permitting, lyrics would be provided with recorded music. The proposed bills were withdrawn in response to the new agreement. But such political horse trading did not deter some of the more vocal critics of rap, who saw this music from the inner-city as more of a threat pushed for direct action by law enforcement.

One such crusader was Jack Thompson, a Florida lawyer and wannabe mini-Comstock who made it a personal mission to see that 2 Live Crew would be prosecuted for obscenity. Thompson was a Christian fundamentalist and self-described vigilante who fancied himself as Batman. He sometimes sent adversaries photocopies of his driver's license with Batman's visage superimposed over his photo. Thompson would later become an anti-video game crusader (before being disbarred in 2008), but in 1990 he put his law practice on hold to make sure that foul-mouthed rappers would be put behind bars. He wrote a letter to then-Florida Governor Bob Martinez, which helped prompt a criminal investigation into whether distribution of 2 Live Crew records might violate state racketeering and obscenity laws. Thompson followed this by sending letters containing 2 Live Crew lyrics to every other governor in the USA, and to prosecutors and sheriffs' departments throughout Florida.

This campaign spurred Broward County Sheriff Nick Navarro to action. He obtained an order from a local judge finding probable cause that 2 Live Crew's album *As Nasty As They Want to Be* violated Florida obscenity laws. Navarro promptly delivered the order to music retailers, warning them against any further distribution of the album. Not surprisingly, the recording was promptly withdrawn from store shelves throughout the county. The band and its record label then filed suit against Navarro's office, seeking a ruling that these actions violated the First Amendment. After a bench trial, Judge Jose Gonzalez issued a split decision: The Sheriff's actions in coercing record stores to cease distribution of the album imposed an unconstitutional prior restraint in violation of the First Amendment, but the 2 Live Crew album was found to be legally obscene.

Judge Gonzalez's lengthy opinion read like an extended treatise on obscenity law, the first section of which was devoted to a defense of the concept of obscenity. He observed that obscenity "is as much against the law as assault, rape, kidnapping, robbery, or any other form of behavior which the legislature has declared criminal," (except, of course, that the essence of the offense – a "prurient interest" in sex – is entirely in the mind), and he railed against "absolutists" who would do away with obscenity altogether. "The absolutists and other members of the party of Anything Goes," he wrote, "should address their petitions to the Florida Legislature, not to this court." As to the album itself, Judge Gonzalez drew on his personal knowledge of local community standards and ruled that *As Nasty As They Want to Be* crossed the line: "It is an appeal directed to 'dirty' thoughts and the loins, not to the intellect and the mind." The opinion sent shock waves across the nation and prompted other law enforcement actions, including a prosecution of 2 Live Crew's members for an "obscene" performance.

But the court of appeals made short work of it. In a very brief unsigned opinion, a three-judge panel of the US Court of Appeals for the Eleventh Circuit reversed Judge Gonzalez's obscenity finding. The appellate court said that it could not assume that the district court judge's "artistic or literary knowledge or skills" were sufficient to decide the ultimate question dictated by the Supreme Court in *Miller* v. *California* – whether a work "lacks serious artistic, scientific, literary or political value." But the panel's most significant pronouncement touched on a far broader question that was not presented (or decided) in the case. Noting that this was the first time a court of appeals had been asked to decide whether the *Miller* obscenity test could be applied to a musical composition, the panel wrote that it tended to agree with 2 Live Crew's contention that "because music possesses inherent artistic value, no work of music alone may be declared obscene." The Supreme Court denied review.

The Eleventh Circuit ruling finally ended the efforts to prosecute 2 Live Crew, but much happened in the two years between the district court and appellate court rulings – none of which was good news for the prosecutors or the regulators. Within a week of Judge Gonzalez's obscenity ruling, the Broward County Sheriff made two arrests, one of a record store owner who had publicly vowed to continue selling 2 Live Crew albums, and another of the band itself after it performed at Club Futura in Hollywood, Florida. But juries largely saw these efforts to sanitize the culture as a waste of time. 2 Live Crew band members were acquitted, as were members of another band, Too Much Joy, who had separately been arrested for performing 2 Live Crew songs to protest the government's actions. After this, the state's attorney dropped the charges against Club Futura for hosting 2 Live Crew.

An Alabama jury earlier that year had voided a store owner's conviction for selling *As Nasty As They Want to Be*, and, in Texas, a county court judge dismissed criminal charges brought against a retailer for selling the album. Meanwhile, a federal court enjoined the town of Westerly, Rhode Island from revoking the entertainment license for a planned concert by 2 Live Crew, holding that it violated the First and Fourteenth Amendments. As a result, even before the Eleventh Circuit's broad pronouncement about First Amendment protection for music, the *Miami Times* reported that "the campaign to prosecute purveyors of raunchy music ... [had] rolled to a halt" like "a freight train finally running out of steam."

The same fate befell actions by state legislators. Although most states had backed away from efforts to regulate music sales after RIAA cut its record-labeling deals, Washington State in 1992 adopted an "Erotic Sound Recordings" statute which made it a crime to display or sell to minors recorded music deemed "erotic." The law would have allowed prosecutors to obtain court orders to require retailers of record-ings or publications to label as "adults only" material deemed "harmful to minors," and to prohibit the exhibition, sale, or distribution to minors of labeled material. The law never went into effect, however, because the King County Superior Court declared that it was unconstitutional and the Washington Supreme Court affirmed. The Court held that the law imposed a prior restraint in violation of the First Amendment and that its procedures violated due process.

The outcome is usually the same whenever the extravagant claims of activists and the measures adopted by politicians are subjected to legal or constitutional scrutiny. Insinuations that heavy metal music causes teen suicide, such as those made in the 1985 "porn rock" hearings, were rejected in a pair of cases in the early 1990s. In *Vance v. Judas Priest*, a Nevada state court held that the plaintiff failed to prove that alleged subliminal commands (including "fuck the Lord," "sing my evil spirit," and "do it") had been intentionally placed in the Judas Priest album or that such "commands," if placed, could cause a person to perceive the message and act on it. An almost identical claim against Ozzie Osbourne's "Suicide Solution" was tossed for the same reason. The court could find no subliminal message in the song, only "garbled and unintelligible" lyrics that, in any event, could not be considered an incitement.

POLITICS AND THE CENSOR'S DILEMMA

Perhaps the lessons of these cases had been absorbed by the sponsors of the 1994 "gangsta rap" hearings, or maybe they honestly sought to explore a current controversial issue. There was no extended discussion of the law during the proceedings (other than C. Delores Tucker's uninformed assertion that "gangsta rap" was obscene and her plea that the USA should follow Canadian law). Whatever the reason, the hearings were remarkably free of political bluster or veiled threats, and no deals were struck by cowed record producers. As a result, the "gangsta rap" hearings did not become a cultural touchstone as did PMRC's 1985 production. Of course, the "porn rock" hearing was a tough act to follow, since it had all the ingredients of a first-rate Washington circus: well-connected Washington wives on a mission to save children from eternal peril, salacious stories of sex and satanism, celebrity guests who could be cast as villains, and grandstanding politicians to save us through exhortations of moral outrage. Who could ask for more? Joe Lieberman (and others) tried to revive the show in the late 1990s through the turn of the millennium, but just couldn't match the star power and cultural resonance of the original.

This explains why the 1985 hearing has remained a topic of interest, with retrospectives regularly published on notable anniversaries. Twenty years after the hearings, National Public Radio (NPR)'s *All Things Considered* looked back through Tipper Gore's eyes in a piece that was little more than a promotion for her 1987 book Raising PG Kids in an X-Rated Society. Five years later, *Vulture* recalled the "infamous" hearings and cheekily observed, "And from that moment on, no youngster ever heard anything filthy again," quickly adding, "Oh, wait: One of the big songs of this summer is called 'Fuck You.' Sorry, cancel that last conclusion."

At thirty years out, *Newsweek* ran a major piece it described as "An Oral History of PMRC's War on Dirty Lyrics." By then, Tipper Gore declined to be interviewed. And Twisted Sister's Dee Snider was amused. He pointed out that the 2012 movie *Rock of Ages*, which parodied the controversy, had the leader of the PMRC-type group (played by Catherine Zeta-Jones) belt out a version of "We're Not Gonna Take it" when confronting the profane rock star (played by Tom Cruise). This, of course, was the Twisted Sister song played at the 1985 hearings to illustrate the downfall of civilization. Snider called this "irony in its purest form." Gore did provide a comment for *Rolling Stone*'s short piece commemorating the thirty-year mark for the hearing, saying she thought that PMRC's campaign was still relevant, but adding somewhat sheepishly, "In this era of social media and online access, it seems quaint to think that parents can have control over what their children see and hear."

But it didn't take the Gores three decades to begin their strategic retreat. That started almost immediately, when Al ran for President in 1988. He and Tipper began paving the way the year before with what was, in essence, an "apology tour" to mend fences and raise money from entertainment moguls. In a private meeting with industry executives in LA (that was secretly recorded and written up in *Daily Variety*), they called the 1985 hearing "a mistake" that "sent the wrong message." A campaign spokesperson explained that Tipper Gore had never favored censorship and that the California meeting had been requested by supporters to "clear up misperceptions about Mrs. Gore's position." Even before this awkward meeting, Tipper had already been exploring ways to distance them both from the hearing. Al had not requested the "porn rock" hearing, she wrote in her 1987 book, and claimed that they'd both had reservations about it.

Journalists Alexander Cockburn and Jeffrey St. Clair were singularly unimpressed with the Gores' election-year effort to paint themselves as innocent bystanders who just happened to be present at the time. If not for the efforts of Tipper and PMRC, there would not have been a hearing; as one target of their campaign recalled, the ladies of PMRC "came on like Joe McCarthy in drag." And as for Al, Cockburn and St. Clair reported that most other senators floated in and out of the hearing (as members tend to do), but Gore stayed for the duration, questioning every witness and suggesting at one point that record company executives should be compelled to testify. And he did not hesitate to spout PMRC's line, observing that the record companies were simply being irresponsible in "promoting suicide and all the other things we have heard about here." If Gore had any reservations, they must have been at a Capitol Hill restaurant, for he displayed none at the hearing.

PMRC'S LEGACY

Much as with Comstock's legacy, the efforts of the would-be music censors became the subject of parody and their censorship campaigns turned out to be great advertising for the taboo material. It also was evident that the public at large did not buy in to the deathly serious, blood-and-thunder "end-of-civilization" pronouncements of the anti-music crusaders (as was obvious from the popularity of the forbidden music itself). One sign of this disconnect came on the first day of the 2 Live Crew obscenity trial, when the jury sent a note to the judge asking if it was alright to laugh in the jury box. After the group was acquitted, one juror told the *Washington Post*: "[W]e took the whole thing as a comedy." She added that she didn't yet have their record but was thinking about buying it after the trial and attending a 2 Live Crew show.

The artists themselves made record ratings (and riffing on the idea of the "voluntary" label) part of their marketing. As with most things, Frank Zappa was ahead of the curve. The year before the "porn rock" hearing, his albums *Them or Us* and *Thing-Fish* had their own label on the inner sleeve guaranteeing that the lyrics would "not cause eternal torment in the place where the guy with the horns and the pointed stick conducts his business." George Carlin released a comedy album titled *Parental Advisory: Explicit Lyrics* where the entire cover was an enlarged version of the PMRC label with Carlin's steely eyes peering over it (Figure 6.2). The liner notes

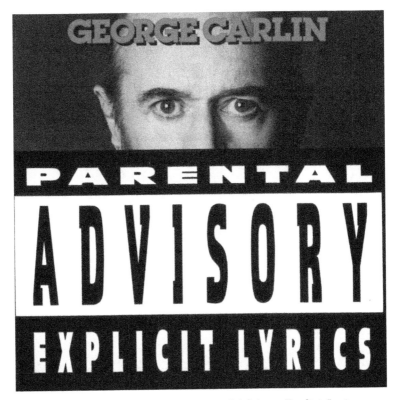

FIGURE 6.2 Cover of album *Parental Advisory: Explicit Lyrics*
Source: Amazon.com, used by permission of Kelly Carlin on behalf of the George Carlin Estate.

warned: "This recording contains no backmasking or subliminal suggestions. All messages from the Devil are recorded clearly and audibly in standard American English."

Other record companies followed a similar strategy. A compilation of ten cuts by top rap artists (including Ice Cube, 2 Live Crew, Ice-T, N.W.A., Eazy-E, Geto Boys, Too Short, and M.C. Choice) was released under the title *Parental Advisory – Explicit Rap*, and, much like the Carlin album, the entire cover was a blow-up of the PMRC label. Another release was titled *Barsha's Explicit Lyrics*, and the cover sported the warning "NOTICE: This is a rap record which contains street language and sexual innuendo." 2 Live Crew's album that followed its obscenity trial, entitled *Banned in the U.S.A.*, was the first to bear the standardized warning label that had been worked out in the deal between PMRC and the record industry. Given the notoriety of the trial and the hype surrounding the newly minted warning label, the album literally flew off the shelves. Atlantic Records reported that it received orders for more than a million copies *even before the title was released* (Figure 6.3).

As the bands learned – and just as many had predicted – having a PMRC warning label was hardly bad for business. *Newsweek* reported that Jane's Addiction's *Ritual de lo Habitual* went twice platinum despite having a sticker and Dr. Dre's debut album, *The Chronic*, also stickered, hit triple platinum. Red Hot Chili Peppers' 1991

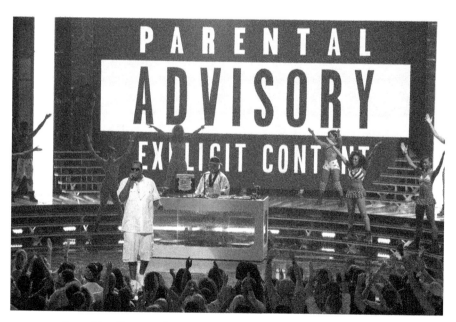

FIGURE 6.3 2 Live Crew performs onstage at the 2010 Vh1 Hip Hop Honors at the Hammerstein Ballroom, New York City on June 3, 2010
Source: Photo by Michael Loccisano/FilmMagic.

album *Blood Sugar Sex Magik* sold tens of millions of copies, and Ice Cube's *The Predator* hit No. 1 in 1992. The following year, Snoop Dogg's *Doggystyle* (a favorite target of C. Delores Tucker at the "gangsta rap" hearings) likewise soared to the top of the charts.

The warning label remains an iconic symbol, but it is hard to imagine that it any longer has much of an effect, either good or bad. As *Newsweek* observed on the thirtieth anniversary of the "porn rock" hearing, "[i]f the Parental Advisory label isn't quite dead, it's too ubiquitous and too much of a relic to carry much weight. It's just part of the scenery, like landline phones or TV guides." The notion of putting physical stickers or labels on albums or CDs is anachronistic in an age where people obtain most music from online stores and streaming services. On iTunes, songs with harsh lyrics carry a red "EXPLICIT" label (which is also embedded in the song metadata), but it is the uncommon parent who can navigate such services as adeptly as his or her kids. So, after all the moral panics over ragtime, jazz, rock, and rap, we live in a time when rock has gone classic, rap is mainstream, and kids have access to it all on demand on their portable devices. Yet, somehow, civilization has not come to an end.

7

The Vast Wasteland

On May 9, 1961, Newton Minow, JFK's youthful FCC Chairman, strode confidently to the podium at the NAB Convention and, in his first speech as chairman, delivered a stinging rebuke of his hosts' business. Right there, in the very Belly of the Beast, Minow branded television with a label that still resonates after the passage of more than half a century: TV, he said, is a "vast wasteland" of "game shows, violence, audience participation shows, formula comedies about totally unbelievable families, blood and thunder, mayhem, violence, sadism, murder, western badmen, western good men, private eyes, gangsters, more violence, and cartoons" (Figure 7.1). The move was bold, the speech pithy, and, in every important respect, wrong.

The television marketplace at the time was neither vast nor as much of a wasteland as Minow claimed. More importantly, the speech itself was an exercise in "public interest piracy" – a naked effort to coerce broadcasters indirectly into doing what the government could not compel directly. It is the kind of speech that puts the bully in the bully pulpit. The message itself was pretty unremarkable if you don't think about who delivered it, and where. After all, you don't have to be all that smart to know that TV can be dumb. As the popular euphemisms of the time made clear – like "idiot box" and "boob tube" – the ideas in the speech were hardly original. Noted personages of the day also had made the same point: Frank Lloyd Wright called TV "chewing gum for the eyes." Ernie Kovacs said that television is called a medium "because it is neither rare nor well done." And David Frost said that television is an invention "that permits you to be entertained in your living room by people you wouldn't have in your home." But the message carries far more weight when delivered not by an architect, a comic, or a journalist but by the head of the agency that grants and, more to the point, can deny broadcast licenses.

The expression itself – "vast wasteland" – is positively Churchillian. Like "Iron Curtain," it is rich with imagery and can fit on a bumper sticker. And it is absolutely breathtaking to combine this memorable turn of phrase with the master stroke of delivering such an unwelcome message at the annual celebration of commercial broadcasting. The *Vast Wasteland Speech*, as it has come to be known, is nothing less than the regulator's manifesto. For those who think the government should have

FIGURE 7.1 FCC chairman Newton Minow kneeling beside a TV set, a medium he
considers to be a "vast wasteland," Chicago, Illinois, 1961
Source: Photo by Walter Bennett/The *Life* Picture Collection via Getty Images.

a significant role in controlling what we see on TV and hear on the radio, the speech
was the background theme for the march to *Red Lion Broadcasting Co.* v. *FCC*, the
1969 Supreme Court ruling that upheld the federal government's authority to
regulate broadcasting content.

The idea that the federal government should play such a role is a pretty radical
proposition given the First Amendment's command that "Congress shall make no
law ... abridging the freedom of speech, or of the press," particularly since the
Constitution's framers adopted the amendment in substantial part as a reaction to
England's repressive history of press licensing. But those who advocate for greater
broadcast regulation, like Chairman Minow, believe that the promise of freedom of
the press cannot be realized fully unless the federal government licenses broadcast
stations and uses the FCC's licensing process to exert control over the programming
content. That paradoxical argument emerged from historical practice and the
incremental way that First Amendment protections in the United States have

been extended to new technologies – those newer than the printing press, that is. But the regulator's claim that free expression is actually *bolstered* through government control has not shielded its proponents from the censor's dilemma. If anything, it has added to their defensiveness.

And so it was with Minow, whose *Vast Wasteland Speech* reached Shakespearian heights of rationalization. Perhaps unconsciously, Minow paraphrased Marc Antony's funeral oration from *Julius Caesar* ("I have come to bury Caesar, not to praise him"), claiming: "I am in Washington to help broadcasting, not to harm it; to strengthen it, not to weaken it; to reward it, not punish it; to encourage it, not threaten it; to stimulate it, not censor it." That's right. His message was, I am from Washington, and I am here to help you.

But this was hardly a subtle exercise of regulation by raised eyebrow. Minow reminded the broadcasters that their obligation to serve the public trust was imposed by law and that they should not expect automatic renewal of their licenses if their programming failed to improve. "I say to you now: renewal will not be *pro forma* in the future. There is nothing permanent or sacred about a broadcast license." He also scoffed at those who asked the FCC to establish clear standards to qualify for license renewal. "My answer is: Why should you want to know how close you can come to the edge of the cliff?"

Minow insisted that he was not seeking to impose his personal programming preferences on broadcasters. Heavens, no. That would be censorship, which, he said, "strikes at the tap root of our free society." Rather, the Chairman said he wanted to hold public hearings on license renewals to determine "whether the community which each broadcaster serves believes he has been serving the public interest." In such hearings, Minow said he wanted "the people who own the air and the homes that television enters to tell you and the FCC what's been going on"; that it would be up to the people "to make notes, document cases, tell us the facts."

What could be more democratic than that? Well, people's actual viewing preferences, for one thing. However, what interests the public has never been of much interest to "public interest" regulators. As Chairman Minow told the assembled broadcasters, "[y]ou will get no argument from me if you say that, given a choice between a western and a symphony, more people will watch the western." "But," he added, "your obligations are not satisfied if you look only to popularity as a test of what to broadcast." Accordingly, he warned, "[i]t is not enough to cater to the nation's whims – you must also serve the nation's needs."

This is the enduring dilemma that confronts the "public interest" regulator. In order to avoid the well-founded charge that governmental mandates about programming quality would violate basic First Amendment principles, he must claim that he is not imposing his own tastes but is merely regulating on behalf of "the people." The hitch in this argument is that the facts refuse to cooperate. In reality, people's choices are so, well, *disappointing* to the refined mind of the regulator. As theater critic Clive Barnes put it, "[t]elevision is the first truly democratic culture – the first culture available to everybody and entirely governed by what people want. The most terrifying thing is what the people want." Writer Paddy Chayefsky was even blunter: "[T]elevision is democracy at its ugliest." Accordingly, the theory goes, it is the regulator's job to ensure that broadcasters rise above mere public "whims" and offer programs that meet the people's "needs." The problem, according to Professors Thomas Krattenmaker and Lucas A. Powe, is that "viewers will watch or read what critics and regulators like with insufficient frequency and will enjoy too often what commissioners and columnists abhor."

So, rather than determining the public interest by asking what shows people actually want to watch, the determined regulator seeks to divine what the public *should* see through administrative hearings in which the loudest pressure groups set the agenda. This may not represent the direct imposition of "bureaucratic tastes," which Minow eschewed, but it is awfully far removed from people's actual preferences. In such a scheme, the public interest is determined by governmental selection from among the various views presented at public hearings and in written comments. While it is true that most license renewals have never led to hearings, the FCC's public interest determinations nevertheless are institutionalized in the form of administrative decisions and rules that apply to all broadcasters.

Come to think of it, this pretty much *is* the imposition of "bureaucratic tastes." In the regulator's mind, the public interest should be gauged not by the desires of those rubes who watch TV but by the views of an enlightened "public" that cares about television but would not be caught dead watching it – or at least, wouldn't want to admit watching, much less liking it. No FCC commissioner would be so rude as to say these things, but the true "public interest" regulator certainly believes them. One giveaway is the lack of any discernible difference between the personal tastes of the typical reform-minded FCC commissioner and those of the idealized viewers he or she claims to represent. It is little wonder that the trade press at the time began to refer to Minow as the "culture czar."

It was a sore point with Minow, who would attempt time and again over the course of his long career to try to explain why a government bureaucrat who threatened broadcast license revocations should not be considered a censor. Three months after the *Vast Wasteland Speech*, Minow spoke at a Northwestern University conference to point out that "the censorship alarm has been sounded, or shouted, or whispered, or printed," and he wanted to use the occasion "to discuss it in depth." It was a stunningly Comstockian display of the censor's dilemma at work: simultaneously belittling concerns about government control of an important medium of communication while declaring that "nobody – least of all me – wants to be put in the role of censor."

Conflating editorial choice with censorship, Minow claimed that broadcasters were the real censors, because they base programming decisions on ratings (aka, what the audience wants), and because they strive to air only nonoffensive programming. This, he said, is censorship "in its most pernicious form," and he wondered "what would have been the fate of the world's great dramatists if they were solely dependent upon television for performance of their plays?" Minow expressed concern that literary giants like Ibsen, Shakespeare, and Shaw would be considered too provocative for television and "too concerned with morals and conflicts of their times" to make the grade. But then, in the very next breath, he decried "the amount of violence, murder, mayhem and sadism on TV shows" because "in somebody's opinion . . . the ratings demand a jolt."

So, what was the complaint exactly? Was it that broadcast programming was too offensive, or not provocative enough? And what was the FCC's role in this, given that it enforced indecency rules patterned after the Comstock law – the very law that had been used to threaten and prosecute the works of Shaw and other writers who dared to explore the "morals and conflicts of their times?" Minow did not say.

But he bollixed the very concept of censorship by insisting that the FCC "clearly does *not* censor anything" because it does not restrict particular programs. He went on: "We don't censor rock and roll, or Westerns or quiz shows or even overdoses of brutality." Leaving aside for a moment the fact that the FCC to this day exercises precisely the kind of censorship authority that Minow said does not exist (a subject explored in greater detail in Chapter 8), his speech was not so much an effort to deny censorship as it was to redefine it. From the beginnings of First Amendment jurisprudence, the Supreme Court explained that freedom from prior restraint "cannot be deemed to exhaust the conception of the liberty guaranteed by the state and federal constitutions." Freedom of speech and press also prevents the government from inflicting subsequent punishment on speech that fails to measure up to government standards.

So, what Minow was really saying is that the type of program supervision undertaken by the FCC may be censorship as traditionally understood, but it is not *censorship* when applied to broadcasters. He approvingly quoted legislators responsible for the Radio Act of 1927 and the Communications Act of 1934 who made clear that they had no intention of extending true freedom of speech and press to radio. Citing Senator Wallace White, who Minow described as one of the "fathers of the Communications Act," he said that broadcasters who wanted to be treated like newspapers were "indulging in dreams," and that "Congress will not stand . . . for any such interpretation." A quotation he attributed to Senator Edwin Johnson was even pithier: To say that "radio presents a direct analogy to the press" is "as far-fetched as comparing an elephant to a flea."

Despite his denials about censorship, Minow embraced the role of program supervision with gusto. He described this type of eat-your-vegetables, the-government-knows-what-is-good-for-you regulation as "the very reverse of censorship." The former FCC Chairman proudly described having denied a license application for an FM radio station applicant who had proposed to provide only "standard" broadcasting service and put broadcasters on notice that he expected more of them if they wanted to keep their licenses. Renewal applications submitted to Minow's FCC would require more information on local programming, coverage of controversial issues, educational programs, political and news shows, and children's programming.

Minow had wanted to go even further – to require stations to set forth the hours and time slots for public affairs programs made available by networks; if not aired, an explanation from the local affiliate for why the programming was rejected; and what was put in its place. Broadcasters who failed to satisfy the government's expectations would face nonrenewal of their licenses – not because of their programming, Minow claimed, but because a failure to justify their scheduling choices would show that they lacked sufficient "character" or "fitness" to be licensees. But, euphemisms aside, of course, it *was* all about the programming, and Minow did more than just make speeches about it. In the year following the *Vast Wasteland Speech*, fourteen broadcast stations were put on "probation" and received only short-term license renewals. The Commission also scheduled eight stations for renewal hearings, thus clouding their future tenure as licensees.

Minow returned to these themes over three decades later in a 1995 book entitled ABANDONED IN THE WASTELAND, proving that it is possible for a person to dine out on one metaphor for too long. His principal theme was that more "public interest" regulation should be employed to protect children from televised depictions of violence, to reduce salacious programming, and to require more educational programs for children. What about First Amendment concerns? "Surely if ever a word were in need of rest," he wrote, "'censorship' is that word," along with "its frequent advance man, 'chilling.'" He recounted his usual arguments for why control of a communications medium in the name of the "public interest" is not "censorship." For good measure, he added that the First Amendment "must be read in a special way" when children are involved, and that this diminished level of protection "is especially important in broadcast television." He called his interpretation "the child's First Amendment." It was aptly named, for only a child could believe it.

FACT-CHECKING THE "WASTELAND"

In a time of a seemingly unlimited choice of video options ranging from streaming video to cable and satellite TV, it is tempting to think of the *Vast Wasteland Speech* as simply a period piece that belongs to an era when there were only three television networks and the broadcast day began at 6 a.m. and ended at midnight. But the continuing appeal of Minow's words transcends the limited media landscape of the early 1960s. The main attraction of the speech has very little to do with facts and everything to do with mindset. Its attitude is that if television is bad, it is the government's job to make it better. Or, in the language of the speech – broadcast licensees have an obligation to make it better . . . or else. The speech rhapsodizes the broadcast medium's second-class status under the First Amendment, a condition that persists even now.

Given Minow's premise, perhaps a look at the facts might be instructive. A network executive who accepted his challenge in 1961 to "sit down in front of your television set when your station goes on the air ... and keep your eyes glued to that set until the station signs off" would find a quite different picture from the one sketched in the *Vast Wasteland Speech*. On May 14, 1961, five days after the speech, a viewer in New York would have had to choose between *Washington Conversation* on WCBS-TV, featuring none other than FCC Chairman Newton Minow, and *Meet the Professor* on WABC-TV, in which the former president of Sarah Lawrence College discussed American education. The third (and only other choice) in that time slot was devoted to televangelist Oral Roberts on WOR-TV.

Later on that same day, a viewer in that market would have had the following programming choices in addition to the three just mentioned: *Let's Look at Congress* with Senator Kenneth B. Keating and guest (WOR-TV); *Camera Three*, featuring Mozart's comic opera *The Impresario* (WCBS-TV); *Accent*, with a discussion among architects (WCBS-TV); *Dorothy Gordon's Youth Forums*, discussing whether the Peace Corps will serve a purpose (WNBC-TV); *UN International Zone*, a tour of the United Nations headquarters with Alistair Cooke (WNBC-TV); *Directions '61*, discussing rare books and manuscripts from the vaults of the Jewish Theological Seminary of America (WABC-TV); *Catholic Hour*, exploring man's dignity in the face of death as described in modern dramas (WNBC-TV); *Direct Line*, a discussion with the New York State Housing Commissioner (WNBC); *Congressional Conference*, with Representative John V. Lindsay (WOR-TV); *Youth Wants to Know*, with Senator Henry Jackson of Washington (WABC-TV); *WCBS-TV Views the Press*, with Charles Collingwood (WCBS-TV); *Open Mind*, with reflections on the social, political, and economic changes of the past fifty years by theologian Dr. Reinhold Niebuhr, Socialist Party leader Norman Thomas, NAACP counsel (and future Supreme Court Justice) Thurgood Marshall, and Professor Eric F. Goldman (WNBC-TV); *Eichmann on Trial*, featuring highlights of the week's war crimes tribunal sessions (WABC-TV); *American Musical Theatre*, with Alan J. Lerner discussing his career (WCBS-TV); *Issues and Answers*, with Treasury Secretary Douglas Dillon (WABC-TV); *College Bowl*, pitting Johns Hopkins University against Montana State University (WCBS-TV); *Chet Huntley Reporting*, showing a Cuban propaganda newsreel about the Bay of Pigs invasion (WNBC-TV); *Meet the Press*, with an interview of Dr. Jonas Salk, inventor of the polio vaccine (WNBC-TV); *Recital Hall*, featuring baritone Theodor Uppman (WNBC-TV); *On Call to a Nation*, reporting on socialized medicine in Great Britain (WNTA); *A Way of Thinking*, with Dr. Albert Burke (WNEW-TV); *Between the Lines*, discussing issues involving parochial schools (WNTA); *Open End*, exploring the pros and cons of "the New Frontier" (WNTA); and *Winston Churchill* (WABC-TV).

Admittedly, these programming choices were on a Sunday, the day of the week when most issues-oriented and educational programming was clustered. Yet during the week, when entertainment predominated, the commercial networks also presented news reports and commentary, as well as special reports. WABC, for example, broadcast a report on the Nuremburg war crimes trials each evening at 6:30, just before the 7 p.m. newscast. While some well-meaning FCC commissioners no doubt would have preferred that every day's programming schedule be more like the one on Sunday, this was no "wasteland." Nor was it vast. In 1961, the largest media marketplace in the world – New York – had seven television stations, only five of which were full-time (which means that they signed off at 1 or 2 a.m. with the national anthem before beginning the next broadcast day at 6 a.m.). At that time, all of New York City's television stations combined presented fewer *programs* in a given week than there were different *channels* by the end of the millennium.

HOW DID WE GET HERE?

To understand the paradox of a government licensing system for the broadcast medium in a country with a constitutional prohibition barring abridgment of freedom of the press, it is necessary to review some First Amendment history. Broadcasting did not exist when the USA was founded, of course, and the only mass medium the Constitution's framers knew was the printing press. Protections for the press may have been written into the First Amendment, but courts were baffled as to how those protections should apply to newer media when, in the twentieth century, they finally began interpreting the First Amendment.

The question first came to the Supreme Court when in 1915 it was asked to determine whether First Amendment protections extended to cinema. The Court concluded that "the exhibition of moving pictures is a business, pure and simple, originated and conducted for profit, like other spectacles, not to be regarded . . . as part of the press of the country or as organs of public opinion." It found, as a matter of "common sense," that protections for a free press did not apply to this new medium, because "there are some things which should not have pictorial representation in public places and to all audiences," and the technology of film posed a special danger that "a prurient interest might be excited and appealed to." Accordingly, it upheld the authority of state censorship boards to subject moving pictures to prior review and censorship.

Courts followed much the same approach when similar questions began to arise for the new medium of radio as it emerged through the 1920s and 1930s. Congress developed a licensing regime for broadcasting in the Radio Act of 1927, superseded by the Federal Communications Act of 1934, but the constitutional status of this new medium had not yet been determined. So, when the Federal Radio Commission (the "FRC," predecessor to the FCC) revoked a radio station license in 1931, the agency argued that, just as with cinema, First Amendment protections did not extend to radio.

The United States Court of Appeals for the District of Columbia Circuit didn't go quite that far, but it upheld the license revocation in *Trinity Methodist Church, South* v. *Federal Radio Commission*, because of the station owner's intemperate attacks on public officials in broadcasts considered "sensational rather than instructive." The court described radio as a mere "instrumentality of commerce" and upheld the FRC's action as simply "application of the regulatory power of Congress in a field within the scope of its legislative authority." This was a stark indicator of how differently the First Amendment was applied to new technologies such as film and radio than to newspapers. The FRC decision to revoke a station license upheld in *Trinity Methodist Church, South* came just after the Supreme Court *invalidated* a similar action against a newspaper publisher in the seminal case *Near* v. *Minnesota*.

The problem in *Near* was almost identical to the one facing the FRC in *Trinity Methodist Church, South*. Both cases involved intemperate attacks on public officials for alleged corruption and malfeasance in office. Jay Near's *Saturday Press* accused Minneapolis police of looking the other way as "Jewish gangsters" ran gambling, racketeering, and bootlegging operations. But when the newspaper's publication was enjoined under a Minnesota "Gag Law" barring "malicious, scandalous, and defamatory" news reports, the Supreme Court held that the First Amendment prohibited such prior restraint, and Chief Justice Charles Evans Hughes described power to enjoin publication as "the essence of censorship."

The result was entirely different for the new medium of radio. In *Trinity Methodist Church, South*, the Reverend "Fighting Bob" Shuler had attacked local corruption on radio station KGEF in his weekly sermons and on shows such as the "Bob Shuler Question Hour" and "Bob Shuler's Civic Talk." His charges included allegations that the mayor had allowed gangsters to run the city, that the chief of police knowingly let vice run rampant, and that the district attorney took bribes. In this case, however, the DC Circuit saw no First Amendment problem in revoking Reverend Shuler's radio station license because of his "sensational" broadcasts. The landmark ruling in *Near* had come down just a few months earlier, but the DC Circuit only mentioned it in passing, and it held that the FRC's action was easily within the power of Congress. No "essence of censorship," here.

The fact is that the courts were reluctant to tackle the question of how the First Amendment might apply to new technologies. As noted economist Ronald Coase later observed, it was "in the shadows cast by a mysterious technology that our views on broadcasting policy were formed." William Howard Taft, who served as Chief Justice of the United States from 1921 to 1930, confirmed that he had "dodged" the question of radio's constitutional status and wrote that he consciously avoided taking cases like *Trinity Methodist Church, South*. He observed that "interpreting the law on this subject is something like trying to interpret the law of the occult." To him, it seemed like dealing with something "supernatural," and he added, "I want to put it off as long as possible in the hope that it becomes more understandable before the court passes on the questions involved." Taft got his wish.

The Supreme Court would not take up the issue of constitutional protections for radio until more than a decade after Taft retired, and when it did, it fashioned a legal fiction that is still employed to justify the differential regulation of radio programming, a fiction that Minow and other regulatory-minded policymakers would enthusiastically embrace. The theory supporting this upside-down notion of press licensing is that "airwaves" are a scarce resource and that chaos would prevail if the government refrained from exerting control and rationing their use. If the feds failed to take charge, radio broadcasters would jump frequencies and constantly interfere with other signals, thus making the new medium useless. According to this narrative, government control of radio promotes freedom of speech, because if it did not regulate, there would be no broadcast speech for anyone. The equation is simple: regulation = freedom.

CHAOS BY DESIGN

The Supreme Court adopted this spectrum scarcity theory in *National Broadcasting Company* v. *United States*, a 1943 case that upheld the FCC's "chain broadcasting" rules. The rules were designed to regulate the business arrangements between national radio networks and their affiliates, governing such issues as the duration of affiliation agreements, the right of affiliates to reject network programs, and the right to set their own advertising rates. NBC and CBS – the two then-existing nation radio networks – challenged the constitutionality of the rules, arguing (among other things) that the regulatory standard of the Communications Act, empowering the FCC to adopt rules to further "the public interest, convenience, and necessity," was too vague and indefinite to survive First Amendment scrutiny. The Court disagreed.

Justice Felix Frankfurter's opinion for the Court traced the development of radio and of the various attempts to exert some control, leading to the Radio Act of 1927 and eventually the Communications Act of 1934. He wrote that the radio spectrum was not sufficient to accommodate all those who might want to engage in broadcasting, and that experience prior to 1927, when the federal government could not deny radio licenses, had resulted in chaos. Accordingly, he concluded that regulation of radio was "as vital to its development as traffic control was to the development of the automobile." It was evident that some system of allotment was required, but Justice Frankfurter didn't stop there.

He wrote that the FCC's authority was not limited to policing the "technical aspects" of radio to prevent interference between stations. Frankfurter added that Congress did not limit the Commission merely to the supervision of radio traffic but also to "determining the composition of that traffic." Thus, in the name of preserving freedom of speech, Congress could regulate broadcasting content. Or, more specifically, it was empowered to delegate that authority to the FCC.

This origin story for broadcast regulation has been used for nearly a hundred years to justify a different level of First Amendment protection for broadcast speech, yet it has been dismissed by leading economists and broadcast historians as pure folklore. Radio as a public medium began developing in 1920 in the aftermath of World War I, and it quickly became a national sensation, with more than 500 stations popping up in just 2 years. The emerging medium was operating relatively smoothly, governed largely by industry cooperation and enforcement by the Commerce Department of prior rights of frequency use. But Herbert Hoover, then Secretary of Commerce and future president, was dissatisfied. He had been advocating for a system of "public interest" regulation in which the government would allocate frequencies for radio and control licenses, but he lacked a crisis that would spur congressional action.

The Commerce Department had been enforcing the rights of station owners to use the frequencies for which they were licensed under the Radio Act of 1912, using well-understood common-law property-rights concepts based on prior use. But then in 1923, the US Court of Appeals for the DC Circuit held, in *Hoover v. Intercity Radio Co.*, that Hoover lacked discretion to deny applications for broadcast licenses, although he could still regulate frequencies and hours of use. The ruling was "good news–bad news" for Hoover. It meant that he had no choice but to grant licenses when applications were made to the Commerce Department, but he still could manage the times and frequencies of broadcasts in order to avoid interference.

But Hoover wanted more. In a series of four Radio Conferences beginning in 1922, Hoover had begun advocating for what would become "public interest" regulation of radio. The conferences enabled the Secretary of Commerce to meet with industry representatives to work out various forms of voluntary self-regulation, but, from the beginning, Hoover also used them as a platform to advocate for greater governmental control over the medium. At the 1922 Radio Conference, he described radio as a "great national asset" and said that "it becomes of primary public interest to say who is to do the broadcasting, under what circumstances, and with what type of material." The Department of Commerce reported that the "sense of the conference" was that radio communication "is a public utility and as such should be regulated and controlled by the Federal government in the public interest."

Radio's popularity continued unabated and led to concerns about spectrum congestion, but at the 1923 Radio Conference, Hoover took the position that he had full authority "to regulate hours and wavelengths of operation of stations when such action is necessary to present interference detrimental to the public good." Based on this assertion of authority, Hoover followed up by creating different power levels for stations, reallocating frequencies for Navy and maritime use, and moving commercial stations to the designated spectrum. As a result, the trade magazine *Radio Broadcasting* reported that the interference problem had been "suddenly remedied" without the passage of a new law.

This approach, based on industry cooperation and minimal regulation, worked to mitigate the most serious interference problems through the mid-1920s. Hoover opened the 1925 Radio Conference by announcing: "We have … developed, in these conferences, traffic systems by which a vastly increasing number of messages are kept upon the air without destroying each other." However, this relative equilibrium was not spurring Congress to pass the type of regulation Hoover wanted, and various legislative proposals had languished in committee. At the same time, radio technology was improving, with new receivers making it possible to reduce interference when tuning in stations. Some kind of emergency was needed to get Congress to act – and Hoover was just the guy to deliver one.

The opportunity arose in 1925, when Zenith Radio Corporation defied a frequency assignment for its Chicago station that it believed was unsatisfactory. The Commerce Department challenged the action but was rebuffed when the federal district court held in *United States* v. *Zenith Radio Corp.* that, under the Radio Act of 1912, Hoover had authority only to issue licenses and assign frequencies but not to enforce restrictions on operations. Hoover could have appealed that ruling. After all, the DC Circuit had held just three years earlier in *Hoover* v. *Intercity Radio Co.* that the Secretary of Commerce *did* have authority to enforce frequency assignments. So why did the Commerce Department act like the inferior court's ruling was the definitive word on its lack of authority?

It was because Hoover saw this as a chance to further his agenda. Rather than appeal the *Zenith* decision, he instead solicited a legal opinion from the Acting Attorney General (Acting AG) in support of *the case he had just lost*. The Acting AG, William J. "Wild Bill" Donovan, just happened to be a Hoover protégé, and he delivered the opinion the Secretary wanted – that the *Zenith* decision was correct and *Intercity Radio* was wrong – and that Hoover's authority was strictly limited. Donovan first shared the opinion privately with Hoover, and the two agreed not to publicize it (unless they needed to) while radio legislation was pending in Congress. When the legislative session ended without a bill being passed, Hoover gave Donovan the go-ahead and the entire Justice Department opinion was published in the *New York Times*. The following day Hoover announced that the Commerce Department was out of the business of regulating radio.

This choreographed retreat produced exactly the emergency Hoover needed to nudge congressional action. Within 6 months, 200 new radio stations took to the air, joining the 550 stations already operating, and existing broadcasters no longer felt constrained to stay on their assigned channels. The predicable result, as the Supreme Court would later find, was chaos. But, then, chaos was the point. It led Congress to finally act on proposed radio legislation that had been languishing for over four years, ever since the first Radio Conference. As former FCC Chief Economist Thomas Hazlett has written, "interference was not the issue, interference was the opportunity."

The problem was not a scarcity of frequencies so much as the fact that there was now no legal mechanism for preventing one broadcaster from using the same frequency as another. Commenting on the Supreme Court's subsequent review of history that led to the Radio Act, Hazlett observed that "[t]he chaos and confusion that supposedly made strict regulation necessary were limited to a specific interval – July 9, 1926, to February 23, 1927. These conditions were triggered by Hoover's own actions as a key part of his legislative quest. In effect, he created a problem in order to solve it, with tools that afforded policy makers far broader regulatory discretion than was needed to restore order."

The chief sponsor of the radio bill, Senator Clarence C. Dill of Washington, described Hoover's actions as being "almost like an invitation for broadcasters to do their worst." And he certainly understood the opportunity it presented, noting at the time that "the one principle regarding radio that must always be adhered to, as basic and fundamental, is that government must always retain complete and absolute control of the right to use the air." This had been Hoover's conception from the beginning. As he told the assembled broadcasters at the first Radio Conference, it is a primary tenet of the public interest for the government "to say who is to do the broadcasting, under what circumstances, and with what type of material."

THE PEOPLE'S AIRWAVES

The Radio Act of 1927 was adopted as a result of these maneuvers, and its first priority was to ensure federal control by prohibiting private ownership of radio frequencies. This wasn't only a reaction to Hoover's induced chaos. Congress also acted quickly to exert control because this brief window of opportunity created by the *Zenith* decision, and Hover's abdication of responsibility, was at risk of being closed. Improvements in radio technology, including more precise tuners, were helping diminish interference, and courts began to develop common-law solutions to frequency jumping by stations.

Just a few months after Hoover announced that the Commerce Department was out of the radio regulation business, a state court in Illinois enjoined a broadcaster from interfering with the transmissions of another station. In *Tribune Company v. Oak Leaves Broadcasting*, Cook County Magistrate Francis S. Wilson issued an order holding that Tribune Broadcasting had established a legally enforceable right through prior use of the spectrum for its station WGN, and that Oak Leaves Broadcasting could not operate closer than 50 kilocycles to that channel. Magistrate Wilson employed a property rights theory holding that Tribune acquired rights in its use of the spectrum through productive use of the frequency that "priority of time creates a superiority of right." The ruling meant that Oak Leaves Broadcasting could not interfere with WGN within a 100-mile radius.

The decision only resolved one local controversy, but federal policymakers took note and understood its significance. The Commerce Department's Solicitor General observed that other courts following this precedent would protect against "wavelength piracy," while the sponsors of radio legislation discussed the case in the

Congressional Record, predicting that it was inevitable that courts would move toward a solution to the interference problem where "the use of a wave length established a priority of right."

This should have been taken as good news, because it meant that courts were finding a way to cope with the radio interference problem. But that is not how things work in Washington. In a town where policymakers had been jockeying for pole position in the four-year-long race for getting control over radio (with Hoover atop the lead pony), this development was viewed as a threat. If Congress failed to act quickly, the opportunity to exert federal control might slip away and Hoover's orchestrated crisis would come to nothing. So, within days of the Illinois ruling, Congress passed an emergency measure requiring all wireless operators to waive any vested rights in radio frequencies or face immediate termination of the right to broadcast if they failed to do so.

This prohibition on the notion of property rights in spectrum became a key part of the opening section of the Radio Act, which became law on February 23, 1927. It authorized the United States "to maintain the control" over "all the channels of interstate and foreign radio transmission" and to "provide for the use of such channels, but not the ownership thereof, by individuals, firms, or corporations, for limited periods of time, under licenses granted by Federal authority," and it provided that "no such license shall be construed to create any right, beyond the terms, conditions, and periods of the license." The same concepts were incorporated into the Communications Act of 1934, which seven years later supplanted the Radio Act.

Thus, the two defining characteristics of broadcasting law from 1927 to the present are that (1) no one may engage in broadcasting without a license from the federal government and (2) the grant of a license is for a limited period and it confers no ownership rights on the licensee. This only makes sense, right? After all, the public owns the airwaves, which are a unique and scarce resource.

Well, no, actually – nothing about that statement is correct. For starters, there is no such thing as an "airwave." It is merely a colloquial term for the electromagnetic spectrum, the properties of which allow the transmission of information. The public does not "own" the airwaves any more than it does any other aspect of physics; Congress merely passed a law prohibiting use of the spectrum for broadcasting without permission, which comes in the form of a government license. In that sense, the government by legislative fiat merely nationalized use of the spectrum for broadcasting. Finally, as a resource, the spectrum is neither unique nor scarce in an economic sense that distinguishes it from any other input to a publishing venture. If anything, it has been made scarce by operation of federal policy.

The myth of spectrum scarcity was debunked in a 1959 article by Nobel Prize-winning economist Ronald Coase. What Justice Frankfurter had described in the *NBC* decision as "unique" aspects of the radio spectrum, Coase explained were "a commonplace of economics," that "almost all resources used in the economic system (and not simply radio and television frequencies) are limited in amount and scarce, in that people would like to use more than exists."

Of course, there would have to be some method of allocating resources among competing claimants, but, as Coase pointed out, in a free society that is normally accomplished through legal protections for property interests and market pricing. Otherwise, the obvious result is interference, for "if no property rights were created in land, so that everyone could use a tract of land, it is clear there would be considerable confusion .... If one person could use a piece of land for growing a crop, and then another person could come along and build a house on the land used for the crop, and then another person could come along, tear down the house, and use the space as a parking lot, it would no doubt be accurate to describe the resulting situation as chaos." Of course, the same is true of the use of radio frequencies – two broadcasters cannot productively occupy the same space at the same time.

To address this problem, Congress chose government control and licensing to the exclusion of a property-based system of allocation. But what of the rest of the package that came with "public interest" regulation of radio? To say that the interference problem must be solved does not answer the First Amendment problem of how much control the government may have over a given medium, particularly when it comes to regulating its content. If the federal government nationalized lumber production and rationed limited amounts of lumber for use as newsprint, it supposedly could make the same claim – that it was in control of a scarce resource and those who wanted to publish had no choice but to deal with the designated agency. But doing so would say nothing about the constitutional legitimacy of regulating a newspaper's editorial policies.

Accordingly, Coase observed that "[t]he situation in the American broadcasting industry is not essentially different in character from that which would be found if a commission appointed by the federal government had the task of selecting those who were to be allowed to publish newspapers and periodicals in each city, town, and village of the United States." He added that such a proposal would be "rejected out of hand as inconsistent with the doctrine of freedom of the press." Perhaps it would be, but not by the determined "public interest" regulator.

THE PUBLIC INTEREST IN ACTION

This was illustrated in 1987 when two former FCC chairmen, Newton Minow and Charles Ferris, testified before Congress to support the FCC's authority to regulate news programming. "We all forget history," Minow told the congressional panel. Broadcasting was regulated in the first place, he explained, because "all the public was getting was static," so broadcasters came to Washington and told the Secretary of Commerce, "Mr. Hoover, you have got to do something to regulate us, you have got to do something so the public can hear the radio." Ferris agreed. He said that public interest regulation was necessary because "[b]ack then, anyone who could put up a transmitter could broadcast, and the result was chaos." This wasn't quite what happened, of course, but the explanations were close enough for government work.

Minow and Ferris at least were correct that the events following the breakdown of the Commerce Department's authority led to passage of the Radio Act of 1927 and the establishment of the Federal Radio Commission. And the Act vested the government with far greater authority than just assigning frequencies and granting licenses. The Commission was also authorized to make licensing decisions based on its notions of what types of programming best served the public interest. Even though Section 29 of the Radio Act promised that "nothing in this Act shall be understood or construed to give the licensing authority the power of censorship over the radio communications or signals transmitted by any radio station," the FRC was "unable to see that the guaranty of freedom of speech has anything to do with entertainment programs as such." It thus assumed the power to "consider the program service rendered by the various applicants to compare them, and to favor those which render the best service." It also exerted broad control over news and political programming as well.

Mission accomplished, right? Nationalization of the radio spectrum and the imposition of "public interest" requirements should have led to the regulatory nirvana that Minow advocated. But, in practice, the scheme reduced radio service to the public, limited the diversity of voices being broadcast, and homogenized the budding industry. The Commission could have accommodated all those who wanted to broadcast at the time – and then some – by expanding the frequencies allocated to radio, but it opted not to do so and instead went in the opposite direction. According to Professor Robert McChesney, government officials were convinced that "the success of radio broadcasting lay in doing away with small and unimportant stations." Thus, as a result of the FRC's policies, more than a hundred small stations were off the air within a year of the Radio Act's adoption.

The first to go were nonprofit and educational stations. In a scheme described by one scholar of broadcast history as "Machiavellian manipulation," the Commission packed smaller stations more closely together on the radio dial, restricted their hours of operation, and forced them into frequency sharing arrangements. Conditions were so unfavorable that many stations voluntarily relinquished their licenses. In 1927, ninety-five radio stations were affiliated with colleges and universities, but, after the FRC's initial purges, by 1930 that number was cut by more than half. As Professors Krattenmaker and Powe put it, "[t]he first step slayed the weak; the second banished the different."

Accordingly, the next stations on the block were those operated by union activists or those with unorthodox political views. In 1929, the FRC limited Chicago station WCFL to daytime-only operation as a condition of its license renewal. The station had been launched in 1926 to promote union causes by the Chicago Federation of Labor, but the FRC restricted its operation on grounds that there was not enough space on the dial to accommodate "every school of thought, religious, political, social, and economic." The station gained the ability to operate full-time only after phasing out its labor programming and affiliating with NBC. A similar fate befell WEVD, a Queens, New York station started by the Socialist Party and named for Eugene V. Debs, who ran for president five times under the socialist banner. In 1929 the FRC moved WEVD to a new frequency and required it to share time with three other stations, thus limiting its operation to fifty hours per week. The station was unable to sustain itself, and its political orientation faded away after the Commission admonished the station to "operate with due regard for the opinions of others."

The FRC took an even more extreme approach to the Reverend "Fighting Bob" Shuler, denying license renewal for station KCEF based on a finding that his station had become a "forum for outrageous and unfounded attacks on public officials." That decision (*Trinity Methodist Church, South*), which was described earlier, was the first to find that there was no conflict between "public interest" regulation and the First Amendment. Never mind that many of Fighting Bob's allegations about corrupt officials were true; the government had decided that it was fake news and took action to shut him down.

Through its actions, the Commission defined the public interest as essentially making radio stations generic. To win the favor of regulators, stations were required to offer "a well-rounded program," offering "entertainment, consisting of music of both classical and lighter grades, religion, education and instruction, important public events, discussions of public questions, weather, market reports, and news of interest to all members of the family." Federal policy thus disfavored diversity and sought to make every station be all things to all people. As Tom Hazlett put it, the FRC decreed that radio programs "were best delivered not via specialty shops but by department stores."

The Federal Communications Commission (FCC) replaced the FRC in 1934 and it continued the policy of promoting a homogeneous broadcasting service. In 1960, the year before Minow took the helm at the agency, the FCC reaffirmed its generalized approach to defining acceptable programming, listing fourteen categories of programs generally considered necessary to serve the public interest. These included programs that provided an opportunity for local self-expression, programs that used local talent, children's programs, religious programs, educational programs, public affairs programs, editorials, political broadcasts, agricultural programs, news, weather and market reports, sports programs, service to minority groups and (finally) entertainment programming.

It should have come as no surprise to anyone – least of all to Minow – that if broadcasting was thought to be bland, focused on a mass audience, and its news programming timid, it was the regimentation of "public interest" regulation that helped make it so. In fact, television producers in the 1960s complained that pitches for new shows began to contain what they called a "Minow paragraph," to explain why, "[l]ike Latin and spinach, these shows are supposed to be good for you." Responding to federal oversight, network executives avoided controversy by gravitating toward the formulaic and the innocuous, which, according to Professor Paul Cantor, helped make the 1960s "arguably the blandest decade of American television." Veteran TV producer Roy Huggins said that for the first time in television's then-brief history, there was a decline in both the quality and the spirit of programming. He attributed the change to Minow's policies as FCC Chairman for a simple reason: "Imagination does not flourish in a climate of coercion."

By favoring large broadcasters, enforcing rules promoting a uniform broadcasting service, and chasing less mainstream voices from the air, the Commission through the decades helped create what Minow would call a "wasteland." Except it was less "vast" than it might have been because regulators limited the amount of the spectrum available for broadcasting and more a wasteland due to federal control over programming. But, still, Minow thought that the answer was to be found in more regulation, not less.

The problem was that, as First Amendment law began to evolve, it was getting harder to justify direct regulation of programming, even for broadcasting. No doubt, courts had been quite forgiving of the FCC's authority to regulate broadcasting more intensively than the traditional press, and would become even more so in the 1969 Supreme Court decision *Red Lion Broadcasting Co.* v. *FCC*. But First Amendment law was developing rapidly in the mid-twentieth century, and many began to anticipate that the fundamental illogic of treating broadcasting differently could not last forever. By 1960, even some at the FCC had become more aware of the tensions between the First Amendment and the Commission's public interest decrees, so the agency shied away from some specific programming mandates.

Such considerations led the Commission to conclude that it could not "condition the grant, denial or revocation of a broadcast license upon its own subjective determination of what is or is not a good program." To do so, it understood, would "lay a forbidden burden upon the exercise of liberty protected by the Constitution." Further, it decided that "as a practical matter, let alone a legal matter, [its role] cannot be one of program dictation or program supervision." But there are other ways of exerting control. Every FCC commissioner knows that a few well-chosen words can be enough to condition broadcasters' behavior, especially when they come from the landlord for the "people's airwaves." As the operator of a protection racket might put it, "You got a nice business here. It would be a shame if anything were to happen to it."

BIG BROTHER'S RAISED EYEBROW

Newton Minow's *Vast Wasteland Speech* is the paradigm for what came to be known as "regulation by raised eyebrow." FCC commissioners know that broadcasters are beholden to them for favorable regulatory rulings and license renewals, and many have not been shy about demanding concessions from station owners that would be awfully hard to defend in court if made by official decree. Former commissioner Glen O. Robinson described "regulation by the lifted eyebrow" as a "Sword of Damocles" over the broadcaster's head. "If the sword does not often fall, neither is it ever lifted, and the *in terrorem* effect of the sword's presence enables the Commission to exercise far-reaching powers of control over the licensee's operations." Hence, the coercive point of Minow's speech at the NAB convention was clear, where he told broadcasters that their shows suck, and demanded that they make things better.

The twitch of the regulator's brow is why radio stations across the country immediately dropped songs from their playlists in the early 1970s after the FCC issued an informal warning against songs with suspected "drug lyrics." One commissioner appended a statement to the FCC's public notice on the subject saying that he wanted to "discourage, if not eliminate, the playing of records which tend to promote and/or glorify the use of illegal drugs." A few weeks later, an FCC staff member just happened to leak a Pentagon-inspired list of twenty-two recordings that supposedly included "so-called drug-oriented song lyrics." That's all it took for many stations to interpret the FCC's action as a blacklist and to drop listed songs by such artists as The Beatles, Bob Dylan, and Peter, Paul and Mary, among others. No formal action was taken, nor was any needed to get broadcasters to react.

Raised eyebrow regulation generally is accomplished off-the-books and in the shadows. The whole point is not to leave fingerprints or – god forbid – develop an administrative record that a reviewing court could examine to determine the legality of agency actions. Former DC Circuit Chief Judge David Bazelon has noted how the Commission's ability to exert "*sub silentio* pressure" on broadcasters can lead to "wide-ranging and largely uncontrolled administrative discretion in the review of telecommunications programming." He described a variety of methods for exerting control "that are by now familiar to FCC practitioners." They can include a prominent speech by a commissioner, a notice of inquiry, an official statement of licensee responsibility couched in general terms but directed against specific programming, forwarding listener complaints to a licensee and requiring the station to respond, summoning network executives for meetings with the Chairman or other officials, and other informal methods.

Judge Bazelon explained: "When the right to continue to operate a lucrative broadcast facility turns on periodic government approval, even a governmental 'raised eyebrow' can send otherwise intrepid entrepreneurs running for the cover of conformity." That is, such methods lead to the very type of governmental bullying that the First Amendment was designed to prevent.

FORGET ABOUT THE FIRST AMENDMENT; WE'LL LET THE COURTS WORRY ABOUT THAT

Just how informal FCC regulation works, and how insidious it can be, was laid bare when the FCC set out to force the broadcast industry to adopt what came to be known as the "family viewing policy" in the mid-1970s. Concern over excessive sex and violence in television programs had been a perennial obsession with activists and members of Congress ever since the mid-1950s, back when prevailing broadcast standards decreed that married couples should be depicted as sleeping in twin beds. Fredric Wertham, when he wasn't focused on comic books, also decried depictions of violence on television as a cause of juvenile delinquency, and Senator Estes Kefauver held hearings on TV violence as well as on comics. Despite the political potency of the issue, no one found a solution after more than a decade, and Congress finally lost its patience.

Both the House and the Senate Appropriations Committees directed the FCC to submit a report "outlining the specific positive actions taken or planned by the Commission to protect children from excessive violence and obscenity." The House directive came first, and it set a deadline of December 31, 1974, for the FCC to issue its report. The Senate committee acted a couple of months later, and it instructed the FCC to "proceed vigorously and as rapidly as possible" to comply. This was serious stuff for the Commission because these committees control its budget. The FCC's Chairman, Richard E. Wiley, tried to beg off the assignment, writing to Senator John Pastore that the Department of Health, Education, and Welfare was conducting a study on TV violence and that "the time is not now" for FCC action. But the House Appropriations Committee's directive was blunt: "The Committee is reluctant to take punitive action to require the Commission to heed the views of the Congress, and to carry on its responsibilities, but if this is what is required to achieve the desired objectives, such action may be considered."

The FCC was not given an option. But Dick Wiley was no Newt Minow. He was not a regulatory enthusiast and he harbored serious doubts about the FCC's statutory or constitutional authority to get directly involved in dictating programming content. However, he was caught between a rock (Congress) and a hard place (constitutional limits), and the message that Congress sent to Wiley, as recounted by those involved in the negotiations, boiled down to this: "Forget about the First Amendment; we'll let the courts worry about that." So, Chairman Wiley directed his staff to find ways to comply with the congressional demands.

Roughly eight months later, the Commission submitted its report to Congress and announced that the three major broadcast networks, along with NAB, would administer a policy under NAB's Television Code in which entertainment programming "inappropriate for viewing by a general family audience" would not be shown during the first hour of prime time (before 9 p.m. Eastern, but earlier in other time zones). This "family viewing policy" was adopted without any formal FCC action or rule. The report acknowledged that Chairman Wiley had initiated talks with the three networks "to serve as a catalyst for the achievement of meaningful self-regulatory reform" and concluded: "[T]his new commitment suggests that the broadcast industry is prepared to regulate itself in a fashion that will obviate any need for governmental regulation in this sensitive area."

So, Congress got its report and the broadcast industry was able to avoid onerous new regulation of entertainment programming. The trouble was, the deal Wiley brokered was not well-received in Hollywood, where program producers who made the shows for network television were not prepared to accept the idea that prime time was about to shrink by about a third. Well, perhaps not "shrink," but approximately one-third of prime-time programming was to be bowdlerized. This would affect such network hits as *All in the Family*, *M*A*S*H*, and *Barney Miller*, and so the creative community went to court to challenge the family viewing policy. In the meantime, many TV shows were rescheduled, certain storylines were scrapped, and scripts were censored.

The resulting litigation in *Writers Guild of America, West v. FCC* exposed the mechanics of regulation by raised eyebrow like no case before or since. The record included weeks of trial testimony, hundreds of exhibits, and thousands of pages of deposition testimony. At the end of it all, Judge Warren J. Ferguson produced a scholarly and meticulously documented 223-page opinion in which he found that "the Commission deliberately set about to suppress material it considered objectionable and succeeded in its aim." This was accomplished through a combination of threats, pressure to secure commitments, and promises to publicize noncompliance, which, taken together, Judge Ferguson concluded, were per se violations of the First Amendment. This was more than just a crooked eyebrow. Judge Ferguson characterized the FCC's tactics as "backroom bludgeoning."

The district court opinion in *Writers Guild of America, West* gives a meeting-by-meeting, memo-by-memo account tracing how the policy emerged from congressional demands and ended in broadcast industry commitments. It set forth details of three public speeches in which Chairman Wiley exhorted the industry to undertake its own action and suggested that if it did not do so, the FCC would; five meetings between Wiley or members of his staff with industry representatives to discuss specific proposals; various telephone calls between the Chairman and various network heads; and communications between Wiley and representatives of NAB. In one meeting with network officials, Chairman Wiley suggested the possibility of issuing a policy statement, or perhaps adding questions to license renewal forms regarding station policies on the acceptance and scheduling of programs with sex and violence.

Judge Ferguson rejected the FCC's defense that the quest for a "family viewing hour" was just a "personal initiative" by the Chairman as a "concerned parent" and found that it was instead "a virtually unprecedented orchestration of regulatory tools by the FCC." The pressure that the agency exerted was "persistent, pronounced, and unmistakable." The root of the Commission's power, he explained, was "the uncertainty of the relicensing process and the vagueness of the standards which govern it." In this regard, the public interest standard has always been the "regulator's friend," because it means whatever the agency wants it to mean at any point in time. The judge also found that such decisions often result from political whims as much as from any desire to find effective solutions to problems, and that "the family viewing policy is in large part a public relations gimmick."

NAB suspended the operation of its Television Code in response to the ruling, and the FCC appealed it to the US Court of Appeals for the Ninth Circuit. The appellate court vacated the district court opinion, but not because the appellate court doubted Judge Ferguson's account of what had happened. Quite to the contrary, the court of appeals agreed that "the activities of Chairman Wiley are beyond dispute" and that "the use of these techniques by the FCC presents serious issues involving the Constitution, the Communications Act and the [Administrative Procedure Act]." But, much like Chief Justice Taft in the 1920s, the appellate court was not eager to get involved in constitutional issues involving broadcasting, and it looked for a way to duck the question.

It found an out via a procedural rule called the "primary jurisdiction doctrine" and held that the plaintiffs should have presented their concerns first to the expert administrative agency before going to court. The Ninth Circuit said that "the district court should not have thrust itself so hastily into the delicately balanced system of broadcast regulation" and that the lower court lacked jurisdiction over a matter that should have first been presented to the FCC, given its expertise in the field. This made little sense. In addition to the fact that the Commission has no special expertise in constitutional questions, the Ninth Circuit's solution was to have the FCC be the judge of whether it had violated the First Amendment. Fox, meet henhouse.

This raised more questions than it answered. What were the plaintiffs supposed to challenge, exactly? A report to Congress? The FCC had expressly eschewed adopting a rule or taking any other official action on the pretext that voluntary self-regulation made doing so unnecessary. Were the affected program producers supposed to challenge a "nonaction?" And if they did bring such a matter to the Commission, how would they disprove the FCC's explanation that the meetings and calls that resulted in the family viewing policy were anything more than Chairman Wiley's "personal initiative" based on his concerns as a parent?

If the challenge had been presented to the FCC, there would have been no discovery into the events that led to the FCC's "report" – no document production, no depositions, and certainly no trial testimony to establish a record to show what really happened. And when the FCC rejected the challenge, as it inevitably would have done, there would have been no way to demonstrate to an appellate court that the agency was lying. The Ninth Circuit's invocation of the primary jurisdiction doctrine effectively doomed the ability to challenge regulation by raised eyebrow.

This did not bring back the family viewing policy, however. After the NAB Code was suspended, the Carter Administration added to the self-regulatory body's woes by mounting an antitrust challenge, and the Code's operation was enjoined. The industry abandoned the Code in 1983.

What was the lesson to be drawn from this? To Minow, it was simple: More regulation was the answer. Twenty years after the family viewing policy debacle, he acknowledged that the FCC's actions had pushed quality programs like *All in the*

Family, *M*A*S*H*, and *Barney Miller* "to the fringes of prime time." These were the very types of program that Minow had said the public interest should foster because they dealt with the "morals and conflicts of their times." He was forced to admit that the "reforms" of the 1960s and 1970s, "however just or well intentioned, had done little to clarify the meaning and application of the public interest standard" and in some respects "had made matters worse." Undaunted by embarrassing regulatory failure, Minow nevertheless advocated giving the FCC even greater authority to regulate programming and to extend its power to new technologies beyond broadcasting.

According to Minow, public interest requirements should include specific mandates for children's educational programming (or require broadcasters to pay fees to support such programming), ban advertising during children's programming, enact an antitrust exemption to allow broadcast associations to enforce programming codes (like the family viewing policy), and take more action to curb televised violence. But doubling down on (and ratcheting up) the regulations that had done nothing to improve broadcasting hardly exhausted this reservoir of bad ideas. Writing just as the World Wide Web was emerging, Minow argued that the same public interest concepts should be applied to what he called the "SuperTube" – digital, computer-driven video servers on the "Information Superhighway" that "will expand exponentially the power of individual viewers to manipulate information." So, the issue for Minow was not about "scarcity" after all but just his enthusiasm for regulatory solutions.

Regulate the Internet using the same watered-down First Amendment protections that have hobbled radio and television? Who would consider such a thing? Senator James Exxon, for one, who, the same year Minow was writing about the "SuperTube," proposed that the Communications Decency Act (CDA) should impose broadcast indecency rules online.

IN ALL FAIRNESS ...?

The vast difference between the FCC's conception of the "public interest" and traditional protections for journalism is crystalized in a Commission policy called the "fairness doctrine." This policy, which existed between 1949 and 1987, purported to require broadcast stations to cover "controversial issues of public importance" in their communities and to do so with "balance." Although the doctrine on its face sounds like nothing more than a statement of sound journalistic principles, it failed to take into account the distorting effect of empowering the government to police the news. It was enforced by complaints to the FCC from disgruntled viewers and listeners about news stories that bugged them, and letting politically appointed bureaucrats decide whether news coverage had been "fair." What could possibly go wrong?

Imagine a president who believes that the press is out to get him and that he ought to have the power to determine what news is "fake" and to punish broadcasters who veered into that dangerous territory. A crazy notion, perhaps, but just consider the possibility. Less than a moment's reflection should be enough to convince most people of the nation's good fortune that the FCC repealed the fairness doctrine three decades before Donald Trump was elected President. Not that the fairness doctrine ever conveyed that kind of personal authority to the President, but Trump didn't know that. And he never hesitated to brand news organizations he disliked the "enemy of the people," to demand FCC sanctions against broadcasters who made fun of or criticized him, or to call for the revocation of station licenses affiliated with networks he disparaged. Nor did he hesitate to use other powers of his office to exact – in his words – "retribution" on his perceived enemies in the press.

It is a problem as old as the Republic. When the USA was a new nation, a major challenge arose from attempts to shield the administration of President John Adams from sharp criticism by a hostile press. The Sedition Act of 1798 thus made it a crime to "write, print, utter or publish . . . any false, scandalous and malicious writing or writings against the government" with the intent to defame Congress or the President. The law was intended, and was used, to exact revenge by federalist lawmakers against the republican newspapers they felt had been slandering them. At least a dozen Sedition Act prosecutions were instituted against editors of news-papers in major cities like Philadelphia, New York, and Boston, as well as in smaller towns in Connecticut and Vermont. As a result, five republican papers were shuttered or ceased publication for at least some period during this time. Many of these prosecutions targeted what an irresponsible (or stupid) politician today might call "fake news."

The Sedition Act expired by its own terms on the last day of the Adams Administration and was never tested in court, but the consensus of history is that it was fundamentally at odds with the First Amendment. As newly elected President Thomas Jefferson put it as he pardoned and remitted the fines of those convicted under the law, "I considered . . . that law to be a nullity, as absolute and as palpable as if Congress had ordered us to fall down and worship a golden image." The Supreme Court would later observe that this formative experience with the federal govern-ment's effort to criminalize false speech "first crystallized a national awareness of the central meaning of the First Amendment." That may be so, but lessons unlearned or forgotten must be repeated. And so it was with the fairness doctrine, which was plagued with a legacy of partisan wrangling and political abuse.

Legendary newsman Fred Friendly (who with Edward R. Murrow helped expose Senator Joseph McCarthy as a fraud and a bully) documented this unfortunate history in his 1975 book THE GOOD GUYS, THE BAD GUYS, AND THE FIRST AMENDMENT. He revealed that in the 1960s, when Minow was at the helm of the FCC, President Kennedy approved a plan to coordinate fairness doctrine complaints to target radio stations that aired right-wing editorials and to focus on small market stations that could not afford to respond. Supported by a secret fund handled by the Democratic National Committee (DNC), a monitoring program was established to demand response time for any commentary considered to be "irrationally hostile to the President and his programs."

The avowed purpose was to "harass right-wing broadcasters and hope the challenges would be so costly to them that they would be inhibited and decide it was too costly to continue." A confidential report to the DNC stressed that the principal targets were "small rural stations ... in desperate need of broadcast revenues" and that a continuing effort would force stations to drop certain programs from their broadcast schedule. The campaign was a smashing success and was continued under LBJ. One of the primary voices the DNC sought to still, a conservative radio preacher named Carl McIntire, was dropped by nearly 400 radio stations. Others were silenced as well.

Such official abuse of broadcast regulations has not been limited to one side of the political divide. Those in control, regardless of partisan stripe, have used the FCC to help maintain their power. The White House taping system that was revealed during the Watergate investigation recorded President Nixon threatening to take action against broadcast stations owned by the *Washington Post* in retaliation for its coverage of the scandal, and he arranged for political allies to challenge license renewals of "unfriendly" broadcast stations. Internal White House memoranda written by Nixon's Special Counsel Charles Colson that later came to light described meetings with the chief executives of the three major broadcast networks for the purpose of threatening enforcement of FCC regulations so as to achieve "an inhibiting impact on the networks and their professed concern with achieving balance." Colson set forth a plan to achieve this objective that included establishing "an official monitoring system through the FCC" in order to generate "official complaints" to the Commission.

Nixon used political allies to exert pressure on broadcasters. His minions worked with a conservative media watchdog group, Accuracy in Media (AIM), to bring fairness doctrine complaints to discipline stations that aired critical news reports. Colson partnered with AIM to bring fairness complaints against programs like the CBS documentary *The Selling of the Pentagon* because it criticized US policies in Vietnam, as well as complaints against programs on PBS. AIM also filed a fairness doctrine complaint against NBC for a documentary criticizing private pension plans entitled *Pensions: The Broken Promise*. As one Nixon aide put it, working through AIM was perfect because it was "a mechanism under which private non-governmental pressures can be brought to bear." This wasn't so much "regulation by raised eyebrow" as it was regulation with a wink ... and a raised fist.

Notwithstanding their rhetoric decrying big government, a number of prominent conservatives continued to support the fairness doctrine into the 1980s. Republican activist Phyllis Schlafly was a vocal proponent because of what she described as "the outrageous and blatant anti-Reagan bias of the TV network newscasts," and she testified at the FCC in support of retaining the policy "to serve as a small restraint on the monopoly power wielded by Big TV Media." Conservative Senator Jesse Helms of North Carolina was another long-time advocate of the fairness doctrine. Various groups on the political right, like AIM and the American Legal Foundation, continued to actively pursue fairness complaints at the FCC against network-owned stations during this period. Even the CIA got in on the act, filing fairness doctrine complaints against ABC and its affiliates for a *World News Tonight* story about an alleged plot to assassinate a former agent. The American Legal Foundation filed in support of the CIA's effort, and filed its own fairness complaints against CBS for the documentary *The Uncounted Enemy: A Vietnam Deception* and for an episode of a news special called *Pentagon Underground.*

Despite this enthusiasm for the fairness doctrine among some conservatives, the Reagan Administration's FCC eliminated the policy as part of a wave of deregulatory actions in the 1980s. Reagan's FCC Chairman, Mark Fowler, championed what he called "a marketplace approach to regulation," in which he proposed applying the same First Amendment standards to broadcasting as to traditional media. The FCC under Fowler conducted a major study of the fairness doctrine and reported to Congress that the policy, in operation, "actually inhibits the presentation of controversial issues of public importance to the detriment of the public and in degradation of the editorial prerogative of broadcast journalists." The 110-page report viewed the doctrine as a "governmentally imposed regulation affecting the content of speech," which no longer served the public interest and was constitutionally suspect.

With conclusions like that, one might think that the FCC would immediately repeal its malfunctioning rule. But it didn't . . . at least not right away. As it turns out, many powerful members of Congress like the idea of having a federal agency at their disposal that has power over broadcast journalism. And notwithstanding the fact that the President is the one who appoints FCC commissioners, Congress views the Commission as *its* agency.

This was summed up in a story that Minow liked to tell about when he was up for Senate confirmation as FCC chairman. Minow, a habitual name-dropper, recalled his first meeting with legendary Speaker of the House Sam Rayburn: Rayburn draped his arm around the shoulders of the young would-be bureaucrat and told him, "Son, just remember one thing. You work for the Congress, . . . you are part of the Congress. Just remember that and we are going to get along fine." FCC chairmen are unlikely to forget such fatherly advice, as the agency is beholden to Congress for its budget, and its commissioners are routinely summoned to the Hill for oversight hearings.

Chairman Dick Wiley learned this lesson in the mid-1970s after floating a proposal to refrain from enforcing the fairness doctrine against radio stations in larger markets. The idea was to keep the rule in place for television and small market radio stations, but to let competition balance things out in larger markets, where radio stations were more numerous. A day after Wiley suggested the experiment in a speech, he was called to account by an angry Senator John Pastore, the powerful chairman of the Subcommittee on Communications of the Senate Commerce Committee. Pastore demanded that Wiley explain what he was suggesting in the speech, pointedly adding, "Before you do anything, you will inform the Congress." It was not a request.

Chairman Wiley's experiment never took place.

It would be another dozen years before the FCC eliminated the fairness doctrine, and that happened only because the Commission had the support of President Reagan and because of some nudging by the courts. The reason for the FCC producing a "report" in 1985, and not a decision to repeal the rule, was because of direct threats from influential members of Congress. When the FCC issued a Notice of Inquiry in 1984 seeking comment on whether it should reconsider the rule, Tim Wirth, then Chairman of the House Subcommittee on Telecommunications, Consumer Protection, and Finance conducted oversight hearings and warned Fowler not to "meddle in my way" by taking up the fairness doctrine. If the agency did so, Wirth added (perhaps unnecessarily), "you will see a very vehement reaction from Congress." The point was not subtle, and Fowler simply responded, "Yes, sir, I understand exactly what you are saying."

Key members of the Senate likewise warned Fowler, albeit in Senator Fritz Hollings' typically folksy way. Hollings chaired the powerful Senate Committee on Commerce, Science, and Transportation, and, during budget reauthorization and oversight hearings, referred back to previous threats he had made on various FCC issues. He went on: "I have often said there is no education in the second kick of a mule" and "the Chairman of the FCC proved that old adage correct. He, however, appears to be showing that three kicks might do the trick."

It did the trick, indeed. The FCC's 1985 fairness doctrine inquiry produced only a "report" and not an order repealing the rule. The report noted "intense congressional interest" in the policy, and explained that the agency had elected to "defer" to Congress. It forwarded copies to the relevant committees to "afford Congress an opportunity to review the fairness doctrine in light of the evidence adduced in this proceeding." Right. Who's your daddy? The message to the FCC from Congress had been clear: when we want your opinion, we'll give it to you.

But Congress does not always get the final say, particularly when constitutional questions are in play. As it happens, the FCC was continuing to rule on fairness doctrine complaints filed with the agency during the same time that it was considering repealing the rule. In the case of WTVH, a Syracuse, New York TV station, it found that the station had failed to provide balanced coverage in stories about the proposed construction of the Nine Mile Point II nuclear power plant. The station owner appealed the FCC's decision and asked what most people thought was a pretty reasonable question: How can an agency enforce a rule that it has concluded doesn't work and very likely infringes the First Amendment?

Judges of the US Court of Appeals for the District of Columbia Circuit were keen to hear the answer to that question in the appeal brought by WTVH and in a companion case brought by the Radio-Television News Directors Association. This led to some particularly awkward moments at oral argument for Jack Smith, the Commission's General Counsel. Why was the FCC still enforcing the fairness doctrine if it believed that it operated to undermine First Amendment values? Smith responded: "Congress has told [the Commission] in no uncertain terms by [a] statement agreed to by both Houses, you shall not advance on this proceeding" to repeal the rule. When one judge noted that congressional expressions of personal pique were not actual legislation, the hapless General Counsel had to admit that he was not arguing law. "We are not talking law school enforcement, legal textbook arguments," he said. "We're talking political reality here."

The court was not impressed. It sent the matter back to the FCC to consider the First Amendment implications of the rule, observing: "[W]e are aware of no precedent that permits a federal agency to ignore a constitutional challenge to the application of its own policy merely because the resolution would be politically awkward."

The remand forced the FCC to tackle the First Amendment problem, but Congress was not yet finished with the issue. Galvanized by the court's action, it passed the Fairness in Broadcasting Act of 1987 to codify the rule, but President Reagan vetoed the legislation as "inconsistent with the First Amendment and with the American tradition of independent journalism." Only then, after being prodded by the court of appeals and backed by the White House was the FCC able to terminate the main provisions of the fairness doctrine and cease enforcement.

THE LION KING

The FCC's action sparked outrage in Congress, which toyed with the idea of imposing budget restrictions on the agency to prevent implementation. But it refrained from doing so to avoid another confrontation with the White House. The Commission's order thus nudged broadcast regulation toward a constitutional standard more in line with traditional First Amendment law. Doing so required the FCC to explain why it was not bound by the Supreme Court's decision in *Red Lion Broadcasting Co. v. FCC*, which had upheld the constitutionality of the agency's personal attack rule (a corollary of the fairness doctrine).

Red Lion, decided in 1969, was still the law, and it was based on the same theory of spectrum scarcity that the Supreme Court has espoused in earlier cases. The Court was aware that the fairness doctrine could not survive traditional First Amendment scrutiny, but it observed: "Where there are substantially more individuals who want to broadcast than there are frequencies to allocate, it is idle to posit an unbridgeable First Amendment right to broadcast comparable to the right of every individual to speak, write, or publish." Consequently, it held that, because of scarcity, "the Government is permitted to put restraints on licensees in favor of others whose views should be expressed on this unique medium."

The *Red Lion* case, which grew out of a fairness complaint tied to the Kennedy Administration's surreptitious campaign to suppress right-wing commentary, was a stark reminder of just how anemic constitutional protections were for broadcasting compared to newspapers. A further illustration of this gulf came just five years after *Red Lion* in another Supreme Court case, *Miami Herald Publishing Company* v. *Tornillo*. That case involved a Florida "right of reply" law that required newspapers to print a candidate's response – free of charge – if the paper published anything that assailed the candidate's personal character or official record. That law was analogous to a fairness doctrine for print media, and its defenders tried to justify its constitutionality on the basis of scarcity – arguing that media concentration in recent years and the economic factors that led to the disappearance of vast numbers of metropolitan newspapers supported the imposition of a "fiduciary duty" to provide balanced coverage of political affairs.

Despite the fact that the Supreme Court had found similar arguments persuasive just a few years earlier in *Red Lion*, it invalidated the Florida law, unanimously holding that it violated the First Amendment. Chief Justice Warren Burger's opinion for the Court stressed that any compulsion for papers to publish that which "'reason' tells them should not be published" is unconstitutional. But what of fairness? Burger explained that "[a] responsible press is an undoubtedly desirable goal, but press responsibility is not mandated by the Constitution and like many other virtues it cannot be legislated." He went on:

> The choice of material to go into a newspaper, and the decisions made as to limitations on the size and content of the paper, and treatment of public issues and public officials – whether fair or unfair – constitute the exercise of editorial control and judgment. It has yet to be demonstrated how governmental regulation of this crucial process can be exercised consistent with First Amendment guarantees of a free press as they have evolved to this time.

The difference in approach between *Red Lion* and *Tornillo* could not have been more pronounced. The Court in these two cases addressed the same First Amendment question based on essentially the same economic rationale, yet it came to opposite conclusions. And it did so in *Tornillo* without even mentioning *Red Lion*. Not even Justice Byron White, who wrote *Red Lion*, cited his prior opinion when he concurred in *Tornillo*. Regarding the constitutional shortcomings of the Florida law, he wrote: "We have learned, and continue to learn, from what we view as the unhappy experiences of other nations where government has been allowed to meddle in the internal editorial affairs of newspapers." With broadcasting, however, those lessons were taking longer to sink in.

The *Red Lion–Tornillo* divide was like a replay of *Near* v. *Minnesota* and *Trinity Methodist Church, South* v. *FRC* from decades earlier: Two sets of court decisions on parallel First Amendment issues but reaching opposite conclusions without even acknowledging the conflicting precedent. It was as if the law was developing in different dimensions. And, in a way, it was. Broadcasting was simply considered to be a "non-First Amendment zone," or, perhaps more accurately, an "attenuated First Amendment zone," where the existence and shape of protected rights is uncertain and fuzzy.

Despite *Red Lion*, however, it wasn't long before courts began to recognize that the government's authority over broadcasting was not without constitutional limits. It was like a case of buyer's remorse, as if the Supreme Court sensed that it had gone too far. In a relatively short span of time, it held that the government couldn't compel licensees to accept editorial advertising, or ban editorials by public broadcasters. Even when it came to the fairness doctrine – *Red Lion*'s core issue – lower courts started to come around. After the FCC's fairness doctrine report, the DC Circuit held that the Commission could not ignore a station's First Amendment concerns.

Once the FCC was forced by the courts to deal with the fairness doctrine's constitutional problems, it concluded that "the concept of scarcity – be it spectrum or numerical – is irrelevant" in determining "the appropriate First Amendment standard to be applied to the electronic press." It accordingly eliminated the fairness doctrine, and observed that "the extraordinary technological advances that have been made in the electronic media since the 1969 *Red Lion* decision, together with a consideration of fundamental First Amendment principles, provide an ample basis for the Supreme Court to reconsider the premise or approach of its decision in *Red Lion*."

Despite this invitation, the Supreme Court has yet to confront *Red Lion* directly. Even though spectrum scarcity is a legal fiction, the plausibility of which has long since been in tatters, the Court has been extremely reluctant to reexamine its different constitutional treatment of broadcasting. Justice Alito highlighted this trepidation during oral argument in a 2012 case in which the broadcast networks asked the Court to overturn *Red Lion* and other broadcast precedent as obsolete. Alito observed that broadcasting was being overtaken by newer media, and asked, "Well, so, why not just let this die a natural death? Why do you want us to intervene?" It was as if he were channeling former Chief Justice Taft, who in the 1920s dodged ruling on radio's constitutional status because he considered the technology "supernatural." This time, however, the Court was dodging the question because broadcasting was thought to be passé.

THE WASTELAND, CONTINUED ...

It was never about scarcity, really. The drive to implement "public interest" regulation over broadcasting content had always been about power. This point was made most forcefully by Minow himself in a 1991 address commemorating the thirtieth anniversary of the *Vast Wasteland Speech*. Noting the advent of new programming services and VCRs (video cassette recorders), Minow said: "[Y]ou can watch a program when you want to see it, not just when the broadcaster puts it on the schedule. If you are a sports fan, a news junkie, a stock-market follower, a rock-music devotee, a person who speaks Spanish, a nostalgic old-movie buff, a congressional-hearing observer, a weather watcher – you now have your own choice." He observed: "The FCC objective in the early 1960s to expand choice has been fulfilled – beyond all expectations."

But no amount of improvement will ever be sufficient to blunt the zeal of a determined "public interest" regulator. As Minow noted in his 1991 speech: "[T]o many of us, this enlarged choice is not enough to satisfy the public interest." Quite to the contrary, in gearing up for this retrospective, he observed: "[I]n several key respects the wasteland had grown only vaster, the prospects for serving the public interest even dimmer."

Minow rejected what he called the "ideological view that the marketplace will regulate itself and that the television marketplace will give us perfection." He challenged "the men and women in television ... to make it a leading institution in American life rather than merely a reactive mirror of the lowest common denominator in the marketplace." In this view of the world, the technological developments running up to that point, including satellite television, DVDs (digital video discs), the Internet, and personal video recorders, simply made no difference. In the mind of the public interest regulator, there will always be a reason to regulate broadcast content. Even after the emergence of the Internet, Minow sounded the same themes, arguing that "public interest" requirements should be applied to digital, computer-driven video servers on the "Information Superhighway." Once a censor, always a censor.

MINOW'S LEGACY

Newton Minow's legacy boils down to two words: vast wasteland.

Looking back, Minow described these buzzwords from his 1961 speech as "television's first enduring sound bite." After delivering it, he was invited to appear on *Meet the Press* and his picture graced the cover of *Time*. The expression has appeared in Bartlett's Familiar Quotations, picked up in countless newspaper and magazine headlines, and even been the answer to questions on the game show *Jeopardy* and in the board game Trivial Pursuit. Plugging the term into a Google search today still retrieves nearly 200,000 hits. Minow would later claim that he considered it a failure that the term "vast wasteland" was the takeaway from his speech. "The two words I wanted people to remember from that speech were not 'vast wasteland,'" he wrote. "The two words I cared about were 'public interest.'"

Nonsense. Without the slogan "vast wasteland," Minow was just another bureaucrat. Had he not coined this memorable catchphrase, it is unlikely that many outside his field would remember him. And Minow seemed well aware of it, because he traded on those words the rest of his career. His 1991 retrospective on the speech was titled *How Vast the Wasteland Now?* and his 1995 book advocating more regulation for children's television was called ABANDONED IN THE WASTELAND. He wrote an article for *The Atlantic* to mark the fiftieth anniversary of the speech. The title? *A Vaster Wasteland.* One might have thought that if the words he wanted people to remember were "public interest," he might have worked them into a title at some point.

But Minow had a great run based on the speech, and in 2016 President Barrack Obama awarded him the Medal of Freedom, the nation's highest civilian award. It was a capstone to an illustrious career, but it came at a time when most of his lifetime's work of promoting "public interest" regulation of broadcast content had ceased to have much relevance.

When Minow was the Commission's chairman, licenses had to be renewed every three years through a process that required cumbersome community "ascertainment" surveys to assess programming needs and, if he had gotten his way at the time, would have required more detailed programming reports. That's all gone now after a wave of deregulation in the 1980s streamlined or eliminated many of these requirements. While the FCC still issues and must renew broadcast licenses (now every eight years), the process is far more streamlined and less intrusive into licensees' programming choices. At one time, public interest advocates had even argued that the FCC was required to hold hearings whenever a radio station license transfer involved a change in entertainment formats, but that effort to expand content regulation failed. The fairness doctrine was repealed decades ago, and remaining broadcast programming regulations are being reconsidered. Minow himself noted the many changes affecting media and suggested in 2016 that perhaps it was time to auction off broadcast frequencies. Hmmm. If only someone had thought of that in 1926 . . . .

These changes also affect an area of the FCC's rules of particular interest for Minow: children's television. Since 1996, the Commission had required commercial television stations to provide three hours per week of regularly scheduled educational programming for kids to avoid getting more intensive scrutiny of their licenses at renewal time. It was a classic "raised eyebrow" approach. The FCC was keenly aware that a direct three-hour programming mandate would raise First Amendment concerns, so it made three hours of programming a "guideline," which, if not met, triggered heightened review of license renewal applications.

By 2018, the Commission wondered if even this made sense. It initiated a proceeding to take a "fresh look" at its rules after noting dramatic changes in the media environment over two decades, including the emergence of multiple media platforms (cable, satellite, and over-the-top alternatives such as Netflix, Hulu, Amazon Prime, and others) that provide a "vast array" of new programming offerings. FCC Commissioner Michael O'Rielly suggested that this meant that it was time to eliminate the ineffective and burdensome requirements.

Such developments highlight that regulation based on "scarcity" is a quaint anachronism in a media world rocked by succeeding revolutions in how video programming reaches consumers. Going from over-the-air television, to cable and satellite services, to DVD distribution, and now to streaming on-demand, the television industry is marked by so much choice that viewers are hard-pressed to keep up. For the most part, these newly emerged services are free from regulation, and none have had the type of intensive review of programming that was long associated with broadcasting. The result? There has been a renaissance of artistic creativity in the video medium that many have called the "new Golden Age of television."

For those paying attention, these developments confirm that the track record for public interest regulation of broadcast content has not been all that great. Nationalization of the spectrum in 1927 was not necessary to solve the frequency allocation problem and resulted in an immediate diminution of nonstandard viewpoints on the air; FCC meddling in programming quality and promotion of "family viewing" dampened creativity and resulted in blander programming; and rules to ensure news "fairness" didn't improve broadcast journalism and provided government officials with a weapon they abused to silence critical voices. Maintaining this system of regulation over the past nine-plus decades created divergent lines of constitutional law that the courts have never been able to reconcile and that even now do not want to confront.

Now *there's* a wasteland for you.

THE WASTELAND STRIKES BACK

Newton Minow didn't suffer from the same ridicule that dogged Anthony Comstock for much of his career. Perhaps that's because he had only a fraction of the impact on American life and law that Comstock had. Or maybe Minow escaped much of the criticism as a perk of being an "eat-your-vegetables" style of censor rather than the "fire-and-brimstone" kind. But he wasn't entirely free of it, either.

The best example came as a coded put-down in a silly situation comedy that was precisely the kind of TV show that Minow criticized in his famous speech to NAB. The ill-fated charter ship in *Gilligan's Island*, lost on a storm-tossed three-hour tour, was christened the SS *Minnow* (Figure 7.2). Although the ship's name was spelled like the little fish and not like the surname of the self-satisfied bureaucrat, the connection was intentional. Sherwood Schwartz, the show's producer, revealed that he named the boat as a swipe at the FCC chairman, who he believed undermined creativity on television with a "disastrous" speech.

This is pretty mild satire when you consider the kind of abuse heaped on the likes of Comstock and Fredric Wertham. Even those who remember *Gilligan's Island* are unlikely to get the connection, so it was more of a private joke than a public shaming. Still, the snarky reference turned up in several books and scholarly articles, and

FIGURE 7.2 Circa 1966, American actors, left to right, Bob Denver, Alan Hale
Jr. (1918–1990), and Russell Johnson (1924–2014) attempt to use a homemade CB radio to
contact civilization in a still from the television comedy show *Gilligan's Island*
Source: Photo by CBS/Getty Images.

Minow was well aware of it. He even called the naming of Gilligan's boat his
"favorite response" to the *Vast Wasteland Speech*, and wrote to one author: "The
S.S. *Minow* has made me immortal."

Maybe Minow's reaction was sincere; who knows? But it had much the same
hollow sound as when Comstock said he considered George Bernard Shaw's barbed
use of the term "Comstockery" to be a tribute. As the author of one law review article
observed: "It is rather ironic that Minow's brilliant legal career may ultimately be
overshadowed by his unflattering connection with *Gilligan's Island.*" This, no
doubt, is an overstatement, if only because few are aware of the "unflattering
connection." But it may not be an exaggeration to say that the cultural influence
of *Gilligan's Island* will exceed that of the one-time FCC chairman.

The vast wasteland-era sitcom that aired on network television for just three years
has been described as one of the most influential television shows of all time. It was
immensely popular in syndication, and episodes of *Gilligan's Island* have been

shown more often and in more places than any television show in history, including *I Love Lucy*. This prompted one scholar to gush that it is "impossible to overstate the influence of *Gilligan's Island* on American life," pointing out that it has been the subject of academic theses and college classes, discussed in serious pieces in publications as diverse as *The New Yorker* and the *Los Angeles Times*, referred to in comic strips like *B.C.*, *Tumbleweeds*, and *Bloom County*, and inspired the names of pets and even children.

By comparison, Newton Minow gave a catchy speech and dined out on it the rest of his career. And the type of content regulation he advocated failed to achieve its objectives and is fading from relevance. As is so often the case, the intended subject of censorship eventually prevails and even flourishes, while the would-be censor is destined for obscurity.

8

New Age Comstockery: The Indecency Wars

Brent Bozell was in his element. The president of the Parents Television Council (PTC) and career anti-media activist had been given a platform from which he could rail against the Sodom and Gomorrah of network television and he took full advantage of the opportunity. Testifying before the Subcommittee on Telecommunications and the Internet of the House Energy and Commerce Committee, Bozell said he was there to speak "on behalf of tens of millions of parents" because "[i]ndecencies and obscenities are now *everywhere* on broadcast TV," (italics his) and it was time to stop the "assault on the American family." The networks, he claimed, were "laughing at the public and at everyone in this room" because "the FCC will not lift a finger to penalize them," and that had to stop. Congress needed to force the Commission to actively monitor what was on the air, crank up the fines for violating indecency rules, and "get serious about revoking station licenses for those who refuse to abide by standards of decency."

Bozell had founded PTC nine years earlier, but up to this point had not made much headway in stemming what he described as a tidal wave of filth pouring into America's living rooms and poisoning children's minds. But 2004 promised to be his year. He was called to testify about the FCC's lack of enforcement of the indecency rules after the Commission staff declined to penalize NBC for its live telecast of the 2003 *Golden Globe Awards* after an unplanned and inadvertent use of the word "fuck" had made it to air. An overly exuberant Bono had declared it was "fucking brilliant" that his band U2 was being honored, and the network's Standards and Practices team had failed to catch the split-second gaffe. This prompted congressional resolutions, legislation proposing to make certain words per se violations of the indecency rules, and – of course – oversight hearings. Bozell was a star witness, invited to attest to the agency's dereliction of duty, and a chastened FCC Enforcement Bureau chief was offered up by the agency to pledge changes in Commission policy (Figure 8.1).

By the time of this hearing in late January 2004, sufficient political heat already was being directed at the FCC to kick-start one of its periodic spasms of indecency enforcement. But no one could have anticipated that, just a few days later, Janet Jackson and Justin Timberlake would give a performance at the Super Bowl that

FIGURE 8.1 DC House Energy and Commerce subcommittee hearing on the FCC's
Enforcement of Broadcast Indecency Rules
Source: Photo by Susan Biddle/The Washington Post via Getty Images.

would shift the regulatory demands into hyper-drive. In an unauthorized and unscripted maneuver, Timberlake ended their halftime show performance of the song "Rock Your Body" by snatching a piece from Janet Jackson's bodice, revealing her right breast for nine-sixteenths of a second, just in time for the lyric "gonna have you naked by the end of this song." Most viewers of the show weren't quite sure what they had seen. The incident was so brief, and the camera shot had pulled back so that the performers were no longer in close-up. But in Washington, DC, the reaction to what Timberlake later called a "wardrobe malfunction" was immediate, and the shock waves seismic (Figure 8.2).

The resulting panic led to a wholesale revision of the FCC's indecency standards, record fines for network television broadcasts as well as for radio shows, and eight years of litigation that included two trips to the Supreme Court. Congress cranked up the oversight machine and held multiple hearings, eventually passing legislation to boost the cost of indecency fines tenfold. And Bozell was at the center of it all. His

FIGURE 8.2 The wardrobe malfunction
Source: Getty Images.

PTC operation became the primary generator of FCC indecency complaints, and his organization set the agenda for the political feeding frenzy over the Commission's rules. Yes, 2004 promised to be a banner year.

COMSTOCK'S "MINI ME"

If ever there were a spiritual heir to Anthony Comstock it is Leo Brent Bozell, III. Like Comstock, Bozell's entire career had been devoted to political and religious activism (although one difference is that Comstock actually held down a job as a dry goods clerk before becoming a full-time reformer). Bozell would never personally exercise direct governmental authority to censor his targets as Comstock did – few ever acquire such power. He had to settle for advocating government restrictions and pulling levers behind the scenes, much like Oz, the Great and Powerful. But there was no doubt he was Comstock's psychic offspring.

Prior to creating PTC as a vehicle to focus specifically on broadcast indecency, Bozell founded the Media Research Center (MRC) in 1987 to (as MRC's website puts it) "expose and neutralize the propaganda arm of the Left: the national news media." Before that he worked with the National Conservative Political Action Committee, heading that group for a time until he started MRC. He has spun off various related organizations over the years. He founded the Conservative Communications Center in 1998 to provide more of a conservative slant on the news because he believed the mainstream media were downplaying coverage of Clinton White House scandals. In 2010 he founded ForAmerica to take his conservative message to social media. That organization describes itself as the Right Wing's "Facebook Army." Bozell is a syndicated columnist and a prolific author of a number of books, including such polemics as the ironically titled COLLUSION: HOW THE MEDIA STOLE THE 2012 ELECTION – AND HOW TO STOP THEM FROM DOING IT IN 2016.

Like Comstock, Bozell's many crusades have a distinctly theocratic theme. In 2006, he set up the Culture and Media Institute as a branch of MRC devoted to restoring "America's culture, character, traditional values, and morals against the assault of the liberal media elite, and to promote fair portrayal of social conservatives and religious believers in the media." Bozell also serves on the board of the Catholic League for Religious and Civil Rights, an organization that "monitors the culture" and acts "as a watchdog agency and defender of the civil rights of all Catholics." He uses these platforms to chastise news organizations for covering sex crimes and pervasive cover-ups in the Catholic Church and to condemn network entertainment programs for engaging in what he believes is irreligious propaganda and anti-Catholic bias. In one tweet, for example, he advocated defunding National Public Radio (NPR), asserting that journalists "use scandals to undercut the moral authority of churches . . . to promote their secular leftist agenda."

Bozell literally was born to this work. The intellectual godfather of the conservative movement, William F. Buckley, Jr., was his uncle, and his father (L. Brent Bozell, Jr.) was Buckley's teammate at the Yale debating society. The senior Bozell and Buckley collaborated on projects after college, including a book defending Senator Joseph McCarthy entitled MCCARTHY AND HIS ENEMIES. But the two grew apart over time as Bozell became more involved in fringe Catholic activism, denouncing conservatism as "an inadequate substitute for Christian politics." Young Brent absorbed it all, and made it his mission to reform not just conservative politics and religion but the larger culture as well.

Bozell did more than follow Anthony Comstock's career path, he appeared to adopt Comstock's very persona. Gruff, pugnacious, and with a perpetual air of sanctimony, Bozell's default tone is seething outrage. Like Comstock, this ginger-bearded decency crusader describes his opponents not just as wrong or misguided but as evil incarnate. More than any other reformer, Bozell fully embraced the ethos and all of the lessons from the Comstock playbook for the morals entrepreneur.

Through PTC's website, he presented his own "chamber of horrors" in the form of salacious clips from network programs he wanted regulators to sanction. His organization mastered the art of spamming the FCC with torrents of complaints (most of them duplicates) about particular shows, which would then be taken as "proof" that the agency was ignoring the will of the people. And he demanded that the FCC begin revoking broadcast station licenses by enforcing a legal standard for indecency indistinguishable from the long-discredited *Hicklin* rule from the Comstock era. But don't you *dare* call him a censor.

WHO'S A CENSOR? *I'M* NOT A CENSOR!

The *raison d'être* of PTC was to foster increased FCC enforcement of the federal criminal law prohibiting broadcast indecency. The activity PTC was created to promote is the dictionary definition of censorship, of course, but PTC will tell you that just ain't so. According to its website, "PTC does not censor." Rather, it claims its actions "are actually a classic case of the First Amendment at work." The organization and its members merely are exercising their "right to speak out" about "the potential abuse of broadcasting privileges," and it compares this to the activities of other groups, such as the NAACP of the Anti-Defamation League, who, it claims, "often attempt to manipulate or alter television portrayals of, or references to, members of their constituencies." Whether or not the comparison to the activities of other organizations passes the laugh test, this exercise in "whataboutism" is no answer to the fact that PTC's entreaties to use federal law to control television programming are naked demands for government censorship.

PTC also tries to pressure advertisers to pull their sponsorship of shows it believes are sinful, which is a type of advocacy that the First Amendment protects. But that is not where PTC devoted most of its energies during this period. Instead, it was fixated on flooding the FCC with complaints and lobbying Congress to legislate harsher penalties for broadcasters. In annual reports, the group described these efforts to spur enforcement of the law as the "major part of the . . . battle to keep the airwaves free of offensive content." PTC's claim that it "has neither the power to forbid programming nor the desire for the government to ban legal programming" rings hollow to the extent that it was actively petitioning the federal government to prohibit a broad swath of entertainment shows and seeking to vastly expand what is considered illegal programming. Thus, PTC's 2006 annual report boasted that members of seven chapters filed petitions with the FCC to revoke the licenses of seventeen television stations they claimed aired programs that violated broadcast indecency standards. As a consequence, it reported enthusiastically, "these stations' broadcasting licenses could be revoked at any time, resulting in the stations being abruptly put out of business."

So there it is. The argument is not, and never has been, that PTC does not advocate the use of *governmental* authority to punish and restrict speech. Instead, its argument is that broadcasting is a medium the government gets to regulate more heavily than others, and the speech PTC dislikes does not deserve constitutional protection anyway. Like all would-be "public interest" speech regulators, PTC does not deny an interest in promoting censorship; it merely seeks to redefine what censorship means. Ultimately, PTC's argument that it merely is exercising its First Amendment rights is the same one used by Newton Minow when he claimed that FCC content regulation is "the very reverse of censorship." As PTC points out, "[i]t has never been supposed by the Supreme Court that broadcasters have an absolute right to air whatever they wish with no responsibility to the public interest." Yet it is a bit hard to maintain the fig leaf argument that this is a "classic case of the First Amendment at work," when some of PTC's targets were the most acclaimed and popular shows on television, and when, as viewed through Bozell's eyes, "[i]ndecencies and obscenities are now *everywhere* on broadcast TV."

HOW DID WE GET HERE?

PTC did not create the broadcast indecency rules, of course; they have been part of broadcasting law from the beginning. The prohibition against transmitting "obscene, indecent, or profane language by means of radio communication" was first enacted as Section 29 of the Radio Act of 1927, and later incorporated into the Communications Act of 1934. The statutory prohibition was transferred without change to the US Criminal Code in 1948, which provides that violators "shall be fined under this title or imprisoned not more than two years, or both." The law was adopted without any statutory definition of its key terms or clear indication of congressional intent. The scant legislative history suggests "'obscenity' was the concern of those members of Congress who spoke" about the provision.

This is not surprising; the law was written at a time before First Amendment doctrine developed to vanquish *Anthony* Comstock's view of the Constitution, and when the terms "obscene," "indecent," and "profane" were treated as essentially synonymous. It was not until 1957 – three decades after Congress enacted the Radio Act – that the Supreme Court confirmed that the First Amendment limits the scope of obscenity law. In this undeveloped state of jurisprudence, the government had wide latitude to prohibit a great deal of speech that is unquestionably protected under current law. In one 1931 case, for example, the Ninth Circuit held that the prohibition of "profane" speech on radio extended to blasphemy (notwithstanding the First Amendment's separate prohibition against establishing religion), and that the defendant could be punished for referring to an individual as "damned," for using "the expression 'By God' irreverently," and for announcing his intention "to call down the curse of God upon certain individuals." But even as First Amendment law developed in the latter half of the twentieth century for other forms of communication, these antiquated views remained firmly in place when it came to broadcasting.

The FCC had the leading role in enforcing the law, but it had no set definitions for the statute's terms. As a result, the Commission's decisions were haphazard, reflecting pretty much the temper of the times. This was illustrated in an early case involving the sultry actress Mae West, known for her use of double entendre (generally involving her sexual proclivities), and Charlie McCarthy, the wise-cracking alter ego of ventriloquist Edgar Bergen. In December 1937, NBC's *Chase and Sanborn Hour* presented a two-part sketch with the first bit set in the Garden of Eden. Mae West's Eve, quickly bored with the tranquility of the garden, seduces the serpent to get the forbidden fruit so that she and Adam can "leave this dump." Part two involves a dialogue with McCarthy that includes West inviting the puppet to "come on home with me, honey. I'll let you play in my wood pile."

This was just too much for the Catholic Legion of Decency, which launched a coordinated campaign to express outrage about the broadcast. One typical editorial would have been right at home on PTC's website today: "The home is our last bulwark against the modern over-emphasis on sensuality, and we cannot see why Miss West and others of her ilk should be permitted to pollute its precincts with shady stories, foul obscenity, smutty suggestiveness, and horrible blasphemy." This prompted an FCC investigation, and the Commission concluded that the sketch was indeed "vulgar and indecent, and against all proprieties." It wasn't that the script contained anything the FCC could point to as indecent, but the agency believed West's inflections were too bawdy and suggestive (Figure 8.3).

Although the FCC didn't issue formal sanctions, Chairman Frank McNinch wrote to NBC President Lenox Lohr to remind him of broadcasters' responsibility to protect their audience "against features that are suggestive, vulgar, immoral, or of such other character as may be offensive to the great mass of right-thinking, clean-minded American citizens." He told the press that the Commission would hold the broadcast against each of the fifty-nine NBC affiliates when their licenses were up for renewal unless "in the next few months they aired nothing else that was offensive." This was not government censorship, McNinch would later say in a speech to the NAB, but merely an acknowledgment that broadcast-ers had an obligation to censor themselves. But the FCC would be watching, he told them, and if programming aired "that might reasonably be anticipated to give offense," he reminded them, it was "the duty of the Commission to do something about it." The incident did nothing to define the indecency standard, but the chilling effect on station owners kept Mae West off the radio for the next fourteen years.

The tumult of the 1960s was reflected in the FCC's decisions as well. One jolt came early in the decade, when the FCC under Chairman Minow denied license renewal for WDKD, a radio station in Kingstree, South Carolina owned by actor Edward G. Robinson. The problem was caused by a DJ known as Uncle Charlie whose on-air banter was considered by the Commission to be "flagrantly and patently offensive ... and thus contrary to the public interest." The host's offending language was impossibly

FIGURE 8.3 Dummy Charlie McCarthy with Mae West
Source: Photo by Bettmann/Contributor/Getty Images.

tame by today's (or any day's) standards – using such expressions as "let it all hang out" and using nicknames for local towns, like "Bloomersville" for Bloomville, and "Ann's Drawers" for Andrews – but to the FCC the case presented a "flagrant situation calling for drastic administrative action."

Of course, this was not *censorship*, according to the Commission, which claimed to be acting "with great circumspection in this sensitive area." It acknowledged that the government could not under the First Amendment "set itself up as a national arbiter of taste," but suggested "the greater danger to broadcasting would be in our failure to protect the public interest." The FCC still lacked a legal definition for indecency, but had no difficulty deciding that Uncle Charlie's shtick was "coarse, vulgar, suggestive, double-meaning programming" and "smut." To Newton Minow's Commission, this wasn't even a close case. In fact, the FCC emphatically rejected the initial hearing examiner's conclusion that the case was difficult, and denied license renewal "in order to set an example to the industry." Pretty strong stuff for an agency that doesn't want to be the "national arbiter of taste."

Then came the counter-culture. Everything changed in the 1960s – what people wore, the music they listened to, and the language they used. The FCC struggled to keep up and to apply Depression Era law to the Woodstock Generation. It got its chance to do that after noncommercial FM station WUHY aired an extended interview with Grateful Dead guitarist Jerry Garcia that was far less inhibited than anything Uncle Charlie might have said. In the fifty-minute interview Garcia discussed his views on ecology, music, philosophy, and interpersonal relations, and frequently interspersed the words "fuck" and "shit" in his comments (as one does) "as adjectives, or simply as an introductory expletive." Neither the station nor the FCC received a single complaint about the broadcast. The agency became aware of it only by happenstance, thus triggering an enforcement action.

What was the reaction? Did the FCC immediately suspend the license or impose ruinous fines? Did Congress schedule emergency oversight hearings or introduce punitive legislation? Not quite. The FCC issued a $100 fine just to ensure that the decision could be reviewed in court. It explained that there was a lack of precedent construing the law, and that "a most crucial peg underlying all Commission action in the programming field is the vital consideration that the courts are there to review and reverse any action which runs afoul of the First Amendment." It applied a test for indecency, roughly based on the Supreme Court's obscenity standard set forth in *Roth* v. *United States* and *Memoirs* v. *Massachusetts*, that identified indecency generally as material that is patently offensive by contemporary community standards and utterly without redeeming social value.

Even with the negligible fine and somewhat protective (but amorphous) legal standard, some commissioners thought the agency had gone too far. Commissioner Kenneth Cox wrote that it hardly promoted the public interest to "narrow our concept of the use of radio in order to protect the sensibilities of those who seem more concerned with suppressing words and pictures they find offensive than with solving the problems that are tearing our society apart." Commissioner Nicholas Johnson dissented, claiming that the FCC was talking sides in a culture war, that it was employing a vague standard where what speech might be prohibited was "anyone's guess," and – weirdly – was claiming to uphold "community standards" although "neither the station nor the FCC received a single complaint about the broadcast in question." Far from promoting the wider and more effective use of radio, Johnson wrote that it was "no coincidence that this Commission has often moved against the programming of innovative and experimental stations."

Commissioners Cox and Johnson made good points, but the fine imposed on WUHY was a far cry from the "drastic administrative action" the FCC took only eight short years earlier to silence the cornball antics of Uncle Charlie. In that time the nation's sensibilities had shifted, and, notwithstanding the Supreme Court's 1969 decision in *Red Lion Broadcasting Co.* v. *FCC*, some courts began to express concern about the different First Amendment standards that were being applied to broadcasting. Commissioners Cox and Johnson were like the municipal court judge who, in 1935, refused to censor a book even though the law had not changed since Comstock's days, observing, "[w]hether we like it or not, the fact is that the public concept of decency has changed." It was in this period that some came to worry about the absence of a specific legal test for indecency (as opposed to obscenity) and the courts had not yet specifically addressed the issue.

TOPLESS RADIO

One who worried about the lack of an indecency standard was FCC Chairman Dean Burch. A conservative, Burch was not troubled in the least by the fine imposed for the Jerry Garcia interview, and, if anything, wished it had been higher. He was especially bothered by certain trends in radio at the time, including what was called "topless radio," a nickname for daytime talk shows where bored housewives would call in to discuss their sex lives and ask questions. Burch's response was to unleash a coordinated campaign of "raised eyebrow" regulation to drive the format from the air. In March 1973 the FCC initiated a notice of inquiry into allegations of indecent broadcasts by eight radio stations, and the same day (not by coincidence) the NAB Board adopted a resolution condemning "tasteless and vulgar program content, whether explicit or by sexually-oriented innuendo."

The next day, Burch gave the annual chairman's speech at the NAB convention (the same venue as Minow's *Vast Wasteland Speech*) and blasted the "prurient trash that is the stock-in-trade of the sex-oriented radio talk show, complete with the suggestive, coaxing, pearshaped tones of the smut-hustling host." Burch was not subtle. He reminded his audience of various proceedings pending either in Congress or before the FCC in which broadcasters were seeking greater stability in the license renewal process, longer license terms, and less detailed intrusion into journalistic discretion, and broadly suggested that favorable consideration depended "on the notion of the responsible public trustee." He added, unnecessarily, that the price of ignoring his concerns "may be high."

If this warning seemed too obscure, Burch drove home the point: He told the audience that the Commission had issued the notice of inquiry on topless radio and threatened to "take further action in this difficult field if necessary." And he added with extortionate flair: "It is my hope and the purpose of this statement to make further government action moot." To top it off with an exclamation point, about a week later the FCC issued a $2,000 notice of apparent liability against Sonderling Broadcasting Company for airing a program called *Femme Forum* (the top-rated show in the Chicago radio market), which it found to be "titillating and pandering." Lacking a working definition of indecency, the Commission concluded that the racy talk about sex and use of double entendre was obscene.

The *Topless Radio Speech* hardly has the same ring as the *Vast Wasteland Speech*, so law reviews don't publish retrospectives on the speech as they did with Minow's magnum opus, and no one remembers it today. But it sure got results. The day after

Burch's speech, Storer Broadcasting Company ended all sexual discussions on a widely syndicated talk show it transmitted from Los Angeles; WHN radio in New York dropped the sex-talk format; and WDEE in Detroit followed suit. Sonderling Broadcasting did the same, but it was too late to forestall the FCC fine. Not surprisingly, by June 1973 the NAB found that such sexual discussion programs had vanished from the radio.

Sonderling quickly paid the $2,000, but an ACLU affiliate, the Illinois Citizens Committee for Broadcasting, appealed on behalf of viewers and listeners. The court of appeals did not disturb the FCC's findings, however, and was not overly concerned about Chairman Burch's heavy-handed tactics. This, the majority explained, was "not FCC action at all," but was merely "the unofficial expression of the views of one member of the Commission." David Bazelon, Chief Judge of the DC Circuit, was troubled by the FCC's behavior, and described the episode as "a classic example illustrating a whole range of 'raised eyebrow' tactics." But he lacked the support of the rest of his court to review the matter *en banc*.

The case, argued around the time the Supreme Court was grappling with revising the obscenity standard in *Miller* v. *California*, highlighted the awkwardness of trying to apply to the broadcast medium a standard designed to address hard-core, patently offensive depictions of sexual activity that lacked serious value. The banter on topless radio unabashedly was about sex and it was designed to titillate, but it was far from obscene. The DC Circuit majority touched on this only lightly, and was able to avoid delving too deeply since the licensee had thrown in the towel. But Judge Bazelon dissected the agency's analysis and found that "the FCC has demonstrated what one can most charitably describe as a total ignorance of the constitutional definition of obscenity." Ignorant or not, the FCC's decision prevailed (in large part because the broadcaster mounted no legal defense), but the episode highlighted the pressing need for the Commission to come up with a separate legal test for indecency.

THE SEVEN DIRTY WORDS

Burch had won this round, but knew it wouldn't last unless the Commission could devise a working definition of indecency that was distinct from obscenity. It was no small task, and Burch turned to the FCC's former general counsel (and his former special advisor) Henry Geller, to come up with something. Geller, a seasoned FCC veteran and brilliant lawyer, knew the difficulty of devising a legal test that could survive rigorous First Amendment scrutiny, largely for the reasons Judge Bazelon had outlined in the *Sonderling* case. He told Burch the effort would likely fail. No matter, the Chairman was determined. To him, the question was not *whether* to create a new legal standard; it was simply a matter of finding the proper vehicle for announcing it.

The opportunity presented itself in the form of a complaint concerning an October 1973 broadcast on Pacifica station WBAI in New York. The program involved was a regularly scheduled discussion show that analyzed contemporary society's attitudes toward language. Near the end of the show, the host, Paul Gorman, played an eleven-minute, forty-five-second cut from the George Carlin album *Occupation: FOOLE* to illustrate his point about the varied uses of language in society (Figure 8.4). The bit, entitled "Filthy Words," was about "the words you couldn't say on the public airwaves." Eureka! This was the perfect confluence of opportunity and irony, and the FCC seized on it to issue a declaratory ruling to define what words "you couldn't say on the public airwaves."

Congress had no clue what particular speech should be included when it prohibited "obscene, indecent, and profane" broadcasts, and the Commission acknowledged that "the term 'indecent' has never been authoritatively construed by the Courts." So this left Carlin pretty free to riff on what the law meant, which he boiled down to seven words that he said will "curve your spine, grow hair on your hands and ... maybe, even bring us, God help us, peace without honor." The words he came up with were shit, piss, cunt, fuck, cocksucker, motherfucker, and tits. Why is "tits" on the list, you might ask? It is because the word serves as a monosyllabic exclamation point to end the list and it is *funny*.

Well, funny to *most* people. Out of all the listeners in the New York metro region, the FCC received one letter of complaint about WBAI's program, and even that one didn't arrive at the Commission until six weeks after the broadcast. John R. Douglas, a member of the national planning board of Morality in Media, a religious anti-porn group, complained that he had heard the Carlin monologue "while driving with his young son" and demanded that the FCC take action. Douglas neglected to mention his affiliation with Morality in Media or to note that his "young son" was a teenager

FIGURE 8.4 Comedian George Carlin, circa 1975
Source: Photo by Michael Ochs Archives/Getty Images.

of fifteen (who inexplicably was not in school at 2 p.m. on a weekday), but none of those details mattered. The FCC now had its vehicle for announcing a new standard for indecency.

In response to the complaint, the Commission in 1975 issued a declaratory ruling to set forth its new definition of indecency. The FCC's order traced its previous decisions, including *WUHY* and *Sonderling Broadcasting*, noting that they were based on the Supreme Court's obscenity rulings, but that the law was in a state of flux and that indecency needed its own separate standard. The Commission concluded that the Carlin monologue clearly met the new test, but that it was not prepared to fine the station. While it said that it could have imposed administrative sanctions, the Commission instead placed the order in the station's license file and said that it would use the controversy "to clarify the applicable standards." "Clarify" might not have been exactly the right word, for the standard the FCC announced left most people scratching their heads about what speech is covered. Debate about the standard continues to rage nearly a half-century later.

The FCC's *Pacifica Broadcasting* ruling "reformulated" the concept of indecent speech as "language that describes, in terms patently offensive as measured by contemporary community standards for the broadcast medium, sexual or excretory activities and organs, at times of day when there is a reasonable risk that children may be in the audience." This definition sounds something like the Supreme Court's description of obscenity in *Miller* v. *California*, and, in fact, was inspired by it, but in substance it is very different. What is missing are all of the constitutional safeguards that evolved following Anthony Comstock's decades-long crusade to wipe out anything he deemed to be smut.

Unlike the *Miller* test for obscenity, the FCC's new indecency standard is not concerned with the "average person" in the community but focuses instead on the imagined impact of sexually oriented material on children (who are present only in about one-third of US households); it does not require the Commission to consider the work "as a whole," or ask whether the material appeals "primarily to the prurient interest"; and it is not a complete defense that the material has serious literary, artistic, political or scientific value. In substance, the FCC's indecency test is virtually indistinguishable from the Victorian Era rule from *Regina* v. *Hicklin*, which asked only "whether the tendency of the matter charged as obscenity is to deprave and corrupt those whose minds are open to such immoral influences." And the paradox is even weirder: According to the Commission, the indecent speech subject to this lax test is *protected* by the First Amendment, unlike obscenity, which is not. This means that the FCC could regulate such speech but could not ban it entirely.

In short, what separated the FCC from Anthony Comstock under this new policy was not the particular elements of the legal test; it was a consciously articulated policy of restraint. The Commission said that it could not impose a ban on speech; it could only "channel" it to late-night hours. It would confine its enforcement actions only to "flagrant" violations, and would not penalize stations for mishaps or insubstantial incidents. It explained that inadvertent, isolated or fleeting transmissions of "indecent" language would not violate law because it would be inequitable to hold a licensee responsible for indecent language when "public events likely to produce offensive speech are covered live, and there is no opportunity for journalistic editing."

The DC Circuit was not much impressed with the FCC's promise to be good, and it reversed the declaratory ruling. Noting that the new legal standard was both vague and overly broad, it explained that what *could* happen under the Commission's policy was the very type of thing that *did* happen under Comstock. Under this amorphous test the FCC could "prohibit the broadcast of Shakespeare's *The Tempest* or *Two Gentlemen of Verona*" along with "certain passages of the Bible" as well as the "works of Auden, Becket, Lord Byron, Chaucer, Fielding, Greene, Hemingway, Joyce, Knowles, Lawrence, Orwell, Scott, Swift, and the Nixon tapes." Accordingly, the court explained that "[t]o whatever extent . . . the Commission errs in balancing its duties, it must be in favor of preserving the values of free expression and freedom from governmental interference in matters of taste." This meant that the question of the legal status of George Carlin's seven dirty words was headed to the Supreme Court.

But there was a hitch. The Justice Department by now agreed with the Court of Appeals that the indecency standard was unconstitutional, and refused to defend this frail and untested theory in the Supreme Court. This required the FCC to use one of its own staff attorneys to bring the appeal, and for this task it turned to Assistant General Counsel Joseph Marino. An experienced appellate litigator, Marino was all too aware of the weakness of the FCC's position, and he understood that his best chance of success lay in framing the Commission's order as narrowly as possible. Thus, he argued that the decision should not be considered the announcement of a broad policy (even though that is *precisely* what the FCC intended) but instead should be limited to the facts of the case. Marino argued that the Commission decision "must be read narrowly," limited to George Carlin's seven words "'as broadcast' in the early afternoon." He emphasized "the deliberate repetition of these words" and noted that the case involved "prerecorded language with the words repeated over and over [and] deliberately broadcast."

The strategy worked. The Supreme Court narrowly upheld the FCC on a five–four vote, and the majority stressed that its review was "limited to the question whether the Commission has the authority to proscribe this particular broadcast" in a "specific factual context." As Justice Powell explained in his concurring opinion, the Court approved "only the Commission's holding that Carlin's monologue was indecent 'as broadcast' at two o'clock in the afternoon, and not the broad sweep of the Commission's opinion."

The Court acknowledged that the indecency test would be unconstitutional if applied to more traditional media, such as books or magazines, but upheld it on a limited basis for the medium of broadcasting. This time, it relied not on the supposed scarcity of the electromagnetic spectrum but on other attributes it said made broadcasting different. First, the Court noted that "the broadcast media have established a uniquely pervasive presence in the lives of all Americans," and that "prior warnings cannot completely protect the listener or viewer from unexpected program content." Second, it described broadcasting as "uniquely accessible to children" and observed that "[o]ther forms of offensive expression may be withheld from the young without restricting the expression at its source."

The FCC was astonished. It had fully expected to lose. And why not? Henry Geller had told Chairman Burch that it was unlikely that the FCC could concoct a standard that would survive judicial review; the DC Circuit bore out his prediction; and the Justice Department refused to defend the indecency test in the Supreme Court. But now, by a single vote, the Court held that it was not unconstitutional for the FCC to place a warning letter in a radio station's license file on the basis of a specific set of facts that involved the afternoon broadcast of a comedian's routine that the majority characterized as "verbal shock treatment." And it did so only after the FCC pledged to use its authority only in extreme cases and even then with the utmost restraint.

What was the lesson here? Could the FCC apply its test more broadly? And what if it failed to exercise restraint? Could it impose fines on stations? Deny license renewals? The *Pacifica* decision answered none of these questions. But the FCC did not wait to find out how far it could go in enforcing the indecency rules. Through various announcements and actions, it made clear that it would enforce its policy only against the seven words of the George Carlin monologue, making the "seven dirty words" the only legal standard ever devised by a stand-up comic. One law review article on this area of law is even entitled "George Carlin, Constitutional Law Scholar."

A POLICY OF RESTRAINT

By the time the Supreme Court decided *Pacifica*, the FCC had a new chairman appointed by President Carter – Charles D. Ferris – who wasted no time assuring broadcasters that the Commission was serious about its pledge of restraint. In a speech to the New England Broadcasters Association just a few weeks after the decision came down, Ferris said: "I do not intend to devote my limited powers under the Communications Act to censoring speech. I do not intend to become an arbiter of taste." He added that the FCC was "far more dedicated to the First Amendment premise that broadcasters should air controversial programming than we are worried about an occasional four-letter word." It wasn't so much that Ferris was generally opposed to content regulation. He was, after all, an avid proponent of the fairness doctrine. But he just didn't perceive indecency to be a pressing problem. As he put it to the New England broadcasters, a case like *Pacifica* was "about as likely to occur again as Halley's Comet."

And Ferris backed up his words with action. Around the same time as his speech to the broadcasters, the Commission rejected a petition to deny the renewal of the license for WGBH, Boston's premier public television station. The activist group Morality in Media had challenged renewal on grounds of alleged indecency, and submitted to the Commission "five and one-half pages of characterizations of programs and/or words and phrases" from programs it characterized as "offensive, vulgar and otherwise . . . harmful to children."

The offending shows on WGBH included an unidentified installment of *Masterpiece Theater* described in the petition as "a story principally concerned with adultery expressing a philosophy that approved of adulterous relationships," and a program called *The Thin Edge*, that assertedly "espoused a hedonistic attitude about guilt resulting from adultery and fornication." The petition also targeted episodes of *Monty Python's Flying Circus*, which it said "relies primarily on scatology, immodesty, vulgarity, nudity, profanity and sacrilege" for humor, and a program entitled *Rock Follies*, which it described as "'vulgar' and as containing 'profanity' (i.e., 'The name of God (six times)'), 'obscenities' such as 'shit,' 'bullshit,' etc., and action indicating some sexually-oriented content in the program."

It was as if Anthony Comstock had risen from the grave. The Morality in Media complaint targeted precisely the kind of works the old crusader had condemned to the flames. This, then, was a good test of the FCC's resolve to show the self-discipline it had promised, since the legal standard the FCC articulated in *Pacifica* would have permitted it to take action had it not pledged restraint. This time, the Commission kept its word. It explained: "We intend strictly to observe the narrowness of the *Pacifica* holding," which emphasized that the language at issue in that case "had been repeated over and over as a sort of verbal shock treatment." The Commission order concluded: "[W]e cannot base the denial of a license renewal application upon the 'subjective determination' of a viewer, or group of viewers, as to what is or is not 'good' programming."

Under Ferris, the FCC determined that the indecency rules would be enforced *only* against the seven Carlin words (unless their use was fleeting or inadvertent, in which case the complaint would be considered "not actionable"). This seemed fair, given that the Commission's defense in *Pacifica* was confined to the specific facts of the case. Justice Brennan's dissent in *Pacifica* had even suggested that the FCC was legally barred from going beyond the Carlin monologue, given the position it had taken before the Court. And the Commission was fine with this, at least for a time. The FCC enforced its policy only against the Carlin words for nearly a decade, but that eventually changed. Such, of course, is a predictable consequence of basing compliance with the Constitution on political promises rather than specific legal standards.

GENERICALLY SPEAKING

The 1980s saw the rise of the radio "shock jocks" like Howard Stern and, along with it, demands for the FCC to get tough on indecency. Mark Fowler, the deregulatory-minded FCC chairman who championed the elimination of the fairness doctrine, had become the target of protests and behind-the-scenes machinations by pro-censorship groups who believed he had been too lax on indecency. Morality in Media conducted a letter-writing campaign directed at members of Congress to block his reappointment for another term as chairman, and in 1986, its members picketed on the street outside the FCC. The National Federation of Decency likewise opposed Fowler's renomination. Patrick Buchanan, the former White House Communications Director, political activist (and future presidential candidate), publicly advised President Reagan that the FCC should deny a broadcast license or two over indecency infractions in order to mend fences with the religious right. Fowler got the message, and he directed the Commission's general counsel, Jack Smith, to work with anti-indecency activists to help craft effective complaints. Smith went so far as to recommend which complaints would be most likely to succeed.

The campaign paid off for the anti-indecency activists, and the FCC decided to take action. But it could not do much if its policy was still focused on just the "Carlin words." So, in 1987, the FCC modified its construction of the law to include a "generic definition" of the statutory term "indecent" that was not limited to the "seven dirty words." In three declaratory rulings issued on the same day (some based on complaints for which the Commission's general counsel acted as informal advisor), the Commission set forth what it described as a "clarification" of its construction of the statutory term to apply to "a broader range of material than the seven specific words at issue in *Pacifica*." It did not alter the indecency standard it had articulated in that case, but decided to use the words of the Carlin monologue only as "examples of, rather than a definitive list of, the kinds of words" that may be considered indecent. In all other respects, the FCC claimed that it would adhere to its "restrained" approach to enforcement.

The US Court of Appeals for the DC Circuit upheld this change in policy, but tried to keep the FCC on a fairly short leash. Then-Judge Ruth Bader Ginsburg, writing for the Court of Appeals, stressed that "the FCC has assured this Court . . . that it will continue to give weight to reasonable licensee judgments when deciding whether to impose sanctions in a particular case." Quoting Justice Powell's "expectation that Commission will continue to proceed cautiously," Judge Ginsburg predicted that "the potential chilling effect of the FCC's generic definition . . . will be tempered by the Commission's restrained enforcement policy." She emphasized that "the FCC may regulate [indecent] material only with due respect for the high value our Constitution places on what the people say and hear."

But the court balked at the FCC's decision to shrink the late-night hours to which indecent speech was to be relegated (the so-called safe harbor period) to after midnight. It held that indecency regulation could not be accomplished constitutionally "unless the FCC adopts a reasonable safe harbor rule." Congress saw things differently, however, and in 1989 passed a budget rider that would have eliminated the safe harbor entirely. But the court reiterated that it meant what it said, and in a subsequent ruling held that the First Amendment precludes the government from imposing a total ban on indecent broadcasts and that Congress could not constitutionally repeal the safe harbor. After that, the court ultimately approved a safe harbor rule that allowed indecent broadcasts between 10 p.m. and 6 a.m.

But there was a bigger problem with the FCC's "generic" approach to indecency beyond the times of day during which such material must be kept off the air. When the definition of "indecent" speech was limited to George Carlin's "seven dirty words," the law presented little question of interpretation. The law may not have made much sense, but at least its boundaries were clear. But once the Commission adopted the generic standard, it had to develop its meaning "on a case-by-case basis," and the policy lacked any definite limits or analytic precision. To make matters worse, most indecency rulings are never made public, so the FCC was operating under a body of secret, non-binding law. Well over 90 percent of its indecency decisions were unpublished, informal letter rulings that are stored in individual complaint files at the FCC. In short, the FCC's case-by-case approach clarified nothing, and the agency hardly went out of its way to make things better.

HICKLIN RIDES AGAIN

After the FCC adopted its generic standard, there was no longer any real answer to the DC Circuit's original concern that the indecency rules might be used to ban broadcasts of classic literature, including works by Shakespeare, Chaucer, Hemingway, and James Joyce. This presented a problem once again for Pacifica Radio, whose edgy format included readings from James Joyce's ULYSSES to mark "Bloomsday," the annual celebration of the writer's life each June 16 (the date of the events described in the book). Could the reading go forward under the FCC's new indecency standard? Pacifica's lawyer, John Crigler, decided to find out, and he wrote a letter to the Commission that quoted passages from ULYSSES and asked whether the broadcast would run afoul of the rules.

This presented the FCC with a dilemma. Was it prepared to declare that the indecency rules banned an on-air reading from a literary classic that had been the center of free speech controversies half a century earlier? In 1934 – the same year the FCC was created – courts had ruled that publication of ULYSSES could not be prohibited under Comstock-era obscenity law. Would the FCC now confirm the DC Circuit's worst fears by saying officially that the indecency standard revived the *Hicklin* rule? On the other hand, the Commission had just "clarified" its indecency rules in response to extreme political pressure. How could it realistically green-light a broadcast that included numerous references to "sexual or excretory organs or activities" as well as a number of the Carlin words?

The task of responding to Pacifica's request fell to James McKinney, the FCC's Media Bureau chief, and he did what any seasoned bureaucrat would do. He punted. The FCC could not issue declaratory rulings in advance of a broadcast, he explained in a letter to Pacifica, because the First Amendment does not permit the government to engage in prior restraint. Normally, this is sound constitutional advice, but it rings a bit hollow when espoused by a federal agency that threatens penalties up to license revocation for indecency infractions, yet provides neither a coherent standard nor guidance when particular problems arise. McKinney's letter said that Pacifica should decide for itself whether to take a chance on airing the Bloomsday reading using the "generic" definition as its guide. The full Commission affirmed McKinney's decision not to issue a declaratory ruling, leaving broadcasters generally in the dark about how the standards apply to particular cases. This illustrates why the rule of thumb for compliance with the indecency rules is "when in doubt, leave it out."

This message is reinforced by the very existence of the indecency rules even when the FCC declines to take action. The vagueness of the standard, and its inability to take artistic merit into account, explains how the Commission's policy effectively banned from American television a seven-hour Peabody Award-winning BBC mini-series entitled *The Singing Detective*. The show aired on various public television stations between 1988 and 1990, and had received almost universal praise as a masterpiece. Steven Bochco, creator of *Hill Street Blues* and *NYPD Blue*, called *The Singing Detective* "seven of the best hours I have ever seen on a television set." Marvin Kitman of *Newsday* called it the kind of program that "extends the parameters of what TV drama can do and reclaims TV as a creative medium." Vincent Canby and John J. O'Connor of the *New York Times*, in separate reviews, wrote that *The Singing Detective* "set[s] a new standard for all films," and "opened up the boundaries of TV drama, making the special form as challenging and compelling as the very best of film and theater."

None of this praise mattered when the FCC received an indecency complaint. San Francisco's KQED had presented a *Singing Detective* marathon on New Year's Day 1990, and one viewer complained to the FCC. He sent fuzzy videotapes of the five minutes or so he claimed were indecent, depicting brief images of nudity (of a cadaver) and a short scene in which a child is shown witnessing a nongraphic sexual encounter. The Commission should have been able to make short work of the matter, and if it had a coherent legal standard, could have done so. The critical acclaim, the Peabody Award, and the serious content should easily have outweighed the few allegedly offensive moments in the seven-hour production. But the FCC did not consider artistic merit or the program as a whole. In fact, the Commission did not even know what the show was about. Its staff evaluated the program based solely on the few moments of video that accompanied the complaint.

The investigation lasted more than a year and led to discussions at the agency's highest levels. Staff members of all five commissioners watched the tape and then met to discuss the fate of KQED. Unlike the situation with Pacifica's Bloomsday request, the FCC was not being asked for an assessment in advance of the broadcast, and could not avoid answering the question by claiming that it would amount to prior restraint. So, in the case of *The Singing Detective*, the agency was paralyzed. The matter languished for months, during which time KQED was in regulatory limbo. The station had other matters pending at the Commission and could not afford the black mark of an indecency fine, so it hired Washington counsel and spent thousands of dollars defending the program. The complaint ultimately came to nothing, but the long investigation served as an object lesson for KQED or any other station that might consider presenting groundbreaking programming.

Neither broadcasters nor the FCC staff could figure out the limits of the generic indecency standard. In 2001, the Commission issued a policy statement designed to help clarify the standard by providing "interpretive guidance" to licensees, but it provided little help. Within weeks of its release, the FCC's Enforcement Bureau issued a $7,000 proposed fine to Portland, Oregon's noncommercial radio station KBOO-FM for the broadcast of a rap song entitled "Your Revolution." The song, written and performed by award-winning poet and performance artist Sarah Jones, was a loose reworking of Gil Scott-Heron's classic poem, "The Revolution Will Not Be Televised." According to Jones, "*Your Revolution* was written as a response to music on mainstream radio which often treats women as sex objects and play things."

Although "Your Revolution" had been performed for junior-high and high-school students in educational programs coordinated through the New York City Board of Education, the FCC concluded that the song was indecent because it contained "unmistakably patently offensive sexual references." It was not swayed by KBOO's arguments that the sexual references in "Your Revolution" must be evaluated in context as contemporary social commentary, and expressly "rejected an approach to indecency that would hold that material is not *per se* indecent if the material has merit." Eventually, however, and (not coincidentally) after Sarah Jones showed a willingness to pursue the matter in court, the Commission reconsidered its position. The Enforcement Bureau reversed itself in February 2003 – nearly eighteen months later – but did so without offering any coherent reason why it changed its mind, much less any explanation as to how the indecency standard was supposed to work. It said only that the broadcast presented "a very close case" and that, "on balance and in context, the sexual descriptions in the song are not sufficiently graphic to warrant sanction."

And so it went. During this same period, the Enforcement Bureau recommended another $7,000 fine, this time for a commercial station's broadcasts of a "radio edit" of the Eminem song "The Real Slim Shady." Although the station played a version of the song that omitted offensive language through muting and overdubbing, the

Commission found even the edited version "contains unmistakable offensive sexual references." Six months later, however, the Bureau reversed itself, describing the sexual references in the song as "oblique," and not "expressed in terms sufficiently explicit or graphic enough to be found patently offensive." It rescinded the proposed fine, but left the meaning of indecency even more opaque. So much for clarifying the generic standard "case-by-case."

Broadcasters could be certain only of this: If any part of a broadcast dealt with sex or excretory references, it could trigger a fine or other sanction if the FCC considered it "patently offensive." The content of the work "as a whole" didn't matter and neither did artistic or literary merit. All that mattered was how the material struck the regulators at a particular point in time. The Commission's generalized explanations provided no clues as to why "Your Revolution" was thought to contain "unmistakably patently offensive sexual references" on first hearing but eighteen months later the same references were "not sufficiently graphic to warrant sanction." Nor was there any way to tell why the FCC found Eminem's graphic (but muted) references "oblique," where six months earlier they had been "sufficiently explicit or graphic" to warrant sanction.

The only things that kept the FCC's indecency regime somewhat in check were the remnants of the restrained enforcement policy the Commission had pledged the Supreme Court in *Pacifica*. These included forbearance from regulation where indecent references were fleeting, isolated, or inadvertent; the nighttime "safe harbor"; the relative infrequency of indecency findings; and moderation on the level of fines. But those barriers to more muscular enforcement were about to come crashing down.

OF FLEETING EXPLETIVES AND WARDROBE MALFUNCTIONS . . .

This was the fight Brent Bozell had been spoiling for. Ever since founding PTC in 1995, he had been looking for the opportunity to attack the television networks and to show up the FCC as a toothless watchdog. Politically, the timing was perfect. Ever since the *Pacifica* decision, indecency enforcement at the FCC had tended to be cyclical. The Commission would announce some policy or initiative only to be brushed back from the plate (but not benched) by the courts. Things would then simmer on the back burner until something happened to turn up the political heat. That had been the pattern since *Pacifica*, when the Commission first announced its restrained enforcement policy, and again nine years later with adoption of the generic policy. By 2003, almost a decade had passed since the courts last decided a case on the indecency rules, and so the issue was ready to pop. All it needed was for someone to light the fuse.

Bozell was all too happy to volunteer. He had not made much of a splash since creating PTC a number of years before, but an opportunity presented itself with NBC's January 2003 telecast of the *Golden Globe Awards*. Bono's spontaneous exclamation that it was "fucking brilliant" to be a winner had escaped the network censor's bleep, and Bozell knew just what to do. He fused a family knack for marketing (his grandfather helped found a leading advertising firm and coined the slogan "pork – the other white meat") with his father's passion for religious and political activism, and mounted a campaign directed at the FCC. Within a matter of days, PTC was responsible for flooding the agency with 18,000 complaints.

Bozell's group was able to do this because it had just created what it proudly touted as the "first-ever web-driven complaint form." In the old days, someone who wanted to file an FCC complaint had to grab a pen and paper or warm up the old typewriter and fire off a missive via the US Postal Service. Some groups would organize letter-writing campaigns when they got their members sufficiently riled up, but the process was difficult and time-consuming. PTC, however, was born at the dawn of the Internet Age, and Bozell's skillset included the use of more modern methods of getting the agency's attention. PTC's website became – in its words – "the 'go-to' spot for online activism against television violence, sex, and profanity." PTC's annual reports described this as "a massive, coordinated and determined campaign" to lobby the FCC to punish programming it deemed to be "indecent" and/or "profane." And Bozell lobbied to manipulate the FCC's internal processes to make the public response seem even more significant than it was.

FUN WITH NUMBERS

This was classic Comstockery – using numbers to make the group's methods seem scientific and to inflate the issue to make it appear that the American public was clamoring for censorship. But, in fact, it was just a well-oiled machine of Bozell's creation to Astroturf the issue. PTC staff members monitored and recorded TV shows to find examples of indecent programming and used their findings to stoke email campaigns to generate complaints against particular programs. The group boasted that the "Internet has provided the PTC with the ability to recruit and mobilize an army. . . . With a click of a mouse, information and action calls can be sent nationwide."

As PTC described its operation, "[e]very day, the PTC's trained analysts record detailed information about each and every prime time broadcast series (as well as a significant portion of original cable programming) in a highly sophisticated, custom-built computer database, ETS (Entertainment Tracking System)." The group's "analysts" used standardized logs to note scenes and language: "under the category 'Sex' there are 94 possible entries, including 'sexual innuendo,' 'non-marital,' 'pregnancy,' 'ejaculate,' and 'phone sex.'" The possible entries for foul language numbered "in the hundreds, ranging from 'Ass' to 'Whore.'" Using such data – which appeared to focus more on Bozell's moralistic proclivities than any discernible legal standard – PTC would send out email alerts seeking to gin up FCC complaints.

As part of the campaign, PTC operated a website entitled "Cleanup TV," with its online complaint form as its centerpiece. The forms were already filled out with information listing the shows PTC had decided to target – all a person had to do was add his or her name and address. PTC reassured its recruits that it was quite alright if the "complainant" had never seen the show, or knew nothing about it. As the website emphasized, *"You do not have to experience an indecent broadcast firsthand in order to become outraged and file a complaint with the FCC!"* The campaign got results, and the number of complaints sent to the FCC skyrocketed. According to FCC statistics, the agency received only 111 indecency complaints in 2000 and 346 in 2001. But as PTC became more active – and especially after it implemented its online complaint system – the numbers jumped to 13,9 20032 in 2003, and 1,068,802 in 2004.

But the statistics were deceptive. No doubt, PTC and other advocacy groups had gotten people to file many complaints, but Bozell wanted more. He successfully pressured the Commission to change the way the complaints were tallied. After his January 2004 congressional testimony (and in the wake of the Super Bowl fiasco), the FCC began to count submissions received by the five commissioners' offices and those filed through the agency's general email address as separate complaints (on top of those submitted directly to the Enforcement Bureau). Because PTC's website was structured to forward its indecency complaints simultaneously to all of these offices, it meant that every PTC-generated complaint was counted five, six, or even seven times. The FCC even acknowledged that this "change in method" largely "explained the increase in complaints" between 2003 and 2004, although that key fact was buried deep in the footnotes in one of the Commission's periodic reports. In other words, the difference between the 200,000-some complaints the FCC reported in 2003 and the million-plus it clocked in 2004 was mainly a matter of accounting.

Whatever the actual numbers, this hardly represented a groundswell of actual public sentiment. According to FCC statistics obtained through the Freedom of Information Act (FOIA), 99.8 percent of the 202,032 indecency complaints reported in 2003 came from PTC, and in 2004 the reported percentage was even higher – 99.9 percent. PTC would later denounce these numbers, with Tim Winter (Bozell's successor as PTC president) testily claiming: "Whoever gave that number at the FCC was a liar." Winter's consternation may be understandable, as knowledge of the actual source of complaints reveals how PTC's claim about a national uprising of concerned parents was pure hype.

But it is a little difficult to credibly express outrage after years of annual reports describing PTC's "online activism" as the centerpiece of its efforts, and stressing that complainants need not have actually seen the offending TV shows in order to contact the FCC. PTC even admitted this in 2005, when curious reporters tried to figure out why the number of indecency complaints sent to the FCC dropped 96 percent between the first and second quarters of that year, from 157,016 to just 6,161. They called Melissa Caldwell, PTC's director of research, who helpfully explained the decline by noting that her group had "orchestrated fewer complaint campaigns this year than in previous years."

Another incident a couple of years later further illuminated PTC's outsized role in manufacturing faux outrage. A January 2007 Fox Network telecast of a football game between the Philadelphia Eagles and the New Orleans Saints included a crowd shot that, for a second or two, showed one spectator wearing a T-shirt with the slogan "Fuck da Eagles" (Figure 8.5). It was the kind of live TV moment that never would have led to FCC action under the restrained enforcement policy that excused fleeting, isolated, and inadvertent expletives.

But things were different in the post-*Golden Globes* era of indecency enforcement, and PTC leapt into action. It created an online complaint form with information on the telecast already filled in, and sent email alerts to its network of activists, asking that they bombard the FCC to vent their outrage (Figure 8.6). As with PTC's earlier campaigns against network shows, the tactic got quick results. The FCC received a total of 148,281 indecency complaints in January 2007 alone. While Commission statistics didn't identify how many of the complaints were about the Saints–Eagles game, the totals for the year tell the story: This was the only such campaign PTC organized that year, and January was the only month the FCC received more than 4,000 indecency complaints. In fact, the average monthly total in 2007 was just over 500 complaints. So, as it happens, the month PTC mounted its anti-"Fuck da Eagles" campaign, the FCC received 96 percent of all complaints for all programs for the entire year.

The same thing played out a couple of years later when PTC mounted a jihad against the animated sitcom *Family Guy*, a show that frequently lampooned PTC

FIGURE 8.5 Screenshot from New Orleans Saints versus Philadelphia Eagles football game
Source: YouTube (www.youtube.com/watch?v=7upg4sn1TZs).

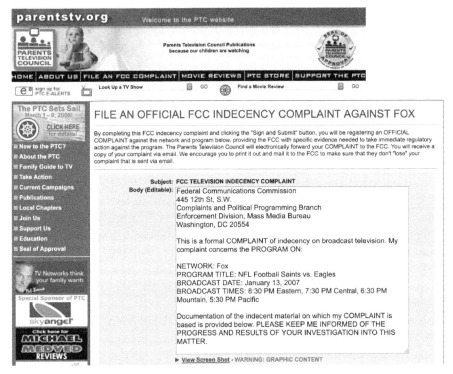

FIGURE 8.6 Parents Television Council online complaint form
Source: https://web.archive.org/web/20071013083822/https://www.parentstv.org/PTC/action/
FoxFootball/main.asp.

and other anti-indecency crusaders. PTC sent out an action alert about a March 2009 episode and managed to generate nearly 180,000 complaints (by the FCC's inflated count). This represented 99.4 percent of the complaints the Commission had received for the year to that point. And so it went during the years of PTC's most intensive activism.

Whether or not PTC was responsible for most of the indecency complaints flooding the FCC, its crusades certainly didn't reflect most viewers' preferences. Far from it. PTC grew out of Bozell's stated intention to "change the culture," so its main targets were among the most popular and critically acclaimed shows at the time. Series that regularly made PTC's "worst of TV" lists (and complaint campaigns) were considered the best of TV for everyone else, including such shows as *C.S.I.: Crime Scene Investigation, Friends*, and *Will & Grace*.

C.S.I., the second-most popular network program during the 2003–2004 season with a weekly average of 25 million viewers, won the People's Choice Award for "Favorite Television Dramatic Series" in both 2003 and 2004. *Friends*, still a favorite in syndication, was ranked fourth and fifth in the ratings those years with an average weekly audience of nearly 22 million viewers, winning the Emmy for "Outstanding Comedy Series" in 2002. *Will & Grace* was among the top fifteen most-watched programs at the time, with an average audience of 16 million viewers. It won an Emmy for "Outstanding Comedy Series" in 2000 and the People's Choice Award for "Favorite Comedy Series" each year between 2000 and 2004. The combined totals of all PTC's complaint campaigns (even when inflated by the FCC's multiple counting) represented but a tiny sliver of the numbers of viewers who regularly tuned to, and enjoyed, what PTC believed were the "worst" programs.

Of course, none of this mattered to PTC, which had its own notions of what programming disserves the public interest. In its view, a show like *Will & Grace*, which it described as a comedy "about the friendship between a gay man and his best friend, a quirky straight woman," had unacceptable levels of "crude innuendo," including "both hetero- and homosexual." PTC's campaign against *Will & Grace* was merely an updated version of the Mae West–Charlie McCarthy flap, tinged with Bozell's pronounced antagonism toward homosexuality. In this way, the FCC was enlisted into the culture war with the battle lines drawn by advocacy groups like PTC, the American Family Association, the Family Research Council, and others.

All of this was done in plain sight. Publicly available information from FCC reports, agency responses to FOIA requests, and press coverage of the issue highlighted the role of activist groups in manufacturing the indecency "crisis," but this did not deter Congress and FCC officials from acting as though it were real. The Commission had been under increasing pressure from Congress ever since the *Golden Globe Awards* telecast, and after the Super Bowl debacle it chose to go with the political flow. Everyone at the agency knew the complaint numbers were false, but that was irrelevant. That's just how things work in Washington.

THE NEW ABNORMAL

The FCC had been the original source of the revelation that PTC's campaigns had spawned 98.6 to 99.9 percent of indecency complaints beginning in 2003, but that hardly deterred the agency from overhauling its policies based on what it claimed was a "direct response to the increase of public complaints." Although it knew better, the Commission observed that "during the last few years ... we have witnessed increasing public unease with the nature of broadcast material" and that "Americans have become more concerned about the content of television programming." So, beginning in 2004, the FCC embarked on a series of actions to redefine the indecency standard, eliminate any notion of a "restrained" approach to enforcement, and vastly ratchet up the penalties for violations. As then-Chairman Michael Powell testified to the Senate Commerce Committee, the Commission had embarked on "the most aggressive enforcement regime in decades" and taken a series of steps "to sharpen our enforcement blade."

He wasn't kidding. Although the PTC complaints were ersatz, the policy changes were quite real. In a series of decisions, the Commission overruled key precedents that had been the basis of its restrained approach to enforcing the law both before and after the Supreme Court's *Pacifica* ruling. The FCC proposed fines or extracted settlement payments from broadcast stations and networks amounting to nearly $8 million in 2004 alone – almost four times the total of all proposed fines in the previous ten years combined. It issued twelve notices proposing stiff fines for presumed indecency violations and reversed the Enforcement Bureau's *Golden Globe Order*, thus eliminating the policy immunizing "fleeting expletives" from penalties.

But that was just the opening round. In 2006, Congress passed the Broadcast Decency Enforcement Act, which not only ratified the FCC's radical approach to enforcement but boosted the level of fines tenfold. The FCC already had used various ploys to jack up the level of fines even before the law passed, including treating each indecent word in a broadcast as a separate violation and fining each network affiliate separately. But under the new law, the aggregate fine to a network for a single, fleeting instance of indecent speech could approach $100 million. There was also mounting pressure for the FCC to begin revoking broadcast licenses.

The flash-points were pretty predictable. There was the Super Bowl incident, of course, which everyone knew would result in a stiff fine. Hundreds of thousands of manufactured complaints and congressional ire insisted on it, regardless of the law or any explanations from the network about how it happened. The FCC got in line (as it always does) and announced the largest indecency fine ever for a single incident (up to that point), of $550,000 for twenty-three CBS-owned stations. The announcement came in what FCC procedure dubs a "Notice of Apparent Liability," or NAL. The broadcaster who receives an NAL has the right to contest the sanction, but if the FCC doesn't change its mind, it ripens into a "forfeiture," or, in plain English, a "fine." It took a while for the Super Bowl to work through the FCC's administrative processes – no one believed the agency might change its mind in response to legal arguments – and the Commission announced its final decision to impose a fine in February 2006.

After the Super Bowl NAL was announced, and the Commission grew more comfortable flashing what Chairman Powell called its "enforcement blade," no record for "highest fine" would stand for long, and no amount would seem too high. Shortly thereafter, the FCC announced a $1.2 million fine for a Fox reality show called *Married by America*. Later, when the FCC issued the Super Bowl forfeiture order, it simultaneously announced fines in other cases totaling $355,000 for six programs, found that four other shows had violated the rules (but proposed no fines), and dismissed various other complaints. These combined decisions were part of what the FCC called its "*Omnibus Order*," which it said was to provide "guidance and clarification" for its new approach to regulating indecency.

Mainly it had the opposite effect. The *Omnibus Order* was a tableau of arbitrary and almost random outcomes. The FCC found that the isolated use of the word "bullshit" in episodes of ABC's *NYPD Blue* was indecent, but the use of the words "dick" and "dickhead" were not. It found that uses of the words "fuck" and "shit" by the subjects of the Martin Scorsese documentary *The Blues: Godfathers and Sons* were indecent, even though it had previously found that similar uses of the same words in an unedited broadcast of the film *Saving Private Ryan* were not. The FCC also found indecency in the utterance of the word "bullshitter" during a news interview on the CBS morning program *Early Show*.

The FCC also used the *Omnibus Order* to amplify its new approach to live broadcasts (after Bono's overly enthusiastic acceptance of a Golden Globe). It targeted brief, unscripted comments on 2002 and 2003 Fox Network telecasts of the *Billboard Music Awards*. In the 2002 broadcast, Cher accepted an award and exulted: "'People have been telling me I'm on the way out every year, right? So fuck 'em.'" In 2003, presenter Nicole Richie ad-libbed: "Have you ever tried to get cow shit out of a Prada purse? It's not so fucking simple."

The FCC was on a roll. Now under the leadership of Chairman Kevin Martin, it issued an NAL that proposed a $3.35 million fine for CBS stations that broadcast an episode of the prime-time program *Without a Trace*. The episode, inspired by a *Frontline* documentary, sought to address the unhealthy and negative results of unsupervised after-school teen activities and sexuality. The dramatization included two brief scenes that suggested, but did not depict, sexual activity among teenagers. But this was too much for the Commission (and, more to the point, PTC). Taking on the role of "super editor" for the networks, the FCC ruled that the sixty seconds or so that were the subject of the complaint went "well beyond what the story line could reasonably be said to require."

The Commission's reaction would have been difficult to rationalize even in isolation. But it was nearly impossible to understand when compared to its ruling about an episode of *The Oprah Winfrey Show* just weeks earlier in the *Omnibus Order*. The episode of *Oprah* had covered the same subject as *Without a Trace*, and included graphic descriptions of teen sex at after-school parties and frank exchanges about specific sex acts. But this was just fine, the FCC found, because if the material is shocking, "it is due to the existence of such practices among teenagers rather than the vulgarity or explicitness of the sexual depictions or descriptions." Plus, it "would have been difficult to educate parents regarding teenagers' sexual activities without at least briefly describing those activities." So, the difference between a $3.35 million fine for *Without a Trace* and a pass for *Oprah* was the federal government's editorial and artistic judgment about a scene that lasted less than a minute.

This schizophrenic response would have been inexplicable but for one thing – *Without a Trace* had been the target of one of PTC's focused complaint campaigns, while *Oprah* had not. This was the second airing of the *Without a Trace* episode, and PTC was loaded for bear. The show aired at 10 p.m. on New Year's Eve,

2004, and within two weeks PTC had sent out an "E-Alert" to drum up complaints. Because the show aired after 10 p.m. Eastern, in the "safe harbor" hours, PTC urged its followers in the Central or Mountain time zones "to flood the FCC with thousands of complaints about this outrageous episode." And it wasn't shy about revealing both its purpose and its methods. The E-Alert made clear that PTC's goal was to put "pressure on the FCC to make sure they start punishing broadcasters for airing this smut," and that the way to do this was to artificially inflate the numbers. It urged its members to forward the email to "friends, relatives and colleagues in your email address book" to ensure that the "protest will be multiplied many, many times over!" PTC would later claim credit for ginning up some 12,000 complaints with this appeal. It was but a tiny sliver of the 19 million actual viewers of the show, but that was more than enough for the FCC.

The same treatment once again would befall ABC's highly rated and award-winning police drama *NYPD Blue*. PTC and other activist groups had complained about an episode that ran in 2003 in which "an adult woman's nude buttocks" were depicted "for slightly less than seven seconds" in a nonsexual context that illustrated the awkwardness of new family situations. The Commission acknowledged that *NYPD Blue* was an award-winning series written for adult audiences in the final hour of prime time, that the scene in question "related to a broad story line of the show," and that the episode had been preceded by a parental advisory and rating. No matter, the Commission ruled. "On balance," it found the program "patently offensive under contemporary community standards for the broadcast medium" and fined the fifty-two ABC-owned or affiliated stations for airing the episode. The tab for this one came to $1.43 million, which was a relative bargain because the episode aired before Congress jacked up the indecency fines. Under the new law, the total would have been $16.9 million.

One by-product of this campaign of intimidation was that it gave the networks no real choice but to seek a showdown in court. As a rule, broadcasters don't like to sue the FCC. They need to maintain a good relationship with the agency on which they depend for license renewals and a host of other regulatory decisions that affect day-to-day operations. But this feeding frenzy over indecency was out of control, and there was no end in sight since the FCC had all but abdicated the process to the political demands of Congress and anti-indecency activists. Inevitably, litigation ensued involving the four major broadcast networks in multiple cases that, over a span of years, would result in two Supreme Court arguments.

THE BIG CHILL

As the drama played out in court, broadcasters struggled to live with a harsh and increasingly erratic enforcement regime. It was not a time for taking chances. Given the FCC's aggressive actions against award show ad libs, gaffes during sporting events, and even mishaps in newscasts, one of the first casualties of the enforcement campaign was live programming, particularly by smaller broadcasters. Phoenix television stations cut live coverage of a memorial service for Pat Tillman, the former pro football player killed in Afghanistan, when grief-stricken family members uttered profanities during the event. A Vermont station refused to carry a political debate because one of the local politicians had previously used expletives on air. A Pennsylvania station dropped all live news coverage that was not directly related to public safety. These broadcasters were not just being overly cautious. In this environment almost anything could be the subject of a complaint, and there was no telling what the FCC might do.

NBC's broadcast of the 2004 Olympics Games was the subject of complaints because the opening ceremonies incorporated a representation of a nude male in the style of an ancient Greek sculpture (actually an actor in a unitard). Rather than dismiss the complaint outright, as a rational agency would have done, the FCC demanded that NBC submit tapes of its Olympic coverage. The Fox network opted to pixilate the bare butt of a *cartoon* character in its prime-time animated series *Family Guy* because the show was a frequent PTC target, and the FCC seriously considered even such obviously frivolous complaints.

There were various ripple effects. When NASCAR star Dale Earnhardt Jr. blurted out the expletive "shit" in a live interview on NBC following his fifth win at Talladega, PTC demanded that the FCC "impose the maximum fine allowable by law against every NBC affiliate that aired this offense" and that the FCC "consider license revocation." NASCAR fined Earnhardt $10,000 and stripped him of his first-place standing, explaining that drivers had been warned to speak carefully "because the Federal Communications Commission would be watching and listening."

The chill affected radio and television stations alike. Some radio stations stopped covering live news events altogether or tried to keep their microphones far from crowds to avoid picking up random profanities. A Boston station declined to provide live coverage of protests at the 2004 Democratic National Convention for fear the demonstrators might utter "indecent" or "profane" language. Many stations abandoned live in-studio performances by musicians, speakers, and comics. Others curtailed live interviews, with some stations placing certain categories of interviewees "off limits" (e.g., no comedians of any kind) rather than making individualized judgments. Call-in shows on topical issues, including local government, state and national politics, sports and religion, became particularly dicey. As the general manager of two radio stations put it: "You have to watch the theme to make sure you're not offending someone, whether you are discussing gay marriages or the disabled or African-Americans. . . . We really don't want to go there anymore."

But it wasn't just live programming that got curtailed. Anything that touched on "dangerous" subject matter was under the gun, and this often affected the more literary programs – the very stuff Newton Minow harangued broadcasters to air back in the 1960s. Public broadcaster WNET determined that it could not risk showing several highly regarded movies, including *The Cotton Club, Fargo,* and the works of Fellini. Its *Great Performances* series likewise dropped plans to televise *Avenue Q,* the 2004 Tony winner for "Best Musical." PBS edited certain expletives from a documentary on the life of poet and educator Piri Thomas for its *Independent Lens* series, even though the deleted words are essential components of the subject's poetry. Some public broadcasting systems, such as Nebraska Public Television, dropped the documentary altogether. WBAI, Pacifica Radio's flagship station, declined to transmit on air a fiftieth anniversary reading of Allen Ginsberg's classic beat poem "Howl" in 2007, even though an effort to declare it obscene had failed in 1957.

The FCC's cryptic approach to news programming was particularly problematic. In the past it had treated news programs as effectively exempt from the indecency policy – even when one (or many) of the seven "Carlin words" was involved – because the Commission didn't consider the context to be salacious or titillating. So, in 1991, it had dismissed an indecency complaint against NPR for a news story about the trial of mob boss John Gotti which included a clip from a wiretap played in court in which Gotti was heard to repeat the words "fuck" or "fucking" ten times in thirty seconds. No more.

In the *Omnibus Order,* the FCC found the solitary use of the word "bullshitter" in a CBS *Early Show* segment to be particularly "shocking and gratuitous" because it occurred "during a morning news interview." The Commission reconsidered its position once it found that it would have to defend this decision in court, and rescinded its initial indecency finding, explaining that it needed to consider the context and would "defer to CBS's plausible characterization of its own programming" as news. The FCC did not pause to explain how material that it previously considered to be indecent *because* it was presented in a news program also could be exonerated because it *might* be news. But lest broadcasters attempt to derive any guidance from this case, the Commission eliminated that possibility by adding: "To be sure, *there is no outright news exemption from our indecency rules.*" Message to news directors: you are on your own in figuring out the rules.

Needless to say, broadcasters were not reassured. In 2006, CBS affiliates serving roughly 10 percent of US households decided to preempt airing the network's Peabody Award-winning 9/11 documentary on the fifth anniversary of the September 11 terrorist attacks, or to delay its start until after 10 p.m., because the program contained expletives actually spoken in real time by the participants in those tragic events. The network and its affiliates had broadcast the same documentary twice before without incident, but many stations would not take that risk in 2006 after the FCC adopted its more restrictive indecency policy.

Other news and documentary programs were affected as well. Most public broadcast stations declined to air an unedited documentary about troops stationed in Iraq entitled *A Company of Soldiers.* Only 48 of the 349 PBS affiliates requested the unedited version of the documentary because it contained the unvarnished

FIGURE 8.7 Screenshot of WJLA newscast promotion
Source: Internet Archive (https://archive.org/details/WJLA_20110404_210000_ABC_7_News
_at_500/start/1980/end/2040).

language of the troops. Similar examples became commonplace: A *Frontline* report on al-Qaeda was edited to delete an utterance by a horrified onlooker as the second plane hit the World Trade Center, and footage on *NOVA* of a bomb blast during the Iraq war was altered because a soldier's shouts included expletives.

In 2011, Washington, DC, television newscasts were perplexed in how to cover a deranged woman's attack at the National Gallery of Art on Paul Gauguin's 1899 masterpiece *Two Tahitian Women*. The attacker, who later told police that the CIA had implanted a radio in her head, had tried to pull the painting off the wall, calling it "evil" and "very homosexual." Local newscasts variously obscured the Tahitian women's naked breasts, some by pixilating the offending body parts, and others by using a banner as a cover (Figure 8.7). Maybe the FCC would have been in an understanding mood if the stations had declined to Bowdlerize the painting, and then again, maybe not. There was no way to tell, and the stakes were high for any news director who cared to second-guess the Commission's reaction.

THE SPIELBERG EXCEPTION

That broadcasters viewed the Commission's decisions as erratic, random, and utterly lacking in guidance was highlighted in 2004 when ABC decided to re-air the Stephen Spielberg film *Saving Private Ryan*. The movie had been broadcast uncut on Veteran's Day in 2001 and 2002 and had drawn some complaints from another anti-indecency group, the American Family Association. After all, the film's dialogue is peppered with "soldier talk," including fuck and variations thereof (at least twenty-one times); shit, bullshit, and variations thereof; bastard; and hell. But the FCC staff had dismissed the complaints, explaining that *Saving Private Ryan* was neither indecent nor profane because "[t]he expletives used by some characters, in context, do not appear to depict or describe sexual or excretory organs or activities." Even before that, the Commission had approved the unedited airing of Spielberg's *Schindler's List*, even though one scene depicted frontal nudity. But that was then. Since the *Golden Globes* decision, such staff dismissals didn't count for much; the FCC had said explicitly that broadcasters could no longer rely on them.

So it came as little surprise that under the Commission's "get tough" approach to indecency enforcement, stations across the USA in 2004 were loath to take a chance on airing *Saving Private Ryan*, even though it was presented with a special introduction by Senator John McCain, Chairman of the Senate Judiciary Committee (and occasional anti-indecency hawk). Despite this symbolic assurance, 66 out of 225 ABC affiliates refused to broadcast *Saving Private Ryan*, and the Oscar-winning film was preempted in approximately 30 percent of the United States. The film was not seen on the air in major markets such as Atlanta, Boston, and Orlando. In its place, some stations aired the made-for-TV *Andy Griffith Show* reunion *Return to Mayberry*, or in other cases a country/western music special.

This was embarrassing. The Commission had insisted repeatedly that the indecency policy did not amount to censorship, and that it was intended only to go after shock jocks, trash-talking celebrities, and purveyors of gratuitous sex on TV. It was not supposed to restrict modern classics (and patriotic ones, at that). The agency had hoped it could avoid saying anything about it one way or the other. Some stations asked the FCC for guidance in advance to determine whether the broadcast might contravene the FCC's rules – not an unreasonable request in light of the fact that the FCC had twice before denied complaints against *Saving Private Ryan*. However, the Commission refused to respond, claiming (as it had years earlier for ULYSSES) that to do so would constitute a prior restraint. But its bid to avoid saying anything about the issue was thwarted when the American Family Association, taking a page from PTC's playbook, sent out an action alert to its members and generated several thousand complaints after the movie was aired.

Now, the FCC not only had to face the fact that its indecency policy had a demonstrably pernicious chilling effect on quality programming, it also had to explain if *Saving Private Ryan* was different from shows it had fined, and (more problematically) in what way. Predictably, it denied the complaints – upholding them would only have made matters worse – but had no clue how to explain its decision coherently. The Commission acknowledged that the film "includes at least one word (i.e., 'fuck' and its variations) which fall within the first prong of our indecency definition," while saying nothing about whether other language in *Saving*

Private Ryan also triggered the test, including "shit," "bullshit," "shitty," "bastard," "ass," "asshole," "crap," "son of a bitch," "bastard," "prick," "pee," "cocksucker," "smart ass," "thought you liked it in the ass," "hard on," and "hell." It focused instead on whether the complained-of material was "gratuitous" or "in any way intended or used to pander, titillate or shock," and concluded that it was not.

The FCC pointed to a number of factors to explain why *Saving Private Ryan* was different: the film had "social, scientific or artistic value" and won both Golden Globe and Academy Awards in 1999; it was a realistic depiction of the fierce combat during the Normandy invasion," and the expletives "realistically reflect[ed] the soldiers' strong human reactions to . . . unspeakable conditions"; deleting or bleeping the language "would have altered the nature of the artistic work and diminished the power, realism and immediacy of the film experience for viewers"; the broadcast was designed "to honor American veterans on the national holiday specifically designed for that purpose" and "was introduced by a surviving veteran of the D-Day landing at Normandy and by Senator John McCain"; it was "not intended as family entertainment" and was preceded by TV ratings and viewer advisories.

The FCC's explanation was all very reasonable and rational but for one thing: it contradicted pretty much everything the Commission had said about its indecency rules since the *Golden Globes* reversal. Except for the bit about the McCain introduction, the agency had rejected every argument that it now latched onto for explaining why *Saving Private Ryan* should not be considered indecent. Before this, it hadn't mattered that a show addressed important subjects and had won awards, nor had the fact that the program warned viewers with advisories and used TV ratings. Appeals to "realism" had been rejected; the very concept of indecency rested on the premise that "serious merit" was not enough to save broadcasters from indecency fines. The more the FCC said about its indecency rules, the less understandable they became.

The one constant was this: The FCC was almost certain to impose a heavy sanction if key members of Congress insisted on it, but it would not do so if key legislators indicated that it was okay to take a pass. The fact that John McCain had blessed *Saving Private Ryan* was therefore the most important factor in the FCC's decision. Yet, even with McCain's on-air endorsement, the Commission was unwilling to dismiss the complaints without first lofting a trial balloon. To ensure that it had political cover, someone at the agency leaked to the press its intention to clear the broadcast several weeks before it released the order. It was the sort of maneuver that serves the FCC's political purpose but does not play so well when judges get involved.

BROADCASTERS' DAY IN COURT

Challenges to the FCC's bulked-up indecency regime came from several angles. CBS appealed the Super Bowl "wardrobe malfunction" order, but had to pay the

$550,000 fine to be able to proceed to the US Court of Appeals for the Third Circuit in Philadelphia. Fox, joined by the other networks, challenged the *Omnibus Order* in the Second Circuit in New York, taking the lead in that case because of the FCC findings regarding the Cher and Nicole Richie ad libs from the *Billboard Music Awards*. ABC would later add another appeal in the Second Circuit, challenging the $1.43 million fine for *NYPD Blue*. Meanwhile, the Department of Justice was pursuing an action against Fox in federal district court to collect the fine for *Married by America*.

The litigation would drag on for six more years, and in each case (but one) courts ruled that the FCC had gone too far. Although the primary problem with the FCC's policy is that it infringes the First Amendment, the initial decisions did not take that issue on directly. As a matter of judicial restraint, courts generally try to avoid declaring a law or policy unconstitutional if there is a narrower way to decide the case. And so the appellate courts first threw out the *Omnibus Order* and the Super Bowl fine by holding that the FCC had failed to adequately explain its change in policy, and that the new rules were "arbitrary and capricious" in violation of the Administrative Procedure Act. The Second Circuit also said that it was skeptical that the FCC could come up with an explanation that would survive First Amendment scrutiny, but sent the matter back to the agency to give another try.

The Bush Administration didn't wait for a better explanation, however, and took the matter to the Supreme Court, which held five–four that the FCC's reasons for its change in policy were good enough for government work. Justice Antonin Scalia's opinion for the fractured Court said that the agency was not required to give reasons why its new policy was "better" than the old one – that it need only be "rational" – which is to say, not crazy. It's a pretty low bar. Justice Scalia discounted concerns expressed by dissenting justices that the new policy would place special burdens on small-town stations, which, he wrote, "generally cannot afford or cannot attract foul-mouthed glitteratae from Hollywood." Justice Scalia noted that the Court needn't deal with the First Amendment questions just yet, adding that whether the policy is unconstitutional "will be decided soon enough, perhaps in this very case."

This was significant foreshadowing, especially given the opinions of the other justices. Justice Stevens, who wrote the *Pacifica* opinion back in 1978 that narrowly upheld the indecency standard, observed that the FCC's current interpretation "bears no resemblance to what *Pacifica* contemplated," and, "[m]ost distressingly, the Commission appears to be entirely unaware of this fact." Justice Ginsburg added that there was "no way to hide the long shadow the First Amendment casts over what the Commission has done." Even justices in the majority, who concurred in the result, raised doubts about whether the indecency policy could survive constitutional review. Justice Thomas joined the majority "as a matter of administrative law," but said that the Court's precedents including *Red Lion* and *Pacifica* were incoherent and led to a "deep intrusion into the First Amendment rights of broadcasters." Justice Kennedy, widely acknowledged as a First Amendment stalwart, joined the majority only in part, and made a point of reserving judgment on whether the FCC's action was constitutional.

The Supreme Court decision was the very definition of a Pyrrhic victory for the FCC. The case was being sent back to the court of appeals with instructions that it rule on the First Amendment challenge after a majority of justices had hinted pretty broadly that the new indecency policy was unconstitutional. What did the FCC think would happen on remand?

The appellate judges didn't leave the agency in suspense. When the case arrived at the court of appeals, Judge Rosemary Pooler grinned as FCC lawyer Jake Lewis approached the lectern. "Welcome back to the Second Circuit," she said. It was a pure New York greeting, and after that beginning, matters only deteriorated for the Commission. Judges Pierre Leval and Peter Hall picked up where Judge Pooler had left off, peppering Lewis with hypothetical questions about the FCC's inconsistencies and what programs it would approve. They were in no mood for sugar-coating the argument with euphemisms or the FCC's "f-word" baby talk. When Judge Pooler wanted to know if the FCC had exempted news programming from indecency sanctions, she asked if a station would get in trouble for covering a zoning board meeting where a citizen complained that the board "fucked up my house."

Lewis gamely sparred with the judges, but the Commission had given him few good cards to play. And this was reflected in the decision, this time focusing on the indecency rules' First Amendment problems. The court found "little rhyme or reason to [the Commission's] decisions," leaving broadcasters "to guess at whether an expletive will be deemed 'integral' to a program or whether the FCC will consider a particular broadcast [acceptable]." It scoffed at how the Commission could believe that "the words 'fuck' and 'shit' were integral to the 'realism and immediacy of the film experience for viewers'" in *Saving Private Ryan* but not for the Martin Scorsese documentary *The Blues*. Highlighting irony with sarcasm, it noted: "We query how fleeting expletives could be more essential to the 'realism' of a fictional movie than to the 'realism' of interviews with real people about real life events." And it suggested that the FCC "was simply more comfortable with the themes in 'Saving Private Ryan,' a mainstream movie with a familiar cultural milieu, than it was with 'The Blues,' which largely profiled an outsider genre of musical experience."

The Second Circuit was equally unimpressed with the FCC's waffling about whether news programs were exempt from the indecency rules. It pointed to the Commission's flip-flop over the use of the word "bullshitter" on CBS's *The Early Show*, noting that the agency first said that the word was "shocking and gratuitous" because of its use on a morning news show and then excused it because – you guessed it – the word was used in a news interview. "In other words," the court dryly observed, "the FCC reached diametrically opposite conclusions at different stages of the proceedings for precisely the same reason – that the word 'bullshitter' was uttered during a news program." Yet still the Commission insisted there was no "news exemption," because it wanted to keep its enforcement options open.

With such arbitrary rules (if you even could call them rules), it was no mystery to the Second Circuit why broadcasters erred on the side of self-censoring programming when faced with the prospect of heavy fines or threats to their licenses. It noted that CBS affiliates had declined to air the rebroadcast of the 9/11 documentary out of fear of indecency complaints, the curtailment of live and local programming, and the impact on network entertainment shows, and concluded that the policy as formulated by the FCC violated the First Amendment. It was careful to note that it was not saying "that the FCC could not create a constitutional policy," but this surely was not it.

The challenges to the Super Bowl and *NYPD Blue* fines followed a similar course, but not with quite the same punch as the Second Circuit's demolition of the FCC's policy. The Third Circuit reaffirmed its decision to strike down the Super Bowl fine because the agency had penalized CBS stations for a broadcast that took place *before* the change in policy in *Golden Globes*. A separate Second Circuit panel threw out the *NYPD Blue* fine, and simply adopted the reasoning of the decision voiding the FCC policy as being unconstitutionally vague. This set up two new bids for Supreme Court review: one from the Second Circuit (combining the appeals from the *Omnibus Order* and the *NYPD Blue* fine) and a second one from the Third Circuit *Super Bowl* decision.

The Supreme Court took up the Second Circuit appeal first, and this time it agreed that the FCC's actions were invalid. The decision was unanimous but limited. Once again, the Court declined to reach the ultimate First Amendment question. Instead, it held that applying the fleeting expletives policy to network broadcasts that took place before the *Golden Globes* reversal was a violation of due process and fundamentally unfair. While this left the FCC's indecency policy in place, it didn't approve it, either. Justice Kennedy's opinion concluded with the most important point of all: The FCC "is free to modify its current indecency policy in light of its determination of the public interest and applicable legal requirements," but he added that the opinion also "leaves the courts free to review the current policy or any modified policy in light of its content and application."

Translation: The Supreme Court wasn't ready just yet to pull the plug on broadcast indecency regulations. But if the FCC were to continue enforcing the rules this way, the lower courts were empowered to deal with it, and the agency should expect a repeat of what it experienced in the Second and Third Circuits.

MOPPING UP AT THE FCC

After the Supreme Court decision, the FCC's remaining enforcement actions fizzled as well. The Supreme Court declined review of the Third Circuit's *Super*

Bowl decision, and the FCC had to write a $550,000 refund check to CBS. The Department of Justice also abandoned its bid to collect a fine for the Fox show *Married by America*. That effort had already been handicapped by the revelation, made by journalist Jeff Jarvis, that all but two of the complaints were near-identical form complaints, and that most did not even come from the viewing areas of the stations named. The Commission's NAL proposed a fine of $1.18 million levied against 169 stations, but, when it was shown that far fewer stations actually received complaints, the FCC lowered the fine to $91,000 (to be collected from 13 stations). After the Supreme Court decision, the Department of Justice scuttled even this more modest effort. FCC Chairman Julius Genachowski explained at the time that the Commission was reviewing its indecency enforcement policy "to ensure that the agency carries out Congress's directive in a manner consistent with vital First Amendment principles." In the meantime, he directed the FCC's Enforcement Bureau to focus only on what he called "egregious indecency violations."

At this point, the FCC had to decide what to do with the million and a half complaints clogging its files that were mainly leftovers from spam email campaigns mounted by PTC and other like-minded groups. It took the Commission nearly a year after the Supreme Court decision, but it finally got around to purging most of the complaints and announcing its intention to take a fresh look at the indecency policy. In an April 2013 Public Notice, the FCC announced that more than a million complaints were being dropped because they were beyond the statute of limitations, otherwise deficient, or "foreclosed by settled precedent."

By this time, it had already taken steps to choke off the inflow of carbon-copy spam email complaints from groups like PTC by eliminating its email inbox for receiving such complaints. After 2011, disgruntled listeners and viewers had to go to the trouble of submitting individualized complaints using a drop-down menu on the FCC's website. Not surprisingly, the volume of complaints plummeted back to normal levels of about 2,000 per year.

The Commission's 2013 Public Notice also opened a proceeding to reform the indecency standard and asked for public input on its indecency policies "to ensure they are fully consistent with vital First Amendment principles." The Commission received over 102,000 comments in response, but, as of the publication of this book, it still has taken no action to modify or clarify its policy. And, it has initiated next to no indecency enforcement actions. Its prime directive appears to be keeping indecency questions as far from federal courts as possible.

One notable exception to the Commission's retreat came in 2015, when it issued an NAL proposing a $325,000 fine – the statutory maximum and the largest ever for a single station – against WDBJ, a Roanoke, Virginia television station, for a 2012 newscast that the FCC said was one of those "egregious" cases. The three-minute, ten-second piece told the story of a former adult film actress (porn name: Harmony Rose) who had joined the volunteer rescue squad in the Roanoke County community of Cave Spring. This sparked a local controversy, and the Fire Chief advocated terminating the young woman's employment because of her shady past.

WDBJ's story explored the diverse community reactions and illustrated the story with material drawn from Internet sources, including Harmony's website. Due to equipment limitations, however, station personnel were unable to see the full screen of the online material during editing, and the eventual broadcast inadvertently displayed a small image of an erect penis at the extreme margin of the screen. The tiny image that appeared covered only 1.7 percent of the screen at the far-right edge and was visible for only 2.7 seconds. Station management was quite naturally mortified once it became aware of the mishap, and took immediate corrective action by replacing its news editing equipment and retraining its staff.

Although the FCC never acted to clarify and refine its indecency rules, it evidently believed that this case was the perfect vehicle to "show" but not "tell" what constituted an "egregious" violation. It issued the record-breaking NAL and even put out a press release bragging that "[t]his enforcement action would be the highest fine the Commission has ever taken for a single indecent broadcast on one station." The agency concluded that WDBJ had not taken adequate steps to prevent the glimpse of nudity from reaching the air, and it reminded the broadcaster that it had explicitly ruled that there is "no news exemption from the indecency law."

Schurz Communications, Inc., WDBJ's owner, opposed the fine and made the same constitutional arguments that had worked in the previous cases (but that the Supreme Court had put off deciding). It described in detail the FCC's failure to reform or explain its policy, how the indecency standard was incoherent and obsolete, and why the proposed fine violated the First Amendment and was inconsistent with FCC precedent. This put the Commission in a rather touchy position. If it rejected Schu as it had to do to save face), it would quickly find itself explaining its decision to a skeptical appellate court. And if the Commission thought the courts were inhospitable half a decade earlier, the reception promised to be far worse now, after the agency had promised – and failed – to revise its indecency rules to be "fully consistent with vital First Amendment principles."

There was only one way out: blackmail.

As it turned out, Schurz was in the process of selling fifteen television stations to Gray Television Group., Inc., a transaction that required FCC approval. An outstanding NAL, like the WDBJ fine, is the type of thing that can hold up such a deal, but in past cases the FCC had permitted licenses to pay proposed fines to allow the deal to close, while preserving the right to appeal. Not this time. FCC Enforcement Bureau Chief Travis LeBlanc, known for his heavy-handed use of the Commission's forfeiture authority, refused to consider any arrangement that would permit Schurz to retain its right to go to court over the WDBJ fine. This effectively blocked a $450 million deal unless Schurz agreed to pay the fine and walk away from any appeal. Given little choice, Schurz paid the $325,000 for the indecency NAL so that it could get the FCC to act on the sale. By threatening to block the transaction, the FCC once again dodged judicial scrutiny of its policy, and the FCC's ten-page order approving the assignment of station licenses to Gray Television was silent about the WDBJ fine.

THE DECLINE OF PTC

PTC's Tim Winter denounced the FCC's 2013 announcement that it would pursue only "egregious" indecency cases as an "outrage" that "unnecessarily weakens a decency law that withstood a ferocious, ten-year constitutional attack waged by the broadcast industry." These were defiant words from the head of a lobbying group on the decline, for Winter had to be aware that the indecency standard did not survive the constitutional challenge. Not really. True enough, the Supreme Court stopped short of delivering a definitive ruling on the FCC's policy. Justice Alito probably crystalized the majority's reluctance to get into the First Amendment issue when he asked at oral argument: "[W]hy not just let this die a natural death? Why do you want us to intervene?" But the reality was that the indecency standard was effectively obsolete after the Supreme Court's decision, and so was PTC.

The decline began several years earlier, around the time that the indecency battleground shifted from the FCC and Congress to the courts. Once the FCC issued appealable orders beginning in 2006, the more important decisions would be made by judges who interpret and apply the law, not legislators and regulators who are prone to be swayed by PR campaigns and political gimmicks. In the judicial arena, florid rhetoric and bogusly inflated complaint counts mean very little, and actually proved to be a detriment. When the Third Circuit voided the Super Bowl fine, for example, it quoted CBS's brief, pointing out that "over 85 percent [of the complaints were] generated by single-interest groups" and "[a]pproximately twenty percent of the complaints are duplicates, with some individual complaints appearing in the record up to 37 times."

Brent Bozell may have sensed this shift when he stepped away as PTC's president at the beginning of 2007, handing the keys to Tim Winter. In many ways, it was like the transition from Anthony Comstock to John Sumner at the New York Society for the Suppression of Vice. Sumner certainly was more presentable, and was less prone to spittle-flecked rants than Comstock, but he lacked the messianic fire that gave the organization its reason to exist. Bozell actually acknowledged the need for a less polarizing figurehead for PTC, noting: "When you have someone that outspoken on that side of the political spectrum, it's hard to shake the appearance of being partisan." He saw Winter's succession as an opportunity "to allow folks of different political stripes to listen more intently to what we have to say."

Winter's credentials certainly suggested that he fit the bill – a lawyer and regis-tered Democrat who previously worked at media companies, including fifteen years at NBC (on the business side). But Winter's balanced résumé and more reasonable demeanor would not be enough to prevent PTC's withering, any more than John Sumner could save the New York Society for the Suppression of Vice. Neither successor could ever fill his predecessor's shoes. It was like casting Bob Newhart to take on a role previously played by Nicholas Cage. Sumner was the one who eventually turned off the lights and locked up when the New York Society (since renamed the Society to Maintain Public Decency) closed forever in 1950. And so it will be with Winter and PTC.

2006 – Bozell's last year as president – was PTC's biggest year. The FCC issued unprecedented indecency fines based on the group's complaint campaigns and Congress enacted the Broadcast Decency Enforcement Act. The group had lobbied aggressively for the bill, and Bozell attended the White House signing ceremony at the invitation of President Bush. By every measure, PTC appeared to be a group on the rise. It had a staff of about thirty, plus a dozen or so interns, in DC and Los Angeles offices. It had just experienced a record year for contributions – nearly $5.2 million according to tax records – and its annual report boasted of having over a million members, with grassroots chapters across the United States.

It seemed like an opportune time to pass the torch. Bozell's departing message said that the strain of running his other organizations, MRC and the Culture and Media Institute, plus his responsibilities to his large family, had "simply become too much." So he handed the reins to Winter with the confident prediction that "Tim will do a better job than I in leading the PTC into the future."

It was all downhill from there.

PTC's 2017 annual report revealed that contributions had plummeted about 65 percent over the previous decade, to about $1.9 million; in 2019, it reported to the IRS total contributions of just over $2.2 million (and expenses of more than $2.3 million). PTC had long since closed its DC office, and it no longer lists staff numbers in its annual reports. Although PTC claimed that it had a dozen employees as of 2020, its website provides information only on PTC's "leadership team," which consists of Winter, a chief financial officer, and a program director. This diminished state of affairs has persisted for some time. One critical 2012 article noted PTC's staff shrinkage and even suggested at the time that the group had only three employees left, including Winter. Its takeaway: Any reporter who quotes PTC as a significant source in the debate over indecency "is committing journalistic malpractice."

The question of PTC's continuing relevance has dogged the group since Bozell's departure. A March 2007 piece in *Variety* posed the question, "How Will Org Survive without Founder Bozell?" A 2010 *New York Times* article described PTC as an organization "on the defensive," observing: "These are difficult times for the indecency police." It detailed PTC's dwindling finances (by then, down to $2.9 million) and sharp staff reductions, and reported an accusation by Patrick W. Salazar, PTC's former vice president for development, that the group had been soliciting donations with a promise to forward donors' complaints to the FCC, but was simply pocketing the money and doing nothing more. PTC vigorously disputed Salazar's claims, and said that he had tried to extort the organization in exchange for his silence. It complained to the Los Angeles Police Department, but, after an investigation, the city attorney declined to bring charges, saying that Salazar had committed no crimes.

Salazar also revealed how PTC had puffed up its membership claims. The group had long boasted of having more than a million members (and by 2010 was claiming 1.3 million), but Salazar explained that PTC had been counting as a "member" anyone who had ever donated or signed a petition since the group's founding. Measured instead by contributions to annual fundraising appeals, PTC's actual "membership" was closer to 12,000. A 2012 article analyzed PTC's contribution levels compared to reported revenue and placed membership at 10,000.

This habit of using inflated numbers – reminiscent of the Comstock playbook – seemed to permeate every aspect of PTC's operations. Like an insect that puffs up its appearance to seem more fearsome, PTC claimed the authority to speak for millions of Americans when in fact it had managed to agitate only a few thousand disgruntled viewers. Its membership numbers were bogus, its complaint tallies were manipulated to multiply the count by many times, and even its various reports on the media were methodologically flawed advocacy pieces masquerading as "studies." In each case, PTC used numbers to make its presence seem larger, its actions more important, and its findings more scientific.

But after the indecency battle moved to court and out of the political arena, numbers were no longer PTC's friends. Once the FCC changed its complaint procedures to require individuals to actually fill out a form in order to file a complaint, the days of PTC's massive spam campaigns were over. PTC still criticizes particular shows from time to time, and it provides a link to the FCC's complaints page, but it can no longer generate the type of interest it once could with its "Action Alerts" where form complaints were forwarded to multiple offices within the FCC with the click of a mouse.

As a result, PTC has not initiated a mass complaint campaign against a broadcast program for indecency since 2015. A section of PTC's website that lists the group's "Broadcast Indecency Campaigns" lists forty such efforts between 2004 and 2015, with the last one being against *Family Guy* on February 8, 2015. In fact, the Seth MacFarlane animated sitcom was PTC's most frequent target, with six out of the forty complaint campaigns devoted to that show alone. Another MacFarlane cartoon sitcom, *American Dad*, was the subject of two other PTC campaigns, which means that 20 percent of PTC's online efforts were directed toward stamping out cartoons by one guy. For his part, MacFarlane compared being on the receiving end of a PTC campaign to getting "hate mail from Hitler." PTC had earlier claimed this online activism as the "centerpiece" of its mission. Once that program effectively ended, it raised the question of what was left for the organization.

PTC also produces reports on various issues involving the media, generally to stoke some panic and motivate donors, but even those have petered out. As early as

2010, the *New York Times* noted a marked slowdown in the reports (with titles like *MTV Smut Peddlers* and *The Rap on Rap*) that had been a staple of PTC's lobbying and fundraising efforts. A 2008 "special report," *Happily Never After*, for example, purported to show how "Hollywood favors adultery and promiscuity over marital intimacy in prime time programming" by simply counting the number of references to marital versus nonmarital sex in TV shows. Its 2010 report, *Habitat for Profanity*, issued to influence the FCC's litigation strategy in the indecency cases, purported to show a sharp increase in the use of profanity on network TV shows after the Second Circuit struck down the FCC's indecency standard, comparing programs aired in 2010 with those in 2005. The result? PTC found a 69.3 percent increase in profanity.

Shocking! With such precise numbers, there *must* be a real crisis, right? The "statistic" was featured in PTC's press statements and got picked up in news stories from Washington to LA. But, as usual, there was a problem with PTC's stats. The study methodology revealed that PTC had counted as "profane" any use of coarse language it found offensive, whether or not it had any connection with "indecency" as the FCC defined it. As malleable as the indecency standard had become, it did not begin to reach the words PTC counted in this study, which included a list of eighteen bleeped and unbleeped terms (including "crap," "damn," "hell," "ass," "bitch," "bastard," and "boobs"). Even for these less-than-mortifying examples, the PTC's count showed that the largest increase in such language came after 10 p.m., during the "safe harbor" period for indecency – the time of the broadcast day when profanity is already permitted under FCC rules. PTC's studies were designed to be just flashy enough to survive a news cycle, but not good enough to withstand any real scrutiny.

In recent years, even the studies slowed to a trickle of about two per year (if you include what PTC calls "mini studies"). In 2019, PTC issued only one such report, and it was a masterful blend of shallowness, irony, and historical ignorance. Entitled *Not for Kids Anymore*, the report found that comic-book-themed TV shows on the major networks feature dark and violent themes that are unfit for children, unlike the comics that inspired them. As PTC explained it, "broadcast TV's representations of comic-book characters are no longer the bright, colorful, and optimistic figures of the past." Its promotional email touting the report exclaimed in bold letters: "You can't imagine what the broadcast networks have done with these characters." The cover of the report says all you need to know about the "study." It is designed to resemble a comic book cover, and features a child dressed as Superman walking down an empty, rain-swept city street toward a violent lightning storm and dark clouds (Figure 8.8). The "study" itself is nothing more than a content analysis of seven years of superhero and other comic-themed shows that adds up the number of violent acts and instances of inappropriate dialogue. Mainly, the PTC report just reproduces descriptions and dialogue from shows it finds the most reprehensible and purports to find 6,000 incidents of violence, over 500 deaths, and almost 2,000 profanities.

FIGURE 8.8 Cover of Parents Television Council report "Not for Kids Anymore"
Source: https://go.parentstv.org/comic-books/.

Paging Dr. Wertham! PTC seemed to be utterly unaware that we have been through all this before. Its feigned nostalgia for the "bright, colorful, and optimistic figures of the past" would take us right back to the very comic books that Fredric Wertham and two congressional committees believed were the source of most juvenile delinquency in America. It is the same type of cluelessness that permeated the Parents Music Resource Center, whose representatives told the Senate Commerce Committee in 1985 that "porn rock" was unprecedented, and that it was nothing like the fun and playful rock 'n' roll of the 1950s. One clear sign that a pro-censorship group has outlived its usefulness is when it can't even competently recycle a moral panic.

PTC's website features an "Indecency Timeline" that purports to trace the issue from its origin with the 1934 Communications Act through the current policy. What the group chooses to put on the timeline is idiosyncratic and interesting, but what is most revealing is where it leaves off. PTC's timeline ends in 2006 with passage of the Broadcast Decency Enforcement Act. Nothing is listed for the period covering the next decade and a half, and none of the judicial decisions that invalidated FCC enforcement orders are mentioned. It is fitting that PTC stopped cataloguing events on its indecency timeline in 2006, for that is the year the group became irrelevant.

BOZELL'S LEGACY

Brent Bozell got out while the getting was good when he ended his day-to-day management of PTC after 2006. But in many ways not that much changed for him. His job is pretty much what it has always been – spewing out an endless stream of invective about the networks and how they are destroying the culture with liberal ideology. An August 2019 column ranted about how the *MTV Music Video Awards* and network news coverage provided a platform for Taylor Swift to trash "anyone still dissenting from the LGBTQ agenda." He frequently blames network news and entertainment shows for promoting homosexuality and for "eroding America's moral character on 'gay marriage.'" And he regularly blasts the networks and "media elites" for anti-Catholic bias for, among other things, continuing coverage of sex abuse scandals in the Church, and for airing disrespectful sitcoms during Christian holidays.

Bozell's creation and leadership of PTC between 1995 and 2006 was just one front in his lifelong war against the Forces of Darkness, which in his mind include anything that smacks of liberalism, hints at sex, or questions Catholic doctrine. But while PTC turned out to be a high-profile failure, it would be wrong to suggest that Bozell's efforts to harness the power of the FCC to transform broadcast network programming had no lasting impact. Quite the opposite is true. Bozell's legacy will be that his activism resulted in neutering the FCC's indecency standard and placing it on the path to extinction.

For over two decades, it has been pretty clear to the First Amendment community that if a case arose in which the Supreme Court had no choice but to rule on the legality of the indecency standard, it would find the law to be unconstitutional. You don't have to be Nostradamus to know this; it isn't a prediction. The Court issued just such a unanimous ruling in 1997 when it invalidated legislation that extended broadcast-style indecency regulations to the Internet, a holding that was echoed in federal courts across the country striking down similar state laws.

Congress first became aware of Internet dangers in the mid-1990s through the efforts of James Exon, a Democratic senator from Nebraska, who, in the manner of Anthony Comstock, brought a "Blue Book" to the floor in a salacious bit of "show and tell" to warn his colleagues of the horrors of Internet porn. He tacked on an amendment to a major rewrite of the Communications Act, and the Communications Decency Act (CDA) was born. The CDA's main provision imposed the same indecency standard on the Internet that historically had applied to broadcasting. However, the law never went into effect because the courts enjoined enforcement and made short work of the defective standard. The Supreme Court held that the law's definition of indecency "lacks the precision that the First Amendment requires when a statute regulates the content of speech" and that no speaker could comfortably assume that the law would not criminalize (among other things) a serious discussion of birth control practices, the consequences of prison rape, homosexuality, or even a discussion of the George Carlin monologue in the Court's *Pacifica* decision. Other courts reached the same conclusion when they struck down "mini CDAs" in New York, New Mexico, Michigan, Arizona, Vermont, Virginia, South Carolina, and Ohio.

The only argument for sustaining broadcasting rules that employ the same standard in the face of so many contrary decisions has been to say that this medium is different. The government's claim is not that the concept of indecency somehow becomes constitutionally clear or precise when applied to broadcasting as opposed to the Internet; it is that the courts have tolerated rules for television and radio that would not survive judicial scrutiny in any other context. In the days of *Pacifica*, the FCC argued that broadcasting was "pervasive" and uniquely accessible to children in ways that other media are not. However, the logic of this position crumbles in an era where most young people watch television from sources other than broadcasting (such as streaming video), don't know the difference between over-the-air channels and cable or satellite channels (that are not subject to indecency rules), and rarely watch TV in real time. The assumption of the indecency rules – that kids are in bed after 10 p.m. – makes no sense at all if people can get video on demand or record shows from all hours on their DVRs and watch them whenever they want.

PTC's crusades did the FCC no favors by forcing the agency to explain the logic of its rules to federal judges. The Supreme Court indicated that it wasn't quite ready to upset the apple cart and found ways to decide the cases arising from PTC's activism without dealing with the First Amendment problem. But the next time, the Commission is unlikely to be so lucky, and the lower courts have not shown the same reticence. The FCC's response for nearly a decade has been to avoid the issue, to confine enforcement to "egregious" cases (whatever those may be), and to strive at all costs to keep indecency cases out of court.

Another sign of Bozell's declining influence is that Tim Winter struck up a friendship with *Family Guy* creator Seth MacFarlane, a man whom Bozell once described as "the guy scribbling graffiti in the bathroom stall." The odd-bedfellows relationship was profiled in the *LA Times* in 2019. If nothing else, it shows that we have come a long way from the days when PTC's website had a button that said "[t]o help the PTC fight Seth MacFarlane's filth, click here," to now, where PTC recommends that advertisers buy time on MacFarlane's sci-fi show, *The Orville*. The fact that Winter and MacFarlane can find common ground may be a positive thing in a reality where civility and reason prevail, but it is anathema in Bozell's alternate universe of the fire-and-brimstone anti-media crusader.

A final nail in the coffin was evident in PTC's reaction to the 2020 Super Bowl halftime show that featured sexy performances by headliners Jennifer Lopez and Shakira. There was no wardrobe malfunction this time. The costumes, decidedly on the skimpy side, performed just as designed. One outraged conservative commentator described J-Lo's outfit as "a two-sided thong and buttless chaps," and fumed that Shakira was wearing "an imitation of a skirt," and that the "cameramen could not stay away from her crotch." The writer demanded that the FCC impose harsh fines on the Fox network for airing the broadcast. Many viewers agreed, and more than 1,300 complaints poured in to the FCC, some of which called the halftime show "soft porn." So, where was PTC on all this? It sent an email to those still on its mailing list, saying "let's keep the Super Bowl family friendly," and calling on its members to sign a petition to that effect to NFL Commissioner Roger Goodell. Gone are the days of the spam FCC complaint campaigns, the congressional lobbying efforts, and the demands for government crackdowns. PTC's guillotine has been supplanted by a squirt gun.

So, in the end, what hath Bozell wrought? PTC is a shell of its former self and its pronouncements no longer strike fear in the hearts of media executives; it cannot manufacture mass complaint campaigns anymore, and even if it could, courts are on to the game; cases launched based on PTC's efforts only made judges more skeptical of FCC authority in this area, and the FCC was forced to refund every indecency fine that was challenged in court during this period. Neither Bozell's continuing activism nor PTC can hold back a changing culture any more than King Canute could hold back the tides. But their efforts laid bare the fragility of the FCC indecency standard as a weapon in the culture wars.

9

The Anti-free Speech Movement

Herbert Marcuse, a Frankfurt School philosopher of the mid-twentieth century, is to political discourse what Anthony Comstock was to cultural purity. Marcuse championed political repression to advance truth as he saw it. While Comstock was on a mission from god to wipe out all sources of lust and impiety, Marcuse argued the necessity of "conditioning" (that is, restricting) political argument so that the people would be capable of understanding the "real" truth. To do so would require the government to abandon its traditional impartiality toward political ideas so that society could be freed from "the prevailing indoctrination." That is, to permit the people to be autonomous and think freely, "they would have to get information slanted in the opposite direction."

What do these abstractions mean in practice? In his 1965 essay *Repressive Tolerance*, Marcuse acknowledged that to establish true democracy "may require apparently undemocratic means." This would mean restricting the rights of speech and assembly for "groups and movements which promote aggressive policies, armament, chauvinism, discrimination on the grounds of race and religion, or which oppose the extension of public services, social security, medical care, etc." As he put it, "the restoration of freedom of thought may necessitate new and rigid restrictions on teachings and practices in the educational institutions which, by their methods and concepts, serve to enclose the mind within the established universe of discourse and behavior – thereby precluding a priori a rational evaluation of the alternatives." The "restoration of freedom of thought" would also require censorship of "scientific research in the interest of deadly 'deterrents,' of abnormal human endurance under inhuman conditions, etc." In this view, "liberating tolerance" means "intolerance against movements from the Right and toleration of movements from the Left."

As Marcuse put it, "tolerance cannot be indiscriminate and equal with respect to the contents of expression" and "it cannot protect false words and wrong deeds" that "contradict and counteract the possibilities of liberation." In short, to guarantee the blessings of liberty, "certain things cannot be said, certain ideas cannot be expressed, certain policies cannot be proposed, certain behavior cannot be permitted without making tolerance an instrument for the continuation of servitude."

Who is to be the arbiter of this system of enforced truth? According to Marcuse, there is only "one logical answer" regarding who is qualified "to make all of these distinctions, definitions, [and] identifications for the society as a whole" – it is "the democratic educational dictatorship of free men." However, in a society currently governed by the power elite, indoctrination, and capitalism, those qualified to identify and to enforce the right ideas "would be a small number indeed." Somehow, this core group of the intelligentsia would have to break "the tyranny of public opinion and its makers in the closed society" by such means as "cancellation of the liberal creed of free and equal discussion."

Let's ponder that for a second. What does it say about a person if, when asked, "Who should be the guardians of truth and the final censors for all social discourse?," he or she answers, "Me and a few guys just like me."? To state Marcuse's argument is to discredit it, but some bad ideas just keep coming back.

MARCUSE'S REVENGE

Marcuse's ideas found expression in campus speech codes and some local ordinances adopted in the late 1980s and early 1990s. Harvey Silverglate and Alan Kors highlighted the issue in their 1998 book THE SHADOW UNIVERSITY, where they described the assaults on free speech and academic freedom on college campuses as "Marcuse's revenge." The predominant purpose of the speech codes was to balance free speech rights with a right to be free from verbal "assault" for students who fell into designated categories of disadvantaged or marginalized groups, but doing so required a redefinition of the First Amendment, which historically has been premised on content and speaker neutrality.

Academic writers at the time who followed in Marcuse's intellectual footsteps included Richard Delgado, Mari Matsuda, Charles R. Lawrence III, and Kimberlé Williams Crenshaw, who, in their 1993 book WORDS THAT WOUND, argued that "defenders of the status quo have discovered, in the first amendment, a new weapon." They called for a conception of "the substance of freedom" that does not protect "a right to degrade and humiliate another human being any more than it implicates a right to do physical violence to another." Another like-minded scholar, Catherine MacKinnon, similarly equated words with actions, "tantamount to ... saying 'ready, aim, fire' to a firing squad." She advocated "a new model for freedom of expression" in which "free speech does not most readily protect the activities of Nazis, Klansmen, and pornographers, while doing nothing for their victims." She advocated the censorship of sexual speech (in particular) to prevent discrimination.

While some academics sought to reconceptualize freedom of speech (and thereby rationalize censorship), others more provocatively appeared to embrace the horror. Professor Stanley Fish thus defended censorship in his book THERE'S NO SUCH THING AS FREE SPEECH, AND IT'S A GOOD THING, TOO, in which he advanced the notion that those who are clearly right ought to be able to impose their collective will and silence the other side. He dismissed talk of the value of free expression for its own sake as an empty piety and suggested that the debate over the protection of speech has always been about promoting messages that one side wants heard and censoring ideas that they want silenced. And he is fine with that because, after all, everybody does it. Or, more fundamentally, he is fine with it because, in his view, all First Amendment arguments amount to nothing more than a contest of opposing political wills.

Thus, according to Professor Fish, public universities should be able to impose speech codes on their students and the government should be able to prohibit "hate speech" (however one might define that nebulous concept) because that's the side he has chosen. (Years later, Fish would expand on these views to acknowledge that "hate speech" is incapable of precise definition and that laws attempting to ban such speech are doomed to fail, but at the same time he reaffirmed his claim that there is no "free speech principle.") According to his thesis, censorship is good, if done for the "right" reasons or by the "right" people. But then, everyone has their reasons, don't they?

For Fish to point out the existence of intellectual inconsistency ("free speech for me, but not for thee") has never been much of an argument, and it is far from a justification for speech restrictions. To say that most people can name some kind of speech they want to suppress while zealously guarding their own makes a case for remedial education, not censorship. In any event, one might hope that a robust defense of censorship would be more intellectually satisfying than hearing Mick Mulvaney, President Donald Trump's acting Chief of Staff, defiantly telling the press that the United States makes quid pro quo demands of foreign governments all the time, and people should just "get over it." Likewise, the academy should be able to do better in marshalling its arguments than the Nixon loyalists who rationalized the abuses of Watergate by claiming that all politicians engage in dirty tricks.

For that reason, courts that first confronted various policies inspired by these "new model[s] for freedom of expression" (as Catherine MacKinnon described them) were not impressed. The US Court of Appeals for the Seventh Circuit in 1985 struck down an anti-pornography ordinance drafted by MacKinnon and feminist activist Andrea Dworkin as an exercise in "thought control" and flatly inconsistent with the First Amendment. The ordinance had defined "pornography" as "the graphic sexual subordination of women, whether in pictures or in words," based on MacKinnon's theory that men who see women as subordinate are likely to treat them so. Thus, "pornography" (as defined by the ordinance) could be prohibited regardless of serious merit and without consideration of the predominant theme of the work as a whole because, as MacKinnon explained, "pornography is not an idea; pornography is the injury." This was a throwback to a Comstockian view of "pornography" with a feminist veneer, and the district court rejected it on traditional First Amendment grounds. It held that the law was unconstitutional because its terms were vague, its scope overly broad, and because it established a prior restraint.

The flaws of the Indianapolis ordinance were so fundamental that the court of appeals held that it needn't even reach questions of the law's vagueness or prior restraint. It found that the law was an exercise in "thought control" because it banned speech only if it promoted the "wrong" attitudes or beliefs. Indianapolis did not employ established legal standards for obscenity (including graphic depictions that appeal to a "prurient interest" in sex that violates contemporary community standards of "patent offensiveness"), and the court observed that, under the city's new definition, there was no limit to how graphic and patently offensive a work could be so long as women were not "subordinated" or "humiliated."

The court directly confronted the claim that porn promotes sexist thinking: "If the fact that speech plays a role in a process of conditioning were enough to permit governmental regulation, that would be the end of freedom of speech." It noted that the world is filled with bad ideas, and that speech that may "influence the culture and shape our socialization," ranging from bigotry and anti-Semitism to televised violence, is all is protected as speech because "[a]ny other answer leaves the government in control of all the institutions of culture, the great censor and director of which thoughts are good for us." The Supreme Court affirmed the decision without opinion.

Regulation of campus expression through "speech codes" based on like-minded theories met the same fate. A federal court struck down a University of Wisconsin policy drafted by a group of professors that included Richard Delgado, holding that its prohibition of "discriminatory comments, epithets, or other expressive behavior" (among other things) was vague, overly broad, and did not fall within the First Amendment exception for "fighting words." Drawing on the Seventh Circuit's holding invalidating MacKinnon and Dworkin's anti-porn ordinance, it held that the First Amendment does not permit "balancing" the value of speech (or lack thereof) against the possibility of causing offense. The decision echoed an earlier ruling that rejected a similar policy at the University of Michigan. It found that a ban on "discriminatory harassment" failed to provide "any principled way to distinguish sanctionable from protected speech," and, consequently, "the University had no idea what the limits of the policy were and it was essentially making up the rules as it went along." In 2018, Delgado looked back at these and other cases and acknowledged that such campus speech codes are almost always struck down when challenged in court.

THE RISE OF POLITICS

While the courts have recognized and applied strong First Amendment principles, the same cannot be said of those among Marcuse's "democratic educational dictatorship of free men." Support for free expression has waned among certain academics – including some who devote special attention to First Amendment scholarship – as the subjects of protection veered away from issues traditionally associated with progressive politics. Earlier, as First Amendment law developed during the 1930s through the 1970s, liberal academics generally could be counted on to provide a full-throated defense of free speech when it came to supporting the labor movement, the struggle for civil rights, battles over academic freedom, opposing restrictions on obscenity, defending anti-war protests, and the like. During this period, liberals primarily supported free expression claims while conservative intellectuals generally were far more skeptical.

This began to change in the 1980s, as a certain faction of feminists like MacKinnon began to advocate restrictions on pornography as civil rights law. At the same time, academics espousing "critical race theory" (like Delgado and Matsuda) drew on MacKinnon's work and argued for adoption of various types of "speech codes." The trend picked up after political conservatives began to perceive legal threats to a variety of issues important to them, and found that they had a First Amendment shield as well. As courts grew increasingly receptive to their arguments, it was now the progressives – particularly within the legal academy – who claimed that the First Amendment had gone too far. This picked up steam after *Citizens United* v. *Federal Election Commission*, in which the Supreme Court struck down restrictions on "electioneering communications" and the use of corporate funds to support political candidates.

Today, scholarship increasingly reflects the same political polarization that infects the public at large. In this charged environment, some academic writers question the value of free speech itself. For example, Cornell University Law Professor Steve Shiffrin complains about the First Amendment's "dark side" and bitterly asks, "[W]hat's wrong with the First Amendment?" He criticizes a number of Supreme Court decisions as overprotecting speech, and argues that both liberal and conservative judges "have turned free speech into a fetish." More specifically, Shiffrin decries decisions of the Roberts Court striking down prohibitions on "crush videos," lying about military honors, and the sale or rental of violence-themed video games to minors (among others) as "loathsome," representing "a form of First Amendment stupidity." Shiffrin suggests that, rather than impose strict First Amendment scrutiny on restrictions on expression, courts should instead engage in an ad hoc balancing of interests and should feel free to expand the categories of unprotected speech. Too much protection, he suggests, represents the "sin" of "First Amendment idolatry" that is at odds with human dignity.

If he could have his way, Shiffrin would crack down on pretrial publicity, forbid the publication of information on rape victims, prohibit "crush videos" and violent video games (at least as to minors), restrict pornography (however that slippery concept might be defined), punish racist speech, prohibit demonstrations near funerals, limit commercial speech that substitutes "consumer pleasure for human flourishing," and – of course – limit political speech by corporations. There simply would not be enough hours in the day for the speech police to do its work.

Shiffrin is far from alone among contemporary First Amendment scholars. Professor Burt Neuborne of NYU Law School takes much the same position as Shiffrin (albeit in more temperate language), arguing that the Supreme Court has elevated "useless or harmful speech to undeserved heights of protection" while downplaying or ignoring democratic values. Neuborne maintains that liberals were fully aligned with strong First Amendment protections through the mid-twentieth century, when they believed that freedom of speech promoted largely progressive causes – what he calls "the First Amendment era of good feelings." But once the Court began extending the same protections to conservative speakers as well, "some progressives began to suspect they had made a bad First Amendment bargain."

If ever there were any room for doubt about the role of political ideology underlying this shift in academic thinking, it evaporated with Professor Louis Michael Seidman's 2018 article *Can Free Speech Be Progressive?* Seidman answered his own question with an emphatic "no," because he sees no potential under current First Amendment doctrine for progressives to "weaponize free speech" (his words) to convert the First Amendment into "a powerful sword that would actually promote progressive goals." This is because recognizing constitutional protection for opposing positions does not further his definition of progressivism, which is "the modern political stance favoring an activist government that strives to achieve the public good, including the correction of unjust distributions produced by the market and the dismantling of power hierarchies based on traits like race, nationality, gender, class, and sexual orientation."

The problem with modern free speech doctrine, according to Seidman, is the freedom part. As he sees it, "[t]he doctrine is dominated by obsession with government restrictions on speech and with government interference with listener autonomy." The First Amendment, with its commitment to neutral principles, cannot be progressive in his estimation, because "progressivism is not neutral." Rather, in an ironic nod to Oliver Wendell Holmes, Seidman describes progressivism as "a fighting faith committed to a particular and controversial outcome." Neutrality is a "sham," he argues, because the law favors the status quo, which entrenches the rich and powerful. Thus, he concludes, "constitutionalizing the right of freedom of speech leads to an anti-liberal mindset," and "[s]o long as we imagine that the Constitution is the common ground that people of all political persuasions can adhere to, it cannot be progressive."

Seidman is not wrong in this respect: It's hard to fashion a coherent argument for activist government from an amendment that starts with the words "Congress shall make no law." Undaunted by this, Seidman's view of free expression melds the messianic zeal of Anthony Comstock with the asymmetrical rights theory of Herbert Marcuse and adds layers of the obfuscations about which Orwell warned. He merely replaces Comstock's Christian god with "progressivism," which he describes as "neutral," in that "all sensible and humane people should favor that program."

Seidman justifies suppressing speech by everyone else, asking (in the style of Stanley Fish) "[i]f speech law is inevitably going to be biased one way or the other, then why not bias it toward progressives?"

Professor Fish defends such result-oriented theorizing by claiming that free speech advocates engage in the same instrumentalist thinking. His 2019 book, THE FIRST: HOW TO THINK ABOUT HATE SPEECH, CAMPUS SPEECH, RELIGIOUS SPEECH, FAKE NEWS, POST-TRUTH, AND DONALD TRUMP, expands on his original thesis that all free speech battles are nothing more than a contest between opposing political wills. Fish argues that First Amendment arguments "are never made in the name of the abstraction itself but in the name of some agenda to which free speech rhetoric has been successfully attached." He asserts that there is no general free speech principle and that "the label of free speech is applied by polemicists to affirm the values they already hold" in order to defend expression *that should be uttered without restrictions because it says things I agree with*" (his emphasis). He concludes that free speech has no intrinsic value and that (again, his emphasis) *"the First Amendment is a participant in the partisan battle, a prize in the political wars, and not an apolitical oasis of principle."*

But Fish goes further and asserts that censorship actually *promotes* freedom of speech. This is because some types of speech undermine what commonly are thought of as "free speech values" – promoting deliberative democracy, the search for truth, informative (rather than corrupting) speech, etc. – and that regulating such "bad" speech therefore "is an act of fidelity" to the First Amendment. Fish argues that any answer to the question "What is free speech for?" logically leads to censorship somewhere down the line "because your understanding of the amendment's purpose will lead you to regulate or suppress speech which serves to undermine that purpose." Consequently, he concludes, "censorship is not a violation of the First Amendment but the necessary vehicle of its implementation."

This is a neat trick, to suggest that censorship *is* free speech. It ranks up there with Oceania's slogan that "freedom is slavery," Rudy Giuliani's claim that "freedom is about authority," and Fredric Wertham's assertion that "true freedom is regulation." But it follows quite naturally from Marcuse's concept of "repressive tolerance," which holds that censorship must be employed to put down ideas or institutions that impede human liberation. Using this logic, unfettered expression is a tool of suppression, while censorship by the correct people promotes "freedom of thought." So, presto change-o, censorship is not really *censorship*; it is merely using the tools of censorship to battle the larger repressions of the established order. And, as translated by Professor Fish, censorship actually *enforces* the First Amendment when used to suppress speech that is antithetical to the "First Amendment values" that he ironically insists do not exist.

So, we are to free the mind through censorship? Somewhere, Big Brother is beaming with pride.

POLITICS VERSUS PRINCIPLE

The academic notion that freedom of speech is nothing but a political argument employed opportunistically to promote some agenda would come as a surprise to actual First Amendment advocates who have devoted careers to defending freedom of expression, including speech (and speakers) they find repugnant. Professor Aryeh Neier, the former National Executive Director of the ACLU, who was vilified in the late 1970s for defending the First Amendment rights of Nazis to march in Skokie, Illinois, certainly would disagree. Few have more justifiable reason to hate Nazis and all that they espouse than Neier, who narrowly escaped the Holocaust with his immediate family, while many members of his extended clan perished. But as he explained in his book DEFENDING MY ENEMY, "I supported free speech for Nazis when they wanted to march in Skokie in order to defeat Nazis. Defending my enemy is the only way to protect a free society against the enemies of freedom."

Neier's defense of the free speech rights of Nazis was not an exercise in the use of high-sounding platitudes to support speakers or philosophies he favors (as Fish understands First Amendment advocacy); it was based on the principle that "[t]he alternative to freedom is power" and that "[t]o defend myself, I must restrain power with freedom, even if the temporary beneficiaries are the enemies of freedom." Fish actually seems to get this point, when he (finally) concludes that "hate speech" laws will always fail because "if you are lucky enough to prevail in an election, you may be able to get your enemy's speech labeled 'hateful.' But when political fortunes turn (as they always will), your enemies will then do to you and your speech what you have done to them." And it is hard to plausibly claim that the defense of speech you hate is unprincipled when doing so comes at significant personal cost. Not only was Neier targeted with thousands of hateful letters but the ACLU lost about 30,000 members (and about $500,000 in contributions – not an inconsiderable sum in 1977 dollars) over its defense of free speech principles in the Skokie case.

Nadine Strossen, former ACLU president (and daughter of a Holocaust survivor), made the same point, even in the post-Charlottesville environment. In her 2108 book HATE: WHY WE SHOULD RESIST IT WITH FREE SPEECH, NOT CENSORSHIP, Strossen explains how traditional free speech principles that include a strict requirement of content neutrality are essential to protecting vulnerable members of the population and members of minority groups. It is only through strict adherence to free speech principles – not politics – that such groups can be protected, and she marshals numerous examples, both in the USA and abroad, confirming that laws restricting speech inevitably are used to punish the very groups they ostensibly were enacted to protect.

It is a straightforward matter of logic: In democracies, policies are made and enforced by the majority. And, unless the rules are made by Marcuse's "democratic educational dictatorship of free men," minorities simply have to trust that the majorities in charge will protect them. Even then, history provides little cause for optimism, as the experience in Europe illustrates. In Turkey, for example, it is illegal to say that the Armenian genocide occurred, while in France it is a crime to deny it. In the USA, the very point of having constitutional protections from majority rule, with the assurance that any speech regulation must be content-neutral, is to prevent majorities from suppressing disfavored and powerless minorities. That is why First Amendment advocates have defended even the speech they hate – as a matter of principle, not out of political expediency.

So Professor Fish makes a good point when he identifies scholars who seek to circumscribe First Amendment protections as champions for their particular causes. He aptly labels Catherine McKinnon an "antipornography crusader," and describes like-minded scholars as "polemicists." For example, in a 2012 book, THE HARM IN HATE SPEECH, Professor Jeremy Waldron borrows from MacKinnon's view of the First Amendment and applies it to support laws against hate speech. Although he acknowledges multiple examples of minority rights being trampled by government, Waldron discounts the problem of majoritarian oppression and asserts that hate speech laws somehow are an exception to the general rules of politics. He asserts that many countries have hate speech laws that are administered responsibly "by and large," meaning, apparently, close enough for government work. But even this modest claim is rebutted by Nadine Strossen's in-depth study of such laws, which finds that they are at best ineffective and in many cases counterproductive.

Fish may be overstating the case in calling Waldron a "polemicist," since he wrote his book "not to condemn or reinterpret the U.S. constitutional provisions" but more to "come to terms with the best that can be said for hate speech regulations." Waldron forthrightly acknowledges that his position is a straight-up policy choice, admitting that "a restriction on hate speech or on group defamation is a restriction on speech on account of its content, and that it is the content that explains the restriction." The "polemicist" label is more accurate when applied to academics whose policy preferences come first and constitutional rationalizations are just the tail wagging the dog.

A major tell is that many such theorists are activists who work to implement their policies and propound their constitutional theories to serve those ends. For such academic writers, Stanley Fish is on point when he describes their methodology as first identifying "First Amendment values" and thereby creating a rationale for censoring any speech that falls outside that privileged construct as they have defined it. The tag certainly is apt for such theorists as MacKinnon, who with Andrea Dworkin drafted the Indianapolis anti-pornography ordinance, and others, like Richard Delgado and Mari Matsuda, who advocated for university speech codes and devised constitutional theories to support them. Thus, Delgado and his co-authors describe their work as part of a "liberation pedagogy" that is "avowedly political" involving "ongoing engagement in political practice." In a 2018 book, Delgado offers what he describes as "a guide for activist lawyers and judges."

The approach of these advocate-academics ignores both the design of the First Amendment and the way in which the law of free speech evolved. The First Amendment is a prohibition of censorship, not a promise of democratic civic engagement, virtue, artistic excellence or individual self-realization. Those aspirations likely will be advanced by strong protections for freedom of expression, or at least we hope they will, but any failure to achieve these presumed *values* does not change the nature of the constitutional *prohibition* of censorship. The relevant question is not what does the First Amendment promote but what was it designed to prevent? Rather than searching for constitutional "values" or "effects," Professors Jane and Derek Bambauer have observed that sound theories of free expression all contain "a necessary assumption about what makes the political process *bad*." That is, the First Amendment was premised on the core insight that "humans are incompetent at designing good rules of censorship."

The framers of the Bill of Rights were pretty up front about it. Even if they failed to explain the full meaning of the forty-five words that make up the First Amendment, it seems they were clear in their purpose to deny government the power to interfere with the ability of individuals to develop and express their ideas.

James Madison, who introduced the Bill of Rights in Congress, initially proposed a more descriptive version of what became the First Amendment, not only protecting freedom of religion but also providing that "the full and equal rights of conscience" shall not be "in any manner, or on any pretext infringed." His initial draft provided that the people "shall not be deprived or abridged of their right to speak, to write, or to publish their sentiments; and the freedom of the press, as one of the great bulwarks of liberty, shall be inviolable." Finally, his proposed language provided that the people "shall not be restrained from peaceably assembling" nor from petitioning the government. As Madison explained when he introduced the amendment in June 1789, "[t]he rights of conscience [and] liberty of the press . . . should be so secured, as to put them out of the power of the Legislature to infringe them." The point was to limit government power, not to promote a particular policy or value, and the First Amendment as finally adopted did not alter that essential design.

The purpose of quoting the Father of the Bill of Rights is not to suggest an originalist view of the First Amendment that claims that its full meaning was cemented at its inception. Nor does this set forth a reading of the First Amendment as an absolute prohibition on any government regulation of the use of words. Quite to the contrary, the meaning of the First Amendment is something that developed over time as a response to real-world episodes of censorship. First Amendment principles evolved through this process of solving censorship problems as they emerged, not from academic navel-gazing seeking to define free speech "values." What became "First Amendment principles" were developed case-by-case by confronting censors in the wild; they were not hatched in an ivory tower.

The First Amendment is not self-defining. It has been the job of the courts to work out the meaning of the various legal terms of art the amendment contains, including "abridging," "the freedom of speech," or "of the press," among others. That inquiry is more easily understood when considered in the context of particular controversies (say, Anthony Comstock seeking to silence Margaret Sanger) and with the understanding that the amendment was adopted to cabin the government's power to muzzle speech. Decide enough of those cases and you get a doctrine; issue opinions covering a diverse array of speakers in different circumstances, you get First Amendment jurisprudence. And that's what happened through the twentieth century, leading to increasing levels of protection for speech across the board.

After the reign of Anthony Comstock ended, the age of free speech in America took off. Comstock's death was not the cause of this – his influence had begun to wane long before he died in 1915 – which was still more than a decade before the Supreme Court began the laborious task of creating First Amendment doctrine. Things changed in large part because the culture moved on. Victorian mores faded away and society, as well as judges, began to accept the arguments that free speech advocates had been making for decades.

Supreme Court Justices Oliver Wendell Holmes and Louis Brandeis started the ball rolling with notable dissents that set forth principles of free expression, and the Court finally began to apply those ideas to cases in the 1930s. This process was slow but inexorable. In those cases and during the ensuing decades, the Court recognized free speech protections for news publishers, political radicals, union organizers, religious proselytizers, Communists, filmmakers, booksellers, pornographers, academics, civil rights activists, anti-war demonstrators, students, gay rights agitators, women's rights proponents, Klansmen, Nazis, advertisers, pro-choice activists, antichoice activists, and so on.

Professor Stuart Jay traced this evolution case-by-case, and observed that "[t]he principle of government neutrality regarding expression did not blow in from the desert. Rather it encapsulates an attitude about the relationship between citizen and state" that grew out of specific cases of censorship. During the formative years of First Amendment jurisprudence, "the Court was presented with an assortment of cases in which individuals were arrested for literally doing nothing other than expressing an unpopular view, or simply being in a place that authorities deemed off limits to those who bucked the established order." Harvard Professor (and former US Solicitor General) Charles Fried has written that this yielded the basic building blocks of First Amendment law:

> The principal lines of doctrine are clear. Government may not suppress or regulate speech because it does not like its content – unless it is obscene or demonstrably defamatory. If government regulates the time, place or manner of speech, it must regulate in a way that does not take sides between competing ideas. And if government regulation directed at other ends has the effect of restricting speech, that regulation too must be neutral.

Academic critics of this evolution argue that it extends protection to the wrong speakers, or to bad speech, and that the resulting jurisprudence is not sufficiently consistent to suit their preferences. Such critiques are to be expected among those who see the First Amendment as nothing more than a struggle between competing political goals, and particularly from those who have been unable to impose their vision of what constitutes "valuable" speech. It is an "eye of the beholder" problem, pure and simple.

STILL A DILEMMA?

But what about the censor's dilemma? Contrary to the thesis of this book, current trends in academia suggest that there is no longer any reticence about censorship, particularly among those who embrace the notion that the First Amendment does indeed go "too far." Such unapologetic endorsements of the need to suppress disagreeable expression seem to contradict the premise that censors in a free society are embattled and defensive. Are these the exceptions that prove the rule?

Not at all. To begin with, exceptions don't prove rules – they test them – and, in this instance, First Amendment critics, in the words of the Bard, "doth protest too much." Condemnatory rhetoric about First Amendment "stupidity" and talk of constitutional "sin" reveal a fundamental defensiveness in the sense that such scholars evidently believe that the best defense is a loud offense. In other words, although a number of academic writers advocate restrictions on a broad range of speech, they nevertheless recoil from the mantle of "censor" by claiming that the Supreme Court has defined the concept of free expression too broadly. *That's* not speech, they sniff, or, at least, not the kind of speech the Constitution's framers had in mind. Who's a censor? *I'm* not a censor.

Ever since Comstock sullied the name, no one wants to be known as a censor. This is particularly true of those who advocate, or seek to exercise, censorial power. It also is why certain academics disparage "First Amendment values" and devise elaborate theories to explain how their proposals for government to restrict the speech they dislike does not make them "censors." It is manifest in Stanley Fish's insistence that censoring speech actually *implements* the First Amendment and his complaint that, "in our legal culture as it is now constituted, if one yells 'free speech' in a crowded courtroom and makes it stick, the case is over." It is illustrated by the lament of Richard Delgado and his co-authors that writers from across the political spectrum, "from George Will to Nat Hentoff have attacked our efforts," unjustly in their view, by describing it as "the work of 'thought police,' 'leftist censors,' and 'first amendment revisionists.'" They *cannot* be censors, Delgado insists, because "when the government regulates hate speech, it enhances and adds to potential social dialogue, rather than subtracts from it."

But censors are as censors do. Chapter 4 explored the tactics of censorship through the vehicle of "Comstock's Playbook," which summarized the tried and true strategies of the alpha morals crusader. They include exhibiting absolute moral certainty about the righteousness (and primacy) of the cause, branding opponents as lovers of vice, reviling adversaries in various other ways as well (such as branding them as criminals), blaming "the other," poisoning the debate with invective, touting pseudoscience, cranking up the publicity machine, exaggerating the threats from speech, over-hyping accomplishments, and playing the victim. The same strategies have been employed ever since by censors and their apologists to varying degrees. Apart from tactics, what are the censor's defining characteristics?

KNOWING THEM WHEN YOU SEE THEM

There may be a way to cut through the pretense and define more precisely when the label "censor" fits. One approach is inspired by stand-up comedian Jeff Foxworthy, a member of the Blue Collar Comedy Tour, who is famous for (among other things) his series of one-liners that start with "You might be a redneck if . . .." Examples: "You might be a redneck if you own a home that is mobile and fourteen cars that aren't"; "You might be a redneck if an episode of *Walker, Texas Ranger* changed your life"; or "You might be a redneck if you've been married three times and have the same in-laws."

Somewhat ironically, Foxworthy's use of stereotype could make him a criminal under the hate speech laws proposed by Delgado and others if his jokes were thought to be disparaging of a "protected" group. But Foxworthy's target audience is not among the favored categories, Delgado explains, because "'[c]racker,' although disrespectful, still implies power, as does 'redneck.'" This claim that rednecks and crackers are people of "power" or privilege would come as a real surprise to the residents of rural America, who largely feel disempowered and disrespected. But I digress . . .. The point is that Foxworthy has come up with a million of these lines because they often ring true. This same rhetorical device can be employed to help identify who has the mind and the soul of a censor, which may not be funny but can be just as telling.

Here are just a few suggestions:

1 *You Might Be a Censor if You Dismiss Support of Free Speech as Empty Dogma*

It is pretty easy to devalue free speech if you can portray its advocates as just a pack of mindless acolytes who mouth First Amendment platitudes as articles of faith. The writings of free speech antagonists are littered with such rhetoric. Academics such as Delgado, Matsuda, Lawrence, and others cannot bring themselves to describe free speech proponents without disparaging them as "absolutists," "purists," "totalists," or "First Amendment fundamentalists." It used to be conservatives like Robert Bork who would complain about "the lunacies of America's rights-crazed culture." But after court decisions increasingly made clear that speech was protected even if the cause was not "progressive," some academic writers became alarmed that they could no longer count on a First Amendment monopoly for "their" issues.

They called the drift in free speech thinking away from right-wing moralists and toward libertarians "the new conservative First Amendment Kool-Aid," referring to the 1978 massacre in Guyana when cult followers of the Reverend Jim Jones drank cyanide-laced Flavor-Aide (a Kool-Aid imitator) in a mass suicide. In line with this tack, Professor Mary Anne Franks devotes her book THE CULT OF THE CONSTITUTION to the proposition that First Amendment advocates are unthinking fundamentalists, akin to back-country religionists, who worship at the altar of white male supremacy. Meanwhile, Steve Shiffrin labels First Amendment "idolatry" a "fetish."

A corollary of this strategy is to wave away the First Amendment jurisprudence that evolved through decades of combatting various forms of censorship as mechanical, wooden, or unprincipled. Jeremy Waldron argues that "First Amendment 'jurisprudence'" is nothing more than a collection of "traditional myths and slogans" and that law school professors caught in its grip merely teach their students "to spout the mantra 'the marketplace of ideas.'" MacKinnon grumbles that Americans are taught to revere freedom of speech "by about the fourth grade and continue to absorb it through osmosis from everything around them for the rest of their lives, including law school, to the point that those who embrace it think it is their own personal faith, their own original view." Stanley Fish calls free speech law nothing more than "a grab bag of analogies, invented-for-the-occasion arguments, rhetorical slogans, shaky distinctions, and ad hoc exceptions" that, in his estimation, "overprotect speech."

What is their proposed solution? Delgado and Jean Stefancic insist that "First Amendment doctrine needs to move beyond mechanical tests, such as no content regulation, and thought-ending clichés such as 'the best cure to bad speech is more speech.'" Shiffrin advocates abandoning "frozen categories" of speech considered outside the First Amendment's protection and suggests that courts should be free to expand the range of unprotected speech. In other words, the way to fix the First Amendment is to excise all those troublesome "rule of law" bits.

Ironies abound, of course. It is more than a little problematic to complain about "absolutists" and at the same time argue that traditional First Amendment doctrine is complicated because it recognizes exceptions. Actually, as Shiffrin and others make clear, their argument is that First Amendment law recognizes *too few* exceptions. If the First Amendment isn't absolute, they say, then it should be able to accommodate the added exceptions they prefer. But this ignores the century of case-by-case development that led to the current state of the law (that explains the exceptions). It is neither seamless nor perfectly consistent, as it is constantly evolving, but it has led to a certain degree of predictability and ever-increasing protections for freedom of expression in the United States. Accordingly, when Stanley Fish is asked what he would replace it with, he candidly admits, "I have no answer at all."

2 *You Might Be a Censor if Your Opposition to Free Speech Can Be Summed Up with a Bumper Sticker Slogan*

Negative sloganeering is a familiar ploy in the era of Donald Trump, where reasoned argument took a back seat to labeling. The twice impeached former president routinely disparaged any story he perceived to be unflattering as "fake news" and repeatedly tarred journalists with the Stalinist tag "enemy of the people" for the same reason. This isn't argument, it's branding. Like the endless list of dopey nicknames Trump conjured for his adversaries, the point was to use an unflattering handle in the hope of undermining his opposition's credibility. Trump candidly admitted the purpose underlying his attacks in an interview with *60 Minutes* correspondent Lesley Stahl: "I do it to discredit you all and demean you all, so when you write negative stories about me no one will believe you."

Academic critics of strong free speech protections follow the same strategy, albeit in a more erudite and refined way than our reality TV ex-president. One such label that has become popular in recent years is the claim that the First Amendment has been "weaponized." The term went viral after a 2018 *New York Times* piece appeared with the headline "How Conservatives Weaponized the First Amendment." The *Times* article itself was a balanced analysis by Adam Liptak of how liberals have become increasingly disenchanted with current trends in free speech jurisprudence, but the headline was inspired by Justice Elena Kagan's use (in a dissent) of the vogue term "weaponizing the First Amendment." Justice Kagan, in turn, apparently drew on the current academic popularity of this turn of phrase. In 2016, for example, the American Constitution Society hosted a panel at its Washington, DC, conference on *The Weaponized First Amendment*.

The use of this metaphor in the First Amendment context may be traced to MacKinnon's quite literal claims from her writings in the 1990s that words are themselves weapons, and from Delgado's argument that "the defenders of the status quo have discovered, in the first amendment, a new weapon." By 2019, MacKinnon jumped further onto the rhetorical bandwagon, writing that the "weaponization of 'speech' for unequal ends ... has increasingly occurred over the past seventy or so years – prominently for White supremacist and male-dominant sexual ends." Apparently, in her view, pretty much all modern First Amendment jurisprudence has been "weaponized" from its inception.

The term itself is rather meaningless. Like candidate Trump's 2016 threat to "open up the libel laws," the rhetorical device says little more than that the speaker dislikes the current state of the law. "Weaponization" certainly has come a long way from its origins in the 1950s, when rocket scientists like Werner von Braun coined the term to describe the placement of nuclear warheads on ballistic missiles. Now, everything is "weaponized." In December 2019, Representative Jim Jordan of Ohio complained that the impeachment process had been "weaponized" against President Trump.

In a 2016 essay for *Slate*, John Kelly observed that the term had become the "metaphor *du jour*," and that the presidential contest that year had become a hotbed of weaponization. The term perfectly captures the mood of a polarized culture, where "*weaponize* is at the center of this fight between microaggressions and dog whistles, between trigger warnings and P.C. backlash, between the collective sacrifices required of pluralism and the conservatism of privilege, where nuance, complexity, and civil engagement are getting kicked in the ribs." Watching the trendlines, Kelly concluded: "[W]e've weaponized *weaponize*." It is now one of the most hackneyed expressions used by critics of the First Amendment.

Another cliché is the more wonkish academic criticism that the Roberts Court has "*Lochnerized* the First Amendment," a charge sometimes combined with the claim that free speech has been "weaponized." The term comes from the discredited 1905 decision *Lochner* v. *New York*, in which the Supreme Court struck down a state law that limited bakers to sixty-hour work weeks. The ruling was sharply criticized at the time in dissents by Justices John Marshall Harlan and Oliver Wendell Holmes, and was later overturned to make way for New Deal-era economic regulation. The *Lochner* era has been reviled as a time in which conservative activist judges imposed their own economic views to strike down government regulations based on substantive due process rights not found in the Constitution's text. Accordingly, Lochnerism has been described as "'one of the worst charges that can be leveled against a doctrine or constitutional interpretation, an unequivocal repudiation' of what the court has done."

For this reason, the *Lochner* tag has become a popular theme among academics who disfavor First Amendment protection for commercial speech or who believe that the courts have too willingly protected business interests. But the connection between *Lochner* and the First Amendment is tenuous, where protections for freedom of speech are part of the Constitution's text, while the substantive due process rights at issue in *Lochner* were not. While people can and do debate the merits of particular First Amendment cases involving business or corporate speech, Professor Howard Wasserman has noted that "slapping the *Lochner* tag" on a given decision "does not advance the discussion." It is merely "a pejorative term whose meaning we do not know and cannot agree upon and whose assumed meaning runs a broad range." Consequently, those who tend to rely on such pejorative labeling as a substitute for argument reveal their inner Comstocks.

3 *You Might Be a Censor if You Equate Defense of Freedom to Express Disagreeable Ideas with the Endorsement of Bad Speech*

Anthony Comstock simply could not believe that anyone who opposed his crusade to cleanse the culture of immoral influences could possibly be acting out of high principle or good motives. He denounced those who opposed him as being innately depraved and insisted that they were seeking merely to protect "their dear obscenity." Such "free lusters," as he called them, "naturally favor the impure and base" and just want to "tear down the pure and holy." He described those who opposed "his" law as a "howling, ranting, blaspheming mob of repealers," and asserted that "*no sect or class*, as a sect or class, has ever publicly sided with the smut-dealer, and defended his nefarious business, except the Infidels, the Liberals, and the Free Lovers." Comstock, like most political activists, divided the world into two camps – those for his cause and those against it – and he was incapable of separating his opponents from the vice he was working so tirelessly to vanquish. H. L. Mencken observed that "moral gladiators" like Comstock all "know the game" of tarring their adversaries as "apologists for . . . evil."

Some modern anti-speech activists exhibit the same trait. Echoing Comstock, Catherine MacKinnon has written that "it is difficult to avoid the conclusion that the First Amendment is construed as it is so men can have their pornography." Mary Anne Franks employs almost identical language in attacking the ACLU because of its opposition to overly broad and poorly drafted laws against so-called "revenge porn" (which is Franks' special project). She writes: "It is difficult to avoid the conclusion that [the ACLU's] motivation for doing so has to do with the gender dynamics of the abuse." It makes sense that Franks would sound like MacKinnon, as she formerly served as the latter's research assistant. But she more closely resembles Comstock in his score-settling polemics of the 1880s. According to Franks, the ACLU has prioritized "white men's free speech rights" over others' because it is "a deeply conservative, and fundamentalist, organization." She goes on: The ACLU's First Amendment advocacy is "defined by consumerism" which has "endeared it to the pornography industry, which found ways to return the favor." I guess *that* will teach groups like the ACLU not to oppose Ms. Franks' legislative proposals.

In the same vein, some advocates of hate speech laws suggest that those who defend Nazis and white supremacists are themselves racist (either consciously or unconsciously). Richard Delgado and Jean Stefancic claim to distinguish groups like the ACLU from "the rest of us, who despise racism and bigotry," and proclaim that "the ACLU and conservative bigots are hand in glove." Far from acting out of principle, they suggest that such First Amendment advocates "prefer defending Nazis to defending their victims," and that "[s]ometimes, defending Nazis is simply defending Nazis." Charles Lawrence asks "which side the civil libertarians are on," and wonders if "the reluctance to regulate hate speech is related to unconscious racism." Meanwhile, Franks charges that free speech advocates are "strangely eager to embrace a narrative that validates prejudices against women, minorities, and fellow liberals."

The tactic of falsely equating the defense of free speech with the ideas being defended – and using it as a way to silence a speaker – was on full display when protestors shouted down an ACLU lawyer at the College of William & Mary in October 2017. Those who disrupted the event were upset that the ACLU had defended the First Amendment right to hold the "Unite the Right Rally" in Charlottesville, Virginia. The protestors stormed the stage brandishing signs with slogans like "Your Free Speech Hides Beneath White Sheets" and "Liberalism Is White Supremacy." Tactics like this descend directly from Comstock, who branded those who traded in, or defended, obscenity (as he broadly defined it) "moral cancer planters."

4 *You Might Be a Censor if Your First Amendment Theories Perfectly Match Your Political Causes*

Anthony Comstock was fortunate in at least one respect: he didn't have to concoct any theories of free expression to support his chosen pursuits. First Amendment doctrine did not yet exist. Being the Victorian-era white male patriarch that he was, Comstock could rely on the parsimonious conceptions of free speech borrowed from English law to prosecute discussions of sex, birth control, literature, art, and anything that pushed the boundaries of traditional womanhood. He believed that the decision in *Regina* v. *Hicklin* was divinely inspired, for it allowed him to suppress "the evil effect of certain matter, whether printed, written, engraved, drawn, or painted." This had to be what the Constitution's framers intended, he reasoned, for it would "libel our forefathers" to suggest that the Constitution contained a right "to debauch the morals of the young." Those genuinely concerned about fundamentalism would find it here – quite literally – if they cared to look.

Strangely, modern activists who decry "First Amendment fundamentalism" advocate constitutional interpretations that are eerily reminiscent of Comstock's view of free expression. It is no coincidence that doing so supports their policy proposals. But, unlike Comstock, they have to contend with a century of case law development that has gotten in their way. Dr. Fredric Wertham faced this problem in the 1950s, because emerging free speech jurisprudence was impeding his crusade against horror comics, which he believed caused crime, and superhero comics – like Batman and Wonder Woman – that he believed turned kids gay. So he insisted that the Constitution's framers never intended to protect such rubbish, calling the invocation of the First Amendment against his activism a "fatal misuse of a high principle." He scoffed at those who cited the First Amendment as "their Magna Charta [*sic*]," and instead pointed to Comstock-era court decisions as setting the proper standard.

During the mid-twentieth century, most liberals (other than Wertham) were comfortable with the evolution of First Amendment law so long as the Constitution was being interpreted to protect leftist political radicals, union organizers, anti-war protestors, and civil rights activists. But once the same rights were recognized for conservatives and corporate entities, then the whole thing went wrong because, as Seidman and others concluded, the First Amendment could not be considered reliably "progressive." Some, like Seidman, Neuborne, and Shiffrin, cast a wide net, arguing that First Amendment law should be reinterpreted across the board to be more in line with their political preferences and so it would not "overprotect speech." Others picked their shots more narrowly, and spun theories focusing more on their particular causes. For academics like Delgado, MacKinnon, and Franks, the targets are hate speech, pornography, and "revenge porn." For theorists like Professor Tamara Piety and others, the problem to be overcome involves protections for commercial speech.

One common refrain among academic critics of the First Amendment is that the courts have become result-oriented in their free speech decisions and are actively pushing a partisan agenda. But it rings hollow to complain about result-oriented decision-making when your principal beef is that the courts have failed to advance *your* preferred policies. Seidman's argument that the First Amendment is insufficiently "progressive" is a prime example. Likewise, Shiffrin says it is time to stop "the mechanical privileging of free speech" because it "has led us to plainly unacceptable *results*." Professors Jane and Derek Bambauer critiqued the trend among certain academics who have written that the Supreme Court's hostility to speech regulation has ushered in a free speech *Lochner*ism. They observe that "[t]hese scholarly critiques are ... guilty of the same instrumentalism of which they accuse the Court. Their agenda is the mirror image of the alleged new *Lochner*ism" and "depends entirely on one's political leanings."

It almost sounds like Stanley Fish may be right when he argues that the battle about freedom of speech is just a contest between opposing political factions, except for this: None of the anti-speech theorists propose interpretations of the First Amendment that would limit speech by anyone with whom they are ideologically aligned, while civil liberties groups, like the ACLU, historically have advocated protections even for those with whom they disagree. Weighing the two sides of this debate, the anti-speech position is, in the end, just a variation of "free speech for me but not for thee" with a scholarly gloss.

5 *You Might Be a Censor if You Are Certain That There Is No "Value" in the Expression You Want to Suppress*

Anthony Comstock was dead certain of many things, but above all he knew that there was no value in the speech he spent his career trying to suppress. How else could a person justify criminal sanctions for a speech crime? He pursued prosecutions of classic literature and art schools, observing that "'art' and 'classic' are made to gild some of the most obscene representations and foulest matters" that "cater[] to the animal in man." And even if the works might possess some vestigial element of merit, Comstock knew that censorship still was the answer because "[a]rt is not above morals. *Morals stand first.*" Judge Robert Bork – another man of great certitude – said the same thing about suppressing flag burning as a form of political protest. With such an act, he wrote, "no idea was being suppressed but merely a particularly offensive mode of expression."

Modern anti-speech activists make the same arguments. Catherine MacKinnon proclaims that the "pornography industry does not produce art or literature, nor are the pornography pimps artists or literary writers." Beyond that, she says, pornography conveys no "ideas" except the subordination of women. Delgado, Waldron, and many others argue that racist speech does not promote the search for truth and is "far from the core of political expression." Such "low-value speech" in their view contributes nothing to the marketplace of ideas, and is immune to any curative effect of "more speech." Charles Lawrence argues that racist speech "advances none of the purposes of the first amendment," and concludes that "the time has come to put an end to the ringing rhetoric that condemns all efforts to regulate racist speech." Mary Anne Franks claims that the Trump era "exposed the hollowness of liberal free speech platitudes: the belief that truth will eventually prevail, that the best answer to bad speech is more speech, and that protecting the free speech rights of the worst people in society is necessary to protect the free speech of all."

Such arguments are brought to life by events of the recent past. The "Unite the Right Rally" in Charlottesville is an example of speech at its ugliest, and it makes the value of free speech hard to discern. Tensions had been brewing throughout the summer of 2017 over the city's plan to remove a statue of Confederate General Robert E. Lee from a public park, which led to a call by white supremacist Richard Spencer, neo-Nazi groups, and the Ku Klux Klan to organize a "Unite the Right" rally that August. It was kicked off by the repulsive spectacle of a procession through the University of Virginia campus by 250 tiki-torch-wielding marchers who chanted neo-Nazi slogans including "Blood and Soil" and "Jews Will Not Replace Us" (Figure 9.1). The following day, confrontations between white supremacists and counter-demonstrators, made more dangerous by an inadequate police response, resulted in multiple injuries and the tragic death of a young woman named Heather Heyer, when twenty-year-old James Alex Fields, Jr. plowed his car into a group of counter-protesters.

Another illustration involves the speech of the Westboro Baptist Church, a peculiar family cult of religious fundamentalists that believes that their god hates the United States because of the nation's tolerance of homosexuality, among other things. The Westboro cultists had chosen as a principal venue for its hateful message the funerals of servicemen, with picket signs such as "Thank God for Dead Soldiers," "Fags Doom Nations," and "God Hates Fags." The Supreme Court found that the First Amendment protects such speech in an eight-to-one decision, even as it acknowledged that the incoherent messages "fall short of refined social or political commentary." In reaching this conclusion, the Court was aware that such speech "can stir people to action, move them to tears of both joy and sorrow, and . . . inflict great pain."

To this, Professor Shiffrin responds that the Westboro protestors made no valuable contribution to the public debate and thus deserve no First Amendment protection. But such arguments about the Charlottesville and Westboro Baptist Church protests miss the point. The First Amendment does not contain literacy or civility tests

FIGURE 9.1 White supremacists march with torches in Charlottesville
Source: Photo by Samuel Corum/Anadolu Agency/Getty Images.

wherein the state can dictate what speech qualifies for protection according to whether it possesses sufficient merit and has the right temperament. Protection does not depend on the "value" of the speech involved, or on the possibility that the views of Nazis, white supremacists, and religious bigots might one day be vindicated. Constitutional immunities are based not on the chance that Nazis may be proven right but on the proposition that the government lacks the authority or competence to declare who is wrong and who must be silent. Freedom includes the right to be wrong. Moreover, the value of such speech does not lie in its potential "truth." Some participants in the marketplace of ideas serve mainly as bad examples, and society is worse off when deprived of them. As John Stuart Mill wrote in ON LIBERTY, the benefit of false speech, for both current and future generations, is to provide a "clearer perception and livelier impression of truth, produced by its collision with error."

While the Westboro picketers may have intended to send a message of intolerance through Old Testament-style retribution, no one honestly believes that they persuaded anyone of the rightness and necessity of their views. It is hard to imagine anyone seeing their hateful displays and thinking, "Hmmm, maybe those rude and angry people have a point." By most accounts, those who witnessed their bizarre and distasteful signs were repulsed, and left to wonder what could produce such callousness and intolerance. The group's anti-American messages likely did more to rekindle a sense of patriotism among those who saw the church's crude denunciations of the United States. Plus, the counter-demonstrations they attracted were often funny and invariably more persuasive (Figure 9.2).

But one thing is absolutely clear: Allowing this fringe group to propagate its idiotic and mean-spirited views did not make Americans less tolerant of gay people or impede the drive toward marriage equality. Four years after the Supreme Court held that the First Amendment protects the Westboro protest, it decided *Obergefell* v. *Hodges*, affirming a constitutional right to gay marriage. Reactions to the violent clashes in Charlottesville tell a similar story. A week after the Unite the Right rally, 40,000 people turned out in Boston in response to a repeat event. This time, however, police were well prepared, and the event took place with few arrests and no major incidents of violence.

The outpouring illustrates the type of response that the marketplace of ideas invites. If the best remedy for bad ideas is good ones, some might take comfort from the fact that counter-demonstrators marching in opposition to racism and white nationalism outnumbered the protest organizers in Boston by an estimated 800 to 1, and that the event came off without any serious injuries or property damage. Likewise, a Unite the Right rally planned in Washington, DC, on the first anniversary of Charlottesville fizzled and was an embarrassment. Only twenty to thirty white

FIGURE 9.2 Protests against the Westboro Baptist Church's demonstration outside the Long Beach, CA Performing Arts Center on May 15, 2010
Source: Photo by Jeff Gritchen/Digital First Media/Orange County Register via Getty Images.

nationalists turned up, and were greatly outnumbered by thousands of counter-protestors. Susan Bro, the mother of Heather Heyer, (who died in the violent confrontations in Charlottesville) saw this as the value of combatting hate with speech, not censorship. She observed of the Washington, DC, rally, "they showed up in very small numbers and they were met with counter-protesters who were in a very large number, saying go home, go away." This was the best way to deal with hate, she observed, because "once we take away the right to free speech, we may never get it back."

6 *You Might Be a Censor if You Equate Speech with Conduct and Believe That It Must Be Restricted Because of Its Bad Tendencies*

Anthony Comstock saw no distinction between evil thoughts or words and evil deeds. All fell into the category of sin. He considered any writings that touched on sex "a deadly poison, cast into the fountain of moral purity" that necessarily polluted society. Comstock believed that "evil reading" was a disease worse than yellow fever or smallpox. There was no need to raise a fuss about cause and effect. It was perfectly obvious to him that bad books "breed vulgarity, profanity, loose ideas of life, impurity of thought and deed." By this reasoning, he equated pornography, contraception, and abortion as products of the same original sin: Illicit images and stories cause lust, which leads to sex, which is facilitated by contraceptives, and, when they fail, abortion.

Modern anti-speech activists use the same logic. Catherine MacKinnon does a spectacular Comstock impression: "Pornography is masturbation material. It is used as sex. It therefore is sex." She even ups the rhetorical ante, asserting that pornography is a "technologically sophisticated form of trafficking in women," and that hate speech and pornography are "racial and/or gender-based terrorism." Stanley Fish describes such tactics like this: If you want to prohibit pornography or hate speech, "what you have to do is deny its status as speech and move it over into the category of action." Hence, all that talk of weaponization.

Some take the concept even further. In a 2017 *New York Times* article, psychology professor Lisa Feldman Barrett argued that certain speakers, such as confrontationally conservative (and gay) former *Breitbart News* editor Milo Yiannopoulos, should be banned from campus appearances because, "[f]rom the perspective of our brain cells," some types of speech are "literally a form of violence." Think of it as a form of transubstantiation, but for censors: speech doesn't just cause violence, it *is* violence. Dr. Barrett based her conclusion on the thesis that chronic stress can affect the body's immune system and that certain speech can produce negative health effects. Speech that is merely offensive – such as listening to a scholarly debate on eugenics – would be okay because it would promote long-term learning. By contrast, an appearance by a "hatemonger" like Milo would be something else entirely, she wrote, because "[h]e is part of something noxious, a campaign of abuse." She added: "There is nothing to be gained from debating him, for debate is not what he is offering."

Arguments like this are nothing more than attempts to invoke science to justify political preferences. Needless to say, stress can affect the human body. But it is quite a stretch to link the type of chronic stress that, say, growing up in poverty can cause, to an adverse emotional reaction to a provocative speaker. It is even more difficult when trying to draw a line between "offensive" speech, which can be unpleasant but potentially educational, and "abusive" speech, which under this theory is not considered expression at all. Barrett offers no analytical tools for drawing such distinctions, and those who seek to silence speakers in the real world usually make no attempt at all to do so. But the tactic of trying to convert obnoxious speech into something else that can be regulated is a familiar one, and it is one defining characteristic of the censor. Jeremy Waldron, for example, describes hate speech as "pollution" of the social environment that can be banned (the same argument made by both Comstock and Fredric Wertham).

While few go so far as to make the literal-minded claim that speech "is" the evil thing the state may prohibit, most censors are quite comfortable assuming cause and effect. Ultimately, they are merely reviving the "bad tendency" test. This was the theory that informed First Amendment law in Comstock's time, and it is the one that was rejected a century ago, beginning with the writings of Holmes and Brandeis. Successive court decisions abandoned the bad tendency test because experience showed that it was all too easy to suppress speech by authors, radicals, and dissenting minorities if all the government had to prove was that the speech *might* have bad effects.

Another problem with the bad tendency approach is that it operates as a universal solvent for First Amendment rights. Thus, MacKinnon invokes it not just to revise First Amendment protections for sexually oriented or racially charged speech but to undo legal barriers to defamation suits (or, as Trump would say, "open up the libel laws"). She complains that because *New York Times* v. *Sullivan* "made it easier for newspapers to publish defamatory falsehoods," individuals "from subordinated groups who take on dominant interests in public are left especially exposed – sexually libeled feminists who oppose pornography, for example." Such efforts to relabel words as actions (or "weapons") and to regulate them because of their tendency for evil are part of a tradition that harkens back to Comstock as a way to undermine First Amendment protections across the board.

7 You Might Be a Censor if You Can't Argue about Free Speech Issues without Using Euphemisms and Apocalyptic Metaphors

Euphemism has always been a tool favored by censors; it is doubtful that they could do their work without it. Anthony Comstock was the unparalleled master of the apocalyptic mixed metaphor. To him, licentious publications were worse than the plagues of Egypt that, "like the fishes of the sea, spawn millions of seed, and each year these seeds germinate and spring up to a harvest of death." Reading an unclean book was "a worse evil than yellow fever or small pox." Dime novels were "products of corrupt minds [that] are the eggs from which all kinds of villainies are hatched," and bawdy theaters were the "recruiting stations for hell." Fredric Wertham was a piker by comparison, but he did his best. Wertham compared the comics industry to Hitler and said that comic books were akin to communicable diseases, asserting: "You cannot resist infantile paralysis in your own home alone. Must you not take into account the neighbor's children?"

Modern anti-speech activists embrace this technique, as it is a corollary of relabeling speech as conduct. As with many of these indicia, MacKinnon leads the pack. She denounces pornography (as she broadly defines it) as "terrorism," "the original fake news," and "lies, pure and simple, about women's and children's sexuality." Of course, the other side of the euphemistic coin of saying that speech isn't speech is to use metaphor to suggest that censorship isn't censorship. Thus, Professor Waldron's response to the argument that hate speech laws might be used to punish fringe or unpopular views is to assert that "[o]ne might as well say that laws against drinking-and-driving represent an attack on the discrete minority of drunk drivers." This echoes Fredric Wertham's claim that a comic book ban "is no more a restriction of freedom of speech than not selling whiskey to children is a restraint of trade." Delgado and Stefancic similarly seek to distance hate speech laws from "speech" regulation by analogizing them to managing an electric grid. They posit that hate speech is not a "core" First Amendment value, so it is a misallocation of resources to defend it, just as it would be wasteful to divert primary energy production to peripheral uses (like enabling "teenagers and young adults to recharge their cell phones"). Such is the rhetoric of the censor: Use exaggerated metaphor to hype the danger to be conquered while minimizing any connection to restricting speech.

8 You Might Be a Censor if You Believe That Silencing Speech You Dislike Is the Exercise of Your Rights

This was another thing about which Anthony Comstock harbored no doubt; his mission to crush immorality was not just ordained by his god, it was his holy mission and the exercise of his fundamental rights. And, just as certainly, the targets of his crusade were exercising no "rights" of their own. Comstock knew in his bones that "[f]reedom to speak or print does not imply the right to say or print that which shocks decency, corrupts the morals of the young, or destroys all faith in God." And he complained about free thinkers who believed that free speech meant that they had the right to do and say as they pleased "without regard to the rights, morals or liberties of others." In the words of Jazz Age writer Ring Lardner, "'Shut up,' he explained."

This is the ethos of "cancel culture" and the disinvitation movement on college campuses, which has picked up steam in recent years. Brandeis University, named for the Supreme Court justice who once wrote that the "freedom to think as you will and to speak as you think are means indispensable to the discovery and spread of political truth," cravenly rescinded its offer of an honorary degree to rights advocate Ayaan Hirsi Ali because of protests over her statements condemning Islam and its treatment of women. Student protests in 2014 caused Christine Lagarde, the first woman to head the International Monetary Fund (IMF), to withdraw as commencement speaker at Smith College, and Condoleezza Rice, former Secretary of State, to cancel as commencement speaker at Rutgers University. Others targeted for disinvitations at various schools included conservative columnist George Will, former Secretary of State Madeleine Albright, former US Attorney General Eric Holder, and comedian Bill Maher. Between 2000 and 2017, there was a sevenfold increase in efforts to cancel speakers. According to the Foundation for Individual Rights in Education (FIRE), which tracks such matters, there were 379 efforts to block speakers on US college campuses during this period, and almost half – 46 percent – were successful.

But aren't such student protests examples of "more speech" that First Amendment advocates claim to crave? No, not when the purpose is to silence the speaker through intimidation or violence, or when authorities are enlisted to enforce their demands. Then it becomes the "heckler's veto," a term coined by Professor Harry Kalven, Jr. in the 1960s to describe segregationists who acted to silence civil rights demonstrators, usually with the backing of the police. Brookings Institute scholar Jonathan Rauch explains the difference: Those who practice free speech values seek to add information to the debate with their message of protest, while cancel culture seeks to shut down disfavored views. "The goal here is for a group, usually a self-defining group, to express its solidarity in contrast to another group who it hates – preferably by shutting it down or shutting it up." The other purpose is not to add to public discussion but to engage in "virtue signaling." Still, there are gradations of culpability. Those who merely agitate to silence speakers they dislike have the soul of the censor; those who seek to coerce the result are the actual censors.

Some theorists claim that silencing a speaker because of hateful or discriminatory rhetoric is not the heckler's veto; it is an act of liberation that frees up the voices of the oppressed. Focusing just on the First Amendment reads the Constitution too narrowly, they argue, because the Fourteenth Amendment promises equality. These different constitutional guarantees are in tension, according to this view, because enforcing First Amendment protections for speech that denigrates women, minorities, or other groups undervalues the Fourteenth Amendment interest in equality. According to Delgado and Stefancic, speech and equality are "opposite sides of the same coin," which is another way of describing the protection of rights as a zero-sum game – to get more of one, you must have less of the other. MacKinnon argues that "[t]he law of equality and the law of freedom of speech are on a collision course," and that when "equality is mandated, racial and sexual epithets, vilification, and abuse should be able to be prohibited, unprotected by the First Amendment." Thus, in the name of equal protection of the law, some speakers must be treated differently and silenced. This is necessary to facilitate speech by members of historically disadvantaged groups who otherwise might feel discouraged from participating in the marketplace of ideas.

These theorists assert that speech must be restricted by law for it to be "truly free," and that legal protections must apply differently to individuals based on their constituent groups in order to achieve "equality." However, this theory of free speech is predicated on a fundamental misreading of the Constitution. Both the First and the Fourteenth Amendments are limits on *governmental* power. The First Amendment prohibits the use of law to abridge speech; the Fourteenth Amendment, among other things, guarantees each citizen equal protection of the laws. But to read the Equal Protection Clause as an affirmative grant of governmental power to restrict speech by individuals who say things that advocate (or result in) inequality is constitutional gibberish. As Charles Fried has written, such reasoning is based on a foundational error that mistakes "an effect of the principle for the principle itself."

With this characteristic, the way to recognize censors is by their Orwellian reasoning and Marcusian proposals. Their diagnoses of the problems and their prescriptions for solutions are pure Newspeak. Just as Oceania declared "Freedom is Slavery," these theorists insist that free speech is censorship. According to MacKinnon, those who make First Amendment arguments represent "a replay of McCarthyism"; Seidman claims that "the assertion of a constitutional right to freedom of speech is dictatorial" and "at war with free thought." As in the allegorical ANIMAL FARM, where the leaders proclaimed that "All animals are created equal; Some animals are more equal than others," these theorists assert that the path to equality is through enforcing asymmetrical speech rights. They would thus employ the "tools of censorship" to restrict "regressive" speakers in the name of freedom of speech.

9 *You Might Be a Censor if You Believe in Forcefully Suppressing Speech to Stop the* Real *Censors*

For some, getting a speaker disinvited from a venue is just not enough. Those who disrupted a free speech presentation by the ACLU's Claire Guthrie Castañaga at the College of William & Mary did more than register their displeasure about the ACLU of Virginia's role in helping secure permits for the "Unite the Right" rally in Charlottesville. The placard-wielding demonstrators forced Castañaga off the stage, shouting slogans like "ACLU, You Protect Hitler Too" and "The Revolution Will Not Uphold the Constitution." When Castañaga tried to engage with some students to answer questions, the protestors blocked this, too, threateningly encircling the ousted speaker and shouting more loudly. If you are willing to engage in this sort of bullying, you just might be a censor.

A similar confrontation occurred in 2017 at Middlebury College, when angry students disrupted a presentation by conservative sociologist Charles Murray, injuring Professor Allison Stanger, the faculty interlocutor for the event. Students had attempted to cancel Murray's speaking invitation because of continuing controversy over his 1994 book THE BELL CURVE (coauthored with Richard Herrnstein). Controversial from the time it was published, the book suggested, among other things, that differences in IQ scores may be explained in part by genetic factors, including race. When the disinvitation bid failed, protestors crowded the room and shouted Murray down, pounded the walls, and pulled fire alarms. A mob pursued Murray and Stanger when they tried to escape campus, and Professor Stanger sustained a whiplash injury and concussion in the resulting scuffle.

Earlier the same year, masked demonstrators at Berkeley shattered windows and set fires to block the appearance of the confrontationally conservative former *Breitbart News* editor Milo Yiannopoulos. The rioting caused an estimated $100,000 in damage (Figure 9.3). Yiannopoulos, whose entire shtick is to provoke and offend, had already had appearances disrupted at several other universities. Two months after his Berkeley speech was canceled, threats of violence at the school led to rescheduling, and ultimately cancellation, of a speech by right-wing provocateur Ann Coulter. In the ensuing weeks, acts of violence and threats led campus officials to cancel speakers at Auburn University, Claremont McKenna College, and (again) Berkeley.

FIGURE 9.3 Violent protests erupt at UC Berkeley against controversial speakers
Source: Photo by Elijah Nouvelage/Getty Images.

The self-described (and ironically named) "anti-fascist" activists (now, with the new, improved label *antifa*!) argue that they may justifiably silence political opponents by using violence if necessary, as an act of "self-defense." As Mark Bray puts it in his 2017 book ANTIFA: THE ANTI-FASCIST HANDBOOK, "[i]nstead of privileging allegedly 'neutral' universal rights, anti-fascists prioritize the political project of destroying fascism and protecting the vulnerable regardless of whether their actions are considered violations of the free speech of fascists or not." Bray's conclusion is drawn from a hodge-podge of arguments that speech isn't truly free under the current system, that the fascists (or their defenders) would restrict far more speech than would the protestors, and the claim of a moral obligation to suppress speech they know to be wrong. The conclusion? Violent suppression equals free expression. Bray asserts that "the antiauthoritarian position held by the majority of antifa is actually *far more pro-free speech* than that put forward by the liberals." The argument is nothing more than bargain-basement Marcuse based on the same Orwellian meme – that freedom may be achieved through censorship.

10 *You Might Be a Censor if You Equate Speech You Oppose with Mental Illness*

Anthony Comstock didn't need to call his adversaries crazy because he knew they were something far worse – they were sinful. But in modern times psychiatry has a stronger grip on most people than does religion, so one tactic used by censors to discredit and delegitimize their opponents is to challenge their mental stability. A 2019 *Psychology Today* article asks whether "Trump Derangement Syndrome," an instinctive negative reaction to all things Trumpian, is a real mental condition. Spoiler alert: It isn't. Do politicians evoke strong negative visceral or emotional reactions? Of course they do. Given the reptilian state of politics today, it would be irrational *not* to have such feelings. But is it deranged? No. Nor is it a new thing to brand as a "syndrome" the strong opposition to a polarizing political figure. Since the "derangement syndrome" neologism was coined by columnist Charles Krauthammer in 2003 in describing reactions to President George W. Bush, it has been applied successively to politicians across the political spectrum ranging from Sarah Palin to Barack Obama, the Clintons, and Al Gore.

Outside the United States, the medicalization of political opposition is more than just partisan histrionics and has a much darker history. After Stalin's death in 1953 and the closure of forced labor camps, the Soviet Union committed thousands of political dissidents to institutions for "treatment" after diagnosing them with such ailments as "sluggish schizophrenia." Disagreement with Communist dogma was diagnosed as "philosophical intoxication" or "delusion of reformism" and those with such "non-standard beliefs" were involuntarily committed. A 2014 report to the European Parliament raised concerns that such repressive measures were making a comeback in Vladimir Putin's Russia. In China, punitive psychiatry was used against religious groups, political dissidents, and whistle blowers, with abuses reaching a peak during the Cultural Revolution from 1966 to 1976. It has been estimated that millions of people were declared "mentally sick" under Mao's rule, and official documents suggest that in the 1980s, 15 percent of forensic psychiatric cases had political connections.

Although the United States has been spared such abuses, the notion that having the wrong ideas is a mental illness (and is susceptible to forced reeducation or medical treatment) is not unknown to us. In a 2016 book, ARE RACISTS CRAZY? HOW PREJUDICE, RACISM, AND ANTISEMITISM BECAME MARKERS OF INSANITY, historian Sander Gilman and sociologist James M. Thomas examine historic efforts to unravel the psychological origins of racism. Starting with discredited research from the eighteenth and nineteenth centuries that purported to link race and psychological disorders, they trace scholarship through the twentieth century suggesting that prejudice is a "group sickness" that could be subject to "treatment." They point to the increased use of pathological language around racism in conference presentations, scholarly articles, and treatment protocols, and discuss a 2012 Oxford University study in which subjects were given a pill to moderate "implicit bias." In one 2005 example they cite, California prison inmates were administered antipsychotic drugs to combat what the divisional chief psychologist for the state prison system called "delusional disorders" of racism and homophobia. In this way, moral shortcomings are medicalized.

We are a long way from China's Cultural Revolution, but vestiges of it may be found in mandatory orientation programs on university campuses in the United States. Alan Kors has written that, through such programs, "some form of moral and political re-education has been built into freshman orientation and residential programming." The purpose is to "cure" the various "isms," including racism, sexism, and classism. Similarly, the vocabulary of mental illness, with terms like homophobia and Islamophobia, has crept into common discourse about what should be seen as moral and ethical problems. Psychoanalyst and philosopher Erich Fromm objected to efforts to classify Nazis as mentally ill, observing that doing so was "a substitute for valid ethical concepts" and it tended to "weaken the sense of moral values, by calling something by a psychiatric term when it should be called plainly evil." A habit of branding those with bad ideas as sick and in need of "treatment" or "reeducation" might make you a censor.

THE FOXWORTHY SCALE

As explained in Chapter 1, this book does not present a new theory of the First Amendment; nor does it engage directly in the ongoing scholarly debates over its interpretation. Those discussions are ably presented in the many books, law review articles, and academic conferences that address the jurisprudence of free expression. The ideas that emerge from such works often are incorporated into the court decisions that make up the body of precedent in this area. This debate over constitutional meaning is unending, as is case law development. The more modest goal of this book is to examine the role that censors have played in this development, and to suggest ways to recognize them when they are in our midst. If the point of the First Amendment is to prevent censorship, having a sense of how to identify censors may help avoid mistakes of the past and provide direction for the future.

If a "Censor-o-Meter" existed to gauge where First Amendment critics fall on the censorship scale, it might measure whether the advocate more resembles Oliver Wendell Holmes or Anthony Comstock. Those exhibiting the most moral certitude, who are convinced of their own infallibility (as well as the venality of their opponents), and who enthusiastically propose government coercion to enforce their preferences would register on the Comstock (Figure 9.4) side of the meter; those who are not too sure that they are right, who believe that the search for truth is an ongoing process, and who are skeptical of the government's ability to dictate truth would fall on the Holmes side. Let's call it the "Foxworthy Scale." At one end of the scale is the spirit of liberty; at the other is "the spirit that ignited the fires of the Inquisition" (as Ezra Heywood said of Comstock). A person's score would depend on how many of the "you-may-be-a censor-if ..." characteristics he or she has, with bonus points for those who fancy themselves "activists" directly involved in suppressing speech.

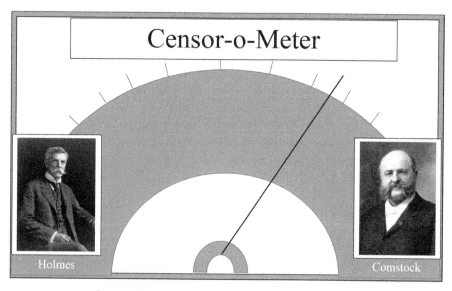

FIGURE 9.4 Censor-o-Meter – Oliver Wendell Holmes to Anthony Comstock

Of course, any proposal to restrict speech must stand or fall on its own merits, based on the strength of its animating ideas and its consistency with First Amendment law. But it might also help round out the analysis by examining how proponents of such measures score when examined for their authoritarian tendencies. On the Foxworthy Scale, some armchair First Amendment skeptics, like Stanley Fish or Lawrence Seidman, may barely move the needle. Activists like Fredric Wertham, Brent Bozell, and Catherine MacKinnon, on the other hand, who worked directly with government authorities to censor speech, would "go to eleven," in the meme popularized in the 1984 mockumentary *This Is Spinal Tap*.

History teaches that people with dictatorial tendencies cannot be trusted to make decisions about what speech should be censored. Marcuse's "democratic educational dictatorship of free men" is an authoritarian's fantasy. Zechariah Chafee, the prominent early academic scholar of free expression, wondered what type of person might be suited to the task of censor. He concluded that "you are likely to get volunteers of the Comstock temperament who are morbidly sensitive about the morals of others. Constant preoccupation with questionable books or plays [or social attitudes, for that matter] is not good for any man. It throws him off his balance, and takes away his sense of proportion (Figure 9.5)." Comstock's biographer, Heywood Broun, was even blunter:

FIGURE 9.5 St. Anthony Comstock, the Village nuisance, L. M. Glackens, *Puck*, 1906.

A case of sorts can be made out for censorship in any field, if you can imagine the job being administered by the wisest man in the world, or one of his five or six closest rivals. But no wise man would ever accept such a post. As things are constituted, it is pretty safe to assume that any given censor is a fool. The very fact [that] he is a censor indicates that.

It therefore pays to know censors when you see them. Using past experience to identify the mind of the censor may be one way to help keep censorship from recurring in our future.

10

Freedom of Speech and the Spirit of Liberty

The American identity and the development of First Amendment law are inextricably intertwined. As First Amendment doctrine evolved and emphasized constitutional protection for individual rights against state power, an antiauthoritarian ethos supporting free expression and the law of free speech became mutually reinforcing. Lee Bollinger, a leading First Amendment expert and President of Columbia University, described it this way:

> Freedom of speech has become so much more than just a legal principle. It has become part of the national identity, and in so many ways we have learned to define ourselves as a people through the process of creating the principle itself. To talk about free speech is ultimately to talk about the ends of life – about the mentality underlying censorship, about what we hope to achieve through human intellect and discussion, and about what speech can do that's evil and harmful and how we must learn to deal with that reality.

The great First Amendment scholar Professor Harry Kalven, Jr., wrote of the culture of free expression in much the same way, describing it as a "worthy tradition" in which cases decided by the courts "carry a compulsion and inspiration that goes beyond literal holdings."

In the United States, the divergence of law from culture is a principal source of the censor's dilemma. Anthony Comstock failed because the culture around him changed and courts eventually caught up as First Amendment law evolved. The same is true for those who have trailed along in his broad wake. Not only were they unable to use the law to serve their various causes over the long haul but, ultimately, they were shamed, their ideas rejected, or both.

Is this inevitable? What if cultural attitudes shifted in another direction, and governmental actions now barred by the courts as censorship were demanded by the public at large as a matter of public policy and social justice? To an extent, such a shift shouldn't make any difference since the protections of the Bill of Rights are counter-majoritarian by design. Writer Kevin Williamson has suggested that "[t]he Bill of Rights ought to be titled 'A List of Things You Idiots Don't Get to Vote On,

Because They Aren't Up for Negotiation.'" Or, on a somewhat loftier plane, albeit expressing the same sentiment, Justice Robert Jackson memorably wrote: "One's right to life, liberty, and property, to free speech, a free press, freedom of worship and assembly, and other fundamental rights may not be submitted to vote; they depend on the outcome of no elections."

But if legal protections for free speech expanded through the twentieth century in part because the law tracked cultural shifts regarding what expression people were willing to tolerate, is there any good reason to believe that they might not contract if social attitudes were to change in the opposite direction? In other words, is the First Amendment safe if the censor's dilemma fades?

THE SPIRIT OF LIBERTY

Legendary jurist Learned Hand, whose legal opinions helped loosen Comstock's grip on the literary world, recognized the interplay of cultural norms and legal protections. But, just as he understood that twentieth-century judges and juries should not interpret the law based on mid-Victorian morals, he also questioned whether constitutional protections could long endure in the face of public antipathy or indifference. He made this point during World War II in a 1944 speech entitled *The Spirit of Liberty*. As Judge Hand saw it: "Liberty lies in the hearts of men and women; when it dies there, no constitution, no law, no court can save it; no constitution, no law, no court can even do much to help it." He suggested that the foundation of our rights depends on "the spirit of liberty," which flows from "the conscience and courage of Americans who create it." He described it as "the spirit which is not too sure that it is right; the spirit of liberty is the spirit which seeks to understand the minds of other men and women; the spirit of liberty is the spirit which weighs their interests alongside its own without bias."

Hand was not speaking just about freedom of speech, but his words have special meaning resonance when it comes to understanding a culture of free expression. Yet he was only half right. Rights may start with "the conscience and courage" of those who seek to exercise and protect them, but it is not enough for liberty to reside just "in the hearts of men and women." There must also be a legal system that recognizes and protects individual rights. It is of little use if the spirit is willing but the Constitution is weak. The long-term security of free speech depends on both a culture that recognizes the value of diverse and unsettling voices backed by legal protections that thwart the majority's natural impulse to silence them.

A culture of free expression requires the ongoing questioning of all things, and this includes a perpetual debate about the value and importance of free speech itself. A sentiment frequently attributed to philosopher Bertrand Russell holds that "in all affairs[,] it's a healthy thing now and then to hang a question mark on the things you have long taken for granted." The attribution of the quote to Russell may be apocryphal, but the truth of the proposition is ironclad. If anything, it understates the case. The perpetual question mark is not just healthy – it is necessary.

In his book KINDLY INQUISITORS, writer and Brookings Institute scholar Jonathan Rauch has described the moral foundations of the system of free expression as a form of liberal science governed by two basic principles: (1) No one gets the final say – meaning no ideas are immune from challenge – and it is never legitimate to end the discussion, and (2) no one has personal authority, which means that anyone can be in error and no person or institution can prescribe the answers to life's great questions (or even its little ones). His point is that, just as with the search for scientific truth, any search for answers on political and social questions is an ongoing process that cannot assume final conclusions, and one in which no one gets to be the ultimate arbiter of truth. In short, in all things, the debate never ends.

Rauch's ideas echo and reinforce the writings of John Stuart Mill and Oliver Wendell Holmes, who were instrumental in developing the American concept of free expression. Mill's ON LIBERTY posited the idea that the exercise of power over individuals is unacceptable, particularly in matters of free inquiry, in large part because "there is no such thing as absolute certainty." Holmes studied and followed Mill's tenets, and infused his free speech philosophy with concepts drawn from the scientific method. In his 1918 essay *Natural Law*, Holmes wrote, "Certitude is not the test of certainty," and he recognized that we "have been cock-sure of many things that were not so."

Professor Vincent Blasi sums up Holmes' scientific approach to freedom of expression as positing that "all propositions are subject to perpetual testing," and that process "must always hold out at least the possibility that prior understandings will be displaced." Political scientist Wayne Batchis describes Holmes' philosophy thusly:

> For Holmes, the First Amendment's approach to truth was more about *journey* than it was about *destination*. It was an end without an end, a vision of truth that was inherently progressive. It does not rest. The search for truth requires constant motion. Indeed, the most significant threat to truth was the stasis advocated by those who were so foolishly confident that they had achieved it. The search-in-perpetuity is facilitated by the First Amendment of the United States Constitution.

This stands in sharp contrast with the mindset of the censor, who claims that the time for debate is over on the subject (or subjects) about which he would silence speech. Anthony Comstock, for example, believed that his work was ordained by the Christian god and described the laws enacted based on his crusades "the most righteous laws ever enacted." He believed that wide-scale censorship was the only thing that could save America's youth from "moral death." Such is not the language of doubt.

Ideas and values that cannot be questioned are nothing but dogma. They hold sway only so long as people are willing to accept them as revealed truths prescribed by their respective gods, great leaders, or founding documents. Where values are protected from questioning and debate, they cannot be handed down to succeeding generations as ideas but only as the memory of ideas. That is why each generation must have access to the entire debate, not just the conclusions derived from earlier intellectual clashes. Societies stagnate if individuals aren't free to search for truth on their own, and that cannot happen if they are told just to memorize and follow some predetermined truth. That includes the need for each generation to discover the value of free speech itself, for, as Holmes wrote, the human impulse for censorship is "perfectly logical" so long as "you have no doubt of your premises or your power." It is also why Learned Hand's spirit of liberty is "the spirit which is not too sure that it is right; the spirit of liberty is the spirit which seeks to understand the minds of other men and women." It is a spirit that is constantly put to the test as new free speech challenges come and go.

WHITHER THE SPIRIT?

Americans constantly debate the value and limits of free speech. We are in the midst of such a debate now, in a time of political polarization and high passions, where the very notion of solving problems through civil discourse seems quaint. On a range of political and cultural issues, partisans argue that their freedoms are under siege while the other side has exceeded the bounds of what free speech should permit. And it is happening at a time when everyone has a voice via social media, yet the fact that we are all connected by an unprecedented global communications medium is increasingly seen as a problem. More speech is enabled for more people than at any time in the history of the world, yet there seems to be less actual communication than ever before. In such an environment will the culture's support for freedom of expression persist?

Historic trends in the United States suggest that support for freedom of speech can be resilient even in times of crisis. The Freedom Forum's First Amendment Center has since 1997 conducted an annual survey of American attitudes toward the First Amendment. The resulting "State of the First Amendment" report addresses various topics, including issues of the day. One question that has remained constant from the beginning asks whether the First Amendment "goes too far in the rights it guarantees." The answer to that question often depends on current events and on the issues that concern respondents most at the time of the survey. In the first report following the terrorist attacks of September 2001, for example, almost half of those surveyed – 49 percent – agreed with the statement that the First Amendment goes too far.

But it says a great deal that, even in the shadow of 9/11, most Americans – if only a bare majority – believed that the First Amendment does *not* go too far in the rights it protects. In years not marked by a national crisis, the solid majority of Americans disagree that the First Amendment's protections are excessive. On average, over more than twenty years of surveys, slightly less than 27 percent responded that the First Amendment provides too much freedom, which means, typically, about three-quarters of Americans are comfortable with broad legal protections for expression – including potentially dangerous speech.

After one of America's most divisive years for politics that saw the election of Donald Trump as President, the 2017 survey found that 69 percent of respondents disagreed that "the First Amendment goes too far," and in 2018 the number was back up to 74 percent despite continuing political turmoil. In some years, the number is even higher, like in 2012 when 81 percent said that the First Amendment does not go too far, and only 13 percent said that it does. Even with the ongoing ideological warfare of the past several years, only 29 percent of respondents in 2019 said they believed that the First Amendment does go too far.

Of course, public opinion polls have their limits. What, exactly, do they measure? According to the survey results, most people cannot name the five freedoms protected by the First Amendment – freedom of religion, freedom of speech, freedom of the press, freedom of assembly, and freedom to petition the government. The Freedom Forum regularly finds that a sizeable minority of the respondents, ranging from 29 to 40 percent, cannot name *a single one* of the rights that the First Amendment guarantees. Most are aware, however, that freedom of speech is constitutionally protected. But this result puts an interesting spin on the question of whether the First Amendment goes too far. How can a person believe that a constitutional guarantee provides "too much" protection if he doesn't know the subject it protects? "Too much" of what? The only reason the answer to the overall question is intelligible at all is because the respondents are read the text of the First Amendment before being asked to opine on whether it provides too much freedom.

Before succumbing to despair over the overall state of ignorance about some of our most basic rights as Americans, it is useful to keep in mind that people live their lives based on general understandings of pretty much everything, from nutrition to traffic laws. Most people are not constitutional experts, nor need they be in order to be good citizens (although it wouldn't hurt). In this context, the average person's *general* reactions based on *general* understandings of constitutional rights are meaningful (although probably not optimal). Perhaps it is more accurate to think of what is being measured as an instinct rather than an understanding, since it is not based on a deep knowledge of the subject matter. But the Freedom Forum "State of the First Amendment" surveys suggest that most Americans instinctively support freedom of expression. As Morris Ernst wrote nearly ninety years ago in recounting the failure of sex censors: "We have always been a people of anarchistic tendencies." Columnist Kathleen Parker observed that this has not changed, writing in 2019 that dissenting from authority "is in our DNA."

General conceptual support only goes so far, however. Censorship proposals arise not as general referenda on the abstract value of free speech but as concrete propositions. Not surprisingly, most surveys tend to find a higher tolerance for censorship in response to questions that pose specific hypotheticals (e.g., "Should a local movie theater be allowed to show *The Last Temptation of Christ?*") as opposed to general propositions (e.g., "Should local movie theaters be censored?"). People naturally are most enthusiastic about free speech when it comes to views they support, or most outraged about censorship when their side is silenced or suppressed. That's just human nature. But it is still disturbing that one 2018 survey found – despite the fact that 85 percent of respondents agreed that "freedom of the press is essential to American democracy" – that a plurality of self-identified Republicans (43 percent) agreed that "the president should have the authority to close news outlets engaged in bad behavior," and 48 percent believed that "the news media is the enemy of the American people."

Of course, all demagogues have their followers, and it should come as no surprise that Donald's Trump's endless road show of rallies and incessant tweet-storms declaring war on an independent press had some effect. Throughout history, opportunistic politicians and morals entrepreneurs have exploited ignorance and stoked fears by peddling simplistic answers to complex problems. The important question is whether such appeals to censorship gain traction over the long haul.

Here, there is cause for some optimism. Surveys that measure long-term trends suggest that public support for free speech among Americans has tended to rise over time, even when the respondents are asked about specific types of "controversial" speakers. For nearly a half-century, the General Social Survey conducted by the National Opinion Research Center at the University of Chicago has asked respondents whether five hypothetical speakers should be allowed to give a public address in their communities – a communist, a homosexual, a supporter of military overthrow of the government, an anti-theist, and a racist. Generally, the longitudinal data show that a majority of respondents support the right of each one to speak, and that the level of support has increased over time (except for the racist).

Such surveys are encouraging but far from conclusive. To surmise that support for free speech is increasing, you have to assume that the audience is predisposed to object to the postulated categories of speech, and that the social acceptability of speakers in those categories has not changed over time. Do the surveys measure an increasing tolerance for objectionable speech, or do they show that some speakers or topics have become less controversial after several decades? Based on the data, it is impossible to say, but either possibility may help explain why censors have an uphill battle in this country.

THE MILLENNIAL CHALLENGE

Such attitudes, even though they have persisted over time, may to a certain extent be generational. Or, at least, they may be influenced by the free speech controversies that raged when older survey recipients came of age. Baby boomers, whose reactions were conditioned by such events as the civil rights movement, anti-Vietnam War protests, and efforts to free entertainment from pervasive censorship, likely have a different instinctive reaction to "free speech" as a concept than younger people who see the issue represented by morons with tiki torches spouting racist nonsense like "Jews will not replace us." For the younger set, and particularly among those who have never felt the heavy hand of government censorship, free speech may be seen as less of a positive value.

Greg Lukianoff, the president and CEO of the Foundation for Individual Rights in Education (FIRE), an organization that defends First Amendment rights at universities, has observed a shift in student attitudes in recent years in matters involving free speech. The most noticeable change, he has written, is that "students often demand freedom *from* speech rather than freedom of speech." This was expressed through a growing concern about "micro-aggressions," subtle or unintended uses of language perceived by some hearers as demeaning or offensive, and calls for such remedies as "trigger warnings" and "safe spaces." Advocates of "trigger warnings" seek advance notice of curricular material that may be upsetting or offensive. And those who seek "safe spaces" want designated areas in which they will not be exposed to whatever it is that may upset them. This phenomenon was also represented by an uptick in the demands to "de-platform" certain speakers or to "disinvite" individuals whose views offend a segment of students.

Just as politics has become more polarized, the debate over freedom of speech has become divided between those claiming a license to offend versus those seeking a right not to be offended. Some speakers from the right, like Richard Spencer, Milo Yiannopoulos, and Ann Coulter, sought out campus venues under a banner of free speech with a seeming intent to do nothing more than provoke angry reactions. The tactic produced predictable results. Speeches were canceled, lawsuits filed, and battle lines drawn. The stereotype that emerged depicted leftist students as "social justice warriors" and "snowflakes" who could not tolerate divergent opinions while those who provoked them were simply attempting to uphold free speech principles. Certainly, there is no shortage of examples to support the stereotypical depictions, of both provocative speakers and would-be censors. But, as with almost everything, the reality is far more nuanced than the simplified explanation suggests.

Lukianoff and social psychologist Johnathan Haidt explore the phenomenon in their 2018 book THE CODDLING OF THE AMERICAN MIND, and find that something indeed is going on with college students that is affecting their attitudes about freedom of speech. But it isn't something that can be explained just by political orientation, nor is it a problem primarily of Millennials. Rather, they conclude that the shift in attitudes showed up in the generation of students that entered universities beginning around 2013, and by then, most Millennials (the generation born roughly between the years 1982 and 2000) had finished college. Younger people (what some refer to as "Generation Z," "Zillennials," or "iGen," for Internet Generation) were making up a growing proportion of the student population.

Lukianoff and Haidt suggest that students of this generation were conditioned by a confluence of factors that includes overprotective parenting that led to fragility and a tendency to equate mental or emotional discomfort with physical danger, social media that distracted from real-life interactions, and a polarized political environment that cultivated identity politics and "us versus them" thinking. They conclude that the result is a generation that grew up more slowly and was less prepared to cope with the challenges of adult life by the time its members entered college. They cite research showing that members of this age group suffer from higher rates of anxiety, depression, and suicide than previous generations (including Millennials). As a consequence, these students place a higher premium on emotional "safety" and seek adult supervision to ensure it. This has been manifested in concerns over "micro-aggressions" and demands for safe spaces and trigger warnings. Lukianoff and Haidt document the fact that demands to silence speakers in this environment have come from both the political left and the right.

University of California Berkeley Law School Dean Erwin Chemerinsky and Howard Gillman, Chancellor of the University of California, Irvine, similarly note differences in today's college students, suggesting that this is the first generation that was taught from an early age not to bully, and they often equate demands for freedom of speech with bullying, an understandable reaction in the Age of Trump. For them, the "historic link between free speech and the protection of dissenters and vulnerable groups is outside [their] direct experience, and it was too distant to affect their feelings about freedom of speech." Also, having grown up with the Internet as an omnipresent reality, they cannot imagine the government effectively suppressing the speech they favor. Although Chemerinsky and Gillman take issue with some of the ways that Lukianoff and Haidt describe students, they agree that the current generation's "instinct" is to "trust the government, including the public university, to regulate speech to protect students and prevent disruptions of the educational environment."

Polling data tend to support this notion of a generational shift. The Freedom Forum's 2019 poll asked several questions that probed this issue and found that the respondents' age significantly affected attitudes toward free speech. It asked in what circumstances public institutions should "disinvite" controversial speakers, and found widely varying answers based on whether the respondents were in the eighteen to forty-nine age group or the over-fifty group. When asked whether a speaker who has been accused of sexual harassment should be disinvited, half of those over fifty said yes, but for those aged eighteen to forty-nine, the number jumped to two-thirds. For a speaker whose remarks would likely offend some groups or individuals, 42 percent of the over-fifties supported disinvitation, while for the eighteen to forty-nine group, the number was 50 percent. Where a speaker's remarks were expected to provoke large-scale protests, 46 percent of older respondents favored disinvitation, while the number grew to 55 percent for younger respondents. And if the speaker actually sought to incite violence or threaten public safety, then a majority of both groups favored disinvitation – 65 percent of those over fifty and 76 percent of the younger respondents.

Of course, no survey can fully capture the extent to which attitudes toward free speech vary with age, and this one has some significant limitations. To begin with, the division of age groups into over and under fifty doesn't focus on the attitudes of Millennials or Zillennials. Yet, even with this reservation, it suggests a generally higher tolerance for censorship among younger people.

Other surveys have produced similar findings. A 2016 study sponsored by the John S. and James L. Knight Foundation and the Newseum Institute, and conducted by Gallup, Inc., found relatively high support among students for free speech in the abstract, but less enthusiasm when asked about particular examples. Seventy-eight percent said that college campuses should promote learning by exposing students to all types of speech and viewpoints, yet 69 percent of students supported policies to restrict racial slurs or other language that is intentionally offensive to certain groups, and 63 percent supported banning the wearing of costumes that stereotype certain racial or ethnic groups.

But even general support for free speech is not a given. A survey released in late 2015 by Yale's William F. Buckley, Jr. Program found that 51 percent of US college students support campus speech codes, and 72 percent favor disciplinary action against "any student or faculty member who uses language that is considered racist, sexist, homophobic *or otherwise offensive.*" A 2017 survey of college students similarly found that 58 percent agreed that it is "important to be part of a campus community where I am not exposed to intolerant and offensive ideas." The Knight Foundation, which found a general support for free speech among students, also reported that students increasingly place a higher value on diversity and inclusion than on free speech. In 2018 it found that 53 percent said that diversity was more important (compared to 46 percent for free speech), while in 2019 it found those numbers flipped – 53 percent favored free speech as a higher value compared to 46 percent placing as a higher priority promoting an inclusive and welcoming society. These shifting numbers suggest that students may be reacting to a range of complex and ever-changing events.

Naturally, the review of such data cannot escape polarized interpretations. Several writers have challenged such survey findings, claiming that they fail to support a narrative that portrays college campuses as increasingly illiberal enclaves where progressive faculty and students shout down offensive speakers and demand refuge from any offensive speech. In an online essay entitled *Who's Afraid of Free Speech in the United States?*, Justin Murphy analyzed the General Social Survey data and concluded that "extreme liberals" and the "far left" "have always been, and generally remain, the *most supportive* of free speech." Citing Murphy's analysis and taking the point even further, Matthew Yglesias, writing in *Vox*, concluded that "[e]verything we think about the political correctness debate is wrong." Citing data showing general sentiment in favor of free speech, he dismisses particular examples of campus censorship by progressives as anecdotal, concluding that "[p]eople on the political right are less supportive of free speech than people on the left," and that "[c]ollege graduates are more supportive than non-graduates."

Framing the debate in political terms misses the point, but it does illustrate the censor's dilemma. When the dispute boils down to who favors censorship and the claim is made that "it's not our side – it's you guys," the one point on which all agree is that censorship is bad. Or, at least, being labeled a censor must be avoided. A 2019 report by Pen America, an international organization that protects the rights of writers and journalists, reviewed the various surveys on campus speech and found that "[v]ery few students are willing to come out and say they are against free speech."

On the whole, the Pen America study found strong support for free expression and the First Amendment generally, but that many students' views began to look different when asked specific questions about hot button issues. It observed that "many students today see hateful expression as not just hurtful but downright dangerous," and found it "interesting that so many students simultaneously advocate censorship and free speech." While it concluded that the problem is not confined to college campuses, the Pen America report foresaw "a looming danger that our bedrock faith in free speech as an enduring foundation of American society could give way to a belief that curtailing harmful expression will enable our diverse population to live together peaceably."

Ultimately, the issue is more generational than political. A closer look at the data from multiple surveys (including from the General Social Survey) that focus specifically on respondents born after 1995 (and who began entering college around 2013) shows a greater willingness among students of this age group to silence disfavored speakers. Zillennials are more prone to agree that "colleges have an obligation to protect students from offensive speech and ideas that could create a difficult learning environment," that "people who don't respect others don't deserve the right to free speech," and that "supporting someone's right to say racist things is as bad as holding racist views yourself." And who would they censor? Well, that depends on the eye of the beholder.

In a 2017 FIRE survey, a majority of current college students who identified as "very liberal" agreed that the following speakers should not be allowed a platform at their school: one who claims that men are better at math than women, a person who argues that whites and Asians have higher IQs than other racial groups, and an advocate of deporting illegal immigrants. For those claiming to be "very conservative," nearly half would disinvite a speaker who asserts that all white people are racist, one who says that Christians are backwards or brainwashed, or a speaker who criticizes and disrespects the police. This research found somewhat more intolerance of speakers by left-leaning respondents for these particular examples, but the results depended heavily on the description of the hypothetical speaker or the speech involved. Pretty much equal numbers of conservative and liberal students (around

20 percent) would support a disinvitation depending on whether the speaker was Barack Obama versus Sarah Palin. And the same mirror-image results obtained if the proposed speaker was a Black Lives Matter activist as opposed to a pro-police Blue Lives Matter advocate. Human nature being what it is, people tend to favor free speech in the abstract, until someone pisses them off.

A number of observers have made the good point that this generation of students simply has not been educated about how and why strong First Amendment protections evolved. As Chemerinsky and Gillman write, the students that they have observed "knew little about the history of free speech in the United States, and had no awareness of how important free speech had been to vulnerable political minorities." They simply did not know how "the power to punish speech has been used primarily against social outcasts, vulnerable minorities, and those protesting for positive change," and thus tended to see free speech more as a shield for online bullies than as an essential protection for the likes of "Eugene Debs, Anita Whitney, John Thomas Scopes, Jehovah's Witnesses who refused to say the Pledge of Allegiance, leftists during the McCarthy Era, civil rights activists who were beaten and even killed, Lenny Bruce, draft card burners, or George Carlin." And they certainly would know nothing of Anthony Comstock and his trainload of literary convicts that included artists, feminists, birth control advocates, and freethinkers.

It is no doubt true that iGen students for the most part lack lived experience of the types of censorship that previous generations had to overcome. But the same may be said of earlier generations, to some degree. Baby boomers came of age at the dawn of the Free Speech Movement and experienced the speech suppression that accompanied the Vietnam War and civil rights protests. But they lacked direct experience of the struggles that preceded them – particularly the ones that came before First Amendment law began to turn in their favor. Students of that generation learned about the free speech fights from the time before the First Amendment wind was at their back by doing what any Zillennial could do now – by opening a book. So ignorance is only a partial defense.

WHERE DOES THIS LEAVE US?

Polling results alone say very little about the current state of the spirit of liberty or what this may portend for the First Amendment's future. Results vary widely depending on how questions are framed and presented, contemporary news events, sample size, and demographics. But opinion polls can roughly identify general trends that should be kept in mind as a background for current and future debates over freedom of expression, particularly when efforts to silence speech follow those trends.

Despite all the uncertainty and differences in their findings, polls over the long term illustrate two things that are undeniably true: First, basic rights cannot be left to depend on current political fashions. It is a damn good thing that fundamental rights – and especially the five freedoms protected by the First Amendment – are not subject to popular will or left to voters' whims. Moral panics and demagogues come and go, but rights lost during times of heightened passions are not easily regained. Second, there is a pressing need for increased education in civics (including American history and government), media literacy, and critical thinking skills. We live in a time of information overload. With the marriage of smart phone technology and the Internet, most Americans have instant access to a vast repository of human knowledge. Whether that access will make a positive difference depends on whether most people are motivated to find the information they need, can critically evaluate it, and will use it in their daily lives and for political decisions. Our current political landscape is hardly cause for optimism on that score, but the wretched state of our public discourse may also provide the needed spark to make things better.

Despite concerns that younger people have less appreciation for strong First Amendment protections, there is reason to be optimistic that some current attitudes will not translate to long-term erosion of free speech rights. To begin with, we have seen far worse, in terms of both the levels of threatened censorship and the public's reactions to those threats. The system has been resilient – and free speech protections have remained strong (and in many cases expanded) – notwithstanding the challenges of Comstockery, Jim Crow, McCarthyism, Nixon, and the inanities of Donald Trump. Progress is not automatic; the system requires ongoing maintenance. But there is much more to work with today to maintain a robust system of free expression than when Anthony Comstock jump-started his career as a professional censor.

Perhaps the best reason for optimism is the pessimism of those who would weaken First Amendment protections if only they could. Professor Shiffrin laments: "It has become part of the American identity to protect the speech we hate, and it would take a significant shift to turn the country from its individualist liberty-loving preference for free speech back to the recognition that other important values may outweigh free speech values." Let's hope he is right.

Epilogue

The initial manuscript for this book was completed at the beginning of 2020, before the COVID-19 pandemic closed the world, before demonstrations for social justice and riots roiled American cities, and before the presidential election further divided a polarized nation, culminating in turmoil and an attempted insurrection. It was a year in which the need for freedom of speech was vitally important yet at the same time greatly misunderstood. Well, perhaps not misunderstood so much as distorted by identity politics, with advocates from both the left and the right demanding "free speech for me but not for thee." Each side insisted that the rhetoric and tactics used by their opponents were illegitimate and exceeded the bounds of free speech; that they should be suppressed by law (or canceled by informal means). Who's a censor? *I'm* not a censor.

This book has focused more on the history of cultural censorship than on political censorship, but the basic impulses flow from a common source. The drive to censor stems from the belief that one side is categorically right, the other side is entirely misguided or evil (or both), and the need for debate is over. Or, worse, that debate in and of itself is harmful. Perhaps no one put this more succinctly than Vladimir Ilyich Ulyanov (better known by his adopted name, Vladimir Lenin). As a revolutionary in czarist Russia, Lenin complained about a lack of free speech but adopted a very different attitude once he took power:

> Why should freedom of speech and freedom of press be allowed? Why should a government which is doing what it believes to be right allow itself to be criticized? It would not allow opposition by lethal weapons. Ideas are much more fatal things than guns. Why should any man be allowed to buy a printing press and disseminate pernicious opinions calculated to embarrass the government?

A similar philosophy was cooked up by Herbert Marcuse fifty years later, and it has been echoed by others who insist that speech *is* violence. They combine faith in the infallibility of their cause with metaphorical allusions to violence and rationalize suppression of others as an act of self-defense.

Arguments for silencing opponents or to rationalize the use of actual violence to preempt perceived aggressions was on full display in 2020. The collection of cranks, white supremacists, and gullible followers who stormed the US Capitol on June 6, 2021, called themselves patriots and claimed that they were only reacting to an illegitimate election. They had been stoked with such nonsense since before Election Day and were urged to believe that a forceful reaction was justified. Texas Congressman Louie Gohmert, who signed on to one of the many frivolous lawsuits that sought to overturn the 2020 election – this one filed by the Attorney General of Texas asking to invalidate all the votes from Wisconsin, Georgia, Pennsylvania, and Michigan – reacted to the inevitable dismissal of that case by declaring on television: "You gotta go to the streets and be as violent as Antifa and BLM [Black Lives Matter]." Calls for such direct action were rampant, and Gohmert was far from the only public official making reckless and irresponsible statements. On January 6, then-President Trump himself told his followers that the vote against him was "a criminal enterprise," and he urged the crowd "to march on the Capitol" and "if you don't fight like hell, you're not going to have a country anymore." At the same time, Rudolph Giuliani, the increasingly erratic former New York mayor turned Trump lawyer, called for "trial by combat."

Those from the opposite end of the political spectrum have also rationalized censorship and violence as political tactics. For example, in his 2020 book, Is Free Speech Racist?, Gavan Titley argued that "racist speech" (however one might define it) should not be protected as a matter of self-defense. He concluded that censorship is justified because far-right and fascist speech "is action oriented toward furthering a violent politics of domination, there is no possibility of democratic debate. Instead, all forms of fascist activity constitute attempts at mobilization which must be defeated before they achieve traction." The philosophy is concisely summed up by journalist P. E. Moskowitz in his book The Case Against Free Speech: "[A]nyone whose political philosophy involves the oppression of others[] does not deserve a right to speak."

This later book is pretty typical of the anti-free speech movement genre, if a bit shallower than most. Moskowitz took it even further than the "free speech for me but not for thee" trope to suggest that violence is an acceptable means of "persuasion" for me but not for thee. Writing about the 2017 riot in Charlottesville, he described the alt-right as "an armed and dangerous nationalist group," compared to Antifa counter-protestors, who he reasoned had no choice but to "take things into their own hands." He described the counterprotestors preparing for the confrontation, "putting on their face masks and helmets," some carrying "batons," while a "leftist group called Redneck Revolt … showed up with rifles." And, in the grand scheme of things, apparently this is all justified. He ended the book by writing that "[r]ealizing a meaningful definition of free speech … will likely require massively overhauling our government through illegal actions, and perhaps violence. Only then will free speech apply to all."

So, extremists of all political stripes apparently believe that violence is an accept-able form of expression, so long as it is used to suppress the other guy (who is the real threat to free speech). As I wrote at the beginning of this epilogue, there is much confusion here. But all rationalizations aside, one thing must be made clear: violence is not speech, and speech is not violence. Those who stormed the US Capitol because they disliked the election result committed crimes that call for prosecution, regardless of any political message they might have intended. And those freelance socialists who destroyed property and looted stores under the cover of demonstrations for social justice deserve the same treatment. The First Amendment protects heated rhetoric even when it is hateful and irresponsible, but it has never protected acts of violence and destruction.

But what of incitement? Former President Trump's abhorrent actions after the election and his incendiary words on January 6 rekindled an old debate. That debate centers on what kind of speech can be a direct catalyst for violence and therefore is beyond constitutional protection. The House of Representatives voted to impeach Trump a second time – the first US president to be impeached twice – this time for, among other things, "inciting violence against the government of the United States." The Senate failed to convict the former president of incitement to violence, although it certainly had ample grounds to convict for his utter failure to protect and defend the Constitution and to ensure that the laws are faithfully executed. But to pose the question of what constitutes incitement raises an important issue that requires careful consideration. Impeachment is more a political question than a legal one, and deciding to impeach a president or not to impeach does not resolve whether Trump's words met the legal test for incitement that would place them outside the First Amendment. However, this sordid episode in American history underscores the importance of politically neutral protections for free speech.

Relaxing the legal test for incitement may seem like a good idea to some in the heat of the moment – particularly for so irresponsible a figure as Trump – but doing so would have far-reaching consequences. Suzanne Nossel, the chief executive of Pen America, an organization dedicated to protecting freedom of expression, wrote in the *New York Times* that broadening the legal concept of incitement to include Trump's diatribe "could make it more perilous for future dissenters and reformers to hold the powerful to account." She observed that First Amendment doctrine had evolved through the twentieth century, at first failing to protect peace advocates during World War I whose words were claimed to have a "bad tendency" to encourage lawlessness but growing in protection through a series of decisions that protected all but those whose words were intended to, and were likely to, result in imminent violence. The strict standard that emerged has protected the fiery advocacy not just of right-wing activists but also of those on the left, including civil rights advocates, socialists, and anti-war protesters.

Nossel's argument against "conflating what is impeachable with what is illegal" was not the product of sympathy for Donald Trump. Far from it. Her organization sued Trump while he was still in office for violating the First Amendment by threatening and retaliating against news organizations and reporters whose coverage he disliked, or who failed to show him "proper" respect. But she warned against expediently altering the legal doctrine of incitement "to meet the moment" in ways that would undermine free speech protections in the long run.

You don't have to look very far to see why this is so. In 2020, the Supreme Court took up the case of *Mckesson* v. *Doe* to determine whether a Black Lives Matter organizer could be held liable for the injury of a police officer who had been hit in the face by "a piece of concrete or similar rock-like object" during a demonstration. Under First Amendment principles established in earlier cases like *NAACP* v. *Claiborne Hardware*, the rally's organizer should not have been legally liable for violence committed by others unless he specifically intended and advocated for it to occur. However, a fractured decision of the US Court of Appeals for the Fifth Circuit allowed the police officer's case to proceed against the protest organizer. The Supreme Court accepted review and, even before hearing argument, sent the case back to the state courts of Louisiana. The Court's unsigned opinion explained that the Fifth Circuit "should not have ventured into so uncertain an area of tort law – one laden with value judgments and fraught with implications for First Amendment rights" without first determining whether such a claim could be made under state law.

The debate over freedom of speech will go on, as it must. But, if one point of clarity can be drawn from the dumpster fire of 2020, it is this: these difficult issues will not be resolved by declaring one side or the other of our deepest political or cultural conflicts the victor and giving in to the mind of the censor. Of course, such a mindset always demands more – that is the censor's pathology. As Floyd Abrams, America's most celebrated First Amendment lawyer, warned decades ago: "The problem with censorship is that it leads to more censorship. It leads to a censorial mentality, to a state of affairs which is, in the most real sense, un-American."

References

CHAPTER 1

1. and made himself the first of its kept professors." H. L. Mencken, A BOOK OF PREFACES 255 (New York: Alfred A. Knopf, 1917).
1. that marks American prudishness. Heywood Broun and Margaret Leech, ANTHONY COMSTOCK: ROUNDSMAN OF THE LORD 229–230 (New York: Albert & Charles Boni, Inc., 1927) ("Broun and Leech").
1. the television medium they so love is nothing but a "vast wasteland." Newton N. Minow, *Television and the Public Interest*, Speech Before the National Association of Broadcasters (May 9, 1961) ("*Vast Wasteland Speech*"). *See also* Robert Corn-Revere, *Avast Ye Wasteland: Reflections on America's Most Famous Exercise in "Public Interest" Piracy*, 55 FED. COMM. L. J. 481 (2003).
2. because of their attractiveness and manner of exhibition." *Mutual Film Corp. v. Ohio Industrial Commission*, 236 US 230 (1915).
2. protected in the same way as newspapers and books, *Joseph Burstyn, Inc. v. Wilson*, 343 US 495 (1952).
2. to censor expression in advance of publication – was strictly limited; *Near v. Minnesota*, 283 US 697 (1931).
2. discussions of intimate subjects could be banned only if they were "prurient" and utterly lacked redeeming social value. *Roth v. United States*, 354 US 476 (1957).
3. to "sharpen our enforcement blade." Testimony of Michael K. Powell, Chairman, Federal Communications Commission, Before the United States Senate, Committee on Commerce, Science and Transportation, at 3 (Feb. 11, 2004).
3. that penalty was thrown out as "arbitrary and capricious," and the fine was refunded. *CBS Corporation v. FCC*, 663 F. 3d 122 (3rd Cir. 2011), *cert. denied*, 132 S. Ct. 2677 (2012).
   and the most searched event online according to Google. Ben Charney, *Jackson's Super Bowl Flash Grabs TiVo Users*, CNET, Feb. 2, 2004 (www.cnet.com/news/jacksons-super-bowl-flash-grabs-tivo-users/); *Janet's Breast Makes Net History*, BBC NEWS, Feb. 5, 2004 (http://news.bbc.co.uk/2/hi/technology/3461459.stm).
3. was a waste of taxpayer dollars. Will Lester, *Poll: Janet Jackson Act Not a Federal Case*, ASSOCIATED PRESS, Feb. 21, 2004 (https://web.archive.org/web/20040312001041/http://customwire.ap.org/dynamic/stories/A/AP_POLL_JANET_JACKSON?SITE=NJASB&SECTION=HOME&TEMPLATE=DEFAULT).

4. but it wasn't *illegal* censorship. *Donald Sterling Banned for Life by the NBA for "Deeply Disturbing" Comments*, CBS NEWS, Apr. 29, 2014 (www.cbsnews.com/news/donald-sterling-banned-for-life-by-the-nba-for-deeply-disturbing-comments/).

4. (although the league later vacillated on that policy). Amelia McDonell-Parry, *Why the NFL Put Its New Kneeling Policy on Hold*, ROLLING STONE, Jul. 20, 2018 (www.rollingstone.com/culture/culture-sports/why-nfl-put-new-kneeling-protest-policy-on-hold-701802/).

    that was another matter entirely. *Knight First Amendment Institute at Columbia University* v. *Trump*, 928 F. 3d 226 (2nd Cir. 2019); *Karem* v. *Trump*, 960 F.3d 656 (DC Cir. 2020); *CNN* v. *Trump*, No. 18-cv-2610 (DDC Nov. 16, 2018); *Pen America* v. *Trump*, 448 F. Supp.3d 309 (SDNY 2020).

5. "fake news" (as is done under European law). E.g., Mary Minow, *The Changing Ecosystem of News and Challenges for Freedom of the Press*, 64 LOYOLA LAW. REV. 499 (2018); Tim Wu, *Is the First Amendment Obsolete?*, 117 MICH. LAW. REV. 547 (2018).

5. to prevent them from enforcing such policies on their own. David French, *Josh Hawley's Internet Censorship Bill Is an Unwise, Unconstitutional Mess*, REASON.COM, Jun. 20, 2019 (www.nationalreview.com/2019/06/josh-hawley-internet-censorship-bill-unconstitutional/).

6. "Self-assurance has always been the hallmark of a censor." *Florida Bar* v. *Went For It, Inc.*, 515 US 618, 645 (1995) (Kennedy, J., dissenting).

6. "[t]heir very cocksureness is their chief source of strength." Mencken, A BOOK OF PREFACES, *supra*, at 245.

6. in politics, nationalism, religion, or other matters of opinion." *West Virginia Board of Education* v. *Barnette*, 319 US 624, 642 (1943).

6. by an official smacks of an ideology foreign to our system." *Hannegan* v. *Esquire*, 327 US 146, 158 (1946).

6. "one man's vulgarity is another man's lyric." *Cohen* v. *California*, 403 US 15, 25 (1971).

6. to persuade them of the need for his 1873 federal obscenity law. J. C. Schwartz, FEDERAL CENSORSHIP: OBSCENITY IN THE MAIL (New York: The Free Press of Glencoe, Inc., 1961); Marjorie Heins, NOT IN FRONT OF THE CHILDREN 31–32 (New York: Hill & Wang, 2001).

7. and the suppressor is gratified by finding his vice." *See* Broun and Leech, *supra*, at 273.

7. examples of such public hypocrisy "are too multitudinous to permit a detailed inventory." Morris L. Ernst and William Seagle, TO THE PURE – A STUDY OF OBSCENITY AND THE CENSOR 14 (New York: Viking Press, 1928).

7. because of a habit of masturbation." Morris L. Ernst and Alan U. Schwartz, CENSORSHIP – THE SEARCH FOR THE OBSCENE 29–30 (New York: The McMillan Co. 1964) ("Ernst and Schwartz").

7. sex is a weak second." Nat Hentoff, FREE SPEECH FOR ME BUT NOT FOR THEE: HOW THE AMERICAN LEFT AND RIGHT RELENTLESSLY CENSOR EACH OTHER 1 (New York: Harper Collins, 1992).

8. so is euphemistic evasion. François de La Rochefoucauld, SENTENCES AND MORAL MAXIMS, No. 218.

8. [employed in] defense of the indefensible." George Orwell, *Politics and the English Language*, reprinted in THE ORWELL READER 355, 366 (San Diego: Harcourt, Inc., 1984).

9. cede to lawful authority a great deal of discretion about what you do." *"Freedom Is about Authority": Excerpts from Giuliani Speech on Crime*, NEW YORK TIMES, Mar. 20, 1994 (www.nytimes.com/1994/03/20/nyregion/freedom-is-about-authority-excerpts-from-giuliani-speech-on-crime.html).

9. Sigma Alpha Mu canceled the fundraiser. Catherine Rampell, *Today's Lesson on Campus: "Controversy Prevention,"* WASHINGTON POST, Apr. 21, 2017, A21.

10. truth is the only ground upon which their wishes safely can be carried out." *Abrams v. United States*, 250 US 616, 630 (1919) (Holmes, J., dissenting).

10. made it critical that the Supreme Court create doctrine defining freedom of speech. Zechariah Chafee, Jr., Free Speech in the United States 3 (Cambridge, MA: Harvard University Press, 1941); Erwin Chemerinsky and Howard Gillman, Free Speech on Campus 36 (New Haven: Yale University Press, 2017); Wayne Batchis, The Right's First Amendment: The Politics of Free Speech & The Return of Conservative Libertarianism 13 (Stanford, CA: Stanford University Press, 2016).

10. any publication that tended to incite crime or disrespect for the law. *Fox v. Washington*, 236 US 273 (1915); *Patterson v. Colorado*, 205 US 454 (1907); *Halter v. Nebraska*, 205 US 34 (1907); *United States ex rel. Turner v. Williams*, 194 US 279 (1904); *Ex Parte Rapier*, 143 US 110 (1892); *Ex Parte Jackson*, 96 US 727 (1878).

10. a "verbal act," not protected expression. *Gompers v. Buck's Stove & Range Co.*, 221 US 418 (1911).

10. for circulating anti-draft pamphlets, *Schenck v. United States*, 249 US 47 (1919).

10. a newspaper publisher for articles that criticized the war effort, *Frohwerk v. United States*, 249 US 204 (1919).

10. Eugene Debs for purportedly obstructing the draft. *Debs v. United States*, 249 US 211 (1919).

11. unless "an immediate check is required to save the country." *Abrams v. United States*, 250 US 616, 630 (1919) (Holmes, J., dissenting).

11. wager our salvation upon some prophecy based upon imperfect knowledge." *Id.*

11. 140 years after the Bill of Rights was ratified. *Stromberg v. California*, 283 US 359 (1931); *Near v. Minnesota*, 283 US 697 (1931).

12. even with the mandate or approval of a majority. *United States v. Playboy Entertainment Group, Inc.*, 529 US 803, 818 (2000).

12. anonymities to turn the color of legal litmus paper." *Abrams v. United States*, 250 US 616, 629 (1919) (Holmes, J., dissenting).

CHAPTER 2

14. "a fella could have a pretty good weekend in Vegas with all that stuff." Stanley Kubrick, *Dr. Strangelove Or: How I Learned to Stop Worrying and Love the Bomb* (Columbia Pictures, 1964).

14. to demonstrate the perils of "evil reading." Craig L. LaMay, *America's Censor: Anthony Comstock and Free Speech*, Communications and the Law (Sept. 1997), at 1–59; James C. N. Paul, and Murray L. Schwartz, Federal Censorship: Obscenity in the Mail 18–24 (New York: The Free Press of Glencoe, Inc., 1961) ("Paul and Schwartz"); Heins, *supra*, at 31–32; Edward deGrazia, Girls Lean Back Everywhere 3–4 (New York: Random House, 1992).

15. Be that as it may, I am sure that the world is better off without them." Broun and Leech, *supra*, at 192.

15. showing off his collection to the horror of many legislators. Broun and Leech, *supra*, at 131.

15. on almost any kind of laws for which their vote might be solicited." D. M. Bennett, Champions of the Church: Their Crimes and Persecutions 1016 (New York: Liberal and Scientific Publishing House, 1878).

15. Comstock always called it "my law." Paul and Schwartz, *supra*, at 22.

15. "Anthony Comstock himself *was* the Comstock Act." Scott Matthew Dix, *When Contraception Was Outlawed!* (editor's preface to Outlawed! How Anthony Comstock

FOUGHT AND WON THE PURITY OF A NATION xv–xxii (Middletown, DE: Western Conservatory of the Arts and Sciences, 2013) (reprinting Charles Galludet Trumbull, ANTHONY COMSTOCK, FIGHTER (1913)).

15. Comstock didn't exactly cut a dashing figure. Paul and Schwartz, *supra*, at 18–19.

15. They disgrace our land and *yet* consider themselves ladies. Broun and Leech, *supra*, at 134.

15. and *New York Sun* publisher Moses S. Beech. Paul S. Boyer, PURITY IN PRINT 5–7 (New York: Charles Scribner's Sons, 1968).

16. an independent organization, the New York Society for the Suppression of Vice. LaMay, *supra*, at 15–17; Margaret A. Blanchard, *The American Urge to Censor: Freedom of Expression Versus the Desire to Sanitize Society – From Anthony Comstock to 2 Live Crew*, WILLIAM & MARY LAW REVIEW 741–851 (1992); Margaret A. Blanchard and John E. Semonche, *Anthony Comstock and His Adversaries: The Mixed Legacy of This Battle for Free Speech*, COMMUNICATIONS LAW & POLICY 317–366 (Summer 2006).

16. stressing their "personal interest" in the legislation. Allan Carlson, Pure Visionary, Touchstone – A Journal of Mere Christianity (Jun. 2009).

16. and Senator William Windom introduced it in the Senate. Broun and Leech, *supra*, at 129–132; Paul and Schwartz, *supra*, at 22.

16. took the bill home to work on it and to combine it with other legislative proposals. Anna Louise Bates, WEEDER IN THE GARDEN OF THE LORD: ANTHONY COMSTOCK'S LIFE AND CAREER 81–84 (Lanham, MD: University Press of America, Inc., 1995).

17. supported resolutions that would have allowed legal presumptions to enforce Christian morality. Amy Werbel, LUST ON TRIAL 67 (New York: Columbia University Press, 2018).

17. The bill that emerged was all encompassing. Paul and Schwartz, *supra*, at 22–23; Charles Galludet Trumbull, Anthony Comstock, FIGHTER 85–91 (1913).

17. very few men here that the young men of today can safely pattern after. Broun and Leech, *supra*, at 138–139.

17. But he was not criticized publicly – at least not by the politicians. Paul and Schwartz, *supra*, at 22.

17. They knew he was there at the behest of powerful benefactors. Boyer, *supra*, at 5–10.

17. a joint-stock company organized to finance the building of the transcontinental railroad. Broun and Leech, *supra*, at 129–132; Paul and Schwartz, *supra*, at 18.

18. Comstock's purity campaign was just the ticket." Blanchard, *The American Urge to Censor, supra*, at 747.

18. All this made talking about smut a welcome distraction. Molly H. McGarry, *Spectral Sexualities: Nineteenth-Century Spiritualism, Moral Panics, and the Making of U.S. Obscenity Law*, JOURNAL OF WOMEN'S HISTORY 8–29 (Summer 2000); Kat Long, *The Forbidden Apple*, NEW YORK TIMES, Apr. 3, 2009.

18. it was combined with 15 other proposals that were adopted in a vote at two a.m. LaMay, *supra*, at 16; Blanchard, *The American Urge to Censor, supra*, at 748.

18. despite the fact that, as Congressman Niblack observed, it is "now Sunday morning." James A. Morone, HELLFIRE NATION 229 (New Haven, CT: Yale University Press, 2003).

18. the clock in the chamber was stopped to preserve the fiction that it was still Saturday night. Ernst and Schwartz, *supra*, at 31.

18. affixing his signature as quickly as an attendant could hand him each one, and without the slightest examination. Bennett, CHAMPIONS OF THE CHURCH, *supra*; Judith Giesburg, SEX AND THE CIVIL WAR 92–95 (Chapel Hill: University of North Carolina Press, 2017).

18. including two boys aged eleven and thirteen. Anthony Comstock, TRAPS FOR THE YOUNG (Cambridge, MA: Harvard University Press 1883/1967) (editor's introduction by Robert Bremner); Broun and Leech, *supra*, at 83–84.

19. any indecent or immoral use or nature ... shall be carried in the mail." An Act for the Suppression of Trade in, and Circulation of, Obscene Literature and Articles of Immoral Use, ch. 258, sec. 2, 17 stat. 598, 599 (1873).

19. carried not just the power to arrest but also free passage on all rail lines that carried the mail. Patricia Schroeder, *Gifts of Speech*, Sept. 24, 1996 (http://gos.sbc.edu/s/schroeder .html).

19. will soon be in the strong grip of government." Carlson, *supra*.

19. will be forgiven to a Congress which thus powerfully sustains the cause of morality." Broun and Leech, *supra*, at 144.

19. During his first ten months as a special agent, he traveled 23,000 miles in search of contraband. Carlson, *supra*.

19. he had made fifty-five arrests and obtained twenty convictions under the new federal law. Blanchard, *The American Urge to Censor, supra*, at 748.

19. 60,300 "rubber articles," and 3,150 boxes of pills and powders. Broun and Leech, *supra*, at 153.

19. the numbers of people arrested and convicted, and even their nationalities. LaMay, *supra*, at 21–22, 34.

19. He also took credit for destroying 160 tons of obscene literature and 4 million pictures. Blanchard, *The American Urge to Censor, supra*, at 758; Broun and Leech, *supra*, at 15–16; LaMay, *supra*, at 2; Morone, *supra*, at 230; David M. Rabban, Free Speech in Its Forgotten Years (London: Cambridge University Press, 1997).

19. "to the length of 565 years, 11 months, and 20 days" and fines amounting to $237,134.30. Mary Alden Hopkins, *Birth Control and Public Morals: An Interview with Anthony Comstock*, Harper's Weekly, May 22, 1915, at 489–490.

20. He openly boasted of causing at least fifteen suicides. LaMay, *supra*, at 18; Morone, *supra*, at 230.

20. 88,000 newspapers with ads for "sexual materials," and 20,000 "figures and images." New York Society for the Suppression of Vice, Forty-Second Annual Report (1916).

20. twenty-four states adopting what were called "mini-Comstock" statutes by 1885. McGarry, *supra*; Blanchard, *The American Urge to Censor, supra*; Carlson, *supra*, at 751.

20. By 1920, all but two states had passed such laws. Bates, *supra*, at 2.

20. in cities such as Philadelphia, Cincinnati, Louisville, Chicago, St. Louis, and San Francisco. New York Society for the Suppression of Vice, Fifth Annual report (1879); Morone, *supra*, at 230; Boyer, *supra*, at 5; Neil Miller, Banned in Boston 4 (Boston: Beacon Press, 2010).

20. the first was the New York Society for the Suppression of Vice, also known as "the Comstock Society." Mencken, A Book of Prefaces, *supra*, at 259.

20. he finally was able to quit his day job as a dry goods salesman. LaMay, *supra*, at 17.

20. the list read "like a *Who's Who* of the day." Boyer, *supra*, at 6.

20. and the YMCA wanted some distance from the fray. Blanchard, *The American Urge to Censor, supra*, at 750.

21. which may hereafter be enacted for the suppression" of vice. Act of Incorporation, New York Society for the Suppression of Vice, May 16, 1873.

21. and bring before any court ... offenders found violating the provisions of any" state or federal obscenity law. New York Law Sec. 1145; Blanchard, *The American Urge to Censor, supra*, at 751.

21. we must not trust to the ordinary officers of the law, and the police to deal with it." New York Society for the Suppression of Vice, Second Annual Report 9 (Jan. 27, 1876).

22. "Congress shall make no law . . . abridging the freedom of speech, or of the press." Neil H. Cogan, ed., The Complete Bill of Rights: The Drafts, Debates, Sources, & Origins 83 (New York: Oxford University Press, 1997).

22. they would have framed an iron-bound section to prevent it." Comstock, Traps for the Young, *supra*, at 223.

22. Ovid's Art of Love and Henry Fielding's Tom Jones (both of which Comstock unsuccessfully tried to suppress in 1894). Ernst and Schwartz, *supra*, at 34; *Anthony Comstock Overruled*, New York Times, Jun. 22, 1894; LaMay, *supra*, at 28.

22. "[a]ll of the early Presidents enjoyed the frankness and vulgarity of fleshly novels." Morris L. Ernst and William Seagle, To The Pure 256–257 (New York: Viking Press, 1928).

22. bulged their cheeks in naughty giggles when reading the works of Fielding or Sterne." Morris L. Ernst, *Sex Wins in America*, The Nation, Aug. 10, 1932, at 122.

22. but they hardly bothered our Constitution's framers. Ernst and Schwartz, *supra*, at 7.

22. an obscene, impudent, and indecent posture with a woman." *Commonwealth* v. *Sharpless*, 2 Serg & Rawle 91 (Pa. Sup. Ct. 1815).

23. the same would be offensive to the court here, and improper to be placed upon the records thereof." *Massachusetts* v. *Holmes*, 17 Mass. 336 (1821); Ernst and Schwartz, *supra*, at 15–16.

23. *Regina* v. *Hicklin* would set that standard for obscenity, not just in Great Britain but also in the USA. Heins, *supra*, at 32.

23. Comstock quickly picked up on the *Hicklin* rule and successfully applied it in numerous prosecutions. E.g., *United States* v. *Bennett*, 24 F. Cas. 1093 (2nd Cir. 1879).

23. until the Supreme Court finally abandoned it in 1957 because of evolving First Amendment concerns. *Roth* v. *United States*, 354 US 476 (1957).

23. "depraves and corrupts those whose minds are open to such immoral influences." *Regina* v. *Hicklin*, LR 3 QB 360 (Queen's Bench, 1868).

23. the test was "laid down before our society ever started." Anthony Comstock, Morals Versus Art 17, 26 (New York: J. S. Ogilvie & Company, 1887).

23. holding that the titles alone were enough to support a conviction. Bennett, Champions of the Church, *supra*, at 1018.

24. "I know it when I see it." *Jacobellis* v. *Ohio*, 378 US 184, 197 (1964) (Stewart, J., concurring).

24. ten years later would abandon even that idea as unconstitutional, *Paris Adult Theatre I* v. *Slayton*, 413 US 49, 73–74 (1974) (Brennan, J., dissenting, joined by Justices Stewart and Marshall).

24. Comstock considered the danger of "evil reading" to be worse than yellow fever or smallpox. Comstock, Traps for the Young, *supra*, at 5–6.

24. you will have a bid for a life of self-gratification and sin." Comstock, Traps for the Young, *supra*, at 14–16.

24. As Comstock put it, "infidelity and obscenity occupy the same bed." Anthony Comstock , Frauds Exposed; Or, How the People are Deceived and Robbed, and Youth Corrupted 443 (New York: Cosimo Classics, 1880/2009).

24. to hide the fact of the extra- or nonmarital relations from public view. Nicola Beisel, Imperiled Innocents: Anthony Comstock and Family Reproduction in Victorian America 36–42 (Princeton, NJ: Princeton University Press, 1997).

24. And if contraceptives fail, abortion then becomes necessary. Trumbull, *supra*, at 4041; LaMay, *supra*, at 45.

24. and an additional 900,000 abortions over a thirty-year period.) Brief Amicus Curiae of 100 Scholars of Marriage in Support of Respondents, *Obergefell* v. *Hodges*, No. 14-556 (Supreme Court, 2015), at 3, 22.

25. he must do it in a decent and lawful manner or not at all." Comstock, FRAUDS EXPOSED, *supra*, at 408–409.

25. while "what they intend leads directly to sin and shame." Bates, *supra*, at 128.

25. in his mind, they "added hypocrisy to vice," Rabban, FREE SPEECH IN ITS FORGOTTEN YEARS, *supra*, at 31.

25. he used such terms as "infidel," "free luster," and "abortionist's pimp" interchangeably. Bremner, *supra*, at xvii.

25. "the howling, ranting, blaspheming mob of repealers." Comstock, FRAUDS EXPOSED, *supra*, at 393.

25. as pretext in order to close down publications that offended his religious sensibilities. Susan Jacoby, FREETHINKERS 209 (New York: Metropolitan Books, 2004); Susan Jacoby, THE GREAT AGNOSTIC 100 (New Haven, CT: Yale University Press, 2013).

26. to overthrow every social restraint. New York Society for the Suppression of Vice, FOURTH ANNUAL REPORT (1878); Beisel, *supra*, at 89–90.

26. corrupts the morals of the young, or destroys all faith in God." Comstock, TRAPS FOR THE YOUNG, *supra*, at 199.

26. he considered them utterly immoral and anti-Christian. Beisel, *supra*, at 85–98.

26. It also was reputed at the time that the widower Vanderbilt became Tennie's lover. Bates, *supra*, at 72; Heins, *supra*, at 31; Werbel, LUST ON TRIAL, *supra*, at 60.

27. addressing the House Judiciary Committee in 1871 on behalf of the Women's Rights Association. Bates, *supra*, at 72; Broun and Leech, *supra*, at 95, 111.

27. "servitude of the hardest kind, and just for board and clothes, at that." Myra MacPherson, THE SCARLET SISTERS: SEX, SUFFRAGE, AND SCANDAL IN THE GILDED AGE 63–64 (New York: Twelve Books, 2014).

27. she proclaimed, "We mean treason!" Bates, *supra*, at 72–73.

27. the iniquity and morbidness in which she now wallows for existence." Bates, *supra*, at 72–73.

27. neither you nor any law you can frame have any right to interfere. Victoria Woodhull, *And the Truth Shall Make You Free: A Speech on the Principles of Social Freedom* (Address at Steinway Hall, New York, Nov. 20, 1871).

28. the first American newspaper to publish Karl Marx's COMMUNIST MANIFESTO. Bates, *supra*, at 71.

28. "burst like a bombshell into the ranks of the moralistic social camp." Victoria Woodhull, *The Beecher-Tilton Scandal Case*, THE WOODHULL AND CLAFIN WEEKLY, Nov. 2, 1872.

28. preaching one set of values while practicing another. Woodhull, *The Beecher-Tilton Scandal Case*, *supra*; Debby Applegate, THE MOST FAMOUS MAN IN AMERICA: THE BIOGRAPHY OF HENRY WARD BEECHER 422 (New York: Image Books, 2006); Broun and Leech, *supra*, at 100; Beisel, *supra*, at 85–86.

28. and that he shared them with numerous friends. Woodhull, *The Beecher-Tilton Scandal Case*, *supra*; Broun and Leech, *supra*, at 102; Bates, *supra*, at 73.

28. and second-hand copies fetched as much as $40 apiece. MacPherson, *supra*, at 185; Applegate, *supra*, at 422; Bennett, *supra*, at 1022; Broun and Leech, *supra*, at 116.

28. thus invoking the jurisdiction of federal law. MacPherson, *supra*, at 186; Broun and Leech, *supra*, at 102.

28. a Plymouth Church parishioner and friend of Reverend Beecher. MacPherson, *supra*, at 186; James C. N. Paul and Murray L. Schwartz, FEDERAL CENSORSHIP: OBSCENITY IN THE MAIL 20 (New York: The Free Press of Glencoe, Inc., 1961).

28. the women were whisked off to the Ludlow Street jail, where they languished for weeks. Broun and Leech, *supra*, at 105; Paul and Schwartz, *supra*, at 20.

28. and destroyed 3,000 copies of the *Weekly*. Heins, *supra*, at 31.
29. the carriage attracted a growing procession of onlookers. Bates, *supra*, at 74.
29. more sedate in appearance, and of a less lovely turn." Broun and Leech, *supra*, at 103.
29. a gentleman whom the whole country reveres," the Reverend Henry Ward Beecher. Broun and Leech, *supra*, at 103.
29. "the sensational comedy of free love." MacPherson, *supra*, at 190; Broun and Leech, *supra*, at 105.
29. because they refused to cease selling their newspaper. Bates, *supra*, at 76.
29. where she denounced the prosecution as a violation of freedom of the press. MacPherson, *supra*, at 193.
29. but was immediately taken into custody. *Woodhull and Blood*, THE BROOKLYN DAILY EAGLE, Jan. 10, 1873, 2; Bates, *supra*, at 77; Broun and Leech, *supra*, at 116–118.
29. the sisters and Colonel Blood were assessed $80,000 in bail. Bennett, CHAMPIONS OF THE CHURCH, *supra*, at 1022.
29. for running Tammany Hall's corrupt political machine. MacPherson, *supra*, at 196; Broun and Leech, *supra*, at 120.
29. a drama that "has seldom been surpassed for filthiness of detail." MacPherson, *supra*, at 190–191.
30. Comstock's fumbling responses were roundly mocked in the press. Bates, *supra*, at 77; Broun and Leech, *supra*, at 118–119.
30. applied to books, pamphlets, and pictures, but not to newspapers or advertisements. Rabban, FREE SPEECH IN ITS FORGOTTEN YEARS, *supra*, at 29; Beisel, *supra*, at 80; Broun and Leech, *supra*, at 122.
30. had inspired him to lobby Congress for expanded authority. Bates, *supra*, at 76.
30. The *Brooklyn Eagle* dubbed the case "An Inglorious Failure." MacPherson, *supra*, at 204; Broun and Leech, *supra*, at 122.
30. what should have been a matter of local concern. Bates, *supra*, at 76.
30. "a dastard's blow at liberty and law in the United States." Broun and Leech, *supra*, at 124–125.
30. Why should I be?" Bates, *supra*, at 76; Broun and Leech, *supra*, at 15.
30. as well as various radical causes. MacPherson, *supra*, at 72–73.
30. dictator of a new government he wanted to form for America. Bates, *supra*, at 126; Broun and Leech, *supra*, at 108–109, 111.
31. he was leery of her free love position. Bates, *supra*, at 75.
31. and later some salacious passages from the Old Testament under sensational headlines. Bennett, CHAMPIONS OF THE CHURCH, *supra*, at 1023; Broun and Leech, *supra*, at 108–110.
31. "disgusting slanders on Lot, Abraham, Solomon and David." Broun and Leech, *supra*, at 110.
31. Train could pay his bail, yet he refused to do so. Bennett, CHAMPIONS OF THE CHURCH, *supra*, at 1023.
31. but the court declined to accept a conditional plea. Broun and Leech, *supra*, at 110–111.
31. playfully dubbed "the Train matinees." Broun and Leech, *supra*, at 112.
31. "This," Comstock proclaimed, "is Free Love." Bates, *supra*, at 126; Broun and Leech, *supra*, at 112.
31. who insinuated that Comstock had acted as a paid informer. Bates, *supra*, at 126–127; Broun and Leech, *supra*, at 112–113.
32. he slipped away to board a ship bound for England. Bates, *supra*, at 126–127; Broun and Leech, *supra*, at 111–114.
32. by comparing his illicit affair to a naval battle. Beisel, *supra*, at 86.

32. the satisfaction that had eluded him after the Train fiasco. Bennett, CHAMPIONS OF THE CHURCH, *supra*, at 1023–1024; Bates, *supra*, at 127–128.

32. decried the strictures of matrimony and extolled the virtues of sexual freedom. Heins, *supra*, at 32–33.

32. a "dull little sociological treatise." Broun and Leech, *supra*, at 171.

32. to very much less than men get for the same work." Ezra H. Heywood, *Cupid's Yokes* 21 (Princeton, MA: Co-Operative Publishing Co., 1876).

32. committing adultery, and Comstock for despotism and cruelty. Rabban, FREE SPEECH IN ITS FORGOTTEN YEARS, *supra*, at 33.

33. falsity with which 'great men' endeavor to appease, cajole, and defy equivocal public opinion." Heywood, *supra*, at 10.

33. "This is clearly the spirit that ignited the fires of the Inquisition." Heywood, *supra*, at 11–12; Broun and Leech, *supra*, at 193.

33. Heywood to be the "chief creature" promoting the "vile creed" of free love. Comstock, TRAPS FOR THE YOUNG, *supra*, at 163; Rabban, FREE SPEECH IN ITS FORGOTTEN YEARS, *supra*, at 35; Broun and Leech, *supra*, at 172–173.

33. an erudite man who was respected in his community that so incensed Comstock. Broun and Leech, *supra*, at 170–171.

33. Mr. Heywood must be crushed out and sent to prison." Bennett, CHAMPIONS OF THE CHURCH, *supra*, at 1060.

33. "Thus, reader," Comstock boasted, "the devil's trapper was trapped." Comstock, TRAPS FOR THE YOUNG, *supra*, at 163–166.

33. and a medical text entitled SEXUAL PHYSIOLOGY. Broun and Leech, *supra*, at 172–174.

34. selected passages were provided to jurors as they entered the jury room. Broun and Leech, *supra*, at 174; Rabban, FREE SPEECH IN ITS FORGOTTEN YEARS, *supra*, at 36; Beisel, *supra*, at 91.

34. "Massachusetts would become a vast house of prostitution." New York Society for the Suppression of Vice, FIFTH ANNUAL REPORT 14 (1879); Broun and Leech, *supra*, at 174; Bates, *supra*, at 135–136.

34. to exclude immoral materials from the US mail. *Ex Parte Jackson*, 96 US 727, 736 (1877).

34. now by their good service has been settled in our favor." New York Society for the Suppression of Vice, FIFTH ANNUAL REPORT 14 (1879).

34. who had strong political connections that extended even to the White House. New York Society for the Suppression of Vice, FIFTH ANNUAL REPORT, *supra*, at 6–9; Broun and Leech, *supra*, at 177; Bates, *supra*, at 129; Beisel, *supra*, at 92; Rabban, FREE SPEECH IN ITS FORGOTTEN YEARS, *supra*, at 38.

34. who had made final revisions to the bill that became the Comstock Act. Broun and Leech, *supra*, at 177; Bates, *supra*, at 139.

35. freedom of the press and to the great hurt of the learned professions." Beisel, *supra*, at 92.

35. Butler "presented" the petition without endorsing its substance. Paul and Schwartz, *supra*, at 29.

35. "backed by one of the basest conspiracies ever concocted against a holy cause." Comstock, TRAPS FOR THE YOUNG, *supra*, at 192; Blanchard and Semonche, *supra*, at 328–332.

35. the opposition by publishing injurious insinuations against the agent." New York Society for the Suppression of Vice, FIFTH ANNUAL REPORT, *supra*, at 6–7.

35. not established to carry instruments of vice, or obscene writings, indecent pictures, or lewd books." Beisel, *supra*, at 92.

35. but no action was taken. Broun and Leech, *supra*, at 179.

35. drawing nearly six thousand people to protest Heywood's conviction. Proceedings of the Indignation Meeting Held in Faneuil Hall, Thursday Evening, Aug. 1, 1878 (Boston: Benj. R. Tucker, 1878).

35. demanded total repeal of the Comstock law as opposed to more moderate reforms. Rabban, FREE SPEECH IN ITS FORGOTTEN YEARS, *supra*, at 38; Bates, *supra*, at 135–136.

35. six months into Heywood's sentence. Broun and Leech, *supra*, at 170; Beisel, *supra*, at 94–95.

35. "it is no crime by the laws of the United States to advocate the abolition of marriage." Beisel, *supra*, at 94–95.

35. "obscene, lascivious, lewd, or corrupting in the criminal sense." Blanchard and Semonche, *supra*, at 333.

35. destroy all that is lovely and of good report, and who openly boast of their crimes." New York Society for the Suppression of Vice, FIFTH ANNUAL REPORT, *supra*, at 9.

35. a great hindrance to the further enforcement of the law." Broun and Leech, *supra*, at 174–175; Bates, *supra*, at 137–138.

35. which led to additional arrests and prosecutions. Bates, *supra*, at 131.

36. puckishly called the "Comstock Syringe." Broun and Leech, *supra*, at 183–184; Beisel, *supra*, at 98–99; Bates, *supra*, at 143.

36. he ceased publishing contraceptive advertisements in *The Word*, lest he be arrested again. Bates, *supra*, at 143.

36. charges were dropped by the US attorney. Beisel, *supra*, at 101.

36. "fuck," "penis," "womb," "semen," and "vagina." Blanchard and Semonche, *supra*, at 338.

36. Heywood served all but two months of his sentence. Bates, *supra*, at 143; Beisel, *supra*, at 101.

36. "who will in the future be classed with murderers." Bates, *supra*, at 144.

36. and who published the leading free-thought journal of the day. Jacoby, FREETHINKERS, *supra*, at 209.

37. everything that degrades or burdens mankind mentally or physically." Bennett, CHAMPIONS OF THE CHURCH, *supra*.

37. "the mouthpiece of these moral cancer planters." Comstock, FRAUDS EXPOSED, *supra*, at 396. Comstock was moved to arrest Bennett in November 1877. Bates, *supra*, at 138–139.

37. which mankind could well spare, losing nothing by its rejection?" D.M. Bennett, *An Open Letter to Jesus Christ* (New York: The Truth Seeker Co., 1876); Beisel, *supra*, at 90–91.

37. without regard to the rights, morals or liberties of others." Broun and Leech, *supra*, at 175.

37. the case was hastily dropped in early January 1878 notwithstanding a grand jury indictment. Bennett, CHAMPIONS OF THE CHURCH, *supra*, at 1066.

37. Ingersoll had campaigned for President Rutherford B. Hayes in 1876. Jacoby, FREETHINKERS, *supra*, at 209.

37. a "monstrous conspiracy" to undo his divinely inspired law. Comstock, FRAUDS EXPOSED, *supra*, at 388–515.

37. a "foul-mouthed libertine" and an "apostle of nastiness." Comstock, FRAUDS EXPOSED, *supra*, at 495–496.

38. a first-class Torquemada, Calvin, Alva, Charles IX, or Matthew Hopkins." Bennett, CHAMPIONS OF THE CHURCH, *supra*, at 1009.

38. who has labored with more resolution and zest" than Comstock. Bennett, CHAMPIONS OF THE CHURCH, *supra*, at 1010, 1064.

38. to Washington in 1878 to lobby against the repeal petition. Comstock, FRAUDS EXPOSED, *supra*, at 430.

38. it could be used as a contraceptive when combined with salicylic acid. Bates, *supra*, at 139, 141; Beisel, *supra*, at 94.
38. boycotted its products on principle. Broun and Leech, *supra*, at 189.
38. not just of embarrassment but of unwanted pregnancies. Jacoby, FREETHINKERS, *supra*, at 208.
38. and was arrested under state law. Broun and Leech, *supra*, at 180; Bates, *supra*, at 141.
38. to send *Cupid's Yokes* to anyone who wanted it. Rabban, FREE SPEECH IN ITS FORGOTTEN YEARS, *supra*, at 36–37.
38. advertise Cupid's something or other, you know what I mean." Paul and Schwartz, *supra*, at 25–26; Broun and Leech, *supra*, at 180.
39. and not just based on portions the prosecutor selected to read to the jury. *United States v. Bennett*, 24 F. Cas. 1093, 1099–1100 (2nd Cir. 1879).
39. improper to be placed on the court records." *United States* v. *Bennett*, 24 F. Cas. at 1094.
39. passages of the book marked by the prosecutor, which were read to the jury. *United States* v. *Bennett*, 24 F. Cas. at 1098–1099.
39. the United States is one great society for the suppression of vice." Broun and Leech, *supra*, at 89; Bremner, *supra*, at xxix.
39. It is the prosecution of the United States." *United States* v. *Bennett*, 24 F. Cas. at 1101.
39. "if it would suggest impure and libidinous thoughts in the young and the inexperienced." *United States* v. *Bennett*, 24 F. Cas. at 1101–1102; Rabban, FREE SPEECH IN ITS FORGOTTEN YEARS, *supra*, at 37–38; Blanchard, *The American Urge to Censor*, *supra*, at 755–756; Paul and Schwartz, *supra*, at 26–28.
39. Bennett's counsel and friends boasted that a pardon would be granted within ten days. Comstock, FRAUDS EXPOSED, *supra*, at 485; Bates, *supra*, at 141.
39. as the petition reportedly garnered 200,000 signatures. Comstock, FRAUDS EXPOSED, *supra*, at 496.
39. for the same crime for which Heywood had been pardoned? Broun and Leech, *supra*, at 182.
40. "[h]e was pardoned because facts were suppressed." Comstock, FRAUDS EXPOSED, *supra*, at 485–486.
40. Hayes denied the pardon petition. Broun and Leech, *supra*, at 182; Bates, *supra*, at 141–142; Beisel, *supra*, at 95; Rabban, FREE SPEECH IN ITS FORGOTTEN YEARS, *supra*, at 40–41.
40. "evidences of this man's character." Comstock, FRAUDS EXPOSED, *supra*, at 496–498.
40. "The Defender of Liberty and Its Martyr." Broun and Leech, *supra*, at 182–183.
40. *Morals stand first.*" Comstock, MORALS VERSUS ART, *supra*, at 5.
41. during the year [1875], but 17 were Americans." New York Society for the Suppression of Vice, SECOND ANNUAL REPORT, *supra*, at 11.
41. to help "keep undesirable classes from our shores." New York Society for the Suppression of Vice, THIRTY-FIFTH ANNUAL REPORT 16 (1909); Blanchard and Semonche, *supra*, at 346; LaMay, *supra*, at 34–35.
41. a quarter of Comstock's prosecutions in 1915 represented these nationalities. LaMay, *supra*, at 22.
41. referring to Shaw as some "Irish smut-dealer." Broun and Leech, *supra*, at 230.
42. to deify this 'companion of every other crime.'" Comstock, TRAPS FOR THE YOUNG, *supra*, at 168–169.
42. comes in its most insidious, fascinating and seductive form." Comstock, MORALS VERSUS ART, *supra*, at 4–5.
42. making the lascivious conception only the more insidious and demoralizing." New York Society for the Suppression of Vice, EIGHTH ANNUAL REPORT 6 (1882).

42. perhaps to avoid the embarrassment of a high-profile loss at his home base. Blanchard and Semonche, *supra*, at 344; Beisel, *supra*, at 167.

42. enjoyed phenomenal sales because of the controversy. Blanchard and Semonche, *supra*, at 342–344; Beisel, *supra*, at 165; Boyer, *supra*, at 15.

42. "The Boston fools have already made me more than $2,000." Miller, BANNED IN BOSTON, *supra*, at 14–17.

42. so prostituted from what has heretofore been thought to be their proper and legitimate place." New York Society for the Suppression of Vice, FIFTH ANNUAL REPORT, *supra*, at 15–17.

43. "little better than histories of brothels and prostitutes, in these lust-cursed nations." Comstock, TRAPS FOR THE YOUNG, *supra*, at 172, 179.

43. "death-dealing powers of strychnine are the same whether administered as a sugar-coated pill or in its natural state." Comstock, TRAPS FOR THE YOUNG, *supra*, at 168, 182–183.

43. simply because clothed in smooth verse or choice rhetoric." Anthony Comstock, *Vampire Literature*, THE NORTH AMERICAN REVIEW 165–166 (Aug. 1891).

43. only the Italian original could properly be considered a classic. Comstock, TRAPS FOR THE YOUNG, *supra*, at 173–176.

44. "Fifth Avenue has no more rights in this respect than Centre Street or the Bowery." Broun and Leech, *supra*, at 223.

44. the greatest educational benefit to the community." Beisel, *supra*, at 172–173.

44. "subversive to the best interests both of art and morality." Amy Werbel, *The Crime of the Nude*, WINTERTHUR PORTFOLIO (2014), at 266.

44. galvanized opposition from prominent artists, public intellectuals, and respectable organizations. Werbel, *The Crime of the Nude*, *supra*, at 264–266.

44. in character and effect a very different thing." Comstock, MORALS VERSUS ART, *supra*, at 9–10; Beisel, *supra*, at 176–177.

44. the siren song of titillating art could be confined in galleries. Comstock, MORALS VERSUS ART, *supra*, at 8–9.

44. it served the interests of his wealthy benefactors. Beisel, *supra*, at 185–187.

45. "a social nuisance almost as pestilent as that which he exists to abate." *Mr. Comstock's Censorship*, NEW YORK TIMES, Mar. 24, 1888, at 4; Beisel, *supra*, at 190.

45. released Comstock's letters and his response to the press. Werbel, LUST ON TRIAL, *supra*, at 192193; Beisel, *supra*, at 178–189.

45. "he was not dissuaded from his campaign against the arts." Broun and Leech, *supra*, at 225; Beisel, *supra*, at 176, 187–193.

46. "influencing 60,000 young girls annually to turn to lives of shame." Werbel, *The Crime of the Nude*, *supra*, at 251, 255, 271; Werbel, LUST ON TRIAL, *supra*, at 268–272, 277.

46. a nineteen-year-old bookkeeper who handed him a copy of the journal. Werbel, *The Crime of the Nude*, *supra*, at 250–251; Werbel, LUST ON TRIAL, *supra*, at 272.

46. destroyed somewhere between 2,500 and 3,650 copies of the League's pamphlet. Bates, *supra*, at 178–179; Werbel, *The Crime of the Nude*, *supra*, at 272; Werbel, LUST ON TRIAL, *supra*, at 278.

46. "to anyone who happened to call for them." Trumbull, *supra*, at 130–131.

46. whenever they could find space on a wall for a sketch." Broun and Leech, *supra*, at 216–219; Werbel, *The Crime of the Nude*, *supra*, at 256; Werbel, LUST ON TRIAL, *supra*, at 272–274.

46. with even *Life* magazine getting in on the fun. Werbel, *The Crime of the Nude*, *supra*, at 256–257; Werbel, LUST ON TRIAL, *supra*, at 273–274.

46. "preposterous pruriency." Werbel, *The Crime of the Nude*, *supra*, at 268.

47. after the League's lawyer cut a backroom deal to allow destruction of the journals. Trumbull, *supra*, at 175–179; Werbel, *The Crime of the Nude, supra*, at 272–273; Werbel, LUST ON TRIAL, *supra*, at 277.

47. even before the trial began. Werbel, *The Crime of the Nude, supra*, at 273.

47. but when they break out, they must be suppressed." Bates, *supra*, at 179.

48. I'll confiscate your whole stock." *Comstock Dooms September Morning*, NEW YORK TIMES, May 11, 1913, at 1.

48. if I have to spend the value of my entire stock in contesting the point with Mr. Comstock." *Comstock Dooms September Morning, supra*, at 1.

48. because the crowds around the display window kept paying customers from entering the shop. *Wearies of Waiting a Comstock Arrest*, NEW YORK TIMES, May 15, 1913, at 7.

48. the Fair's committee of "Lady Managers," no further action was taken. *Cairo Dances to Go*, NEW YORK WORLD, Aug. 5, 1893, at 3; Broun and Leech, *supra*, at 225–228.

48. can be viewed on YouTube to this day. Little Egypt 1896 (http://youtu.be/zxZoXJBILbc).

49. Comstock's objection was that the book dealt with sexual anatomy. Bates, *supra*, at 79.

49. "more offensive to decency" than the smut he suppressed. Comstock, TRAPS FOR THE YOUNG, *supra*, at 158.

49. "no reputable physician has ever been prosecuted under these laws." Hopkins, *Birth Control and Public Morals: An Interview with Anthony Comstock, supra*, at 489–490.

49. Abbey was convicted and given a light sentence, although it was never carried out. D. M. Bennett, *An open Letter to Samuel Colgate* 30–32 (New York: D. M. Bennett, Liberal Publisher, 1879).

49. provided information on birth control in his publications. Rabban, FREE SPEECH IN ITS FORGOTTEN YEARS, *supra*, at 39; Bates, *supra*, at 155.

50. to oppose his 1872 legislative proposal to the New York assembly for an obscenity law. Janice Ruth Wood, THE STRUGGLE FOR FREE SPEECH IN THE UNITED STATES 1872–1915 3–4, 62–83 (New York: Routledge Press, 2008).

50. Comstock ordered a copy of a Foote pamphlet entitled *Words in Pearl*. Bates, *supra*, at 155–156.

50. Comstock obtained a copy of the pamphlet using a decoy letter and arrested Foote. Wood, *supra*, at 53–56.

50. it would "afford an easy way of nullifying the law." *United States* v. *Foote*, 25 F. Cas. 1140 (SDNY 1876).

50. Foote was convicted and fined $3,500. Bates, *supra*, at 156; Bennett, CHAMPIONS OF THE CHURCH, *supra*, at 1039.

50. (although some suggest that he just became more subtle about it). Wood, *supra*, at 36.

50. 300,000 copies of his popular home guide MEDICAL COMMON SENSE between 1858 and 1876. Rabban, FREE SPEECH IN ITS FORGOTTEN YEARS, *supra*, at 40.

50. (or the blame, depending on your outlook). Wood, *supra*, at 5, 62–64.

50. continued to wage battles for freedom of expression in the early twentieth century. Wood, *supra*, at 76–81.

50. in 1873 alone he arrested thirty-five people for advocating contraceptives and secured twenty-five convictions. Bates, *supra*, at 154.

51. beginning with her 1878 arrest for selling "a certain article . . . made of India Rubber and sponge." Bates, *supra*, at 166; Wood, *supra*, at 89.

51. once again the district attorney declined prosecution. Bennett, *An Open Letter to Samuel Colgate, supra*, at 35–36.

51. As before, the grand jury cleared her of the charge. Bates, *supra*, at 166–168.

51. Sieckel was sentenced to a $500 fine and a year in prison. Bates, *supra*, at 103–104.

52. "Is it not time to defy this law?" Margaret Sanger, THE WOMAN REBEL (Jul. 1914), at 5; Bates, *supra*, at 198.

52. "No Gods or Masters." *William Sanger to Fight in Court for Birth Control*, NEW YORK TIMES, Sept. 5, 1915.

52. not just deemed unmailable; they were confiscated. Margaret Sanger, *Comstockery in America*, INTERNATIONAL SOCIALIST REVIEW (1915), at 46–49.

52. Sanger had 100,000 copies of the small pamphlet distributed to factories and mines throughout the country. Sanger, *Comstockery in America, supra.*

52. Can't everybody, whether rich or poor, learn to control themselves?" Broun and Leech, *supra*, at 249.

52. I decided to take an indefinite postponement and left for London." Sanger, *Comstockery in America, supra*; Bates, *supra*, at 198–199.

52. he looked for a copy "as a special favor to a friend of his wife." *William Sanger to Fight in Court for Birth Control*, NEW YORK TIMES, Sept. 5, 1915.

52. the man returned with Comstock, who promptly arrested Sanger. Sanger, *Comstockery in America, supra*; Bates, *supra*, at 198–199; LaMay, *supra*, at 54–55.

52. Sanger "lived separate from his family with many artists in the house." Bates, *supra*, at 199.

52. including Alexander Berkman and labor activist Elizabeth Gurley Flynn, later a founding member of the ACLU. *Disorder in Court as Sanger Is Fined*, NEW YORK TIMES, Sept. 11, 1915.

53. they would be rendering society a greater service." *Disorder in Court as Sanger Is Fined*, NEW YORK TIMES, Sept. 11, 1915; Broun and Leech, *supra*, at 249.

53. "a heinous criminal who sought to turn every home into a brothel." LaMay, *supra*, at 54–55; Bates, *supra*, at 200.

53. I have disregarded the threat." *Disorder in Court as Sanger Is Fined*, NEW YORK TIMES, Sept. 11, 1915.

53. *Family Limitation* was indecent, immoral, and a menace to society. Bates, *supra*, at 200.

53. "Then," Judge McInerney responded, "you will go to jail." *Disorder in Court as Sanger Is Fined*, NEW YORK TIMES, Sept. 11, 1915; Broun and Leech, *supra*, at 250; Bates, *supra*, at 200.

54. struggled to clear the crowd into the corridor. *Disorder in Court as Sanger Is Fined*, NEW YORK TIMES, Sept. 11, 1915.

54. far short of the one-year imprisonment and $1,000 fine that could have been imposed. *William Sanger to Fight in Court for Birth Control*, NEW YORK TIMES, Sept. 5, 1915.

54. "as fast as one circulator was arrested[,] another would step forward and take his place." *Disorder in Court as Sanger Is Fined*, NEW YORK TIMES, Sept. 11, 1915.

54. on September 21, 1915, the old crusader died. Broun and Leech, *supra*, at 258–259; Bates, *supra*, at 200.

54. "and from his successful efforts to convict William Sanger." *Anthony Comstock Dies in His Crusade*, NEW YORK TIMES, Sept. 22, 1915, at 1.

CHAPTER 3

55. "served for forty years as the national line between virtue and vice." Amy Werbel, *Searching for Smut*, COMMON-PLACE (Oct. 2010).

55. and made himself the first of its kept professors." Mencken, A BOOK OF PREFACES, *supra*, at 255, 260.

55. "the foremost policeman of private vices in America's Gilded Age." Craig L. LaMay, *America's Censor: Anthony Comstock and Free Speech*, 1 COMMUNICATIONS AND THE LAW 41 (Sept. 1997).

55. "over most of the civilized world." Mary Alden Hopkins, *Birth Control and Public Morals: An Interview with Anthony Comstock*, HARPER'S WEEKLY, May 22, 1915, at 489–490.

55. a fallen "soldier of righteousness," Broun and Leech, *supra*, at 259.

55. "the most spectacular crusader against vice that America has known." LaMay, *supra*, at 1–2.

55. his crusades against books, pictures and plays that he deemed indecent." *Anthony Comstock Dies in His Crusade*, NEW YORK TIMES, Sept. 22, 1915, at 1.

55. "served a good cause with tireless devotion." Paul S. Boyer, PURITY IN PRINT 29 (New York: Charles Scribner's Sons, 1968).

56. a conspiracy of silence against certain of the major concerns of mankind." Carl Van Doren, *Why the Editorial Board Chose This Book*, 3 WINGS (New York: The Literary Guild of America, Inc., 1927).

56. fornication, adultery, pornography, contraception, easy divorce, abortion, and sodomy." Allan Carlson, Pure Visionary, Touchstone – A Journal of Mere Christianity (Jun. 2009); Allan Carlson, (Forward to OUTLAWED! HOW ANTHONY COMSTOCK FOUGHT AND WON THE PURITY OF A NATION xi (Middletown, DE: Western Conservatory of the Arts and Sciences, 2013) (reprinting Charles Galludet Trumbull, ANTHONY COMSTOCK, FIGHTER (1913)).

56. This analysis compels the conclusion that same-sex couples may exercise the right to marry. *Obergefell* v. *Hodges*, 135 S. Ct. 2584, 2598 (2015).

57. so many joking comments by people in Europe as Comstockery in America." Sanger, *Comstockery in America*, *supra*, at 46–49.

57. "the historical image of Anthony Comstock is more comic than threatening." Heins, *supra*, at 29.

57. "the whipping boy of present day public opinion." John Collier, *Anthony Comstock – Liberal*, SURVEY, Nov. 6, 1915, at 127.

57. a mail clerk smarted under the reprimands of this irascible superior." Broun and Leech, *supra*, at 145.

57. at considerable expense, to remove the garment. *Comstock at Princeton*, NEW YORK TIMES, Mar. 31, 1888; Bates, *supra*, at 185.

57. depicting a time in which Comstock's influence caused even horses, dogs, and birds to wear trousers. Charles Dana Gibson, *A Scene in the Moral Future*, LIFE, Jan. 12, 1888.

58. the advertiser was thrilled by the notoriety. *A Shock to Sir Anthony*, NEW YORK TIMES, Dec. 28, 1895.

58. "not at all libidinous." *Cairo Dances to Go*, THE WORLD, Aug. 5, 1893, at 5; Broun and Leech, *supra*, at 227.

59. "at best, laughable," and "at worst, revolting." H. L. Mencken, *The Emperor of Wowsers*, NEW YORK HERALD TRIBUNE, Mar. 6, 1927.

59. single-handedly fought the battle for national purity ... and won." Kevin Peeples, *Anthony Comstock: Fighter* (2014).

59. HOW ANTHONY COMSTOCK FOUGHT & WON THE PURITY OF A NATION. Charles Galludet Trumbull, ANTHONY COMSTOCK, FIGHTER 85–91 (1913); OUTLAWED! HOW ANTHONY COMSTOCK FOUGHT AND WON THE PURITY OF A NATION, *supra*.

59. he dramatically curtailed the pornography industry, and nearly eliminated both abortion and contraception." Scott Matthew Dix, *When Contraception Was Outlawed!* (editor's preface to OUTLAWED! HOW ANTHONY COMSTOCK FOUGHT AND WON THE PURITY OF A NATION, *supra*, at xviii, xxi).

59. "makes for wickedly amusing reading today." Comstock, FRAUDS EXPOSED, *supra*, at 443.

60. Comstock "both embodied and caricatured the moral sense of his epoch." Comstock, TRAPS FOR THE YOUNG, *supra*, at xxxi).

61. halfway between that enjoyed by phrenology and that enjoyed by homosexuality." Mencken, *The Emperor of Wowsers, supra.*

61. America is a provincial place, a second rate country town civilization after all." Broun and Leech, *supra,* at 229–230.

61. for personally covering up advertisements for the Metropolitan Museum of Art that offended him. *Comstockery,* NEW YORK TIMES, Dec. 12, 1895; LaMay, *supra,* at 29–30; Broun and Leech, *supra,* at 231.

61. exercised their talents on the noted Secretary of the Society for the Suppression of Vice." *Anthony Comstock Dies in His Crusade, supra,* at 1, 6.

61. "[m]ost people don't even like the word – especially the censors." Gerald Gardner, THE CENSORSHIP PAPERS xi (New York: Dodd, Mead & Co., 1987).

62. far more harm to women than pornographic pictures." Bates, *supra,* at vii.

62. everyone wants to know how you got into the business." Jack Vizzard, SEE NO EVIL 9 (New York: Simon and Schuster, 1970).

62. "strange or hypocritical to mention freedom of expression in the same breath with censorship." Alfred Schneider, THE GATEKEEPER 5 (Syracuse, NY: Syracuse University Press, 2001).

62. if we have the eyes to read them." Broun and Leech, *supra,* at 192.

62. the ridicule that was heaped on Comstock began at the very outset of his vigilante career. *Anthony Comstock Dies in His Crusade, supra,* at 6.

63. "if the policy of suppression is pushed to extremes." *The Suppression of Vice,* THE NORTH AMERICAN REVIEW 484–501 (Nov. 1882).

63. whose methods were displeasing to saints." Bremner, *supra,* at xvi.

63. did not always sit well with other reformers. Blanchard and Semonche, *supra,* at 317–366.

63. he thinks no one has the right to work for social purity without first obtaining permission from him." Bremner, *supra,* at xxvi–xxvii.

63. depicted a Victorian gentleman stoking a bonfire with books. Boyer, *supra,* at 250.

63. changed its name to the Society to Maintain Public Decency. Jay A. Gertzman, *John Saxton Sumner of the New York Society for the Suppression of Vice: A Chief Smut-Eradicator of the Interwar Period,* 14 JOURNAL OF AMERICAN CULTURE 41–47 (Jun. 1994).

63. and whose self-hatred stemmed from an obsession with masturbation Ernst and Schwartz, *supra,* at 29–30.

63. the "hard, incontrovertible experience of a Puritan farm-boy, in executive session behind the barn. Mencken, *The Emperor of Wowsers, supra.*

63. the impulses of cruelty arise concurrently with the stirrings of sex emotion." Bates, *supra,* at 191.

63. the laws he had made his especial concern." Broun and Leech, *supra,* at 191.

64. instead each prayer or Hymn seemed to add to my misery." Broun and Leech, *supra,* at 39.

64. the zealot treated anything remotely connected with sex as a public danger. Broun and Leech, *supra,* at 201.

64. compared them to "wild animals" that must be "caged." Bates, *supra,* at 179.

64. and it became a lifelong habit. Robert W. Haney, COMSTOCKERY IN AMERICA 19 (Boston: Beacon Press, 1960).

64. some man of desperate fortunes and ambiguous character." D. M. Bennett, CHAMPIONS OF THE CHURCH: THEIR CRIMES AND PERSECUTIONS 1014 (New York: Liberal and Scientific Publishing House, 1878).

64. destructive to individual rights guaranteed by the Constitution of our country." Bennett, CHAMPIONS OF THE CHURCH, *supra,* at 1014.

65. many thousands of people had seen the photos that otherwise would have been unknown to them. *What Is the Streisand Effect?*, THE ECONOMIST, Apr. 16, 2013; *Streisand v. Adelman*, SC-077-257 (Cal. Super. Ct., Dec. 31, 2003).

65. her name is now forever associated with comically misguided censorship efforts. Paul Rogers, *Streisand's Home Becomes Hit on Web*, SAN JOSE MERCURY NEWS, Jun. 24, 2003.

65. and described the encounter as "sad and ludicrous." Comstock, *Vampire Literature*, *supra*, at 160–161; LaMay, *supra*, at 29.

65. put art on page one." Amy Werbel, *The Crime of the Nude*, WINTERTHUR PORTFOLIO (2014), at 267.

65. "the advertising agents of sex." Morris Ernst, *Sex Wins in America*, THE NATION, Aug. 10, 1932, at 123.

66. to see which one can excel the others in unclean stories." Comstock, *Vampire Literature*, *supra*, at 160–161.

66. invited Comstock to attend rehearsals at the Garrick Theatre. *Comstock at It Again*, NEW YORK TIMES, Oct. 25, 1905.

66. Comstock went to court to block the "obscene" performances, but was unsuccessful. Broun and Leech, *supra*, at 232–234.

66. with overflow audiences and tickets fetching premium prices. Blanchard and Semonche, *supra*, at 349.

66. city police had to call out the reserves to manage the crowds. Broun and Leech, *supra*, at 232.

66. a confrontation captured in a tongue-in-cheek front-page *New York Times* account. Broun and Leech, *supra*, at 238.

66. that story mutated and eventually took on a life of its own. *Comstock Dooms September Morning*, NEW YORK TIMES, May 11, 1913, at 1.

66. was said to spiral from $35 to $10,000. Bates, *supra*, at 181.

67. a lithograph that had been rejected as a brewer's calendar became an overnight sensation. Harry Reichenbach, PHANTOM FAME: THE ANATOMY OF BALLYHOO (New York: Simon and Schuster, 1931).

67. he was not looking for work at the time but was already an established publicist, WASHINGTON POST, Aug. 24, 1913; *The September Morn Hoax* (http://hoaxes.org/archive/permalink/the_september_morn_hoax).

67. to prosecute a small art store for selling copies of the print. *September Morn Pits Her Beauty Against Censors*, CHICAGO DAILY TRIBUNE, Mar. 21, 1913, at 1; *September Morn Wins Case*, CHICAGO DAILY TRIBUNE, Mar. 22, 1913, at 3.

67. but was rebuffed by the courts. Broun and Leech, *supra*, at 238; James Doherty, *The Story of Bathhouse John*, CHICAGO SUNDAY TRIBUNE, May 24, 1953, at 6.

67. "might work havoc in the minds of her pupils passing that way." *September Morn Stirs Mr. Comstock*, THE LA CROSSE TRIBUNE, May 13, 1913.

67. people went into the print publishing business merely for the sake of handling this picture." Broun and Leech, *supra*, at 239.

67. copies of the print were on sale in every part of the United States. *Anthony Comstock Dies in His Crusade*, *supra*, at 6.

67. one of the most famous and popular paintings of the twentieth century. *The September Morn Hoax* (http://hoaxes.org/archive/permalink/the_september_morn_hoax).

68. it grew over time to include mainstream publishers, artists, doctors, and merchants. Werbel, *The Crime of the Nude*, *supra*, at 250.

68. as to reach and corrupt the young and inexperienced." Comstock, *Vampire Literature*, *supra*, at 167–168.

68. according to conscience, men may be found ready to fight and suffer." Broun and Leech, *supra*, at 188–189; Werbel, *The Crime of the Nude*, *supra*, at 266, 269.

69. the insidious repression of the liberties of the people." Comstock, TRAPS FOR THE YOUNG, *supra*, at 189–190.

69. to end the Comstock Act and to defend those prosecuted under it. Rabban, FREE SPEECH IN ITS FORGOTTEN YEARS, *supra*, at 40.

69. to violate the true and constitutional liberty of the press." National Liberal League, *Indignation Meeting Minutes* 6 (Boston, MA: Benjamin R. Tucker, 1878).

69. by their own particular opinion or notion of morality and immorality." Bennett, CHAMPIONS OF THE CHURCH, *supra*, at 1016.

70. still this would be no protection to the next vendor of the book." Theodore S. Schroeder, OBSCENE LITERATURE AND CONSTITUTIONAL LAW: A FORENSIC DEFENSE OF FREEDOM OF THE PRESS 313–314 (New York, 1911).

70. and not to dwell just on what prosecutors thought were the naughty bits. *United States v. Bennett*, 24 F. Cas. 1093, 1099–1100 (2nd Cir. 1879).

70. to protect free speech for all, regardless of viewpoint. Rabban, FREE SPEECH IN ITS FORGOTTEN YEARS, *supra*, at 44–45.

70. and essential to our existence as a free people." *Free Speech or Slavery*, LUCIFER: THE LIGHT BEARER, Jun. 22, 1905, at 327.

70. was an organizer and major funder of the League. Janice Ruth Wood, THE STRUGGLE FOR FREE SPEECH IN THE UNITED STATES 1872–1915 62–83 (New York: Routledge, 2008); Rabban, FREE SPEECH IN ITS FORGOTTEN YEARS, *supra*, at 47–49.

70. a principled commitment to free expression for all viewpoints on all subjects." Rabban, FREE SPEECH IN ITS FORGOTTEN YEARS, *supra*, at 76.

71. having "done more for free expression in America than any other." Boyer, *supra*, at 41; Rabban, FREE SPEECH IN ITS FORGOTTEN YEARS, *supra*, at 54.

71. blasphemy, censorship of the mails, the Alien and Sedition Acts, free speech for radicals, advertising, and sex censorship. THEODORE SCHROEDER ON FREE SPEECH: A BIBLIOGRAPHY 1–24 (Nancy E. Stankey-Jones, ed., Free Speech League, 1919); Boyer, *supra*, at 41–43.

71. "to increase intellectual hospitality to the end that more truth will prevail." Theodore S. Schroeder, METHODS OF CONSTITUTIONAL CONSTRUCTION, THE SYNTHETIC METHOD ILLUSTRATED ON THE FREE SPEECH CLAUSE OF THE FEDERAL CONSTITUTION 41 (Free Speech League, 1914); LaMay, *supra*, at 35–36.

71. was well ahead of its time. Schroeder, OBSCENE LITERATURE AND CONSTITUTIONAL LAW: A FORENSIC DEFENSE OF FREEDOM OF THE PRESS, *supra*.

71. New York City Bar Association and of the British Museum. Theodore S. Schroeder, A CHALLENGE TO THE SEX CENSORS 19 (New York: Free Speech League, 1938); Rochelle Gurstein, THE REPEAL OF RETICENCE 101 (New York: Hill & Wang, 1996).

71. a gathering of social reformers billed as a united national effort to promote public virtue. *The Elementary School Teacher* (Sept. 1906–Jun. 1907), at 100.

71. debated the legitimacy of obscenity laws via extensive correspondence. Blanchard and Semonche, *supra*, at 364; Rabban, FREE SPEECH IN ITS FORGOTTEN YEARS, *supra*, at 74.

71. even Biblical quotations and passages from UNCLE TOM'S CABIN were not safe from the censors. Theodore S. Schroeder, FREEDOM OF THE PRESS AND "OBSCENE" LITERATURE: THREE ESSAYS 732 (Free Speech League, 1906).

71. He was said to be too ill to attend. *Purity Debate One-Sided: Anthony Comstock Fails to Meet His Opponent*, CHICAGO DAILY TRIBUNE, Oct. 11, 1906, at 2.

71. to prevent "suppression of any scientific and educational purity literature." Schroeder, FREEDOM OF THE PRESS AND "OBSCENE" LITERATURE, *supra*, at 7–32.

72. "a new epoch among purity workers." B. O. Flower (editorial), reprinted in FREE SPEECH ANTHOLOGY 167–171 (New York: Free Speech League, 1909) (Theodore S. Schroeder, ed.); Gurstein, *supra*, at 128.

72. by the words, 'obscene, lewd, or lascivious.'" *United States* v. *Kennerley*, 209 F. 119, 120–121 (SDNY 1913); Broun and Leech, *supra*, at 241–242.

72. The jury ultimately acquitted the publisher of the obscenity charge. Boyer, *supra*, at 46–48.

73. that spawned Comstock's New York Society for the Suppression of Vice decades earlier. Laura Weinrib, *The Sex Side of Civil Liberties: United States* v. *Dennett and the Changing Face of Free Speech*, UNIVERSITY OF CHICAGO PUBLIC LAW & LEGAL THEORY WORKING PAPER, No. 385 (2012), at 340–341, 344.

73. "much chaste poetry and fiction, as well as many useful medical works would be under the ban." *United States* v. *Dennett*, 39 F. 2d 564, 568–569 (2nd Cir. 1930).

73. "it must always be remembered that his locale was Celtic and his season spring." *United States* v. *One Book Called "Ulysses"*, 5 F. Supp. 182, 183–184 (SDNY 1933).

74. because it was not written with "pornographic intent." *One Book Called "Ulysses,"* 5 F. Supp. at 183–184.

74. "does not affect the tendency of a book or picture" to corrupt. Comstock, MORALS VERSUS ART, *supra*, at 4, 26.

74. "if sold in such a manner as to reach and corrupt the young and inexperienced." Comstock, *Vampire Literature*, *supra*, at 167.

74. and that, Judge Hand concluded, could not be what Congress had in mind. *United States* v. *One Book Entitled Ulysses by James Joyce*, 72 F. 2d 705, 706–708 (2nd Cir. 1934).

74. They are protected by law, while art, if unclean, is not." Comstock, MORALS VERSUS ART, *supra*, at 4–5.

74. and his book as "an amazing tour de force." *One Book Called "Ulysses,"* 5 F. Supp. at 184.

75. It turned a cultural insurgency into a civic virtue of a free and open society." Kevin Birmingham, THE MOST DANGEROUS BOOK 12 (New York: Penguin Press, 2014).

75. the right to experiment with a new technique." *One Book Entitled Ulysses by James Joyce*, 72 F. 2d at 706, 708.

75. it was his duty "to act as observer and recorder, not as regulator." *People on Complaint of Sumner* v. *Miller*, 155 Misc. 446, 446–448 (City Magistrate's Court of New York, 1935).

75. sold by the retailers and reviewed by the press." Morris Ernst, *Sex Wins in America*, THE NATION, Aug. 10, 1932, at 124.

76. it is one of the vital problems of human interest and public concern." *Roth* v. *United States*, 354 US 476, 487 (1957).

76. have the full protection" of the First Amendment." *Roth*, 354 US at 484, 489–490.

76. "no such verdict could convince me, without more, that these books are 'utterly without redeeming social importance.'" *Roth*, 354 US at 498 (Harlan, J., dissenting in part).

77. "literature should not be suppressed merely because it offends the moral code of the censor." *Roth*, 354 US at 509–514 (Douglas, J., dissenting).

77. it lives on, albeit in a greatly diminished form. Jennifer Kinsley, The Myth of Obsolete Obscenity, 33 Cardozo Arts & Entertainment L. J. 607 (2015).

77. "I know it when I see it." *Jacobellis* v. *Ohio*, 378 US 184, 197 (1964) (Stewart, J., concurring).

77. can reduce the vagueness to a tolerable level." *Paris Adult Theatre I* v. *Slayton*, 413 US 49, 84 (1973) (Brennan, J., dissenting).

77. to grapple with hard questions about obscenity's relevance to a global medium. Robert Corn-Revere, *Cyberspace Cases Force Court to Reexamine Basic Assumptions of Obscenity and Child Pornography Jurisprudence*, CATO SUPREME COURT REV. 115–148 (2002).

77. prosecutions can be used to limit the availability of adult entertainment and to force local businesses to shut down. Kinsley, *supra*, at 639–642.

78. a law that threatened "to torch a large segment of the Internet community." *Reno v. ACLU*, 521 US 844, 875, 882 (1997).

78. at least to the younger generation – a "joke" and a "scapegoat." Broun and Leech, *supra*, at 244.

78. "You are nothing but a little boy trying to tell me my business!" Broun and Leech, *supra*, at 251–252.

78. had struck Comstock in response to being called a liar. Broun and Leech, *supra*, at 252–253.

78. Sumner would later write that he had been hired to replace the crotchety crusader. LaMay, *supra*, at 42–43.

78. They also wanted someone who avoided publicity. Broun and Leech, *supra*, at 256, 258.

78. impressed everyone with his even temper. Gertzman, *supra*; Boyer, *supra*, at 30.

78. naturally, he and Comstock fought often. LaMay, *supra*, at 43.

78. remained in that post for thirty-five years. Gertzman, *supra*.

79. Sumner had taken on the role of running the organization. *Anthony Comstock Dies in His Crusade, supra*, at 6; Broun and Leech, *supra*, at 257–258.

79. his wife's pro-birth control pamphlet, *Family Limitation*. Bates, *supra*, at 199.

79. the old man's fraying reputation and buoying his sagging spirits. Broun and Leech, *supra*, at 258; Bates, *supra*, at 199; Boyer, *supra*, at 28.

79. within ten days died of pneumonia. *Anthony Comstock Dies in His Crusade, supra*, at 1, 6.

79. Comstock dictated notes for use by the Society up until the day before his death. Broun and Leech, *supra*, at 259.

79. documenting Comstock's deep-rooted neuroses. Broun and Leech, *supra*, at 46–58, 63–74, 77–78, 131–144, 178, 261; Ernst and Schwartz, *supra*, at 29–30.

79. to keep them from "falling into the wrong hands." Richard Christian Johnson, ANTHONY COMSTOCK: REFORM, VICE, AND THE AMERICAN WAY 5, n. 4 (unpublished PhD dissertation, University of Wisconsin, 1973); LaMay, *supra*, at 4.

80. The bad news, of course, was that he never rose again. Schroeder, A CHALLENGE TO THE SEX CENSORS, *supra*, at 16–17.

80. Hopkins died of tuberculosis, at home and in his bed.) James Sharpe, *Hopkins, Matthew (d. 1647)*, DICTIONARY OF NATIONAL BIOGRAPHY (online ed.) (London: Oxford University Press, 2004).

80. no longer even mentions Comstock. The Evergreen Cemetery (www.theevergreenscem etery.org/).

CHAPTER 4

81. simplistic and quick-fix solutions. Stanley Cohen, FOLK DEVILS AND MORAL PANICS 1 (London: Routledge, 3rd ed., 2002).

81. "may trace the commencement of their career in crime to their attendance in Penny Theatres." James Grant, SKETCHES IN LONDON (1838); John Springhall, YOUTH, POPULAR CULTURE AND MORAL PANICS 9, 38–58, 75, 93 (New York: St. Martin's Press, 1998).

81. blame dime novels for virtually all the antisocial behavior exhibited by the youth of the period. Margaret A. Blanchard, *The American Urge to Censor: Freedom of Expression Versus the Desire to Sanitize Society – From Anthony Comstock to 2 Live Crew*, 33 WILLIAM & MARY LAW REV. 741–851 (1992).

81. we can expect campaigns to ban or censor it. Springhall, *supra*, at 7.

81. the cycle of outrage in the typical moral panic. Kirsten Drotner, Modernity and Moral Panics, in Media Cultures: Reappraising Transitional Media 52 (Michael Skovmand Schroder and Kim Christian, eds., 1992).

82. fund the American Museum of Natural History. Paul S. Boyer, PURITY IN PRINT 12–16 (New York: Charles Scribner's Sons, 1968).

82. normal fixtures on the philanthropic landscape. Boyer, *supra*, at 12–16.

82. are to be relentlessly proscribed." Julia Ward Howe, *The Influence of Literature Upon Crime*, PAPERS AND LETTERS PRESENTED AT THE FIRST WOMEN'S CONGRESS OF THE AMERICAN ASSOCIATION FOR THE ADVANCEMENT OF WOMEN 13, 15, 17 (New York: American Association for the Advancement of Women, 1874).

82. "standards of propriety are sometimes those of an earlier and grosser age." Arthur E. Bostwick, *The Librarian as Censor*, LIBRARY JOURNAL 264 (1908).

82. in praising the campaign against "salacious literature." Boyer, *supra*, at 24–25.

82. to cleanse newsstands and drugstore magazine racks of 'objectionable' material." Comstock, TRAPS FOR THE YOUNG, *supra*, at vii.

82. on social media and in Washington today." Annalee Newitz, *The Original Anti-Feminist Crusader*, NEW YORK TIMES, Sept. 22, 2019, at SR-10.

83. firmly believed "in himself and in his work to the end." Broun and Leech, *supra*, at 244, 259.

83. a "barrier between youth and moral death." Comstock, FRAUDS EXPOSED, *supra*, at 425.

83. "contrary not only to the law of the State, but to the law of God." Broun and Leech, *supra*, at 249.

83. "in the hope that the blind be made to see and the erring to correct their ways." Comstock, *Vampire Literature*, *supra*, at 171.

83. neither the intellect nor [the] judgment to decide what is wisest and best for themselves." Comstock, TRAPS FOR THE YOUNG, *supra*, at 6.

83. "I cannot expect to have better treatment than our blessed Master." Comstock, FRAUDS EXPOSED, *supra*, at 7.

83. "you have no doubt of your premises or your power and want a certain result with all your heart." *Abrams v. United States*, 250 US 616, 630 (1919) (Holmes, J., dissenting).

83. is by their level of self-assurance *Florida Bar v. Went For It, Inc.*, 515 US 618, 645 (1995) (Kennedy, J., dissenting).

83. "Eternal vigilance is the price of liberty." Monticello.org (www.monticello.org/site/jeffer son/eternal-vigilance-price-liberty-spurious-quotation).

83. "eternal vigilance is the price of moral purity." Comstock, FRAUDS EXPOSED, *supra*, at 433.

84. according to Comstock, "defending 'this, their dear obscenity.'" Comstock, FRAUDS EXPOSED, *supra*, at 508; Broun and Leech, *supra*, at 191.

84. their actions were based on "revenge, avarice, and innate depravity." Comstock, FRAUDS EXPOSED, *supra*, at 393.

84. "naturally favor the impure and base." Comstock, FRAUDS EXPOSED, *supra*, at 196–197.

84. the "enemies of moral purity." Comstock, FRAUDS EXPOSED, *supra*, at 418.

84. a means of persecution, terrorism and blackmail." Mencken, A BOOK OF PREFACES, *supra*, at 251.

84. Comstock bragged that he was responsible for at least fifteen suicides. Broun and Leech, *supra*, at 192–193; LaMay, *supra*, at 18; James A. Morone, HELLFIRE NATION 230 (New Haven, CT and London: Yale University Press, 2003).

85. asserted that some of the names on the petition were forgeries. Comstock, TRAPS FOR THE YOUNG, *supra*, at 192–193, 226.

85. describing his advocacy as "sneering, scoffing, and blasphemous lectures." Comstock, TRAPS FOR THE YOUNG, *supra*, at 187.

85. "a scoundrel whom I caught committing a felony." Comstock, TRAPS FOR THE YOUNG, *supra*, at 194.

85. created merely "to defend those so charged." Comstock, TRAPS FOR THE YOUNG, *supra*, at 185.

85. to help "keep undesirable classes from our shores." New York Society for the Suppression of Vice, SECOND ANNUAL REPORT 11 (Jan. 27, 1876); New York Society for the Suppression of Vice, THIRTY-FIFTH ANNUAL REPORT 16 (1909); LaMay, *supra*, at 34–35; Blanchard and Semonche, *supra*, at 346.

85. "little better than histories of brothels and prostitutes, in those lust-cursed nations." Comstock, TRAPS FOR THE YOUNG, *supra*, at 179.

85. "see no reason why we should have the sewerage of Great Britain dumped on our shores." Broun and Leech, *supra*, at 224, 248–249.

85. a "foreign writer of filth." Broun and Leech, *supra*, at 18, 235–236; Boyer, *supra*, at 24–25.

86. all the invective that his violent nature and colorful imagination suggested." Broun and Leech, *supra*, at 150.

86. a post he shared with "rattlesnakes and other poisonous dangers." Broun and Leech, *supra*, at 19.

86. protect the young of our land from the leprosy of this vile trash." Broun and Leech, *supra*, at 123.

86. more dangerous beasts of prey than rabid dogs. Broun and Leech, *supra*, at 42–43, 86.

86. Its breath is fetid, and its touch moral prostration and death." Comstock, MORALS VERSUS ART, *supra*, 11–12.

86. or lighting matches in a powder magazine. Comstock, TRAPS FOR THE YOUNG, *supra*, at 228.

86. while he was just a "weeder in the garden of the Lord." Comstock, FRAUDS EXPOSED, *supra*, at 396, 414; Bates, *supra*, at 3.

86. away from the 'Lamb of God which taketh away sins of the world.'" Mary Alden Hopkins, *Birth Control and Public Morals: An Interview with Anthony Comstock*, HARPER'S WEEKLY, May 22, 1915, at 490; Broun and Leech, *supra*, at 416–417.

86. "open to every insidious teacher, and subject to every bad influence." Comstock, *Vampire Literature*, *supra*, at 162; Comstock, FRAUDS EXPOSED, *supra*, at 416–417.

87. the filth will all pour in and the degradation of youth will follow." Hopkins, *supra*, at 489–490.

87. "cursed as thousands of the present day are, with secret vices." Anthony Comstock, MORALS VERSUS ART, *supra*, at 9.

87. "seventy-five if not ninety percent of our young men are victims of self-abuse." Comstock, TRAPS FOR THE YOUNG, *supra*, at 154.

87. including "[l]ocal congestions, nervous affections and debilities." Allan C. Carlson, *Comstockery, Contraception, and the Family: The Remarkable Achievements of an Anti-Vice Crusader*, THE FAMILY IN AMERICA (2009) (http://profam.org/pub/fia/fia.2301.htm).

87. the very best medical advice and for the protection of women's health." Carlson, *supra*.

87. break down the health of women and disseminate a greater curse than the plagues and diseases of Europe." Hopkins, *supra*, at 489–490.

87. from the infection or seduction of this class of crime-breeding publications." Comstock, TRAPS FOR THE YOUNG, *supra*, at 26–37.

88. theories about the pernicious effects of dime novels. Boyer, *supra*, at 17–18.

88. courts would be unable to keep up with the literature-induced crime wave. Comstock, TRAPS FOR THE YOUNG, *supra*, at 26–37; Comstock, *Vampire Literature*, *supra*, at 164–166.

88. which was very frequently, that fact was bruited about." Mencken, *The Emperor of Wowsers*, *supra*.

88. a thing "from which to weave headlines." Broun and Leech, *supra*, at 244.

88. "if one may borrow a stage term, 'created' his unique position." Hopkins, *supra*, at 489–490.

88. have been in reality the accomplishments of Mr. Comstock." Hopkins, *supra*, at 489.

89. are invaded by the evil of licentious literature." Comstock, TRAPS FOR THE YOUNG, *supra*, at 41, 133, 136.

89. "a devil-trap to captivate the child by perverting taste and fancy." Comstock TRAPS FOR THE YOUNG, *supra*, at 6, 12, 28.

89. associated with thieves, murderers, libertines, and harlots." Comstock, TRAPS FOR THE YOUNG, *supra*, at 13, 15–16.

89. make foul-mouthed bullies, cheats, vagabonds, thieves, desperados, and libertines." Comstock, TRAPS FOR THE YOUNG, *supra*, at 21, 25.

89. "should be named 'recruiting stations for hell.'" Comstock, TRAPS FOR THE YOUNG, *supra*, at 48–49.

89. the harvest of this seed-sowing of the Evil one." Broun and Leech, *supra*, at 80–81.

89. then reaching out like immense cuttlefish, draw in, from all sides, our youth to destruction." Comstock, TRAPS FOR THE YOUNG, *supra*, at 133, 136.

90. although there is no telling who said it first. Mark Twain, *Chapters from My Autobiography* – XX, THE NORTH AMERICAN REVIEW 471 (1907).

90. to fill a long passenger train of more than sixty coaches, Broun and Leech, *supra*, at 15–16; Blanchard, *supra*; LaMay, *supra*; Morone, *supra*, at 230; Rabban, FREE SPEECH IN ITS FORGOTTEN YEARS, *supra*.

90. almost 3,000 people for a total of "565 years, 11 months, and 20 days." Hopkins, *supra*, at 489–490.

90. other times he would say that it was eighty-one or as low as ten. David M. Oshinsky, A CONSPIRACY SO IMMENSE: THE WORLD OF JOE McCARTHY 103–113 (New York: Oxford University Press, 2005); Richard Cohen, *Trump Is a Modern-Day McCarthy*, WASHINGTON POST, Feb. 7, 2018, at A21; *McCarthy Says Communists Are in State Department*, *This Day in History* (www.history.com/this-day-in-history/mccarthy-says-communists-are-in-state-department).

90. This works out to a conviction rate of 73 percent. Mencken, A BOOK OF PREFACES, *supra*, at 254, n. 1.

91. 3,697 prosecutions and 2,740 convictions, for a success rate of around 74 percent. Rochelle Gurstein, THE REPEAL OF RETICENCE 126 (New York: Hill & Wang, 1996); Hopkins, *supra*, at 489–490.

91. "while the father of lies lives and his horde of followers inhabit the earth." Comstock, FRAUDS EXPOSED, *supra*, at 5–6, 442.

91. and ruin a good man's name and reputation." Comstock, FRAUDS EXPOSED, *supra*, at 392.

91. was to see who could say the bitterest things against the present writer." Comstock, TRAPS FOR THE YOUNG, *supra*, at 185.

91. yet I have received nothing but misrepresentation, odium, and abuse." Comstock, Frauds Exposed, *supra*, at 5–6.

91. the Society that has dared to confront this evil." Comstock, Frauds Exposed, *supra*, at 434.

CHAPTER 5

93. "a card-carrying member of the liberal intelligentsia" Fredric Wertham, Seduction of the Innocent (New York: Main Road Books, Inc., 2004 ed.) (Introduction to 2004 ed. by James E. Reibman, at xxx); James E. Reibman, *Ralph Ellison, Fredric Wertham, M.D., and the LaFargue Clinic: Civil Rights and Psychiatric Services in Harlem*, 26 Okla. City Law. Rev. 1041, 1053 (Fall, 2001).

94. "which have brought him to the penitentiary or the State's prison." Comstock, Traps for the Young, *supra*, at 26–37.

94. stories of deeds of bloodshed, lust or crime." New York Penal Law § 1141(2).

94. photographs of criminals and their victims. David Hajdu, The Ten-Cent Plague: The Great Comic Book Scare and How It Changed America 96 (New York: Picador, 2008).

94. 'vehicles for inciting violent and depraved crimes.'" *Winters* v. *New York*, 333 US 507, 510, 519–520 (1948).

95. "not only inspire evil but suggest a form for evil to take." *Puddles of Blood*, Time, Mar. 29, 1948.

95. compared to the sadistic drivel pouring from the presses today." Sterling North, *A National Disgrace*, Chicago Daily News, May 8, 1940 21. *See* John E. Twomey, *The Citizens' Committee and Comic Book Control: A Study of Extragovernmental Restraint*, 20 Law & Contemporary Problems 621, 622 (1955).

96. moral panics that even predated Comstock. John Springhall, Youth, Popular Culture and Moral Panics 1–97 (New York: St. Martin's Press, 1998).

96. a "national crime against our children." Hajdu, *supra*, at 11–13.

96. no respectable newspaper would think of accepting." *A National Disgrace*, *supra*.

96. anti-comic book hysteria trace its roots to these articles. Bart Beaty, Fredric Wertham and the Critique of Mass Culture 113–114 (Jackson: University Press of Mississippi, 2005); Karen Sternheimer, Pop Culture Panics 77 (New York: Routledge, 2015); Hajdu, *supra*, at 39–45.

96. Superman in 1938 and Batman in 1939. Sternheimer, *supra*, at 73, 76.

96. sold or traded each month reached 75 million copies. Springhall, *supra*, at 122, 124. *See* Hajdu, *supra*, at 45; Bradford W. Wright, Comic Book Nation 88–89, 155 (Baltimore: Johns Hopkins University Press, 2001); Note, *Crime Comics and the Constitution*, 7 Stanford Law. Rev. 237 (1955).

96. 91 to 95 percent of children between the ages of six and eleven. Note, *Regulation of Comic Books*, 68 Harvard Law. Rev. 489, 489–90 (Jan. 1955).

96. "the greatest mass influence on children." Fredric Wertham, *The Comics ... Very Funny!*, The Saturday Review of Literature, May 29, 1948, at 8.

97. "Words and the Comics." Paul Witty, *Children's Interest in Reading the Comics*, 10 Journal of Experimental Education 100–104 (1941); Paul Witty, *Reading the Comics: A Comparative Study*, 10 Journal of Experimental Education 105–109 (1941); Robert L. Thorndyke, *Words and the Comics*, 10 Journal of Experimental Education 110–113 (1941).

97. "Reading the Comics in Grades IV – XII." Paul Witty, Ethel Smith, and Anne Coomer, *Reading the Comics in Grades IV – XII*, 28 EDUCATIONAL ADMINISTRATION AND SUPERVISION 344–353 (1942).

97. could make kids prone to daydreaming or becoming "a loafer." James D. Lansdowne, *The Viciousness of the Comic Book*, 12 JOURNAL OF EDUCATION 14–15 (1944).

97. was that such super beings "defy natural laws." Hajdu, *supra*, at 81; Sternheimer, *supra*, at 7778.

97. to right the wrongs of the German state." Robert E. Southard, *Parents Must Control the Comics*, ST. ANTHONY MESSENGER, May 1944; Hajdu, *supra*, at 79–80.

97. such as no Nazi could ever aspire to." Gershon Legman, *The Comic Books and the Public* (remarks as the Mar. 19, 1948 symposium on The Psychopathology of Comic Books), printed in 2 American Journal of Psychotherapy 475 (1948). *See* Jill Lepore, THE SECRET HISTORY OF WONDER WOMAN 264 (New York: Alfred A. Knopf, 2014); Wright, *supra*, at 91–92.

97. the Superman myth is becoming a kind of international monster." Philippe Bauchard, A REPORT ON PRESS, FILM AND RADIO FOR CHILDREN 37–38 (Paris: UNESCO, 1952). *See* Mark Strauss, *That Time the United Nations Condemned Superman (in Real Life)*, GIZMODO (Jun. 19, 2014) (https://io9.gizmodo.com/that-time-the-united-nations-condemned-superman-1592310861).

97. causing drug use and juvenile delinquency. Wright, *supra*, at 86–87.

97. and (incidentally), "bred juvenile delinquency." *Comic Books Held Harmful to Youth*, NEW YORK TIMES, May 5, 1948, at 35; Sternheimer, *supra*, at 81; Lepore, *supra*, at 264–271.

98. "intellectual marijuana" and harbingers of cultural doom. Marya Mannes, *Junior Has a Craving*, NEW REPUBLIC, Feb. 17, 1947, at 20–23; Wright, *supra*, at 91.

98. their loathing of such popular culture was unbounded. Carol L. Tilley, *Seducing the Innocent: Fredric Wertham and the Falsifications That Helped Condemn Comics*. 47 INFORMATION & CULTURE: A JOURNAL OF HISTORY 404 (2012); Springhall, *supra*, at 132–133; Hajdu, *supra*, at 231; Sternheimer, *supra*, at 75; Wright, *supra*, at 91–94; Nyberg, *supra*, at 94.

98. "the same undercurrent of homosexuality and sadomasochism." Gershon Legman, LOVE AND DEATH: A STUDY IN CENSORSHIP (New York: MW Books, 1949); Legman, *The Comic Books and the Public*, *supra*, at 476; Springhall, *supra*, at 133.

98. published in 2 AMERICAN JOURNAL OF PSYCHOTHERAPY 472–490 (1948).

98. the August 1948 issue of READER'S DIGEST. Fredric Wertham, *The Comics . . . Very Funny!*, READER'S DIGEST, Aug. 1948. *See* Wright, *supra*, at 94.

98. unabashed admiration for public burnings of comic books. Wertham, *The Comics . . . Very Funny!*, THE SATURDAY REVIEW OF LITERATURE, *supra*.

99. off the newsstands and out of the candy stores." Judith Crist, *Horror in the Nursery*, COLLIERS, Mar. 27, 1948, at 22; Hajdu, *supra*, at 100–103; Wright, *supra*, at 94–95.

99. every home in this country where there are children." Hajdu, *supra*, at 103.

99. sit on committees and decide the fate of children from a distance." Crist, *Horror in the Nursery*, *supra*; Hajdu, *supra*, at 100–103.

99. read comics of various kinds, and discuss them with their children. Harvey Zorbaugh and Mildred Gilman, *What Can YOU Do about Comic Books?*, FAMILY CIRCLE, Feb. 1949 at 61–63.

100. for increasing the level and intensity of juvenile crime. Fredric Wertham, *What Parents Don't Know about Comic Books*, LADIES' HOME JOURNAL, Nov. 1953, at 50–53, 215–217.

100. prowl on the streets and dismember beautiful girls." Wertham, *What Parents Don't Know about Comic Books*, *supra*, at 219–220.

100. in Spencer, West Virginia garnered national press coverage. Wright, *supra*, at 86–87; Hajdu, *supra*, at 115–127.

101. they had the full support of church and school authorities. Hajdu, *supra*, at 118–119, 120–127; Sternheimer, *supra*, at 82.

101. a rally to burn comic books was sponsored by a community police captain. Twomey, *supra*, at 624.

101. lighting the bonfire in Victory Park. Hajdu, *supra*, at 148.

102. to stay away from retail establishments where such are sold." Hajdu, *supra*, at 148–149.

102. children would prefer to burn comic books than read them. Wertham, *The Comics . . . Very Funny!*, THE SATURDAY REVIEW OF LITERATURE, *supra*.

102. if the language of the statute is sufficiently precise to pass constitutional muster. *Winters*, 333 US at 520.

102. a long list of specified crimes from murder to "mayhem." Hajdu, *supra*, at 104–108. *See Regulation of Comic Books, supra*, at 501, n. 92.

102. than not selling whiskey to children is a restraint of trade." Wertham, SEDUCTION OF THE INNOCENT, *supra*, at xi n. 17, 302–305.

102. would lead to comprehensive state legislation. Hajdu, *supra*, at 108; *Objectionable Books of Comics Disappear from Los Angeles Stands after New Law*, NEW YORK TIMES, Oct. 4, 1948, at 26.

102. publications depicting such crimes as the Lincoln assassination could be prohibited by the law. *Regulation of Comic Books, supra*, at 501; *People* v. *Dickey*, No. CR-A-2528 (Cal. Super. Ct., App. Dep't, Dec. 27, 1949).

102. Lincoln's time and life that would be far more instructive." Wertham, SEDUCTION OF THE INNOCENT, *supra*, at 326; Wertham, *What Parents Don't Know about Comic Books*, LADIES' HOME JOURNAL, Nov. 1953, at 219.

103. at least fifty US cities would attempt to regulate the sale of comics. Hajdu, *supra*, at 150; Lawrence Kutner and Cheryl K. Olson, GRAND THEFT CHILDHOOD 50 (New York: Simon & Schuster, 2008). *See Regulation of Comic Books, supra*, at 501–503; *Crime Comics and the Constitution, supra*, at 257–260.

103. or by withdrawing it afterwards." *Regulation of Comic Books, supra*, at 495–496.

103. efforts almost never saw the inside of a court. Clay Calvert, *Of Burning Houses and Roasting Pigs: Why Butler* v. *Michigan Remains a Key Free Speech Victory More Than a Half-Century Later*, FED. COMM. L. J. 247, 254 (2012).

103. anything blacklisted under this quasi-informal system. Calvert, *supra*, at 253; Wright, *supra*, at 98; Hajdu, *supra*, at 75–79; *Regulation of Comic Books, supra*, at 495–496; *Crime Comics and the Constitution, supra*, at 243–244.

103. Indianapolis "persuaded" local news dealers to drop twenty-five comic book titles. Wright, *supra*, at 98.

103. to advise law enforcement agencies about which publications should be investigated or restricted. *Regulation of Comic Books, supra*, at 495–496.

103. "legal proceedings which might impose limitations on these practices are extremely rare." *Regulation of Comic Books, supra*, at 496; *Crime Comics and the Constitution, supra*, at 243–244.

104. to strike down the renewed comic book ordinance under the First Amendment. *Katzev* v. *County of Los Angeles*, 52 Cal. 2d 360 (1959).

104. applied *Winters* and other Supreme Court precedent, and voided the law. *Adams* v. *Hinkle*, 51 Wash. 2d 763, 779 (Wash. 1958).

104. books like CATCHER IN THE RYE, FROM HERE TO ETERNITY, and GOD'S LITTLE ACRE. *Regulation of Comic Books, supra*, at 504; Twomey, *supra*, at 621 n. 6.

104. a paperback novel, THE DEVIL RIDES OUTSIDE, to a Detroit police inspector. Calvert, *supra*, at 253–255.

104. "is to burn the house to roast the pig." *Butler v. Michigan*, 352 US 380, 383 (1957).

104. striking down state laws regulating sale of comic books. *Adams v. Hinkle*, 51 Wash. 2d at 779.

105. functioned as an "instrument[] of regulation independent of the laws." *Bantam Books, Inc. v. Sullivan*, 372 US 58, 62–63 & n. 5, 67–70 (1963).

105. aimed at "the cause of a psychological mutilation of children." Assem. Int. No. 2799, Pr. No. 2944. *See* Springhall, *supra*, at 132.

105. said that the bill violated the First Amendment. *People v. Bookcase, Inc.*, 201 N.E.2d 14, 15–16 (NY 1964). *See* Wright, *supra*, at 157.

105. He had vetoed an earlier bill on the same grounds. Wright, *supra*, at 104–106; Sternheimer, *supra*, at 85.

105. the verdict has frequently been arrived at in advance." Louis Menand, *The Horror*, THE NEW YORKER, Mar. 31, 2008 (www.newyorker.com/magazine/2008/03/31/the-horror).

105. in some of the first ever televised congressional hearings. Hajdu, *supra*, at 171–174; Sternheimer, *supra*, at 61–63, 74, 85–87; Wright, *supra*, at 157.

105. was voted one of America's ten most admired men. Special Committee on Organized Crime in Interstate Commerce, Notable Senate Investigations, US Senate Historical Office, Washington, DC (www.senate.gov/artandhistory/history/common/investiga tions/Kefauver.htm).

105. "don't you want to be vice president?" Hajdu, *supra*, at 172.

106. and public officials, such as FBI Director J. Edgar Hoover. US Senate Special Committee to Investigate Organized Crime in Interstate Commerce, *A Compilation of Information and Suggestions Submitted to the Special Senate Committee to Investigate Organized Crime in Interstate Commerce Relative to the Incidence of Possible Influence There-on of So-Called Crime Comic Books During the Five-Year Period 1945 to 1950*, 81st Cong., 2nd Sess. (1950) ("1950 Special Committee Report"). *See* Hajdu, *supra*, at 172.

107. certainly not in the interests of the public." Wertham, SEDUCTION OF THE INNOCENT, *supra*, at 342.

107. if crime comic books of all types were not readily available to children." 1950 Special Committee Report, *supra*, at 2–8 (Statement of FBI Director J. Edgar Hoover).

107. no demonstrable connection between the reading of comic books and juvenile delin-quency." 1950 Special Committee Report, *supra*, at 109–114 (Statement of Hon. Louis Goldstein, Chairman, Board of County Judges, County Court, Kings County, Brooklyn, NY); Hajdu, *supra*, at 173.

107. "comics have very little to do with juvenile delinquency." 1950 Special Committee Report, *supra*, at 191–192 (Statement of Dr. Harvey Zorbaugh, Professor of Education, New York University).

107. "no direct connection between the comic books dealing with crime and juvenile delinquency." *Crime and the Comics*, NEW YORK TIMES, Nov. 14, 1950, at 30; United Press, *Comics Held No Factor in Delinquency*, WASHINGTON POST, Nov. 12, 1950, at M20; Janet Pinkley and Kaela Casey, *Graphic Novels: A Brief History and Overview for Library Managers*, LIBRARY LEADERSHIP & MANAGEMENT, May 2013, at 5; Wright, *supra*, at 157.

107. Kefauver had developed a taste for the show. Sternheimer, *supra*, at 86–87; Wright, *supra*, at 157; Hajdu, *supra*, at 250–251.

107. "the increasing emphasis on sex and crime in public entertainment." Hajdu, *supra*, at 250–251.

108. vetoed the bills on First Amendment grounds. Wright, *supra*, at 157.

108. in newspapers, and even on billboards across the USA. Menand, *supra*, (www.newyorker .com/magazine/2008/03/31/the-horror); Pinkley & Casey, *supra*, at 5; Beaty, *supra*, at 155–156.

108. from SEDUCTION OF THE INNOCENT. Hajdu, *supra*, at 228–230.

108. *Comic Books – Blueprints for Delinquency.* Fredric Wertham, *Comic Books – Blueprints for Delinquency*, READER'S DIGEST, May 1954, at 24–29.

108. described as the "primer of the American campaign" against comics. Amy Kiste Nyberg, SEAL OF APPROVAL: THE HISTORY OF THE COMICS CODE 50 (University Press of Mississippi, 1998).

109. "an angry man, who has good reasons for anger." C. Wright Mills, *Nothing to Laugh At*, NEW YORK TIMES, Apr. 25, 1954, at BR20.

109. the most difficult types of problems in the whole of social psychology." Mills, *supra*, at BR20.

109. "a formidable indictment" against comics that was "practically unanswerable." John B. Sheerin, *Crime Comics Must Go!*, CATHOLIC WORLD, Jun. 1954, at 162; Wolcott Gibbs, *Keep Those Paws to Yourself, Space-Rat!*, THE NEW YORKER, May 8, 1954, at 137; Wright, *supra*, at 164; Hajdu, *supra*, at 243–244.

109. most of his problematical behavior can be explained in terms of comic books." Robert S. Warshow, *The Study of Man: Paul, the Horror Comics, and Dr. Wertham*, COMMENTARY, Jun. 1, 1954; Sternheimer, *supra*, at 93.

109. "a tissue of troublesome points." Reuel Denney, *The Dark Fantastic*, NEW REPUBLIC, May 3, 1954, at 18–19; Hajdu, *supra*, at 242–243; Wright, *supra*, at 164.

109. his preconceived conclusions about comics. Springhall, *supra*, at 125; Nyberg, *supra*, at 96.

109. the conjectures are biased, unreliable, and useless." *Seduction of the Innocent: The Great Comic Book Scare*, in MILESTONES IN MASS COMMUNICATION RESEARCH 262, 264 (Shearon Lowery and Melvin DeFleur, eds., 1983).

109. implicitly or explicitly assumed unmediated modeling effects." Patrick Parsons, *Batman and His Audience: The Dialectic of Culture*, in THE MANY LIVES OF THE BATMAN: CRITICAL APPROACHES TO A SUPERHERO AND HIS MEDIA 82 (Roberta E. Pearson and William Uricchio, eds., 1991); Nyberg, *supra*, at 85, 96–97.

110. "became perhaps disconnected from the kids that he was treating and observing." Dave Itzkoff, *Scholar Finds Flaws in Work by Archenemy of Comics*, NEW YORK TIMES, Feb. 23, 2013, at C1; Tilley, *supra*, at 383–413. *Project MUSE*, doi:10. 1353/lac. 2012. 0024; Dusty Rhodes, *BAM! WAP! KA-POW! Library Prof Bops Doc Who K.O.'d Comic Book Industry*, Blog Post, Feb. 11, 2013 (http://news.illinois.edu/view/6367/204890); Sternheimer, *supra*, at 93–94.

110. three-quarters of the American public believed that comic books caused juvenile delinquency. Menand, *supra* (www.newyorker.com/magazine/2008/03/31/the-horror).

110. "one of the great documents of legal and social philosophy of our time." Wertham, SEDUCTION OF THE INNOCENT, *supra*, at 330–333.

110. an example of "burn[ing] the house to roast the pig." *Butler*, 352 US at 383.

111. "but I did think that there would be at least some kind of investigation." Wertham, SEDUCTION OF THE INNOCENT, *supra*, at 333, 340–342.

111. helped develop the questionnaire to be sent to experts. Nyberg, *supra*, at 54.

111. "strange" for vetoing anti-comics legislation on constitutional grounds. Wertham, SEDUCTION OF THE INNOCENT, *supra*, at 343–351; Beaty, *supra*, at 156.

112. "real freedom of expression." Wertham, SEDUCTION OF THE INNOCENT, *supra*, at 386–389; Nyberg, *supra*, at 93.

112. the Democratic nomination for president in 1956. Nyberg, *supra*, at 53.

112. some of the experts it employed were consultants to comic-book publishers. Peter Kinss, *Senator Charges "Deceit" on Comics*, NEW YORK TIMES, Apr. 23, 1954, at 29; Wright, *supra*, at 171.

112. providing body counts along the way. US Congress, *Juvenile Delinquency (Comic Books): Hearings before the Subcommittee on Juvenile Delinquency*, 83rd Cong., 2nd Sess. 4–10 (Apr. 21–22 and Jun. 24, 1954) ("*1954 Senate Hearings*") (Statement of Richard Clendenen); Nyberg, *supra*, at 56–57; Wright, *supra*, at 165–166; Hajdu, *supra*, at 257–260.

113. "incontrovertible evidence of the pernicious influences on youth of crime comic books." *1954 Senate Hearings*, *supra*, at 81–82 (Testimony of Dr. Fredric Wertham).

113. any doubt of his status as a doctor. Hajdu, *supra*, at 263.

113. "on this subject there is practically no controversy." *1954 Senate Hearings*, *supra*, at 16–17, 81–82 (Testimony of Dr. Fredric Wertham); Nyberg, *supra*, at 20.

114. The same thing with crime." *1954 Senate Hearings*, *supra*, at 87 (Testimony of Dr. Fredric Wertham).

114. "teach complete contempt of the police" *1954 Senate Hearings*, *supra*, at 85 (Testimony of Dr. Fredric Wertham).

114. Must you not take into account the neighbor's children?" *1954 Senate Hearings*, *supra*, at 84 (Testimony of Dr. Fredric Wertham).

114. "Hitler was a beginner compared to the comic-book industry," he proclaimed. *1954 Senate Hearings*, *supra*, at 95 (Testimony of Dr. Fredric Wertham). *See* Wright, *supra*, at 166–167.

114. to help members nudge the doctor toward more mainstream views. Nyberg, *supra*, at 77.

115. should be measured in the "thousands." *1954 Senate Hearings*, at 93 (Testimony of Dr. Fredric Wertham).

115. "investigating" Communists in the US Army. Beaty, *supra*, at 156.

116. an effort to forestall any inquiry into the comic book industry. *1954 Senate Hearings* at 58–59, 108. *See* Wright, *supra*, at 169; Hajdu, *supra*, at 260.

116. claimed that the Tennessee Democrat was "coddling Communists." *1954 Senate Hearings*, at 92; Nyberg, *supra*, at 74–75.

116. as it would to explain the sublimity of love to a frigid old maid." *1954 Senate Hearings* at 97–98 (Testimony of William Gaines).

117. How could it be worse? *1954 Senate Hearings* at 103 (Testimony of William Gaines). *See* Hajdu, *supra*, at 265–271; Wright, *supra*, at 167–171.

117. including in a front-page NEW YORK TIMES story. Peter Kihss, *No Harm in Horror, Comics Issuer Says, Comics Publisher Sees No Harm in Horror, Discounts "Good Taste,"* NEW YORK TIMES, Apr. 22, 1954, at 1; *Horror Comics*, TIME, May 31, 1954, at 78; Nyberg, *supra*, at 62–63; Wright, *supra*, at 168–169; Hajdu, *supra*, at 271–272; Beaty, *supra*, at 159.

117. adopting a "voluntary" code of self-regulation. Nyberg, *supra*, at 79; Wright, *supra*, at 169.

118. at least in the short term, would disrupt the comics industry. *Comic Books and Juvenile Delinquency*, Interim Report of the Committee on the Judiciary, S. Rep. No. 84-62, at 1, 7, 23, 32 (1955) ("*Senate Report*").

118. "[a] competent job of self-policing within the industry will achieve much." *1954 Senate Hearings*, *supra*, at 310; Nyberg, *supra*, at 79.

118. Murphy would serve as the "comics czar." Wright, *supra*, at 172–173; Nyberg, *supra*, at 83–84; Beaty, *supra*, at 161–162.

118. but he turned it down. Nyberg, *supra*, at 110; Hajdu, *supra*, at 285–286.

118. after the inking stage to ensure that they conformed. Hajdu, *supra*, at 291–292; Nyberg, *supra*, at 166–169.

119. prior approval by code authorities. Thomas Doherty, Hollywood's Censor: Joseph I. Breen & the Production Code Administration 31–37, 41–47 (New York: Columbia University Press, 2007).

119. in substantial part a paraphrase of the Hays Office code. Doherty, *supra*, at 342.

120. only three publishers remained as members. Nyberg, *supra*, at 35–36, 104–106, 165; Wright, *supra*, at 103–104p; Hajdu, *supra*, at 129–131.

120. who refused to carry nonapproved comics. Nyberg, *supra*, at 127–128; Wright, *supra*, at 173–174.

120. rejected 126 stories and 5,656 individual drawings. Wright, *supra*, at 174; Hajdu, *supra*, at 286–287.

120. purged from the industry, and they were. Springhall, *supra*, at 140.

120. gone by the following year. Beaty, *supra*, at 161; Springhall, *supra*, at 140–141.

120. to focus his energies on *Mad* magazine. Hajdu, *supra*, at 287–290; Sternheimer, *supra*, at 90.

120. declined by more than half. Hajdu, *supra*, at 314–315, 326–327; Sternheimer, *supra*, at 99.

120. and associated employees lost their jobs as a result. Menand, *supra*; Hajdu, *supra*, at 337–351.

120. that lacked CMAA's seal of approval. Hajdu, *supra*, at 295–303.

120. no new publishers entered the comic book market. Nyberg, *supra*, at 124–128.

120. brought under control by voluntary compliance with the code of ethics." Sternheimer, *supra*, at 90.

120. Senators are more informed about subversion than about perversion." Fredric Wertham, *It's Still Murder*, The Saturday Review of Literature, Apr. 9, 1955, at 11.

121. for the proposition that "True freedom is regulation." Wertham, *It's Still Murder*, *supra*, at 11, 46–48. *See* Beaty, *supra*, at 163–164.

121. "I detest censorship." 1954 *Senate Hearings*, *supra*, at 91 (Testimony of Dr. Fredric Wertham).

121. actually *not* democracy; it is anarchy." Wertham, Seduction of the Innocent at 326–327.

121. "moral bankruptcy in publishers hiding behind the First Amendment." Seduction of the Innocent, *supra*, at vii. (introduction to 2004 ed. by James E. Reibman).

121. can be construed in *any* way as a threat to free expression for adults." Seduction of the Innocent, *supra*, at xi–xi n. 17 (introduction to 2004 ed. by James E. Reibman).

121. was angered by those who called him a censor. Seduction of the Innocent, *supra*, at xxvii (introduction to 2004 ed. by James E. Reibman).

121. professed opponent of censorship." Wright, *supra*, at 98. *See also* Hajdu, *supra*, at 99.

121. "[c]rime comics are a severe test of the liberalism of liberals." Wertham, Seduction of the Innocent, *supra*, at 339.

122. "think in terms of general precaution and spray the whole field." Wertham, Seduction of the Innocent, *supra*, at 2–3.

122. "the devil's ally." Tilley, *supra*, at 407.

123. "one of the most iconic censors in modern history." Tilley, *supra*, at 391; Comic Book Legal Defense Fund, *History of Comics Censorship, Part 1* (http://cbldf.org/resources/history-of-comics-censorship/history-of-comics-censorship-part-1/).

123. The rest of his career was described almost as an afterthought. Bayard Webster, *Fredric Wertham, 86, Dies; Foe of Violent TV and Comics*, New York Times, Dec. 1, 1981.

123. social science communities, cultural critics, and comic book fans. Beaty, *supra*, at 207.

123. unfairly blamed for the demise of comic books. SEDUCTION OF THE INNOCENT, *supra*, at xxix (introduction to 2004 ed. by James E. Reibman).

123. stature as a scholar has been erased. Beaty, *supra*, at 3, 195–197.

123. the censorious, the narrow-minded, and the ill-informed." SEDUCTION OF THE INNOCENT, *supra*, at xxviii (introduction to 2004 ed. by James E. Reibman).

123. even falsified evidence to support his dubious conclusions. Tilley, *supra*, at 386.

123. collects and preserves covers of the many comics he condemned. SEDUCTION OF THE INNOCENT (www.lostsoti.org/).

123. including numerous unflattering portrayals in comics. SEDUCTION OF THE INNOCENT, *supra*, at xxix (introduction to 2004 ed. by James E. Reibman). *See* SEDUCTION OF THE INNOCENT (www.lostsoti.org/).

123. reprinted in other books at least four times over the following decades. *See* SEDUCTION OF THE INNOCENT (www.lostsoti.org/).

123. kept a framed copy of the *Mad* article in his office. Beaty, *supra*, at 104–105.

124. Wonder Woman creator William Moulton Marston. SEDUCTION OF THE INNOCENT (www.lostsoti.org/).

124. "For Heaven's sake, gentlemen, let us move on." Michael Chabon, THE AMAZING ADVENTURES OF KAVALIER & CLAY 613–616 (2000).

124. illegal drug use, explicit sexuality, and even horror. Roger *Sabin, Going Underground, Comics, Comix & Graphic Novels: A History of Graphic Art* (London: Phaidon Press, 1996), 92, 94–95, 103–107, 110, 111, 116, 119, 124–126, 128; WIKIPEDIA, *Underground Comix* (https://en.wikipedia.org/wiki/Underground_comix).

124. We could do whatever we wanted." *Sabin, Going Underground, supra.*

124. including works by Crumb and others. Paul Richard, *Walter Hopps, Museum Man with a Talent for Talent*, WASHINGTON POST, Mar. 22, 2005.

126. a darker and more sophisticated form of graphic storytelling. Sebastian T. Mercier, *"Truth, Justice and the American Way": The Intersection of American Youth Culture and Superhero Narratives*, 1 IOWA HISTORICAL REVIEW 21, 49–58 (2008).

126. by 2011 the organization ceased to exist. *Comics Code Authority*, WIKIPEDIA (https://en .wikipedia.org/wiki/Comics_Code_Authority#Abandonment).

126. Peter Cushing and Joan Collins as characters in the various stories. IMDb, *Tales from the Crypt* (www.imdb.com/title/tt0069341/).

126. *Tales from the Crib*, by Canadian band d.b.s. Wheeler Winston Dixon and Richard Graham, A BRIEF HISTORY OF COMIC BOOK MOVIES 13 (Palgrave Macmillan, 2017); *Tales from the Crypt*, WIKIPEDIA (https://en.wikipedia.org/wiki/Tales_from_the_Crypt).

126. Zorro, Tarzan, and Flash Gordon. Dixon and Graham, *supra*, at 1–3.

126. the many television series that were spun off. *List of Films Based on English-Language Comics*, WIKIPEDIA (https://en.wikipedia.org/wiki/List_of_films_based_on_English-language_comics).

126. that together pulled $3.4 billion globally. Michael Cavna and David Betancourt, *An All-Inclusive Wakanda: Kids and "Black Panther" Costumes*, WASHINGTON POST, Oct. 31, 2018, at C1, C3.

126. grossing $1.2 billion worldwide its opening weekend. Michael Cavna, *Record $1.2 Billion Debut for "Avengers: Endgame,"* WASHINGTON POST, Apr. 29, 2019, at C1.

126. and the University of Toronto, among others worldwide. *E.g.*, University of Florida Comics Studies, Department of English (www.english.ufl.edu/comics/study.shtml); University of Toronto, Visual Culture Studies (www.utm.utoronto.ca/dvs/programs/vis ual-culture-studies).

126. collections of underground comics. *E.g.*, Moore Collection of Underground Comix, Robert E. Kennedy Library, California Polytechnic State University (http://lib.calpoly .edu/support/findingaids/ms052-moore-comix/); Frank Stack Collection, University of Missouri Libraries (http://libraryguides.missouri.edu/stack).

126. which has been held annually since 1995. International Comic Arts Forum (www .internationalcomicartsforum.org/about-icaf.html).

126. teachers and librarians likewise attend comic book conventions. Tilley, *supra*, at 405.

127. grossed more than $17.5 billion globally. Alexander F. Remington and Michael Cavna, *Marvel Star Gave Spider-Man His Angst, Iron Man His Snark*, Washington Post, Nov. 13, 2018, at A22; Michael Cavna, *Stan Lee: A Marvel to Behold*, Washington Post, Nov. 13, 2018, at C1.

CHAPTER 6

129. so that "the whole issue can be brought to the attention of the American people." *Record Labeling*, Hearing Before the Senate Committee on Commerce, Science, and Transportation, 99th Cong., 1st Sess., Sept. 19, 1985, at 1 (Statement of Chairman John C. Danforth) ("*Record Labeling Hearing*").

129. "half the original 20 PMRC members [were] married to 10% of the Senate." Dennis McDougal, *"Porn Rock": The Sound Draws Fury*, LA Times, Nov. 1, 1985.

129. and had gotten nowhere with the record companies. *Record Labeling Hearing*, *supra*, at 88, 92 (Statement Millie Waterman, National PTA Vice President for Legislative Activity); John Pareles, *Debate Spurs Hearing on Rating Rock Lyrics*, New York Times, Sept. 18, 1985.

129. commitments from twenty-four RIAA members, who collectively released 80 percent of prerecorded music sold in the USA, to put warning labels on record albums. *Record Labeling Hearing*, *supra*, at 95, 99 (Statement of Stanley Gortikov, President of the Recording Industry Association of America).

130. He chided them, "Ladies, how dare you?" *Record Labeling Hearing*, *supra*, at 53 (Statement of Frank Zappa).

130. Or, as Zappa asked simply, "Is this private action?" *Record Labeling Hearing*, *supra*, at 58.

130. such a "voluntary" initiative "in no way infringes on First Amendment rights." *Record Labeling Hearing*, *supra*, at 67.

130. her organization "would in no way encourage nor support censorship of the music industry." *Record Labeling Hearing*, *supra*, at 89, 91 (Statement Millie Waterman, National PTA Vice President for Legislative Activity).

130. there was "zero chance of legislation." *Record Labeling Hearing*, *supra*, at 89, 91.

130. under the "classic legal definition," only "prior restraint of publication constitutes censorship." *Record Labeling Hearing*, *supra*, at 4 (Opening Statement of Senator Paul S. Trible, Jr.).

130. First Amendment abridgments may come in many forms, and not just by previous restraint. *Near v. Minnesota*, 283 US 697 (1931).

131. not seeking "a Government role of any kind whatsoever." *Record Labeling Hearing*, *supra*, at 4 (Opening Statement of Senator Albert Gore, Jr.).

131. "may well be the most important hearing conducted by the Commerce Committee this year." *Record Labeling Hearing*, *supra*, at 4 (Opening Statement of Senator Paul S. Trible, Jr.).

131. what is the reason for these hearings in front of the Commerce Committee?" *Record Labeling Hearing, supra,* at 49.

131. "I want to hold that threat . . . over the head [of those] trying to accomplish some free enterprise volunteerism that most people have agreed to." *Record Labeling Hearing, supra,* at 72.

131. "trying our level best to limit and control [this music] as best we can, for the tender young ears of America." *Record Labeling Hearing, supra,* at 2–3 (Opening Statement of Senator Ernest F. Hollings).

132. we are going to be forced somewhere with regulations, through the FCC or otherwise." *Record Labeling Hearing, supra,* at 68–70.

132. certain four-letter words, and did not offend the producer's sense of art in the production itself." *Record Labeling Hearing, supra,* at 60, 76–77.

133. an effort "to balance the need for voluntary industry restraint with a strong sensitivity to first amendment concerns." *Record Labeling Hearing, supra,* at 132–133 (Statement of Edward O. Fritts, President, National Association of Broadcasters).

133. some form of legislation may be appropriate." *Record Labeling Hearing, supra,* at 135–138 (Statement of William J. Steding, Executive Vice President, Central Broadcast Division, Bonneville International Corp.).

133. to exercise "responsibility" in deciding whether to air "drug-oriented" music. *In re Licensee Responsibility to Review Records Before Their Broadcast,* 28 FCC 2d 409 (1971), *Memorandum Opinion and Order,* 31 FCC 2d 377 (1971), *Reconsideration denied,* 31 FCC 2d 385 (1971).

133. to "discourage, if not eliminate, the playing of records which tend to promote and/or glorify the use of illegal drugs." *In re Licensee Responsibility to Review Records Before Their Broadcast,* 28 FCC 2d at 410 (Statement of Commissioner Robert E. Lee). *See Yale Broadcasting Co. v. FCC,* 478 F. 2d at 603 (Bazelon, C. J.) (dissenting from denial of rehearing *en banc*).

133. and the whimsical "Puff, the Magic Dragon" by folk trio Peter, Paul and Mary. Ben Fong-Torres, *FCC Discovers Dope, Does Darndest Thing, Rolling Stone,* Apr. 1, 1971. *See* Margaret A. Blanchard, *The American Urge to Censor: Freedom of Expression Versus the Desire to Sanitize Society – From Anthony Comstock to 2 Live Crew,* 33 WILLIAM & MARY LAW. REV. 741, 806 (1992).

133. "the management could not interpret the lyrics." *Yale Broadcasting Co. v. FCC,* 478 F. 2d at 603 (Bazelon, C. J.) (dissenting from denial of rehearing *en banc*); Tom Wheeler, *Drug Lyrics, the FCC, and the First Amendment,* 5 LOYOLA LAW. REV. 329, 348 (1972); Blanchard, *supra,* at 806.

133. "could jeopardize his license by failing to exercise licensee responsibility in this area." *Memorandum Opinion and Order,* 31 FCC 2d at 379.

134. songs that in the Commission's judgment were somehow 'drug-related.'" *Yale Broadcasting Co. v. FCC,* 414 US 914 (1973) (Douglas, J.) (dissenting from denial of certiorari).

134. "We're Not Gonna Take It" by Twisted Sister. *Record Labeling Hearing, supra,* at 10–17, 85.

134. the band members of Twisted Sister who proceed to discipline "daddy." *Record Labeling Hearing, supra,* at 10, 14, 85.

134. "I looked into that." *Record Labeling Hearing, supra,* at 2 (Opening Statement of Senator Ernest F. Hollings).

134. to compensate the industry for music piracy. *Record Labeling Hearing, supra,* at 53.

134. in a committee chaired by Strom Thurmond. Dennis McDougal, *"Porn Rock": The Sound Draws Fury,* LA TIMES, Nov. 1, 1985; *Record Labeling Hearing, supra,* at 18; Patrick

Goldstein, *Parents Warn: Take the Sex and Shock Out of Rock*, LA Times, Aug. 25, 1985; Steve Pond, *Industry Said Fearful of PMRC's Sway*, Washington Post, Oct. 30, 1985 (www.washingtonpost.com/archive/business/1985/10/30/industry-said-fearful-of-pmrcs-sway/1194b3f8-8255-4f25-a7d3-235161ae14fa/?utm_term=.f228d0705c81).

134. Mrs. Thurmond, as it turned out, was a PMRC member. *Record Labeling Hearing, supra,* at 53; Dennis McDougal, *"Porn Rock": The Sound Draws Fury*, LA Times, Nov. 1, 1985.

135. Tipper Gore would later refer to Gortikov as her "secret ally" in the record industry. Alexander Cockburn and Jeffrey St. Clair, Al Gore: A User's Manual 102–103 (London: Verso Press, 2000).

136. such bands as AC/DC, Twisted Sister, Ozzie Osbourne, Judas Priest, KISS, Great White, WASP, and Mötley Crüe. *Record Labeling Hearing, supra,* at 13–17 (Statement of Jeff Ling).

136. to "needlessly use expressions that may be in bad taste." *Record Labeling Hearing, supra,* at 2 (Statement of Chairman Danforth).

136. Golden Showers." *Record Labeling Hearing, supra,* at 17 (Statement of Jeff Ling).

136. it had previewed the material for committee members before the hearing. *Record Labeling Hearing, supra,* at 2 (Statement of Senator Hollings).

136. it was not the most pleasant of experiences to read some of the lyrics in public." *Record Labeling Hearing, supra,* at 51.

136. described the lyrics as "poison." *Record Labeling Hearing, supra,* at 5–10, 50 (Statement of Senator Paula Hawkins).

136. Thank you. I think that statement tells the story to this committee." *Record Labeling Hearing, supra,* at 61.

137. a young man in a small Texas town "took his life while listening to the music of AC/DC." *Record Labeling Hearing, supra,* at 11–12.

137. "Absolutely," she responded. *Record Labeling Hearing, supra,* at 48.

137. that the Night Stalker was a "fan" of AC/DC. *Record Labeling Hearing, supra,* at 13–14.

137. "I think it has great effect." *Record Labeling Hearing, supra,* at 46.

137. but not to the levels that existed in the mid-1980s. Centers for Disease Control, *QuickStats: Suicide Rates for Teens Aged 15–19 Years, by Sex – United States*, 1975–2015 (www.cdc.gov/mmwr/volumes/66/wr/mm6630a6.htm).

137. among the most frequently cited correlates, among numerous factors. *Teenage Suicide in the United States* (http://en.wikipedia.org/wiki/Teenage_suicide_in_the_United_States); *Causes of Teen Suicides* (www.buzzle.com/articles/facts-about-teen-suicide-causes-of-teenage-suicide.html#causes); Robert Olson, *Suicide, Rock Music and Moral Panics*, Centre for Suicide Prevention (www.suicideinfo.ca/resource/musicandsuicide/).

137. has never been listed by legitimate researchers as a "cause" of teen suicide. K. R. Scheel and J. S. Westefeld. *Heavy Metal Music and Adolescent Suicidality: An Empirical Investigation*, Adolescence 253–273 (Summer, 1999); Litman, R. and Farberow, N., *Pop-Rock Music as Precipitating Cause in Youth Suicide*, 39 Journal of Forensic Sciences 494–499 (1994).

138. the rate at which teens have sex or have abortions has declined as well. Eileen Patten and Gretchen Livingston, *Why Is the Teen Birth Rate Falling?* Pew Research Center (Apr. 29, 2016) (www.pewresearch.org/fact-tank/2016/04/29/why-is-the-teen-birth-rate-falling/).

138. that the crime rate for rape was cut in half between 1975 and 1985. Karen Sternheimer, Pop Culture Panics 126 (New York: Routledge, 2015).

138. "[s]ubtleties, suggestions, and innuendo" had been replaced by "descriptions of often violent sexual acts, drug taking, and flirtations with the occult." *Record Labeling Hearing, supra,* at 6.

138. the media's impact on children as "historically unique." *Record Labeling Hearing, supra,* at 12.

138. categorically different from previous forms of popular music." *Record Labeling Hearing, supra,* at 117 (statement of Dr. Joe Stuessy).

138. should be "suppressed by press and pulpit." John E. Semonche, CENSORING SEX: A HISTORICAL JOURNEY THROUGH AMERICAN MEDIA 144 (Lanham, MD: Roman & Littlefield Publishers, Inc., 2007).

138. "take a united stand against the Ragtime Evil as we would against bad literature." *See, e.g.,* Peter Blecha, TABOO TUNES: A HISTORY OF BANNED BANDS & CENSORED SONGS 17 (San Francisco: Backstreet Books, 2004).

138. those convicted of being "jazzily intoxicated shall go before the Superior Court and be sent to an insane asylum." Blecha, *supra,* at 23.

139. Mass-staria! Meredith Willson, *Ya Got Trouble,* THE MUSIC MAN (1957).

139. only the instrumental version of Cole Porter's "Love for Sale" could be aired. Blanchard, *supra,* at 824.

139. Asbury Park, New Jersey, Santa Cruz, California, and Birmingham, Alabama. Sternheimer, *supra,* at 105.

139. who opined that rock and roll was a "contagious disease." *"Rock 'n' Roll" Stage Show Frantic, Noisy,* LA TIMES, Nov. 4, 1955, B9.

139. called rock "cannibalistic and tribalistic," comparing it to a "communicable disease." Glenn C. Altschuler, ALL SHOOK UP: HOW ROCK 'N' ROLL CHANGED AMERICA 6 (New York: Oxford University Press, 2003).

139. "primitive quasi-music that can be traced back to prehistoric cultures." Sternheimer, *supra,* at 112. *See Renowned Psychiatrist Francis Braceland Dies,* LA TIMES, Feb. 28, 1985; Eric Pace, *Jules Masserman, 89, Leader of Psychiatric Group, Is Dead,* NEW YORK TIMES, Nov. 15, 1994, D29.

140. the world's most famous rock 'n' roll song. Dave Marsh, LOUIE LOUIE (Ann Arbor, MI: University of Michigan Press, 1995/2004).

140. How can we stamp out this menace? ? ? ? Letter from complainant (name redacted) to Attorney General Robert F. Kennedy, Feb. 7, 1964 (reprinted in Eric Predoehl, *The FBI Investigation of the Song "Louie, Louie"* (1984) (collection of FBI reports obtained through FOIA request).

140. he announced a statewide ban on both radio play and live performances of the song. Gil Faggen, *Indiana Gov. Puts Down 'Pornographic' Wand Tune,* BILLBOARD, Feb. 1, 1964, at 3. *See* Marsh, *supra,* at 124–125; Blecha, *supra,* at 98.

140. to make sure that the record was not played in his state.). Alexis Petridis, *Louie, Louie: The Ultimate Rock Rebel Anthem,* THE GUARDIAN, Jan. 23, 2014 (www.theguardian.com/music/2014/jan/23/louie-louie-ultimate-rock-rebel-anthem). *See* Marsh, *supra,* at 124–125.

140. involved efforts by six FBI field offices, several US attorneys, and the FCC into the supposedly corrupting lyrics of "Louie, Louie." *See* Predoehl, *The FBI Investigation of the Song "Louie, Louie," supra.*

141. involved (although this may have been a subconscious nod to Anthony Comstock). Marsh, *supra,* at 114–138.

141. and therefore could not make any decision concerning the matter." Letter to SAC, Tampa, Feb. 28, 1964, Re: Phonograph Record "Louie, Louie." Predoehl, *The FBI Investigation of the Song "Louie, Louie," supra.*

141. no one knows for sure how it all started. Marsh, *supra,* at 118.

141. "with this type of rock and roll music, a listener might think he heard anything being said that he imagined." FBI Memo, Nov. 2, 1965. Predoehl, *The FBI Investigation of the Song "Louie, Louie," supra.*

142. "it is obvious [that] the lyrics to this record are not pornographic or objectionable in any way." FBI LA Field Office Memo, Aug. 31, 1965. Predoehl, *The FBI Investigation of the Song "Louie, Louie," supra.*

142. Get that Broad out of here! Lyric sheet submitted to FBI Laboratories along with recording of *Louie, Louie*, Mar. 27, 1964. Predoehl, *The FBI Investigation of the Song "Louie, Louie," supra.*

143. they had heard something "bad," no matter what words had been sung. Letter to J. Edgar Hoover from [identity redacted], Jun. 18, 1965. Predoehl, *The FBI Investigation of the Song "Louie, Louie," supra.*

143. *Poison for Our Youth*, and *Combatting Merchants of Filth: The Role of the FBI*. Letter from J. Edgar Hoover to [identity redacted], Jun. 25, 1965. Predoehl, *The FBI Investigation of the Song "Louie, Louie," supra.*

143. "by no stretch of the imagination is the obscene lyric audible." Letter to J. Edgar Hoover from [identity redacted], Jul. 14, 1965. Predoehl, *The FBI Investigation of the Song "Louie, Louie," supra.*

143. "nothing derogatory concerning correspondent." Report to FBI Director from Detroit Office, Jul. 20, 1965; Letter from J. Edgar Hoover to [identity redacted], Jul. 27, 1965. Predoehl, *The FBI Investigation of the Song "Louie, Louie," supra.*

143. memo from the FBI Labs to the New York office returning the recording and lyrics sheet. Memo to SAC New York, Oct. 10, 1966. Predoehl, *The FBI Investigation of the Song "Louie, Louie," supra.*

143. the accidentally improvised expletive stayed in, indistinct and in the background. Marsh, *supra*, at 97. *See* Mike Masnick, *FBI Spent Years "Researching" the Lyrics to "Louie, Louie" Before Realizing the Copyright Office Must Have Them*, TECH DIRT, May 6, 2015 (www.techdirt.com/articles/20150503/22075130880/fbi-spent-years-researching-lyrics-to-louie-louie-before-realizing-copyright-office-must-have-them.shtml); Anwen Crawford, *Is This the Dirtiest Song of the Sixties?* THE NEW YORKER, May 6, 2015 (www.newyorker.com/culture/cultural-comment/jack-ely-louie-louie-the-dirtiest-song-of-the-sixties).

144. offered a $1,000 reward to anyone who could substantiate the reported obscenity. FBI Memorandum, Sept. 7, 1965. Predoehl, *The FBI Investigation of the Song "Louie, Louie," supra*; Marsh, *supra*, at 137–138.

144. "[i]f a record isn't played at the suggestion of the state's chief executive, it has been banned." Marsh, *supra*, at 124–125; *Was 'Louie, Louie' Banned in Indiana?* (www.agecon.purdue.edu/crd/Localgov/Topics/Essays/Louie_Louie.htm).

144. Superintendent Dawning ultimately relented. Petridis, *supra*; Semonche, *supra*, at 138–142.

144. a public official's constitutional obligation not to succumb to a heckler's veto were factors. Eric Predoehl, *The Marching Band Story*, THE LOUIE REPORT BLOG (www.louielouie.net/blog/?p=4); Eric Predoehl, *Follow-up on the Michigan Marching Band Story*, THE LOUIE REPORT BLOG (www.louielouie.net/blog/?p=15).

145. Washington Governor Christine Gregoire danced to the tune at her Inaugural Ball in 2005. *Louie, Louie* (https://en.wikipedia.org/wiki/Louie_Louie); Jim Abbott, *"Louie, Louie" Still Fighting Bad Image*, THE SPOKESMAN-REVIEW, May 22, 2005 (www.heraldpalladium.com/localnews/louie-louie-still-banned-for-benton-harbor-band/article_do46b4b7-b6f6-54f4-a74d-514ab4bdccoe.html).

145. in Washington, DC, Klan members decked out in their robes and hoods picketed a Beatles concert. Blecha, *supra*, at 42–44; Sternheimer, *supra*, at 120–121; Randall J. Stephens, THE DEVIL'S MUSIC 102–145 (Cambridge, MA: Harvard University Press, 2018).

145. ordered the wholesale burning of Jewish and Arabic texts. Robert Corn-Revere, *Bonfires of Insanity: A History of Book Burnings from Nazis to ISIS*, THE DAILY BEAST, Feb. 28, 2015 (www.thedailybeast.com/bonfires-of-insanity-a-history-of-book-burnings-from-nazis-to-isis). *See generally* Haig Bosmajian, BURNING BOOKS (London: McFarland & Co., 2006).

146. Similar events were held throughout Germany in the 1930s and 1940s. Corn-Revere, *supra*; Bosmajian, *supra*, at 212.

146. claimed to have destroyed ten million dollars' worth of records and tapes. Blecha, *supra*, at 46; Sternheimer, *supra*, at 122–124; Shoshana D. Samole, *Rock & Roll Control: Censoring Music Lyrics in the '90s*, ENT. & SPORTS LAW REV. 175, 176 (1995–1996); Cockburn and St. Clair, *supra*, at 109.

146. getting "the rock 'n['] roll wrecking ball swinging in the right direction." Cockburn and St. Clair, *supra*, at 109.

147. to eliminate "all immoral and foreign racial elements in the arts." Sternheimer, *supra*, at 108; Blecha, *supra*, at 23.

147. described as "hot music," from the air. Blecha, *supra*, at 24.

147. "jungle music," "cannibalistic," and "primitive." Sternheimer, *supra*, at 110–115; Blecha, *supra*, at 25–27.

147. classified by *Billboard* magazine as "race records." Sternheimer, *supra*, at 109.

147. pull the white man down to the level of the negro." Blecha, *supra*, at 25.

147. focused on their real concerns by banning interracial dancing. Altschuler, *supra*, at 20–21; Sternheimer, *supra*, at 110; Blecha, *supra*, at 31.

147. the unwelcome attention of policymakers. Blanchard, *supra*, at 827–830.

147. had been introduced in more than twenty states. *Music Lyrics and Commerce*, Hearings before the Subcommittee on Commerce, Consumer Protection, and Competitiveness of the House Energy and Commerce Committee (Feb. 11, 1994) ("*Gangsta Rap Hearings I*"), at 2.

148. more black males in jail than we have in college." *Gangsta Rap Hearings I*, *supra*, at 5 (testimony of C. Delores Tucker).

148. "more important to ban speech that is dehumanizing to women than to protect free speech." *Gangsta Rap Hearings I*, *supra*, at 6 (testimony of C. Delores Tucker).

148. to confiscate or detain materials from more than half of the feminist bookstores in that country. Nadine Strossen, DEFENDING PORNOGRAPHY 229–244 (Scribner: New York, 1995).

148. "something must be done to stop the production of violent, misogynistic material." *Gangsta Rap Hearings I*, *supra*, at 4 (statement of Hon. Cliff Stearns).

149. almost as an afterthought. *Music Lyrics and Commerce*, Hearings Before the Subcommittee on Commerce, Consumer Protection, and Competitiveness of the House Energy and Commerce Committee (May 5, 1994) ("*Gangsta Rap Hearings II*"), at 129–132 (testimony of Hillary Rosen).

149. if "a parent wants his child to listen to this music, that is a parent's responsibility." *Gangsta Rap Hearings II*, at 73; *Gangsta Rap Hearings I*, *supra*, at 56–57.

149. "evil propaganda stands virtually unopposed in today's public debate over rap music." *Gangsta Rap Hearings II*, at 63–65 (statement of Rep. Maxine Waters).

149. "these companies have the blood of children on their hands." Blecha, *supra*, at 172–173; Jason C. Bivins, RELIGION OF FEAR: THE POLITICS OF HORROR IN CONSERVATIVE EVANGELISM 121–122 (New York: Oxford University Press, 2008); David Hinckley, *Rap Takes the Rap for Our Real Problems*, NEW YORK DAILY NEWS, Jun. 4, 1996 (www.nydailynews.com/archives/nydn-features/rap-takes-rap-real-problems-article-1.716781).

149. "little boys are raping little girls." Barry Glassner, THE CULTURE OF FEAR: WHY AMERICANS ARE AFRAID OF THE WRONG THINGS 122–123 (New York: Basic Books, 1999).

150. Gingrich urged people to boycott radio stations that played any rap music at all. Blecha, *supra*, at 172–173; Bivins, *supra*, at 121–122; Hinckley, *supra*; Mark Landler, *Coalition Challenges Time Warner over Gangsta Rap*, New York Times, Jun. 1, 1995, at B10.

150. there is a danger [that] those very rights will be endangered." Blecha, *supra*, at 173–174.

150. the use (or misuse) of ratings in the entertainment industry constituted a "deceptive trade practice." Federal Trade Commission, Marketing Violent Entertainment to Children: A Review of Self-Regulation and Industry Practices in the Motion Picture, Music Recording & Electronic Game Industries (Sept. 2000) ("FTC Ratings Report"); Federal Trade Commission, Marketing Violent Entertainment to Children: A Six-Month Follow-up Review of Industry Practices in the Motion Picture, Music Recording & Electronic Game Industries (Apr. 2001) ("FTC Ratings Follow-up").

150. guide their children's exposure to entertainment media with violent content." Letter from Chairman Robert Pitofsky to Senator John McCain, Nov. 20, 2000; FTC Ratings Follow-up, at iii.

150. mandatory uniform ratings scheme for labeling "violent content in audio and visual media products." S. 792, Media Marketing Accountability Act of 2001, 107th Cong., 1st Sess.; H. R. 1916, The 21st Century Media Responsibility Act of 2001, 107th Cong., 1st Sess.

151. The proposed bills were withdrawn in response to the new agreement. Blanchard, *supra*, at 826–827; David P. Gaertner, 2 *Live Crew and Judge Gonzales Too – 2 Live Crew and the Miller Obscenity Test*, 18 J. Legislation 105, 107, 113 (1991).

151. he put his law practice on hold to make sure that foul-mouthed rappers would be put behind bars. Chuck, Philips, *The "Batman" Who Took On Rap: Obscenity: Lawyer Jack Thompson Put His Practice on Hold to Concentrate on Driving 2 Live Crew Out of Business. In Southern Florida, He Is Loved and Loathed*, LA Times, Jun. 18, 1990 (http://articles.latimes.com/1990-06-18/entertainment/ca-87_1_jack-thompson); *Jack Thompson (activist)*, Wikipedia (https://en.wikipedia.org/wiki/Jack_Thompson_(activist)).

151. and to prosecutors and sheriffs' departments throughout Florida. Hunter Schwartz, 25 *Years Ago, 2 Live Crew Were Arrested for Obscenity. Here's the Fascinating Back Story*, Washington Post, Jun. 11, 2015 (www.washingtonpost.com/news/the-fix/wp/2015/06/11/25-years-ago-2-live-crew-were-arrested-for-obscenity-heres-the-fascinating-back-story/?noredirect=on&utm_term=eb19a003c8fd).

151. promptly withdrawn from store shelves throughout the county. Gaertner, *supra*, at 106.

151. but the 2 Live Crew album was found to be legally obscene. *Skyywalker Records, Inc.* v. *Navarro*, 739 F. Supp. 578 (S. D. Fla. 1990), *rev'd sub nom, Luke Records, Inc.* v. *Navarro*, 960 F. 2d 134 (1992), *cert. denied*, 506 US 1022 (1992). *See* Laura Parker, *Federal Judge Finds Rap LP Obscene*, Washington Post, Jun. 7, 1990, at A1.

151. "should address their petitions to the Florida Legislature, not to this court." *Skyywalker Records, Inc.*, 739 F. Supp. at 586.

151. "It is an appeal directed to 'dirty' thoughts and the loins, not to the intellect and the mind." *Skyywalker Records, Inc.*, 739 F. Supp. at 589–591.

152. whether a work "lacks serious artistic, scientific, literary or political value." *Luke Records, Inc.*, 960 F. 2d at 138.

152. no work of music alone may be declared obscene." *Luke Records, Inc.*, 960 F. 2d at 135.

152. a county court judge dismissed criminal charges brought against a retailer for selling the album. Gaertner, *supra*, at 105–110; Schwartz, *supra*; Blanchard, *supra*, at 831.

152. holding that it violated the First and Fourteenth Amendments. *Atlantic Beach Casino, Inc.* v. *Morenzoni*, 749 F. Supp. 38, 39 (D.R.I. 1990).

152. like "a freight train finally running out of steam." Schwartz, *supra*.

153. a prior restraint in violation of the First Amendment and that its procedures violated due process. *Soundgarden v. Eikenberry*, 123 Wash. 2d 750, 777–778 (1994) (*en banc*).

153. could cause a person to perceive the message and act on it. *Vance v. Judas Priest*, 1990 WL 130920 *19 (Nev. Dist. Ct.).

153. could not be considered an incitement. *Waller v. Osbourne*, 763 F. Supp. 1144, 1149 (M. D. Ga. 1991), *aff'd mem.* 958 F. 2d (11th Cir.), *cert. denied*, 506 US 916 (1992).

153. her 1987 book Raising PG Kids in an X-Rated Society. Robert Siegel, *Tipper Gore and Family Values*, All Things Considered, Jan. 11, 2005 (www.npr.org/templates/story/story.php?storyId=4279560?storyId=4279560).

153. Sorry, cancel that last conclusion." Bryan Reesman, *25 Years after Tipper Gore's PMRC Hearings, the Opposing Sides Aren't So Far Apart*, Vulture, Sept. 20, 2010 (www.vulture.com/2010/09/pmrc_25_anniversary.html).

154. "irony in its purest form." Zach Schonfeld, *Parental Advisory Forever: An Oral History of the PMRC's War on Dirty Lyrics*, Newsweek, Sept. 19, 2015 (www.newsweek.com/2015/10/09/oral-history-tipper-gores-war-explicit-rock-lyrics-dee-snider-373103.html).

154. control over what their children see and hear." Kory Grow, *Tipper Gore Reflects on PMRC 30 Years Later*, Rolling Stone, Sept. 14, 2015 (www.rollingstone.com/politics/politics-news/tipper-gore-reflects-on-pmrc-30-years-later-57862/).

154. and claimed that they'd both had reservations about it. Gwen Ifill, *Gores Change Tune on Rock-Lyric Hearings*, Washington Post, Nov. 5, 1987 (www.washingtonpost.com/archive/politics/1987/11/05/gores-change-tune-on-rock-lyric-hearings/ad8b1435-c301-46aa-8138-46e618c4508b/?utm_term=157a924da95b); Cockburn and St. Clair, *supra*, at 107–108.

154. "promoting suicide and all the other things we have heard about here." Cockburn and St. Clair, *supra*, at 101, 108–109. Record Labeling Hearings, *supra*, at 4–5, 70–71, 111–114.

155. asking if it was alright to laugh in the jury box. *Rappers Released* (Editorial), Washington Post, Oct. 28, 1990, at C6.

155. was thinking about buying it after the trial and attending a 2 Live Crew show. Laura Parker, *Rap Group Acquitted in Florida*, Washington Post, Oct. 21, 1990, at A1.

156. recorded clearly and audibly in standard American English." Zach Schonfeld, *Does the Parental Advisory Label Still Matter?* Newsweek, Nov. 10, 2015 (www.newsweek.com/does-parental-advisory-label-still-matter-tipper-gore-375607).

156. contains street language and sexual innuendo." Richard Harrington, *The Sticker, Selling Records*, Washington Post, Oct. 31, 1990, at C7.

156. more than a million copies *even before the title was released*. Blanchard, *supra*, at 830; *Gone Platinum*, Newsweek, Jul. 30, 1990, at 57.

157. likewise soared to the top of the charts. Zach Schonfeld, *Does the Parental Advisory Label Still Matter?* Newsweek, Nov. 10, 2015 (www.newsweek.com/does-parental-advisory-label-still-matter-tipper-gore-375607).

157. like landline phones or TV guides." Schonfeld, *supra*.

CHAPTER 7

158. private eyes, gangsters, more violence, and cartoons." Newton N. Minow, *Television and the Public Interest*, Speech delivered at the National Association of Broadcasters Convention, Washington, DC, May 9, 1961 (the "*Vast Wasteland Speech*").

158. by people you wouldn't have in your home." The Portable Curmudgeon 268–269 (Jon Winokur, ed., New York: New American Library, 1987).

159. upheld the federal government's authority to regulate broadcasting content. *FCC* v. *Red Lion Broadcasting Co.*, 395 US 367 (1969).

161. "[T]elevision is democracy at its ugliest." THE PORTABLE CURMUDGEON, *supra*, at 269–270.

161. enjoy too often what commissioners and columnists abhor." Thomas G. Krattenmaker and L. A. Powe, Jr., *Converging First Amendment Principles for Converging Communications Media*, 104 YALE LAW J. 1719, 1725–1726 (May 1995).

161. to refer to Minow as the "culture czar." Paul A. Cantor, *The Road to Cultural Serfdom: America's First Television Czar*, in BACK ON THE ROAD TO SERFDOM: THE RESURGENCE OF STATISM 172 & n. 3 (Thomas E. Woods Jr., ed., Wilmington, DE: ISI Books, 2011).

161. "nobody – least of all me – wants to be put in the role of censor." Newton Minow, EQUAL TIME 73 (New York: Atheneum, 1964).

162. "in somebody's opinion ... the ratings demand a jolt." Minow, EQUAL TIME, *supra*, at 74–76, 92.

162. or even overdoses of brutality." Minow, EQUAL TIME, *supra*, at 76.

162. the conception of the liberty guaranteed by the state and federal constitutions." *Near* v. *Minnesota*, 283 US 697, 714–715 (1931).

162. "as far-fetched as comparing an elephant to a flea." Minow, EQUAL TIME, *supra*, at 88–89.

163. lacked sufficient "character" or "fitness" to be licensees. Minow, EQUAL TIME, *supra*, at 90–94.

163. thus clouding their future tenure as licensees. Mary Ann Watson, THE EXPANDING VISTA: AMERICAN TELEVISION IN THE KENNEDY YEARS 216–217 (New York: Oxford University Press, 1990); Cantor, *supra*, at 172 & n. 3.

163. It was aptly named, for only a child could believe it. Newton N. Minow and Craig L. LaMay, ABANDONED IN THE WASTELAND 108–109, 122–132 (New York: Hill & Wang, 1995).

164. televangelist Oral Roberts on WOR-TV. *TV Listings*, NEW YORK TIMES, May 14, 1961, X14–X16.

164. and *Winston Churchill* (WABC-TV). *TV Listings*, NEW YORK TIMES, May 14, 1961, X14–X16.

165. to subject moving pictures to prior review and censorship. *Mutual Film Corp.* v. *Industrial Comm'n of Ohio*, 236 US 230, 242 (1915).

166. as simply "application of the regulatory power of Congress in a field within the scope of its legislative authority." *Trinity Methodist Church, South* v. *Federal Radio Comm'n*, 62 F. 2d 850, 851 (DC Cir. 1932).

166. "the essence of censorship." *Near*, 283 US at 713.

166. let vice run rampant, and that the district attorney took bribes. L. A. Powe, AMERICAN BROADCASTING AND THE FIRST AMENDMENT 13–21 (Berkeley: University of California Press, 1987).

166. before the court passes on the questions involved." Ronald Coase, *The Federal Communications Commission*, 2 J. LAW & ECON. 1, 40 (1959) (quoting Clarence C. Dill, RADIO LAW 1–2 (1938)). *See* Thomas G. Krattenmaker and Lucas A. Powe, Jr., REGULATING BROADCAST PROGRAMMING 33 (Cambridge, MA: The MIT Press, 1994).

167. The Court disagreed. *NBC* v. *United States*, 319 US 190 (1943).

167. to the development of the automobile." *NBC* v. *United States*, 319 US at 213.

168. "determining the composition of that traffic." *NBC* v. *United States*, 319 US at 215–126.

168. a crisis that would spur congressional action. Thomas Winslow Hazlett, THE POLITICAL SPECTRUM 36–46 (New Haven: Yale University Press, 2017); Jonathan W. Emord, FREEDOM, TECHNOLOGY, AND THE FIRST AMENDMENT 153–156 (San Francisco: Pacific Research Institute for Public Policy, 1991).

168. he could still regulate frequencies and hours of use. *Hoover* v. *Intercity Radio Co.*, 286 F. 1003 (DC Cir. 1923). *See* Krattenmaker and Powe, *supra*, at 9.

168. under what circumstances, and with what type of material." Herbert Hoover, Minutes of Open Meetings of Department of Commerce Conference on Radio Telephony, Feb. 27, 1922 (Herbert Hoover Presidential Library, West Branch, Iowa, Box 496); Krattenmaker and Powe, *supra*, at 8.

168. should be regulated and controlled by the Federal government in the public interest." Tentative Report of Department of Commerce Conference on Radio Telephony (Mar. 1922). Herbert Hoover Presidential Library, West Branch, Iowa, Box 496.

168. necessary to present interference detrimental to the public good." Krattenmaker and Powe, *supra*, at 10.

168. "suddenly remedied" without the passage of a new law. Krattenmaker and Powe, *supra*, at 10; Powe, *supra*, at 57–58.

169. are kept upon the air without destroying each other." Hazlett, THE POLITICAL SPECTRUM, *supra*, at 41.

169. with new receivers making it possible to reduce interference when tuning in stations. Powe, *supra*, at 58.

169. but not to enforce restrictions on operations. *United States* v. *Zenith Radio Corp.*, 12 F. 2d 614 (N. D. Ill. 1926).

169. in support of *the case he had just lost.* 35 Op. Att'y Gen 126 (1926).

169. that Hoover's authority was strictly limited. Hazlett, THE POLITICAL SPECTRUM, *supra*, at 41–42.

169. the entire Justice Department opinion was published in the *New York Times*. Philip T. Rosen, THE MODERN STENTORS: RADIO BROADCASTERS AND THE FEDERAL GOVERNMENT, 1920–1934 101–102 (Westport, CT: Greenwood Press, 1980); *Text of Ruling Denying Radio Control*, NEW YORK TIMES, Jul. 10, 1926.

169. the Commerce Department was out of the business of regulating radio. Powe, *supra*, at 60; Krattenmaker and Powe, *supra*, at 11–12; Hazlett, THE POLITICAL SPECTRUM, *supra*, at 41–42.

169. broadcasters no longer felt constrained to stay on their assigned channels. Krattenmaker and Powe, *supra*, at 11–12.

169. "interference was not the issue, interference was the opportunity." Thomas W. Hazlett, *The Rationality of Regulation of the Broadcast Spectrum*, 33 J. LAW & ECON. 133, 162 (1990).

170. mechanism for preventing one broadcaster from using the same frequency as another. Jora A. Minasian, *The Political Economy of Broadcasting in the 1920's*, J. LAW & ECON. 391, 402–403 (Oct. 1969).

170. afforded policy makers far broader regulatory discretion than was needed to restore order." Hazlett, THE POLITICAL SPECTRUM, *supra*, at 38. *See also* Emord, *supra*, at 155–156.

170. "almost like an invitation for broadcasters to do their worst." Douglas B. Craig, FIRESIDE POLITICS: RADIO AND POLITICAL CULTURE IN THE UNITED STATES 1920–1940 49 (Baltimore: Johns Hopkins University Press, 2005).

170. retain complete and absolute control of the right to use the air." Clarence C. Dill, *A Traffic Cop for the Air*, 75 REVIEW OF REVIEWS 181, 184 (1927).

170. under what circumstances, and with what type of material." Krattenmaker and Powe, *supra*, at 19.

170. could not interfere with WGN within a 100-mile radius. *Tribune Company* v. *Oak Leaves Broadcasting Station*, Cook County, Ill. Circuit Court (Nov. 17, 1926), reprinted in 68

CONG. REC.-SENATE 215–219 (Dec. 10, 1926). *See* Rosen, *supra*, at 102–103; Krattenmaker and Powe, *supra*, at 15–16.

171. "the use of a wave length established a priority of right." CONG. REC.-HOUSE 2579 (Jan. 29, 1927). *See* Hazlett, THE POLITICAL SPECTRUM, *supra*, at 43; Emord, *supra*, at 156–157.

171. or face immediate termination of the right to broadcast if they failed to do so. Hazlett, THE POLITICAL SPECTRUM, *supra*, at 43.

171. beyond the terms, conditions, and periods of the license." Radio Act of 1927, Pub. L. No. 632, 69th Cong., 2nd Sess. Ch. 169.

171. which seven years later supplanted the Radio Act. 47 USC § 301.

172. it would no doubt be accurate to describe the resulting situation as chaos." Ronald Coase, *The Federal Communications Commission*, 2 J. LAW & ECON. 1, 14 (1959).

172. inconsistent with the doctrine of freedom of the press." Coase, *supra*, at 7.

172. you have got to do something so the public can hear the radio." Hearing Before the Subcommittee on Telecommunications and Finance of the Committee on Energy and Commerce on H. R. 1934, House of Representatives, 100th Cong. 64 (Apr. 7, 1987) (Testimony of Newton Minow) ("*House Fairness Doctrine Hearings*").

173. and the result was chaos." *House Fairness Doctrine Hearings* at 62 (Testimony of Charles Ferris).

173. censorship over the radio communications or signals transmitted by any radio station," 47 USC § 109 (1927).

173. has anything to do with entertainment programs as such." Louis Caldwell, *Censorship of Radio Programs*, 1 J. RADIO LAW 441, 467 (1931).

173. and to favor those which render the best service." *Rosen, supra*, at 138.

173. but it opted not to do so and instead went in the opposite direction. Federal Radio Commission, FIRST ANNUAL REPORT 13 (1927).

173. "the success of radio broadcasting lay in doing away with small and unimportant stations." Robert McChesney, TELECOMMUNICATIONS, MASS MEDIA & DEMOCRACY: THE BATTLE FOR THE CONTROL OF U.S. BROADCASTING, 1928–1935 19 (New York: Oxford University Press, 1995).

173. more than a hundred small stations were off the air with a year of the Radio Act's adoption. Hazlett, THE POLITICAL SPECTRUM, *supra*, at 50; Powe, *supra*, at 63; Rosen, *supra*, at 134–137.

173. many stations voluntarily relinquished their licenses. Rosen, *supra*, at 136–137.

173. by 1930 that number was cut by more than half. McChesney, *supra*, at 30–31; Hazlett, THE POLITICAL SPECTRUM, *supra*, at 50.

173. "[t]he first step slayed the weak; the second banished the different." Krattenmaker and Powe, *supra*, at 21.

174. religious, political, social, and economic." Federal Radio Commission, THIRD ANNUAL REPORT 32 (1929); Krattenmaker and Powe, *supra*, at 23–24.

174. phasing out its labor programming and affiliating with NBC. Hazlett, THE POLITICAL SPECTRUM, *supra*, at 55–57.

174. "operate with due regard for the opinions of others." Federal Radio Commission, SECOND ANNUAL REPORT 156 (1928); Krattenmaker and Powe, *supra*, at 23; Hazlett, THE POLITICAL SPECTRUM, *supra*, at 57–58.

174. outrageous and unfounded attacks on public officials." *Trinity Methodist Church, South v. Federal Radio Comm'n*, 62 F. 2d 850, 851 (DC Cir. 1932); Powe, *supra*, at 16; Hazlett, THE POLITICAL SPECTRUM, *supra*, at 53–54; Emord, *supra*, at 177–179; Krattenmaker and Powe, *supra*, at 24–25.

174. and news of interest to all members of the family." *Great Lakes Broadcasting Co.*, 3 FRC Ann. Rep. 32; Federal Radio Commission, THIRD ANNUAL REPORT 34 (1929); Krattenmaker and Powe, *supra*, at 23–24; Hazlett, THE POLITICAL SPECTRUM, *supra*, at 54.

174. "were best delivered not via specialty shops but by department stores." Hazlett, THE POLITICAL SPECTRUM, *supra*, at 54.

174. and (finally) entertainment programming. *Report and Statement of Policy re: Commission En Banc Programming Inquiry*, 44 FCC 2303, 2314 (1960).

175. "arguably the blandest decade of American television." Cantor, *supra*, at 171–187.

175. "Imagination does not flourish in a climate of coercion." Cantor, *supra*, at 177–178. Watson, *supra*, at 51.

175. its own subjective determination of what is or is not a good program." *En Banc Programming Inquiry*, 44 FCC at 2308.

175. [its role] cannot be one of program dictation or program supervision." *En Banc Programming Inquiry*, 44 FCC at 2308–2309 (quoting *Cantwell v. Connecticut*, 310 US 296, 307 (1940)).

176. to exercise far-reaching powers of control over the licensee's operations." Glen O. Robinson, *The FCC and the First Amendment: Observations on 40 Years of Radio and Television Regulation*, 52 MINN. LAW REV. 67, 119 (1967).

176. tend to promote and/or glorify the use of illegal drugs." *In re Licensee Responsibility to Review Records Before Their Broadcast*, 28 FCC 2d 409 (1971), *Memorandum Opinion and Order*, 31 FCC 2d 377, 410 (1971) (Statement of Commissioner Robert E. Lee), *Reconsideration Denied*, 31 FCC 2d 385 (1971).

176. such artists as The Beatles, Bob Dylan, and Peter, Paul and Mary, among others. Ben Fong-Torres, *FCC Discovers Dope, Does Darndest Thing*, ROLLING STONE, Apr. 1, 1971. *See* Margaret A. Blanchard, *The American Urge to Censor: Freedom of Expression Versus the Desire to Sanitize Society – From Anthony Comstock to 2 Live Crew*, 33 WILLIAM & MARY LAW REV. 741, 806 (1992).

176. uncontrolled administrative discretion in the review of telecommunications programming." David L. Bazelon, *FCC Regulation of the Telecommunications Press*, DUKE LAW J. 213, 215 (1975).

176. even a governmental 'raised eyebrow' can send otherwise intrepid entrepreneurs running for the cover of conformity." David L. Bazelon, *The First Amendment and the "New Media" – New Directions in Regulating Telecommunications*, 31 FEDERAL COMMUNICATIONS LAW J. 201, 206 (1979).

177. and Senator Estes Kefauver held hearings TV violence as well as comics. *See Hearings for the Investigation of Juvenile Delinquency in the United States*, Subcomm. to Investigate Juvenile Delinquency of the Senate Comm. on the Judiciary, 84th Cong., 1st Sess. (1955) and 83rd Cong., 2nd Sess. (1954).

177. to "proceed vigorously and as rapidly as possible" to comply. H. Rep. No. 1139, 93rd Cong., 2nd Sess. 15 (1974); S. Rep. No. 1056, 93rd Cong., 2nd Sess. 19 (1974).

177. such action may be considered. H. Rep. No. 1139, 93rd Cong., 2nd Sess. at 15.

177. "Forget about the First Amendment; we'll let the courts worry about that." *Writers Guild of America, West v. FCC*, 423 F. Supp. 1064, 1111 (C.D. Cal. 1976), *vacated and remanded on jurisdictional grounds sub nom. Writers Guild of America, West v. ABC*, 609 F. 2d 355 (9th Cir. 1979), *cert. denied*, 449 US 824 (1980).

177. will obviate any need for governmental regulation in this sensitive area." *Report on the Broadcast of Violent, Indecent, and Obscene Material*, 51 FCC 2d 418, 420, 422 (1975).

178. TV shows were rescheduled, certain storylines were scrapped, and scripts were censored. David W. Rintels, *Why We Fought the Family Viewing Hour*, NEW YORK TIMES, Nov. 21, 1976, at 107.

178. were per se violations of the First Amendment. *Writers Guild of America, West*, 423 F. Supp. at 1073, 1142, 1151.

178. Judge Ferguson characterized the FCC's tactics as "backroom bludgeoning," *Writers Guild of America, West*, 423 F. Supp. at 1142.

178. communications between Wiley and representatives of NAB. *Writers Guild of America, West*, 423 F. Supp. at 1094–1119; *Writers Guild of America, West v. FCC*, 609 F. 2d at 359–360.

178. on the acceptance and scheduling of programs with sex and violence. *Writers Guild of America, West*, 423 F. Supp. at 1100–1101.

178. "persistent, pronounced, and unmistakable." *Writers Guild of America, West*, 423 F. Supp. at 1094, 1098–1099.

178. the vagueness of the standards which govern it." *Writers Guild of America, West*, 423 F. Supp. at 1146.

178. "the family viewing policy is in large part a public relations gimmick." *Writers Guild of America, West*, 423 F. Supp. at 1149 n. 138.

179. serious issues involving the Constitution, the Communications Act and the [Administrative Procedure Act]." *Writers Guild of America, West v. FCC*, 609 F. 2d at 364–365.

179. should have first been presented to the FCC, given its expertise in the field. *Writers Guild of America, West v. FCC*, 609 F. 2d at 365–366. Page 264

179. and the Code's operation was enjoined. *United States v. National Ass'n of Broadcasters*, 536 F. Supp. 149 (D. D.C. 1982).

180. to extend its power to new technologies beyond broadcasting. Minow and LaMay, *supra*, at 99–100; Minow, EQUAL TIME, *supra*, at 92, 152–175.

180. and take more action to curb televised violence. Minow and LaMay, *supra*, at 152–175.

180. the power of individual viewers to manipulate information." Minow and LaMay, *supra*, at 63, 65, 67, 153.

181. the revocation of station licenses affiliated with networks he disparaged. *E.g.*, David Shepardson, *Trump Suggests Challenging TV Network Licenses Over "Fake News,"* REUTERS, Oct. 11, 2017 (www.reuters.com/article/us-usa-trump-media/trump-suggests-challenging-tv-network-licenses-over-fake-news-idUSKBN1CG1WB); Thomas Winslow Hazlett, *Making the Fairness Doctrine Great Again*, REASON.COM (Mar. 2018) (https://reason.com/archives/2018/02/15/making-the-fairness-doctrine-g).

181. "retribution" on his perceived enemies in the press. *E.g.*, William Cummings, *"It's called the First Amendment": Pundits Decry Trump Call for "Retribution" against "SNL,"* USA TODAY, Feb. 18, 2019 (www.usatoday.com/story/news/politics/onpolitics/2019/02/17/trump-attack-saturday-night-live-reactions/2899634002/).

181. with the intent to defame Congress or the President. Sedition Act of 1798, 1 Stat. 596.

181. the republican newspapers they felt had been slandering them. Eric Burns, INFAMOUS SCRIBBLERS: THE FOUNDING FATHERS AND THE ROWDY BEGINNINGS OF AMERICAN JOURNALISM 356 (New York: Public Affairs, 2006).

181. five republican papers were shuttered or ceased publication for at least some period during this time. Philip I. Blumberg, REPRESSIVE JURISPRUDENCE IN THE EARLY AMERICAN REPUBLIC 101 (Cambridge: Cambridge University Press, 2010); Charles Slack, LIBERTY'S FIRST CRISIS 233 (New York: Atlantic Monthly Press, 2015).

181. as palpable as if Congress had ordered us to fall down and worship a golden image." 4 JEFFERSON'S WORKS 555–556 (Washington ed.) (Letter to Abigail Adams, Jul. 22, 1804).

181. a national awareness of the central meaning of the First Amendment." *New York Times* v. *Sullivan*, 376 US 254, 273 (1964).

182. "irrationally hostile to the President and his programs." Fred W. Friendly, THE GOOD GUYS, THE BAD GUYS, AND THE FIRST AMENDMENT 32–42, 78–83 (New York: Vintage Books, 1975); Fred Friendly, *What's Fair on the Air?* NEW YORK TIMES, Mar. 30, 1975 p. 177. *See House Fairness Doctrine Hearings*, at 67–68 (Testimony of FCC Chairman Mark Fowler).

182. Others were silenced as well. Friendly, THE GOOD GUYS, THE BAD GUYS, AND THE FIRST AMENDMENT, *supra*, at 32–42, 78–83.

182. to challenge license renewals of "unfriendly" broadcast stations. Bazelon, *FCC Regulation of the Telecommunications Press*, *supra*, at 214, 216 & n. 9, 239.

182. "an official monitoring system through the FCC" in order to generate "official complaints" to the Commission. Bazelon, *FCC Regulation of the Telecommunications Press*, *supra*, at 244–248. *See* Final Report, Senate Select Committee on Presidential Campaign Activities, S. Rep. No. 981, 93rd Cong., 2nd Sess. 149 (1974).

182. as well as complaints against programs on PBS. *Accuracy in Media, Inc.* v. *FCC*, 521 F. 2d 288 (DC Cir. 1975); *In the matter of Complaints Concerning Columbia Broadcasting System, Inc., Program "The Selling of the Pentagon,"* 30 FCC 2d 149 (1971). *See* Nicole Hemmer, *Trump Wants to Make the Media "Fair." He's Not the First GOP President to Try It*, WASHINGTON POST, Aug. 29, 2018 (www.washingtonpost.com/outlook/2018/08/29/trump-wouldnt-be-first-gop-president-try-make-media-fair/?utm_term=.08f4e64d2ce7).

182. criticizing private pension plans entitled *Pensions: The Broken Promise*. *See* Hemmer, *supra*.

182. the monopoly power wielded by Big TV Media." *House Fairness Doctrine Hearings* at 247–248 (Testimony of Phyllis Schlafly).

183. and for an episode of a news special called *Pentagon Underground*. Robert L. Corn, *Broadcasters in Bondage*, REASON, Sept. 1985, 31–34; Robert Corn–Revere, *Fairness 2.0: Media Content Regulation in the 21st Century*, CATO INSTITUTE POLICY ANALYSIS NO. 651, Nov. 10, 2009 (www.cato.org/publications/policy-analysis/fairness-20-media-content-regulation-21st-century).

183. applying the same First Amendment standards to broadcasting as to traditional media. Mark Fowler and Daniel L. Brenner, *A Marketplace Approach to Broadcast Regulation*, 60 TEXAS LAW REV. 207 (1982).

183. which no longer served the public interest and was constitutionally suspect. *Inquiry into Section 73. 1910 of the Commission's Rules and Regulations Concerning General Fairness Doctrine Obligations of Broadcast Licensees*, 102 FCC 2d 143, 147–149 (1985) ("1985 *Fairness Doctrine Report*").

183. Just remember that and we are going to get along fine." *House Fairness Doctrine Hearings*, at 64–65 (Testimony of Newton Minow). *See* Friendly, THE GOOD GUYS, THE BAD GUYS, AND THE FIRST AMENDMENT, *supra*, at 215.

184. "Before you do anything, you will inform the Congress." Friendly, THE GOOD GUYS, THE BAD GUYS, AND THE FIRST AMENDMENT, *supra*, at 214–215.

184. "Yes, sir, I understand exactly what you are saying." Federal Communications Commission Oversight Hearings Before the Subcomm. on Telecommunications, Consumer Protection, and Finance of the House Comm. on Energy and Commerce, 98th Cong., 2nd Sess. 53 (1984).

184. three kicks might do the trick." *Reauthorization and Oversight of the FCC*, Hearing Before the Subcomm. on Communications of the Senate Comm. on Commerce, Science, and Transportation, 99th Cong., 1st Sess. 2–3 (1985).

184. in light of the evidence adduced in this proceeding." 1985 *Fairness Doctrine Report*, 102 FCC 2d at 247.

184. the proposed construction of the Nine Mile Point II nuclear power plant. *In re Complaint of Syracuse Peace Council*, 99 FCC 2d 1389 (1984).

185. "We're talking political reality here." *Meredith Corp. v. FCC*, 809 F. 2d 863, 873 (DC Cir. 1987).

185. because the resolution would be politically awkward." *Meredith Corp. v. FCC*, 809 F. 2d at 874.

185. and with the American tradition of independent journalism." President Ronald Reagan, Veto Message for S. 742, the Fairness in Broadcasting Act of 1987, Jun. 19, 1987. *See* Veto of Fairness in Broadcasting Act of 1987, 23 WEEKLY PRES. COMP. DOC. 715 (Jun. 29, 1987).

185. terminate the main provisions of the fairness doctrine and cease enforcement. *Complaint of Syracuse Peace Council*, 2 FCC Rcd. 5043 (1987), *aff'd, Syracuse Peace Council v. FCC*, 867 F. 2d 654 (DC Cir. 1989).

185. avoid another confrontation with the White House. *See* Susan Low Bloch, *Orphaned Rules in the Administrative State: The Fairness Doctrine and Other Orphaned Progeny of Interactive Deregulation*, 76 GEORGETOWN LAW J. 59, 83–84 (1987).

185. in favor of others whose views should be expressed on this unique medium." *Red Lion Broadcasting Co. v. FCC*, 395 US 367, 388, 390 (1969).

186. to provide balanced coverage of political affairs. *Miami Herald Publ'g Co. v. Tornillo*, 418 US 241, 250–252 (1974).

186. First Amendment guarantees of a free press as they have evolved to this time. *Tornillo*, 418 US at 258.

186. where government has been allowed to meddle in the internal editorial affairs of newspapers." *Tornillo*, 418 US at 259 (White, J., concurring).

187. couldn't compel licensees to accept editorial advertising, *CBS, Inc. v. Democratic National Committee*, 412 US 94 (1973).

187. or ban editorials by public broadcasters. *FCC v. League of Women Voters of California*, 468 US 364 (1984).

187. the Commission could not ignore a station's First Amendment concerns. *Meredith Corp.*, 809 F. 2d at 873.

187. to reconsider the premise or approach of its decision in *Red Lion.*" *Complaint of Syracuse Peace Council*, 2 FCC Rcd. at 5048, 5055.

187. Why do you want us to intervene?" *FCC v. Fox Television Stations, Inc.*, No. 10-1293, Transcript of oral argument, Jan. 10, 2012, 33–34 (www.supremecourt.gov/oral_argu ments/argument_transcripts/2011/10-1293.pdf).

187. because he considered the technology "supernatural." Coase, *supra*; Krattenmaker and Powe, *supra*, at 33.

188. "[T]o many of us, this enlarged choice is not enough to satisfy the public interest." Newton Minow, *How Vast the Wasteland Now?* Address at the Freedom Forum Media Studies Center, Columbia University, May 9, 1991.

188. the prospects for serving the public interest even dimmer." Minow and LaMay, *supra*, at vii.

188. the lowest common denominator in the marketplace." Minow, *How Vast the Wasteland Now?*, *supra*.

188. should be applied to digital, computer-driven video servers on the "Information Superhighway." Minow and LaMay, *supra*, at 174–175.

188. "The two words I cared about were 'public interest.'" Minow and LaMay, *supra*, at 3–4.

189. The title? *A Vaster Wasteland*. Newton Minow, *A Vaster Wasteland*, THE ATLANTIC (Apr. 2011) (www.theatlantic.com/magazine/archive/2011/04/a-vaster-wasteland/308418/).

189. streamlined or eliminated many of these requirements. *Deregulation of Radio*, 84 FCC 2d 968 (1981), *aff'd. in part and remanded in part, Office of Communication of the United Church of Christ v. FCC*, 707 F. 2d 1413 (DC Cir. 1983); *Revision of Programming and Commercialization Policies, Ascertainment Requirements, and Program Requirements for Commercial Television Stations*, 98 FCC 2d 1078 (1984); *Revisions of Programming Policies and Reporting Requirements Related to Public Broadcasting Licensees*, 96 FCC 2d 74 (1984).

189. but that effort to expand content regulation failed. *FCC v. WNCN Listeners Guild*, 450 US 582 (1981).

189. perhaps it was time to auction off broadcast frequencies. Minow, *A Vaster Wasteland, supra*.

189. triggered heightened review of license renewal applications. Robert Corn-Revere, *Regulation in Newspeak: The FCC's Children's Television Rules*, Feb. 19, 1997 (www.cato.org/publications/policy-analysis/regulation-newspeak-fccs-childrens-television-rules).

189. a "vast array" of new programming offerings. Notice of Proposed Rulemaking, *In the Matter of Children's Television Programming Rules*, FCC 18-93 (Jul. 13, 2018), at 15–16.

189. it was time to eliminate the ineffective and burdensome requirements. Commissioner Michael O'Rielly, *It's Time to Reexamine the FCC's Kid Vid Requirements*, Jan. 26, 2018 (www.fcc.gov/news-events/blog/2018/01/26/its-time-reexamine-fccs-kid-vid-requirements).

190. that many have called the "new Golden Age of television." Ian Leslie, *Watch It While It Lasts: Our Golden Age of Television*, FINANCIAL TIMES, Apr. 13, 2017 (www.ft.com/content/68309b3a-1f02-11e7-a454-ab04428977f9); *TV's Golden Age Is Real*, THE ECONOMIST, Nov. 24, 2018 (www.economist.com/graphic-detail/2018/11/24/tvs-golden-age-is-real); Martin Shuster, *The New Golden Age of Television*, AEON, Jun. 17, 2018 (https://theweek.com/articles/776675/new-golden-age-television).

190. undermined creativity on television with a "disastrous" speech. Cantor, *supra*, at 171; Sherwood Schwartz, INSIDE GILLIGAN'S ISLAND xv–xvi, 5, 269 (New York: St. Martin's, 1994).

191. "The S. S. *Minnow* has made me immortal." Minow, *A Vaster Wasteland, supra*.; Robert M. Jarvis, *Legal Tales from Gilligan's Island*, 39 SANTA CLARA LAW REV. 185, 204 n. 113 (1998).

191. overshadowed by his unflattering connection with *Gilligan's Island*." Jarvis, *supra*, at 203–204.

192. and inspired the names of pets and even children. Jarvis, *supra*, at 185 & n. 1, 195–196.

CHAPTER 8

193. for those who refuse to abide by standards of decency." Testimony of L. Brent Bozell, III, *"Can You Say That on TV?": An Examination of the FCC's Enforcement with Respect to Broadcast Indecency*, Hearing Before the Subcommittee on Telecommunications and the Internet of the House Committee on Energy and Commerce, No. 108-67, 108th Cong., 2nd Sess. 26–30 (Jan. 28, 2004) (*"House Indecency Hearings"*).

196. the propaganda arm of the Left: the national news media." *About the MRC* (www.mrc.org/about).

196. downplaying coverage of Clinton White House scandals. Ed Murrieta, *If You Want It Done Right*, WIRED, Jun. 16, 1998 (www.wired.com/1998/06/if-you-want-it-done-right/).

196. as the Right Wing's "Facebook Army." Shane Goldmacher and Tim Alberta, *The Right Wing's Facebook Army*, THE ATLANTIC, Dec. 8, 2014. (www.theatlantic.com/politics/archive/2014/12/the-conservative-digital-army/383526/); The ForAmerica Mission (https://foramerica.org/about/).

196. of social conservatives and religious believers in the media." *About the MRC* (www.mrc.org/about).

196. the civil rights of all Catholics." *Our Mission* (www.catholicleague.org/our-mission/).

196. the moral authority of churches … to promote their secular leftist agenda." *Defund NPR*, May 26, 2018 tweet (http://twitter.com/BrentBozell/status/1000520178327793664).

196. "an inadequate substitute for Christian politics." Linda Bridges and John R. Coyne, Jr., STRICTLY RIGHT: WILLIAM F. BUCKLEY JR. AND THE AMERICAN CONSERVATIVE MOVEMENT 122–123 (New York: John Wiley & Sons, 2007).

197. members of their constituencies." Parents Television Council, *Frequently Asked Questions* (https://w2.parentstv.org/main/About/FAQ.aspx).

197. "major part of the … battle to keep the airwaves free of offensive content." Parents Television Council, 2006 ANNUAL REPORT, at 15.

197. seeking to vastly expand what is considered illegal programming. Parents Television Council, *Frequently Asked Questions* (https://w2. parentstv.org/main/About/FAQ.aspx).

197. resulting in the stations being abruptly put out of business." Parents Television Council, 2006 ANNUAL REPORT, at 16.

198. "the very reverse of censorship." Newton Minow, EQUAL TIME 94 (New York: Atheneum, 1964).

198. with no responsibility to the public interest." Parents Television Council, *Frequently Asked Questions* (https://w2.parentstv.org/main/About/FAQ.aspx).

198. "[i]ndecencies and obscenities are now *everywhere* on broadcast TV." *House Indecency Hearings, supra,* at 26.

198. first enacted as Section 29 of the Radio Act of 1927, Radio Act of 1927, § 29, 44 Stat. 1172–1173.

198. the Communications Act of 1934. Communications Act of 1934, §§ 312, 326, 501, 48 Stat. 1086, 1091 and 1100.

198. imprisoned not more than two years, or both." 18 USC § 1464, 62 Stat. 769, 866.

198. or clear indication of congressional intent. *See, e.g.,* 67 CONG. REC. 12615 (1926) (remarks of Sen. Dill); *id.* at 5480 (remarks of Rep. White); 68 CONG. REC. 2567 (1927) (remarks of Rep. Scott); Hearings on S. 1 and S. 1754 before the Senate Committee on Interstate Commerce, 69th Cong., 1st Sess. 121 (1926); Hearings on H. R. 5589 before the House Committee on the Merchant Marine and Fisheries, 69th Cong., 1st Sess. 26, 40 (1926). *See also* Hearings on H. R. 8825 before the House Committee on the Merchant Marine and Fisheries, 70th Cong., 1st Sess. (1928).

198. members of Congress who spoke" about the provision. *See United States* v. *Simpson*, 561 F. 2d 53, 57 (7th Cir. 1977) (citing legislative history of Radio Act of 1927).

198. "obscene," "indecent," and "profane" were treated as essentially synonymous. *E.g., Swearingen* v. *United States*, 161 US 446, 450–451 (1896); Edythe Wise, *A Historical Perspective on the Protection of Children from Broadcast Indecency*, 3 VILL. SPORTS & ENT. LAW J. 15, 18 (1996).

198. the First Amendment limits the scope of obscenity law. *Roth* v. *United States*, 354 US 476 (1957).

198. "to call down the curse of God upon certain individuals." *Duncan* v. *United States*, 48 F. 2d 128, 134 (9th Cir.), *cert. denied,* 283 US 863 (1931). *See generally* Zechariah Chafee Jr., FREE SPEECH IN THE UNITED STATES 149–152 (2nd ed. 1941).

199. foul obscenity, smutty suggestiveness, and horrible blasphemy." Lindsey Hobbs, *The Mae West Incident: Radio Censorship in the 1930s, The Ultimate History Project* (http://ultimatehistoryproject/mae-west-incident.html); A. Brad Schwartz, BROADCAST HYSTERIA: ORSON WELLES'S WAR OF THE WORLDS AND THE ART OF FAKE NEWS 136–138 (New York: Hill & Wang, 2015).

199. West's inflections were too bawdy and suggestive. Harrison B. Summers, FEDERAL LAWS, REGULATIONS, AND DECISIONS AFFECTING THE PROGRAMMING AND OPERATING POLICIES OF AMERICAN BROADCASTING STATIONS, p. C-10 (Ohio State University, Feb. 1962) (citing contemporary accounts in *Broadcasting Magazine*, Dec. 20, 1937 and Jan. 25, 1938). *See* Heins, *supra*, at 91.

199. "in the next few months they aired nothing else that was offensive." Schwartz, *supra*, at 137.

199. "the duty of the Commission to do something about it." Schwartz, *supra*, at 138.

199. kept Mae West off radio for fourteen years. Hobbs, *supra*; Schwartz, *supra*, at 138.

200. "coarse, vulgar, suggestive, double-meaning programming" and "smut." *Palmetto Broadcasting Co. (WDKD), Kingstree, S. C.*, 33 FCC 250, 256–259, 265–280 (1962), *aff'd on other grounds, Robinson v. FCC*, 334 F. 2d 534 (DC Cir. 1964). *See Heins, supra*, at 92–93; L. A. Powe, AMERICAN BROADCASTING AND THE FIRST AMENDMENT 167–169 (University of California Press, 1987).

200. "in order to set an example to the industry." *Palmetto Broadcasting Co. (WDKD)*, 33 FCC at 258.

201. "as adjectives, or simply as an introductory expletive." *Eastern Educational Radio (WUHY-FM)*, 24 FCC 2d 408, 414 (1970). *See Powe, supra*, at 174–176.

201. and utterly without redeeming social value. *Eastern Educational Radio*, 24 FCC 2d at 412.

201. a single complaint about the broadcast in question." *Eastern Educational Radio*, 24 FCC 2d at 420 (Statement of Commissioner Kenneth A. Cox, concurring in part and dissenting in part).

201. the programming of innovative and experimental stations." *Eastern Educational Radio*, 24 FCC 2d at 422–423 (Statement of Commissioner Nicholas Johnson, dissenting).

202. the fact is that the public concept of decency has changed." *People on Complaint of Sumner v. Miller*, 155 Misc. 446, 446–448 (City Magistrate's Court of New York, 1935).

202. "tasteless and vulgar program content, whether explicit or by sexually-oriented innuendo." *Illinois Citizens Comm. for Broad. v. FCC*, 515 F. 2d 397, 408 (DC Cir. 1974) (Statement of Chief Judge Bazelon on why he voted to grant rehearing *en banc*, quoting NAB resolution).

202. "It is my hope and the purpose of this statement to make further government action moot." *Illinois Citizens Comm. for Broad. v. FCC*, 515 F. 2d 397, 408 (DC Cir. 1974) (Statement of Chief Judge Bazelon quoting speech by FCC Chairman Dean Burch).

202. the Commission concluded that the racy talk about sex and use of double entendre was obscene. *Sonderling Broad., Corp.*, 41 FCC 2d 777 (1973).

203. unofficial expression of the views of one member of the Commission." *Illinois Citizens Comm. for Broad.*, 515 F. 2d at 402, 405–406.

203. he lacked the support of the rest of his court to review the matter *en banc. Illinois Citizens Comm. for Broad.*, 515 F. 2d at 408 (Statement of Chief Judge Bazelon).

203. total ignorance of the constitutional definition of obscenity." *Illinois Citizens Comm. for Broad.*, 515 F. 2d at 418–425 (Statement of Chief Judge Bazelon).

204. has never been authoritatively construed by the Courts." *A Citizen's Complaint Against Pacifica Found. Station WBAI(FM), New York, N.Y.*, 56 FCC 2d 94, 97 (1975) ("*FCC Pacifica Order*").

205. but none of those details mattered. Powe, *supra*, at 186.

205. "to clarify the applicable standards." *FCC Pacifica Order*, 56 FCC 2d at 99.

205. a reasonable risk that children may be in the audience." *FCC Pacifica Order*, 56 FCC 2d at 9798.

205. whose minds are open to such immoral influences." *Regina v. Hicklin*, LR 3 QB 360 (Queen's Bench 1868).

206. no opportunity for journalistic editing." *Petition for Reconsideration of a Citizen's Complaint Against Pacifica Foundation Station WBAI (FM), New York, N.Y.*, 59 FCC 2d 892, 893 n. 1 (1976) ("*Pacifica Reconsideration Order*").

206. from governmental interference in matters of taste." *Pacifica Found. v. FCC*, 556 F. 2d 9, 18 (DC Cir. 1977), *rev'd*, 438 US 726 (1978).

206. with the words repeated over and over [and] deliberately broadcast." Brief for the Federal Communications Commission, *FCC v. Pacifica Found.*, No. 77-528 (Mar. 3, 1978), 1978 WL 206838 at 25–26 (citation omitted).

206. in a "specific factual context." *FCC v. Pacifica Foundation*, 438 US 726, 742 (1978).

206. and not the broad sweep of the Commission's opinion." *Pacifica Foundation*, 438 US at 755–756 (Powell, J., concurring).

207. without restricting the expression at its source." *Pacifica Foundation*, 438 US at 748–749.

207. "George Carlin, Constitutional Law Scholar." Christine A. Corcos, *George Carlin, Constitutional Law Scholar*, 37 STETSON LAW REV. 899 (2008).

208. likely to occur again as Halley's Comet." Charles D. Ferris, Chairman, FCC, Address to New England Broadcasters Assoc. (Jul. 21, 1978).

208. and action indicating some sexually-oriented content in the program." *WGBH Educ. Found.*, 69 FCC 2d 1250, 1251–1252 (1978).

208. what is or is not 'good' programming." *WGBH Educ. Found.*, 69 FCC 2d at 1254.

208. given the position it had taken before the Court. *Pacifica*, 438 US at 772 (Brennan J., dissenting).

209. to recommend which complaints would be most likely to succeed. John Crigler and William J. Byrnes, *Decency Redux: The Curious History of the New FCC Broadcast Indecency Policy*, 38 CATH. U. LAW REV 329, 344–347 (1989);
  Robert Corn-Revere, *New Age Comstockery*, 4 COMMLAW CONSPECTUS 173, 182 (1996).

209. "a broader range of material than the seven specific words at issue in *Pacifica*." *Pacifica Radio*, 2 FCC Rcd. 2698, 2699 (1987), *aff'd on recon.*, *Infinity Broad. Corp. of Pa.*, 3 FCC Rcd. 930 (1987), *aff'd in part, rev'd in part, Action for Children's Television v. FCC*, 852 F. 2d 1332 (DC Cir. 1988) ("*ACT I*"). *See Regents of the Univ. of Cal.*, 2 FCC Rcd. 2703 (1987) (same subsequent history); *Infinity Broad. of Pa.*, 2 FCC Rcd. 2705 (1987) (same subsequent history). *See also New Indecency Enforcement Standards to Be Applied to all Broadcast and Amateur Radio Licensees*, 2 FCC Rcd. 2726 (1987).

209. that may be considered indecent. *Pacifica Radio*, 2 FCC Rcd. at 2699. *See Infinity Broad. of Pa.*, 3 FCC Rcd. at 930.

209. the high value our Constitution places on what the people say and hear." *ACT I*, 852 F. 2d at 133839, 1340 n. 14, 1344.

210. a reasonable safe harbor rule." *ACT I*, 852 F. 2d at 1343 n.18.

210. Congress could not constitutionally repeal the safe harbor. *Action for Children's Television v. FCC*, 932 F. 2d 1504, 1509–1510 (DC Cir. 1991) ("*ACT II*").

210. that allowed indecent broadcasts between 10 p.m. and 6 a.m. *Action for Children's Television v. FCC*, 58 F. 3d 654 (DC Cir. 1995) (*en banc*) ("*ACT III*").

210. letter rulings that are stored in individual complaint files at the FCC. Letter from Chairman Michael K. Powell to Hon. John D. Dingell, Mar. 2, 2004.

210. Chaucer, Hemingway, and James Joyce. *Pacifica Found.* v. *FCC*, 556 F. 2d at 18.

210. could not be prohibited under Comstock-era obscenity law. *United States* v. *One Book Entitled Ulysses*, 72 F. 2d 705 (2nd Cir. 1934).

211. in the dark about how the standards apply to particular cases. Letter from FCC Mass Media Bureau Chief James McKinney, to Counsel for Pacifica Radio (Jun. 5, 1987); *William J. Byrnes, Esq.*, 63 Rad. Reg. 2d 216 (Mass Media Bur. 1987); *Memorandum Opinion and Order, Pacifica Found.*, FCC No. 87-215 (FCC, released, Jun. 16, 1987). See Crigler and Byrnes, *supra*, at 339–340.

211. "seven of the best hours I have ever seen on a television set." Quoted in Stephen Farber, *They Watch What We Watch*, NEW YORK TIMES, May 7, 1989.

211. and reclaims TV as a creative medium." Marvin Kitman, *The Best Unwatched Show Ever*, NEWSDAY, Jan. 21, 1988, at 15; Marvin Kitman, *Riding Potter's Express*, NEWSDAY, Feb. 17, 1989.

211. as challenging and compelling as the very best of film and theatre." Vincent Canby, *Is the Year's Best Film on TV?* NEW YORK TIMES, Jul. 10, 1988; John J. O'Connor, *TV View*, NEW YORK TIMES, Dec. 25, 1988.

211. solely on the few moments of video that accompanied the complaint. Corn-Revere, *New Age Comstockery*, *supra*, at 181–182; Heins, *supra*, at 119.

212. that might consider presenting groundbreaking programming. Corn-Revere, *New Age Comstockery*, *supra*, at 181–182; Heins, *supra*, at 119.

212. but it provided little help. *Industry Guidance on the Commission's Case Law Interpreting 18 U.S. C. § 1464 and Enforcement Policies Regarding Broadcast Indecency*, 16 FCC Rcd. 7999, 8008–8009 (2001).

212. material is not *per se* indecent if the material has merit." *The KBOO Found.*, 16 FCC Rcd. 10731, 10733 (Enf. Bur. 2001).

212. a willingness to pursue the matter in court, the Commission reconsidered its position. *Jones* v. *FCC*, 2002 WL 2018521 (S.D.N.Y. 2002).

212. the sexual descriptions in the song are not sufficiently graphic to warrant sanction." *KBOO Found.*, 18 FCC Rcd. 2472, 2474 (Enf. Bur. 2003).

213. even the edited version "contains unmistakable offensive sexual references." *Citadel Broad. Company*, 16 FCC Rcd. 11,839 (Enf. Bur. 2001).

213. sufficiently explicit or graphic enough to be found patently offensive." *Citadel Broad. Co.*, 17 FCC Rcd. 483 (Enf. Bur. 2002).

214. mounted a campaign directed at the FCC. Michael Learmonth, *Parents Television Council Sees New Era*, VARIETY, Mar. 17, 2007 (https://variety.com/2007/tv/news/par ents-television-council-sees-new-era-1117961334/).

214. flooding the agency with 18,000 complaints. Parents Television Council, *Indecency Timeline* (http://w2parentstv.org/Main/Research/IndecencyTimeline.aspx).

214. the "first-ever web-driven complaint form." 2006 PTC ANNUAL REPORT, *supra*, at 17; 2004 PTC ANNUAL REPORT, *supra*, at 12 (www.parentstv.org/ptc/joinus/AR2004.pdf).

214. "the 'go-to' spot for online activism against television violence, sex, and profanity." 2006 PTC ANNUAL REPORT, *supra*, at 17; 2004 PTC ANNUAL REPORT, *supra*, at 12 (www .parentstv.org/ptc/joinus/AR2004.pdf).

214. programming it deemed to be "indecent" and/or "profane." 2006 PTC ANNUAL REPORT, *supra*, at 17.

214. information and action calls can be sent nationwide." 2006 PTC ANNUAL REPORT, *supra*, at 17.

214. custom-built computer database, ETS (Entertainment Tracking System)." Parents Television Council E-Alert for Feb. 10, 2005: PTC's Latest Victories. See Lynn Smith, *For "Indecency" Watchdogs, Work Is a Day Full of TV; The Parents Television Council*

Monitors Shows and Uses Its Data to Put Pressure on the FCC, LA TIMES, May 10, 2004, at A1; Doug Halonen, *PTC E-mails Generate Results*, TELEVISION WEEK, Oct. 18, 2004, at 51; Chris Baker, *TV Complaints to FCC Soar as Parents Lead the Way*, WASHINGTON TIMES, May 24, 2004.

214. ranging from 'Ass' to 'Whore.'" Todd Shields, *PTC: On the Offensive*, MEDIAWEEK, Feb. 14, 2005.

215. the numbers jumped to 13,922 in 2002, 202,032 in 2003, and 1,068,802 in 2004. *See* www.fcc.gov/eb/broadcast/ichart.pdf.

215. counted five, six, or even seven times. Adam Thierer, *Examining the FCC's Complaint-Driven Broadcast Indecency Enforcement Process* (Nov. 2005), at 7–8 (www.pff.org/issues-pubs/pops/pop12.22indecencyenforcement.pdf).

215. deep in the footnotes in one of the Commission's periodic reports. News Release, *Quarterly Report on Informal Consumer Inquiries and Complaints Released* (Jun. 10, 2004). *See* Kurt Hunt, *The FCC Complaint Process and "Increasing Public Unease": Toward an Apolitical Broadcast Indecency Regime*, 14 MICH. TELECOMM. TECH. LAW REV. 223, 232–233 (2007).

215. the reported percentage was even higher – 99.9 percent. Adam Thierer, *Why Regulate Broadcasting? Toward a Consistent First Amendment Standard for the Information Age*, 15 COMMLAW CONSPECTUS 431, 460 (2007); *Fight the Tyranny of the Minority*, BROADCASTING & CABLE, Dec. 20, 2004, at 28; Todd Shields, *Activists Dominate Content Complaints*, MEDIAWEEK.COM, Dec. 6, 2004; Jake Tapper, *Is Popular Will Behind FCC Crackdowns*, ABC NEWS.COM, Dec. 4, 2004; Sarah McBride, *One Man's Campaign to Rid Radio of Smut Is Finally Paying Off*, WALL STREET JOURNAL, May 13, 2004, at A1.

215. "Whoever gave that number at the FCC was a liar." Clay Calvert and Robert D. Richards, *The Parents Television Council Uncensored: An Inside Look at the Watchdog of the Public Airwaves and the War on Indecency with Its President, Tim Winter*, 33 HASTINGS COMM. & ENT. LAW J. 293, 328 (2011).

216. "orchestrated fewer complaint campaigns this year than in previous years." Thierer, *Why Regulate Broadcasting?*, *supra*, at 459–460.

216. the average monthly total in 2007 was just over 500 complaints. FCC, *Quarterly Reports on Informal Consumer Inquiries and Complaints – 1st and 3rd Quarters 2007* (Jul. 1, 2008).

217. 99.4 percent of the complaints the Commission had received for the year to that point. Adam Thierer, *More Inflated FCC Indecency Complaints*, Sept. 9, 2009 (http://techliberation.com/2009/09/09/more-inflated-fcc-indecency-complaints).

217. including such shows as *C.S.I.: Crime Scene Investigation, Friends*, and *Will & Grace*. Scott Collins, *Television & Radio; Crime Pays for Week's Leader, CBS*, LA TIMES, Oct. 13, 2004, at 12.

218. and FCC officials from acting as though it were real. Adam Thierer, *Why Regulate Broadcasting? Supra*, at 460; *Fight the Tyranny of the Minority*, BROADCASTING & CABLE, Dec. 20, 2004, at 28; Todd Shields, *Activists Dominate Content Complaints*, MEDIAWEEK. COM, Dec. 6, 2004; Jake Tapper, *Is Popular Will Behind FCC Crackdowns*, ABC NEWS. COM, Dec. 4, 2004; Sarah McBride, *One Man's Campaign to Rid Radio of Smut Is Finally Paying Off*, WALL STREET JOURNAL, May 13, 2004, at A1.

218. "direct response to the increase of public complaints." Remarks of Michael K. Powell, Chairman, Federal Communications Commission, at the National Association of Broadcasters Convention, Apr. 20, 2004, Las Vegas, Nevada, at 1, 3, 13–14; Hunt, *supra*, at 229–230.

218. "Americans have become more concerned about the content of television programming." Hunt, *supra*, at 230.

218. and taken a series of "steps to sharpen our enforcement blade." Testimony of Michael K. Powell, Chairman, Federal Communications Commission, Before the United States Senate, Committee on Commerce, Science and Transportation, at 3–4 (Feb. 11, 2004) (www.commerce.senate.gov/pdf/powell021104.pdf).

219. almost four times the total of all proposed fines in the previous ten years combined. *See* www.fcc.gov/eb/broadcast/ichart.pdf (as of Jan. 3, 2005); Thierer, *Why Regulate Broadcasting?*, *supra*, at 463. In 2004 the FCC issued the following Notices of Apparent Liability: *Entercom Kansas City Licensee, LLC*, FCC 04-231 (Dec. 22, 2004) ($220,000 NAL); *WQAM License Ltd. P'ship*, 19 FCC Rcd. 22997 (2004) ($55,000 NAL); *Complaints Against Various Licensees Regarding Their Broadcast of the Fox Network Program "Married by America" on April 7, 2003*, 19 FCC Rcd. 20191 (2004) ($1,183,000 NAL); *Complaints Against Various Television Licensees Concerning Their February 1, 2004, Broadcast of the Super Bowl XXXVIII Halftime Show*, 19 FCC Rcd. 19230 (2004); *Entercom Sacramento*, 19 FCC Rcd. 20129 ($55,000 NAL); *AMFM Radio Licenses, L. L. C.*, 19 FCC Rcd. 10751 ($27,500 NAL), *concurrently rescinded*, 19 FCC Rcd. 10775 (2004); *Clear Channel Broad. Licenses, Inc.*, 19 FCC Rcd. 6773 (2004) ($495,000 NAL); *Infinity Broad. Operations, Inc.*, 19 FCC Rcd. 5032 ($27,5000 NAL); *AMFM Radio Licenses, Inc.*, 19 FCC Rcd. 5005 (2004) ($247,500 NAL); *Capstar TX Ltd. P'ship*, 19 FCC Rcd. 4960 (2004) ($55,000 NAL); *Clear Channel Broad. Licenses, Inc.*, 19 FCC Rcd. 1768 ($755,000 NAL); *Young Broad. of San Francisco*, 19 FCC Rcd. 1751 ($27,500 NAL); *AMFM Radio Licenses, LLC*, 19 FCC Rcd. 5005 (2004) ($247,500 NAL). In addition to these enforcement actions, the FCC entered settlements that resulted in payments totaling $5.5 million to the United States Treasury. *See Viacom, Inc.*, 19 FCC Rcd. 23100 (2004) ($3.5 million); *Emmis Communications Corp.*, 19 FCC Rcd. 16003 (1999) ($300,000); *Clear Channel Communications, Inc.*, 19 FCC Rcd. 10,880 (2004) ($1.75 million).

219. thus eliminating the policy immunizing "fleeting expletives" from penalties. *Complaints Against Various Broadcast Licensees Regarding Their Airing of the "Golden Globe Awards" Program*, 19 FCC Rcd. 4975 (2004).

219. boosted the level of fines tenfold. Broadcast Decency Enforcement Act of 2005, Pub. L. 109–235, 120 Stat. 491 (Jun. 15, 2006), *codified at* 47 USC 503(b)(2)(C)(ii).i.

219. of $550,000 for twenty-three CBS-owned stations. *Complaints Against Various Television Licensees Concerning Their February 1, 2004, Broadcast of the Super Bowl XXXVIII Halftime Show*, 19 FCC Rcd. 19230 (2004).

219. to impose a fine in February 2006. *Complaints Against Various Television Licensees Concerning Their February 1, 2004, Broadcast of the Super Bowl XXXVIII Halftime Show*, 21 FCC Rcd. 6653 (2006).

219. for a Fox reality show called *Married by America. Complaints Against Various Licensees Regarding Their Broadcast of the Fox Network Program "Married by America" on April 7, 2003*, 19 FCC Rcd. 20191 (2004) ($1,183,000 NAL).

219. and dismissed various other complaints. *Complaints Regarding Various Television Broadcasts Between February 2, 2002 and March 8, 2005*, Notices of Apparent Liability and Memorandum Opinion & Order, 21 FCC Rcd. 2664 (2006) ("*Omnibus Order*").

220. stations that broadcast an episode of the prime time program *Without a Trace. Complaints Against Various Television Licensees Concerning Their December 31, 2004 Broadcast of the Program "Without A Trace,"* 21 FCC Rcd. 2732, 2735 (2006).

220. could reasonably be said to require." *Without a Trace NAL*, 21 FCC Rcd. at 2736.

220. without at least briefly describing those activities." *Omnibus Order*, 21 FCC Rcd. at 2705–2706.

221. PTC had sent out an "E-Alert" to drum up complaints. PTC E-Alert, *CBS Reruns Teen Orgy Scene* (Jan. 12, 2005); PTC Press Release, *PTC Chastises CBS/Viacom for Re-Airing Show Featuring Teen Orgy Party* (Jan. 13, 2005).

221. "protest will be multiplied many, many times over!" PTC E-Alert, *CBS Reruns Teen Orgy Scene* (Jan. 12, 2005).

221. before Congress jacked up the indecency fines. *In re Complaints Against Various Television Licensees Concerning Their February 25, 2003 Broadcast of the Program "NYPD Blue,"* 23 FCC Rcd. 3147 (2008).

222. dropped all live news coverage that was not directly related to public safety. *Fox Television Stations, Inc. v. FCC*, 613, F. 3d 317, 335 (2nd Cir. 2010), *aff'd on other grounds*, 567 US 239 (2012).

222. the FCC demanded that NBC submit tapes of its Olympic coverage. Lisa de Moraes, *FCC Wary of Greeks Bearing Gifts at Games*, WASHINGTON POST, Dec. 11, 2004, at C1; Complaints in re EB-04-IH-0570, available at fcc.gov.

222. the FCC seriously considered even such obviously frivolous complaints. Dominic Timms, *Fearful U.S. TV Networks Censor More Shows*, THE GUARDIAN, Jan. 18, 2005.

222. and that the FCC "consider license revocation." PTC Press Release Regarding Dale Earnhardt, Oct. 18, 2004.

222. "because the Federal Communications Commission would be watching and listening." PTC Press Release regarding Dale Earnhardt, Oct. 18, 2004; Viv Bernstein, *Earnhardt Fined for Checkered Language*, NEW YORK TIMES, Oct. 6, 2004, at D2; Ed Hinton, *Curses! Earnhardt Loses Cup Lead; NASCAR Docks Him 25 Points for Expletive on TV*, CHICAGO TRIBUNE, at C1.

222. We really don't want to go there anymore." Diane Toroian Keaggy, *Radio's "Shock" Therapy*, ST. LOUIS POST-DISPATCH, Apr. 11, 2004 (quoting John Kijowski, general manager of WVRV-FM and WSSM-FM); David Hinckley, *DJ Fired for Race Remark*, NEW YORK DAILY NEWS, Mar. 23, 2004; Josh Margolin, *Jersey Radio Stations Clear the Air as Feds Crack Down*, NEWARK STAR-LEDGER, Jun. 27, 2004; Charles Pierce, *Hot Button Issue*, BOSTON GLOBE, Jul. 18, 2004, at 9; Jennifer Davies, *Fine-Wary Broadcasters Toe a Shifting Line; FCC Crackdown on Indecency Is Making Some Gun-Shy*, SAN DIEGO UNION-TRIBUNE, May 29, 2004, at A1; Jacques Steinberg, *Eye on FCC, TV and Radio Watch Words*, NEW YORK TIMES, May 10, 2004, at A1; Matthew Daneman, *WHUR Drops Its Live Radio Programs*, ROCHESTER DEMOCRAT AND CHRONICLE, May 27, 2004, at B1.

223. the deleted words are essential components of the subject's poetry. Press Release, PBS Edits "Offensive" Content from Independently-Produced Documentary *Every Child Is Born a Poet: The Life and Work of Piri Thomas* in Order to Comply with New FCC Indecency Rules, Apr. 6, 2004.

223. even though an effort to declare it obscene had failed in 1957. Patricia Cohen, *"Howl" in an Era That Fears Indecency*, NEW YORK TIMES, Oct. 4, 2007, at E3.

223. "fuck" or "fucking" ten times in thirty seconds. *Letter to Peter Branton*, 6 FCC Rcd. 610 (1991), *petition for rev. dismissed*, 993 F. 2d 906 (DC Cir. 1993).

223. because it occurred "during a morning news interview." *Omnibus Order*, 21 FCC Rcd. at 2699.

223. would "defer to CBS's plausible characterization of its own programming" as news. *Complaints Regarding Various Television Broadcasts between February 2, 2002 and March 8, 2005*, 21 FCC Rcd. 13299, 13327–13328 (2006) ("*Omnibus Remand Order*").

223. *there is no outright news exemption from our indecency rules." Omnibus Remand Order*, 21 FCC Rcd. at 13327 (emphasis added).

223. after the FCC adopted its more restrictive indecency policy. Jeremy Pelofsky, *Profanity Concerns Prompt CBS to Show "9/11" on Web*, REUTERS (Sept. 9, 2006); John Eggerton, *Pappas Won't Air CBS' 9–11 Doc*, BROADCASTING & CABLE (Sept. 7, 2006); John Eggerton, *Sinclair to Delay 9/11 Doc*, BROADCASTING & CABLE (Sept. 1, 2006).

224. was altered because a soldier's shouts included expletives. Dinesh Kumar, *FCC Indecency Guidelines Clear for Some Public TV Stations*, COMMUNICATIONS DAILY, Mar. 2, 2005, at 9–11.

224. and others by using a banner as a cover. Lisa de Moraes, *Some Local Stations Cautious in Gauguin Painting Coverage*, WASHINGTON POST, Apr. 5, 2011, at C1.

225. depict or describe sexual or excretory organs or activities." Letter from Charles W. Kelley, Chief, Investigations and Hearings Division, Enforcement Bureau to Tim Wildmon, Vice President, American Family Association, File No. EB-02-IH-0085/RP, Jun. 7, 2002.

225. one scene depicted frontal nudity. *WPBN/WTOM License Subsidiary, Inc.*, 15 FCC Rcd. 1838 (2000).

225. or in other cases a country/western music special. Frank Rich, *Bono's New Casualty: "Private Ryan,"* NEW YORK TIMES, Nov. 21, 2004; Lisa de Moraes, *"Saving Private Ryan": A New Casualty of the Indecency War*, WASHINGTON POST, Nov. 11, 2004; *ABC Affiliates Pulling "Private Ryan,"* CNN MONEY, Nov. 11, 2004 (http://money.cnn.com/2004/11/11/news/ fortune500/savingpvt_ryan/).

225. claiming (as it had years earlier for ULYSSES) that to do so would constitute a prior restraint. John Eggerton, *Dissing Private Ryan*, BROADCASTING & CABLE, Nov. 12, 2004.

225. "hard on," and "hell." *Complaints Against Various Television Licensees Regarding Their Broadcast on November 11, 2004, of the ABC Television Network's Presentation of the Film "Saving Private Ryan,"* 20 FCC Rcd. 4507, 4510 (2005).

226. and concluded it was not. *Saving Private Ryan*, 20 FCC Rcd. at ¶ 14.

226. was preceded by TV ratings and viewer advisories. *Saving Private Ryan*, 20 FCC Rcd. at ¶¶ 2 & n. 3, 11, 14–16.

226. several weeks before it released the order. *FCC to Deny Private Ryan Indecent – Source*, REUTERS, Jan. 24, 2005; Jeremy Pelofsky, *FCC Chief Urges Denying "Private Ryan" Complaints*, REUTERS, Dec. 13, 2004.

227. in violation of the Administrative Procedure Act. *Fox Television Stations, Inc. v. FCC*, 489 F. 3d 444 (2nd Cir. 2007), *rev'd*, 556 US 502 (2009); *CBS Corp. v. FCC*, 535 F. 3d 167 (3rd Cir. 2008), *cert. granted, vacated, and remanded*, 556 US 1218 (2009).

227. but sent the matter back to the agency to give another try. *Fox Television Stations, Inc.*, 489 F. 3d at 462.

227. "will be decided soon enough, perhaps in this very case." *Fox Television Stations*, 556 US at 517, 527, 529.

227. the Commission appears to be entirely unaware of this fact." *Fox Television Stations*, 556 US at 544 (Justice Stevens, dissenting).

227. the long shadow the First Amendment casts over what the Commission has done." *Fox Television Stations*, 556 US at 545 (Justice Ginsburg, dissenting).

227. a "deep intrusion into the First Amendment rights of broadcasters." *Fox Television Stations*, 556 US at 531–535 (Justice Thomas, concurring).

228. reserving judgment on whether the FCC's action was constitutional. *Fox Television Stations*, 556 US at 538–539 (Justice Kennedy, concurring).

228. the board "fucked up my house." *Fox Television Stations, Inc. Oral Argument,* C-Span (Jan. 13, 2010) (www.c-span.org/video/?291305-1/fox-television-v-fcc).

228. whether the FCC will consider a particular broadcast [acceptable]." *Fox Television Stations, Inc.,* 613 F. 3d at 332.

228. which largely profiled an outsider genre of musical experience." *Fox Television Stations, Inc.,* 613 F. 3d at 333.

229. that the word 'bullshitter' was uttered during a news program." *Fox Television Stations, Inc.,* 613 F. 3d at 332.

229. but this surely was not it. *Fox Television Stations, Inc.,* 613 F. 3d at 335.

229. that took place *before* the change in policy in *Golden Globes. CBS Corp.* v. *FCC,* 663 F.3d 122 (3rd Cir. 2011), *cert. denied,* 567 US 953 (2012).

229. voiding the FCC policy as being unconstitutionally vague. *ABC, Inc.* v. *FCC,* 404 Fed. Appx. 530 (2nd Cir. 2011).

229. any modified policy in light of its content and application." *FCC* v. *Fox Television Stations, Inc.,* 567 US 239, 259 (2012).

230. the FCC had to write a $550,000 refund check to CBS. *CBS Corp.* v. *FCC,* 567 US 953 (2012).

230. most did not even come from the viewing areas of the stations named. Jeff Jarvis, *The Shocking Truth about the FCC: Censorship by the Tyranny of the Few,* Buzzmachine, Nov. 15, 2004 (https://buzzmachine.com/2004/11/15/).

230. the FCC lowered the fine to $91,000 (to be collected from 13 stations). David Oxenford, *A Tale of Two Indecency Decisions – FCC Issues Fines for Married by America and NYPD Blue,* Broadcast Law Blog, Feb. 23, 2008 (www.broadcastlawblog.com/2008/02/articles/a-tale-of-two-indecency-decisions-fcc-issues-fines-for-married-by-america-and-nypd-blue/).

230. to focus only on what he called "egregious indecency violations." John Eggerton, *DOJ, FCC Drop Pursuit of Fox "Married by America" Indecency Fine,* Broadcasting & Cable, Sept. 21, 2012.

230. otherwise deficient, or "foreclosed by settled precedent." Public Notice, *FCC Reduces Backlog of Broadcast Indecency Complaints by 70% (More Than One Million Complaints); Seeks Comment on Adopting Egregious Cases Policy Pleading Cycle Established,* 28 FCC Rcd 4082 (2013) ("*2013 Public Notice*").

230. plummeted back to normal levels of about 2,000 per year. Cynthia Chris, The Indecent Screen 76 (New Brunswick: Rutgers University Press, 2018); *FCC Consumer Complaint Center* (https://consumercomplaints.fcc.gov/hc/en-us).

230. "to ensure they are fully consistent with vital First Amendment principles." *2013 Public Notice,* 28 FCC Rcd at 4082.

230. still has taken no action to modify or clarify its policy. Clay Calvert, Minch Minchin, Keran Billaud, Kevin Bruckenstein, and Tershone Phillips, *Indecency Four Years After Fox Television Stations: From Big Papi to a Porn Star, an Egregious Mess at the FCC Continues,* 54 Univ. of Richmond Law Rev. 329, 349 (2017).

230. one of those "egregious" cases. *In the Matter of WDBJ Television, Inc.,* 30 FCC Rcd. 3024 (2015).

231. the highest fine the Commission has ever taken for a single indecent broadcast on one station." News Release, *FCC Plans Maximum Fine Against WDBJ for Broadcasting Indecent Programming Material During Evening Newscast* (Mar. 23, 2015) (www.fcc.gov/document/fcc-plans-max-fine-against-wdbj-indecent-material-evening-news-0).

231. there is "no news exemption from the indecency law." *In the Matter of WDBJ Television, Inc.,* 30 FCC Rcd. at 3031.

231. and was inconsistent with FCC precedent. Opposition of WDBJ Television, Inc. to Notice of Apparent Liability, File Nos. EB-IHD-14-00016819, EB-12-IH-1363 (filed Jun. 30, 2015); Calvert et al., 54 UNIV. OF RICHMOND LAW REV. at 359–365.

232. was silent about the WDBJ fine. *Schurz Communications, Inc.*, DA 16-154 (rel. Feb. 12, 2016).

232. ten-year constitutional attack waged by the broadcast industry." Press Release, *PTC Responds to FCC's Proposal to Limit Broadcast Decency Enforcement*, Apr. 1, 2013 (http://w2.parentstv.org/Main/News/Detail.aspx?docID=2771); Calvert et al., 54 UNIV. OF RICHMOND LAW REV., at 349.

232. Why do you want us to intervene?" FCC v. *Fox Television Stations, Inc.*, No. 10-1293, Transcript of oral argument, Jan. 10, 2012, 33–34 (www.supremecourt.gov/oral_argu ments/argument_transcripts/2011/10-1293.pdf).

232. some individual complaints appearing in the record up to 37 times." *CBS Corp.*, 663 F. 3d at 135 n. 13.

232. "to allow folks of different political stripes to listen more intently to what we have to say." Michael Learmonth, *Parent's Television Council Sees New Era*, VARIETY.COM, Mar. 17, 2007 (https://variety.com/2007/tv/news/parents-television-council-sees-new-era-1117961334/).

233. over a million members, with grassroots chapters across the United States. Parents Television Council, 2006 ANNUAL REPORT, at 1, 3–5, 14–15, 24–25.

233. "Tim will do a better job than I in leading the PTC into the future." Parents Television Council, 2006 ANNUAL REPORT, at 1.

233. just over $2.2 million (and expenses of more than $2.3 million). Parents Television Council, 2017 ANNUAL REPORT (http://w2.parentstv.org/Main/WebMedia/PDF/ PTC_Annual_2017.pdf); Parents Television Council, IRS Form 990 (2019) (www.cau seiq.com/organizations/view_990/954819071/46f9fbbb398d7649073b03ad2ef2fbc2).

233. and a program director. PTC Leadership Team (http://w2.parentstv.org/main/About/ leadership.aspx).

233. "is committing journalistic malpractice." Rob Eshman, *Howard Stern and the Parent's Television Council Fallacy*, JEWISH JOURNAL May 15, 2012 (https://jewishjournal.com/ opinion/rob_eshman/104052/).

233. "How Will Org Survive without Founder Bozell?" Michael Learmonth, *Parent's Television Council Sees New Era*, VARIETY.COM, Mar. 17, 2007 (https://variety.com/ 2007/tv/news/parents-television-council-sees-new-era-1117961334/).

233. difficult times for the indecency police." Brooks Barnes, *TV Watchdog Group Is on the Defensive*, NEW YORK TIMES, Oct. 24, 2010 (www.nytimes.com/2010/10/25/business/ media/25watchdog. html).

234. Salazar had committed no crimes. Barnes, *TV Watchdog Group Is on the Defensive, supra*, (www.nytimes.com/2010/10/25/business/media/25watchdog.html).

234. placed membership at 10,000. Eshman, *Howard Stern and the Parent's Television Council Fallacy, supra*, (https://jewishjournal.com/opinion/rob_eshman/104052/).

234. to getting "hate mail from Hitler." PTC, Broadcast Indecency Campaign (http://w2 .parentstv.org/Main/Campaigns/Complaints.aspx); Meg James, *"Family Guy's" Seth MacFarlane was attacked by this conservative TV watchdog. Now they're friends*, LA TIMES, May 30, 2019 (www.latimes.com/business/hollywood/la-fi-ct-col1-seth-macfar lane-parents-television-council-tim-winter-20190530-story.html).

234. but even those have petered out. PTC, *Studies and Reports* (http://w2.parentstv.org/ main/Research/Reports.aspx).

235. a staple of PTC's lobbying and fundraising efforts. Barnes, *TV Watchdog Group Is on the Defensive, supra*, (www.nytimes.com/2010/10/25/business/media/25watchdog.html).

235. references to marital versus nonmarital sex in TV shows. PTC, *Happily Never After* (http://w2.parentstv.org/main/MediaFiles/PDF/Studies/Marriagestudy-PDF-4.pdf).

235. picked up in news stories from Washington to LA. Joe Flint, *PTC Study Shows Almost 70% Jump in Ban Language on Broadcast TV*, LA TIMES, Nov. 9, 2010 (https://latimes blogs.latimes.com/entertainmentnewsbuzz/2010/11/ptc-study-shows-almost-70-jump-in-bad-language-on-broadcast-tv.html); Jennifer Harper, *The FCC Bomb*, WASHINGTON TIMES, Nov. 9, 2010 (www.washingtontimes.com/news/2010/nov/9/inside-the-beltway-255624183/).

235. during the "safe harbor" period for indecency. PTC, *Habitat for Profanity* (http://w2 .parentstv.org/main/MediaFiles/PDF/Studies/2010_HabitatforProfanity.pdf).

235. purports to find 6,000 incidents of violence, over 500 deaths, and almost 2,000 profanities. PTC, *Not for Kids Anymore* (http://w2.parentstv.org/main/MediaFiles/PDF/ Studies/Marriagestudy-PDF-4.pdf).

237. with the 1934 Communications Act through the current policy. PTC, Indecency Timeline (http://w2.parentstv.org/Main/Research/IndecencyTimeline.aspx).

237. "anyone still dissenting from the LGBTQ agenda." L. Brent Bozell III and Tim Graham, *Networks Endorse Taylor Swift's "Equality" Lobbying*, MRC NEWSBUSTERS, Aug. 31, 2019 (www.newsbusters.org/blogs/nb/tim-graham/2019/08/31/bozell-graham-column-net works-endorse-taylor-swifts-equality).

237. "eroding America's moral character on 'gay marriage.'" L. Brent Bozell III, *Censoring the "Anti-Gay" Viewpoint*, CNS NEWS.COM, Jun. 19, 2013 (www.cnsnews.com/blog/l-brent-bozell-iii/censoring-anti-gay-viewpoint); L. Brent Bozell III, *Hollywood's Gay Marriage Thank You Card*, CNS News, May 11, 2012 (www.cnsnews.com/blog/l-brent-bozell-iii/ hollywoods-gay-marriage-thank-you-card).

237. and for airing disrespectful sitcoms during Christian holidays. L. Brent Bozell III and Tim Graham, *An Unholy Week for Hollywood*, CNS NEWS.COM, Mar. 25, 2016 (www .cnsnews.com/commentary/l-brent-bozell-iii/unholy-week-hollywood).

238. the George Carlin monologue in the Court's *Pacifica* decision. *Reno v. ACLU*, 521 US 844, 871, 874 (1997).

238. in New York, New Mexico, Michigan, Arizona, Vermont, Virginia, South Carolina, and Ohio. *American Library Ass'n v. Pataki*, 969 F. Supp. 160 (SDNY 1997); *ACLU v. Johnson*, 194 F. 3d 1149 (10th Cir. 1999); *Cyberspace Communications, Inc. v. Engler*, 238 F. 3d 420 (6th Cir. 2000); *American Booksellers Found. v. Dean*, 342 F. 3d 96 (2nd Cir. 2003); *PSI Net Inc. v. Chapman*, 372 F. 3d 671 (4th Cir. 2004); *ACLU v. Goddard*, No. Civ. 00-505-ACM (D. Ariz. 2004); *Southeast Bookseller's Ass'n. v. McMaster*, 371 F. Supp. 773 (DSC 2005); *American Bookseller's Found. v. Strickland*, 2007 WL 2783678 (S. D. Ohio 2007).

239. PTC recommends that advertisers buy time on MacFarlane's sci-fi show, *The Orville*. Meg James, *'Family Guy's' Seth MacFarlane was attacked by this conservative TV watchdog. Now they're friends*, LA TIMES, May 30, 2019 (www.latimes.com/business/ hollywood/la-fi-ct-col1-seth-macfarlane-parents-television-council-tim-winter-20190530-story.html).

239. demanded that the FCC impose harsh fines on the Fox network for airing the broadcast. Megan Fox, *NFL's Raunchy Halftime Show Featuring Jennifer Lopez's A** Should Result in Harsh Fines for Fox*, PJ MEDIA, Feb. 3, 2020 (https://pjmedia.com/lifestyle/ nfl-gross-out-halftime-show-featuring-jennifer-lopezs-a-should-result-in-harsh-fines-for-fox/).

239. some of which called the halftime show "soft porn." Jimmy Traina, *'This Is Soft Porn!' FCC Gets 1,312 Complaints about J-Lo/Shakira Super Bowl Halftime Show*, SPORTS

ILLUSTRATED, Feb. 26, 2020 (www.si.com/extra-mustard/2020/02/26/jennifer-lopez-sha
kira-super-bowl-live-halftime-show-fcc-complaints); Alaa Elassar, *Over 1,300
Complaints Were Sent to the FCC about Shakira and J-Lo's Super Bowl Halftime
Show*, CNN, Feb. 26, 2020 (www.cnn.com/2020/02/25/us/shakira-jlo-super-bowl-half
time-show-fcc-complaints-trnd/index.html).

239. to NFL Commissioner Roger Goodell. What Did You Think of the Super Bowl
Halftime Show? (PTC email to membership list, Feb. 7, 2020).

CHAPTER 9

240. get information slanted in the opposite direction." Herbert Marcuse, *Repressive
Tolerance*, in A CRITIQUE OF PURE TOLERANCE 95–137 (Robert Paul Wolff, Barrington
Moore, Jr., and Herbert Marcuse, eds., Boston: Beacon Press, 1969).

240. toleration of movements from the Left." Marcuse, *Repressive Tolerance, supra.*

240. an instrument for the continuation of servitude." Marcuse, *Repressive Tolerance, supra.*

241. the liberal creed of free and equal discussion." Marcuse, *Repressive Tolerance, supra.*

241. "Marcuse's revenge." Alan Charles Kors and Harvey A. Silverglate, THE SHADOW
UNIVERSITY: THE BETRAYAL OF LIBERTY ON AMERICA'S CAMPUSES 67–96 (New York:
Harper Collins, 1998).

241. it implicates a right to do physical violence to another." Richard Delgado, Mari Matsuda,
Charles R. Lawrence III, and Kimberlé Williams Crenshaw, WORDS THAT WOUND 7,
14–15 (Boulder, CO: Westview Press, 1993).

241. while doing nothing for their victims." Catherine MacKinnon, ONLY WORDS 12, 109
(Cambridge, MA: Harvard University Press, 1993).

242. because that's the side he has chosen. Stanley Fish, THERE'S NO SUCH THING AS FREE
SPEECH, AND IT'S A GOOD THING, TOO 102–133 (1990) ("THERE'S NO SUCH THING AS FREE
SPEECH").

242. reaffirmed his claim that there is no "free speech principle.") Stanley Fish, THE FIRST: HOW
TO THINK ABOUT HATE SPEECH, CAMPUS SPEECH, RELIGIOUS SPEECH, FAKE NEWS, POST-TRUTH,
AND DONALD TRUMP 31–61 (New York: One Signal Publishers, 2019) ("THE FIRST").

242. "get over it." *Mulvaney Confesses to quid pro quo: Get Over It*, CNN, Oct. 18, 2019 (www
.cnn.com/videos/politics/2019/10/18/mulvaney-trump-get-over-it-quid-pro-quo-sot-crn-
vpx.cnn).

242. "pornography is not an idea; pornography is the injury." *American Booksellers Ass'n, Inc.*
v. *Hudnut*, 771 F. 2d 323, 324–328 (7th Cir. 1985), *aff'd mem*, 475 US 1001 (1986).

242. and because it established a prior restraint. *American Booksellers Ass'n, Inc.* v. *Hudnut*,
598 F. Supp. 1316, 1331–1337 (S. D. Ind. 1984).

243. The Supreme Court affirmed the decision without opinion. *Hudnut*, 771 F. 2d at
328–331, *aff'd mem*, 475 US 1001 (1986).

243. against the possibility of causing offense. *The UMW Post, Inc.* v. *Board of Regents of the
University of Wisconsin System* 774 F. Supp. 1163, 1165, 1169–1175, 1178–1181 (E. D. Wisc.
1991).

243. it was essentially making up the rules as it went along." *Doe v. University of Michigan*, 721
F. Supp. 852, 867–868 (E. D. Mich. 1989).

243. are almost always struck down when challenged in court. Richard Delgado and Jean
Stefancic, MUST WE DEFEND NAZIS? 31 (New York: New York University Press, 2018).

244. "have turned free speech into a fetish." Steven H. Shiffrin, *The Dark Side of the First Amendment*, 61 UCLA LAW. REV. 1480 (2014); Steven H. Shiffrin, WHAT'S WRONG WITH THE FIRST AMENDMENT? 1–10 (London: Cambridge University Press, 2016).

244. at odds with human dignity. Shiffrin, WHAT'S WRONG WITH THE FIRST AMENDMENT?, *supra*, at 45.

245. "some progressives began to suspect they had made a bad First Amendment bargain." Burt Neuborne, MADISON'S MUSIC 106–116 (The New Press, 2015).

245. would actually promote progressive goals." Louis Michael Seidman, *Can Free Speech Be Progressive?*, 118 COLUMBIA LAW REV. 2219, 2223 (2018).

245. on traits like race, nationality, gender, class, and sexual orientation." Seidman, *supra*, at 2220.

245. with government interference with listener autonomy." Seidman, *supra*, at 2236.

245. it cannot be progressive." Seidman, *supra*, at 2245, 2247.

246. then why not bias it toward progressives?" Seidman, *supra*, at 2245, 2247.

246. *because it says things I agree with.*" (his italics). Fish, THE FIRST, *supra*, at 11, 19–20.

246. *and not an apolitical oasis of principle.*" Fish, THE FIRST, *supra*, at 4.

246. the necessary vehicle of its implementation." Fish, THE FIRST, *supra*, at 25.

247. to protect a free society against the enemies of freedom." Aryeh Neier, DEFENDING MY ENEMY 12 (New York: E. P. Dutton, 1979).

247. even if the temporary beneficiaries are the enemies of freedom." Neier, *supra*, at 4–5.

247. do to you and your speech what you have done to them." Fish, THE FIRST, *supra*, at 51.

247. over its defense of free speech principles in the Skokie case. Neier, *supra*, at 79.

247. to punish the very groups they ostensibly were enacted to protect. Nadine Strossen, HATE: WHY WE SHOULD RESIST IT WITH FREE SPEECH, NOT CENSORSHIP (New York: Oxford University Press, 2018).

248. while in France it is a crime to deny it. Alan M. Dershowitz, *The Right Shoe of Censorship Is Now on the Left Foot*, WASHINGTON POST, Feb. 4, 2018, at B1, 7.

248. describes like-minded scholars as "polemicists." Fish, THE FIRST, *supra*, at 43–44.

248. "by and large," Jeremy Waldron, THE HARM IN HATE SPEECH 202–203 (Cambridge, MA: Harvard University Press, 2012).

248. and in many cases counterproductive. Strossen, *supra*, at 133–156.

248. the best that can be said for hate speech regulations." Waldron, *supra*, at 11.

248. it is the content that explains the restriction." Waldron, *supra*, at 152.

248. "ongoing engagement in political practice." Delgado et al., WORDS THAT WOUND, *supra*, at 3, 10–11.

248. "a guide for activist lawyers and judges." Delgado, MUST WE DEFEND NAZIS?, *supra*, at 109–133.

249. "humans are incompetent at designing good rules of censorship." Jane and Derek Bambauer, *Information Libertarianism*, 105 CAL. LAW REV. 335, 365–366 (2017).

249. nor from petitioning the government. James H. Read, *James Madison*, THE FIRST AMENDMENT ENCYCLOPEDIA, Middle Tennessee State University, 2009 (https://mtsu.edu/first-amendment/article/1220/james-madison).

249. to put them out of the power of the Legislature to infringe them." Gazette of the US, Jun. 10, 1789, 67, cols. 2–3 (quoted in Neil H. Cogan, THE COMPLETE BILL OF RIGHTS: THE DRAFTS, DEBATES, SOURCES, & ORIGINS 59 (New York: Oxford University Press, 1997)).

250. off limits to those who bucked the established order." Stewart Jay, *The Creation of the First Amendment Right to Free Expression: From the Eighteenth Century to the Mid-Twentieth Century*, 34 WM. MITCHELL LAW REV. 773 (2008).

250. that regulation too must be neutral. Charles Fried, *The New First Amendment Jurisprudence: A Threat to Liberty*, 59 UNIV. OF CHICAGO LAW REV. 225, 226 (1992).

251. and makes it stick, the case is over." Fish, THERE'S NO SUCH THING AS FREE SPEECH, *supra*, at 105; Fish, THE FIRST, *supra*, at 25.

251. and 'first amendment revisionists.'" Delgado et al., WORDS THAT WOUND, *supra*, at 11.

251. rather than subtracts from it." Delgado, MUST WE DEFEND NAZIS?, *supra*, at 94.

252. "You might be a redneck if you've been married three times and have the same in-laws." *See, e.g., Talk: Jeff Foxworthy*, WIKIQUOTE.ORG (https://en.wikiquote.org/wiki/Talk :Jeff_Foxworthy).

252. as does 'redneck.'" Delgado, MUST WE DEFEND NAZIS?, *supra*, at 95.

252. "First Amendment fundamentalists." Delgado, MUST WE DEFEND NAZIS?, *supra*, at 35, 38, 141, 145; Delgado, WORDS THAT WOUND, *supra*.

252. "the lunacies of America's rights-crazed culture." Robert H. Bork, *Thanks a Lot*, NATIONAL REVIEW, Apr. 16, 2007 (http://web.archive.org/web/20130410132839).

253. cyanide-laced Flavor-Aide (a Kool-Aid imitator) in a mass suicide. Wayne Batchis, THE RIGHT'S FIRST AMENDMENT: THE POLITICS OF FREE SPEECH & THE RETURN OF CONSERVATIVE LIBERTARIANISM 174 (Stanford, CA: Stanford University Press 2016).

253. who worship at the altar of white male supremacy. Mary Anne Franks, THE CULT OF THE CONSTITUTION 105–157 (Stanford, CA: Stanford University Press, 2019).

253. First Amendment "idolatry" a "fetish." Shiffrin, WHAT'S WRONG WITH THE FIRST AMENDMENT?, *supra*, at 1–10.

253. wooden, or unprincipled. Shiffrin, WHAT'S WRONG WITH THE FIRST AMENDMENT?, *supra*, at 95.

253. "to spout the mantra 'the marketplace of ideas.'" Waldron, *supra*, at 156–157.

253. their own personal faith, their own original view." MacKinnon, *supra*, ONLY WORDS, at 76–77.

253. that, in his estimation, "overprotect speech." Fish, THE FIRST, *supra*, at 1, 4.

253. clichés such as 'the best cure to bad speech is more speech.'" Delgado, MUST WE DEFEND NAZIS?, *supra*, at 33.

253. courts should be free to expand the range of unprotected speech. Shiffrin, WHAT'S WRONG WITH THE FIRST AMENDMENT?, *supra*, at 71–76.

253. "I have no answer at all." Nico Perrino, *So to Speak podcast transcript: There's No Such Thing as Free Speech, Argues Professor Stanley Fish*, Nov. 5, 2019 (www.thefire.org/so-to-speak-podcast-transcript-theres-no-such-thing-as-free-speech-argues-professor-stanley-fish/).

254. no one will believe you." Eli Rosenberg, *Trump Admitted He Attacks Press to Shield Himself from Negative Coverage, Lesley Stahl Says*, WASHINGTON POST, May 22, 2018.

254. "How Conservatives Weaponized the First Amendment." Adam Liptak, *How Conservatives Weaponized the First Amendment*, NEW YORK TIMES, Jun. 30, 2018, at 1.

254. "weaponizing the First Amendment." *Janus v. American Federation of State, County, and Municipal Employees, Council 31*, 138 S. Ct. 2448, 2501 (Kagan, J., dissenting).

254. have discovered, in the first amendment, a new weapon." MacKinnon, *supra*, ONLY WORDS, at 12; Delgado, *supra*, WORDS THAT WOUND, at 7, 14.

254. for White supremacist and male-dominant sexual ends." MacKinnon, *supra*, *Equality Reading*, at 157.

255. "[W]e've weaponized *weaponize*." John Kelly, *Everything Is Weaponized Now. This Is a Good Sign for Peace*, SLATE, Aug. 30, 2016 (https://slate.com/human-interest/2016/08/how-weaponize-became-a-political-cultural-and-internet-term-du-jour.html).

255. sometimes combined with the claim that free speech has been "weaponized." William Bennett Turner, FREE SPEECH FOR SOME 8 (Berkeley, CA: Roaring Forties Press 2019).

255. that limited bakers to sixty-hour work weeks. *Lochner v. New York*, 198 US 45 (1905).

255. an unequivocal repudiation' of what the court has done." Howard M. Wasserman, *Bartnicki as Lochner: Some Thoughts on First Amendment Lochnerism*, 33 NORTHERN KENTUCKY LAW REV. 421 (2006) (quoting Neil M. Richards, *Reconciling Data Privacy and the First Amendment*, 52 UCLA LAW REV. 1149, 1212 (2005)).

255. the courts have too willingly protected business interests. *E.g.*, Robert Post, *The Constitutional Status of Commercial* Speech, 48 UCLA LAW REV. 1 (2000); Julie Cohen, *The Zombie First Amendment*, WILLIAM & MARY LAW REV. 1119 (2015); C. Edwin Baker, *The First Amendment and Commercial Speech*, 84 Ind. L. J. 981 (2009); Tim Wu, *Machine Speech*, 161 UNIV. OF PA LAW REV. 1495 (2013); Mark Tushnet, *Introduction: Reflections on the First Amendment and the Information Economy*, 127 HARVARD LAW REV. 2234 (2014).

255. and whose assumed meaning runs a broad range." Wasserman, *supra*, at 457.

255. to protect "their dear obscenity." Comstock, FRAUDS EXPOSED, *supra*, at 393, 508; Broun and Leech, *supra*, at 191.

256. and just want to "tear down the pure and holy." Comstock, TRAPS FOR THE YOUNG, *supra*, at 196–197.

256. except the Infidels, the Liberals, and the Free Lovers." Anthony Comstock, FRAUDS EXPOSED, *supra*, at 393.

256. "know the game" of tarring their adversaries as "apologists for . . . evil." Mencken, A BOOK OF PREFACES, *supra*, at 255.

256. construed as it is so men can have their pornography." MacKinnon, *Equality Reading*, *supra*, at 158.

256. so has to do with the gender dynamics of the abuse." Franks, *supra*, at 134.

256. which found ways to return the favor." Franks, *supra*, at 109, 124.

256. defending Nazis is simply defending Nazis." Delgado, MUST WE DEFEND NAZIS?, *supra*, at 109, 161–162.

256. reluctance to regulate hate speech is related to unconscious racism." Charles R. Lawrence III, *If He Hollers Let Him Go: Regulating Racist Speech on Campus*, in Delgado et al., WORDS THAT WOUND, *supra*, at 83; *see also* Delgado et al., WORDS THAT WOUND, *supra*, at 11.

256. that validates prejudices against women, minorities, and fellow liberals." Franks, *supra*, at 140.

257. "Liberalism Is White Supremacy." *Chasm in the Classroom*, *supra*, at 66; Francesca Truitt, *Black Lives Matter Protests American Civil Liberties Union*, THE FLAT HAT, Oct. 2, 2017 (http://flathatnews.com/2017/10/02/black-lives-matter-protests-american-civil-liberties-union/); Robby Soave, *Black Lives Matter Students Shut Down the ACLU's Campus Free Speech Event because 'Liberalism Is White Supremacy*,' REASON.COM, Oct. 4, 2017 (https://reason.com/2017/10/04/black-lives-matter-students-shut-down-th/).

257. or defended, obscenity (as he broadly defined it) "moral cancer planters." Comstock, FRAUDS EXPOSED, *supra*, at 396, 414.

257. engraved, drawn, or painted." Comstock, MORALS VERSUS ART, *supra*, at 17, 26.

257. "to debauch the morals of the young." Comstock, TRAPS FOR THE YOUNG, *supra*, at 223.

257. pointed to Comstock-era court decisions as setting the proper standard. Fredric Wertham, *What Parents Don't Know about Comic Books*, LADIES' HOME JOURNAL, Nov. 1953, at 219–220; Fredric Wertham, SEDUCTION OF THE INNOCENT 330–333 (New York: Rinehart & Company, Inc., 1954) (New York: Main Road Books, Inc., 2004 ed.).

258. involves protections for commercial speech. *E.g.*, Tamara Piety, BRANDISHING THE FIRST AMENDMENT: COMMERCIAL EXPRESSION IN AMERICA (Ann Arbor: University of Michigan Press, 2012).

258. "has led us to plainly unacceptable *results.*" Shiffrin, WHAT'S WRONG WITH THE FIRST AMENDMENT?, *supra*, at 186 (emphasis added).

258. "depends entirely on one's political leanings." Jane and Derek Bambauer, *Information Libertarianism*, 105 CAL. LAW. REV. 335 (2017).

258. "cater[] to the animal in man." Comstock, TRAPS FOR THE YOUNG, *supra*, at 168–169.

258. *Morals stand first.*" Comstock, MORALS VERSUS ART, *supra*, at 5.

258. merely a particularly offensive mode of expression." Robert H. Bork, *An End to Political Judging?*, NATIONAL REVIEW, Dec. 31, 1990, at 30; Batchis, *supra*, at 1.

259. no "ideas" except the subordination of women. MacKinnon, *Equality Reading*, *supra*, at 157; MacKinnon, ONLY WORDS, *supra*, at 21.

259. is immune to any curative effect of "more speech." Delgado, MUST WE DEFEND NAZIS?, *supra*, at 72–74, 94, 146, 155.

259. condemns all efforts to regulate racist speech." Lawrence, *If He Hollers Let Him Go*, in Delgado et al., WORDS THAT WOUND, *supra*, at 57.

259. is necessary to protect the free speech of all." Franks, *supra*, at 16.

259. "Jews Will Not Replace Us." Debbie Lord, *What Happened at Charlottesville: Looking Back on the Rally That Ended in Death*, ATLANTA JOURNAL-CONSTITUTION, Aug. 10, 2018 (www.ajc.com/news/national/what-happened-charlottesville-looking-back-the-anniver sary-the-deadly-rally/fPpnLrbAtbxSwNI9BEy93K/).

259. plowed his car into a group of counter-protesters. Debbie Lord, *What Happened at Charlottesville: Looking Back on the Rally That Ended in Death*, ATLANTA JOURNAL-CONSTITUTION, Aug. 10, 2018 (www.ajc.com/news/national/what-happened-charlottes ville-looking-back-the-anniversary-the-deadly-rally/fPpnLrbAtbxSwNI9BEy93 K/).

259. both joy and sorrow, and . . . inflict great pain." *Snyder* v. *Phelps*, 562 US 443, 453–455,460–461 (2011).

259. thus deserve no First Amendment protection. Shiffrin, WHAT'S WRONG WITH THE FIRST AMENDMENT?, *supra*, at 18–19.

260. produced by its collision with error." John Stuart Mill, ON LIBERTY, Ch. II (1859).

261. a constitutional right to gay marriage. *Obergefell* v. *Hodges*, 135 S. Ct. 2584 (2015).

261. no major incidents of violence. Katie Reilly, *Thousands of Counter-Protestors March Against White Nationalism in Boston a Week after Charlottesville*, TIME, Aug. 19, 2017 (https://time.com/4907681/boston-free-speech-rally-protests-charlottesville/).

261. without any serious injuries or property damage. Chas Danner, *Tens of Thousands March Against Hatred and White Supremacy in Boston, Overwhelm "Free Speech" Rally*, NEW YORK MAGAZINE, Aug. 19, 2017 (http://nymag.com/intelligencer/2017/08/thousands-march-against-right-wing-rally-in-boston.htm).

262. greatly outnumbered by thousands of counter-protestors. German Lopez, *Unite the Right 2018 Was a Pathetic Failure*, VOX.COM, Aug. 12, 2018 (www.vox.com/identities/ 2018/8/12/17681444/unite-the-right-rally-dc-charlottesville-failure); James Bovard, *Pathetic Unite the Right and Angry Antifa Sputter. There's Still Time to Heed Rodney King*, USA Today, Aug. 13, 2018 (www.usatoday.com/story/opinion/2018/08/12/unite-right-sputters-antifa-fails-hopeful-signs-america-column/971952002/).

262. "once we take away the right to free speech we may never get it back." Remarks of Susan Bro at Open Future Festival Chicago, Oct. 5, 2019 (https://youtu.be/_4t12rS6_jo?t=11522).

262. that necessarily polluted society. Broun and Leech, *supra*, at 80–81.

262. impurity of thought and deed." Comstock, TRAPS FOR THE YOUNG, *supra*, at 5–6, 21, 25.

262. It therefore is sex." MacKinnon, ONLY WORDS, *supra*, at 17.

262. "racial and/or gender-based terrorism." MacKinnon, *Equality Reading, supra*, at 141, 157.

262. move it over into the category of action." Fish, THE FIRST, *supra*, at 44–45.

263. for debate is not what he is offering." Lisa Feldman Barrett, *When Is Speech Violence?*, NEW YORK TIMES, Jul. 14, 2017 (www.nytimes.com/2017/07/14/opinion/sunday/when-is-speech-violence.html).

263. an adverse emotional reaction to a provocative speaker. Jesse Singal, *Stop Telling Students Free Speech Is Traumatizing Them*, NEW YORK MAGAZINE, Jul. 18, 2017 (http://nymag.com/intelligencer/2017/07/students-free-speech-trauma.html); Jonathan Haidt and Greg Lukianoff, *Why It's a Bad Idea to Tell Students Words Are Violence*, THE ATLANTIC, Jul. 18, 2017 (www.theatlantic.com/education/archive/2017/07/why-its-a-bad-idea-to-tell-students-words-are-violence/533970/).

263. "pollution" of the social environment that can be banned. Waldron, *supra*, at 16, 33.

263. undo legal barriers to defamation suits (or, as Trump would say, "open up the libel laws"). MacKinnon, *Equality Reading, supra*, at 159–160.

263. who oppose pornography, for example." MacKinnon, ONLY WORDS, *supra*, at 79, 81.

263. "a worse evil than yellow fever or small pox." Comstock, TRAPS FOR THE YOUNG, *supra*, at 6, 12, 28, 41, 133, 136.

264. the "recruiting stations for hell." Comstock, TRAPS FOR THE YOUNG, *supra*, at 21, 25, 48–49.

264. Must you not take into account the neighbor's children?" US Congress, *Juvenile Delinquency (Comic Books): Hearings Before the Subcommittee on Juvenile Delinquency*, 83rd Cong., 2nd Sess. 84 (Apr. 21–22 and Jun. 24, 1954) (testimony of Dr. Fredric Wertham).

264. "lies, pure and simple, about women's and children's sexuality." MacKinnon, *Equality Reading, supra*, at 141, 158.

264. on the discrete minority of drunk drivers." Waldron, *supra*, at 203.

264. not selling whiskey to children is a restraint of trade." Wertham, SEDUCTION OF THE INNOCENT, *supra*, at xi n. 17, 302–305.

264. and young adults to recharge their cell phones"). Delgado, MUST WE DEFEND NAZIS?, *supra*, at 148.

264. or destroys all faith in God." Comstock, TRAPS FOR THE YOUNG, *supra*, at 199.

264. "without regard to the rights, morals or liberties of others." Broun and Leech, *supra*, at 175.

265. to cancel as commencement speaker at Rutgers University. Richard Perez-Pena, *After Protests, I.M.F. Chief Withdraws as Smith College's Commencement Speaker*, NEW YORK TIMES, May 12, 2014; Emma G. Fitzsimmons, *Condoleezza Rice Backs Out of Rutgers Speech after Student Protests*, NEW YORK TIMES, May 3, 2014; Richard Perez-Pena and Tanzina Vega, *Brandeis Cancels Plan to Give Honorary Degree to Ayaan Hirsi Ali, a Critic of Islam*, NEW YORK TIMES, Apr. 8, 2014.

265. Attorney General Eric Holder, and comedian Bill Maher. Greg Lukianoff and Jonathan Haidt, THE CODDLING OF THE AMERICAN MIND 48 (New York: Penguin, 2018).

265. a sevenfold increase in efforts to cancel speakers. Foundation for Individual Rights in Education, *Nationwide: Colleges Across the Country Disinvite Commencement Speakers* (www.thefire.org/cases/disinvitation-season/). *See also Pomp and Circumstances: Booted Speakers Raise Academic Concerns*, NBC NEWS, May 2, 2014 (www.nbcnews.com/news/education/pomp-circumstances-booted-speakers-raise-academic-concerns-n90141).

265. and almost half – 46 percent – were successful. Lukianoff and Haidt, THE CODDLING OF THE AMERICAN MIND, *supra*, at 47.

265. but to engage in "virtue signaling." *So to Speak Podcast: The 100th Episode, The State of Free Speech in America*, Dec. 12, 2019 (www.thefire.org/so-to-speak-podcast-the-100th-episode-the-state-of-free-speech-in-america/).

265. to get more of one, you must have less of the other. Delgado, MUST WE DEFEND NAZIS?, *supra*, at 114–115.

266. unprotected by the First Amendment." MacKinnon, ONLY WORDS, *supra*, at 71, 108.

266. "an effect of the principle for the principle itself." Fried, *supra*, at 226–227.

266. "a replay of McCarthyism;" MacKinnon, ONLY WORDS, *supra*, at 76–77; MacKinnon, *Equality Reading, supra*, at 140, 142.

266. and "at war with free thought." Seidman, *supra*, at 2247.

266. encircling the ousted speaker and shouting more loudly. *Chasm in the Classroom, supra*, at 66; Francesca Truitt, *Black Lives Matter Protests American Civil Liberties Union*, THE FLAT HAT, Oct. 2, 2017 (http://flathatnews.com/2017/10/02/black-lives-matter-protests-american-civil-liberties-union/); Robby Soave, *Black Lives Matter Students Shut Down the ACLU's Campus Free Speech Event Because 'Liberalism Is White Supremacy,'* REASON.COM, Oct. 4, 2017 (https://reason.com/2017/10/04/black-lives-matter-students-shut-down-th/).

267. and concussion in the resulting scuffle. Lukianoff and Haidt, THE CODDLING OF THE AMERICAN MIND, *supra*, at 87–88; Chemerinsky and Gillman, *supra*; Keith E. Whittington, SPEAK FREELY: WHY UNIVERSITIES MUST DEFEND FREE SPEECH 107–108 (Princeton, NJ: Princeton University Press, 2018); *Chasm in the Classroom, supra*, at 30.

267. former *Breitbart News* editor Milo Yiannopoulos. Lucy Pasha-Robinson, *Berkeley Cancels Milo Yiannopoulos Speech after Violent Protests Erupt*, THE INDEPENDENT, Feb. 2, 2017 (www.independent.co.uk/news/world/americas/uc-berkeley-cancels-milo-yiannopoulos-speech-after-violent-protests-erupt-a7559056.html); *Chasm in the Classroom, supra*, at 32–33.

267. had appearances disrupted at several other universities. *Chasm in the Classroom, supra*, at 32–33.

267. a speech by right-wing provocateur Ann Coulter. Joseph Russomanno, *Speech on Campus: How America's Crisis in Confidence Is Eroding America's Free Speech Values*, 45 HASTINGS CONST. LAW QUARTERLY 273, 274 (Winter 2018); Thomas Fuller and Stephanie Saul, *Berkeley Reschedules Coulter, but She Vows to Keep Original Date for Speech*, NEW YORK TIMES, Apr. 21, 2017, at A14.

267. Claremont McKenna College, and (again) Berkeley. Robert Shibley, *Colleges Are Ground Zero for Mob Attacks on Free Speech, Lawyer Says*, WASHINGTON POST, Mar. 7, 2017. *See* Peter Holley, *A Conservative Author Tried to Speak as a Liberal Arts College. He Left Fleeing an Angry Mob*, WASHINGTON POST, Mar. 4, 2017.

268. *far more pro-free speech* than that put forward by the liberals." Mark Bray, ANTIFA: THE ANTI-FASCIST HANDBOOK 144, 148 (Melville House 2017).

268. is a real mental condition. Rob Whitley, *Is "Trump Derangement Syndrome" a Real Mental Condition?*, PSYCHOLOGY TODAY, Jan. 4, 2019.

268. Barack Obama, the Clintons, and Al Gore. *Bush Derangement Syndrome*, RATIONALWIKI (https://rationalwiki.org/wiki/Bush_Derangement_Syndrome).

269. were making a comeback in Vladimir Putin's Russia. Fiona Clark, *Is Psychiatry Being Used for Political Repression in Russia?*, 383 THE LANCET, Jan. 11, 2014 (www.thelancet.com/journals/lancet/article/PIIS0140-6736(13)62706-3/fulltext); *Political Abuse of Psychiatry in the Soviet Union*, WIKIPEDIA (https://en.wikipedia.org/wiki/Political_abuse_of_psychiatry_in_the_Soviet_Union).

269. 15 percent of forensic psychiatric cases had political connections. Robin Munro, DANGEROUS MINDS: POLITICAL PSYCHIATRY IN CHINA TODAY AND ITS ORIGINS IN THE MAO ERA (Human Rights Watch, 2002); *Political Abuse of Psychiatry*, WIKIPEDIA (https://en.wikipedia.org/wiki/Political_abuse_of_psychiatry).

269. "delusional disorders" of racism and homophobia. Sander Gilman and James M. Thomas, Are Racists Crazy? How Prejudice, Racism, and Antisemitism Became Markers of Insanity (New York: New York University Press, 2016); Rebecca Onion, *Is Racism a Disease?*, Slate.com, Nov. 17, 2016 (https://slate.com/news-and-politics/2016/11/is-racism-a-psychological-disorder.html).

269. including racism, sexism, and classism. Alan Kors, *Thought Reform 101: The Orwellian Implications of Today's College Orientation*, Reason.com, Mar. 2000 (https://reason.com/2000/03/01/thought-reform-101-2/#).

269. when it should be called plainly evil." Onion, *Is Racism a Disease?*, *supra*.

270. (as Ezra Heywood said of Comstock). Ezra H. Heywood, Cupid's Yokes 11–12 (Princeton, MA: Co-Operative Publishing Co., 1876).

271. the 1984 mockumentary *This Is Spinal Tap*. Up to Eleven, Wikipedia (https://en.wikipedia.org/wiki/Up_to_eleven).

271. and takes away his sense of proportion." Zechariah Chafee, Jr., Free Speech in the United States 532–533 (Cambridge, MA: Harvard University Press, 1941).

272. The very fact [that] he is a censor indicates that. Heywood Broun, *Broun on Censorship* (epilogue to Broun and Leech, *supra*, at 275).

CHAPTER 10

273. how we must learn to deal with that reality. Lee C. Bollinger and Geoffrey R. Stone, The Free Speech Century 4 (New York: Oxford University Press, 2019).

273. inspiration that goes beyond literal holdings." Harry Kalven, Jr., A Worthy Tradition: Freedom of Speech in America xviii–xix (New York: Harper & Row, 1988).

274. Because They Aren't Up for Negotiation.'" Kevin Williamson, The Smallest Minority: Independent Thinking in the Age of Mob Politics 54 n.4 (Washington, DC: Regnery Gateway, 2019).

274. they depend on the outcome of no elections." *Barnette* v. *West Virginia Board of Education*, 319 US 624, 638 (1943).

274. should not interpret the law based on mid-Victorian morals. *United States* v. *Kennerley*, 209 F. 119 (SDNY 1913).

274. which weighs their interests alongside its own without bias." Irving Dillard (ed.), The Spirit of Liberty: Papers and Addresses of Learned Hand 189–191 (New York: Alfred A. Knopf, 1960).

274. to hang a question mark on the things you have long taken for granted." The quote is attributed to Russell in a 1940 Reader's Digest article, but its origin is disputed (https://en.wikiquote.org/wiki/Bertrand_Russell).

275. answers to life's great questions (or even little ones). Jonathan Rauch, Kindly Inquisitors 31–56 (Chicago: University of Chicago Press, 1993/2013).

275. "there is no such thing as absolute certainty." John Stuart Mill, "On Liberty" and Other Writings 8 (Stefan Collini ed. 1989).

275. we "have been cock-sure of many things that were not so." Oliver Wendell Holmes, *Natural Law*, 32 Harvard Law Rev. 40 (1918).

275. the possibility that prior understandings will be displaced." Vincent Blasi, *Holmes and the Marketplace of Ideas*, 2004 Sup. Ct. Rev. 1, 19 (2004).

275. facilitated by the First Amendment of the United States Constitution. Wayne Batchis, The Right's First Amendment: The Politics of Free Speech & the Return of Conservative Libertarianism 17 (Stanford, CA: Stanford University Press, 2016).

275. that could save America's youth from "moral death." Comstock, FRAUDS EXPOSED, *supra*, at 425.

276. "you have no doubt of your premises or your power." *Abrams v. United States*, 250 US 616, 630 (1919) (Holmes, J., dissenting).

276. that the First Amendment goes too far. Freedom Forum First Amendment Center, *State of the First Amendment Survey 2014* (www.newseuminstitute.org/wp-content/uploads/2014/09/FAC_sofa_2002report.pdf).

277. disagreed that "the First Amendment goes too far." Freedom Forum First Amendment Center, *State of the First Amendment Survey 2017* (www.freedomforuminstitute.org/first-amendment-center/state-of-the-first-amendment/2017-report/).

277. back up to 74 percent despite continuing political turmoil. Freedom Forum First Amendment Center, *State of the First Amendment Survey 2018* (www.freedomforumin stitute.org/first-amendment-center/state-of-the-first-amendment/2018-report/).

277. and only 13 percent said that it does. Freedom Forum First Amendment Center, *State of the First Amendment Survey 2014* (www.newseuminstitute.org/wp-content/uploads/2014/08/FAC_sofa_2012report.pdf).

277. in 2019 said they believed that the First Amendment does go too far. Freedom Forum First Amendment Center, *State of the First Amendment Survey 2019* (www.freedomfor uminstitute.org/wp-content/uploads/2019/06/SOFAreport2019.pdf).

277. "We have always been a people of anarchistic tendencies." Morris Ernst, *Sex Wins in America*, THE NATION, Aug. 10, 1932, at 124.

277. dissenting from authority "is in our DNA." Kathleen Parker, *China Won't Die Laughing. Just Ask "South Park."* WASHINGTON POST, Oct. 9, 2019, at A19.

278. 48 percent believed that "the news media is the enemy of the American people." Sam Stein, *New Poll: 43% of Republicans Want to Give Trump the Power to Shut Down Media*, THE DAILY BEAST, Aug. 7, 2018 (www.thedailybeast.com/new-poll-43-of-repub licans-want-to-give-trump-the-power-to-shut-down-media).

278. the level of support has increased over time (except for the racist). Justin Murphy, *Who's Afraid of Free Speech in the United States?* (https://jmrphy.net/blog/2018/02/16/who-is-afraid-of-free-speech/) (updated Sept. 21, 2019); Matthew Yglesias, *Everything We Think About the Political Correctness Debate Is Wrong*, Vox, Mar. 12, 2018 (www.vox.com/policy-and-politics/2018/3/12/17100496/political-correctness-data).

279. freedom *from* speech rather than freedom of speech." Greg Lukianoff, *Campus Free Speech Has Been in Trouble for a Long Time*, CATO UNBOUND, Jan. 4, 2016 (www.cato-unbound.org/2016/01/04/greg-lukianoff/campus-free-speech-has-been-trouble-long-time).

279. will not be exposed to whatever it is that may upset them. Pen America, *And Campus for All: Diversity, Inclusion, and Freedom of Speech at U.S. Universities* (Oct. 17, 2016), at 18–25; National Coalition Against Censorship, *What's All This about Trigger Warnings?* (Dec. 2015), at 1–5.

279. were making up a growing proportion of the student population. Lukianoff and Haidt, THE CODDLING OF THE AMERICAN MIND, *supra*, at 30, 146–147; Robby Soave, PANIC ATTACK: YOUNG RADICALS IN THE AGE OF TRUMP 7–8 (New York: All Points Press, 2019).

280. demands for safe spaces and trigger warnings. Lukianoff and Haidt, THE CODDLING OF THE AMERICAN MIND, *supra*, at 125–194.

280. have come from both the political left and the right. Lukianoff and Haidt, THE CODDLING OF THE AMERICAN MIND, *supra*, at 133–140.

280. and prevent disruptions of the educational environment." Erwin Chemerinsky and Howard Gillman, FREE SPEECH ON CAMPUS 12–14, 18–19 (New Haven: Yale University Press, 2017).

281. 65 percent of those over fifty and 76 percent of the younger respondents. Freedom Forum First Amendment Center, *State of the First Amendment Survey 2019* (www .freedomforuminstitute.org/wp-content/uploads/2019/06/SOFAreport2019.pdf), at 6.

281. a generally higher tolerance for censorship among younger people. Freedom Forum First Amendment Center, *State of the First Amendment Survey 2019* (www.freedomfor uminstitute.org/wp-content/uploads/2019/06/SOFAreport2019.pdf), at 7.

281. supported banning the wearing of costumes that stereotype certain racial or ethnic groups. Gallup, Inc., FREE EXPRESSION ON CAMPUS: A SURVEY OF U.S. COLLEGE STUDENTS AND U.S. ADULTS 12 (2016).

281. sexist, homophobic *or otherwise offensive.*" Lukianoff, *Campus Free Speech Has Been in Trouble for a Long Time*, *supra*.

281. not exposed to intolerant and offensive ideas." Lukianoff and Haidt, THE CODDLING OF THE AMERICAN MIND, *supra*, at 48.

281. promoting an inclusive and welcoming society. Gallup/Knight Foundation Survey, FREE EXPRESSION ON CAMPUS: WHAT COLLEGE STUDENTS THINK ABOUT FIRST AMENDMENT ISSUES 9 (https://kf-site-production.s3.amazonaws.com/publications/pdfs/000/000/248/ original/Knight_Foundation_Free_Expression_on_Campus_2017.pdf); John. S. and James L. Knight Foundation, FREE EXPRESSION ON COLLEGE CAMPUSES 6 (May 2019) (https://kf-site-production.s3.amazonaws.com/media_elements/files/000/000/351/ori ginal/Knight-CP-Report-FINAL.pdf).

281. generally remain, the *most supportive* of free speech." Justin Murphy, *Who's Afraid of Free Speech in the United States?* (https://jmrphy.net/blog/2018/02/16/who-is-afraid-of-free-speech/) (updated Sept. 21, 2019).

282. and that "[c]ollege graduates are more supportive than non-graduates." Murphy, *Who's Afraid of Free Speech in the United States?*; Yglesias, *Everything We Think about the Political Correctness Debate Is Wrong*, *supra* (www.vox.com/policy-and-politics/2018/3/ 12/17100496/political-correctness-data).

282. "[v]ery few students are willing to come out and say they are against free speech." Pen America, *Chasm in the Classroom: Campus Free Speech in a Divided America* (Apr. 2, 2019), at 61.

282. so many students simultaneously advocate censorship and free speech." Pen America, *Chasm in the Classroom*, *supra*, at 62–63.

282. will enable our diverse population to live together peaceably." Pen America, *Chasm in the Classroom*, *supra*, at 9.

282. a greater willingness among students of this age group to silence disfavored speakers. Sean Stevens and Jonathan Haidt, *The Skeptics Are Wrong Part 1: Attitudes about Free Speech on Campus Are Changing* (Mar. 19, 2018) (https://heterodoxacademy.org/skep tics-are-wrong-about-campus-speech/).

282. as bad as holding racist views yourself." Sean Stevens, *The Skeptics Are Wrong Part 2: Free Culture on Campus Is Changing* (Apr. 11, 2018) (https://heterodoxacademy.org/the-skep tics-are-wrong-part-2/).

283. a pro-police Blue Lives Matter advocate. Sean Stevens, *The Skeptics Are Wrong Part 3: Political Intolerance Levels on Campus Are High, and Here Is Why* (May 11, 2018) (https://heterodoxacademy.org/the-skeptics-are-wrong-part-3-intolerance-levels-are-high/).

283. Lenny Bruce, draft card burners, or George Carlin." Chemerinsky and Gillman, *supra*, at 10–11.

284. may outweigh free speech values." Steven H. Shiffrin, WHAT'S WRONG WITH THE FIRST AMENDMENT? 190–191 (London: Cambridge University Press, 2016).

EPILOGUE

285. who insist that speech *is* violence. Stephen Rohde, *A Failed Case Against Free Speech*, Los Angeles Review of Books, Mar. 17, 2020.

286. "You gotta go to the streets and be as violent as Antifa and BLM [Black Lives Matter]." Luke Mogelson, *Among the Insurrectionists*, The New Yorker, Jan. 15, 2021 (www.new yorker.com/magazine/2021/01/25/among-the-insurrectionists).

286. "you're not going to have a country anymore." David Remnick, *The Inciter-in-Chief*, The New Yorker, Jan. 9, 2021 (www.newyorker.com/magazine/2021/01/18/the-inciter-in-chief).

286. called for "trial by combat." Luke Mogelson, *Among the Insurrectionists*, The New Yorker, Jan. 15, 2021 (www.newyorker.com/magazine/2021/01/25/among-the-insurrectionists).

286. must be defeated before they achieve traction." Gavan Titley, Is Free Speech Racist? (Cambridge: Polity, 2020); Stephen Rohde, *Free Speech and the Question of Race*, Los Angeles Review of Books, Jan. 24, 2021.

286. "anyone whose political philosophy involves the oppression of others, does not deserve a right to speak." P. E. Moskowitz, The Case Against Free Speech 107 (New York: Bold Type Books, 2019).

286. showed up with rifles." Moskowitz, The Case Against Free Speech, at 15–17.

287. for future dissenters and reformers to hold the powerful to account." Suzanne Nossel, Keep Our Free Speech Laws Intact, New York Times, Jan. 17, 2021, Section SR, Page 7.

288. or who failed to show him "proper" respect. *Pen American Center, Inc. v. Trump*, 448 F. Supp. 3d 309 (SDNY 2020).

288. without first determining whether such a claim could be made under state law. *McKesson v. Doe*, 141 S.Ct. 48, 51 (2020).

288. in the most real sense, un-American." Floyd Abrams, *Is a Free Press a Threat to Freedom?*, 2 Communications and the Law 67, 78–79 (1980).

Index